DIAGNOSIS
AND
TREATMENT
OF THE
LOWER EXTREMITIES

NONOPERATIVE ORTHOPAEDIC MEDICINE AND MANUAL THERAPY

DOS WINKEL, PT
Instructor, Scientific Society of Flemish General Practitioners
Antwerp, Belgium
Director, Dutch and German Academy of Orthopaedic Medicine
Delft, the Netherlands and Göttingen, Germany
President, International Academy of Orthopaedic Medicine

OMER MATTHIJS, PT
Instructor, International Academy of
 Orthopaedic Medicine
Instructor, American Academy of
 Orthopedic Medicine, Inc.
Tucson, Arizona

VALERIE PHELPS, PT
Instructor, International Academy of
 Orthopaedic Medicine
Director and Instructor, American
 Academy of Orthopedic Medicine, Inc.
Tucson, Arizona

AN ASPEN PUBLICATION®
Aspen Publishers, Inc.
Gaithersburg, Maryland
1997

Library of Congress Cataloging-in-Publication Data

Winkel, Dos.
Diagnosis and treatment of the lower extremities: nonoperative
orthopaedic medicine and manual therapy / Dos Winkel with Omer Matthijs,
Valerie Phelps.
p. cm.
"Translation and adaptation of material previously published in
Dutch under the titles: Orthopedische geneeskunde en manuele
therapie, Diagnostiek extremiteiten (deel 2c) and Orthopedische
geneeskunde en manuele therapie, Therapie extremiteiten (deel 3b) by
Dos Winkel with Geert Aufdemkampe and Onno G. Meijer; Weke delen
aandoeningen van het bewegingsapparaat, Anatomie in vivo (deel 1) by
Andry Vleeming, Dos Winkel, and Onno G. Meijer"—T.p. verso.
Includes bibliographical references and index.
ISBN 0-8342-0902-0
1. Spine—Diseases—Treatment. 2. Spine—Diseases—Physical
therapy. 3. Spine—Diseases. I. Matthijs, Omer. II. Phelps,
Valerie. III. Winkel, Dos. Orthopedische geneeskunde en manuele
therapie. IV. Vleeming, Andry. Weke delen aandoeningen van het bewegingsapparaat. V. Title.
[DNLM: 1. Leg. 2. Manipulation, Orthopedic—methods.
3. Orthopedics—methods. WE 870 W773d 1997]
RD768.W527 1997
617.5′8—dc21
DNLM/DLC
for Library of Congress
96-36871
CIP

Orders: (800) 638-8437
Customer Service: (800) 234-1660

About Aspen Publishers • For more than 35 years, Aspen has been a leading professional publisher in a variety of disciplines. Aspen's vast information resources are available in both print and electronic formats. We are committed to providing the highest quality information available in the most appropriate format for our customers. Visit Aspen's Internet site for more information resources, directories, articles, and a searchable version of Aspen's full catalog, including the most recent publications: http://www.aspenpub.com
Aspen Publishers, Inc. • The hallmark of quality in publishing
Member of the worldwide Wolters Kluwer group.

The authors have made every effort to ensure the accuracy of the information herein. However, appropriate information sources should be consulted, especially for new or unfamiliar procedures. It is the responsibility of every practitioner to evaluate the appropriateness of a particular opinion in the context of actual clinical situations and with due consideration to new developments. Authors, editors, and the publisher cannot be held responsible for any typographical or other errors found in this book.

Editorial Resources: Ruth Bloom

Library of Congress Catalog Card Number: 96-36871
ISBN: 0-8342-0902-0

Printed in the United States of America

1 2 3 4 5

Table of Contents

Contributors

Geert Aufdemkampe, PT
Physical Therapist
Central Netherlands School of Higher
    Professional Education
Faculty of Health Care Education
Academy for Physical Therapy
Utrecht, The Netherlands

Gaby M. van Meerwijk, PT
Physical Therapist
St. Lucas Hospital
Instructor
Stichting Academy of Physical Therapy
Amsterdam, The Netherlands

Omer Matthijs, PT
Physical Therapist/Manipulative Therapist
Instructor, International Academy of
    Orthopaedic Medicine
Instructor, Academy for Orthopaedic
    Medicine
Göttingen, Germany
Instructor, Association for Physical Therapy
Stuttgart, Germany
Instructor, American Academy of
    Orthopedic Medicine, Inc.
Tucson, Arizona

Onno G. Meijer, PhD, MD
Movement Scientist
Study Group for the Theory and History of
    Movement Science
Free University of Amsterdam
Amsterdam, The Netherlands

Didi G.H. van Paridon-Edauw, PT
Physical Therapist/Manipulative Therapist
Instructor, Academy for Orthopaedic
    Medicine
Göttingen, Germany
Instructor, Association for Physical Therapy
Stuttgart, Germany
Instructor, American Academy of
    Orthopedic Medicine, Inc.
Tucson, Arizona

Valerie Phelps, PT
Physical Therapist/Manipulative Therapist
Instructor, International Academy of
    Orthopaedic Medicine
Instructor, Academy for Orthopaedic
    Medicine
Göttingen, Germany
Instructor, Association for Physical Therapy
Stuttgart, Germany
Director and Instructor, American Academy
    of Orthopedic Medicine, Inc.
Tucson, Arizona

Dos Winkel, PT
Instructor, Scientific Society of Flemish
    General Practitioners
Antwerp, Belgium
Director, Dutch and German Academy of
    Orthopaedic Medicine
Delft, the Netherlands and Göttingen,
    Germany
President, International Academy of
    Orthopaedic Medicine

Foreword

Once again I am pleasantly surprised by the several volume series *Diagnosis and Treatment of the Spine, Diagnosis and Treatment of the Lower Extremities*, and *Diagnosis and Treatment of the Upper Extremities* by Dos Winkel. Practical information has been assembled for the health care professional in an ideal combination of extensive but conveniently organized subject matter and thorough but easy-to-read discussion of various topics. Basic data regarding functional anatomy and biomechanics, followed by thorough descriptions of the clinical examination and thorough discussions of pathology and treatment, make these volumes essential reference books that deserve a place in every medical library. Moreover, the most recent diagnostic techniques are illustrated in every volume.

During our many years of working together, I have gotten to know and appreciate Dos Winkel as an extremely qualified clinician with an analytical mind, which is evident in his approach to clinical problems, during his frequent seminars, and from his many publications and books. I also recognize a friend in Dos Winkel, for whom the writing of this preface is an expression of thanks for our fascinating, cooperative working relationship with the orthopedic patient.

Marc Martens, MD, PhD
Professor and Chief of Orthopedics
O.L.V. Middelares Hospital
Deurne, Belgium
Consultant Orthopedist
University Hospital
Antwerp, Belgium

Preface

Orthopedic medicine is a medical specialty that has gone through enormous changes during past decades. Research is being conducted worldwide in the various fields of movement science. This research includes arthrokinematics and dynamic electromyography, often with the aid of motion pictures. Because of such research, the causes of many disorders have become increasingly apparent, thus facilitating a more causal approach in the treatment of patients. A direct consequence of this is the decrease in the use of injection therapy, arthroscopy, and other surgical procedures. The opposite impression is gained, however, when one is dealing with patients' histories.

I am very grateful to **Valerie Phelps, PT**, Director of the American Academy of Orthopedic Medicine, for the translation of this series of books. This was a monumental task, which she performed with excellence. I am grateful to her as well, and to **Omer Matthijs, PT**, for having updated this series of books from both the Dutch and German versions. Omer Matthijs has for years been one of my closest coworkers and collaborators, as well as a most excellent practitioner and teacher.

In recognition of the fact that improvements in the field are constantly being made, it is necessary to provide updated information as well as hands-on practice via a series of instructional courses designed around the techniques described in these books. Therefore, in addition to individual use, this series of books supports and provides source material for instructional courses organized by the American Academy of Orthopedic Medicine, Inc. For information about these courses, call 1-800-AAOM-305 (1-800-226-6305).

I hope that this series of books will improve the effectiveness of practitioners in diagnoses and providing the appropriate treatment techniques. To everyone who will use these books, I hope you enjoy great success in using this knowledge and these techniques to the benefit of your patients. We look forward to hearing all remarks and considerations that could lead to further improvement of the text.

Dos Winkel
Bonaire (Dutch Antilles)

Acknowledgments

This book would never have come into existence without the help of many experts who have made specific contributions. Didi van Paridon-Edauw and Omer Matthijs, who have been instructors at seminars in orthopedic medicine and manual therapy both nationally and internationally, have had a continuous significant influence on the ultimate contents of this book. I would also like to express my gratitude to Dr. Marc Martens, Dr. Geert DeClercq, and Dr. Peter Hirshfeld for the many illustrations they so willingly contributed. I would also like to thank Aspen Publishers, whose staff again patiently followed and adapted to the process of writing this book.

I would like to acknowledge the contributions of Onno G. Meijer and Geert Aufdemkampe, whose work influenced *Nonoperative Orthopaedic Medicine and Manual Therapy*. In addition, the contribution of Gaby M. van Meerwijk for the thoracic outlet compression syndrome is also gratefully acknowledged.

Introduction

Every day, physicians and physiotherapists see a number of patients disabled by a lesion in the sphere of orthopedic medicine. Sooner or later, in the course of our lives, all of us suffer from nonsurgical disorders of the moving parts, be it, for example, a stiff shoulder or neck, lumbago, or a sprained knee. In these cases an exact diagnosis may be difficult to reach because referred pain and referred tenderness divert attention from the actual site of the lesion. The absence of objective signs puts physicians off, and misleading radiographic appearances add to the confusion.

What the clinician needs is a quick and simple way to examine patients whereby the tissue at fault can be identified with precision. This is exactly what this book offers. The method that it advocates is selective tension. Tension is applied in different ways to each separate structure from which the symptom could originate. After such an examination is adequately performed and correlated with a full and accurate history, exact localization is seldom difficult. The pattern of movements elicited by this means is interpreted on the basis of functional anatomy, and the site of the lesion is singled out.

Dos Winkle has pioneered this work in Holland. His summary of the theory of this approach to pain and the discussions of possible findings in this book greatly facilitate one's arrival at a precise diagnosis. Treatment can now be formulated on factual grounds, often with rapid success, even in cases hitherto regarded as intractable. This method of diagnosis also identifies patients with emotional problems that have been projected to their moving parts. This detection avoids waste of their own and physiotherapists' time in treating the wrong tissue.

All Dos Winkel's colleagues will be grateful to him for publishing this concise account of the fundamental approach to diagnosis. I recommend this book to all professionals facing problems in orthopedic medicine. He imparts, to physicians no less than to physiotherapists, new, essential knowledge—for which no substitute exists—about the proper attitude to the many soft tissue lesions that they encounter so often.

James Cyriax

Editor's Note: This originally appeared as the Foreword in *Soft Tissue Affections of the Musculoskeletal System, Part 2, Diagnostic*, in 1984.

Part I

The Hip

Chapter 1

Functional Anatomy of the Hip

Like the shoulder, the hip is a good example of a ball-and-socket joint. Much recent consideration has been given to both the anatomy and biomechanics of the hip joint. This emphasis is due to the increasing popularity of surgical procedures in which parts of the joint are replaced. These considerations are also important for the nonsurgical clinician because, just as in the knee, the hip joint can present the clinician with many different symptoms caused by a variety of degenerative cartilage conditions.

JOINT MORPHOLOGY

Bony Structures

The joint is formed by the acetabulum, as the socket, and the head of the femur, as the ball. Although at first glance the head of the femur appears to be a true spheroid in structure, upon closer examination it is seen to be more ellipsoid. The head is completely covered with hyaline cartilage, with the exception of the recess, where the ligament of the head of the femur is found.

The acetabulum is not entirely covered with cartilage. There is an incomplete cartilage ring, the facies lunata, with a "pillow" of fat in the middle. The socket of the hip joint is extended by the acetabular labrum, which is similar to the glenoid cavity in the shoulder joint (Figure 1–1).

Capsuloligamentous Structures

The hip joint is surrounded by a thick, fibrous membrane. This fibrous capsule is reinforced by a number of strong ligaments. The capsule is thicker at its proximal and anterior aspects than at the distal and posterior aspects.

At the hip joint, five ligaments can be distinguished: four capsular and one intracapsular (the ligament of the head of the femur; Figures 1–2 and 1–3). The deepest lying ligament is called the orbicular zone and con-

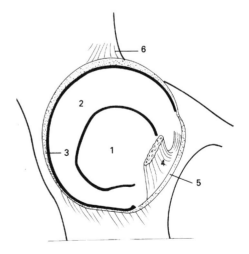

Figure 1–1 Acetabulum of the right hip joint. **1**, Acetabular fossa; **2**, facies lunata; **3**, acetabular labrum; **4**, ligament of the head of the femur; **5**, transverse ligament of the acetabulum; **6**, iliofemoral ligament.

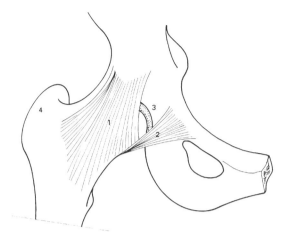

Figure 1–2 Anterior ligaments of the hip joint. **1**, Iliofemoral ligament; **2**, pubofemoral ligament; **3**, acetabular labrum; **4**, greater trochanter.

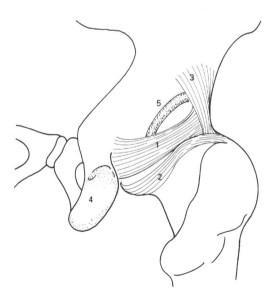

Figure 1–3 Posterior ligaments of the hip joint. **1**, Ischiofemoral ligament; **2**, orbicular zone; **3**, iliofemoral ligament, lateral part; **4**, ischial tuberosity; **5**, acetabular labrum.

sists of circular running fibers that form a sort of collar around the neck of the femur. This ligament, lying on the synovial membrane, does not have a direct attachment to bone. It has a firm connection with the pubofemoral and ischiofemoral ligaments, however.

The iliofemoral ligament is triangular in shape and actually consists of two parts, which together have the form of a Y. This ligament is considered the strongest ligament in the human body. The pubofemoral ligament, like the iliofemoral ligament, lies at the anterior aspect of the joint, but slightly more distally. This ligament is also triangular in form. The ischiofemoral ligament is found at the posterior aspect of the joint and runs in a somewhat spiral course.

The intracapsular ligament is the ligamentum capitis femoris, also called the ligament of the head of the femur. It runs from the central fossa, a recess in the middle of the femoral head, to the acetabulum, where it attaches in two slips. A blood vessel within this ligament, the acetabular ramus, runs from the posterior branch of the obturator artery. The ligament of the head of the femur is rather strong but is not thought to play any role in restricting hip motions. It becomes taut during combined movements of flexion and adduction. The distribution of tension in the hip ligaments, considering their course and attachments, is shown in Table 1–1.

The synovial membrane is extensive and runs over part of the femoral neck. The synovial cavity sometimes has a connection to the iliopectineal (psoas) bursa, which lies on the anterior side of the joint.

Muscles

The hip joint is a three-axis ball-and-socket joint; thus the movements can be interpreted as motions around three main axes. The active motions are guided by the muscles listed in Table 1–2; the major muscles are shown in Figure 1–4.

Table 1–1 Distribution of Tension in Hip Ligaments

Movement	Taut	Relaxed
Flexion		All capsular ligaments
Extension	All capsular ligaments, especially the iliofemoral ligament, pars inferior	
Abduction	Pubofemoral ligament, ischiofemoral ligament	Iliofemoral ligament
Adduction	Iliofemoral ligament, pars superior	Pubofemoral ligament, ischiofemoral ligament
External rotation	Iliofemoral ligament, pars superior; pubofemoral ligament	Ischiofemoral ligament
Internal rotation	Ischiofemoral ligament	Pubofemoral ligament

Other Structures

Bursae

Around the hip joint, a number of clinically important bursae are found. First, there is the iliopectineal bursa (also called the psoas bursa). The iliopsoas muscle runs from the vertebral column to the lesser trochanter and, in so doing, passes over the iliopubic eminence. At this eminence, the muscle makes an angle of approximately 30° as it courses in a dorsodistal direction. Movement in the hip joint creates friction at this site, which is neutralized through the iliopectineal bursa. From superior to inferior, the bursa can have a length of 6 to 7 cm; from medial to lateral, a width of 3 to 4 cm. It is not unusual for this bursa to have a surface area of 20 cm². Sometimes the iliopectineal bursa has a connection to the joint cavity of the hip joint.

The trochanteric bursa of the gluteus maximus muscle lies on the greater trochanter, just underneath the gluteus maximus. This bursa is also rather large, with a surface area of 15 cm². Its position varies with the position

of the leg. With a gradual change in standing posture, when external rotation predominates, the bursa, together with the trochanter, shifts posteriorly.

The ischial bursa of the gluteus maximus muscle is found between the ischial tuberosity and the gluteus maximus. Another bursa is found between the insertions of the gluteus maximus and vastus lateralis of the quadriceps (at the level of the femoral attachment).

Lateral Femoral Cutaneous Nerve

The lateral femoral cutaneous nerve arises from the posterior branch of the ventral rami of the second and third lumbar nerves and runs distally along the edge of the iliopsoas muscle. It gives off branches to the parietal peritoneum and then runs underneath the inguinal ligament to the thigh. The nerve becomes superficial approximately 10 cm distal to the inguinal ligament and provides sensory innervation to an oval section of skin at the lateral side of the thigh extending to the knee.

At the site where the nerve runs through the inguinal canal, the nerve can be com-

Table 1–2 Muscles Involved in Active Hip Movements

Movement	Muscles
Flexion	Psoas major, iliacus, rectus femoris, sartorius (assisted by adductor longus)
Extension	Gluteus maximus, hamstrings
Abduction	Gluteus medius and minimus, tensor fasciae latae, sartorius
Adduction	Adductor longus, adductor brevis, and adductor magnus; gracilis, pectineus
External rotation	Obturator internus and externus, gemelli, quadratus femoris, piriformis
Internal rotation	Tensor fasciae latae, gluteus medius and minimus (anterior fibers, assisted by adductor muscles)

pressed as a result of various causes. Another clinically significant site where compression can occur is 1 to 2 cm medial to the anterior superior iliac spine.

For other clinically important nerves, refer to Chapter 6.

Biomechanics

With regard to joint kinematics, it is important to keep in mind that the hip should be seen as part of a kinetic chain of which the pelvis and lumbar spine are also components. During movement in the hip joint, compensatory movements occur in the other parts of this chain as well. In addition, a number of muscles that influence the hip joint also run over the knee joint.

In the hip, there is a large difference in range between passive and active motion. Active flexion of the hip with an extended knee amounts to approximately 90°. If the knee is flexed, active flexion is approximately 120°. Passive flexion (eg, when the subject pulls the knee to the chest) amounts to about 140°. Range of motion in extension is approximately 15° to 20° when performed actively; passively, it is 30°.

When abduction and adduction are described, use is made of a reference axis that divides the pelvis into equal left and right parts. Because of a tipping of the pelvis in the frontal plane, abduction almost always takes place in both hip joints simultaneously. The maximal amount of motion in this situation is approximately 45°. The maximal range of motion in the adduction direction is about 30°, whereby adduction is combined with flexion or extension, and the pelvis and spine perform compensatory motions.

The amount of motion of external and internal rotation is described from the prone position with the hips straight and the knees in 90° flexion. From this position the available internal rotation is about 30°, and external rotation is approximately 60°.

It should be clear that these values are averages coming from untrained subjects. In dancers, for instance, active abduction of 70° and passive abduction of 90° (splits) is not exceptional. In a split, a forward tilting of the pelvis also occurs, so that the movement is more of a flexion-abduction motion.

The average range of motion during normal walking varies from approximately 40° flexion at the end of the swing phase to about 7° extension at the end of the stance phase.[1] The abduction is maximal just after toe-off and amounts to about 6°. The same degree of ad-

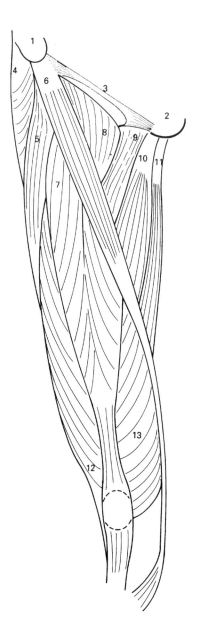

Figure 1–4 Anterior hip (thigh) musculature. **1**, Anterior superior iliac spine; **2**, pubic tubercle; **3**, inguinal ligament; **4**, gluteus medius muscles; **5**, tensor fasciae latae muscle; **6**, sartorius muscle; **7**, rectus femoris muscle; **8**, iliopsoas muscle; **9**, pectineus muscle; **10**, adductor longus muscle; **11**, gracilis muscle; **12**, vastus lateralis muscle; **13**, vastus medialis and vastus medialis obliquus muscles.

duction occurs throughout the entire stance phase; it amounts to about 3°.[2]

The weight of each leg amounts to approximately one sixth of the body weight. Thus the load on both hip joints together is two thirds of the body weight.[3] In standing on one leg, the load on the hip joint of the standing leg is relatively greater because all the various moments increase the reaction forces in the joint.[4] With the help of a so-called free body diagram, the reaction force in the joint in standing on one leg is calculated to be approximately three times the body weight. With the help of other methods of calculation, similar values have been obtained.[3]

It is interesting to note that walking generates much greater reaction forces, and there are differences between men and women in their intensity.[5] In men, a peak value of approximately four times the body weight occurs in the hip joint just after heel strike, and an even greater peak, approximately seven times the body weight, occurs just before toe-off. During the stance phase, the reaction forces decrease to less than body weight. The given values are lower in women: approximately two and a half times the body weight just after heel strike and four times the body weight just before toe-off.

In research by Bullough et al,[6] the relationship between anatomy and the loading pattern of the hip joint was examined. According to these investigators, the acetabular fossa often has no contact with the femoral head. Only when the load increases to more than half the body weight do both joint partners come into direct contact with each other. This occurs particularly in walking, running, or kneeling. Research indicates that the total time an individual loads the hip joint to more than half the body weight averages between 1.2 and 3.2 hours per day; the latter value was derived from a study of mail carriers.

According to Bullough et al,[6] the center part of the acetabulum, which does not have any cartilage, functions as a synovial fluid reservoir. In a joint in which the ball is so firmly grasped by the socket, movement to at least 90° would have to occur for the joint surfaces to be adequately bathed in synovial fluid. Such extremes of motion are rare in the hip joint. The incongruence of the joint surfaces and the presence of this so-called reservoir guarantee that the surfaces of the joint come into contact with sufficient synovial fluid. Radin[7] proposed that the joint surfaces become congruent in loaded situations; thus the prior incongruence has an apparent shock-absorbing effect as well.

In the study by Bullough et al,[6] hip joints in adults were often found to have an increased congruence. Based on the theories of these investigators, this would lead to decreased synovium dynamics, and based on Radin's theory[7] this would result in inadequate shock absorption. Both possibilities can be damaging for the joint.

Chapter 2

Surface Anatomy of the Hip

PALPATION OF THE BONY AND LIGAMENTOUS STRUCTURES IN THE PELVIC AREA

Anterior Superior Iliac Spine

Follow the easily visible fold of the groin in a craniolateral direction. The anterior superior iliac spine, a remarkable bone structure, is located at the end of the fold of the groin (Figures 2–1, 2–3, 2–5, 2–8, and 2–10). Mark the edges of this bony prominence on both sides of the pelvis, and check to see if both are at the same level. The iliac spines are located at the level of the first sacral vertebra. They are used as fixed points from which other structures can be located. During the measuring of the length of the legs, the most caudal part of the anterior superior iliac spine is used as a starting point. When the pelvis is in a normal position, the iliac spines are in the same frontal plane as the pubic tubercle.

Both the sartorius and the tensor fasciae latae muscles originate from the anterior superior iliac spine. This can be easily seen when the hip is actively flexed and slightly abducted in a standing or supine position. An inverse V form is visible, with the tensor fasciae latae forming the lateral leg of the V and the sartorius muscle forming the medial part of the V.

An avulsion fracture of the anterior superior iliac spine is sometimes seen in adolescent boys, particularly in high-level athletes (eg, young sprinters), who place intensive demands on the sartorius.

Anterior Inferior Iliac Spine

The anterior inferior iliac spine can be palpated in the space formed by the sartorius and tensor fasciae latae muscles (lateral femoral triangle) during passive flexion of the hip (Figures 2–1 and 2–3). Exact palpation of this bony structure is difficult, so that it is more an indirect palpation. Forceful palpation can be sensitive because the lateral femoral cutaneous nerve runs through this V-form space.

One of the two origins of the rectus femoris muscle attaches to the proximomedial part of the anterior inferior iliac spine. The main purpose of palpation is to determine whether the teno-osseous connection of this muscle is tender. An avulsion fracture (as mentioned in the discussion of the anterior superior iliac spine) can also occur in this bony structure.

Pubic Tubercle

The pubic tubercle is the first palpable bony structure that is felt when the palpation follows the fold of the groin in a caudomedial direction (Figures 2–2, 2–3, 2–5, and 2–10). Another way to reach this bony structure is by following the tendon of the adductor longus muscle to where the caudal aspect of this tubercle can be felt.

The tuberculi are covered with pubic hair and lie in the same transverse plane as the center of the greater trochanter. Both tuberculi should be at the same level. A fracture of the superior pubic ramus (seen quite often) can disturb the symmetry.

In men it is advisable not to palpate directly over the pubic tubercle but rather to approach it from a cranial or caudal direction to prevent compression on the spermatic cord. Damage to branches of the genitofemoral and ilioinguinal nerves in men and women can be caused by sustained friction on the surface of the tubercle.

The pubic tubercle functions as a reference point in the diagnosis of an inguinal or femoral hernia. An inguinal hernia can usually be palpated cranial and medial to the tubercle. The protrusion of a femoral hernia is almost always lateral to the pubic tubercle. If an extensive femoral hernia protrudes through the saphenous hiatus into the subcutaneous tissue, however, part of it is sometimes palpable cranial to the inguinal ligament.

Inguinal Ligament

The fold of the groin is easily visible in almost every person. On transverse palpation in the fold, a collagenous structure, the inguinal ligament, can be felt (Figure 2–5). This

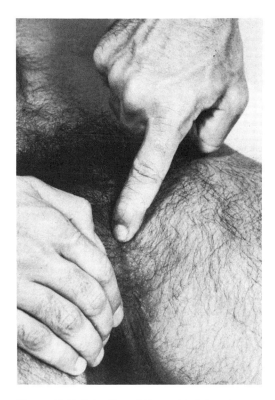

Figure 2–2 Palpation of the pubic tubercle.

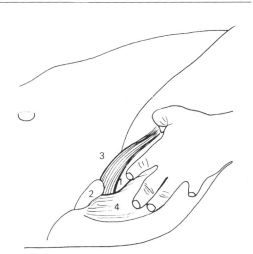

Figure 2–1 Palpation of the anterior inferior iliac spine in the lateral femoral triangle (**1**). **2**, Anterior superior iliac spine; **3**, sartorius muscle; **4**, tensor fasciae latae muscle.

structure runs from the anterior superior iliac spine to the pubic tubercle and is connected with several other structures by minute collagen bridges. The inguinal ligament should not be regarded as an independent structure, but rather as a thickening of the superficial fascia from the abdominal muscles and the fascia lata of the thigh. All the abdominal muscles have connections to or insertions at the inguinal ligament.

Tubercle of the Iliac Crest

To palpate the tubercles of the iliac crest, place the thumbs on the anterior superior iliac spines and the index fingers on the lateral tubercles located proximally 5 cm more cranial and lateral. These tubercles are generally located at the level of the widest place of the pelvis (Figure 2–3). These bony structures are not mentioned in the official anatomic nomenclature, but they are important orientation spots for an understanding of surface anatomy.

Iliac Crest

Palpate and mark the entire iliac crest from the anterior superior iliac spine to the posterior superior iliac spine (Figure 2–3). Determine where the distance between the crests is the widest (for anthropometric evaluation). Inexperienced clinicians quite often estimate the dorsal aspect of the crest too caudally.

The iliac crest has a slightly vaulted S form, in which the highest part is convex to the inside. In corpulent subjects, this highest part (in most people at the level of L4) is not easy to palpate.

Cordlike structures can sometimes be felt on the iliac crest. These cords can be tender in patients with lumbar complaints and are likely to be branches of the lumbar dorsal rami, which can thicken because of cellular infiltration processes.

The so-called lumbar trigone (Petit's triangle) is located between the dorsal end of the iliac crest, the lateral edge of the latissimus dorsi muscle, and the dorsal edge of the external oblique abdominal muscle. This is typically a triangle of variable dimensions that is filled with fatty tissue, and it is the only place where the internal oblique abdominal muscle is not covered with other muscles and can be directly palpated. The presence of only one muscle layer makes the lumbar trigone a weak spot for a hernia, although this occurs infrequently.

Posterior Superior Iliac Spine

The iliac crest thickens at the dorsocaudal aspect to become the posterior superior iliac spine (Figure 2–3). The posterior superior iliac spines are located underneath the pelvic dimples, which are easily visible in women and children.

Palpation of the posterior superior iliac spine is fairly easy, but it is difficult to mark the exact location. It is important to get it right because its location is used to determine whether the pelvis is symmetric from the dorsal aspect. This is important to determine a difference in leg length and for obstetric purposes. Quite often, when the patient complains about pain at the level of the pelvic dimples, it is referred pain. Several disorders in the lumbar and pelvic area can cause this.

A line connecting the caudal aspects of both posterior superior iliac spines identifies the location of the spinous process of S2. This is a consistent reference point which is used to locate the L5 spinous process and other structures.

As a result of the presence of soft tissue, palpating the posterior inferior iliac spines is hardly possible.

The ischial spines are only palpable from a vaginal approach in women who have a narrow pelvis.

Sacrum

Despite its superficial location, palpation of the sacrum is not easy (Figure 2–3). It is often mistakenly thought that the lateral border of the sacrum can be found along an imaginary line connecting the most cranial aspect of the anal cleft to the posterior superior iliac spine. The lateral border of the sacrum, however, can actually be palpated lateral to this connecting line.

In the midline, there are three to four rudimentary spinous processes that can be palpated as a low ridge, the median sacral crest. This ridge is flanked on both sides by the not always palpable lateral sacral crest. Directly caudal and on each side at the end of the median sacral crest, small prominences can be felt. These are the sacral cornua, and the space between them is the sacral hiatus, a location that is important for sacral epidural injections.

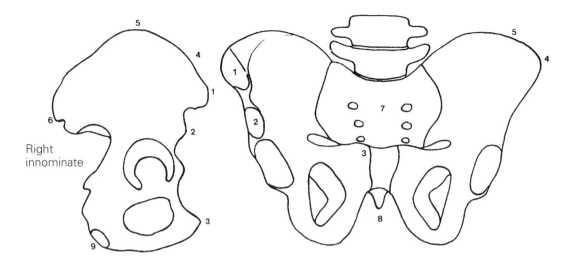

Figure 2–3 Palpable structures of the pelvis. **1**, Anterior superior iliac spine; **2**, anterior inferior iliac spine; **3**, pubic tubercle; **4**, tubercle of the iliac crest; **5**, iliac crest; **6**, posterior superior iliac spine; **7**, sacrum; **8**, coccyx; **9**, ischial tuberosity.

Coccyx

The connection between the sacrum and coccyx can best be palpated by inserting the index finger in the rectum with the thumb on the external aspect of the sacrum (rectal approach; Figure 2–3). This technique is unpleasant for the patient; it should only be done when absolutely necessary and with extreme care. The best position for this procedure is with the patient kneeling and resting the head on the hands. Sterile gloves with a lubricant must be used, and the approach should be performed slowly. This examination may elicit severe pain. Severe pain is especially prevalent after a blow or other trauma to the coccyx. Pain at the level of the coccyx can also be referred pain coming from the lumbar spine. A variety of extreme pain complaints in this area may be categorized under the name *coccygodynia* or *coccygalgia*.

During careful palpation, exostoses (benign growths at the surface of a bone) and

subluxations of the sacrococcygeal joint can sometimes be felt.

Sacroiliac Joint

The sacroiliac joint itself is not palpable. Small motions are possible in this joint and can be seen as rotations around variable transverse axes. These motions are called nutation and counternutation. Attempts to determine sacroiliac motion by palpation are not reliable because of the many soft tissue structures covering these joints. Also, during testing of these joints involving stretching and relaxation, the soft tissues can simulate motions of these joints.

Ischial Tuberosity

The ischial tuberosity is a prominent bony structure coming from the ischial bone in a dorsocaudolateral direction (Figures 2–3 and 2–11). It is palpable at the lower edge of the gluteus maximus muscle, just lateral to the anal cleft. Palpation is easier during flexion of the hip, when the tuberosity is no longer covered by muscle.

The hamstrings insertion at the posterior and lateral aspects of the ischial tuberosity should be palpated for tenderness. Palpation can be performed at the caudal aspect of the tuberosity to test for the possibility of a bursitis.

Sacrotuberal Ligament

The sacrotuberal ligament is usually easy to palpate between the ischial tuberosity and the sacrum. Palpation should be performed with the fingers transverse to the ligament. The sacrospinal ligament is usually not palpable.

Lesser Trochanter

Palpation of the lesser trochanter is difficult and is mostly indirect. It is possible to locate it from a dorsal aspect when the subject is completely relaxed and the clinician positions the leg in extension and internal rotation.

The lesser trochanter is located deeply lateral to the ischial tuberosity. It may be located from a ventral approach when the leg is positioned in external rotation. The clinician palpates the pectineus muscle, gently bringing the fingers deeper. The subject should be in a supine position for both techniques.

Greater Trochanter

The greater trochanter is usually easy to palpate. Accurately marking its location and dimensions may take some practice. During anthropometric evaluation it is common to use the proximal border of the greater trochanter as a reference point (Figure 2–4). When the leg is abducted, an obvious depression above the greater trochanter is visible. The greater trochanter should be in the same

frontal plane as the pubic tubercle, the femoral head, and the coccyx.

PALPATION OF MUSCLES AND OTHER SOFT TISSUE STRUCTURES OF THE PELVIS AND THE THIGH

Note: There is no rigid sequence for palpation of the pelvis and thigh. The method presented here is based on experiences in the clinic and from teaching surface anatomy techniques.

Sartorius Muscle

The sartorius muscle is the longest muscle in the human body (Figures 2–1, 2–5, 2–6, 2–7, and 2–10). Its origin is at the anterior superior iliac spine. This muscle has its own fascial

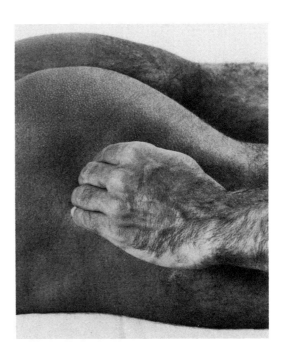

Figure 2–4 Palpation of the greater trochanter. The palpating fingers are moved from the iliac crest in a distal direction until the proximal border of the greater trochanter is felt.

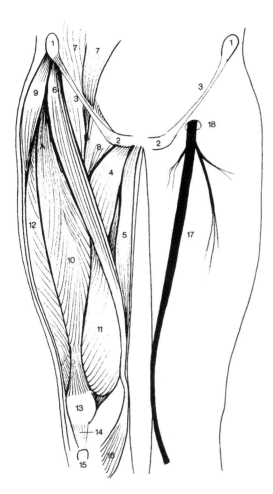

Figure 2–5 Thigh, anterior view. **A**, Lateral femoral triangle; **B**, medial femoral triangle; **1**, anterior superior iliac spine; **2**, pubic tubercle; **3**, inguinal ligament; **4**, adductor longus muscle; **5**, gracilis muscle; **6**, sartorius muscle; **7**, iliopsoas muscle; **8**, pectineus muscle; **9**, tensor fasciae latae muscle; **10**, rectus femoris muscle; **11**, vastus medialis muscle; **12**, vastus lateralis muscle; **13**, patella; **14**, patellar ligament; **15**, tibial tuberosity; **16**, pes anserinus; **17**, great saphenous vein; **18**, saphenous hiatus.

behind the medial femoral condyle and then swings forward again. Together with the gracilis and semitendinosus muscles, the sartorius inserts into the pes anserinus at the tibial tuberosity.

The proximal part the muscle is easily visible when the hip is externally rotated, abducted, and flexed with a flexed knee (cross-legged sitting position). Resistance against this position will make palpation of this muscle easier. For better training, however, it is best to concentrate on learning the palpation when the muscle is relaxed.

Palpation of the sartorius should be performed from proximal to distal using alternating pressure from two fingers. The index and middle fingers are placed at either side of the muscle in a longitudinal direction. During movement in the distal direction, the fingers should apply varying amounts of pressure.

To understand positioning of the sartorius muscle behind the femoral condyle, refer to Chapter 8. The pes anserinus is easily visible in thin people, but it is not possible to differentiate among the sartorius, gracilis, and semitendinosus muscles because they attach via the pes anserinus to the tibial tuberosity.

Lateral Femoral Triangle

Orientation in the area of the hip abductors should begin with location of the lateral femoral triangle (Figures 2–5, 2–6, 2–7, and 2–8). The medial border of this triangle is the sartorius muscle, and its lateral border is the tensor fasciae latae muscle; the apex is formed by the anterior superior iliac spine. The triangle has the form of an inverse V (a V with the tip cranial). It is made visible during active hip flexion and external rotation with slight abduction.

Origin of the Rectus Femoris Muscle

The tendon of the rectus femoris is most clearly palpable in the lateral femoral triangle, approximately 5 cm distal from the anterior

sheath and courses in a spiral fashion down the thigh from proximolateral to distomedial, where it crosses the rectus femoris and adductor longus muscles. The sartorius runs

superior iliac spine, between the tensor fasciae latae and sartorius muscles (Figures 2–5 and 2–6). The best way to perform this palpation is transversely on the fibers. (In the search for the anterior inferior iliac spine, the palpation is longitudinal to the fibers.)

In lesions of the rectus femoris tendon, pain is rarely provoked when the hip is flexed against resistance. The patient almost always experiences pain, however, during resisted knee extension while in a prone position.

Tensor Fasciae Latae Muscle and Iliotibial Tract

The tensor fasciae latae muscle is made visible by bringing the straight leg into abduction with at least 45° of flexion (Figures 2–1, 2–5, 2–6, 2–7, and 2–8). When resistance is applied in this position, the muscle becomes more obvious, and palpation is easier. The muscle is most prominent just distal and lateral to the anterior superior iliac spine. Dorsal to this muscle, a depression is visible in the direction of the gluteus maximus muscle.

The tensor fasciae latae muscle can be palpated from proximal to distal with the use of the alternating finger method, up to the point where it connects with the iliotibial tract. The iliotibial tract is a reinforcement of the fascia lata (the deep fascia of the region), which can be felt on the lateral side of the leg as a bandlike structure. Both sides should be compared, realizing that the iliotibial tract runs at the lateral aspect of the thigh and inserts at the tibia (not at the fibula). In the vicinity of the insertion, care should be taken in differentiating among the iliotibial tract, the biceps femoris tendon, and the lateral collateral ligament; the latter two structures are found

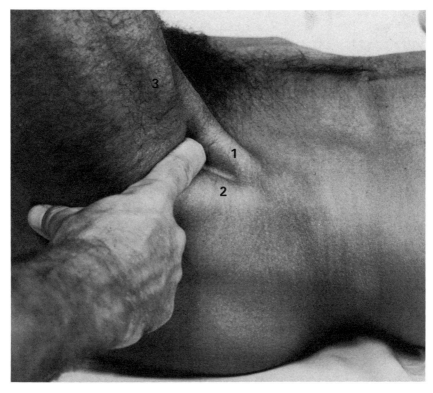

Figure 2–6 Palpation of the rectus femoris tendon. **1**, Sartorius muscle; **2**, tensor fasciae latae muscle; **3**, rectus femoris muscle.

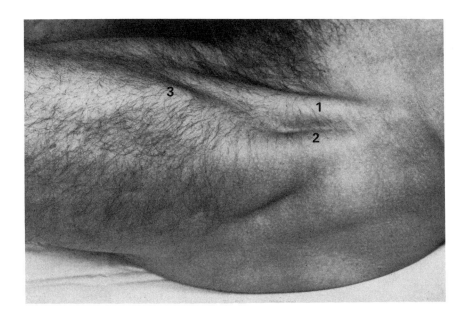

Figure 2–7 Lateral femoral triangle. **1**, Sartorius muscle; **2**, tensor fasciae latae muscle; **3**, rectus femoris muscle.

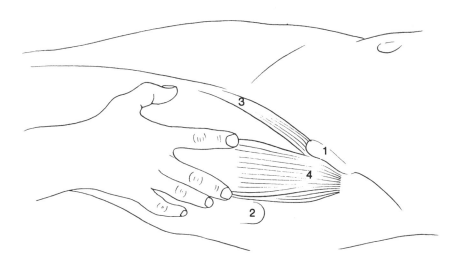

Figure 2–8 Alternating palpation with two fingers of the same hand following the edges of the tensor fasciae latae muscle. Left thigh, anterolateral view. **1**, Anterior superior iliac spine; **2**, greater trochanter; **3**, sartorius muscle; **4**, tensor fasciae latae muscle.

more posterior and have insertions at the fibula (see Chapter 8). The iliotibial tract can be most easily palpated distally with the help of alternating finger palpation.

To evaluate a contracture of the tensor fasciae latae, the patient should lie on the unaffected side. In so doing, the leg being assessed lies on top, and the other leg is positioned in slight extension. The top leg can now be adducted; if there is a contracture of the tensor fasciae latae, this motion is limited.

Gluteus Medius Muscle

Because of its association with the tensor fasciae latae muscle, it is useful to palpate the gluteus medius muscle, even though it does not belong to the area of the lateral femoral triangle. To palpate the gluteus medius muscle, the leg should be abducted with the knee straight. From this position, the anterior part of the gluteus medius can be palpated directly behind the already marked tensor fasciae latae. (Most of the gluteus medius is covered by the gluteus maximus.)

The fibers of the anterior part of the gluteus medius muscle run longitudinally and slightly backward; the fibers from the posterior part run longitudinally and slightly forward. These fiber orientations give the anterior part of this muscle an internal rotating effect on the hip. Because the tensor fasciae latae produces an external rotating effect on the hip, by asking the subject to make alternating internal and external rotation, the borders between the two muscles can be easily palpated.

In cases of a paretic gluteus medius, the pelvis cannot be fixated when the patient is standing on the affected leg. This produces a tilting of the pelvis toward the unaffected side (thus toward the leg that is in the swing phase). At the same time, the hip of the

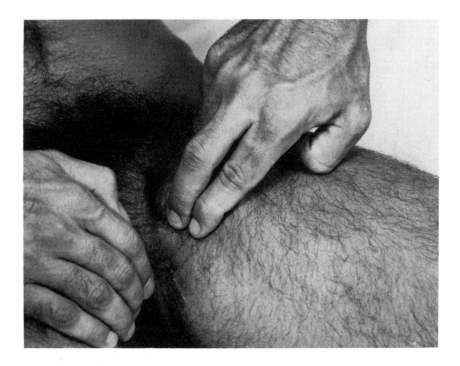

Figure 2–9 Palpation of the edge of the adductor longus muscle.

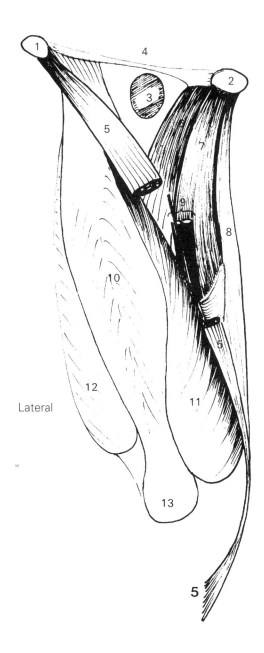

Figure 2–10 Right leg, anterior view. **1**, Anterior superior iliac spine; **2**, pubic tubercle; **3**, iliopectineal bursa (psoas bursa), iliopsoas muscle removed; **4**, inguinal ligament; **5**, sartorius muscle; **6**, pectineus muscle; **7**, adductor longus muscle; **8**, gracilis muscle; **9**, adductor canal (femoral artery and vein, saphenous nerve); **10**, rectus femoris muscle; **11**, vastus medialis muscle; **12**, vastus lateralis muscle; **13**, patella.

Lateral

stance leg shifts outward. The patient appears to "hang" in the lateral ligaments of the affected hip joint. This visible symptom is called the Trendelenburg sign.

The gluteus minimus muscle is completely covered by other muscles and cannot be palpated.

Adductor Longus Muscle

During resisted adduction of the leg, a round cord is visible and palpable distal to the pubic tubercle. This cord is the border of the adductor longus, which is palpable from the pubic tubercle to the point where it crosses underneath the sartorius muscle (Figures 2–9 and 2–10). The pubic tubercle, from which the adductor longus originates, can be reached by following the tendon in a proximal direction. The distal insertion of the adductor longus muscle is not easily palpable.

The origin can be tender during applied pressure. This increased sensitivity is often seen in swimmers, long distance runners, soccer players, and other athletes in whom excessive force is placed on the adductors. Without care or treatment, chronic tendinitis can develop.

Gracilis Muscle

The gracilis muscle is palpable medial and posterior to the adductor longus muscle (Figures 2–5, 2–10, 2–11, and 2–12). The palpation is most effective when the transverse palpation technique is used. This muscle feels like a rolling band and can be followed from the groin to the pes anserinus, where it has a collective insertion with the sartorius and semitendinosus muscles. For a discussion of palpation techniques used behind the medial femoral condyle, refer to Chapter 8.

Adductor Magnus Muscle

This muscle is palpable for only a small portion of its large surface (Figures 2–11 and 2–12). There is a small triangle, in which the muscle is easily palpable, located posterior to the gracilis muscle and anterior to the (still to be discussed) semimembranosus muscle.

The proximal part of the medial femoral condyle can be reached by pushing the palpating fingers deeply along the inner side of the thigh in a distal direction. By using a deep transverse palpation just posterior to the vastus medialis, the clinician can feel a tendinous structure. This is the most distal part of the adductor magnus, which inserts at a bony prominence on the condyle, the adductor tubercle.

Medial Femoral Triangle (Scarpa's Triangle*)

The most ideal position for evaluation of the medial femoral triangle is one that brings the hip in slight flexion, external rotation, and abduction (Figures 2–5 and 2–10). Because it is important that the subject is relaxed, this position can best be achieved passively with the subject supine.

Cranial Border

The cranial border of the medial femoral triangle is the inguinal ligament, seen as a reinforced caudal border of the aponeurosis of the external oblique abdominal muscle. This collagenous thickening of the fascia between the pubic tubercle and the anterior superior iliac spine can be felt by placing a finger in the fold of the groin with palpation parallel and in a cranial direction. It is extremely important during this palpation to avoid compressing the lymph nodes.

Medial and Lateral Borders

The medial border of the triangle is formed by the adductor longus and gracilis muscles. The lateral border is formed by the sartorius muscle. The floor is formed by the iliopsoas and the pectineus muscles, which are difficult to palpate.

The roof can be seen as the superficial fascia, which is continuous with the superficial abdominal fascia and the inguinal ligament. This fascia is separated into layers. Between these layers are lymph nodes and the great saphenous vein. A deeper fascial compartment lies dorsal to the entering vessels, which have their own fascial envelope. These vessels enter the triangle through the femoral sheath. The anterior part of this sheath consists of the continuation of the fascia from the transverse abdominal muscle (the innermost fascia from the abdominal wall). The posterior part of this sheath is a continuation of the fascia from the iliacus muscle. There is an opening between the superficial fascia and the femoral sheath, called the saphenous hiatus, through which the more superficial great saphenous vein empties into the deeper lying femoral vein.

Lacuna Vasorum

A slip of fascia runs from the inguinal ligament to the iliopectineal eminence, separating the space between the inguinal ligament and the innominate bone into two parts: the lateral lacuna musculorum, containing the iliopsoas muscle and femoral nerve, and the medial lacuna vasorum through which the femoral artery and vein run. As already mentioned, the femoral artery and vein have their own fascial sheath, the femoral sheath. A separate lymph node (Rosenmüller's† node) and a certain amount of fatty tissue are located in the lacuna vasorum. The lacuna vasorum is spacious enough to let the femoral vein expand (expansion function).

The lacuna vasorum is a potential site for a hernia (femoral hernia). Care must be taken not to confuse the femoral hernia with the inguinal hernia. The inguinal hernia is located cranial to the inguinal ligament. The protru-

---

*Antonio Scarpa, Italian anatomist and surgeon, 1752–1832.

†Johan Christian Rosenmüller, German anatomist, 1771–1820.

sion of a femoral hernia is located caudo-lateral to the pubic tubercle. An extensive femoral hernia can protrude through the saphenous hiatus, however, in which case part of the contents can be found cranial to the inguinal ligament. Even so, it is not diffi-cult to differentiate between hernias because, in general, with inguinal hernias the contents protrude into the scrotum or the labia majora; this is not the case with femoral hernias.

Femoral Artery, Vein, and Nerve

The femoral artery exits the abdominal cavity through the lacuna vasorum and is pal-pable under the midinguinal point. This pal-pation is a valuable means of orientation. Sometimes slight compression is necessary on this palpation to feel the pulsation of the artery. In most cases only slight pressure is needed.

The femoral vein enters the pelvis through the lacuna vasorum. The vein is located about 1.5 cm medial to the artery. Generally, it is not palpable.

The femoral nerve leaves the pelvis through the lacuna musculorum, just lateral to the femoral artery. This nerve is best pal-pated directly under the inguinal ligament, where it can be felt as a rolling cord. This should be a transverse palpation and done carefully.

Inguinal Lymph Nodes

Numerous lymph nodes are present in the groin region. Many patients will be seen with lymph nodes swollen in this area. This condi-tion does not necessarily mean that serious pathology is present, but further evaluation is needed. Small inflammations of the leg are the most common cause of this condition. If swollen lymph nodes are present, extreme care must be taken during palpation in the area to avoid causing unnecessary pain.

There are both superficial and deep layers of lymph nodes. The superficial layer is ori-ented horizontally and longitudinally. The deep layer lies parallel to the great saphenous vein, draining tissue in the superficial area of the leg. The horizontal layer is directly distal to the inguinal ligament, draining the skin from the back, buttocks, and lower third of the abdomen as well as a part of the perineum, scrotum and penis, the distal part of the vagina, and the distal part of the anus. The superficial lymph nodes have a connec-tion with the deeper nodes, which lie medial to the femoral vein, via the saphenous hiatus.

Palpable swellings may be felt in the medial femoral triangle. Swellings in this area can have different causes. Common causes in-clude inflammations or malignant processes, hernia or varicose conditions, abscesses, a neuroma of the femoral nerve, or an aneu-rysm of the femoral artery.

Great Saphenous Vein

The great saphenous vein enters the upper leg mediodorsal to the medial femoral condyle (Figure 2–5). The topography is vari-able. In its proximal course, the vein runs more ventrally and slightly more medially. In the saphenous hiatus, the vein runs deep to empty into the femoral vein. The saphenous hiatus is an opening in the fascia lata, distal and medial to the midinguinal point. In gen-eral, the hiatus is not easily palpable. In some people, the great saphenous vein is easy to see and palpate; in others, it may be difficult or impossible.

Adductor Canal

From the distal point of the medial femoral triangle, the femoral artery and vein run through the groove formed by the vastus me-dialis and adductor longus muscles (Figure 2–10). For some distance they run together with the sensory branch of the femoral nerve, the saphenous nerve. The roof of the adductor canal (which can be located by indirect palpation) is the sartorius muscle.

Iliopsoas and Pectineus Muscles

Two to three parts of the iliopsoas muscle originate in the pelvis. These are the iliacus, psoas major, and (sometimes) the psoas minor. The iliopsoas muscle runs in the lacuna musculorum under the inguinal ligament and inserts at the lesser trochanter (Figure 2–5. The pectineus muscle has its origin on the pubic bone, runs medial to the iliopsoas muscle, and inserts at the femur (Figure 2–5). Together, the iliopsoas and pectineus muscles form the floor of the medial femoral triangle.

It is advisable, for the palpation of these muscles, to locate the femoral artery first. Lateral to the femoral artery, the iliopsoas muscle is palpable during resisted hip flexion. During resisted hip flexion with slight adduction, the pectineus muscle is palpable medial to the femoral artery.

The iliopectineal bursa, which is located between the hip joint and the iliacus muscle, can cause pain when inflamed (Figure 2–10).

Gluteus Maximus Muscle

The gluteus maximus muscle gives the buttocks its typical round contour (Figures 2–11 and 2–12). The muscle is clearly visible during forceful extension of the hip. The complete surface of the muscle can be palpated. It is difficult for inexperienced clinicians to determine the upper edge of this muscle, and often it is estimated either too high or too low. An effective orienting procedure is to draw a line from the posterior superior iliac spine to the upper edge of the greater trochanter. This line roughly describes the upper border of this muscle. The lower edge is not the fold of the buttocks but rather crosses beyond. To locate it, place the palpating finger in the fold of the buttocks, and palpate from medial to lateral. The exact location of the lower edge is an important prerequisite for finding the sciatic nerve, which is sometimes palpable around this edge. The lateral part of this muscle is easiest to find when the muscle is contracted.

Bursae

Two bursae can be found under the gluteus maximus muscle (Figures 2–11 and 2–12). It is deceptively easy to diagnose complaints of pain in the buttocks area as sciatica when the true cause is a bursitis. Patients complaining of pain in this area often have a history of overtraining or excessive sitting. Deep pressure can be effectively used to localize the most painful spot. In most instances, this will be the location of a bursa.

The ischial bursa of the gluteus maximus is found between that muscle and the most cranial part of the ischial tuberosity. The trochanteric bursa is located between the greater trochanter and the gluteus maximus muscle.

Pain in the buttocks is often a sign of hip disorders. An occlusion of the caudal part of the aorta can cause the exact same complaints. It is easy to tell the difference because in the latter case the complaints will increase significantly *during* activities.

Hamstrings

The hamstrings, with the exception of the short head of the biceps femoris muscle, have a common origin on the ischial tuberosity (Figures 2–11 and 2–12). This origin is visible when the subject is in the prone position and resists knee flexion. Distal to the fold of the buttocks, a muscle elevation is clearly visible.

Semitendinosus Muscle

When the lower leg is flexed and internally rotated, the thin round tendon of the semitendinosus is clearly visible and palpable medially in the back of the knee. Place a finger on each side of the round tendon, and follow the tendon (and muscle belly) in a proximal di-

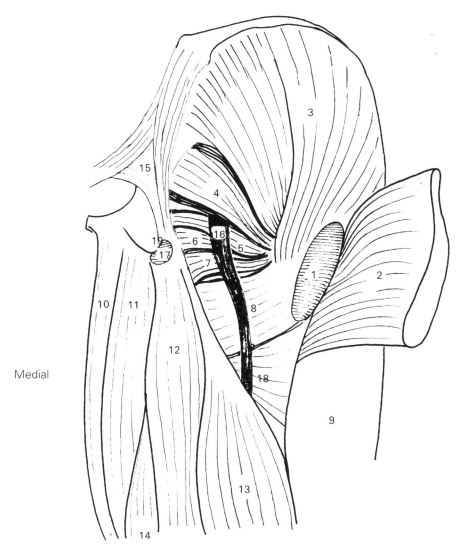

Medial

Figure 2–11 Right leg, posterior view. **1**, Trochanteric bursa of the gluteus maximus muscle; **2**, gluteus maximus muscle; **3**, gluteus medius muscle; **4**, piriformis muscle; **5**, superior gemellus muscle; **6**, obturator internus muscle; **7**, inferior gemellus muscle; **8**, quadratus femoris muscle; **9**, iliotibial tract; **10**, gracilis muscle; **11**, adductor magnus muscle; **12**, semitendinosus muscle; **13**, biceps femoris muscle (long head); **14**, semimembranosus muscle; **15**, sacrotuberal ligament; **16**, sciatic nerve; **17**, ischial bursa of the gluteus maximus muscle; **18**, palpation site for sciatic nerve; **19**, ischial tuberosity.

rection. Without too much pressure, let the fingers glide along the muscle to its origin.

Semimembranosus Muscle

At its distal end, the semimembranosus can be palpated at a deeper level both medial and lateral to the semitendinosus tendon. Its lateral edge can be followed proximally over a relatively small area with the use of a deep palpation starting in the middle of the back of the knee. The entire medial border of the muscle can be palpated. The proper technique is to use the full length of a finger, pal-

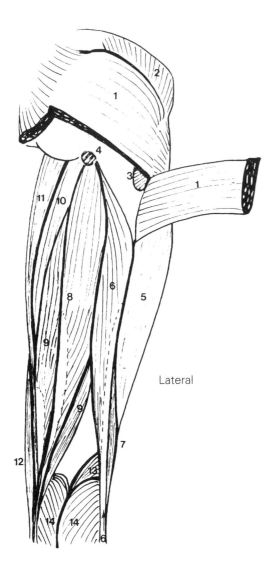

Lateral

Figure 2–12 Right leg; posterior view. **1**, Gluteus maximus muscle; **2**, gluteus medius muscle; **3**, trochanteric bursa of the gluteus maximus muscle; **4**, ischial bursa of the gluteus maximus muscle; **5**, vastus lateralis muscle and iliotibial tract; **6**, long head of the biceps femoris muscle; **7**, short head of the biceps femoris muscle; **8**, semitendinosus muscle; **9**, semimembranosus muscle; **10**, adductor magnus muscle; **11**, gracilis muscle; **12**, sartorius muscle; **13**, plantaris muscle; **14**, gastrocnemius muscle.

pating transversely in the groove between the semitendinosus and semimembranosus muscles.

The semimembranosus does not insert at the pes anserinus but rather at a deeper group of structures located posteromedially in the knee joint. These structures are collectively termed the pes anserinus profundus. The main tendon of the semimembranosus is sometimes palpable at the anteromedial aspect of the knee, just distal to the medial tibial condyle.

Biceps Femoris Muscle

Make the biceps femoris muscle visible by placing the lower leg in flexion and external rotation against resistance. The long head should be easily visible (Figures 2–11 and 2–12).

An effective technique in palpating this muscle is to use the same method as used with the semitendinosus: start at the back of the knee. The biceps femoris is palpable to the point of its insertion on the fibula head. A large part of the long head borders on the vastus lateralis muscle. Protected by the insertion tendon of the biceps femoris, the common peroneal nerve runs medial to this structure through the popliteal fossa, where it is palpable. The short head of the biceps femoris muscle is palpable, at some depth, between the iliotibial tract insertion and the biceps femoris long head, up to the level where the vastus lateralis and biceps femoris meet.

The best place to palpate the sciatic nerve is located by following the lateral edge of the biceps femoris muscle in a proximal direction to just under the edge of the gluteus maximus. On deep palpation, the sciatic nerve can be felt as a large, round cord slightly lateral to the biceps femoris muscle and just distal to the gluteus maximus muscle.

Quadriceps Femoris Muscle

In most people, the quadriceps femoris muscle with its different parts is clearly visible when the knee is forcefully extended against resistance.

Rectus Femoris Muscle

The rectus femoris muscle is best palpated from proximal to distal by placing a finger on both sides of the muscle and palpating with alternating fingers (Figures 2–5 and 2–10). About midthigh, the muscle belly becomes wider; this width is quite often underestimated by the palpating clinician. The tendon takes an hourglass form distally, where it inserts at the tibial tuberosity via the patella.

Vastus Medialis Muscle (and Vastus Medialis Obliquus Muscle)

The vastus medialis muscle is located between the sartorius and rectus femoris muscles and is easily visible at the end phase of active extension (Figures 2–5 and 2–10). The muscle should be palpated from a distal direction. It should be noted that the muscle belly of the vastus medialis runs more distal than the muscle belly of the vastus lateralis.

The muscle inserts at the upper edge of the patella, with fibers running almost horizontally. The lateral part of the muscle has a connection to the medial patellar retinaculum via the patella. The medial part of the muscle, the vastus medialis obliquus, along with the medial patellar retinaculum, is important for stabilization of the patella.

In any kind of knee injury or degeneration, atrophy is visible in this muscle. The vastus lateralis muscle atrophies less quickly. Repetitive measuring of the size of the upper leg at the level of the vastus medialis muscle can be used to gauge improvements or deterioration in the condition of the knee.

Vastus Lateralis Muscle

The vastus lateralis muscle is most easily palpated after the borders of the rectus femoris muscle have been determined (Figures 2–5 and 2–10). The vastus lateralis is palpable directly lateral to the rectus femoris. The muscle is palpable for the most part, although it is partially covered by the iliotibial tract. Its posterior edge can best be palpated after the easily found biceps femoris muscle is marked; the vastus lateralis runs just next to and along the lateral edge of the biceps femoris.

It is remarkable how many inexperienced clinicians "locate" the posterodistal border of the vastus lateralis muscle at the level of the posterior edge of the iliotibial tract. The posterodistal border of the vastus lateralis is difficult to palpate. The best technique is to feel the distal tendon of the iliotibial tract as well as the tendon of the biceps femoris posterior to it. When the palpating finger is placed in the groove between these two structures, the short head of the biceps femoris muscle is felt; just proximal to the knee, where the groove narrows, the posterodistal edge of the vastus lateralis can be palpated.

The tendon of the vastus lateralis muscle is at the level of the proximolateral part of the patella. It feels like a thick cord about 4 cm long. It is easily palpable, especially when the knee is actively extended.

Anatomy and palpation sites for the nerves and blood vessels of the lower extremity are discussed in Appendix A.

Chapter 3

Examination of the Hip

HIP JOINT (ARTICULATIO COXAE)

- **Zero position:** The upper leg is in line with the trunk. A perpendicular line from the anterior superior iliac spine to the middle of the patella makes a right angle with a line connecting the underside of both anterior superior iliac spines.
- **Maximal loose-packed position:** Approximately 30° flexion, 30° abduction, and slight external rotation.
- **Maximal close-packed position**
  1. Ligamentous close-packed position: Maximal extension, internal rotation, and adduction.
  2. Bony close-packed position: Maximal extension, internal rotation, and abduction.
- **Capsular pattern:** Internal rotation has the greatest amount of limitation. Extension, flexion, and abduction have limitations of motion that are about equal. External rotation and adduction are least limited (Figure 3–1).

OVERVIEW OF THE FUNCTIONAL EXAMINATION

Most lesions of the hip joint, but also lesions of many of the periarticular structures, cause pain in the groin. In addition, radiating pain often occurs, particularly in the L3 dermatome (anterior aspect of the thigh, the knee, and part of the lower leg). It should also be kept in mind that pain from hip disorders can be felt in *part* of the L3 dermatome. For example, there is often only anterior knee pain when there is coxarthrosis. In such cases, the functional examination of the knee does not provoke the patient's symptoms, but functional examination of the hip will elicit pain.

The groin region is a meeting point of several dermatomes, such as the T12, L1, L2, L3, S3, and S4 dermatomes. Additionally, groin pain can be seen occasionally in L4 and L5 nerve root syndromes. Making matters even more confusing is the fact that a large number of other disorders can also cause groin pain. Included are such disorders as the various hernias in the groin region (inguinal, femoral, and the rarer obturator), some affections of the urogenital tract, and swelling of the local lymph glands. Groin pain can also be caused by problems occurring in the sacroiliac joint or the pubic symphysis.

Hip pathology can cause pain in the back and in the gluteal region as well. This is in part because the L3 dermatome is found in these regions and additionally because the load on the back can change because of the hip disorders. There are also problems caused in the gluteal region, where there is an overlapping of several dermatomes, including L4 (sometimes), L5, S1, and S2. In most cases, however, pain in the gluteal region is caused by a lumbar problem.

Because of this, it is not always easy to differentiate lesions of the hip joint or periarticular structures from lesions of the lumbar spine, sacroiliac joint and pubic symphysis, or the urogenital tract. The examination with

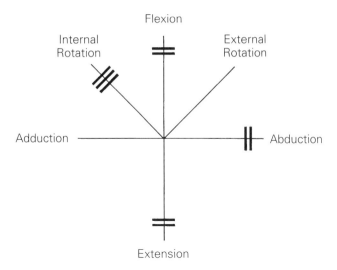

Figure 3–1 Capsular pattern of the hip.

the patient standing and walking, the patient's history, and the functional examination have to be performed carefully and thoroughly.

General Inspection

As the patient enters the room, the examiner should observe the gait pattern, general posture, facial expression, and whether the patient uses assistive devices. Many disturbances in gait are characteristic of specific disorders.

History

(Refer also to "History" in *Diagnosis and Treatment of the Spine*, pp. 153–154.)

Age, Occupation, Hobby, Sport

Many disorders of the hip are only seen at specific ages. Examples include transient synovitis of the hip (coxitis fugax) and Perthes' disease in young children, slipped capital femoral epiphysis in teenagers, osteochondrosis dissecans in adolescents, and coxarthrosis in adults.

Workers in certain occupations put a great demand on the hip joint. Examples of these are people engaged in heavy labor and those who frequently have to carry heavy loads. Soccer, for example, is a sport where groin pain (pubalgia) is often seen.

Chief Complaints

- Pain? Where and when?
- Swelling? With or without fever?
- Paresthesia: Where and when?
- Disturbed gait pattern?

The location of the pain is important in ruling out lumbar disorders. If the pain occurs exclusively in the groin during weight bearing, it is likely that there is indeed a hip problem. Pain that particularly occurs at the beginning of weight-bearing activities can be due to coxarthrosis (early stage) or a tendopathy in young adults. Pain that is especially felt at night can indicate the presence of a tumor.

Swelling in the groin is usually caused by the local lymph glands. It is rare that there is such a severe iliopectineal bursitis that swelling occurs. Swelling in conjunction with a fever can indicate an abscess, which may, for example, be caused by tuberculosis.

Paresthesia at the anterolateral side of the thigh is quite often caused by meralgia paresthetica, a compression neuropathy of the lateral femoral cutaneous nerve at the level of the anterior superior iliac spine. Paresthesia in the groin area itself can be caused by compression of the smaller nerves in that area, such as the obturator or ilioinguinal nerves. Such paresthesia can occur during either sitting or walking, which, taken together with the localization of symptoms, is not characteristic of a lesion of the lumbar spine.

A disturbed gait pattern is rarely the only complaint. Sometimes in small children, however, the parents notice that the child does not walk normally. This may be the result of a subluxation of the hip, for example.

Onset

Conditions surrounding the onset of symptoms are important in determining the causal treatment. If the symptoms are the result of a specific incident, the examiner should try to determine as precisely as possible what exactly happened. If the symptoms arose spontaneously, it is important to acquire as much information as possible about the loads placed on the patient during work or sports activities.

Type of Pain

- Aching?
- Sharp?
- Sharp stabbing, twinges?

Aching pain is often experienced in later stages of coxarthrosis. Patients usually complain of sharp pain during activities when there is a tendinitis, particularly in the third clinical stage. Sharp, stabbing pain can result from tendinitis but is much more often due to loose bodies in the joint.

Duration of the Symptoms

Duration of the symptoms can provide general information as to the severity of the lesion and prognosis. This holds true for joint disorders as well as for lesions of the periarticular structures. The shorter the duration of symptoms and the earlier treatment is initiated, the more successful and the quicker will be the results achieved by therapy.

Involvement of Other Joints

If the patient has problems in joints besides the hip, the possibility of a systemic disease should be considered.

Previous Surgery

Previous hip surgeries, such as an osteotomy, quite often require a second surgery to relieve symptoms. Other surgeries may have been performed for malignant pathology. In this instance, the possibility of metastases needs to be ruled out.

Medications

If the patient is taking anticoagulants, most forms of mechanical therapy, such as transverse friction or manipulation, are contraindicated. If the patient is on nonsteroidal antiinflammatory medication and is getting relief from the symptoms, one should suspect pathology in which inflammation is involved, such as coxarthritis. If the patient is on antihypertensive medication, any exercise program should be closely monitored (specifically, the patient's blood pressure during the exercises). The patient should also be instructed to breathe in a relaxed manner during the exercises and never to hold the breath. If the patient is on antidepressant medication, the symptoms being experienced may be complicated by psychologic factors.

Previous Treatment and Results

The question of previous treatment is important with regard to planning the current treatment program. In general, a treatment that has already been applied and was not successful should not be repeated, unless there is doubt concerning whether the treatment was correctly performed.

Specific Inspection in Standing

(Refer also to Chapter 2.)

The patient is inspected from the front, the back, and both sides. In so doing, the examiner should pay attention to the patient's complete posture:

- position of the feet
- position of the knees
- position of the legs
- position of the pelvis
- leg length
- presence of atrophy, swelling, or changes in color

Before the functional examination, palpation only for local swelling and skin temperature is performed. When swelling is present, its consistency is determined.

Functional Examination

(Refer also to *Diagnosis and Treatment of the Spine*, pp. 153–157.)

Before the functional examination, it should be noted whether the patient is experiencing symptoms at that specific moment. With each test the examiner should observe whether the symptoms change. Procedurally, the affected side should always be compared with the nonaffected side. The nonaffected side is tested first to have an idea of what is normal for the patient. Even though it may be clear from the first part of the clinical examination (general inspection, patient history, palpation, and specific inspection) that there is hip pathology, the examiner should always begin the basic functional examination of the hip with quick tests for the lumbar spine in standing. If the patient's symptoms are pro-

voked on these tests, the examiner should continue with the appropriate tests for the lumbar spine.

In the following sections, the essential tests that comprise the basic functional examination are printed in ***underlined bold italic*** type. The other tests are performed if warranted by the findings in the basic functional examination.

In Standing

Active motions

3.1   ***Quick tests for the lumbar spine (extension, right and left side-bending, and flexion)***
3.2   ***Trendelenburg's test***
3.3   Active internal rotation of both hips
3.4   Active external rotation of both hips

In Supine

Passive motions

3.5   Passive internal rotation of both hips
3.6   Passive external rotation of both hips
3.7   ***Straight leg raise test***
3.8   ***Sacroiliac joint provocation test***
3.9   ***Passive hip flexion***
3.10   Circumduction test
3.11   ***Passive internal rotation of the hip in 90° flexion***
3.12   ***Passive external rotation of the hip in 90° flexion***
3.13   ***Passive hip abduction with extended knee***
3.14   ***Passive hip adduction***

Resisted tests (and iliopsoas stretch test)

3.15   ***Resisted hip flexion in 90° flexion***

3.16   Resisted hip abduction (bilateral)

3.17   Resisted hip adduction in the neutral position (bilateral)

Prone

Passive tests

3.18   Passive hip extension

3.19   Passive hip extension followed by knee flexion (femoral nerve stretch test)

3.20   Passive bilateral internal rotation, with the knees in 90° flexion

Resisted tests

3.21   Resisted internal rotation of the hip, with the knees in 90° flexion (bilateral)

3.22   Resisted external rotation of the hip, with the knees in 90° flexion (bilateral)

3.23   Resisted hip extension

3.24   Resisted knee extension, with the knee in 90° flexion

3.25   Resisted knee flexion, with the knee in 70° flexion

After the functional examination, palpation is again performed for swelling and temperature. Palpation should also include inspection of the suspected affected structure to localize as precisely as possible the site of the lesion.

Occasionally, special tests should be performed to confirm a diagnosis. These tests are discussed in the clinical findings sections for the various disorders in Chapter 4.

Other examinations can also be performed to confirm a diagnosis or to gain further information when a diagnosis cannot be reached based on the functional examination. These include:

- imaging techniques (conventional radiographs, computed tomography [CT], arthrography, CT arthrography, magnetic resonance imaging, and ultrasonography)
- laboratory tests
- arthroscopy
- electromyography

DESCRIPTION OF THE FUNCTIONAL EXAMINATION

- *Active motions:* Active motions are examined to assess the range of motion and the course of movement. The range of motion measured actively is compared with the range of passive motion. Provocation of the patient's symptoms during the test is also noted. Differentiation among a number of conditions, such as lesions of the hip, lumbar spine, sacroiliac joints, pubic symphysis, and internal organs, is important.

- *Passive motions:* Just as with examination of the active motions, when the passive motions are tested particular attention is paid to the range of motion. In instances of limited motions, it is necessary to determine whether the limitations are in a capsular or noncapsular pattern. It is also important to note the end-feel with each passive test and any provocation of the patient's symptoms.

  During the examination of the hip, movement of the lumbar spine cannot be prevented. For instance, in the passive hip flexion test, the lumbar spine flexes as well; in passive internal rotation of the hip, an ipsilateral sidebend of the lumbar spine takes place; and in external rotation, the lumbar spine sidebends contralaterally.

- *Resisted tests:* The resisted tests are performed to assess the contractile structures for strength and painfulness.

Various bursae located around the hip joint, when affected, can become painfully compressed during isometric contraction of specific muscles.

In Standing

3.1   Quick Tests for the Lumbar Spine (not illustrated)

Quick tests for the lumbar spine consist of the following active motions: extension, left and right sidebending, and flexion.

3.2   Trendelenburg's Test

The patient stands on one leg and lifts the other leg up to approximately 90° hip flexion.

The examiner kneels or sits behind the patient and palpates underneath the posterior superior iliac spine bilaterally.

This test is positive when the posterior superior iliac spine on the standing leg rises or the other side sinks, thus indicating weakness of the gluteus medius on the standing leg side. Possible causes for weakness are pathology whereby the origin and insertion of the muscle are brought closer to each other (such as in a slipped capital femoral epiphysis), congenital subluxation or dislocation of the hip, fractures of the greater trochanter, severe forms of coxarthrosis, and various neurologic diseases.

3.3   Active Internal Rotation of Both Hips

The patient is instructed to keep the knees extended and to try to internally rotate the hips as far as possible.

The examiner ensures that the line connecting both anterior superior iliac spines remains in the frontal plane and observes any asymmetry in the range of motion.

The range of motion is compared with that found in supine with the hips in 0° (Test 3.5)

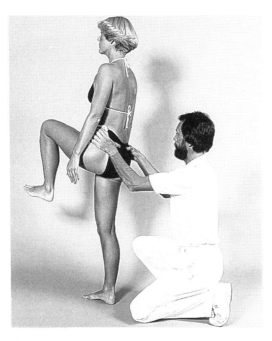

Test 3.2

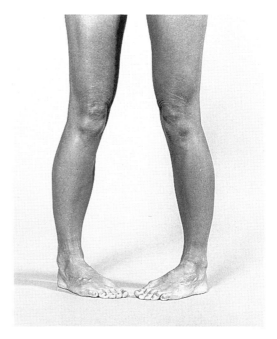

Test 3.3

and 90° flexion (Test 3.11) as well as in prone positions (Test 3.20).

3.4 Active External Rotation of Both Hips

The patient keeps the knees extended and attempts to externally rotate the hips as far as possible.

The examiner ensures that the line connecting both anterior superior iliac spines remains in the frontal plane and observes any asymmetry in the range of motion.

The range of motion is compared with that found in supine with the hips in 0° (Test 3.6) and 90° flexion positions (Test 3.12). Slight asymmetry in the range of motion is almost always observed; in most people, the right hip joint exhibits slightly more external rotation than the left.

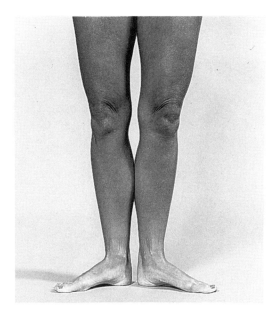

Test 3.4

In Supine

3.5 Passive Internal Rotation of Both Hips (not illustrated)

The examiner grasps the patient's lower legs at the malleoli and maximally internally rotates the patient's hips. The knees remain extended.

Usually there is a pseudoasymmetry in the range of motion as a result of an asymmetric position of the acetabuli.

3.6 Passive External Rotation of Both Hips (not illustrated)

The examiner grasps the patient's lower legs at the malleoli and maximally externally rotates the patient's hips. The knees remain extended.

As with the internal rotation test (Test 3.5), minimal asymmetry in the amount of motion is almost always seen as a result of an almost always present pelvic asymmetry.

3.7 Straight Leg Raise Test

The straight leg raise is a test for pathology of the hamstring muscles and also for the mobility of the nerve roots L4 to S2. (Refer to *Diagnosis and Treatment of the Spine* for interpretation of the straight leg raise test with regard to the lumbar spine.)

The straight leg raise test can be painful and limited in cases of severe pathology of the hip joint. Refer to the section "Sign of the Buttock" in Chapter 4 for more detailed information about this phenomenon.

3.8 Sacroiliac Joint Provocation Test

The patient lies relaxed in a supine position with the legs extended.

The examiner places the hands on the patient's anterior superior iliac spines in such a way that the extended arms are crossed and the shoulders are positioned over the hands. This test puts tension on some ligaments and compresses other ligaments of the sacroiliac joint.

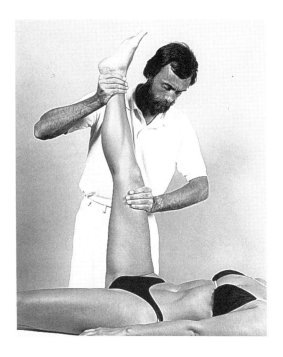

Test 3.7

The test is positive if the patient experiences unilateral pain. This pain can be felt in the abdominal-groin area, the gluteal region, or the leg. If the test is positive, it is repeated with the patient's forearm placed in the small of the back to support the lumbar lordosis. If the test is still positive, sacroiliac pathology is suspected, and the examiner should go on with further testing of the sacroiliac joints. A detailed description of the functional examination of the sacroiliac joints is provided in *Diagnosis and Treatment of the Spine*.

3.9 *Passive Hip Flexion*

The examiner grasps the posterior aspect of the patient's thigh, just proximal to the knee, and flexes the patient's hip as far as possible.

Attention is given to the amount of motion, end-feel (usually soft as a result of soft tissue approximation), and pain provocation. It should be kept in mind that the lumbar spine also flexes during this test. Pain provocation without a limitation of motion usually occurs

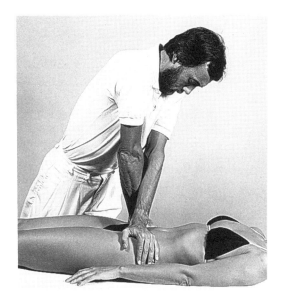

Test 3.8

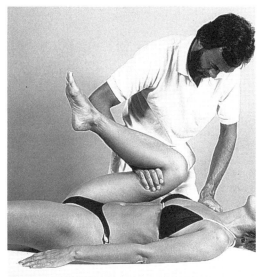

Test 3.9

as the result of compression of an affected structure in the groin region. Limitations of motions can be in a capsular pattern, usually concerning a coxarthrosis, or a noncapsular pattern, which is often due to a loose body.

3.10   Circumduction Test

If the patient's complaints include pain in the groin, the circumduction test should be performed. In the same manner as described in Test 3.9, the examiner maximally flexes the patient's hip (initial position). From this position, the hip is then slowly adducted (hip adduction). In this fashion, the following structures, from lateral to medial, can be compressed:

- insertions of the tensor fasciae latae and sartorius muscles (initial position)
- iliopsoas muscle, iliopectineal bursa, and the neurovascular bundle (mid position)
- insertion of the pectineus muscle
- insertion of the adductor longus muscle (end position)

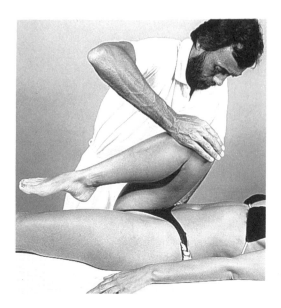

Test 3.10B Mid position

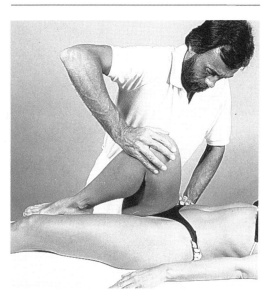

Test 3.10C End position

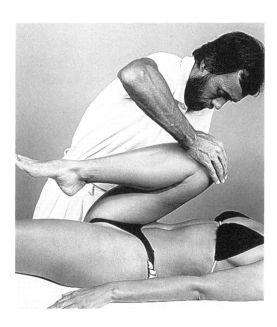

Test 3.10A Initial position

From the position of maximal flexion and adduction, the hip can then be internally rotated (position for internal rotation). If this test provokes the specific symptoms of the patient, a lesion of the acetabular labrum should be suspected (especially if the onset was traumatic).

3.11 *Passive Internal Rotation of the Hip in 90° Flexion*

The examiner grasps the medial aspect of the patient's lower leg with the patient's knee and hip flexed to 90°. The other hand is placed against the anterolateral aspect of the thigh, just proximal to the patient's patella.

The examiner then rotates the lower leg as far outward as possible, while keeping the knee in the same place (internal rotation of the hip). At the end of the range of motion, overpressure is exerted.

Attention is paid to the amount of motion, end-feel, and provocation of pain. The end-feel is usually firm. Limitations of motion are almost always part of a capsular pattern and indicate arthritis or arthrosis of the hip joint. The examiner has to keep in mind that ipsilateral sidebending of the lumbar spine also takes place during this test. Thus in the presence of lumbar pathology, this test could be painful.

3.12 *Passive External Rotation of the Hip in 90° Flexion*

The examiner grasps the lateral aspect of the patient's lower leg with the patient's knee and hip flexed to 90°. The other hand is placed against the anteromedial aspect of the thigh, just proximal to the patient's patella.

The examiner then rotates the lower leg as far as possible inward, while keeping the knee in the same place (external rotation of the hip). At the end of the range of motion, overpressure is exerted.

Attention is paid to the amount of motion, end-feel, and provocation of pain. The end-feel is usually firm. Limitations of motion are usually part of a noncapsular pattern and indicate pathology such as a loose body.

3.13 *Passive Hip Abduction with Extended Knee*

If possible, the patient brings the leg not being tested into abduction to the point where the lower leg hangs over the edge of the table (this position helps fixate the pelvis).

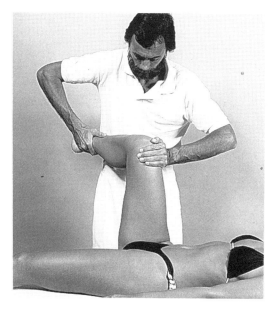

Test 3.11

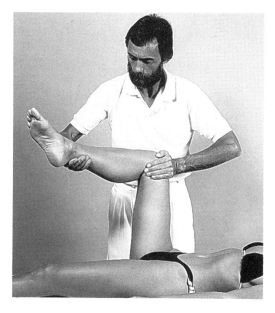

Test 3.12

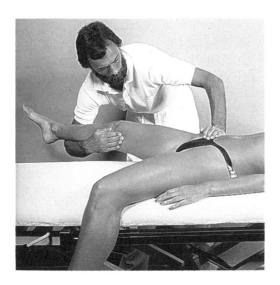

Test 3.13A

In Test 3.13A, the examiner grasps the leg being tested in such a way that the patient's lower leg rests on the volar aspect of the examiner's forearm and the examiner's hand is on the medial aspect of the patient's extended knee. With the other hand, the examiner fixates the patient's pelvis at the lateral aspect, just above the greater trochanter. The examiner abducts the patient's hip on the side being tested, taking care not to bring the patient's hip into flexion. At the end of the range of motion, overpressure is exerted.

Attention is paid to the amount of motion, end-feel, and provocation of pain. The end-feel is usually soft-springy because the motion is normally restricted by increased tension in the hip adductor muscles. Limitation of motion is usually part of a capsular pattern, indicating an arthritis or arthrosis of the hip. Pain without a limitation of motion is usually the result of a lesion of the hip adductors, which are stretched during this test.

If the patient experiences pain during passive hip abduction with extended knee, then, without bringing the hip into flexion, the knee is allowed to flex to 90° (Test 3.13B). In this

manner, the hip is able to abduct further because tension has been momentarily taken away from the gracilis muscle. At the end of the range of motion, overpressure is exerted.

With this procedure, in cases of lesions of the gracilis muscle the following can be observed: Groin pain is provoked during passive abduction with extended knee, which disappears the moment the knee is bent but returns again at the end of the abduction motion. If groin pain is provoked during passive abduction with extended knee and does not disappear the moment the knee is bent, there is more likely to be a lesion of the adductor longus, adductor brevis, or pectineus muscles. In both instances, there is no limitation of motion. In the case of a gracilis lesion, resisted hip adduction and resisted knee flexion must also be painful. In the case of an adductor longus or adductor brevis lesion, resisted hip adduction must be painful. In the case of a pectineus lesion, resisted flexion and resisted adduction of the hip must be painful.

This test can provoke pain in a number of other hip disorders, and therefore it is not specific. If pain is experienced in the greater

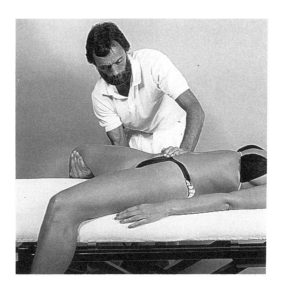

Test 3.13B

trochanter region, however, trochanteric pathology is indicated (eg, a bursitis of one of the bursae found around the greater trochanter).

3.14   *Passive Hip Adduction*

Passive adduction of the hip is only possible if the other leg is flexed or extended in the hip. To achieve this position, the patient places the foot of the side not being tested on the lateral side of the other knee.

The examiner stands opposite the side being tested and grasps the leg being tested from the lateral aspect in such a way that the patient's lower leg rests on the examiner's forearm and the examiner's hand is placed at the lateral aspect of the patient's extended knee. The examiner then adducts the patient's hip as far as possible. Overpressure is exerted at the end of the range of motion.

Attention is paid to limitation of motion, end-feel, and pain provocation. The end-feel is usually soft-springy because the motion is normally restricted by a stretch of the musculature of the pelvic and thigh muscles. Limitations of motion are rarely seen. Pain can be experienced as the result of a stretch of the pelvic and thigh muscles (tensor fasciae latae and iliotibial tract) or compression of the underlying subtrochanteric bursae.

3.15   *Resisted Hip Flexion in 90° Flexion*

The patient is asked to flex the hip to 90°.

The examiner stands at the head of the table on the side being tested. The examiner places one hand against the anterior aspect of the distal thigh, while on the same side the other hand rests on the patient's shoulder.

The patient is instructed to bring the knee in the direction of the ipsilateral shoulder. At the same time, the examiner's extended arm exerts isometric resistance.

In Test 3.15A in particular, the iliopsoas muscle is assessed for strength and pain. Sometimes, even though a lesion of the iliop-

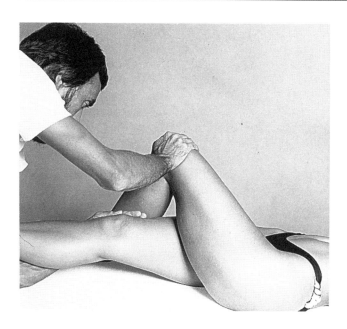

Test 3.14

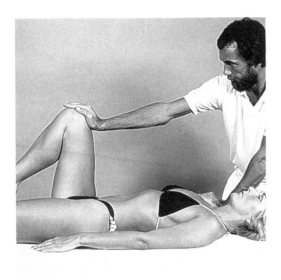

Test 3.15A

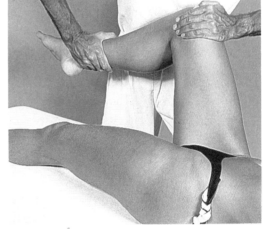

Test 3.15B

soas muscle is suspected, this test is not painful. The muscle can be examined more specifically by means of the tests described below.

The examiner stands next to the side being tested and grasps the medial aspect of the patient's lower leg as distally as possible. The other hand is placed on the anterior aspect of the most distal part of the thigh. The patient flexes the hip to 45°.

The specific function of the iliopsoas, flexion and external rotation of the hip, is tested in Test 3.15B.

The patient is now instructed to move the knee toward the ipsilateral shoulder and simultaneously bring the heel toward the con-

tralateral knee. At the same time, the examiner exerts isometric resistance.

The same test described in test 3.15B can be performed with the muscle in a stretched position. The patient brings the hip to an extended and internally rotated position and tries to move the hip into flexion and external rotation. Again, the examiner exerts simultaneous isometric resistance.

A lesion may cause the iliopsoas to be painful to stretch.

The patient lies in a supine position on the table so that the sacrum is positioned at the short end of the treatment table. The patient brings the side not being tested into maximal flexion by holding the knee to the chest. The leg being tested hangs in a relaxed manner over the edge of the table. The thigh should now lie in the horizontal plane or, if the muscle is "too short," at an angle above the horizontal.

3.16 Resisted Hip Abduction (Bilateral)

The examiner places both hands at the lateral aspect of both of the patient's knees in such a way that the thenar eminences rest just proximal to the joint line.

The patient is asked to bring both legs as forcefully as possible away from each other. At the same time, the examiner exerts isometric resistance.

In this test, the hip abductors are tested for strength and pain.

3.17 Resisted Hip Adduction in the Neutral Position (Bilateral)

The examiner places both hands at the medial aspect of both of the patient's knees in such a way that the thenar eminences rest just proximal to the joint line.

The patient is asked to bring both legs as forcefully as possible toward each other. At the same time, the examiner exerts isometric resistance.

In this test, the hip adductors are tested for strength and pain.

In lesions of the hip adductors, this test alone is not always sufficient to provoke the patient's pain. Because not all patients with a lesion of the hip adductors experience pain when adduction is resisted from this position, the test is repeated with the hips in 45° and 90° flexion. It is not yet clear why some patients with adductor lesions experience pain in 45° but not 0° positions, and vice versa. Empirically, however, if this test is positive a lesion of the gracilis muscle is probable.

The test for resisted hip adduction in 45° hip flexion and 90° knee flexion (bilateral) (not illustrated) is performed in a way similar to that described for Test 3.17A, but now the patient's hips are flexed to 45° with the knees in 90° flexion and the feet resting flat on the table.

Empirically, this test is found to be painful in lesions of the adductor longus or adductor brevis muscles and particularly in pubic symphysis pathology.

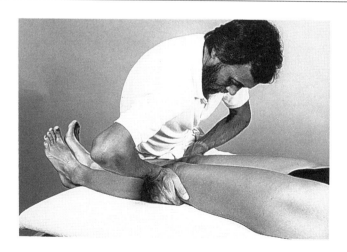

Test 3.16

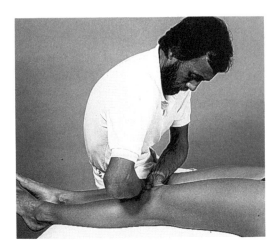

Test 3.17A

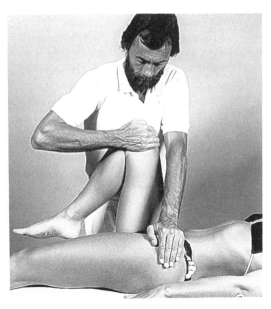

Test 3.17C

For resisted hip adduction in 90° flexion, the patient lies in a supine position and flexes the side being tested to 90° (Test 3.17C).

The examiner stands next to the patient at the side being tested and places one hand at the medial aspect of the patient's knee. The other hand is placed against the anterior aspect of the opposite anterior superior iliac spine.

The patient is now instructed to bring the hip in the direction of the other hip. At the same time, the examiner exerts isometric resistance.

Empirically, this test is less painful in instances of pubic symphysis pathology.

For resisted hip adduction in combination with flexion, with the hip in 70° flexion, the patient lies in a supine position and flexes the side being tested to 70° (Test 3.17D).

The examiner stands next to the patient at the side being tested and places one hand at the medial aspect of the patient's knee. The other hand is placed against the anterior aspect of the opposite anterior superior iliac spine.

From this position of 70° hip flexion, the patient is asked to bring the knee of the side being tested toward the contralateral hip (adduction in combination with flexion).

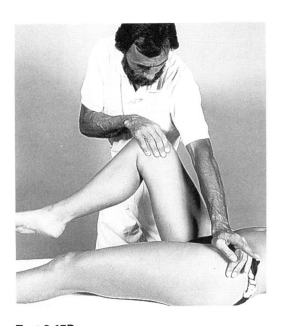

Test 3.17D

This test is specific for assessing strength and painfulness of the pectineus muscle. In instances of a pectineus lesion, Tests 3.13A and 3.13B are usually also painful as a result of stretch, and Tests 3.10A through 3.10C can be painful as a result of compression of the injured muscle.

In Prone

3.18 Passive Hip Extension

The examiner stands on the side to be tested and grasps the distal aspect of the thigh anteriorly just proximal to the extended knee. As a result, the patient's lower leg rests on the examiner's forearm. The thenar eminence of the examiner's other hand is placed against the posterior aspect of the patient's ischial tuberosity.

The examiner brings the patient's leg as far as possible into extension while the proximal hand fixates the patient's pelvis against the treatment table. At the end of the range of motion, the examiner exerts slight overpressure.

Attention is given to the amount of motion, end-feel, and provocation of pain. The end-feel is usually firm. A limitation of motion is usually part of a capsular pattern, indicating an arthrosis or arthritis of the hip joint. Pain without a limitation in motion is usually the result of a stretch of the superficial anterior soft tissue structures (such as the iliopsoas muscle) or compression of the deeper lying soft tissue structures (such as the iliopectineal bursa).

3.19 Passive Hip Extension Followed by Knee Flexion (Femoral Nerve Stretch Test)

From the end-position described in Test 3.18, the examiner slowly flexes the knee of the patient's passively extended hip. This is done by a shifting of the examiner's body in the direction of the patient's head. In so do-

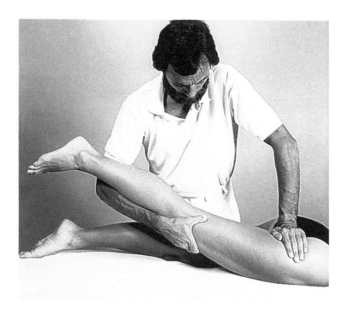

Test 3.18

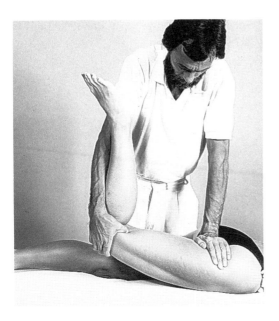

Test 3.19

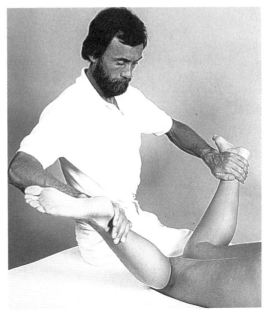

Test 3.20

ing, the examiner's forearm bends the patient's knee.

During this test, the rectus femoris muscle is stretched. Additionally, this is a stretch test for the femoral (L3, L4) nerve. In this instance, the patient experiences pain in the back and possibly in the anterior aspect of the thigh.

3.20   Passive Bilateral Internal Rotation, with the Knees in 90° Flexion

The patient lies in a prone position and flexes both knees to 90°.

The examiner sits at the foot of the table and places both hands at the medial aspect of the patient's lower legs, just proximal to the ankles. The patient's knees contact each other. The examiner brings both of the patient's hips into internal rotation by bringing the patient's lower legs away from each other. At the end of the range of motion, the examiner exerts overpressure.

Small differences in range of motion, and particularly end-feel, can be better assessed

in this test than by internal rotation in the supine position with the hips flexed to 90°. Limitations of motion are almost always part of a capsular pattern and indicate arthritis or arthrosis of the hip joint.

3.21   Resisted Internal Rotation of the Hip, with the Knees in 90° Flexion (Bilateral)

The patient lies in a prone position with the knees flexed to 90°, holding the legs together.

The examiner sits at the foot of the table and grasps each of the patient's lower legs from the lateral direction, just proximal to the ankles.

The patient is now asked to keep the knees together and push the ankles away from each other. At the same time, the examiner exerts isometric resistance.

In this test, the internal rotators of the hip are assessed for strength and painfulness. This test is seldom positive.

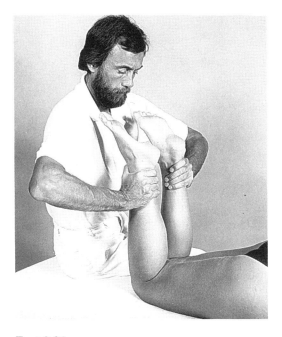

Test 3.21

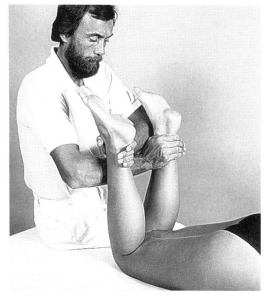

Test 3.22

3.22   Resisted External Rotation of the Hip, with the Knees in 90° Flexion (Bilateral)

The patient flexes the knees to 90° and holds the legs together.

The examiner sits at the foot of the table and grasps each lower leg from the medial sides (arms are crossed), just proximal to the ankles.

The patient is asked to keep the knees together and push the ankles toward each other. At the same time, the examiner exerts isometric resistance.

In this test, the external rotators of the hip are assessed for strength and painfulness. The iliopsoas muscle is more often affected than the sartorius muscle. When there is a lesion of the iliopsoas muscle, Tests 3.15A to 3.15C will also be painful.

3.23   Resisted Hip Extension

The examiner stands opposite the side being tested, at the level of the lower leg, and

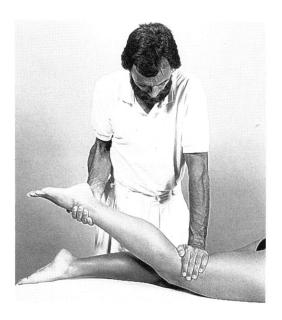

Test 3.23

places one hand on the posterior aspect of the patient's thigh just proximal to the knee. The other hand supports the patient's lower leg from an anterior position, just proximal to the ankle.

The patient is now asked to lift the thigh and simultaneously exert slight pressure with the lower leg in the direction of the treatment table. At the same time, the examiner provides isometric resistance.

This tests the hip extensors for strength and painfulness. Performing the test in this manner provides more reliable information about the gluteal muscles because it prevents the knee flexion function of the hamstrings by requiring simultaneous slight isometric contraction of the quadriceps.

3.24 Resisted Knee Extension, with the Knee in 90° Flexion

The examiner stands next to the side being tested, at the level of the patient's upper body. The patient flexes the knee to 90°.

With one hand, the examiner grasps the anterior aspect of the patient's lower leg just proximal to the ankle and places the other hand on the posterior side of the thigh just proximal to the popliteal fossa.

The patient is now instructed to straighten the knee without lifting the thigh. At the same time, the examiner provides isometric resistance with the extended arm.

Test 3.24

Test 3.25

This tests the quadriceps muscles for strength and painfulness. The rectus femoris muscle plays the most important role in hip pathology.

3.25 Resisted Knee Flexion, with the Knee in 70° Flexion

The examiner stands next to the side being tested, at the level of the patient's upper body. The patient flexes the knee to 70°.

With one hand, the examiner grasps the posterior aspect of the patient's lower leg just proximal to the ankle and places the other hand on the posterior side of the patient's thigh just proximal to the popliteal fossa.

The patient is now asked to bend the knee without lifting the pelvis from the table. At the same time, the examiner exerts isometric resistance.

This tests the hamstrings for strength and painfulness. In cases where there is a hamstring lesion, Tests 3.7 and 3.23 could also be painful.

Chapter 4

Pathology of the Hip

4.1 JOINT PATHOLOGY

PATHOLOGY WHERE MOTIONS ARE LIMITED IN A CAPSULAR PATTERN

ARTHRITIS

Traumatic Arthritis

Traumatic arthritis of the hip is rare. When it occurs, it is seen primarily in athletes, particularly soccer players. The disorder is seldom seen in people younger than 20 years. The trauma usually involves hyperextension, rotation, or combinations of these conditions. A patient with coxarthrosis can develop traumatic arthritis of the hip as the result of overuse or from an accident. Such cases are categorized as being an activated or traumatized arthrosis.

Clinical Findings

The patient complains of groin pain, which can radiate to the anterior aspect of the thigh.

Functional Examination

Passive internal rotation is painful and limited. Sometimes, that is the only finding. Flex-ion, extension, and abduction can be slightly limited as well (capsular pattern).

Treatment

Treatment consists of manual traction of the hip, administered daily for at least 10 minutes, possibly in conjunction with nonsteroidal antiinflammatory medication. The symptoms usually subside within 2 to 3 weeks.

Nontraumatic Arthritis

The most frequently seen nontraumatic arthritides of the hip are rheumatoid arthritis, gout, ankylosing spondylitis, and arthritis resulting from pigmented villonodular synovitis (Figure 4–1). Idiopathic arthritis is also seen in the hip joint (Figure 4–2). The progression of this disorder is analogous to that of idiopathic arthritis of the shoulder. This form of arthritis is self-limited; the symptoms resolve within a period of 1 to 2 years. A unilateral or bilateral arthrokatadysis can occur at any age as the result of some hip joint arthritides. Arthrokatadysis is a sinking in of the floor of the acetabulum, resulting in protrusion of the femoral head through it. When the femoral head protrudes "inward" through the acetabulum, the condition is diagnosed as sec-

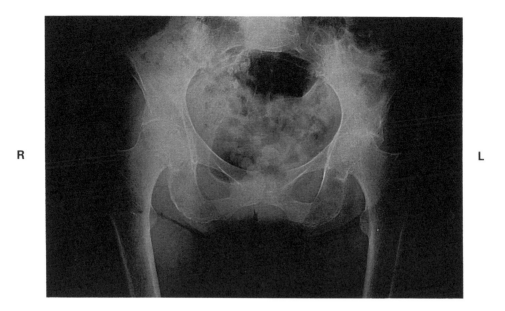

R   L

Figure 4–1 Anteroposterior (AP) conventional radiograph demonstrating severe (rheumatoid) arthritis of the hips, affecting the left hip more than the right. The joint space of the left hip joint has almost completely disappeared, and on the right side there is an obvious narrowing.

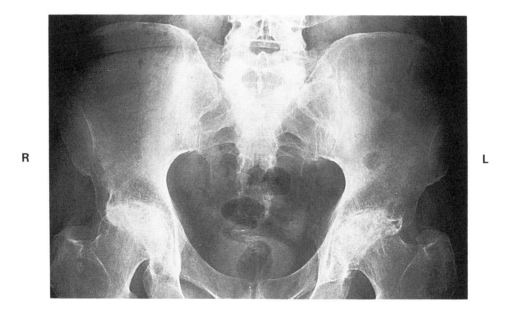

R   L

Figure 4–2 AP conventional radiograph showing bilateral coxitis (arthritis of both hip joints). In this case, the cause is not (yet) known. There is severe narrowing of the joint space bilaterally with subchondral geode (cavity) formation.

ondary arthrokatadysis. The seldom seen primary arthrokatadysis occurs during adolescence; its cause is unknown (Figure 4–3).

Clinical Findings

Activity-related groin pain and limited range of motion are the patient's chief complaints. Patients with severe cases may also experience pain at rest.

Functional Examination

Limitations of motion in the capsular pattern are found. Further examination with a blood work-up and the use of imaging techniques is necessary to determine the cause of the nontraumatic arthritis and to select an appropriate treatment.

Treatment

The idiopathic arthritis is self-limiting and can last for a period of 1 to 2 years. Therapy is restricted to carefully performed manual traction and the administration of nonsteroi-

dal antiinflammatory medication. With the other arthritides, the treatment, usually consisting of medication, depends on the cause. In many cases, when the symptoms of pain subside, slight capsular pattern limitations remain. These can often be alleviated by means of joint-specific manual therapy.

Coxarthrosis

Coxarthrosis is a common hip joint disorder that in most cases does not cause any pain. The diagnosis is often based exclusively on radiographic findings (eg, when the hip joints are visible on colon films). Patients usually do not experience any symptoms from an arthrotic hip joint condition.

The disorder can be classified as either primary or secondary. A classification as primary means that the disorder occurs in a normally formed and positioned joint, as determined by radiography. A classification as secondary means that the disorder is a re-

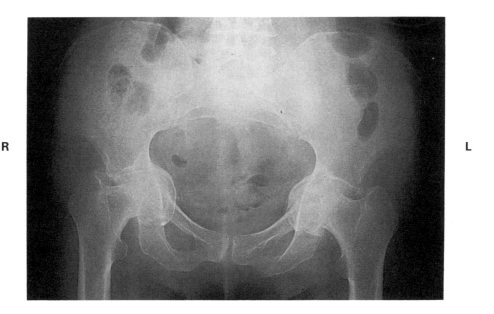

R   **L**

Figure 4–3 Bilateral secondary arthrokatadysis, conventional radiograph. The joint spaces have practically disappeared; the femoral heads are visible on the inner side of the pelvis.

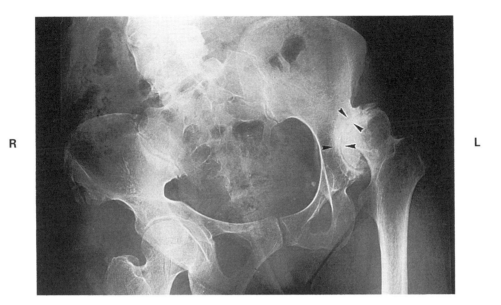

Figure 4–4 AP conventional radiograph of the pelvis. There is a severe obliquity of the pelvis, declined to the right, with an adduction position of the right hip and compensatory lumbar scoliosis. The left hip shows evidence of severe arthrotic changes (arrowheads).

sult of either a deviation in the anatomy of the hip joint (Figure 4–4) or previous disease in the hip joint (Figure 4–5). In the first instance, congenital deviations are usually involved, such as hip dysplasia, subluxation or dislocation, coxa vara, coxa valga, or femoral antetorsion. The second instance usually concerns a slipped capital femoral epiphysis, Perthes' disease, or an arthritis of the hip.

Primary coxarthrosis usually occurs in patients older than 40 years; secondary coxarthrosis is most often seen in patients older than 25. The disorder can occur unilaterally as well as bilaterally and is seen equally in men and women. The progression of coxarthrosis in women is usually much more severe, however. An overweight condition can be an unfavorable factor in this disorder.

Clinical Findings

Initially the patient complains only of pain in the groin or the anteromedial aspect of the thigh. Sometimes, however, pain is felt only at or just distal to the knee. In patients who have only knee pain but for whom the functional examination of the knee is negative, pathology of the hip joint should be suspected, leading to a functional examination of the hip.

In the early stages, pain is only experienced during weight-bearing activities; later, there can also be temporary periods of pain when the hip is at rest. At first, there are long intervals without pain; ultimately these become shorter and shorter.

Many people with coxarthrosis actually experience fewer symptoms over a period of time. Ten years after the onset of symptoms, most patients have less pain but greater limitations of motion. Obviously, only patients with progressive symptoms require intensive medical attention. This would be true for patients who frequently have pain at rest or at night and who can no longer lie on the affected side.

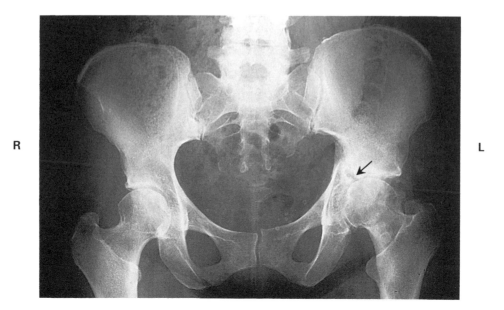

R   L

Figure 4–5 AP conventional radiograph of the pelvis. The left hip shows evidence of sequelae of an earlier acetabulum fracture (arrow). There are early arthrotic changes (secondary coxarthrosis).

Functional Examination

Depending on the severity of the disorder, a slight, moderate, or severe capsular pattern of limited motions can be found.

Conventional radiographs generally confirm the diagnosis. Differentiation is made between the expulsive form and the enclosing form. In the expulsive form, the lateral part of the femoral head appears to be displaced laterally (Figure 4–6). This form usually causes a significant amount of pain with a relatively small amount of motion limitation. In its enclosing form, the hip cavity "grasps" even more of the femoral head. Patients with this form generally have severe limitations of motion and relatively little pain.

It is important to obtain an anteroposterior (AP) view in the standing position because otherwise misleading information can be presented. In a lying position, the joint space can appear to be normal, but with the radiograph taken in the standing position, body weight may reveal the space to have almost disappeared (Figure 4–7).

A number of complications can be caused by coxarthrosis, the most frequent being the loose body. The patient experiences unexpected, brief, sharp pains in the groin, during which standing on the affected leg is impossible. In such cases, the functional examination sometimes presents misleading information because the limitations of motion are not always in the capsular pattern.

Another complication is irritation of the iliopsoas muscle. Additionally, compression neuropathies can occur as a result of the increased tonus in the muscles as they attempt to adapt in a shortened position. This is true of muscles such as the iliopsoas, rectus femoris, adductors, and hamstrings. The most frequently compromised nerves are the lateral femoral cutaneous and obturator nerves. In these instances, the pain reference remains constrained to a rather small area of the thigh. This pain has a burning sensation that is

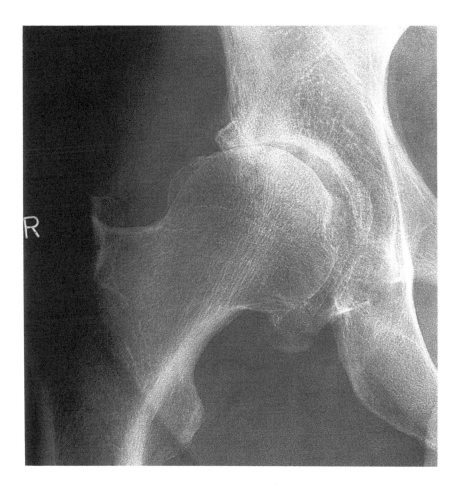

Figure 4–6 AP conventional radiograph of the right hip in a 52-year-old man. Here, the so-called expulsive form of coxarthrosis can be seen. This patient reacted unsuccessfully to conservative therapy and ultimately had the hip joint replaced with an endoprosthesis.

clearly different from the usual pain in a coxarthrosis.

Treatment

Initially, therapy is conservative and depends on the findings on the functional examination. In principle, manual traction is always indicated. Other techniques of manual mobilization can be tried, but in many cases the rotation mobilizations seem to aggravate the symptoms, even when they are carefully performed. Muscle stretching should be considered for the shortened muscles. The therapist has to find a balance between joint mobilization and muscle stretching.

In more severe cases, pressure can be taken off the hip during walking by use of a cane on the nonaffected side. In so doing, the load can be decreased by approximately 60%. If physical therapy does not bring improvement and surgical treatment is not (yet) indicated, an intraarticular injection with a corticosteroid often provides pain relief for an extended period of time.

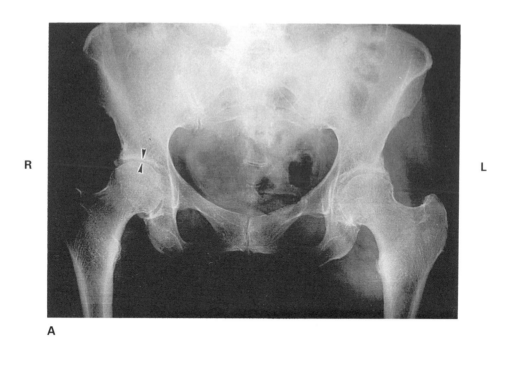

R   L

A

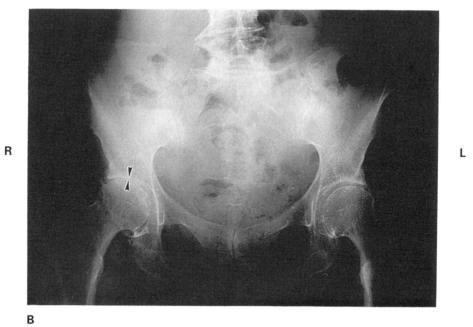

R   L

B

Figure 4–7 AP conventional radiograph of the pelvis in a 60-year-old woman with complaints about the right hip. (**A**) Lying position: The joint space of the right hip appears to have only a minimal amount of narrowing (arrowheads). (**B**) Standing position: Severe narrowing of the joint space and even bony contact (arrowheads) can now be seen.

Symptoms caused by a loose body can often be remedied by a rotation manipulation under traction. Compression neuropathies can be treated by means of perineural injections. As a final alternative, surgical procedures may be needed to remedy severe pain and limitations of motions.

Perthes' Disease (Legg-Calvé-Perthes Disease)

Perthes' disease concerns an aseptic bone necrosis that particularly affects children between the ages of 3 and 10 but can still occur up to the age of 15. The necrosis of the femoral head is the result of imperfect vascularization. The etiology of this condition is as yet unknown. Early diagnosis is of utmost importance because otherwise severe deformation of the femoral head can occur (Figure 4–8).

The most severe deformation particularly occurs in children between 4 and 6 years of age. The disorder can occur bilaterally, but when that is the case one side is affected several months before the other.

Clinical Findings

Symptoms in the early stages are usually minimal. There is a slight deviation in the gait pattern; the child drags the leg, but only slightly. Severe pain develops later, and the child demonstrates a noticeable limp. The pain is felt in the groin and knee and sometimes solely in the knee, a condition that is obviously misleading.

Functional Examination

During the inspection, a slight atrophy of the thigh musculature is sometimes noted. The Trendelenburg test is usually slightly

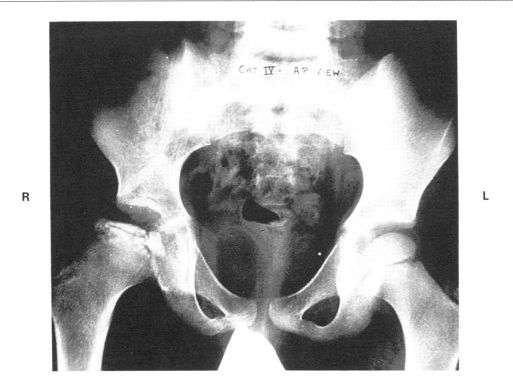

Figure 4–8 AP conventional radiograph of the pelvis. There is severe flattening and widening of the right femoral head and femoral neck. This radiograph is typical of Perthes' disease.

positive (the pelvis tilts slightly toward the nonaffected side when the patient is standing on the affected leg). Usually, motions are moderately limited in a capsular pattern.

The radiograph is diagnostic. In addition to the standard AP view, a film should also be taken in the Lauenstein position (AP view with the hip in flexion–abduction–external rotation). In the early phase of the disease, bone scan or computed tomography (CT) is indicated. In the first stage, an increase in the joint space is observed in comparison with the nonaffected side. In the second stage, a half-moon–shaped subchondral fracture line is visible in the femoral head. This condition is usually visible on radiographs about 4 months after the onset of the symptoms. Progressive stages, revealed by radiography, are characterized by fragmentation and, later, collapse of the femoral head.

Treatment

Treatment is sought from a specialist. The greatest concern is the prevention of collapse and displacement of the femoral head. Depending on the clinical findings and the stage revealed by radiography, treatment can be conservative or operative.

Transient Synovitis (Coxitis Fugax)

Transient synovitis is a disorder of unknown etiology that exclusively affects children younger than 10 years, particularly boys. The hip joint becomes irritated, possibly as a result of trauma or a viral infection. In a number of cases, the expected spontaneous recovery does not occur, and the disorder appears to develop into a severe disease of the hip joint, such as Perthes' disease, juvenile rheumatoid arthritis, or bacterial arthritis. Therefore, it is important to observe such patients over an adequate period of time, even when the symptoms disappear for a short or extended period of time. This condition is termed an observation hip, meaning that radiographs should be repeated after 2 months.

Clinical Findings

The child usually has little pain but walks with some degree of limp. Medical care providers should immediately refer a child with these symptoms to an orthopaedic specialist.

Functional Examination

The functional examination usually demonstrates a slight capsular pattern of limited motions. Plain films of the area usually appear normal.

Treatment

In a pure transient synovitis, the symptoms usually do not last longer than 2 to 3 weeks. As much load as possible should be taken off the hip during this period. Sometimes bed rest is necessary. If the symptoms do not subside within the expected time frame, further examination is necessary.

PATHOLOGY WHERE MOTIONS ARE LIMITED IN A NONCAPSULAR PATTERN

OSTEOCHONDROSIS DISSECANS

Osteochondrosis dissecans is a disorder of unknown etiology that is most commonly seen in the knee and elbow joints. Occurrence in the hip joint is extremely rare. When found in the hip, the lesion is usually located in the femoral head and, less often, the acetabulum.

The disorder is seen particularly in males between the ages of 15 and 25 years. In some cases, the disorder occurs bilaterally. Necrosis of the subchondral bone occurs. A necrotic bony fragment can break loose from the joint surface and end up in the joint as a loose body. Such a fragment usually has a diameter of 1 to 2 cm.

Clinical Findings

The symptomatology is usually vague. The nature of pain depends upon the load placed on the hip and, in the presence of a loose body, can be instantaneous and paralyzing.

Functional Examination

The findings on the functional examination often vary. Usually, there is a limitation of one or more motions, particularly flexion, external rotation, or abduction. Radiographs are used to confirm the diagnosis. CT and magnetic resonance (MR) scans are used to assess the exact size of the lesion.

Treatment

Treatment is tailored to the severity of the clinical findings and information provided by imaging studies. If the bone fragment has not yet broken loose, unloading the hip can eliminate the symptoms. It is recommended that the patient use crutches for at least 2 months. If there is no improvement visible on imaging studies after 3 months, surgical treatment is indicated. Surgery is always indicated in the case of loose bodies.

ISCHEMIC NECROSIS OF THE FEMORAL HEAD

Ischemic necrosis of the femoral head in children is usually the result of Perthes' disease or a slipped capital femoral epiphysis. Ischemic (avascular, aseptic) femoral head necrosis in adults has an unclear clinical picture but can be clearly defined radiographically, particularly with MR imaging (Figure 4–9). The cause of this disorder is still the subject of much discussion.

The disorder involves a subchondral stress fracture, which may result from a general skeletal disease or from an accident (posttraumatic femoral head necrosis). In the latter case, a neck or trochanter fracture is often involved. Necrosis of the femoral head sometimes also occurs after an intertrochanteric osteotomy. In rare instances, this condition may be seen in dysplasias and in dislocations of the hip.

The necrosis can occur early or late with respect to the trauma. So-called early necrosis occurs within a few weeks or months after the accident. So-called late necrosis occurs 1 year or more afterward.

The disorder is also part of the description of decompression sickness (also termed caisson sickness or "the bends"). Other diseases in which necrosis of the femoral head is seen are lupus erythematosus, scleroderma, gout, Cushing's syndrome, pancreatitis, and endocarditis.

Necrosis of the femoral head is seen most frequently in the 25- to 45-year age group. In approximately 60% of all cases, the disorder is bilateral, but it can be months to years before both hips are affected (Figures 4–10 and 4–11).

The etiologic factors listed in Exhibit 4–1 can lead to a decrease in the blood supply of the femoral head.[9] Exhibit 4–2 lists pathologic conditions that can lead to necrosis of the femoral head.[9]

Clinical Findings

The clinical picture varies. Initially there are scarcely any symptoms of pain or limitations of motion. When the symptoms increase (pain in the groin), there is still not always a limitation of motion. Plain films are diagnostic. In early stages, the disorder can be seen on CT scan and particularly on MR images.

As soon as the femoral head becomes deformed, the limitations of motion occur in a noncapsular pattern. Eventually, severe pain and limitations of motion occur in the joint

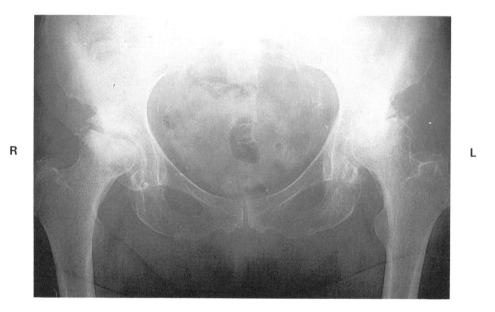

Figure 4–9 AP conventional radiograph of the pelvis. Dysplasia of both hip joints with secondary arthrosis and necrosis at the level of the femoral head are seen. The osteonecrosis has led to severe malformation of the femoral heads.

Exhibit 4–1 Etiologic Factors in Decreased Blood Supply to the Femoral Head

Extensive blood vessel ruptures
- Fracture-dislocation of the femoral neck
- Hip dislocation

External vascular occlusion
- Bone marrow hypertrophy
- Bone marrow injection or transplantation

Increase in intraosseous pressure

Thrombosis
- Vascular pathology
- Altered erythrocyte sedimentation rate

Emboli
- Blood clots
- Fat globules
- Sickle-shaped erythrocytes
- Nitrogen bubbles

Osteopenia with microfractures

Multifactoral

Idiopathic

Exhibit 4–2 Pathologic Conditions Leading to Femoral Head Necrosis

Traumatic
- Fracture of the femoral neck
- Dislocation or fracture-dislocation
- Trauma without fracture or dislocation
- Hip surgeries, particularly osteotomy

Nontraumatic
- Systemic steroid administration
- Alcohol (excessive use)
- Smoking
- Pregnancy
- Kidney transplant
- Collagen diseases (eg, lupus erythematosus)
- Sickle cell diseases and sickle cell variants
- Various hemoglobinopathies and coagulopathies
- Caisson (or decompression) sickness
- Exposure to extremely high altitudes
- Chronic liver diseases
- Pancreatitis
- Ileitis and colitis
- Burns
- Various hyperlipidemias
- Gaucher's disease (glucosylceramide lipidosis)
- Fabry's disease (also known as diffuse angiokeratoma or ceramide trihexosidase deficiency)
- Gout
- Metabolic bone diseases
- Radiation
- Arteriosclerosis and other vessel-narrowing diseases
- Cushing's syndrome
- Sarcoidosis
- Chemotherapy and toxic chemical products
- Tumors
- Idiopathic factors

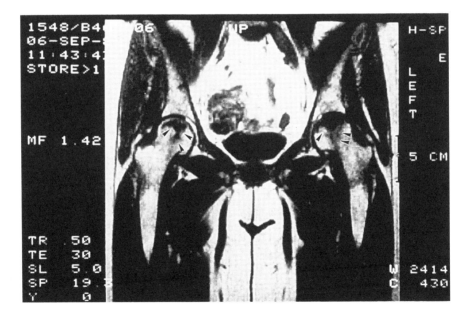

Figure 4–10 MR image demonstrating bilateral necrosis of the femoral heads (arrowheads) in a 36-year-old man who had an onset of hip (groin) pain several months after falling from a horse. The necrosis occurred first on the right and later on the left.

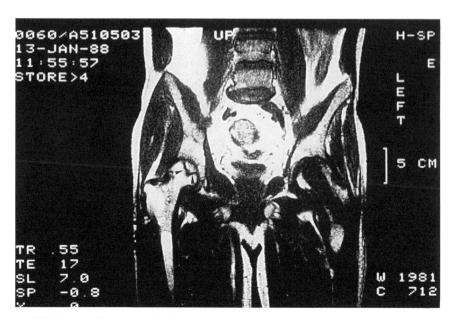

Figure 4–11 MR image demonstrating beginning necrosis of the femoral head on the right (arrowheads) in a 42-year-old woman. This woman had been treated earlier for the same condition on the left side with bone drilling through the femoral head and neck.

with obvious crepitation. The pain can radiate to the gluteal region, the anterior aspect of the thigh, and the knee. Early arthrosis of the joint is the ultimate result.

Treatment

Unloading the affected hip joint is necessary until radiographs confirm complete repair of the femoral head. This process can last many months. In severe cases with persistent pain and dysfunction, surgical treatments such as bone grafting, osteotomy, or total joint replacement may be effective. Good results have recently been reported with the use of electric stimulation.[10] In the final stages of the disorder, the joint can be treated with methods previously described as appropriate for coxarthrosis.

SLIPPED CAPITAL FEMORAL EPIPHYSIS

Slipped capital femoral epiphysis is a sliding off of the femoral head epiphysis from the femoral neck. The cause is most probably a disturbance in the development of the epiphyseal plate in prepuberty. In this phase of life, there is lability of the endocrine balance in regard to the growth and sex hormone metabolism. The smallest disturbance of this endocrine mechanism can lead to a weakening of the epiphyseal plate. This results in a reduction in resistance to mechanical load.

The disorder is seen in girls between the ages of 11 and 13 and in boys between the ages of 13 and 15. The ratio of boys to girls is approximately 6:4. About 70% of all patients are overweight and have a delayed development of the secondary sex characteristics. The other 30% are normal or thin children with normal secondary sex characteristics or children in a "growth spurt."

In about 25% of all cases, it can be determined that a trauma was responsible for the onset of symptoms. Often the other side is also affected but does not always lead to complaints; thus radiographic monitoring becomes necessary. In a large number of cases, an aseptic necrosis of the femoral head occurs as an early complication.

Clinical Findings

Differentiation is made between gradual and acute slipped capital femoral epiphysis.

Gradual slipped capital femoral epiphysis. The first clinical signs are so minimal that they normally do not lead to consultation with a physician. The patient has occasional mild pain in the groin or knee and a slight limping gait pattern. Usually the slipped epiphysis is not yet visible on plain films. Only a slight widening of the epiphyseal plate is generally seen. As soon as the slipping begins, muscle guarding occurs. This muscle guarding lasts until such time as the slipping stops. At every new stage of slipping, the muscle guarding begins again.

With an increase in the slipping of the epiphysis, the mobility of the hip decreases. The internal rotation in particular is severely limited, and the external rotation appears to increase. The flexion motion is not limited but is accompanied by simultaneous external rotation and abduction, the so-called Drehmann sign.

In the final stage, the leg length is shortened by about 2.5 cm. The Trendelenburg test is positive. Often in the final stage, the pain decreases.

Acute slipped capital femoral epiphysis. The patient with acute epiphyseal slipping experiences a sudden onset of symptoms where previously there had been no complaints. The obvious clinical picture consists of a complete inability to put load on the hip, and it will appear as if there is a femoral neck fracture. Radiographs are diagnostic (Figure 4–12). In addition to the standard view, the so-called Lauenstein view (sometimes called the frog-leg position) should also be taken (Figure 4–13).

Treatment

Conservative treatment consists of continuous traction in moderate to maximal ab-duction of the hip, for a duration of 24 hours per day with a pull of 8 to 10 kg, for the first 6 weeks. After that, the pull is gradually decreased to 4 to 6 kg. After 2 months, the pull is again decreased to 2 kg.

This traction therapy can last 2 to 5 months. The child is able to leave the bed with a Thomas splint to keep as much load as possible off the hip joint. The splint should be worn until the epiphyseal plate is completely ossified. Operations in which the epiphyseal plate is fixated surgically are more frequently taking the place of conservative therapy.

LOOSE BODY

In various disorders of the hip, loose bodies can obscure the symptoms of the underlying clinical picture. Loose bodies can also occur without evidence of articular pathology or prior trauma. The following factors can be responsible for the presence of loose bodies:

- trauma
- coxarthrosis
- osteochondrosis dissecans
- ischemic necrosis of the femoral head
- synovial (osteo)chondromatosis (rare)
- idiopathic

Clinical Findings

The most commonly experienced symptom is a sharp, unexpected twinge of pain in the groin. It does not last long and can radiate to the anterior aspect of the thigh. Sometimes, it is felt only in the knee. In such a patient history, plain films should always be taken to rule out serious pathology. If the films are normal, the loose body has no known cause.

Functional Examination

Usually the passive flexion is limited, often with a springy end-feel. Passive external rotation, with the hip in 90° flexion, adduction, and abduction are also often limited. If necessary, the diagnosis can be confirmed by means of arthrography, CT, or MR imaging.

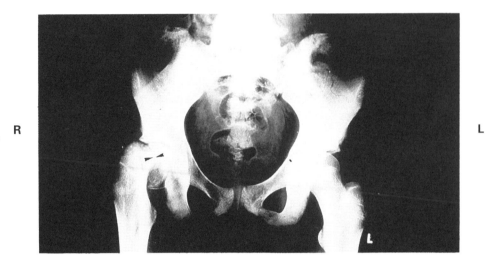

Figure 4–12 AP conventional radiograph of the pelvis. Severe acute slipped capital femoral epiphysis of the right femoral head is seen (arrowheads).

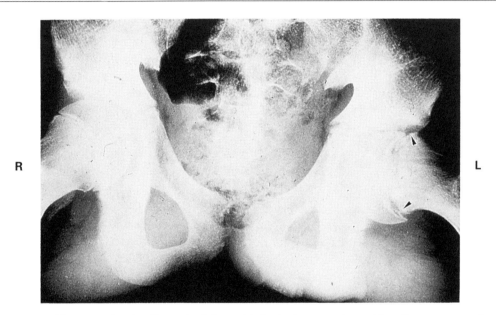

Figure 4–13 AP conventional radiograph of the pelvis in the Lauenstein position. Severe acute slipped capital femoral epiphysis on the left side is seen (arrowheads).

Treatment

A rotation manipulation while pulling on the leg is usually effective when a limitation of motion is found during the functional examination. This treatment is also recommended for patients who have a loose body based on a coxarthrosis. In most cases it can be assumed that a loose body will become encapsulated in the synovial membrane. If the loose body recurs too often, surgical removal is indicated.

4.2 PATHOLOGY OF THE BURSAE

ILIOPECTINEAL BURSITIS (PSOAS BURSITIS)

Iliopectineal bursitis is a lesion that can exist for years without being identified as such. From our patient population, it took several years for some of the cases to be diagnosed.

The bursa is located between the anterior side of the joint capsule of the hip and the musculotendinous junction of the iliopsoas. The bursa has an average dimension of 6×3 cm. In approximately 15% to 20% of all cases, there is a congenital communication with the hip joint. Theories regarding the etiology of this disorder are in dispute. The disorder is seen most often in nonathletic individuals.

Differentiation is made between an acute bursitis and a chronic bursitis. In the first case, the cause is an acute trauma, such as a kick in the groin during soccer. In the second instance, the cause is also traumatic, but here microtrauma plays a role. Biomechanical factors, such as a short leg or an altered position or change in the form of lower extremity parts can eventually lead to irritation of the bursa. A short muscle in the region of the hip joint could be responsible for the development of a bursitis as well. Changes within the hip joint can also cause an irritation of the bursa. As evidence of this, an iliopectineal bursa is often seen in coxarthrosis patients.

Clinical Findings

The patient complains of pain in the groin region, which sometimes radiates to the anterior aspect of the hip. The pain is usually activity related but can also be experienced at rest.

Functional Examination

Passive flexion of the hip is usually the most painful motion. If the hip is simulta-neously adducted, the pain can initially increase and, after about 45°, again decrease (the so-called painful arc). Passive external rotation and passive extension of the hip are also usually painful. Except for severe cases, resisted flexion of the hip is usually not painful. In some patients, there is palpable swelling in the groin.

Treatment

In an acute bursitis, and in the case of obvious swelling, an attempt should be made to aspirate the bursa. In mild cases without palpable swelling, an attempt is made to decrease the symptoms by correcting a possible leg length discrepancy or by changing the position of the leg (eg, by means of an orthotic or heel wedge). If these measures are unsatisfactory, the bursa can be injected with a local anesthetic. When symptoms reoccur, a corticosteroid can be added. Injection of the bursa requires a special technique in order to avoid contact with the femoral artery and nerve (see Chapter 5 for detailed instructions on this injection).

SUBTROCHANTERIC BURSITIS

Subtrochanteric bursitis is a collective term that covers the various bursae around the greater trochanter. The lesion is often difficult to differentiate from pain in the greater trochanter region that is due to an insertion tendopathy either with or without calcification of the gluteus maximus or medius muscles. Frequently, pain at the greater trochanter is caused by irritation of the L4 or L5 nerve roots. The functional examination does not always provide the information needed for a definitive diagnosis.

Generally, three deep bursae lie at the greater trochanter. The largest, the trochanteric bursa of the gluteus maximus muscle, lies between the posterior aspect of the greater trochanter and the gluteus maximus muscle. A second bursa, the intermuscular gluteal bursae (there are often two), is found between the tendon of the gluteus maximus and the tendon of the vastus lateralis muscle. The third bursa lies between the ischial tuberosity and the muscle belly of the gluteus maximus. This bursa of the gluteus maximus muscle is discussed later as the ischial bursa.

The cause of the classic subtrochanteric bursitis is probably traumatic. Not only acute trauma but also microtrauma can lead to irritation and signs of inflammation. Interestingly enough, it is seen in long-distance runners, where it usually involves hypermobile athletes or women runners with a relatively wide pelvis.

Differential Diagnosis

- "Snapping hip" (coxa saltans)
- Scar tissue after hip operations with a posterior incision
- Pain as a result of a loosening of a total hip endoprosthesis

Clinical Findings

The pain is experienced at the greater trochanter and just proximal to it. In many cases, the pain radiates to the lateral side of the thigh and sometimes to the lower leg.

Functional Examination

The patient should be thoroughly examined for variations in leg length and other asymmetries of the legs.

The findings from the functional examination are usually vague. Passive flexion, external rotation, and adduction of the hip can be painful. In such cases, the pain is always felt on the lateral side of the thigh. Resisted abduction of the hip, as well as resisted extension or external rotation, can also be painful as a result of compression of the bursa. Usually there is local tenderness. Ultrasound can differentiate a bursitis from a tendopathy in

many instances. Sometimes calcification of the bursa is visible on plain films.

Treatment

Treatment, if possible, is based on causal factors. If causal treatment provides unsatisfactory results, or if no clear cause for the disorder can be found, an injection with a local anesthetic is the best alternative treatment. In instances of recurrence or unsatisfactory results, a few milliliters of corticosteroid can be added to the local anesthetic. In a number of cases, a caudal epidural anesthetic injection is indicated to rule out lumbar problems. This is sometimes necessary because differentiation between a subtrochanteric bursitis and a lumbar nerve root syndrome is not always easy.

ISCHIAL BURSITIS

An ischial bursitis concerns two different bursae. These are the ischial bursa, lying between the ischial tuberosity and the caudal part of the muscle belly of the gluteus maximus muscle, and the subtendinous bursa, located between the tendons of the biceps femoris and the semimembranosus muscles. Problems with these bursae are usually caused by chronic pressure. This is particularly seen in people who engage in activity that involves a significant amount of sitting (eg, rowing team members).

Differential Diagnosis

- Lumbar nerve root syndrome (S1, S2)
- Insertion tendopathy of the hamstrings (pain during walking; extension of the hip against resistance is painful from a stretched position; a resisted flexion of the knee is painful)
- Hamstrings syndrome (refer to "Lesions of the Sciatic Nerve" in Chapter 6)

Clinical Findings

The patient complains of local pain while sitting, which usually quickly disappears upon standing.

Functional Examination

The functional examination is usually negative. Sometimes the straight leg raise test, passive hip flexion, or resisted hip extension provokes mild symptoms. There is local tenderness to palpation.

Treatment

Treatment is primarily causal, for example padding the (usually too hard) seat in such a way that the pain is no longer felt. An injection with a local anesthetic and eventually a corticosteroid usually provides quick relief.

4.3   PATHOLOGY OF THE MUSCLE–TENDON UNIT

PUBALGIA

Pubalgia is a collective term for all disorders that cause pain in the region of the pubic tubercle and the structures attached to the pubic bone. Often, the pain extends to the pubic symphysis area and the lower abdomen. Pubalgia is typically a sports injury. If the patient does not engage in sports and the functional examination does not produce symptoms, pathology of the hip joint, pubic symphysis, or internal organs should be considered.

The medical literature often lists the most significant cause of pubalgia to be the performance of so-called unipodal movements. Such movements are those where the weight-bearing leg is rotated as the other leg performs a motion. For example, this occurs during the kicking of a ball when abduction-extension of the hip is immediately followed by an adduction-flexion motion. The pelvis and trunk have to be fixated on the weight-bearing leg, and, depending on the force on the moving leg, the abdominal and leg muscles have to provide enormous synergistic activity as well.

During this kind of motion, small shearing movements occur in the pubic symphysis, eventually with dehiscence, or the splitting away of both pubic bones. This set of circumstances is considered one of the possible partial causes of adductor lesions. The symptoms occur particularly after activities that are more vigorous than usual or after inadequate preparation for the sports activity.

A second possible cause of pubalgia is a significant dysbalance between the adductors and the abdominal musculature. This could lead, in an unusually severe way, to the development of a dehiscence of both pubic bones in the pubic symphysis. As a result, severe pain in the adductor muscle bellies or significant irritation of the insertions of the adductors occurs.

Sometimes, the adductor longus completely avulses from the pubic tubercle. This applies particularly to soccer players and usually happens as the result of a trauma, such as one caused by sliding to reach the ball. Such a result, however, is probably only possible in the presence of already existing but symptomless degenerative changes in the tendon. In many cases, an insertion tendopathy of the abdominal muscles occurs as well. The rectus abdominis is more often affected than the oblique abdominal muscles.

Effective warm-up and progressive preparation in training before strenuous sports activity can play an important preventive role. Often in the patient history, there will be a time when the sports participant was unexpectedly required to participate strenuously. This disorder is particularly associated with the following sports: soccer, track and field, distance running, speed skating, and swimming.

Differential Diagnosis

- Stress fractures of the pelvis
- Stress fracture of the femur (usually the neck)

- Calcification in the musculature (post-traumatic)
- Lesion of the hip joint
- Lesion of the pubic symphysis
- Lesion of the lumbar spine or the sacro-iliac joint

In many cases, it appears that the running, skating, or swimming motion is not perfectly performed. Particularly, soccer players tend to have a rather poor running and kicking technique. Thus the adductors are over-loaded, producing microruptures in the muscle belly of the adductor longus and inser-tion tendopathies of the adductor longus and, less often, of the gracilis, adductor brevis, and pectineus muscles. Lesions of the adductor magnus are also seen, but these are rare.

The direct result of the overloading is fa-tigue of the adductors. When this happens, muscle tension increases, leading to muscle shortening and continuous traction on the tendons and their insertions. Because of this, the shearing force acting on the symphysis increases significantly, the cranioventral liga-ments of the pubic symphysis overstretch, and finally an instability of the symphysis oc-curs with irritation of the symphysis disc. These changes are usually partly visible on plain films.

In approximately 70% of all pubalgia cases, a leg length difference of more than 5 mm is found. In contrast, only 5% of athletes with other lesions in the lower extremity have a leg length difference of more than 5 mm.

Clinical Findings

The most significant symptom is pain, which is initially localized to the groin area. With an insertion tendopathy of the abdomi-nal muscles, the pain is also experienced in the lower abdominal area. Localization of pain in the groin can change regularly and can therefore be misleading. For instance, it may appear that the insertion of the adductor lon-gus is affected, but then at the next examina-tion the pain may be more localized at the level of the insertion of the gracilis or

pectineus. The pain occurs particularly dur-ing sprinting, kicking against a ball, and pivot-ing (particularly in soccer). After warming up, the symptoms decrease or even disap-pear. Particularly after exertion, the pain re-turns, often more intensely.

If the abdominal muscles are affected, then in addition to sprinting, kicking, and pivoting motions sneezing and coughing can be pain-ful. Ruling out an inguinal or femoral hernia is important; after exertion there is obvious lo-cal tenderness just cranial to the pubic sym-physis, to the left and right of the middle. If the oblique abdominal muscles are affected, the tender areas are farther lateral.

Four clinical stages are differentiated:

Stage 1: groin pain, short lasting, particu-larly after exertion

Stage 2: groin pain, particularly at the be-ginning of exertion, that returns after 1 day, often more intense, and disappear-ing with rest

Stage 3: groin pain and pain in the lower abdominal region, unilateral, during the entire duration of the exertion and last-ing for several days afterward

Stage 4: chronic pain, increasing with exer-tion, only slightly diminishing with rest

Functional Examination

The functional examination includes the lumbar spine, pelvic motions, and the hip. The examination of the lumbar spine is usu-ally negative; sometimes extension is slightly painful as a result of the stretch of the af-fected abdominal muscles. Examination of the pelvic joints (sacroiliac joints and pubic symphysis) is usually negative, unless there is an instability of the symphysis.

In the hip examination, passive flexion of the hip, particularly combined with passive adduction, is painful in most cases as a result of compression of the origin of the adductors. Passive abduction can be painful with both a straight and a flexed knee as a result of a stretch of the adductors.

Differentiation can be made between lesions of the gracilis and adductor longus, adductor brevis, and pectineus (refer to Test 3.13 in Chapter 3 for detailed information about this test). Adduction against resistance is usually painful as tested in different positions, with the hip in 0°, 45°, and 90° flexion. In 0° hip flexion, the gracilis is usually responsible for complaints of pain. In 45° flexion, the adductor longus and adductor brevis usually provoke pain. The pectineus muscle causes pain particularly when isometric resistance is exerted against the combined motion of flexion and adduction from a position of 90° hip flexion. If the abdominal muscles are affected, the relevant resisted tests are painful.

Palpation makes further specific localization of the lesion possible. When affected, the adductor brevis becomes extremely tender to palpation; palpation is performed deeply between the tendons of the adductor longus and gracilis muscles. In acute cases, the adductor longus appears to be more often affected. In more chronic cases, the gracilis and adductor brevis tend to be affected, either individually or together.

Radiographic examination is indicated for patients who have symptoms lasting longer than 2 months(Figure 4–14). The following classification is useful for interpreting radiographic findings:

0:   normal joint

I: irregular borders of the symphysis

II: the same as I plus abnormally wide joint space of the pubic symphysis

III: the same as I and II plus reactive sclerosis

IV: the same as I to III plus pubic symphysis instability

Radiographic changes, with or without minimal clinical symptoms, are of little significance.

Treatment

The first attempt at treatment is causal. If necessary, the running, kicking, skating, or swimming technique is improved. If necessary, differences in leg length are corrected. Such correction is dependent on the cause of the leg length difference. For instance, the remedy may consist of an orthotic in the shoe to correct a pes plano valgus or a lift underneath the shoe of a clinically established short leg. A heel lift alone should not be used. If necessary, the type of footwear may be changed. Track athletes and skaters should also be allowed to circle the track in the opposite direction (in other words, they should run in a clockwise direction and on the outer edge of the track).

An alternative treatment is local. The treatment of choice is transverse friction. Semilocal treatment consists of stretching the short and long adductor muscles. These exercises should be performed daily at home as well.

As soon as the pain allows, isokinetic strengthening of the adductors should be initiated. The abdominal muscles should be isometrically trained (no sit-ups!). The muscle-strengthening exercises should be performed at least two times per day for 10 minutes each time. In principle, every patient can continue sports activity during the first week of treatment (treatment is given daily). If there is no improvement after the first week, however, activities that provoke the pain have to be avoided or reduced. As long as there is improvement, physical therapy should be continued.

In therapy-resistant cases, the site of the lesion can be injected with a corticosteroid. If this is of no avail and 3 months of rest do not bring about healing, surgical treatment is usually indicated.

TENDOPATHY OF THE RECTUS FEMORIS

As is the case with pubalgia, lesions of the rectus femoris typically result from sport injuries as the result of either chronic or acute overuse. Such trauma is usually from an activity such as kicking the ground during soccer or kicking a ball at the same time that an op-

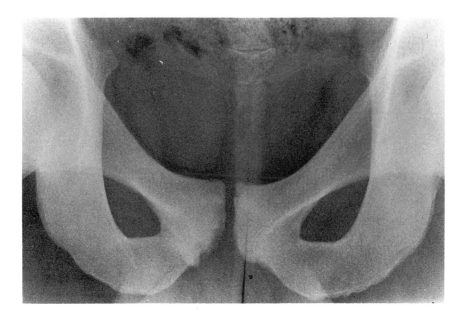

Figure 4–14 AP conventional radiograph of the pubic symphysis in a long-distance runner with groin pain. This patient had a clinical stage IV and a radiographic stage III pubalgia.

ponent blocks the kick. The lesion is also seen in skaters. Lesions of the rectus femoris are usually located either at the level of the origin (on the anterior inferior iliac spine) or just distal to the origin in the body of the tendon.

In children and adolescents, an avulsion fracture of the anterior inferior iliac spine occasionally occurs (Figure 4–15). In adults, a traumatic, complete rupture of the tendon can occur at the level of its insertion (this is seen particularly in soccer players).

Clinical Findings

The patient complains of pain in the groin during sprinting and lifting the knee. A misleading phenomenon is the fact that in many cases the patient indicates that the pain is further proximally than the actual site of the lesion.

Functional Examination

Passive flexion of the hip can be painful as a result of compression of the affected site.

Extension of the knee against resistance, with the knee in 90° flexion and the hip in 0°, is painful. Flexion of the hip against resistance, with the hip in 90° flexion, is only painful in extreme cases. Passive stretch is painful (femoral nerve stretch test). In most cases, the rectus femoris muscle is found to be too short. In the instance of an avulsion fracture or a rupture, the resisted tests are not only painful but also weak.

Treatment

Transverse friction and stretching are effective. Treatment is usually necessary for a period of 2 to 4 weeks. The patient should perform daily stretching exercises. In the third and fourth clinical tendinitis stages, the sports activities should be reduced or, when results are unsatisfactory, completely stopped. When contraction against resistance is no longer painful, isokinetic muscle-strengthening exercises can be initiated. An avulsion fracture and a total rupture should at

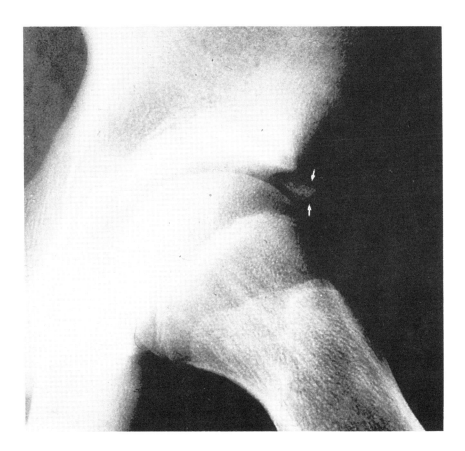

Figure 4–15 AP conventional radiograph of the left hip of a young basketball player. An avulsion fracture of the anterior inferior iliac spine is seen (arrows).

first be treated conservatively. In cases where there is recurrence, surgical treatment may be indicated.

LESIONS OF THE SARTORIUS MUSCLE

Lesions of the sartorius muscle are rare in occurrence, and, as with the previously described lesions, they are seen exclusively in athletes, particularly soccer players. The following lesions are most common: insertion tendopathy, tendinitis, and apophyseal avulsion fracture from the anterior superior iliac spine. The first two lesions are seen mostly in

adult athletes, and the avulsion fracture is seen in children and adolescents.

Clinical Findings

The patient usually complains of local pain. An avulsion fracture usually occurs during sprinting and causes severe pain in the groin. Walking and running are impossible in the acute phase, but after several hours the patient can usually walk again. Strenuous running remains impossible.

Functional Examination

Resisted flexion and external rotation of the hip are painful and, in avulsion fractures,

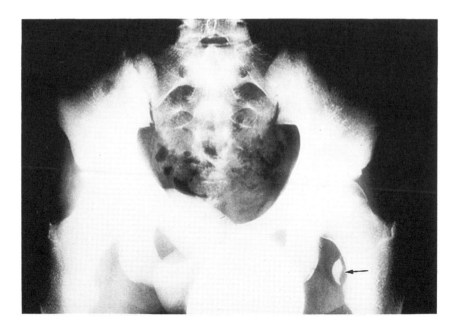

Figure 4–16 AP conventional radiograph of the pelvis of an adolescent soccer player. An avulsion fracture of the left lesser trochanter is seen (arrow).

are also weak. The avulsion fracture is often mistaken for a muscle tear. The radiograph is diagnostic.

Treatment

In a sprain or muscle tear, transverse friction and stretching exercises are usually effective. The athlete should perform the stretching exercises daily at home as well. If treatment is administered daily, the patient is usually completely healed within 1 week.

Generally, an avulsion fracture is not treated. The patient should not participate in sports for about 6 weeks. After this, training should only be reinitiated when the functional examination is completely negative and recovery has been confirmed radiographically.

LESIONS OF THE ILIOPSOAS MUSCLE

Lesions of the iliopsoas muscle almost always concern an overstretching of the muscle belly. It is found particularly in athletes but can also be seen as a complication in patients with coxarthrosis. In children and adolescents, sometimes an avulsion fracture of the lesser trochanter is involved (Figures 4–16 and 4–17).

In the differential diagnosis, an obturator hernia should be considered. In both disorders, resisted hip flexion is painful. In an obturator hernia, however, the pain usually disappears when the patient has lain approximately 10 minutes in Trendelenburg's position (a supine position where the table is tilted downward at an angle of 30° and angulated beneath the knees).

Clinical Findings

The patient complains of pain in the groin, which can radiate to the anterior aspect of the thigh.

Functional Examination

Passive hip flexion can be painful as a result of compression of the affected structure. Resisted flexion and external rotation of the hip are painful. Passive extension of the hip with simultaneous internal rotation can also be painful as a result of a stretch on the affected muscle. Of course, in coxarthrosis patients, limitations of motion in a capsular pattern are also found. The site of the lesion is located by palpation. The affected site is almost always just distal to the inguinal ligament and just medial to the sartorius muscle. In an avulsion fracture of the lesser trochanter, resisted flexion and external rotation of the hip are painful and weak.

Treatment

Good results can be achieved with transverse friction and stretching. This is true for athletes and also for patients with coxarthrosis. The patient should also stretch several times per day at home. An avulsion frac-

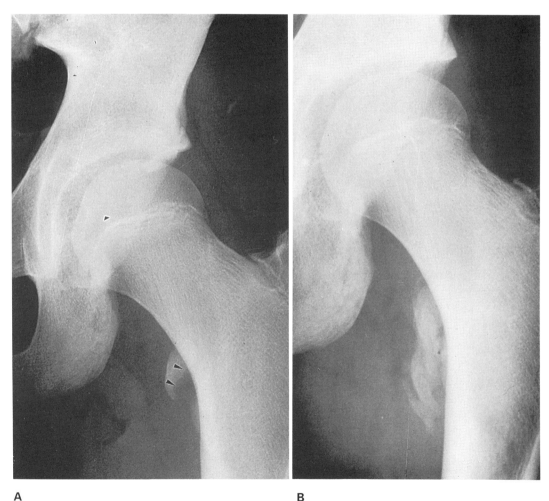

A   **B**

Figure 4–17 (A) AP conventional radiograph of the left hip of a 14-year-old short-track skater who experienced acute pain in the left groin and leg during skating and was no longer able to lift up the leg. An avulsion fracture of the left lesser trochanter is seen (arrowheads). **(B)** The same patient after 6 weeks. The follow-up radiograph shows effective callus formation. When this was taken, the patient was completely free of symptoms.

ture of the lesser trochanter should be treated conservatively.

SPRAIN OF THE ILIOTIBIAL TRACT AND TENSOR FASCIAE LATAE MUSCLE

Lesions of the iliotibial tract and tensor fasciae latae muscle are almost always the result of an explosive abduction movement from a stretched position (hip adduction). These lesions are seen in gymnasts, track and field athletes, and ballet dancers.

Differential Diagnosis

- Subtrochanteric bursitis
- L4 and L5 nerve root syndromes
- Insertion tendopathy (with or without calcification) of the gluteus maximus or gluteus medius muscles
- "Snapping hip"
- Scar tissue (eg, after a hip operation with a posterior incision)
- Pain as the result of a loosened total hip replacement

Clinical Findings

The patient complains of pain on the lateral aspect of the thigh, usually just proximal to the greater trochanter.

Functional Examination

Sidebending of the trunk away from the affected side can be painful as a result of a stretch on the muscle. The pain increases if the leg is simultaneously adducted. If the tensor fasciae latae muscle is affected, resisted hip abduction can also be painful. Sometimes, however, this is only the case when tested from a stretched position.

Treatment

Transverse friction is effective. In most cases only a few treatments are necessary, even when the symptoms are of long duration.

SNAPPING HIP (COXA SALTANS)

A "snapping hip" can be either intra-articular or extraarticular. The cause of the usually nonpainful intraarticular form is unknown. The extraarticular snapping hip can result from an aberration of the iliotibial tract or the iliopsoas muscle. The most often seen aberration of the iliotibial tract is a thickening of the most posterior superior part of the tract or of the most anterior part of the gluteus maximus. This lesion is seen particularly in track and field athletes and ballet dancers, but can also be found in nonathletes.

In most cases, the patient does not have any pain but complains of a snapping sound and feeling at the lateral aspect of the thigh, in the region of the greater trochanter, experienced when walking. This is caused by the snapping of the iliotibial tract over the greater trochanter. The second location for a snapping hip is the pubic pecten. At this site, the iliopsoas can cause the same complaints, but now they are experienced in the groin.

Differential Diagnosis in the Case of Pain

- Subtrochanteric bursitis
- L4 and L5 nerve root syndromes
- Insertion tendopathy (with or without calcification) of the gluteus maximus or gluteus medius muscles
- Sprain of the iliotibial tract and tensor fasciae latae muscle
- Scar tissue (eg, after a hip operation with a posterior incision)
- Pain as the result of a loosened total hip replacement

Clinical Findings

The patient is apprehensive about the snapping sound and feeling.

Functional Examination

The functional examination is negative, but during active hip flexion from a position of extension the snapping at the lateral side of the thigh in the region of the greater trochanter is palpable or audible. In some cases, snapping is only evoked by rotating the hip in a position of adduction and flexion. If the snapping is caused by the iliopsoas muscle, a small snap is palpable deep in the groin during active flexion of the hip from a neutral position.

Treatment

A painless lesion usually does not require treatment; the patient just needs to be assured that there is nothing serious to worry about. If pain is provoked by the snapping hip, attempts can be made to decrease the symptoms by stretching exercises. In unsuccessful cases, there may be a bursitis in this region, which can be expected to respond well to an injection.

LESIONS OF THE MUSCLE BELLIES OF THE QUADRICEPS FEMORIS

Sprains or partial tears of one of the muscle bellies of the quadriceps femoris are most commonly seen in track and field athletes, particularly sprinters and long jumpers, and less often in soccer players. The lesion almost always occurs acutely and can usually be blamed on insufficient warm-up procedures. In almost every case, the lesion occurs at the precise moment when a quick extension motion of the knee is accompanied by hip flexion from a position of knee flexion and hip extension. It is important to note that the rectus femoris muscle is a predilection site for myositis ossificans!

Clinical Findings

The patient can usually make a correct diagnosis and is accurately able to identify the site of the rupture. A hematoma is often visible, and in acute cases a gap can be felt (Figure 4–18). If the pain is localized in the groin, the proximal part of the muscle belly of the rectus femoris is affected.

Functional Examination

In the acute phase, resisted extension of the 90° flexed knee (tested with the hip in neutral), is painful. Extension of the hip combined with flexion of the knee is also painful as a result of a stretch of the injured muscle. The rupture can be seen on ultrasound (Figure 4–19).

Treatment

In acute cases with obvious swelling, the hematoma can be aspirated. Immediately after, it is recommended that a few milliliters of a local anesthetic be injected just above and below the rupture. Starting on the second day of treatment, transverse friction can be cautiously administered to prevent adhesions. This treatment should be performed daily and increased in duration up to 15 minutes, in accordance with the patient's level of tolerance. After each session of transverse friction, active muscle contraction should be performed with the muscle in an approximated position. For instance, in a rectus femoris lesion, the hip is flexed and the knee extended, thereby taking the muscle off stretch and bringing its insertions closer to each other. If active contraction of the muscle is painful, the same effect can be achieved using electrical muscle stimulation. Gentle stretching exercises should also be performed. Treatment should be continued for approximately 2 weeks after clinical recovery; otherwise the risk of recurrence is great (Figure 4–20).

LESIONS OF THE HAMSTRINGS

In lesions of the hamstrings, differentiation is made between insertion tendopathy at the ischial tuberosity and sprain and partial tear of the muscle bellies. In all cases, a sports injury is usually involved. The lesion is seen particularly in track and field athletes and soccer players. Occasionally, an avulsion fracture of the ischial tuberosity is seen in children and adolescents (Figure 4–21).

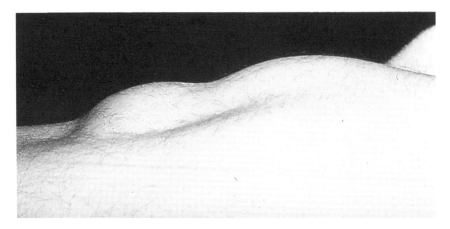

Figure 4–18 Clinical photograph of a typical deformation in the case of a large tear in the quadriceps. Proximal to the muscle tear, there is a lump resulting from contraction of the muscle tissue. At the same time, the gap distal to the tear is evident.

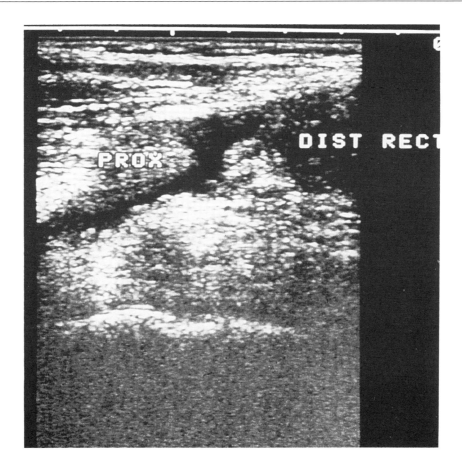

Figure 4–19 Ultrasound showing an obvious rupture (dark zone) in the rectus femoris muscle.

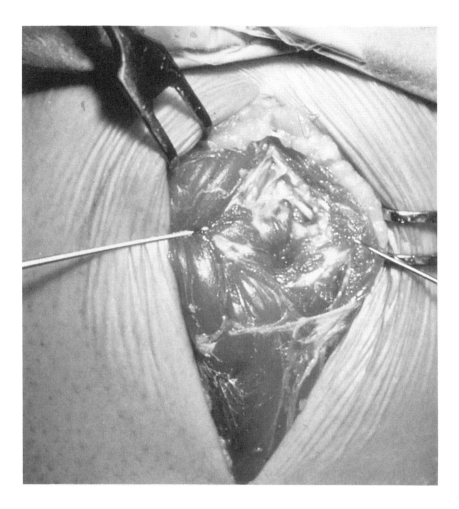

Figure 4–20 Preoperative view of an old rupture of the quadriceps muscle. Fibrotic tissue is evident, as is cystic degeneration, which leads to recurrent injuries and pain.

In the differential diagnosis, consideration should be given to S1 and S2 nerve root syndromes, ischial bursitis, and the hamstring syndrome (refer to Chapter 6).

Clinical Findings

The patient is usually able to locate the exact site of the lesion. There is usually no radiation of pain.

Functional Examination

When the lesion concerns a partial tear of one of the hamstring muscle bellies or an avulsion fracture of the ischial tuberosity, the straight leg raise test is limited and painful. Resisted extension of the hip, in combination with flexion of the knee, is painful. In instances of an insertion tendopathy, the straight leg raise is often the only painful test. The resisted test is painful only in severe cases.

Treatment

In acute cases where there is obvious swelling, the hematoma can be aspirated. Immediately after, injection of a few milliliters of a

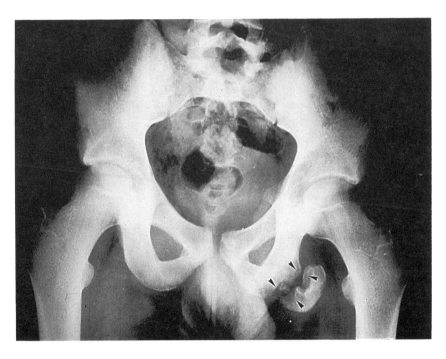

Figure 4–21 Conventional radiograph showing a large avulsion fracture of the ischial tuberosity (arrowheads).

local anesthetic just above and below the rupture is recommended. Starting on the second day of treatment, adhesions can be prevented by the cautious use of transverse friction. This treatment should be performed daily and increased in duration up to 15 minutes, taking into account the patient's tolerance level for pain. After each session of transverse friction, active muscle contraction should be performed with the muscle in an approximated position. If active contraction of the muscle is painful, the same effect can be achieved using electrical muscle stimulation. Gentle stretching exercises should also be performed. Treatment should be continued for approximately 2 weeks after clinical recovery; otherwise the risk of recurrence is great. In cases of insertion tendopathy, transverse friction and stretching exercises are almost always effective. The patient should also perform stretching exercises several times each day at home.

TENDINITIS OF THE GLUTEUS MAXIMUS OR GLUTEUS MEDIUS MUSCLE

Lesions of the gluteus maximus or gluteus medius muscles are rare. The gluteus maximus inserts on the iliotibial tract and on the gluteal tuberosity (distal to the greater trochanter at the posterior aspect of the femur). The gluteus medius inserts more proximally, at the posterior aspect of the greater trochanter.

Differential Diagnosis

- Subtrochanteric bursitis
- Local trauma and, more frequently, brain trauma, after which large calcifications can occur in the gluteal region (Figure 4–22)
- L4 and L5 nerve root syndromes
- "Snapping hip"

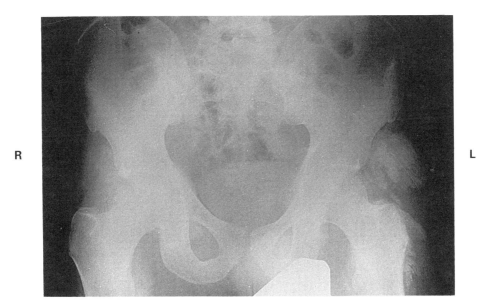

R L

Figure 4–22 Conventional radiograph showing a large calcification in the pelvic region, more on the left than on the right, that occurred after a severe brain trauma.

- Scar tissue (eg, after a hip operation with a posterior incision)
- Pain as the result of a loosened total hip replacement

Clinical Findings

The patient complains of local pain, particularly during strenuous running.

Functional Examination

The functional examination is usually negative, but in some cases resisted hip extension is painful. Sometimes, resisted external rotation or abduction is also painful. There is local tenderness to palpation. If the gluteus maximus is affected, the tenderness is located at the posterior aspect of the greater trochanter. With tendinitis of the gluteus medius, the site is more proximal. A plain film is the best means to detect calcification. The calcium is localized at the level of the gluteal tuberosity. An ultrasound examination is an effective way to differentiate between this lesion and a bursitis.

Treatment

Treatment of a gluteus maximus or medius tendinitis is often difficult. Transverse friction should be tried, but it is seldom effective. In cases where there is calcification, transverse friction is not indicated. Injection with a local anesthetic, with or without the addition of corticosteroid, often leads to a cure. In some cases, surgical treatment is indicated.

4.4   OTHER DISORDERS

GROIN PAIN IN A NEGATIVE FUNCTIONAL EXAMINATION OF THE HIP

If the functional examination of the hip is negative, the lumbar spine and sacroiliac joint should be examined as thoroughly as possible. If these examinations are also negative, the patient should be sent to an internist, urologist or gynecologist. Many internal disorders, such as femoral and inguinal hernias, urethritis posterior, prostatitis, nephrolithiasis, and various gynecologic problems can cause pain in the lower abdomen and groin region.

In some cases, form and position aberrations of the hip, which are often congenital, can also cause pain in the groin region, even in the absence of positive findings in the functional examination. Radiographic examination is then indicated. Such congenital aberrations include hip dysplasias, hip subluxations and dislocations, as well as coxa vara, coxa valga, and femoral antetorsion.

STRESS FRACTURES

The incidence of stress fractures in the hip region has increased with the popularity of jogging and many other sports, such as the very demanding triathlon. Stress fractures can occur in the iliac crest, femoral neck, lesser trochanter, and greater trochanter (rare). The overly enthusiastic athlete often has too little regard for the proper progression in training and the use of appropriate footwear.

The most frequent causes of stress fractures in the hip region are muscle fatigue, inadequate footwear, and biomechanical left–right asymmetry. Such asymmetry may consist of an apparent or true short leg, a unilateral flat foot, or a unilateral varus or valgus position of the knee or calcaneus.

Clinical Findings

Initially, the symptoms are activity related. After a period of time, the pain becomes more localized, and finally severe tenderness develops. The local tenderness is sometimes accompanied by slight local swelling at one point. The pain may also radiate slightly. Plain films are negative in the first 3 to 4 weeks of symptoms.

Treatment

Treatment consists of drastically reducing or stopping the sports activity while isolating and treating the specific causes.

APOPHYSEAL AVULSION FRACTURE IN CHILDREN

An apophyseal avulsion fracture in children occurs between the ages of 11 and 13 years, when muscular forces act upon the apophyseal plate. In this age group, the ligaments and tendons in the region of the growth plates have stronger attachments than the growth plates themselves. In most cases, sports injuries are involved. Predisposition sites in the hip region are ischial tuberosity, anterior superior iliac spine, lesser trochanter, greater trochanter, and iliac crest. Most of these predilection sites have already been discussed with the respective muscle lesions. For more detailed information about the clinical findings for avulsion fractures of the first four sites, refer back to the appropriate sections. Thus, only the apophyseal avulsion fracture of the iliac crest is discussed below.

Apophyseal Fracture of the Iliac Crest

In instances of an apophyseal fracture of the iliac crest, differentiation should be made between a stress fracture and a compression neuropathy of the lateral cutaneous ramus of the iliohypogastric nerve. The latter lesion is seen particularly in adults, however. In adolescent athletes, there can be a radiographically demonstrable pathology of the apophysis of the iliac crest, a condition that differs from an apophyseal avulsion fracture of the iliac crest.

Clinical Findings

The patient complains of pain and tenderness at the level of the iliac crest, which occurs after a period of (relative) overuse. Usually this involves sprinters or jumpers. The tenderness is most pronounced at the junction between the anterior third and the posterior two thirds of the apophysis, which is confirmed on plain films. Some patients also have local swelling.

Functional Examination

In the functional examination, only passive adduction of the hip is painful.

Treatment

The treatment of an avulsion fracture is almost always conservative.

COMPARTMENT SYNDROME (FASCIAL COMPRESSION NEUROPATHY AND COMPARTMENTAL SYNDROME)

Acute Compartment Syndrome

A compartment syndrome can develop as the result of a decrease in the size of the compartment. Such decreases may, for instance, be due to constriction by a cast, scars from surgery (closing fascial defects), arterial thrombosis or emboli, and reconstructive vascular and bypass operations. They can also develop as the result of a constriction of the compartment through edema, hemorrhage, or both.

Clinical Findings

The clinical findings may include pain, swelling, sensory disturbances, motor disturbances, and absence of peripheral pulses accompanied by paleness of the skin.

- *Pain:* The pain is more severe than expected in a fracture or a contusion and is described as a deep, throbbing pressure. The pain does not disappear with immobilization and actually increases if immobilization is achieved by means of casting. In some cases, however, the pain is absent because of a central or peripheral neurologic sensory deficit. In many cases, pain increases on stretching of the muscles of that compartment.
- *Swelling:* Swelling occurs throughout the entire compartment. In addition, the skin is sometimes warm. Palpation is tender.
- *Sensory disturbances:* Because of the increased pressure, ischemia of the nerve(s) within the compartment occurs. The first sign is paresthesia in the area of cutaneous innervation of the affected nerve; later, this evolves to hypesthesia followed by anesthesia.
- *Motor disturbances:* Muscle weakness, secondary to the nerve ischemia, can develop 30 minutes after the occurrence of the ischemia and becomes irreversible after 12 to 24 hours!
- *Peripheral pulsation:* Absence of peripheral pulses with paleness of the skin is a rather rare sign and is certainly not a reliable basis on which to make the diagnosis.

In addition to the clinical diagnostics, a Doppler examination, arteriography, electromyography, CT scan, MR imaging, and intracompartmental pressure measurements can help confirm the diagnosis.

Treatment

Treatment is surgical.

Exertion-Related Compartment Syndrome

The exertion-related compartment syndrome is classified further into acute and chronic forms. In the acute variant, there is a significant increase in the intracompartmental pressure, which makes immediate decompression necessary to prevent necrosis of the intracompartmental structures. The clinical picture is similar to that of the acute compartment syndrome, except that in this case there may be no known external trauma, and the situation arises after heavy exertion. Of these acute types, approximately 100 cases are described in the medical literature.

The chronic compartment syndrome is seen more often, and it is most often seen in the anterior compartment of the lower leg. Compartment syndromes of the thigh are seldom seen. The exact pathogenesis of an exertion-related compartment syndrome is unknown.

Posterior Compartment Syndrome of the Thigh

Posterior compartment syndrome of the thigh is typically a sports disorder that is seen particularly in long-distance runners. The left thigh is more often affected than the right thigh. The biceps femoris, semitendinosus, and semimembranosus muscles run in the posterior compartment, along with the sciatic nerve. The cause is thought to be excessively heavy exertion during training and competitions.

Clinical Findings

In the chronic compartment syndrome, pain is experienced at the posterior aspect of the thigh, sometimes radiating slightly medially during running. Severity of the pain corresponds to the running speed. In sprinting, the pain is experienced quickly. In normal running, the pain comes on gradually. Because of the pain, the athlete is forced to run more slowly.

Functional Examination

The functional examination is negative. There is also no tenderness to palpation.

Treatment

In the first instance, treatment is conservative. Activities are decreased; sudden acceleration and sprinting should be avoided. In addition, warm-up and stretching exercises are emphasized during and after training and competitions. Sharp curves should also be avoided because these increase the pain. In therapy-resistant cases, a fasciotomy is indicated. Results from this procedure are usually good.

Lateral Compartment Syndrome of the Thigh

Lateral compartment syndrome of the thigh concerns chronic compression of the tensor fasciae latae muscle. The patient complains of pain and local swelling of this muscle at the level of the greater trochanter.

The clinical diagnosis is determined by intracompartmental pressure measurements. CT scan can be valuable in assessing the extent of the swelling. In the differential diagnosis, a subtrochanteric bursitis should be considered.

Clinical Findings

The pain can arise during activities as well as while sitting. Sitting causes a decrease in the intrafascial space; movements cause an increase of the muscle volume.

Functional Examination

The functional examination is negative.

Treatment

In this instance, conservative treatment is ineffective. Surgical decompression is the treatment of choice.

"SIGN OF THE BUTTOCK"

The "sign of the buttock" concerns a syndrome in which severe pain is experienced in the gluteal region and sometimes also in the groin.[11] The syndrome can occur traumatically or insidiously. Traumatic onset usually involves a fracture of the sacrum or pelvis. Insidious onsets usually involve an abscess, severe inflammation, or a tumor in the pelvic region.

Clinical Findings

The patient complains of severe pain in the gluteal region, which can radiate to the posterior aspect of the thigh and sometimes all the way to the foot. Normal walking is almost impossible.

Functional Examination

The functional examination demonstrates a characteristic triad:

1. The straight leg raise test is painful and limited.

2. Passive hip flexion (with a flexed knee) is painful and limited, with an empty end-feel.

3. The passive motion tests of the hip demonstrate a noncapsular pattern of limitations.

Laboratory tests and radiologic imaging, along with a bone scan, should be performed to determine the cause of the symptoms.

Treatment

The treatment depends on the cause.

* * *

For an overview of the common pathologies of the hip, refer to Appendix D—Algorithms for the Diagnosis and Treatment of Hip Pathology.

Chapter 5

Treatment Techniques in Lesions of the Hip

ARTHROSIS OR ARTHRITIS OF THE HIP JOINT

Functional Examination

Passive motions are limited in a capsular pattern; internal rotation is more limited than extension, flexion, and abduction (measured in degrees of limitation).

INTRAARTICULAR INJECTION

An intraarticular injection of the hip joint with a corticosteroid is indicated in patients with coxarthrosis when conservative treatment is ineffective and surgery is not yet indicated. This injection is also indicated in rheumatoid diseases when oral medications offer minimal to no results.

Position of the Patient

The patient lies on the treatment table on the nonaffected side.

Position of the Physician

The physician stands next to the long side of the treatment table, behind the patient.

Performance

With one hand, the physician locates the greater trochanter. If this is made difficult by thick subcutaneous tissue, the leg can be passively abducted with one arm while the other hand palpates for the superior edge of the greater trochanter with the leg in the abducted position. In this position, the iliotibial tract is relaxed.

A 5-mL syringe is filled with 2 mL of corticosteroid and 3 mL of local anesthetic. A 10-cm needle is inserted in a mediodistal direction at an angle of approximately 70° to the horizontal, just proximal to the superior edge of the greater trochanter. After passing through the thickened joint capsule, the needle hits the femoral neck close to the femoral head. The needle is then withdrawn slightly and the solution injected (Figure 5–1).

Almost all patients have increased pain for several minutes after the injection, which can return several hours later. It can be expected to last a maximum of 24 hours.

Follow-Up

In the first 3 days after the injection, the joint should be protected as much as possible and restricted to minimal or no weight bearing. Patients with a coxarthrosis may need a second injection when the pain returns, which may occur from 2 to 6 months later. In

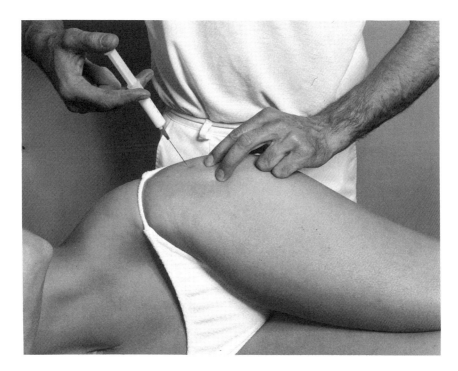

Figure 5–1 Intraarticular injection of the hip joint.

this manner, injections can be given in 3- to 6-month intervals until such time as surgery becomes necessary. The number of injections given in rheumatoid disorders ranges from a few injections to one injection every 6 months.

LOOSE BODY IN THE HIP JOINT

Functional Examination

Passive motions are limited in a noncapsular pattern. The most common combinations of limited motions are external rotation and flexion, and adduction and flexion; every other combination is also possible. In a coxarthrosis patient with a loose body in the hip joint, there will be limitations of motions in a capsular pattern, but then external rotation is often also painful and limited.

MANIPULATION

A rotation manipulation under traction is indicated in the hip both in instances of a loose body without a known cause and in cases of coxarthrosis with "joint mice" (loose bodies) as a complication. The patient history is usually highly diagnostic. The patient complains of sharp shooting pains in the groin that are characterized as being irregularly occurring, short lasting, and momentarily paralyz-

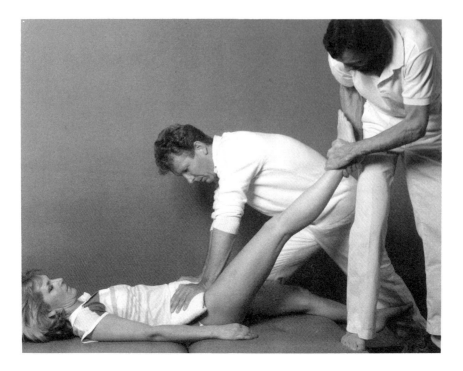

Figure 5–2A Initial position in an external rotation manipulation of the hip joint with a loose body.

ing. This pain can radiate to the anteromedial aspect of the thigh. Lesions of the acetabular labrum can cause similar symptoms. Manipulations can be tried in these instances as well.

Position of the Patient

The patient lies supine on the treatment table. The patient shifts over so that the nonaffected side lies as closely as possible to the edge of the table. The distal half of the patient's lower legs should hang over the foot of the table. The treatment table is lowered as far as possible.

Position of the Therapist

The therapist stands at the end of the table with one bare foot up on the end of the table parallel to the end of the table with the toes pointed toward the closest long side of the

table. (External rotation is described here as an example, but exactly the same principles are followed for internal rotation manipulations.) If the right hip is being treated, the therapist grasps the lower leg of the patient with both hands. The left hand is placed on the anterior aspect of the leg just proximal to both malleoli, and the right hand grasps from the medial aspect. The therapist holds both elbows in about 90° flexion.

Position of the Assistant

Because the therapist exerts traction on the patient's hip, the patient's pelvis has to be fixated. This fixation can be accomplished by means of two mobilization belts, but in view of the force required during this treatment, fixation by an assistant is preferred.

The assistant stands, with legs apart, next to the treatment table on the affected side of the patient. (For the purposes of picture taking, and visibility, the assistant in the pictures here stands on the patient's nonaffected side.) A folded towel or piece of foam is placed across the anterior aspect of the patient's pelvis, and the assistant places both hands on the anterior superior iliac spines, pushing in a cranial and dorsal direction.

Performance

The therapist first exerts traction on the patient's hip and then, from maximal internal rotation, externally rotates the patient's straight, slightly abducted leg. At the same time, the therapist shifts the upper trunk away from the treatment table. The therapist does not slip off the treatment table because the foot remaining on the table is bare.

The external rotation is performed in a manipulative manner, after which the hip is more slowly internally rotated. The external rotation manipulation is repeated two to four times while the therapist brings the body weight farther away from the table. At the same time, the patient's hip is slowly extended. Just when the last external rotation is performed, the therapist places the other foot on the floor (Figure 5–2, A and B).

After the manipulation, the mobility of the hip is retested. If there is improvement, the same manipulation is repeated. If the functional examination has not changed, the manipulation is performed in an internal rotation direction (Figures 5–3 and 5–4).

Until now, we have had the most success with the internal rotation manipulation. The number of treatments varies significantly. Some patients are completely free of symptoms after one treatment, whereas other patients are treated one time per week over a period of several months. If the symptoms continually recur, arthroscopy is indicated. Arthroscopy can also confirm the possibility of a labrum lesion.

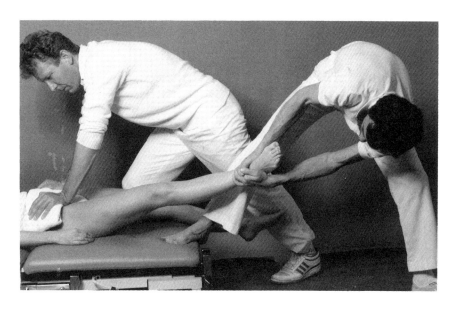

Figure 5–2B End position in an external rotation manipulation of the hip joint with a loose body.

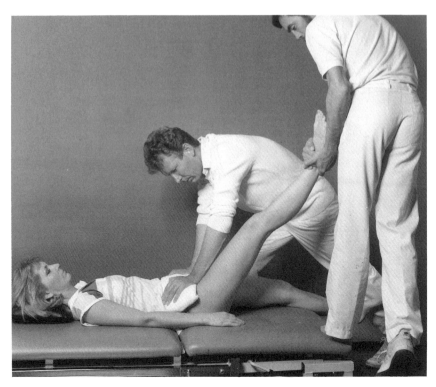

Figure 5–3 Initial position in an internal rotation manipulation of the hip joint with a loose body.

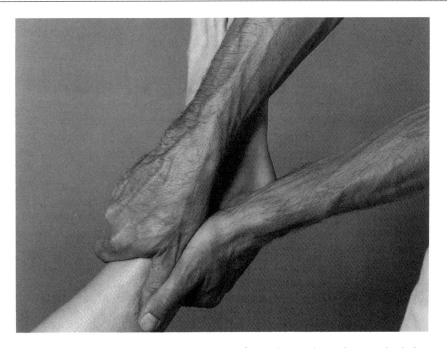

Figure 5–4 Alternative hand position, in this instance, for an internal rotation manipulation.

LESIONS OF THE HIP ADDUCTORS I

Functional Examination

Passive hip flexion is sometimes painful as a result of compression of the affected structures. Passive hip flexion in combination with adduction is often more painful as a result of even more compression of the affected structures. Passive abduction of the hip is sometimes painful as a result of a stretch of the affected structures. Resisted adduction of the hip (with the hip in neutral, 45° flexion, or 90° flexion) is painful.

TRANSVERSE FRICTION

Of the hip adductors, the adductor brevis and gracilis are most susceptible to lesions. The pectineus and adductor longus are less often affected. In Europe, the lesion is most often seen in soccer players, often in combination with a lesion of the rectus abdominis muscle or of the oblique abdominal muscles.

When the adductor brevis is affected, injection is the single choice for local therapy because the muscle lies so deeply and cannot be reached for transverse friction. Stretching exercises and causal treatment are attempted first. Injection is only indicated if the results are unsatisfactory.

Lesions of the adductors can have various causes. In addition to the performance of transverse friction therapy, stretching exercises, and so forth, the primary cause of the lesion should be determined and dealt with. Refer to Chapter 4 for more detailed information.

Transverse Friction of the Insertion of the Gracilis

Position of the Patient

The patient lies supine on the treatment table, with the hip in 60° or more of flexion and the knee flexed accordingly.

Position of the Therapist

The therapist stands next to the treatment table at the patient's affected side, just cranial to the pelvis. If the left hip is being treated, the therapist places the tip of the right index finger as proximal as possible on the most medial part of the tendon of the gracilis. The thumb gives counterpressure and is placed on the lower abdomen parallel to the index finger in a proximal direction (how far cranially depends on the size of the hand).

Performance

The transverse friction is performed with the end phalanx of the index finger. The index finger is reinforced by the middle finger, and the index finger presses the tendon against the inferior pubic ramus. The pressure is exerted in the direction of the thumb, almost directly cranial. The friction phase occurs through an extension of the wrist with slight adduction of the arm (Figure 5–5).

Duration

The transverse friction should be performed daily or at least three times per week, lasting about 15 minutes per session. Along with stretching exercises, which the patient should also perform several times per day at home, abdominal strengthening exercises should be initiated.

In the acute stage, the conservative therapy described here usually provides quick results. If the lesion has been present no longer than 3 months, there is still a good chance that conservative treatment will help, but then the treatment should be combined with rest (the patient has to refrain from activities that put a great demand on the adductors). In most lesions existing longer than 3 months, the results with conservative therapy are disappointing and surgical treatment is necessary if the athlete wants to continue participation in sports.

Figure 5–5 Transverse friction of the insertion of the gracilis on the inferior pubic ramus.

Transverse Friction of the Pectineus and Insertion of the Adductor Longus

If the pectineus is to be treated with transverse friction, the obvious, prominent tendon of the adductor longus must first be located. The pectineus lies directly lateral to this point and has a flat, muscular origin. Palpation is used to locate the most tender site. In this regard, it is important to note that often one or two small cords can be felt running over the muscle. These are lymph nodes and should *not* be subject to friction. During the transverse friction, bone contact should be maintained. In other words, the treating finger should feel the bone of the pubic pectin through the muscle insertion as a way to ensure that the friction is applied to the correct location. The thumb of the hand performing the transverse friction is placed at the patient's ipsilateral anterior superior iliac spine. During this technique, pressure is exerted by the index finger in the direction of the contralateral anterior superior iliac spine, and the transverse friction is performed from medial to lateral over the lesion (Figure 5–6).

In treatment of the adductor longus, most lesions occur at its origin on the pubic tubercle. Sometimes, however, the muscle belly or musculotendinous junction is affected. Treatment of the latter sites is described in the following sections.

As with transverse friction of the pectineus, in the treatment of the adductor longus origin bone contact should be maintained. The thumb of the hand performing the transverse friction is placed at the patient's ipsilateral anterior superior iliac spine. During this technique, pressure is exerted toward the ipsilateral anterior superior iliac spine, and the transverse friction is performed from medial to lateral over the lesion (Figure 5–7).

The same patient and therapist positions as well as the duration of treatment described for transverse friction of the gracilis are applied to transverse friction of the pectineus and adductor longus.

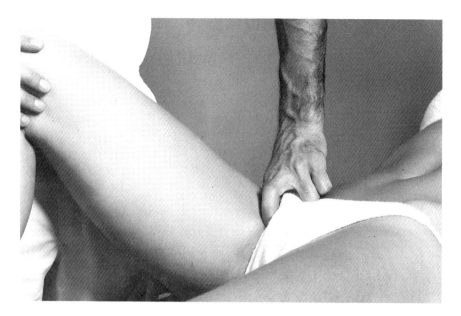

Figure 5–6 Transverse friction of the origin of the pectineus.

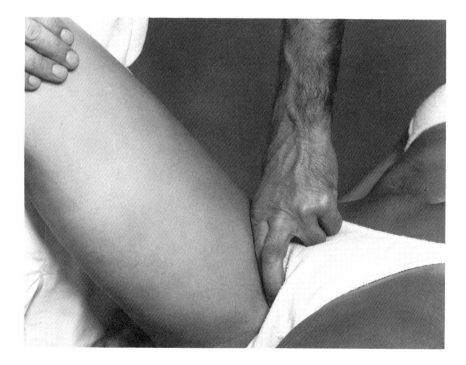

Figure 5–7 Transverse friction of the origin of the adductor longus.

SPRAIN OF THE MUSCLE BELLY OR MUSCULOTENDINOUS JUNCTION OF THE ADDUCTOR LONGUS

Functional Examination

Passive hip abduction is usually painful. Resisted hip adduction is painful.

TRANSVERSE FRICTION

In lesions of the adductor longus, an attempt should be made to determine the primary cause of the lesion and to apply the appropriate treatment. Therefore, transverse friction is only part of the treatment program, which also includes muscle stretching.

Position of the Patient

The patient lies in a supine position with the knee flexed approximately 45°.

Position of the Therapist

The therapist stands next to the treatment table at the patient's affected side, at the level of the patient's thigh. If the right side is to be treated, the therapist grasps the muscle belly of the adductor longus between thumb and index finger of the right hand. The site of the lesion is located by palpating the length of the muscle belly and musculotendinous junction between the thumb and index finger.

Performance

The lesion is held between thumb and index finger. The friction phase consists of a slight extension of the therapist's wrist; in so doing, the thumb and index finger move from lateral to medial over the site of the lesion (Figure 5–8). During the relaxation phase, pressure is not exerted.

Duration

The transverse friction treatment should be given three times per week, in conjunction with stretching exercises. The prognosis in

Figure 5–8 Transverse friction of the muscle belly of the adductor longus.

this lesion is usually good. Symptoms subside in a relatively short time, 3 to 4 weeks. During the treatment period, the patient should refrain from activities that provoke pain.

LESIONS OF THE HIP ADDUCTORS II

STRETCHING OF THE HIP ADDUCTORS

Static stretching of the adductors should be performed not only by the therapist but also by the patient. In treating hip adductor lesions, stretching is only part of the treatment program, which should also include transverse friction and abdominal muscle strengthening. Both the long adductor (gracilis) and the short (monarthric) adductors should be stretched, even in cases, for example, where only the adductor longus is affected.

Stretching of the Gracilis Muscle

Position of the Patient

The patient lies supine on the treatment table, with the head of the table inclined about 30°. The affected leg lies in an extended position on the table. The nonaffected thigh is on the table with the lower leg hanging over the table; in this way, the pelvis is fixated.

Position of the Therapist

The therapist stands with feet apart next to the treatment table, at the patient's affected side. If the right gracilis muscle is to be stretched, the therapist grasps the patient's leg with the right forearm and hand in such a way that the patient's lower leg rests in the hollow of the elbow and the hand is placed at the medial aspect of the extended knee. The other hand is placed on top of the left anterior superior iliac spine.

Performance

Taking into consideration the patient's pain and muscle splinting, the leg is slowly abducted (Figure 5–9). The patient should also stretch several times per day at home.

Stretching of the Monarthric Adductor Muscles

To stretch the monarthric adductors, the biarticular adductor (the gracilis) is relaxed by bending the knee. The therapist now grasps the flexed knee from the medial side and performs the stretch from this position (Figure 5–10).

Self-Stretching Exercises

Performance

The patient can perform self-stretching exercises in a number of different ways. The two types presented here are simple and easy to learn. Figure 5–11 shows stretching of the monarthric adductors. The patient sits on the floor. After placing the soles of the feet together, the patient pulls the feet as closely as possible toward the hips. Both forearms are placed on the medial aspect of the thighs, just above the knees, and they are used to push the knees slowly and gently toward the floor. The lumbar spine must be as upright as possible to get the most benefit from the exercise.

Figure 5–12 demonstrates how the patient can focus stretch on the gracilis muscle. In standing, the trunk is sidebent toward the af-

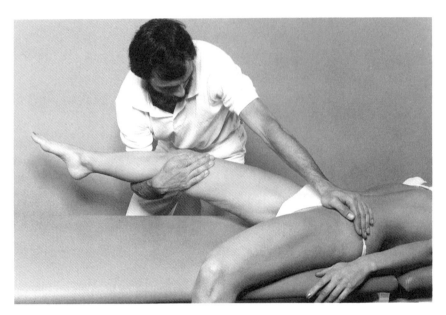

Figure 5–9 Static stretch of the gracilis.

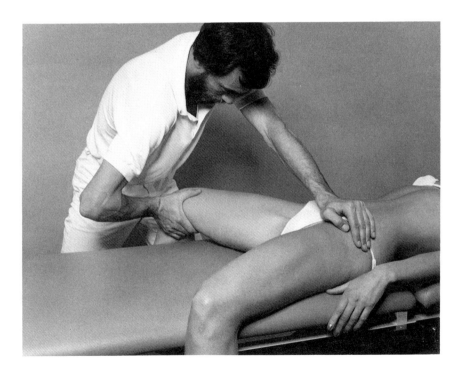

Figure 5–10 Static stretching of the monarthric adductors.

Figure 5–11 Self-stretching for the monarthric adductors.

fected side, with the patient's hand resting on the lateral aspect of the thigh just distal to the anterior superior iliac spine. With this hand, the patient pushes the thigh slowly and gently in a medial direction (the knee remains extended). By pushing the pelvis more forward, emphasis is shifted to a stretch of the more anterior lying adductors. Stretching should be performed on the nonaffected side as well.

INJECTION FOR INSERTION TENDOPATHIES OF THE ADDUCTOR LONGUS AND ADDUCTOR BREVIS

When conservative treatment has only minimal or no effect, injection is the next step before surgery is considered.

Injection of the Adductor Longus

Position of the Patient

The patient lies in a semireclined position with the head of the treatment table inclined about 30°. The thigh is slightly abducted and externally rotated.

Position of the Physician

The physician stands or sits next to the treatment table, at the patient's affected side. With the tip of the index finger, the origin of the adductor longus on the pubic tubercle is located.

Performance

A syringe is filled with 1 mL of corticosteroid. A 3-cm needle is inserted almost horizon-

Figure 5–12 Self-stretching for the gracilis muscle.

tally at the site of the lesion. Directed by the location of the patient's pain, the teno-osseous insertion of the adductor longus is injected in a dropwise fashion (Figure 5–13).

Follow-Up

The patient should decrease weight bearing on the affected leg as much as possible for 1 week. After 2 weeks, the patient's condition should be reassessed. Depending on the findings in the functional examination, a second injection may be given. After 2 more weeks, if necessary, a third injection may given. After each injection, the patient should limit weight bearing on the affected extremity for 1 week.

Injection of the Adductor Brevis

Position of the Patient

If the adductor brevis is being injected, the patient lies supine on the treatment table. The hip is flexed to 90° and is slightly abducted.

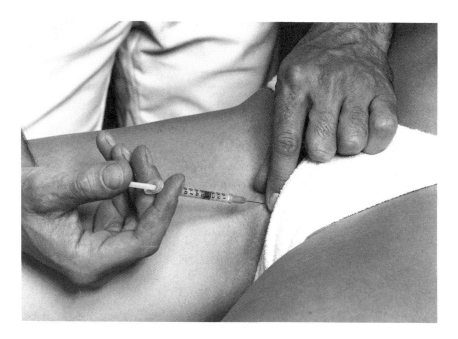

Figure 5–13 Injection of the adductor longus at the pubic tubercle.

Position of the Physician

The physician stands or sits next to the treatment table, at the patient's affected side. The tendon of the adductor longus is located with the tip of the index finger. The adductor brevis lies in the depth just medial from here, between the tendons of the adductor longus and gracilis.

Performance

A syringe is filled with a corticosteroid. A 5-cm needle, as small in diameter as possible, is inserted between the insertions of the adductor longus and gracilis. As determined by pain location, the insertion of the adductor brevis is injected in a dropwise fashion.

Follow-Up

The patient should reduce weight bearing on the affected leg as much as possible for 1 week. After 2 weeks, the patient's condition is reassessed. Depending on the findings in the functional examination, a second injection may be given. After 2 more weeks, if necessary, a third injection may be given. After each injection, the patient should limit weight bearing on the affected extremity for 1 week.

INSERTION TENDOPATHY OF THE RECTUS FEMORIS MUSCLE

Functional Examination

Passive hip flexion is sometimes painful as a result of compression of the affected structure. Resisted flexion of the hip is only painful in severe cases. Resisted knee flexion from the prone position is painful.

TRANSVERSE FRICTION

Lesions of the rectus femoris muscle are most often seen at the insertion on the anterior inferior iliac spine. Occasionally, the tendon of this muscle is affected. Except for the location of the affected site, the transverse friction technique is the same for both lesions.

Position of the Patient

The patient sits on the treatment table and leans against the head of the table, which is inclined approximately 70°. A roll is placed under the knee. In this position, the structures lying on top of the lesion are relaxed, and the origin of the rectus femoris muscle can be more easily reached (Figure 5–14).

This lesion can also be treated with the patient lying on the nonaffected side. The hips are flexed about 90°.

Position of the Therapist

The therapist sits next to the treatment table at the patient's affected side. If the right side is being treated, the therapist places the tip of the left thumb just medial to the lesion (which is just distal to the most prominent part of the anterior inferior iliac spine; the anterior inferior iliac spine is best palpable when the hip is passively brought farther into flexion). The fingers apply counterpressure against the posterior aspect of the thigh.

Performance

The active phase of the transverse friction consists of a radial deviation of the wrist with the tip of the thumb moving from a medial to a lateral direction over the lesion (Figure 5–15, A and B).

Duration

Transverse friction should be performed for 15 minutes daily, or at least three times per week, in combination with stretching exercises. The patient should stretch daily at home. Two to 4 weeks of treatment are generally necessary to achieve complete relief of pain.

STRETCHING

Therapist-Assisted Stretching Exercises

Stretching exercises for the rectus femoris muscle are indicated for insertion tendopathies, both proximal (at the anterior inferior iliac spine) and distal (at the patella), sprains, and partial tears. Stretching can be performed with the assistance of the therapist in conjunction with transverse friction treatments. The patient is also instructed how to perform daily stretching exercises at home.

Position of the Patient

The patient lies supine on the treatment table. The sacrum lies just on the table, the nonaffected leg is maximally flexed at the hip and knee, and the patient maintains this position by pulling the knee to the chest with both hands. The other leg hangs over the table.

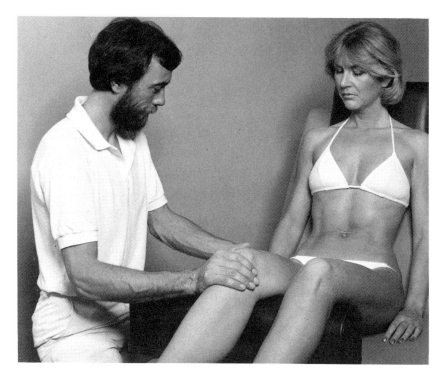

Figure 5–14 Initial position in transverse friction of the origin of the rectus femoris muscle.

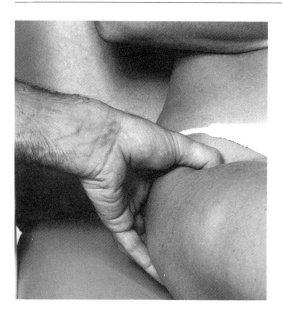

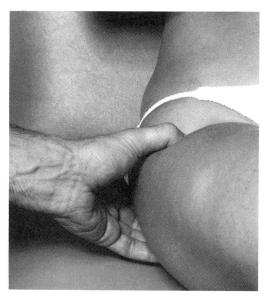

Figure 5–15A Initial position of the hand during transverse friction of the origin of the rectus femoris.

Figure 5–15B End position.

Position of the Therapist

The therapist stands with feet apart at the foot of the treatment table, in line with and facing the patient's nonaffected leg. If the left leg is being treated, the therapist places the left hand in the hollow of the patient's right knee while the other hand grasps the lower leg of the affected side as distally as possible.

Performance

Together with the patient, the therapist fixates the patient's nonaffected leg. The other hand, slowly and without causing pain or muscle splinting, brings the affected leg into hip extension and simultaneous knee flexion (Figures 5–16 and 5–17).

Self-Stretching Exercises

There are many possible ways of performing self-stretching exercises for the rectus femoris muscle. The exercise described below is a simple one in which the low back is not burdened.

Performance

The patient stands on the nonaffected leg and places the hand of that side on a table, wall, or the back of a chair for support. With the other hand, the foot of the affected leg is grasped from dorsal. First the pelvis is tilted maximally backward to fixate the pelvis during the stretch. From this position, the knee is brought slowly into flexion and, if possible, without losing the backward tilt of the pelvis, the hip is brought into extension (Figure 5–18, A and B). To maintain this backward tilt of the pelvis, it is important to contract the abdominal muscles maximally during the stretching exercise. The nonaffected side should also be stretched.

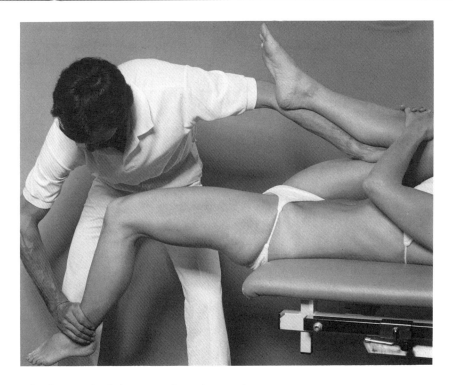

Figure 5–16 Static stretch of the rectus femoris muscle.

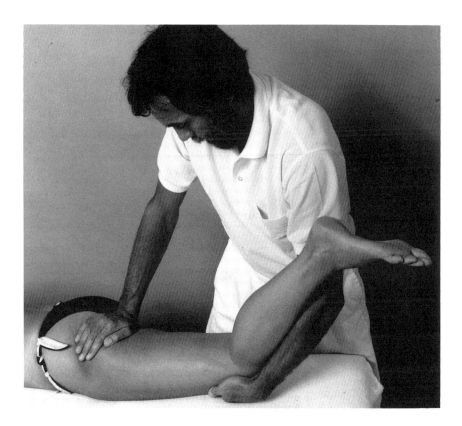

Figure 5–17 Alternative technique: The patient's pelvis is fixated against the treatment table via the ischial tuberosity. The therapist's distal hand extends the patient's hip, and the distal forearm flexes the patient's knee.

The patient should perform the stretching exercise two or three times daily, particularly first thing in the morning and before and after vigorous activities. Athletes should perform a more intensive stretching exercise program; stretching hourly is recommended during the first week of treatment and then every 2 hours in the second week of treatment. In the third week, the athlete should stretch two or three times per day.

This exercise is also performed in later stages of treatment for a partial tear of the muscle bellies of the quadriceps. The same is true in distal insertion tendopathies of the quadriceps in the para-, infra-, and suprapatellar regions.

Figure 5–18A Self-stretching of the rectus femoris, anterior view.

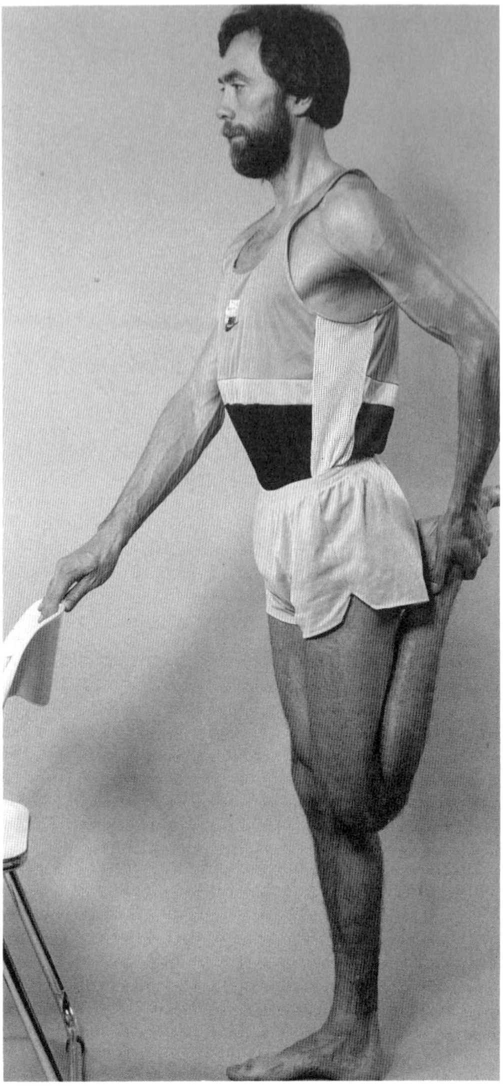

Figure 5–18B Self-stretching of the rectus femoris, lateral view.

STRAIN OR PARTIAL TEAR OF THE MUSCLE BELLY OF THE QUADRICEPS FEMORIS

Functional Examination

Passive flexion of the knee is painful and limited. Resisted knee extension, tested with the patient in a prone position, is painful.

TRANSVERSE FRICTION

This typical sports lesion can occur in different areas in the quadriceps muscle. Swelling and tenderness, and in acute cases even an interruption in the continuity of the muscle, indicate the site of the lesion. Superficial lesions are treated with the tips of the fingers by means of an extension of the wrist during the active phase of transverse friction. Deeper lying lesions, however, are treated in the manner described below.

Position of the Patient

The patient is in a semireclined position on the treatment table, with the head of the table inclined about 45°.

Position of the Therapist

The therapist stands next to the treatment table at the patient's affected side, at the level of the patient's thigh. The therapist grasps the lesion between both thumbs and all fingertips. In so doing, the fingers of both hands are placed at the medial aspect of the lesion, with both thumbs at the lateral aspect.

Performance

During the active phase of the transverse friction, both wrists perform an extension motion (starting from a flexed position). At the same time, the muscle is compressed between the thumbs and fingers (Figure 5–19, A and B). This technique is similar to the transverse kneading techniques used in classic massage. Cryotherapy can be administered before beginning the transverse friction.

Note

In principle, this treatment can be initiated as early as 2 days after the trauma. Depending on the severity of the lesion (sprain, small or large partial tear), the friction treatment should be gentle and last only a few minutes. Each day, the time and intensity of transverse friction can be increased, until approximately 15 minutes of daily transverse friction is performed. After each treatment of transverse friction, active contraction of the muscle should be performed in an approximated position of the muscle to maintain transverse mobility. If active contraction is too painful, as is sometimes the case in acute stages, the contraction can be achieved by means of electrical stimulation. The utmost care must be taken during stretching to avoid provocation of pain or muscle splinting (see previous section, self-stretching exercise for the rectus femoris).

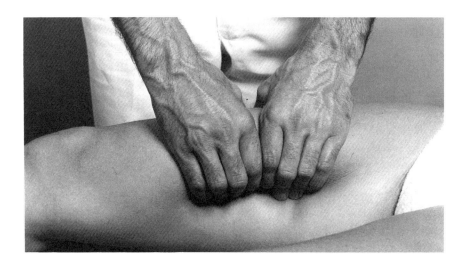

Figure 5–19A Initial position during transverse friction of a more deeply lying lesion in the vastus medialis.

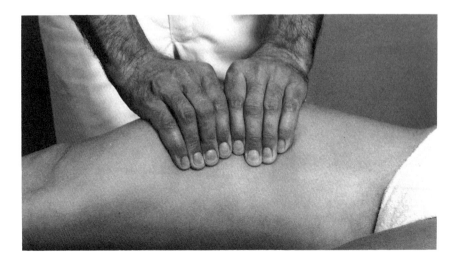

Figure 5–19B End position.

Usually, the functional examination is negative 10 to 14 days after injury. To prevent reoccurrence, the treatment should be continued for another 2 weeks: daily stretching and three times a week of transverse friction. At the same time, the patient should begin a muscle-strengthening exercise program. This can be accomplished using isometric, isotonic, and isokinetic exercises. At the earliest, the athlete can return to sports 2 weeks after the functional examination is found to be negative.

INSERTION TENDOPATHY OF THE HAMSTRINGS

Functional Examination

The straight leg raise test is usually painful at end-range. Resisted knee flexion combined with resisted hip extension is usually painful only after the pain-provoking activity has been performed.

TRANSVERSE FRICTION

It is not always easy to differentiate among an insertion tendopathy of the hamstrings, an ischial bursitis, and an S1–S2 nerve root irritation. In many instances, injecting a local anesthetic at the insertion of the hamstrings can help determine the diagnosis.

Position of the Patient

The patient lies supine on the treatment table with the hips and knees in approximately 90° flexion and with the lower legs resting on a chair or bolster. The treatment can also be given with the patient lying on the nonaffected side with the hips and knees flexed to about 90°.

Position of the Therapist

The therapist sits next to the treatment table, at the patient's affected side and at the level of the patient's trunk. If the left side is being treated, the therapist places the tips of the left index and middle fingers (depending on the size of the lesion, the ring finger is also

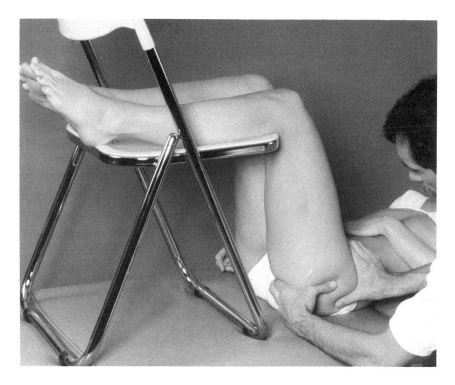

Figure 5–20A Transverse friction of the origin of the hamstrings at the ischial tuberosity.

often used), just medial to the lesion at the level of the lateral aspect of the ischial tuberosity. The thumb applies counterpressure at the lateral side of the thigh.

Performance

The active phase of the transverse friction occurs through an extension of the therapist's wrist with a simultaneous slight adduction of the arm (Figures 5–20, A and B, and 5–21).

Duration

Transverse friction should be performed for 15 to 20 minutes daily or three times per week. It may take 2 weeks, and sometimes up to 8 weeks, to achieve full recovery.

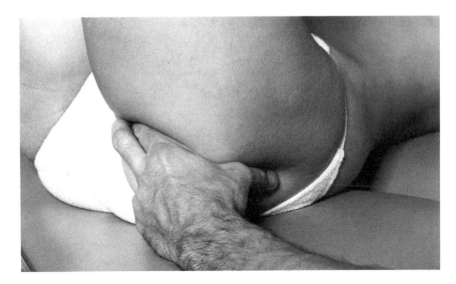

Figure 5–20B Hand position in transverse friction of the origin of the hamstrings at the ischial tuberosity.

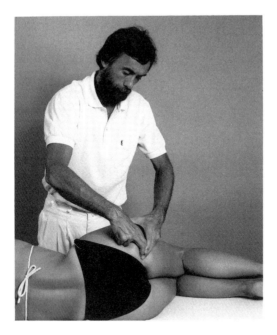

Figure 5–21 Alternative technique, with the patient lying on the side.

STRAIN OR PARTIAL TEAR OF THE HAMSTRINGS MUSCLE BELLY

Functional Examination

The straight leg raise test is painful and limited. Resisted knee flexion combined with resisted hip extension is painful.

TRANSVERSE FRICTION

As with the sprain or partial tear of the quadriceps muscle belly, the sprain or partial tear of the hamstrings muscle belly is a typical sports injury that, in many instances, can be avoided by proper warm-up techniques.

Position of the Patient

The patient lies prone on the treatment table with the knee slightly flexed and with a roll placed underneath the distal part of the lower leg.

Position of the Therapist

The therapist stands or sits next to the treatment table at the patient's affected side, at the level of the patient's thigh. In instances of a superficial lesion (not pictured here), the therapist places the fingertips of the second to fourth fingers just medial to the lesion. The thumb gives counterpressure at the lateral aspect of the thigh. The active phase of the transverse friction is performed through an extension of the wrist.

The initial position pictured in Figure 22A is appropriate for the more often seen deep lesion. The lesion is grasped between the thumbs and index fingers. In so doing, the therapist places the thumbs as close as possible to each other at the lateral aspect of the thigh and all the fingers at the medial aspect of the thigh.

Performance

As with the transverse friction for deep lesions of the quadriceps muscles, both wrists begin in slight flexion. The active phase consists of compressing the injured muscle fibers between the thumbs and fingers and simultaneously performing extension of the wrists. This is similar to transverse kneading techniques used in classic massage. Here, the friction is performed locally (Figure 5–22, A and B).

Duration

As described in the treatment of a sprain or partial tear of the quadriceps femoris muscle group, transverse friction for a hamstrings muscle belly lesion can be initiated as early as the second day after the trauma. Depending on the severity of the lesion (sprain, small or large partial tear), gentle friction should be applied for only a few minutes. The time and intensity of the transverse friction can be increased daily until treatment is established at 15 minutes per session. After each treatment of transverse friction, the muscle should be actively contracted from an approximated position (knee in 90° flexion) to maintain transverse mobility. If active contraction is too painful (as is sometimes the case in acute stages), the contraction can be achieved by means of electric stimulation. The utmost care must be taken during stretching, to avoid the provocation of pain or muscle splinting (see the following section).

Initially, treatment should be given daily and, after 3 weeks, three times per week. As soon as the functional examination is negative, the patient can begin a muscle-strengthening program, progressing from isometric to isokinetic exercises.

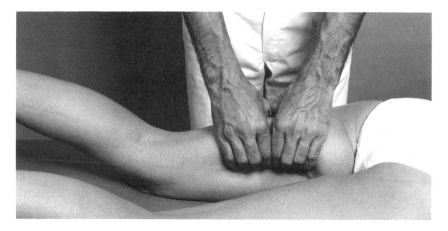

Figure 5–22A Initial position in transverse friction of a deep lesion in the hamstrings muscle belly.

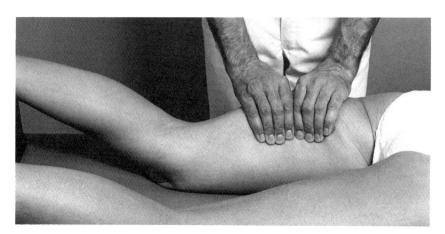

Figure 5–22B End position.

LESIONS OF THE HAMSTRINGS

STRETCHING

Therapist-Assisted Stretching Exercises

Stretching is usually effective for insertion tendopathies, sprains, and partial tears of the hamstrings. The therapist treats these lesions with transverse friction in combination with stretching exercises.

Position of the Patient

The patient lies in a supine position on the treatment table. By means of a mobilization belt placed just proximal to the knee, the nonaffected leg is fixated to the table in the neutral position.

Position of the Therapist

The therapist stands next to the treatment table (not pictured), or kneels on the treat-

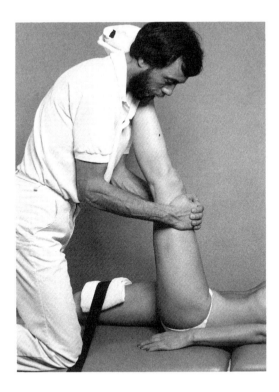

Figure 5–23A Static stretch of the hamstrings.

ment table, at the patient's affected side. The patient's leg, with extended knee, rests on a small pillow or towel on the therapist's shoulder. The therapist places both hands just superior to the patient's patella to keep the patient's knee extended.

Performance

Slowly, to avoid causing pain or muscle splinting, the patient's hip is brought into flexion, without losing the extension in the knee. The same procedure is also performed on the patient's nonaffected side (Figure 5–23, A and B).

Self-Stretching Exercises

There are many self-stretching exercises designed to stretch the hamstring muscles. Two simple exercises are pictured and described here.

Performance

The patient places both hands (with the fingers pointing toward each other) on the thighs, just proximal to the knees, to maintain knee extension. The pelvis is then tilted forward (hollow back) and the patient bends slowly forward (hip flexion; Figures 5–24 and 5–25).

To emphasize one side, the patient places the leg being stretched about 12 inches in front of the other leg. Both hands are placed above the knee, fixating it in extension. As described above, the patient then bends forward (Figure 5–26).

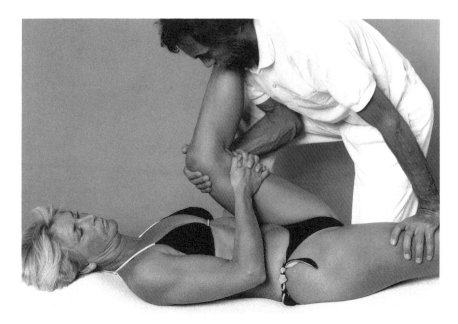

Figure 5–23B Alternative technique: The nonaffected leg is fixated against the treatment table. The patient holds the affected leg in hip flexion. Then the knee is slowly extended.

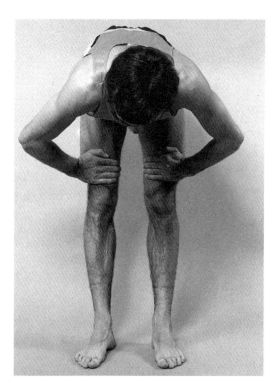

Figure 5–24 Self-stretching exercise for the hamstrings.

Figure 5–25 The lumbar spine should be kept "hollow" while stretching the hamstrings.

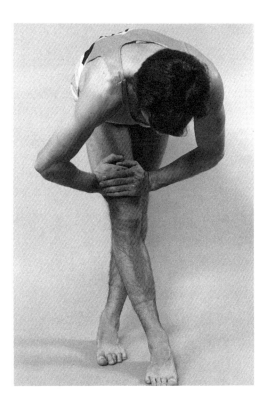

Figure 5–26 More intensive stretch of the hamstrings of one leg.

STRAIN OR OVERUSE OF THE ILIOPSOAS MUSCLE

Functional Examination

Passive hip extension is sometimes painful. Resisted hip flexion is painful. Resisted external rotation of the hip is painful.

TRANSVERSE FRICTION

A lesion of the muscle belly of the iliopsoas can be seen particularly in instances of coxarthrosis. Overuse is a typical sports injury (soccer, track and field). Beware of severe pathology in this region. Refer to "Lesions of the Iliopsoas Muscle" in Chapter 4 for a description of the differential diagnosis for this lesion.

Position of the Patient

The patient sits on the treatment table, with the head of the table inclined. A roll is placed under the knees to bring the hips into slight flexion.

Position of the Therapist

The therapist sits next to the treatment table at the patient's affected side, at the level of the patient's thigh. If the right side is being treated, the therapist places the tip of the right index finger just medial to the lesion (located in the medial femoral triangle, just distal to the inguinal ligament and medial to the sartorius muscle). The therapist's thumb gives counterpressure at the lateral aspect of the thigh.

Performance

The index finger is reinforced by the middle finger. The active phase of the transverse friction is performed through wrist extension. In so doing, the index finger is moved from medial to lateral over the lesion (Figure 5–27, A and B).

Duration

In coxarthrosis patients who also have an irritated iliopsoas, significant pain relief is usually achieved after the first treatment of transverse friction. This treatment is combined with manual traction of the hip joint and muscle stretching (see the following section).

In an overuse syndrome, the iliopsoas usually reacts very well to transverse friction and

Figure 5–27A Initial position of the therapist's hand in transverse friction of the iliopsoas muscle belly.

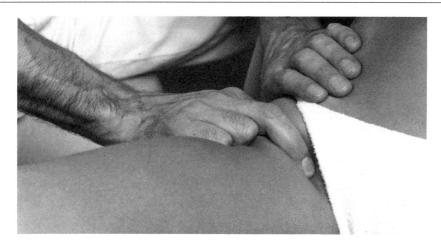

Figure 5–27B End position (the therapist's wrist is extended).

muscle stretching (see the following section). In the first week, transverse friction treatment should be given daily, lasting 10 to 15 minutes. In the second week, treatments should be every other day (three times per week).

LESIONS OF THE ILIOPSOAS MUSCLE

STRETCHING

Therapist-Assisted Stretching Exercises

Stretching of the iliopsoas is indicated where there is irritation of the muscle in patients with coxarthrosis, where there is overuse of the muscle in athletes, and occasionally for patients with complaints of back pain.

Position of the Patient

The patient lies supine on the treatment table. The sacrum lies just on the table, the nonaffected leg is maximally flexed at the hip and knee, and the patient maintains this position by pulling the knee to the chest with both hands. The other leg hangs over the table.

Position of the Therapist

The therapist stands with feet apart next to the foot end of the treatment table, in line with the patient's nonaffected leg and facing the affected leg. If the left leg is being treated, the therapist places the left hand against the posterior aspect of the patient's right thigh. The foot of the patient's same leg rests against the therapist's trunk. The therapist's other hand is placed on the anterior aspect of the thigh of the affected side, just proximal to the knee.

Performance

Together with the patient, the therapist fixates the patient's nonaffected leg. The other hand brings the affected leg slowly into hip extension, without causing pain or muscle splinting. The iliopsoas muscle can be stretched even more by sidebending the trunk away from the affected side and adding internal rotation to the extended hip. An alternative technique for stretching is with the patient lying in a prone position, with the nonaffected leg off the side of the table and in as much hip flexion as possible with the foot resting on the floor. In this position, the therapist can more easily perform internal rotation of the patient's hip (Figure 5–28, A and B).

Self-Stretching Exercises

The patient has many possible ways of independently stretching the iliopsoas muscle. We have no special preferences. Keep in mind that, during the exercise, lordosing of the lumbar spine should be prevented.

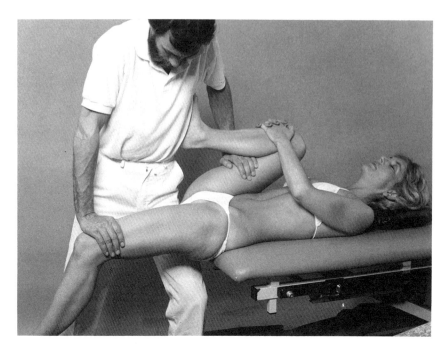

Figure 5–28A Static stretching of the iliopsoas.

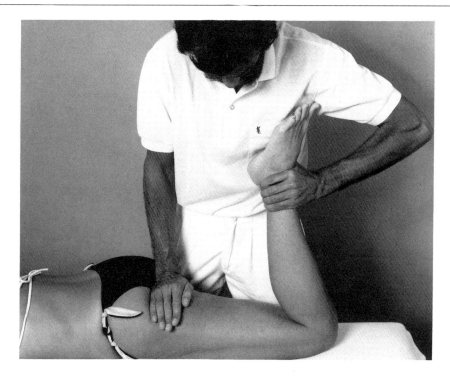

Figure 5–28B Alternative technique with internal rotation of the hip.

LESION OF THE ILIOTIBIAL TRACT

Functional Examination

Passive hip adduction, combined with sidebending of the trunk away from the affected side, is painful.

TRANSVERSE FRICTION

This rare, traumatic lesion is seen almost exclusively in ballet dancers and track and field athletes. Differentiating among a lesion of the iliotibial tract, a subtrochanteric bursitis, or an L4 or L5 nerve root irritation is not always easy. Sometimes a local anesthetic injected into the iliotibial tract at the most painful site can confirm the diagnosis.

Position of the Patient

The patient lies on the nonaffected side on the treatment table. The bottom leg is slightly flexed in the hip and approximately 90° flexed in the knee. The top leg is almost completely extended and slightly adducted.

Position of the Therapist

The therapist stands next to the treatment table, behind the patient. If the left side is affected, the therapist places the tips of the index and middle fingers of the right hand just anterior to the lesion (which lies just proximal to the greater trochanter).

Performance

The active phase of the transverse friction is performed through an extension of the wrist. In so doing, the fingers are moved over the lesion from anterior to posterior (Figure 5–29).

Duration

Usually, three to six treatments are sufficient to achieve complete recovery. The transverse friction should last about 15 minutes per session.

Note

As of the time of this writing, we have never seen a lesion of the tensor fasciae latae muscle.

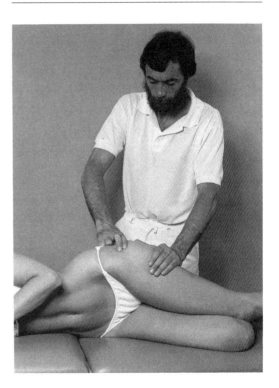

Figure 5–29 Transverse friction of the iliotibial tract, just proximal to the greater trochanter.

ILIOPECTINEAL BURSITIS

Functional Examination

Passive hip flexion is painful as a result of compression of the affected structure. Passive hip extension is sometimes painful as a result of compression of the bursa through a stretch of the iliopsoas muscle. Passive internal rotation of the hip can be painful as a result of compression of the bursa through a stretch of the iliopsoas muscle. Resisted hip flexion and resisted external rotation are sometimes painful as a result of compression of the bursa during the contraction of the iliopsoas muscle.

INJECTION

Because a large number of internal disorders can cause pain in the groin, with or without radiating pain into the thigh, ruling out such disorders is of utmost importance.

Position of the Patient

The patient sits against the inclined head of the treatment table. In this position, the structures lying in the groin are relaxed.

Position of the Physician

The physician stands next to the treatment table at the patient's affected side.

Performance

First, the physician locates the midinguinal point: at this site the pulsation of the femoral artery is palpable. From this point, an imaginary 5 cm long perpendicular line is drawn distally in relation to the inguinal ligament. The insertion point of the needle lies 2 cm lateral to the distal end of this perpendicular line. In this manner, the neurovascular bundle in the groin is avoided during the injection.

A 5-mL syringe is filled with a local anesthetic (for example, 1% lidocaine). An 8-cm needle is inserted in the direction of an imaginary point 5 cm deep underneath the midinguinal point. This means that the needle is at a 45° angle in relation to the horizontal and pointed in a craniomediodorsal direction (Figure 5–30).

As soon as the patient experiences pain, the needle is pushed slightly farther, and then, while the needle is withdrawn, the local anesthetic is injected. Then the needle is withdrawn to the subcutaneous layer and reinserted in a slightly different direction. Again, when the patient experiences pain, after first being pushed slightly farther in, the needle is withdrawn while local anesthetic is injected. In this way, the entire lesion is injected in a fan-shaped manner.

If the functional examination is negative after the injection, the diagnosis is confirmed. The patient should be seen 1 week later for follow-up. If the symptoms have decreased, the injection is repeated. If the symptoms have not changed, however, 3 mL of local anesthetic with 2 mL of corticosteroid are injected. Usually, two or three injections, given at 1- to 2-week intervals, are necessary to achieve complete recovery.

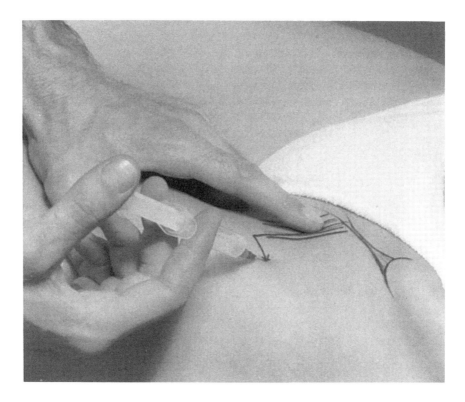

Figure 5–30 Injection of the iliopectineal bursa.

SUBTROCHANTERIC BURSITIS

Functional Examination

Passive hip flexion is sometimes painful. Passive external rotation of the hip can be painful. Passive adduction of the hip is sometimes painful. Resisted hip abduction is sometimes painful. Ultrasound is usually diagnostic.

INJECTION

Differentiating among a subtrochanteric bursitis, a lesion of the iliotibial tract, an L4 or L5 nerve root irritation, and other local causes is usually difficult. Refer to Chapter 4 for further details on the differential diagnosis.

Position of the Patient

The patient lies in a supine position on the treatment table.

Position of the Physician

The physician sits next to the treatment table, next to the patient's affected side.

Performance

The physician locates the most tender site between the patient's greater trochanter and the iliac crest. A 10-mL syringe filled with lo-

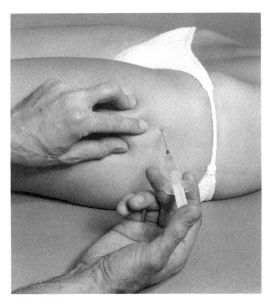

Figure 5–31 Injection of the subtrochanteric bursa.

cal anesthetic and an 8-cm needle is used for this injection. The needle is inserted horizontally into the bursa, and the bursa is injected

in a fan-shaped manner in the area of pain (Figure 5–31). In other words, as soon as the patient experiences pain, the needle is pushed slightly farther, and then, while the needle is withdrawn, the local anesthetic is injected. Then the needle is withdrawn to the subcutaneous layer and reinserted in a slightly different direction. Again, when the patient experiences pain, after first being pushed slightly farther in, the needle is withdrawn while local anesthetic is injected. In this manner, the entire lesion is injected. Often, both the physician and the patient feel the needle go through the wall of the bursa "as if a balloon was punctured."

If the functional examination is negative after the injection, the diagnosis is confirmed. The patient should be seen 1 week later for follow-up. If the symptoms have decreased, the injection is repeated. If the symptoms have not changed, however, 3 mL of local anesthetic with 2 mL of corticosteroid are injected. Usually, two or three injections, given at 1- to 2-week intervals, are necessary to achieve complete recovery.

ISCHIAL BURSITIS

Functional Examination

The functional examination is usually negative. The patient complains of pain during sitting. Rarely is there pain during walking.

INJECTION

Differentiating an ischial bursitis from an S1 or S2 nerve root irritation or an insertion tendopathy of the hamstrings is usually difficult. Refer to Chapter 4 for further details on the differential diagnosis.

Position of the Patient

The patient lies in a prone position on the treatment table. This bursa can also be in-

jected with the patient lying supine on the treatment table with the hips and knees in approximately 90° flexion while the lower legs rest on a chair or bolster. An alternative position is with the patient lying on the nonaffected side with the hips and knees flexed to about 90°.

Position of the Physician

The physician stands next to the treatment table, on either side of the patient.

Performance

The injection is given with 2 mL of local anesthetic and a 5-cm needle. The needle is inserted at the site of most tenderness in the region of the ischial tuberosity (Figure 5–32).

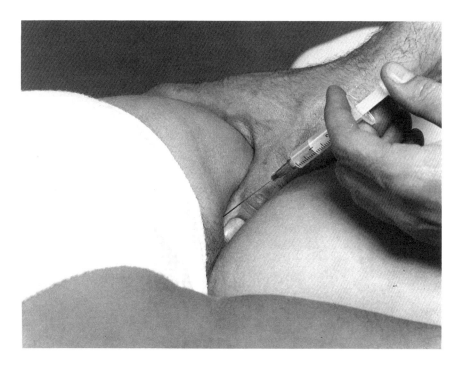

Figure 5–32 Injection of the ischial bursa.

As soon as the patient experiences pain, the needle is pushed slightly farther, and then, while the needle is withdrawn, the local anesthetic is injected. Then the needle is withdrawn to the subcutaneous layer and reinserted in a slightly different direction. Again, when the patient experiences pain, after first being pushed slightly farther in, the needle is withdrawn while local anesthetic is injected. In this manner, the entire lesion is injected.

If the functional examination is negative after the injection, the diagnosis is confirmed. The patient should be seen 1 week later for follow-up. If the symptoms have decreased, the injection is repeated. If the symptoms have not changed, however, 3 mL of local anesthetic with 2 mL of corticosteroid are injected. Usually, two or three injections, given at 1- to 2-week intervals, are necessary to achieve complete recovery.

MERALGIA PARESTHETICA (COMPRESSION NEUROPATHY OF THE LATERAL FEMORAL CUTANEOUS NERVE)

Functional Examination

Passive extension of the hip is sometimes painful. The femoral nerve (L3) stretch test is often painful.

INJECTION

If the cause of the compression neuropathy of the lateral femoral cutaneous nerve is mechanical, attempts should first be made to alleviate the mechanical cause (eg, a short leg or obesity). The perineural injection with a local anesthetic has both diagnostic and therapeutic value in that it might help the sometimes difficult differentiation between neuropathy and an L3 nerve root irritation.

Position of the Patient

The patient lies in a supine position on the treatment table. The head of the table is inclined approximately 30° to take tension off the structures lying at the level of the inguinal ligament.

Position of the Physician

The physician sits or stands next to the treatment table, at the affected side of the patient.

Performance

A 2-mL syringe is filled with a local anesthetic (eg, 1% lidocaine). Depending on the amount of subcutaneous tissue, a 5- to 7-cm needle is inserted vertically at a site 1 cm medial to the anterior superior iliac spine and just cranial to the inguinal ligament (Figure 5–33). As soon as the patient experiences an increase in pain, the needle is slightly withdrawn, and the local anesthetic is slowly injected.

Follow-Up

No specific restrictions are placed on the patient. The patient should be seen for reassessment in 1 week. If necessary, the injection can be repeated several times at weekly intervals.

Note

In instances of recurrence, 1 mL of corticosteroid can be injected. Surgical treatment is rarely indicated.

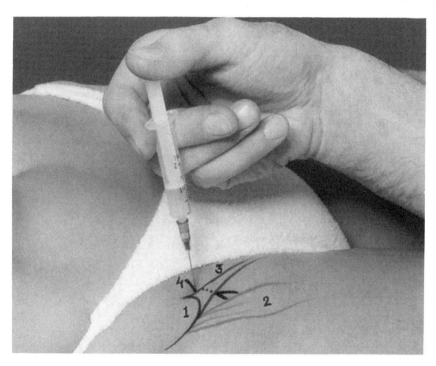

Figure 5–33 Perineural injection of the lateral femoral cutaneous nerve in meralgia paresthetica. **1**, Anterior superior iliac spine; **2**, sartorius muscle; **3**, inguinal ligament; **4**, lateral femoral cutaneous nerve.

Chapter 6

Peripheral Compression Neuropathies in the Pelvis and Hip Region

LESIONS OF THE SCIATIC NERVE

Lesions of the sciatic nerve (L4 to S3) are rarely seen. They can have a wide variety of causes, such as a gunshot wound, pelvic fracture, posterior dislocation of the hip, or surgery in the hip and pelvic region. Sometimes, damage can occur as the result of a wrongly placed intragluteal injection, the so-called injection paralysis. Intragluteal injections should be given in the upper outer quadrant of the gluteal region, with the needle inserted exactly vertical to the skin.

Various schools of manual therapy discuss the piriformis syndrome, which is described as a condition of dysfunction of the sacroiliac joint leading to compression of the sciatic nerve through hypertonia of the piriformis muscle. This diagnosis should really be questioned. Compression of the sciatic nerve as a result of the many anatomic variations in the exiting site of this nerve (such as between the piriformis and superior gemellus muscles or directly through the piriformis) is also unlikely.

Clinical Findings

The sciatic nerve motorically innervates the hamstrings and several muscles of the lower leg and foot. In the functional examination, a deficit condition of the hamstrings is manifested by severe weakness of resisted knee flexion. Only the sartorius and gracilis muscles remain to resist the knee flexion. Walking is still possible to some extent, however, if the gluteal muscles, being extensors and abductors of the hip, still function. In a complete deficit of the sciatic nerve, the foot and toes are entirely paralyzed.

The sciatic nerve provides sensory innervation to a large part of the skin on the lateral and posterior aspects of the lower leg. This nerve also completely supplies the cutaneous innervation of the foot, with the exception of the medial malleolus region and a small strip along the medial edge of the foot, which are innervated by the saphenus nerve.

Treatment

Treatment depends on the cause but will almost always be surgical. In cases of traumatic lesions, good results are usually achieved from primary suturing of the sciatic nerve.

PIRIFORMIS SYNDROME

The piriformis syndrome can occur as the result of a direct trauma to the gluteal region.

Clinical Findings

The patient complains of severe localized pain in the gluteal region radiating to the sacrum, in the direction of the greater trochanter, and sometimes also distally along the posterior aspect of the thigh. Bending and lifting heavy objects cause the pain to increase.

Functional Examination

In the functional examination, passive flexion of the hip and passive internal rotation of the hip are painful. There is severe tenderness to palpation in the region of the greater sciatic foramen.

Treatment

Treatment consists of surgical exploration with resection of adhesions from the piriformis muscle, together with a partial or total transection of the piriformis muscle 4 to 5 cm proximal to its insertion on the greater trochanter.

HAMSTRING SYNDROME

The hamstring syndrome involves a compression neuropathy of the sciatic nerve, usually in the region of the ischial tuberosity, and is seen particularly in athletes such as sprinters, hurdlers, jumpers, and long-distance runners. It affects men three times more often than women. Usually, the symptoms arise without a direct trauma. In approximately half of all cases, however, the patient has had one or more previous incidences of minor tears in the hamstrings.

The symptoms in the hamstring syndrome are caused by a fibrotic cord or fibrosing of all or part of the tendons of the long head of the biceps femoris and semitendinosus, which insert on the ischial tuberosity. These conditions cause an irritation of the sciatic nerve. In some cases, adhesions form between the sciatic nerve and these fibrous cords.

In the differential diagnosis, S1 and S2 nerve root syndromes, ischial bursitis, and a compartment syndrome of the posterior thigh muscles have to be considered. In the S1 and S2 nerve root syndromes, movements of the lumbar spine will be painful. A patient with an ischial bursitis often has pain at rest and is unable to find a comfortable position at night. An individual with a compartment syndrome does not have any pain during sitting. These findings are generally not consistent with findings in a hamstring syndrome.

Clinical Findings

The pain is experienced in the lower gluteal region. From there, it radiates to the posterior aspect of the thigh and to the back of the knee. Typically, the pain is experienced during sitting. Because of the pain, the patient is often forced to stand. Forcefully bringing the affected leg forward, such as during sprinting, jumping, or jumping hurdles as well as when kicking a ball, provokes the most pain. Generally, in long-distance runners the pain is felt at the beginning of a sprint.

Functional Examination

In the functional examination, the straight leg raise test is painful. There is tenderness to palpation just lateral to the ischial tuberosity. Restricted knee flexion is painful as well.

Treatment

Conservative therapy is unsuccessful in most cases. Surgical neurolysis is the preferred treatment.

LESION OF THE FEMORAL NERVE

The femoral nerve (L2 to L4) motorically innervates the iliopsoas muscle and the muscles that extend the knee. It is responsible for the cutaneous innervation of the anterior aspect of the thigh and the medial side of the lower leg.

The nerve runs between the iliopsoas and iliacus muscles, covered by the psoas fascia. Proximal to the inguinal ligament, several branches are given off. These are the muscular ramus for the iliopsoas and a muscular ramus for the pectineus. The femoral nerve then runs together with the iliopsoas through the lacuna musculorum, underneath the inguinal ligament. Distal to the inguinal ligament, the nerve innervates the sartorius, pectineus, and sometimes the adductor longus muscles. However, the most important muscle group innervated by the femoral nerve is the quadriceps femoris.

Intraabdominally, the femoral nerve can be damaged during surgery (such as an appendectomy) or by tumors.

Clinical Findings

If the femoral nerve is damaged proximally in its intrapelvic course, a partial paresis of the iliopsoas occurs. The iliopsoas will not demonstrate a complete deficit because it is also innervated directly through plexus branches from L2 and L3. The patient has difficulty walking, particularly when ascending stairs and inclined surfaces. In the functional examination, weakness is demonstrated during resisted hip flexion.

Lesions of the femoral nerve at the level of the inguinal ligament are seen more frequently. In this instance, paresis of the quadriceps femoris, sartorius, and pectineus muscles occurs. The functional examination indicates weakness during resisted knee extension. Walking is almost impossible. Deficit of the sartorius and pectineus muscles is hardly noticeable, because the other flexors and external rotators, as well as the adductors of the hip, are able almost completely to take over those functions.

Treatment

Treatment is generally surgical.

MERALGIA PARESTHETICA

The term *meralgia paresthetica* denotes symptoms that result from damage to the lateral femoral cutaneous nerve (L2, L3). The nerve is usually affected just mediodistal to the anterior superior iliac spine, where it runs either through or under the inguinal ligament (Figure 6–1).

The cause is usually traumatic. Acute as well as chronic trauma and microtrauma can result in damage to this nerve. An example of damage to the lateral femoral cutaneous nerve is a kick in the groin during soccer or karate. In obese people, chronic pressure from the weight of the fatty tissue can compress the nerve. Meralgia paresthetica can also occur during pregnancy. Sometimes it can be caused by misapplied traction belts during lumbar traction. A leg length difference results in adduction of the longer leg; in this instance, compression of the nerve can occur on that side with each step during walking.

Differential Diagnosis

- L3 nerve root syndrome
- Diabetic neuropathy

Clinical Findings

The patient complains of burning pain and paresthesia at the anterolateral aspect of the thigh. At a later stage, the center of this area can have decreased sensation or become completely numb. The symptoms often occur during prolonged standing. Movement of the leg or flexion of the hip can cause the symptoms to disappear.

Functional Examination

Maximal passive hip flexion sometimes provokes the symptoms. The L3 stretch test often provokes the symptoms. Usually there is tenderness to palpation just medial and slightly distal to the anterior superior iliac spine.

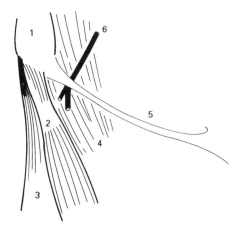

Figure 6–1 Lateral femoral cutaneous nerve (right). **1**, Anterior superior iliac spine; **2**, sartorius muscle; **3**, tensor fasciae latae muscle; **4**, iliopsoas muscle; **5**, inguinal ligament; **6**, lateral femoral cutaneous nerve.

Treatment

Treatment depends on the cause of the symptoms. In many cases there is spontaneous recovery, which can last months to years. Local anesthetic injected at the site of the compression provides good results in most instances. This perineural injection can be repeated 1 to 2 weeks later. If the symptoms still persist after three injections, a corticosteroid can be injected along with the local anesthetic.

LESIONS OF THE ILIOINGUINAL AND ILIOHYPOGASTRIC NERVES

Lesions of the ilioinguinal (T12, L1) and iliohypogastric (L1) nerves are rare. Damage to one of the nerves can occur traumatically as the result of a direct blow or from urogenital surgery. Another possible cause is an extremely weakened abdominal wall in conjunction with a severe coxarthrosis.

The ilioinguinal nerve courses ventrally at the lateral aspect of the psoas major and crosses over the quadratus lumborum muscle. From there, it runs through the in-

guinal canal to its area of cutaneous innervation, the proximomedial thigh and the skin of the scrotum in males or the skin over the mons pubis and the adjacent part of the labia majora in females (Figure 6–2). The nerve innervates the following muscles: internal abdominal oblique and transverse abdominal.

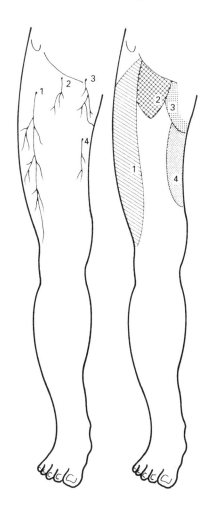

Figure 6–2 The four most clinically important cutaneous nerves in the groin region. **1**, Lateral femoral cutaneous nerve and its area of cutaneous innervation; **2**, genitofemoral nerve and its area of cutaneous innervation; **3**, ilioinguinal nerve and its area of cutaneous innervation; **4**, obturator nerve and its area of cutaneous innervation.

The iliohypogastric nerve runs together with the ilioinguinal nerve for a while, then perforates the iliopsoas muscle and runs farther in a ventrolateral and caudal direction to the iliac crest. The nerve innervates the same abdominal muscles as the ilioinguinal nerve. A cutaneous branch from the iliohypogastric nerve, the lateral cutaneous ramus, innervates the skin at the anterolateral aspect of the proximal thigh (Figure 6–2). Another cutaneous branch, the anterior cutaneous ramus, arises after the innervation of the abdominal muscles and supplies the skin in the pubic symphysis region.

Clinical Findings

The patient complains of neuropathic pain in the cutaneous area of the affected nerve. Rarely is there a deficit in the sensation of that area. Because the abdominal muscles are innervated by both nerves as well as the last two thoracic nerve roots, motor deficits are also rare.

Functional Examination

Usually there are no specific findings in the functional examination; sometimes, passive hip flexion reproduces the patient's symptoms. In rare cases, there is a loss of strength of the oblique abdominal muscles.

Treatment

A local perineural injection at the site of the compression (which is usually tender to palpation) usually offers temporary relief. Ultimately, however, surgical neurolysis is the only treatment method that will provide permanent relief from the symptoms.

LESION OF THE OBTURATOR NERVE

The obturator nerve (L2 to L4) runs on the medial side of the psoas major to the obturator foramen, where it divides into two branches: the anterior and posterior rami (Figure 6–2). The anterior ramus innervates the pectineus, adductor longus, adductor brevis, and gracilis muscles. It ends in a sensory cutaneous ramus. This cutaneous branch runs along the anterior edge of the gracilis through the fascia and innervates the skin at the distal half of the medial aspect of the thigh. The posterior ramus runs between the adductor brevis and adductor magnus, innervating this latter muscle. The obturator nerve lies deep in the abdominal cavity but is quite visible, so that lesions as a result of surgery are rarely seen.

Paresis of the obturator nerve generally results from pelvic fractures, a hernia obturatoria, or metastases in the region of the obturator foramen. Occasionally, during delivery, lesions can occur. Once in a while, an ostitis pubis is seen as a complication after a urologic operation. The swelling that accompanies this disorder can irritate the obturator nerve, with resulting sensory disturbances in its area of cutaneous innervation. A compression neuropathy of the obturator nerve can also develop in instances of severe coxarthrosis.

Clinical Findings

In a paresis of the obturator nerve, weakness of the hip adductors is seen. Sometimes passive hip flexion provokes pain. There are sensory deficits at the medial aspect of the thigh, just above the knee. There is tenderness to palpation at the level of the origin of the pectineus, between the pectineus and adductor longus, or at the exiting site of the cutaneous branch of the anterior ramus.

Treatment

If a compression neuropathy of the obturator nerve is seen as a complication of coxarthrosis, injection therapy is often effective. Initially, the preferred treatment is a local perineural injection with a local anesthetic at the site of greatest tenderness. In a later stage, the injection can be repeated with a corticosteroid. In other cases, surgical neurolysis is usually the only treatment that will offer permanent relief from the symptoms.

LESION OF THE GENITOFEMORAL NERVE

The genitofemoral nerve comprises nerve fibers from the L1 and L2 roots. The nerve divides into a genital ramus and femoral ramus. These branches run caudally, ventral to the psoas muscle and within its fascia. The femoral ramus innervates the skin in the groin and the area just distal to it that corresponds to the medial femoral triangle. The genital ramus innervates the skin of the scrotum and a small zone at the proximomedial aspect of the thigh. It supplies motor fibers to the cremaster muscle. Damage to this nerve can occur during a herniotomy.

Clinical Findings

The patient complains of sensory deficit and sometimes pain, the so-called spermaticus neuralgia.

Functional Examination

In some cases, passive hip flexion is painful. In addition to the sensory disturbances, the cremaster reflex can be absent.

Treatment

Treatment is always surgical.

PART I—HIP REVIEW QUESTIONS

1. List three commonly seen non-traumatic arthritides of the hip.
2. Describe the capsular pattern of the hip.
3. List three complications that can occur with coxarthrosis (osteoarthrosis of the hip).
4. What is Perthes' disease, and in which age group is it generally seen?
5. What is ischemic femoral head necrosis in adults?
6. Between what two types of slipped capital femoral epiphysis can one distinguish? At what age is this pathology usually seen in girls? At what age is this pathology usually seen in boys?
7. List five causes for a loose body in the hip joint.
8. Describe the clinical findings one could expect in a patient with an iliopectineal (psoas) bursitis.
9. It is not always easy to diagnose an ischial bursitis; between which other lesions must one differentiate?
10. Describe the four clinical stages of pubalgia.
11. Describe the clinical findings one could expect in a patient with a rectus femoris tendopathy.
12. Iliopsoas muscle lesions are more often seen in which kind of person? As a result of which other pathology?
13. Besides a strain of the tensor fascia latae muscle or the iliotibial band, what other structures can give symptoms in the same area? (What would you consider a differential diagnosis?)
14. What are two extraarticular causes of a "snapping hip"?
15. Define the hamstring syndrome.
16. Define meralgia paresthetica.
17. List three predilection sites for a stress fracture in the hip area.
18. List four predilection sites for an apophyseal avulsion fracture in the hip area.
19. List and briefly describe the types of compartment syndromes in the thigh.
20. Which ligament, in particular, restrains the adduction motion in the hip?
21. Which muscles internally rotate the hip?
22. What is the maximal close-packed position of the hip?
23. What is the maximal loose-packed position of the hip?
24. Describe a positive Trendelenburg test.
25. List four lesions whereby a patient has a positive Trendelenburg test.
26. Define the "sign of the buttock."
27. Briefly describe the cause of a subtrochanteric bursitis.
28. Give three examples of a possible causal treatment for publagia.
29. How can a lesion occur in the iliotibial band or in the tensor fascia latae muscle?
30. What complication can occur after a partial tear or a total rupture of the rectus femoris muscle belly?

PART I—HIP REVIEW ANSWERS

1. Rheumatoid arthritis, gout, and ankylosing spondylitis.

2. Internal rotation has the greatest limitation of motion; extension, flexion, and abduction are the second most limited motions (these motions are about equally limited); and external rotation and adduction are the least limited motions.

3. Loose body, iliopsoas muscle irritation, and obturator nerve compression neuropathy.

4. It concerns an aseptic bone necrosis of the femoral head as a result of a disturbance in the vascularization of unknown etiology. It is usually seen in children between the ages of 3 and 10 years.

5. It concerns an ischemic aseptic femoral head necrosis in adults. It can be clearly distinguished on plain films but is clinically difficult to define.

6. The gradual and the acute slipped capital femoral epiphysis. It is seen in girls between the ages of 11 and 12 years and in boys between the ages of 13 and 15 years.

7. Idiopathic, traumatic, coxarthrosis (osteoarthritis of the hip), osteochondrosis dissecans, and ischemic femoral head necrosis.

8. The patient complains of pain in the groin and anterior aspect of the thigh. Passive hip flexion is painful; the pain increases when the hip is brought passively from full flexion toward adduction and then decreases after about 45° of adduction in flexion. Passive external rotation and extension are also usually painful.

9. S1 or S2 nerve root syndrome and hamstring insertion tendopathy.

10. *Stage 1*, groin pain of short duration after exertion. *Stage 2*, groin pain at the beginning of exertion that returns in intensity the following day and disappears with rest. *Stage 3*, groin pain and lower abdominal pain during exertion and lasting a few days afterward. *Stage 4*, chronic pain that increases with exertion and barely diminishes with rest.

11. Pain in the groin during running and lifting the knee. Passive hip flexion is sometimes painful. Resisted knee extension with the knee in 90° flexion and the hip in 0° flexion is painful. Passive stretch is painful. The muscle is usually shortened.

12. In athletes and in patients with coxarthrosis (osteoarthrosis of the hip).

13. Subtrochanteric bursitis, L4 or L5 nerve root syndrome.

14. Deflection of the iliotibial band or of the ilipsoas muscle, which "snap" over the greater trochanter or the pubic pecten, respectively.

15. A compression neuropathy of the sciatic nerve at the level of the ischial tuberosity, which is most often seen in athletes. The compression is caused by a fibrotic band or a fibrosis of part of the tendon from the long head of the biceps femoris and the semitendinosus muscles.

16. Burning pain and paresthesia on the anterolateral aspect of the thigh as a result of a compression of the lateral femoral cutaneous nerve.

17. Iliac crest, femoral neck, and lesser trochanter.

18. Ischial tuberosity, anterior superior iliac spine, and greater trochanter and lesser trochanter.

19. An acute compartment syndrome. It occurs as a result of a decrease in the size of the compartment, for example from a cast, a scar, or a thrombosis. In an exertion-dependent compartment syndrome, one differentiates between an acute and a chronic type. The acute type is treated with immediate surgery. The chronic compartment syndrome is seen more frequently and usually concerns the anterior compartment.

20. Iliofemoral ligament, pars superior.

21. Tensor fascia latae muscle, gluteus medius and minimus muscles (the anterior fibers), and partly the adductor muscles.

22. Maximal extension, internal rotation, and abduction.

23. Approximately 30° flexion, 30° abduction, and slight external rotation.

24. When the patient is standing on the affected leg with the other leg in 90° of hip and knee flexion, the posterior superior iliac spine on the side of the standing leg rises and on the other side falls. This indicates weakness of the gluteus medius muscle.

25. Severe coxarthrosis, slipped capital femoral epiphysis, congenital subluxation/dislocation of the hip, and severe forms of Perthes' disease.

26. Painful and limited straight leg raise and equally painful and limited hip flexion with the knee flexed. Sometimes other hip motions are also limited and painful. This usually indicates severe pathology in the hip/pelvis region.

27. Traumatic (acute trauma as well as microtrauma, as in endurance athletes).

28. Replacing the shoes, correcting a difference in leg length, and correcting the running, kicking, skating, or swimming technique.

29. As a result of an explosive abduction movement from a stretched position (hip adduction).

30. Myositis ossificans.

PART I—REFERENCES

1. Murray MP. Gait as a total pattern of movement. *Ann J Phys Med.* 1987;46:290–333.

2. Johnston RC, Schmidt GL. Measurement of hip joint motion during walking: Evaluation of an electrogoniometric method. *J Bone Joint Surg Am.* 1969;51:1083–1094.

3. Frankel VH, Nordin M, Snijders CJ. *Biomechanika van het Skeletsysteem: Grondslagen en toepassingen.* Lochem, Holland: De Tijdstroom; 1984.

4. McLeish MP, Charnley J. Abduction forces in the one-legged stance. *J Biomech.* 1970;3:191–209.

5. Paul JP. *Forces at the Hip Joint.* Chicago, Ill: University of Chicago; 1967. Thesis.

6. Bullough P, Goodfellow J, O'Connor J. The relation between degenerative changes and load bearing in the human hip. *J Bone Joint Surg Br.* 1973;55:746–758.

7. Radin EL. Mechanical aspects of osteoarthrosis. *Bull Rheum Dis.* 1967;26:862–865.

8. Healy EJ, Seybold WD. *A Synopsis of Clinical Anatomy.* Philadelphia, Pa: Saunders; 1969.

9. Steinberg ME, Steinberg DR. Avascular necrosis of the femoral head. In: Steinberg ME, ed. *The Hip and Its Disorders.* Philadelphia, Pa: Saunders; 1991.

10. Aaron RK, Lennox DW, Bunce GE, Ebert T. The conservative treatment of osteonecrosis of the femoral head: A comparison of core decompression and pulsing electromagnetic fields. *Clin Orthop.* 1989;249:209–218.

11. Cyriax J. *Textbook of Orthopaedic Medicine.* 7th ed. London, England: Baillière Tindall; 1978, 1.

PART I—SUGGESTED READING

Aldea PA, Shaw WW. Management of acute lower extremity nerve injuries. *Foot Ankle.* 1986;7:82–94.

Armstrong P, Saxton H. Ilio-psoas bursa. *Br J Radiol.* 1972;45:493–495.

Balaji MR, Deweese JA. Een nieuw gevaar van draven: Trombose van de A. femoralis. *JAMA.* 19XX;245:167–170.

Battista AF, Battista R. The anatomy and physiology of the peripheral nerve. *Foot Ankle.* 1986;7:65–70.

Berman L, Mitchell R, Katz D. Ultrasound assessment of femoral anteversion: A comparison with computerized tomography. *J Bone Joint Surg Br.* 1987;69:268–270.

Bradley J, Wetherill M, Benson MKD. Splintage for congenital dislocation of the hip. Is it safe and reliable? *J Bone Joint Surg Br.* 1987;69:257–262.

Bruns J, Heller M, Knop J. Die Femurkopfnekrose. Vergleichende Untersuchungen über Methoden der Frühdiagnostik. *Z Orthop.* 1988;26:143–148.

Catterall A. What is congenital dislocation of the hip? *J Bone Joint Surg Br.* 1984;66:469–470.

Caudle RJ, Crawford AH. Osteosarcoma at the site of total hip replacement: A case report. *J Bone Joint Surg Am.* 1988;70:1568–1570.

Clain A, ed. *Hamilton Bailey's Demonstrations of Physical Signs in Clinical Surgery.* Bristol, England: Wright; 1965.

Clarke NMP, Karcke HT, McHugh P, et al. Real-time ultrasound in the diagnosis of congenital dislocation and dysplasia of the hip. *J Bone Joint Surg Br.* 1985;67:406–412.

Crawford Adams J. *Outline of Orthopaedics.* 6th ed. London, England: Churchill Livingstone; 1967.

Das De S, Bose K, Balasubramaniam P, et al. Surface morphology of Asian cadaveric hips. *J Bone Joint Surg Br.* 1985;67:225–228.

Davies SJM, Walker G. Problems in the early recognition of hip dysplasia. *J Bone Joint Surg Br.* 1984;66:479–484.

Dee R. Structure and function of hip joint innervation. *Ann R Coll Surg Engl.* 1969;45:357–374.

Delcamp DD, Klaaren HE, Pompe van Meerdervoort HF. Traumatic avulsion of the ligamentum teres without dislocation of the hip: Two case reports. *J Bone Joint Surg.* 1988;70:933–935.

Dubois JL, Halet W, Delcourt P, Wallon P, Raynal L. Pathologie de la bourse séreuse du psoas-iliaque: Bursitis et kystes synoviaux: mise au point et revue de la littérature. *Rev Rheum.* 1968;35:9–20.

Elias N. *Über den Prozeß der Zivilisation.* 5th ed. Baden-Baden, Germany: Suhrkamp; 1978.

Engelhardt P. Die Bedeutung des Zentrumeckenwinkels zur Prognose der Dysplasiehüfte 50 Jahre nach Erstbeschreibung durch G. Wiberg. *Orthopäde.* 1988;17:463–467.

Fairclough J, Colhoun E, Johnston D, Williams LA. Bone scanning for suspected hip fractures: A prospective study in elderly patients. *J Bone Joint Surg Br.* 1987;69:251–253.

Finder JG. Iliopectineal bursitis. *Arch Surg.* 1938;36:519–530.

Francillion MR, Debrunner HA. Orthopädie der Coxarthrose. *Doc Rheumatol.* 1957;13:9–94.

Françon F. Caxarthrose (Ohne orthopädische und chirurgische Behandlung). *Doc Rheumatol.* 1956;9:13–120.

Gardner E, Gray DJ, O'Rahilly R. *Anatomy.* Philadelphia, Pa: Saunders; 1975.

Geller L. Erkrankungen des Hüftgelenks im Kindesalter. *Krankengymnastik.* 1987;39:326–330.

Gillespie R, Torode IP. Classification and management of congenital abnormalities of the femur. *J Bone Joint Surg Br.* 1983;65:557–568.

Goddard NJ, Gosling PT. Intra articular fluid pressure and pain in osteoarthritis of the hip. *J Bone Joint Surg Br.* 1988;70:52–55.

Good C, Walker G. The hip in the moulded baby syndrome. *J Bone Joint Surg Br.* 1984;66:491–492.

Gray H, Williams PL, Warwick R. *Gray's Anatomy.* 36th ed. London, England: Churchill Livingstone; 1980.

Grimm J, Apel R, Higer HP. Der akute Hüftschmerz des Erwachsenen—Abklärungdurch MR-Tomographie. *Orthopäde.* 1989;18:24–33.

Haak A, Steendijk R, de Wijn IF. *De Samenstelling van het Menselijk Lichaam.* Assen, Holland: Van Gorcum; 1968.

Hadlow V. Neonatal screening for congenital dislocation of the hip. *J Bone Joint Surg Br.* 1988;70:740–743.

Hafferl A. *Lehrbuch der topographischen Anatomie des Menschen.* Berlin, Germany: Springer Verlag; 1957.

Hall AJ, Barker DJP, Dagnerfield PH, et al. Small feet and Perthes' disease. *J Bone Joint Surg Br.* 1988;70:611–613.

Hamilton WJ, Simon G, Hamilton SGI. *Surface and Radiological Anatomy.* 5th ed. London, England: Macmillan; 1976.

Hanker GJ, Amstutz HC. Osteonecrosis of the hip in the sicklecell diseases: Treatment and complications. *J Bone Joint Surg Am.* 1988;70:499–506.

Hardcastle P, Nade S. The significance of the Trendelenburg test. *J Bone Joint Surg Br.* 1985;67:741–746.

Harris CM, Baum J. Involvement of the hip in juvenile rheumatoid arthritis: A longitudinal study. *J Bone Joint Surg Am.* 1988;70:821–833.

Hattrup SJ, Wood MB. Delayed neural reconstruction in the lower extremity: Results of interfascicular nerve grafting. *Foot Ankle.* 1986;7:105–109.

Hauzeur JP, Pateels JL, Orloff S. Bilateral non-traumatic aseptic osteonecrosis in the femoral head: An experimental study of incidence. *J Bone Joint Surg Am.* 1987;69:1221–1225.

Heeg M, Visser JD, Oostvogel JM. Injuries of the acetabular triradiate cartilage and sacroiliac joint. *J Bone Joint Surg Br.* 1988;70:34–37.

Heerkens YF, Meijer OG. *Tractus-anatomie.* Amsterdam, Holland: Interfaculty Physical Education; 1980.

Hermans GPH. Liesblessures. *Reuma Wereldwijd.* September 1983:5–7.

Hoppenfeld S. *Physical Examination of the Spine and Extremities.* New York, NY: Appleton-Century-Crofts; 1976.

Hopson CN, Siverhus SW. Ischemic necrosis of the femoral head: Treatment by core decompression. *J Bone Joint Surg Am.* 1988;70:1048–1051.

Hougaard K, Thomsen PB. Coxarthrosis following traumatic posterior dislocation of the hip. *J Bone Joint Surg Am.* 1987;69:679–683.

Ikeda T, Awaya G, Suzuki S, Okada Y, Tada H. Torn acetabular labrum in young patients. *J Bone Joint Surg Br.* 1988;70:13–16.

Ippolito E, Tudisco C, Farsetti P. The long-term prognosis of unilateral Perthes' disease. *J Bone Joint Surg Br.* 1987;69:243–250.

Jackson AM, Hutton PAN. Injection-induced contractures of the quadriceps in childhood: A comparison of proximal release and distal quadricepsplasty. *J Bone Joint Surg Br.* 1985;67:97–102.

Janis JL, Mahl GF, Kagan J, Holt RR. *Personality, Dynamics, Development, and Assessment.* New York, NY: Harcourt Brace & World; 1969.

Johnston RC, Schmidt GL. Hip motion measurements for selected activities of daily living. *Clin Orthop.* 1970;72:205–215.

Kallio P, Ryöppy S, Kunnamo I. Transient synovitis and Perthes' disease. Is there an aetiological connection? *J Bone Joint Surg Br.* 1986;68:808–810.

Karpinski MRK, Piggott H. Greater trochanteric pain syndrome: A report of 15 cases. *J Bone Joint Surg Br.* 1985;67:762–763.

Keret D, Harrison MHM, Clarke NMP, Hall DJ. Coxa plana—the fate of the physis. *J Bone Joint Surg Am.* 1984;66:870–877.

Kinzinger H. Les vices de torsion des membres inferieurs. Historique. Evolution. Clinique. *Acta Orthop Belg.* 1977;43:379–414.

Kummer B. Biomechanischer Aspekt der Luxationshüfte. *Orthopäde.* 1988;17:452–462.

Laméris C. *Loopstoornissen bij kinderen, op basis van torsiestoornisen.* 1982. Thesis.

Landin LA, Danielsson LG, Wattsgard C. Transient synovitis of the hip: Its incidence, epidemiology and relation to Perthes' disease. *J Bone Joint Surg Br.* 1987;69:238–242.

Larsen E, Johansen J. Snapping hip. *Acta Orthop Scand.* 1986;57:168–170.

Lequesne M, Becker J, Bard M, Witvoet J, Postel M. Capsular constriction of the hip: Arthrographic and clinical considerations. *Skeletal Radiol.* 1981;6:1–10.

Lohman AGM. *Vorm en beweging. Leerboek van het bewegingsapparaat van de mens.* 4th ed. Utrecht, Netherlands: Bohn, Scheltema & Holkema; 1977.

Lombardo SJ, Retting AC, Kerlan RK. Radiographic abnormalities of the iliac apophysis in adolescent athletes. *J Bone Joint Surg Am.* 1983;65:444–446.

Lusskin R, Battista A, Lenso S, Price A. Surgical management of late post-traumatic and ischemic neuropathies involving the lower extremities: Classification and results of therapy. *Foot Ankle.* 1986;7:95–104.

Marguery O. Hochleistungs-Tennis-Pubalgie und manuelle Medizin. *Man Med.* 1988;26:100–102.

Matsui M, Ohzono K, Saito S. Painful cystic degeneration of the limbus in the hip: A case report. *J Bone Joint Surg Am.* 1988;70:448–451.

Mau H. Familiäre Hüftdysplasie mit kurzen Pfannendächern. *Z Orthop.* 1988;26:156–160.

Maxted MJ, Jackson RK. Innominate osteotomy in Perthes' disease: A radiological survey of results. *J Bone Joint Surg Br.* 1985;67:399–401.

McAndrew MP, Weinstein SL. A long-term follow-up of Legg-Calvé-Perthes disease. *J Bone Joint Surg Am.* 1984;66:860–869.

McCauley RGK, Wunderlich BK, Zimbler S. Air embolism as a complication of hip arthrography. *Skeletal Radiol.* 1981;6:11–13.

McGuigan LE, Edmonds JP, Painter DM. Pubic osteolysis. *J Bone Joint Surg Am.* 1984;66:127–129.

McMinn RMH, Hutching RT. *A Color Atlas of Human Anatomy.* London, England: Wolfe Medical; 1977.

Mégevand A, Sholder-Hegi P. Das klinishe Bild der Epiphyseolysis capitis femoris. *Acta Rheumatol.* 1964;21:63–84.

Melzer C, Refior HJ. Die Behandlung der instabilen Luxationshüfte im Säuglings-und Kleinkindersalter nach einer modifizierten Fettweis-Methode. *Z Orthop.* 1988;26:195–199.

Miller EH, Benedict FE. Stretch of the femoral nerve in a dancer: A case report. *J Bone Joint Surg Am.* 1985;67:315–317.

Morscher E. Die operative Therapie der Epiphyseolysis capitis femoris. *Acta Rheumatol.* 1964;21:103–132.

Muckle DS. Associated factors in recurrent groin and hamstring injuries. *Br J Sports Med.* 1982;16:37–39.

Murphy SB, Simon SR, Kijewski PK, et al. Femoral anteversion. *J Bone Joint Surg Am.* 1987;69:1169–1176.

Nilsson BE. Klinische symptomatologie en natuurlijk verloop van coxarthrosis en gonarthrosis. *Scand J Rheum.* 1982;43:13–20.

O'Connor DS. Early recognition of iliopectineal bursitis. *Surg Gynecol Obstet.* 1933;57:674–683.

Peltokallio P, Harjula A. The posterior compartment syndrome of the thigh in runners. *Sports Med Track Field Athlet.* 1985:57–59.

Puranen J. The hamstring syndrome: A new diagnosis of gluteal sciatic pain. *Am J Sports Med.* 1988;16:517–621.

Raimann A, Saavedra C, Améstica G, De la Fuente M. Langfristige Beobachtung von 166 operierten Patienten mit angeborener Hüftverrenkung. *Z Orthop.* 1988;26:161–168.

Ranawat CS, Atkinson RE, Salvati EA, Wilson PD. Conventional total hip arthroplasty for degenerative joint disease in patients between the ages of forty and sixty years. *J Bone Joint Surg Am.* 1984;66:745–751.

Richards BS, Coleman SS. Subluxation of the femoral head in coxa plana. *J Bone Joint Surg Am.* 1987;69:1312–1318.

Rolland JJ, Menou P, Le Bourg M, et al. Pubic pain and position of the pelvis. *Anat Clin.* 1982;4:69–72.

Russe O, Gerhardt JJ, King PS. *An Atlas of Examination, Standard Measurements and Diagnosis in Orthopaedics and Traumatology.* Bern, Switzerland: Huber Verlag; 1972.

Rutishouser E, Jacqueline F. Die rheumatischen Koxitiden. Die Beteiligung des Hüftgelenkes bei der Spondylarthritis ankylopoetica: klinische Vorbemerkungen. Die Beteiligung des Hüftgelenkes beim primär-chronischen Gelenkrheumatismus des Erwachsenen: klinische Vorbemerkungen. Primär-chronischer Gelenkrheumatismus des Erwachsenen: vergleichende Untersuchung der Beteiligung des Hüftgelenks mit derjenigen andere Gelenke. Gegenüberstellun der Koxitis bei Spondylarthritis ankylopoetica und beim primär-chronischen Gelenkrheumatismus der Erwachesenen. Eigenschaften, welche de beiden Krankheitsbilder

voneinander unterscheiden. *Doc Rheumatol.* 1959;16:10–109.

Rydholm U, Brun A, Ekelund L, Rydholm A. Chronic compartmental syndrome in the tensor fasciae latae muscle. *Clin Orthop.* 1985;177:169–171.

Saleh M, Morduch G. In defence of gait analysis: Observation and measurement in gait assessment. *J Bone Joint Surg Br.* 1985;67:237–241.

Salter RB, Thompson GH. Legg-Calvé-Perthes disease: The prognostic significance of the subchondral fracture and a two group classification of the femoral head involvement. *J Bone Joint Surg Am.* 1984;66:479–489.

Sartoris DJ, Danzig L, Gilula L, Greenway G, Resnick D. Synovial cysts of the hip joint and iliopsoas bursitis: A spectum of imaging abnormalities. *Skeletal Radiol.* 1985;14:85–94.

Schoenecker PL, Strecker WB. Congenital dislocation of the hip in children: Comparison of the effects of femoral shortening and of the skeletal traction in treatment. *J Bone Joint Surg Am.* 1984;66:21–27.

Scholder-Hegi P. Die konservative Therapie der Epiphyseolyse. *Acta Rheumatol.* 1964;21:87–100.

Schrott E, Holzhauser P. Meralgia paraesthetica bei coxarthrose. *Dtsch Med Wochenschr.* 1982;107:813–818.

Sherlock DA, Gibson PH, Venson MKD. Congenital subluxation of the hip: A long-term review. *J Bone Joint Surg Br.* 1985;67: 390–398.

Sobotta J, Becher PH. *Atlas of Human Anatomy.* 9th English ed. Berlin, Germany: Urban & Schwarzenberg; 1975; 1–3.

Staheli LT. Medial femoral torsion. *Orthop Clin North Am.* 1980;11:39–49.

Staheli LT, Corbett M, Wyss C, King H. Lower extremity rotational problems in children: Normal values to guide management. *J Bone Joint Surg Am.* 1985;67:39–47.

Taillard W. Anatomie und Physiopathologie der Epiphyseolysis capitis femoris. *Acta Rheumatol.* 1964;21:15–60.

Terjesen T, Benum P, Anda S, Svenningsen S. Increased femoral anteversion and osteoarthritis of the hip joint. *Acta Orthop Scand.* 1982;53:571–575.

Tezcan R, Erginer XX, Babacan M. Bilateral traumatic anterior dislocation of the hip: Brief report. *J Bone Joint Surg Br.* 1988;70:148.

Upadhyay SS, Moulton A, Burwell RG. Biological factors predisposing to traumatic posterior dislocation of the hip: A selection process in the mechanism of injury. *J Bone Joint Surg Br.* 1985;67:232–236.

Van Dam BE, Crider RJ, Noyes JD, Larsen LJ. Determination of the Catterall classification in Legg-Calvé-Perthes disease. *J Bone Joint Surg Am.* 1981;63:906–914.

Vischer TL. Hüftschmerzen. *Folia Rheumatologica.* Basel, Switzerland: Ciba-Geigy; 1987.

Wepfer JF, Reed JG, Cullen GM, McDevitt WP. Calcific tendinitis of the gluteus maximus tendon (gluteus maximus tendinitis). *Skeletal Radiol.* 1983;9:198–200.

Wingstrand H, Egund N, Forsberg L. Sonography and joint pressure in synovitis of the adult hip. *J Bone Joint Surg Br.* 1987;69:254–256.

Winkel D, Fisher S. *Schematisch Handboek voor Onderzoek en Behandeling van Weke Delen aandoeningen van het Bewegingsapparaat.* 6th ed. Delft, Netherlands: Nederlandse Akademie voor Orthopedische Geneeskunde; 1982.

Wynne AT, Nelson MA, Nordin BEC. Costo-iliac impingement syndrome. *J Bone Joint Surg Br.* 1985;67:124–125.

Part II

The Knee

Chapter 7

Functional Anatomy of the Knee

The knee joint is the largest joint in the human body. In the lower extremity it takes the central position not only anatomically but also functionally. In describing the morphology and function of the knee joint, two important points should be kept in mind: On one hand, the joint has to have a large amount of stability to accommodate a great amount of load. On the other hand, the joint has to have a lot of mobility to facilitate movements such as walking, squatting, and kneeling. Morphology and function of the joint are such that for these seemingly contradictory requirements, a "solution has been found."

JOINT MORPHOLOGY

Bony Structures

The knee joint comprises the following bones: femur, tibia, and patella. Within the cavity of the knee joint, two functionally different anatomic connections (joints) can be identified: the connection between tibia and femur, and the connection between femur and patella. For the sake of analysis, the connection between tibia and femur can be seen as two condylar joints. These two joints are again divided by the menisci into a medial and lateral meniscofemoral connection, and a medial and lateral meniscotibial connection. The connection between femur and patella can be seen as a saddle joint.

The condyles of the femur appear to be different in form compared to each other when viewed from the front. The medial condyle extends less far distally than the lateral condyle. When the knee is flexed to 90° and the femur is viewed from distal to proximal in an axial direction, the condyles appear as an upside-down V, forming an angle of 50° to 60° in relation to each other (Figure 7–1). The space between the condyles, the intercondylar fossa, is the site where the cruciate ligaments attach.

Viewed from the side, the condyles are spiral in form; they are not purely cylindrical because the posterior curves are sharper. The amount of curve varies interindividually. At the same time, there is an intraindividual difference between the condyles: The lateral condyle is longer in an anteroposterior direction. The joint surfaces on the medial and lateral side of the femur are convex in both the sagittal and the frontal planes. On the anterior aspect, the cartilage surfaces of the femoral condyles are continuous with the patellar groove. In full extension, the patella lies completely against the patellar groove. In flexion, the patella also has contact with the cartilage surfaces of the condyles (Figure 7–2).

In this context, it can be pointed out that the form of the patella has a significant interindividual variance. The five most frequently seen forms have been described by Wiberg[1] (see "Subluxation of the Patella," in Chapter 10).

Joint Capsule and Ligaments

The joint capsule is composed of a fibrous membrane and a synovial membrane. The synovial membrane of the knee joint has a complicated course. From the patella, it runs upward and forms a large synovial space that

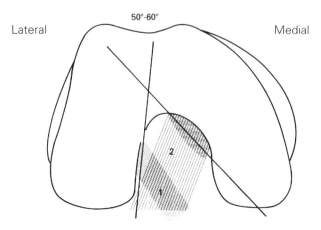

Figure 7–1 Distal view of the femur in a 90° flexed knee. As with the condyles, the attachments of the cruciate ligaments also make an angle of 50° to 60° in relation to each other. **1**, anterior cruciate ligament; **2**, posterior cruciate ligament.

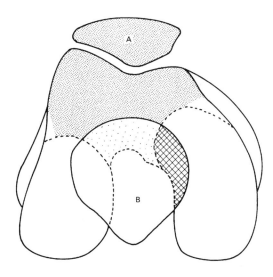

Figure 7–2 Distal view of the femur in a 90° flexed knee showing the position of the patella in relation to the joint surface of the femur. (**A**) In extension, the patella articulates exclusively with the patellofemoral part of the joint surface. (**B**) In maximal flexion, the patella articulates with a part of the femorotibial joint surface as well.

is continuous with the joint cavity. Based on the embryologic development, this space is called the suprapatellar bursa. Clinically, however, it is more often termed the suprapatellar recess (Figure 7–3). During flexion, this space decreases slightly in size (Figure 7–4).

The synovial membrane covers the cruciate ligaments on the anterior aspect and sides but not on the posterior aspect. It is as if the cruciate ligaments push the synovial membrane forward. Thus the position of the cruciate ligaments is described as extrasynovial. Furthermore, through this construction, the most middle part (pars intercondylaris) of the anterior aspect of the posterior capsule is not covered with synovial membrane.

The fibrous part of the capsule (fibrous membrane) is formed as a united bundle around the femoral and tibial parts of the knee joint. The patella is enveloped by the capsule at the anterior aspect of the knee and in this way forms a functional unit.

The ligaments of the joint cannot be seen as solitary structures. They are thick reinforcements of the fibrous membrane and therefore have an accessory function. The lateral collateral (or fibular) ligament is an exception to this rule. The ligament is separated from the fibrous membrane by a small bursa. It runs as

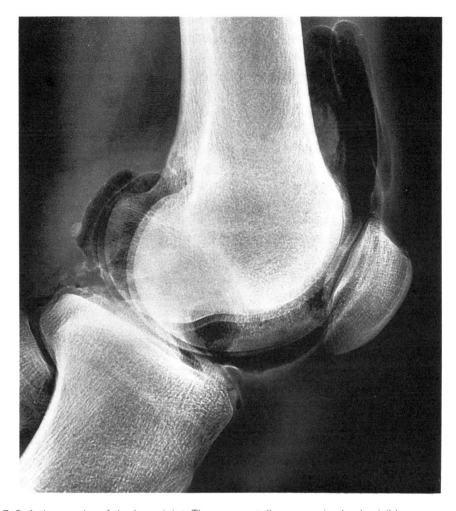

Figure 7–3 Arthrography of the knee joint. The suprapatellar recess is clearly visible.

a cord-shaped band from the lateral femoral epicondyle to the head of the fibula. In addition, there are no connections of the lateral collateral ligament to the lateral meniscus. The other ligaments are part of the collagen of the joint capsule (Figures 7–5, 7–6, and 7–7).

The medial and lateral patellar retinacula, as parts of the patellar ligament, run at the anterior side of the joint capsule. These retinacula, together with the central part of the patellar ligament (the patellar tendon), can be seen as the ventral part of the joint capsule. The retinacula are separated from the synovial membrane by the infrapatellar fat pad. They are designated as the medial and lateral patellotibial ligaments (or retinacula) and the medial and lateral patellofemoral ligaments (or retinacula).

At the medial side, the medial collateral (or tibial) ligament reinforces the fibrous membrane, running from the medial femoral epicondyle to the medial condyle of the tibia. The anterior part of this ligament is separated from the joint capsule by several small bursae. The posterior part (called the posterior medial collateral or posterior ob-

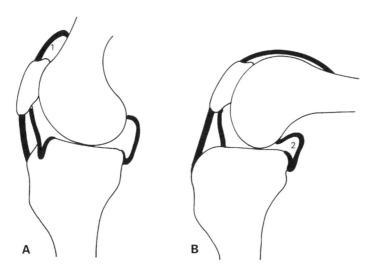

Figure 7–4 The joint capsule during extension **(A)** and flexion **(B)** of the knee. **1,** Suprapatellar recess; **2,** subpopliteal recess.

lique ligament) is closely connected to the capsule.

Both medially and laterally within the joint capsule, the so-called deep collateral ligaments are found. Composed of a separate layer of collagen, these deep collateral ligaments are located closer to the joint cavity and have fibers that run in a different direction than those of the more superficial medial and lateral collateral ligaments. Medially in several places, the collagen fibers of the deep collateral ligament are continuous with the superficial collateral ligament (specifically, the posterior medial collateral ligament). Laterally, the deep and superficial collagenous layers are separated by the already mentioned bursa. These deep ligaments can be further designated according to their relation to the menisci into a meniscofemoral and meniscotibial part. The latter is also called the coronary ligament.

The posterior aspect of the joint capsule is reinforced by a number of more or less obliquely running ligaments. The inserting tendon of the semimembranosus fans out into the posteromedial side of the joint capsule, which is closely connected to the medial meniscus. In so doing, the oblique popliteal ligament is formed as a reinforcement of the posterior capsule (see Figure 7–5).

Within the joint, a number of meniscofemoral ligaments are found that run from the lateral meniscus to the medial femoral condyle. Generally, there is an anterior meniscofemoral ligament (running in front of the posterior cruciate ligament) or a posterior meniscofemoral ligament (running behind the posterior cruciate). Most of the time, the posterior meniscofemoral ligament, also called Wrisberg's ligament, is present (Figure 7–8). Rarely are both ligaments found in the same knee. These ligaments play an important role in the dynamics of the lateral meniscus.

MUSCLES

The knee is not a particularly stable joint, considering the form and arrangement of its bony structures. Thus to a great degree the stability has to be derived from coordinated contraction of the surrounding musculature (Table 7–1). Numerous muscles have a connection with the joint capsule, providing a direct, stabilizing influence.

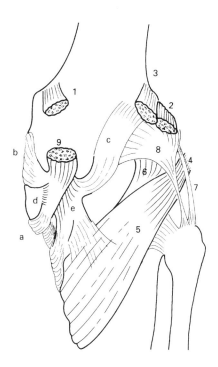

Figure 7–5 Posterior view of the right knee. **1**, Origin of the gastrocnemius muscle, medial head; **2**, origin of the gastrocnemius muscle, lateral head; **3**, origin of the plantaris muscle; **4**, tendon of the popliteus muscle; **5**, popliteus muscle; **6**, popliteus muscle, fibers to the posterior horn of the lateral meniscus; **7**, lateral collateral ligament; **8**, arcuate popliteal ligament; **9**, tendon of the semimembranosus muscle: **a**, to the medial side of the medial tibial condyle; **b**, to the posterior side of the medial tibial condyle; **c**, oblique popliteal ligament; **d**, to the posterior capsule, posterior oblique ligament, and medial meniscus; **e**, to the fascia of the popliteus muscle, posterior tibia, and medial tibia.

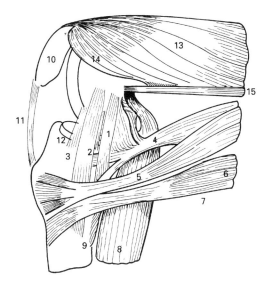

Figure 7–6 Medial view of the right knee. **1**, posterior collateral (or posterior oblique) ligament; **2**, medial collateral ligament (1 and 2 are illustrated separately to show the deep collateral structures; in reality, they are firmly connected); **3**, medial capsuloligamentous structure, consisting of the medial meniscotibial ligament and the medial meniscofemoral ligament; **4**, semimembranosus muscle; **5**, sartorius muscle; **6**, gracilis muscle; **7**, semitendinosus muscle; **8**, gastrocnemius muscle, medial head; **9**, popliteus muscle; **10**, patella; **11**, patellar ligament; **12**, medial meniscus; **13**, vastus medialis muscle; **14**, vastus medialis obliquus muscle; **15**, tendon of the adductor magnus.

Quadriceps Femoris

The four heads of the quadriceps femoris join together in the patellar ligament. The tendon tissue has an attachment to the upper edge of the patella, and a thin superficial layer runs over the patella. From here, the earlier mentioned retinaculum is formed, from which the patellotibial ligaments, in their turn, have a connection with the menisci. The connective tissue (the quadriceps tendon or patellar ligament) that runs from the patella to the tibial tuberosity is again much thicker. In this way, the quadriceps muscle actually forms a part of the joint capsule.

Biceps Femoris

At the lateral side of the joint space, the biceps femoris muscle has contact with the lateral collateral ligament. This ligament appears to divide the distally running fibers of the biceps femoris into a superficial and a deep part.

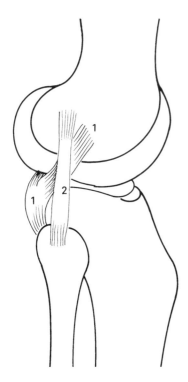

Figure 7–7 Lateral view of the right knee. **1**, Popliteus muscle; **2**, lateral collateral ligament.

Some fibers from the biceps femoris muscle attach to the lateral collateral ligament, and some attach at the posterolateral aspect of the lateral meniscus; these insertions are inconsistent, however (Figure 7–9). Most of the biceps fibers attach to the tibia, between Gerdy's tubercle and the head of the fibula. These latter fibers are rarely affected. Clinically, the most often affected part of the biceps insertion is at the head of the fibula.

Popliteus

Part of the popliteus muscle fans out into the arcuate popliteal ligament (see Figure 7–5). Another part of the popliteus tendon has an attachment to the posterior horn of the lateral meniscus. Thus contraction of the popliteus muscle is partly responsible for the mobility of the lateral meniscus.

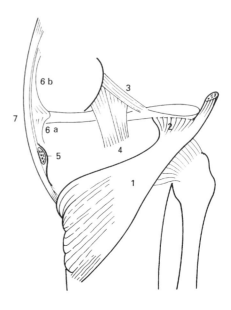

Figure 7–8 Posterior view of the right knee. **1**, popliteus muscle; **2**, insertion of the popliteus muscle on the lateral meniscus; **3**, posterior meniscofemoral ligament (Wrisberg's ligament); **4**, posterior cruciate ligament; **5**, semimembranosus (tendon to the tibia); **6**, medial capsuloligamentous structures: **a**, medial meniscotibial ligament; **b**, medial meniscofemoral ligament; **7**, medial collateral ligament.

Semimembranosus

The semimembranosus muscle splits into a number of tendons at the level of the knee joint. One of the tendons forms the oblique popliteal ligament.

OTHER STRUCTURES

Cruciate Ligaments

The anterior cruciate ligament runs obliquely from anterior on the tibial intercondylar eminence in a posterior and proximal direction to insert at the lateral condyle of the femur in the intercondylar fossa. The posterior cruciate ligament runs obliquely from the

Table 7–1 Active Movements of the Knee Joint

Movement	Muscles
Extension	Quadriceps femoris Tensor fasciae latae (last ~30°)
Flexion	Semimembranosus Semitendinosus Sartorius Gracilis Popliteus Biceps femoris Tensor fasciae latae (after ~30°) Gastrocnemius
External rotation	Biceps femoris Tensor fasciae latae
Internal rotation	Semimembranosus Semitendinosus Sartorius Gracilis Popliteus

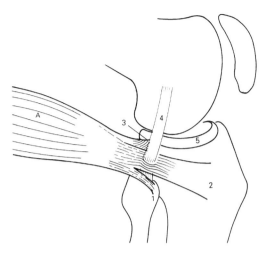

Figure 7–9 Lateral view of the right knee, particularly of the biceps femoris muscle (**A**). **1**, Fibular insertion; **2**, tibial insertion; **3**, insertion at the lateral meniscus; **4**, lateral collateral ligament; **5**, lateral meniscus.

posterior side of the tibial intercondylar eminence in an anterior direction and inserts at the medial condyle of the femur in the intercondylar fossa. Each of these ligaments can be divided into two, or sometimes three, bundles. In their course in the intercondylar fossa, the cruciate ligaments are more cordlike in form; at their distal insertions, they flatten out.

Menisci

In a transverse cross-section, the medial meniscus has the form of a C; the lateral meniscus is smaller and forms almost a complete circle (Figure 7–10). The menisci are found on the tibial plateau, to which they are also connected. Differentiation is made among an anterior horn, a posterior horn, and an arch located between them. The anterior horn and posterior horn are attached to the inter-condylar eminence of the tibia. Through the transverse ligament, the menisci are connected to each other at their anterior aspects. Both menisci are also connected to the joint capsule. The medial meniscus has a firm connection to the tibia via the meniscotibial (coronary) ligament; the arch has a much stronger attachment to the femur through the meniscofemoral ligament.[2] During rotation of the knee, the arch moves with the femur and the horns with the tibia. As a whole, the lateral meniscus is more loosely attached to the capsule and thus can accommodate more movement.

Branches of the medial genicular artery run to the outer edges of the menisci, allowing a large part of the menisci to be directly vascularized.

Plicae

Plicae of the knee are synovial "shelves" that are residual (to a greater or lesser degree) of the embryologically present partitions in the knee joint. Differentiation is made

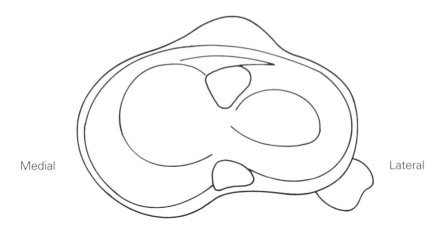

Medial   Lateral

Figure 7–10 Menisci of the right knee joint.

among suprapatellar, infrapatellar, and mediopatellar plicae (Figure 7–11).

Of these structures, the mediopatellar plica is the most clinically important because it is the most often affected. It runs from the distal end of the quadriceps muscle (where the muscle inserts into the base of the patella), over the cartilage of the medial femoral condyle, to the infrapatellar fat pad. In a synovitis of the knee joint, this plica can thicken, thereby causing a disturbance in the joint kinematics. In addition, degeneration of the condylar cartilage can occur as a result of friction from the thickened plica.[3] The suprapatellar plica is a structure that remains from the septum that formed the division between the suprapatellar bursa and the joint cavity. The infrapatellar plica runs more or less in the same direction as the anterior cruciate ligament but, as a whole, lies more anteriorly. This plica is left over from the septum that divided the joint cavity into left and right compartments.

BIOMECHANICS

Characteristics of Movement

There are many models formulated to describe the movements of the knee joint. The most often cited models are the purely mechanical models of Huson,[4] Menschik,[5,6] and Kapandji.[7] These models are based on a system of four rods (Figure 7–12).

Cruciate Ligaments

Central to these models stand the cruciate ligaments and their attachments to the femur and tibia. When flexion and extension movements are performed, the intersection of both lines (representing the cruciate ligaments) shifts in such a way that an imaginary curve can be projected on the femoral condyles. This curve forms the so-called evolute.

Figure 7–12 represents the four rod system. In flexion, the *A–D* line stands more vertical, and the *B–C* line lies more horizontal; the posterior cruciate ligament becomes taut, and the anterior cruciate ligament becomes relatively more relaxed. In extension, the exact opposite happens.

A limitation of such a model is that, in reality, the cruciate ligaments are not lines, and the attachments do not form points. Actually, the fanning out of the cruciate ligaments into the bone is nearly flat. Thus in flexion the anterior part of the posterior cruciate ligament becomes taut, while the posterior part is closer to the tibial plateau and thus relaxes. In contrast, during extension the anterior part

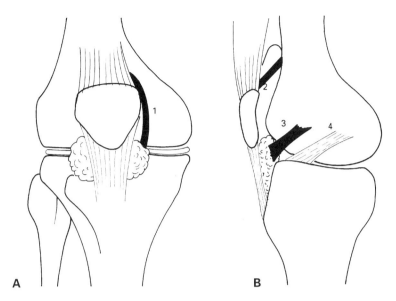

Figure 7–11 (**A**) Anterior aspect of the right knee. (**B**) Sagittal section of the right knee in extension. **1**, Mediopatellar plica; **2**, suprapatellar plica; **3**, infrapatellar plica; **4**, anterior cruciate ligament.

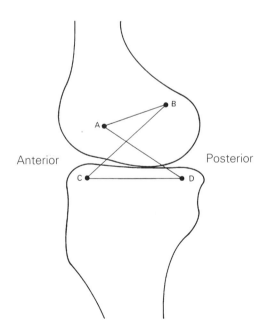

Figure 7–12 Movement of a four-rod system. *A–B*, femur; *C–D*, tibia; *B–C*, anterior cruciate ligament; *A–D*, posterior cruciate ligament.

of the posterior cruciate relaxes, and the posterior part becomes taut. The same is implied for the anterior cruciate ligament: During flexion and extension movements, a part of each of the ligaments is always under tension. In internal rotation, both cruciate ligaments twist around each other and, in so doing, come under even more tension. In external rotation, the tension in both ligaments decreases slightly.

In the clinical setting, the position of the tibia in relation to the femur should always be adjusted in such a way as to test the cruciate ligaments when they are under as little tension as possible. For instance, in 90° flexion, the anterior drawer test for the anterior cruciate ligament can be hindered by tension in the nonruptured part of the ligament. Thus the optimal position for such a test is 10° knee flexion.

Collateral Ligaments

The medial and lateral collateral ligaments are never completely relaxed. Flexion and extension movements of the knee continually bring about tension in different parts of these ligaments: in flexion the anterior part, and in extension the posterior part. In external rotation the tension in the collateral ligaments increases, and in internal rotation it decreases. During flexion, the medial collateral ligament shifts slightly posterior and folds slightly over the posterior medial collateral ligament.

Joint Surfaces

If there were no cruciate ligaments in the knee, during flexion a pure rolling movement of the femoral condyle would occur; after a certain point, the femoral condyle would roll off the tibia. The ligaments act as reins on this system. Thus as the femoral condyle rolls backward on the tibia during flexion, the ligaments hold the joint partners together, resulting in a compensatory simultaneous forward gliding of the femur on the tibia. The ligaments ensure proper alignment of the femur and tibia, and for every knee motion a certain amount of rolling and gliding of the joint partners in relation to each other takes place.

Because of the difference in size between the condyles, in an anteroposterior direction the medial condyle begins to glide after rolling about 15°, the lateral after about 25°. Thus in flexion this difference in behavior between the condyles results in a relative external rotation of the femur in relation to the tibia. In extension, the opposite mechanism occurs. During the last phase of extension, the so-called locking rotation takes place: external rotation of the tibia in relation to the femur.

The normal ratio of rolling and gliding is the same for both femoral condyles. Throughout the various phases of the flexion motion, the ratio of rolling to gliding is about 1:2, and at the end of the motion it is about 1:4.

Menisci

The movement of the menisci can be easily described. In general, the menisci move backward on the tibial plateau during knee flexion; during extension they move forward on the tibial plateau. The lateral meniscus moves more than the medial meniscus. At the end of the flexion motion, the lateral meniscus even tips over the edge of the tibial plateau and is folded, so to speak, over the posterior edge of the tibia.

Movement of the menisci is partly caused by the femoral condyles, which push the menisci posteriorly. The already mentioned meniscotibial ligaments and the activity of the quadriceps, popliteus, biceps femoris, and semimembranosus also play a part in movement of the menisci. Thus in active flexion, as a result of the connection of the medial meniscus with the semimembranosus and the lateral meniscus with the popliteus and biceps femoris muscles, the posterior movement is promoted further. In active extension, the menisci are actively moved forward because of the connection with the extensor mechanism.

During rotations in the joint, the menisci shift over the tibial plateau. The torsion encountered during internal and external rotation of the knee causes the menisci mainly to follow the femoral condyles.

Loading of the Knee Joint

Measuring the load on the knee joint in living subjects is difficult. Researchers must instead depend on analysis of the loads based on models.

There is a difference between static and dynamic loading of the joint. In calculating the static loading, it is easiest to make use of a free body diagram, whereby a part of the extremity is isolated. For instance, in regard to the knee, the lower leg and foot are isolated. Then a simplified calculation is made of the forces and moments acting on that body part.

Frankel and colleagues[8] have determined that, when climbing stairs, a statistical loading of the tibial plateau of the weight-bearing leg is approximately four times the body weight. Morrison[9] used electromyography (EMG) to study the dynamic loading in subjects' knees during walking. The EMG was performed to determine which muscles were most active during peak loading. Morrison calculated that, during the first part of the stance phase, the reaction force on the tibial plateau is two to three times body weight, during which the hamstrings are most active. At midstance, with most activity centered in the quadriceps femoris muscle, the reaction force on the tibial plateau is about two times the body weight. At the end of the stance phase, involving significant activity of the gastrocnemius, the reaction force is between two and four times the body weight.

Chapter 8

Surface Anatomy of the Knee

Considering the significant amount of medical attention devoted to the knee because of the enormous forces it must endure, it is fortunate that many of its bones are easily accessible for palpation. This is because they are superficially located. The extensive variety of traumas sustained by the knee makes good palpation techniques especially important to arrive at a correct diagnosis. The sequence of palpation presented here was chosen for its systematic approach; it starts with the easily recognizable structures and progresses on to the more difficult.

ANTERIOR ASPECT OF THE KNEE

Initial Position

The subject should sit on the treatment table with the thighs resting on the table and the lower legs hanging over the edge. The clinician should sit on a chair in front of the subject, within reach of both knees. Different initial positions are required for some palpations; when that is the case, they are so indicated.

Patella

The patella should be inspected with the subject in the initial position described above. The clinician should look for differences in skin color and notice whether the patella is abnormally shifted or tilted (Figures 8–1 to 8–4). From the patellar apex, palpate both edges in a proximal direction. To make this palpation easier, bring the leg to a position of passive extension; the patella can be moved freely, and its edges can be felt.

Note: The knee should be kept in extension for the following palpations.

Pain complaints can develop on both sides of the patella because of overuse of the extensor mechanism or with relative overuse because of a change in the form of the patella (patellar malalignment).

The parapatellar structures consist of the insertions of the vastus medialis and vastus lateralis muscles together with the various layers of capsule. Again, these are reinforced with ligaments that run between the femur and tibia, medial and lateral to the patella. These ligaments are the medial and lateral patellofemoral and the medial and lateral patellotibial ligaments.

Palpation is performed with the patella moved to the palpating side with pressure from the thumb. With the middle finger, while the whole hand is in supination, the medial or the lateral edge of the patella can be palpated from proximal to distal. During palpation of the medial side of the patella, the clinician should stand at the lateral side of the knee. During palpation of the lateral side, the clinician should switch sides and stand next to the medial side of the knee.

Suprapatellar palpation of the insertion of the rectus femoris muscle is only possible when the patella is tipped slightly forward. This can be accomplished by pushing the apex of the patella in a posterior direction with the other hand, which brings the base of the patella to a more anterior position. The middle finger is used to palpate the upper edge of the patella in a horizontal plane from medial to lateral.

It is significant when the patient complaints of pain distal to the patella during extension of the knee against resistance. This indicates the probable presence of an insertion tendopathy of the quadriceps tendon (patellar ligament) at the patellar apex. Palpation is possible by pressing the base of the patella in a posterior direction, which tilts the apex up. Again, the best palpation can be performed with the middle finger from medial to lateral in a horizontal plane. Generally, the most tenderness will be experienced at the apex.

Patellar Ligament

Palpation of the patellar ligament should start at the distal part of the patella (Figures 8–1 to 8–4). There are two indentations on both sides of the ligament; these may be covered when there is joint effusion. The palpation technique is to follow the ligament distally to the bony elevation on the tibia where the ligament inserts; this is the tibial tuberosity.

Tibial Tuberosity

Palpation and inspection of the tibial tuberosity is not difficult (Figure 8–1). In Osgood-Schlatter disease,* the tibial tuberosity is affected, and, together with the patellar ligament, it is sensitive to pressure. This complaint is most often seen in 10- to 15-year-old boys and increases during activity.

Intense pain of the entire extensor tendon and patella, leaving the patient unable to straighten the leg, can be the sign of a (partial) rupture. Such ruptures can be seen at the level of the proximal edge of the patella,

---

*Robert Bailey Osgood, orthopaedic surgeon from Boston, Massachusetts, 1873–1956. Karl Schlatter, surgeon from Zurich, Switzerland, 1864–1934.

the tibial tuberosity, or the muscle belly of the rectus femoris muscle.

Infrapatellar Bursa

An infrapatellar fat pad (Hoffa's fat pad†) is located between the patellar ligament (anteriorly) and the tibia and anterior joint capsule (posteriorly). Located between the distal part of the patellar ligament and this infrapatellar fat pad is the deep infrapatellar bursa. The superficial infrapatellar bursa is located between the ligament and the skin. These bursae can get irritated and become increasingly sensitive to palpation.

Tendon of the Quadriceps Muscle

Overuse can also irritate this teno-osseous junction of the quadriceps muscle. On palpation from the upper outer edge of the patella in a proximolateral direction, a thick cord can be felt. This is the tendon of the vastus lateralis muscle (Figure 8–2).

In muscular people, the horizontal fibers of the vastus medialis muscle can be palpated at the level of the upper inner edge of the patella. The examining clinician should feel for possible hardening in this muscle. This muscle is a predilection site for myositis ossificans (calcification) after trauma. As a result of knee surgery, the vastus medialis muscle will start to atrophy almost immediately. In all knee disorders, atrophy of this muscle is a valid indicator of the status of the knee joint.

Lateral and Medial Patellar Retinacula

In some individuals, the continuation of the tendon of the vastus lateralis muscle, the lateral patellar retinaculum, can be palpated at the lateral side of the patella (Figures 8–1 and 8–4). The medial patellar retinaculum is much more difficult to palpate because of the

---

†Albert Hoffa, German surgeon, 1857–1919.

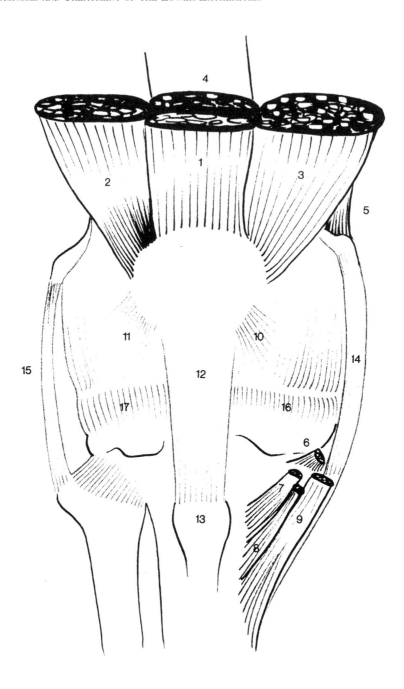

Figure 8–1 Anterior view of the (right) knee joint; the superficial aspect of the capsule is removed. **1**, Rectus femoris muscle; **2**, vastus lateralis muscle; **3**, vastus medialis muscle; **4**, vastus intermedius muscle; **5**, adductor magnus muscle; **6**, semimembranosus muscle; **7**, sartorius muscle; **8**, gracilis muscle; **9**, semitendinosus muscle; **10**, medial patellar retinaculum (patellofemoral part); **11**, lateral patellar retinaculum (patellofemoral part); **12**, patellar ligament; **13**, tibial tuberosity; **14**, medial collateral ligament; **15**, lateral collateral ligament; **16**, medial coronary ligament (medial meniscotibial ligament); **17**, lateral coronary ligament (lateral meniscotibial ligament).

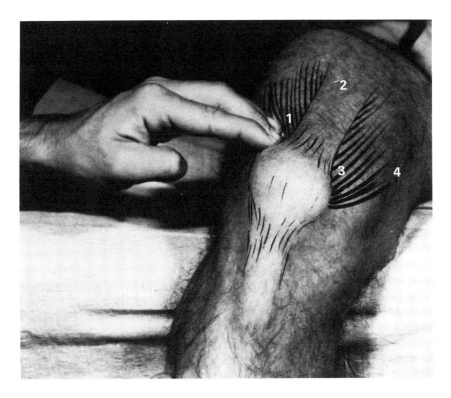

Figure 8–2 Palpation of the insertion of the quadriceps, right knee. **1**, Tendon of the vastus lateralis muscle, proximolateral to the patella; **2**, rectus femoris muscle; **3**, vastus medialis (its insertion is farther distal than that of the vastus lateralis); **4**, vastus medialis obliquus muscle.

more distal insertion of the vastus medialis muscle.

Patellar Groove of the Femur

The larger parts of the femoral condyles can be felt by palpating at the edges of the patella in proximal direction (Figure 8–3). The lateral condyle can be palpated farther proximally than the medial condyle. The clinician should inspect the patellar groove that is formed by the condyles.

MEDIAL ASPECT OF THE KNEE

Initial Position

The starting position is with the subject sitting on the examination table with the knee in 90° flexion and the lower leg relaxed over the edge of the table.

Medial Joint Space

The proper palpation technique is to slide the palpating finger in the medial joint space, starting at the indentation medial to the patellar ligament (Figures 8–3 and 8–5). When this indentation is not visible or not palpable, the patellar apex should be used as a point of reference for the level of the joint space. Inexperienced clinicians commonly make mistakes while palpating the knee. Palpation is made easier when the knee is internally and externally rotated while in the flexed position; this helps the clinician discern between the stationary femur and the moving tibia.

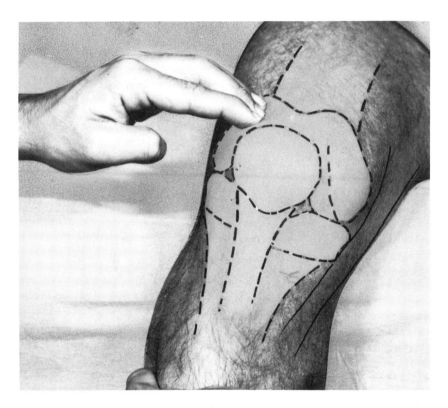

Figure 8–3 Palpation of the patellar rgroove, right knee.

Medial Meniscus

Normally, the anterior part of the medial meniscus is easily palpable in the medial joint space, between the patellar ligament and the anterior edge of the medial collateral ligament, when the knee is passively extended (Figure 8–5). During active and passive flexion of the knee, the medial meniscus moves slightly in a posterior direction. Under normal conditions, the meniscus is not palpable when the knee is flexed beyond 30°.

Increased tenderness to palpation of the joint space often occurs in tears of the meniscus. Medial meniscus tears occur more often than lateral meniscus tears, especially in men. One of the reasons for this is that men have a higher incidence of genu vara than genu valga, exerting more compression force on the medial meniscus.

The medial meniscus is connected to the tibia by a ligament called the medial meniscotibial or coronary ligament. This ligament is palpable anteriorly, proximal to the tibia. (In lesions of the medial meniscotibial ligament, passive external rotation of the knee provokes the patient's pain; sometimes this test is misinterpreted as a meniscus lesion.) Palpation of the medial meniscotibial ligament should be performed with the knee positioned in 90° flexion and maximal external rotation.

Medial Femoral Condyle

The medial femoral condyle can be palpated by following it along the edge of the patella in a proximal direction and then as far

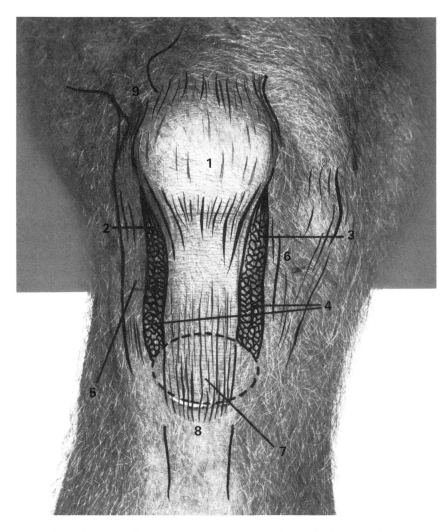

Figure 8–4 Patella and surrounding structures, right knee. **1**, Patella; **2**, lateral indentation; **3**, medial indentation; **4**, Hoffa's fat pad (infrapatellar fat pad); **5**, lateral patellar retinaculum; **6**, medial patellar retinaculum; **7**, deep infrapatellar bursa; **8**, tibial tuberosity; **9**, insertion tendon of the vastus lateralis.

as possible in a posterior direction (Figure 8–3). On palpation of the entire medial side of the condyle, a bony prominence, the medial epicondyle, can be felt. The most proximal point of the medial epicondyle is formed by the adductor tubercle. At the adductor tubercle, the adductor magnus inserts, and the medial collateral ligament originates.

At the level of the joint space, the clinician should palpate the edges of the medial femo-

ral condyle for inconsistencies, such as the formation of osteophytes, indicating gonarthrosis.

Medial Tibial Plateau

The edge of the medial tibial plateau can be palpated from the sartorius muscle to the patellar ligament (Figure 8–3). During this technique, the palpating finger should remain in the joint space. Mark the upper edge of the

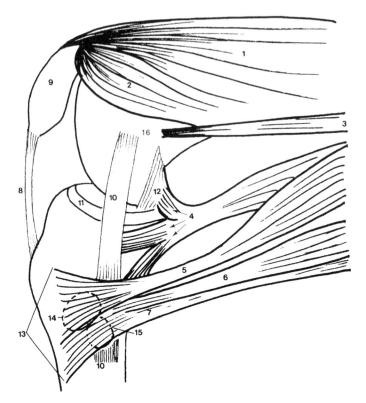

Figure 8–5 Medial view of the (right) knee. **1**, Vastus medialis muscle; **2**, vastus medialis obliquus muscle; **3**, adductor magnus muscle; **4**, semimembranosus muscle with inserting slips (also termed the pes anserinus profundus); **5**, sartorius muscle; **6**, gracilis muscle; **7**, semitendinosus muscle; **8**, patellar ligament; **9**, patella; **10**, medial collateral ligament; **11**, medial meniscus; **12**, part of the posterior capsule; **13**, pes anserinus superficialis; **14**, bursa between the sartorius and gracilis muscles; **15**, bursa between the semitendinosus muscle and the medial collateral ligament; **16**, adductor tubercle.

tibial plateau. Palpating distally, the clinician will feel the plateau going over into the body of the tibia. The exact border between the tibial plateau and the body of the tibia is not discernible.

Medial Collateral Ligament

Sliding a finger deep in the medial joint space from anterior to posterior, the clinician will feel an abrupt elevation. This is a collagen thickening of the capsule called the medial collateral ligament (Figures 8–1 and 8–5). If the palpation is performed roughly, the subject may experience pain because the ligament has an extensive sensory innervation. Proximal to the ligament, a small protuberance on the medial femoral condyle can be felt, where the ligament has its origin on the medial epicondyle.

Medial Muscles

Many muscles insert at the medial side of the knee joint. To make an exact diagnosis, one must be able to differentiate among the muscles. The best way to begin the evaluation of the muscles is by locating the tendon of the semitendinosus muscle at the back of the knee (refer to the section, Posterior Aspect of the Knee).

More deeply, and on both sides of this tendon, the fibers of the semimembranosus muscle can be palpated. The medial edge of the semitendinosus muscle may feel sharp, which helps differentiate it from the round tendon of the gracilis muscle. The tendon of the gracilis muscle can be felt slightly medial and anterior to the medial part of the semimembranosus muscle. More medially and anteriorly, palpation will lead to the sartorius muscle. Both muscles have their insertion in the pes anserinus (superficialis). Sometimes it is difficult to differentiate between these muscles. The gracilis feels like a round tendon, however, whereas the sartorius feels like a flat muscle. Alternating abduction and adduction of the thigh can assist in differentiation: The gracilis contracts during adduction, and the sartorius contracts during abduction.

Palpation in a more anterior direction will lead to the adductor tubercle and the insertion of the adductor magnus muscle. By placing the fingers more lateral from here, the clinician can palpate the vastus medialis muscle. Practice is necessary to be able to identify with certainty the lateral aspect of the semimembranosus, the semitendinosus, the medial aspect of the semimembranosus, the gracilis, the sartorius, the adductor magnus, and the vastus medialis.

Pes Anserinus Profundus and Superficialis

The semimembranosus muscle has three collagenous insertions at the level of the knee joint (Figure 8–5). These three collagenous slips are called the pes anserinus profundus (refer to "Posterior Aspect of the Knee," below). This is not the same as the pes anserinus superficialis. The pes anserinus superficialis is the common insertion of the semitendinosus, gracilis, and sartorius muscles on the proximal anteromedial surface of the tibia, just medial to the tibial tuberosity. Sometimes this fanning out of the pes anserinus superficialis to the tuberosity is visible.

Located between the tendons of the sartorius and gracilis muscles is the subtendinous bursa of the sartorius muscle, also known as the internal superior genual bursa. When this bursa is inflamed, palpation of the anterior and proximal part of the gracilis muscle insertion is painful.

Another bursa is located distal of the tibial condyle, between the medial collateral ligament and the pes anserinus superficialis. Pain at this location indicates irritation of the bursa. Most of the time this is caused by overuse of the tendons of the pes anserinus superficialis (seen in long-distance runners).

LATERAL ASPECT OF THE KNEE

Initial Position

The subject sits on the examination table with the knee in 90° flexion and the lower leg hanging relaxed over the end of the table.

Lateral Joint Space

The lateral joint space of the knee is palpated by moving the finger laterally, starting from the indentation lateral to the patellar ligament (Figures 8–6 and 8–7). To make sure that the palpation remains accurate, an alternating internal and external rotation of the lower leg is performed. The object is to feel the movement of the lateral tibial plateau compared with the stationary lateral femoral condyle.

Lateral Femoral Condyle

Palpation is started in the indentation lateral to the patellar ligament and continues along the entire lateral condyle in the same way as described for the medial side (Figures

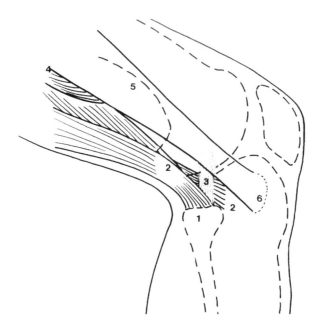

Figure 8–6 Lateral view of the (right) knee. **1**, Fibular head; **2**, insertion of the biceps femoris muscle; **3**, lateral collateral ligament; **4**, vastus lateralis muscle; **5**, iliotibial tract; **6**, Gerdy's tubercle.

8–6 and 8–7). The sides of the condyle should be checked to detect thickenings of the capsule. The lateral condyle can also be followed to a point proximal to the patella.

Lateral Meniscus

The anterior part of the lateral meniscus is best palpated with the knee in an extended position. Compared with the medial meniscus, the lateral meniscus is injured less often. This is probably because the lateral meniscus is more mobile than the medial meniscus.

Tendon of the Biceps Femoris Muscle

The tendon of the biceps femoris muscle is easily visible and will be felt as a round cord lateral to the knee joint (Figure 8–6). This tendon will be used as a reference point for orientation of this area.

Fibular Head

The fibular head can be found by following the tendon of the biceps femoris muscle distally (Figures 8–6 and 8–7). The fibular head is located more distally and posteriorly than most people expect. Thus it is helpful to mark the fibular head, the lateral femoral condyle, and the lateral tibial plateau to get a general impression of local bone relationships.

Lateral Collateral Ligament

The lateral collateral ligament runs from the lateral femoral condyle to the fibular head and can be felt as a thick, round cord (Figures 8–6 and 8–7). It can best be palpated when the hip is maximally externally rotated and the knee is flexed to about 90°. Palpation will be made easier if the subject, who is in a sitting position, brings the distal part of the lower leg over and on top of the distal thigh of

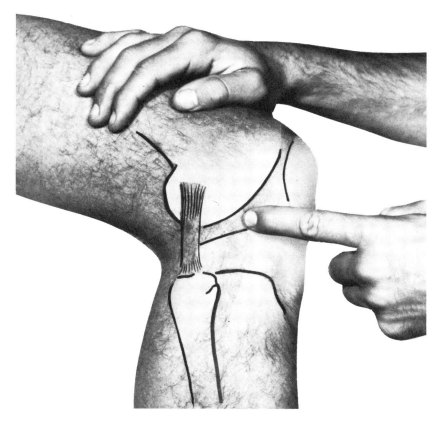

Figure 8–7 Palpation of the lateral joint space, right knee. The palpating finger moves from the indentation lateral to the patellar apex into the joint space.

the other leg. This position is called the "figure-4" position for the right leg and the "reversed 4" for the left leg (Figure 8–8). The correct position will place the ligament 80° relative to the tendon of the biceps femoris muscle. Palpation of the lateral collateral ligament is easier than palpation of the medial collateral ligament.

Lateral Tibial Plateau

The edge of the lateral tibial plateau can be palpated from the lateral collateral ligament to the patellar ligament (Figure 8–7). During this technique, the palpating finger should remain in the joint space. Mark the upper edge of the tibial plateau. Palpating distally, the plateau can be felt going over into the body of the tibia. The exact border between tibial plateau and the body of the tibia is not discernible.

Iliotibial Tract

The iliotibial tract inserts just distal to the lateral tibial plateau (Figure 8–6). If the lateral collateral ligament is palpated as described above, confusion with this structure is unlikely. The iliotibial tract inserts on Gerdy's tubercle, which is generally the largest bony prominence medial to the apex of the fibular head.

The best place to begin palpating the iliotibial tract is just proximal to the joint space.

Figure 8–8 The "figure-4" sign, a position used in palpation of the lateral collateral ligament.

From here, the tract is followed proximally, and then the examination continues across the joint space to the distal insertion. This palpation can be facilitated by bringing the knee into a position of active extension. The insertion of the iliotibial tract can be felt as a firm cord anterior to the lateral collateral ligament, in the area of the lateral patellar retinaculum. The iliotibial tract also has a connection with the lateral patellar retinaculum and with other parts of the knee joint capsule. Note that the space between the prominent iliotibial tract and the lateral edge of the patella edge is filled with radiating fibers coming from the tract. This can have clinical significance in incidences of patellar malalignment syndromes.

Common Peroneal Nerve

The tendon of the biceps femoris muscle is used as the starting point for the palpation of the common peroneal nerve (Figure 8–6). Medial to the tendon of the biceps femoris muscle is a thin, round cord palpable in the popliteal fossa. Bringing the lower leg into 45°

flexion and internal rotation facilitates the palpation. This nerve should not be confused with the tibial nerve, which runs through the middle of the popliteal fossa. Posterior and lateral to the fibular neck, the common peroneal nerve is superficial and easy to palpate.

Because of its superficial position, this nerve can be easily injured. Persons with professions requiring squatting positions, which put stress on the knees, are particularly prone to pinching this nerve. The result may be a diminution of the nerve function with a typical finding of drop foot.

POSTERIOR ASPECT OF THE KNEE

Initial Position

The starting position is with the subject prone.

Popliteal Fossa

Theoretically, the shape of the popliteal fossa is a diamond (Figure 8–9). In fact, however, it is a narrow space that can be seen as

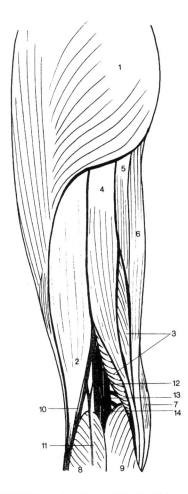

Figure 8–9 Posterior view of the (left) leg showing the popliteal fossa. **1**, Gluteus maximus muscle; **2**, biceps femoris muscle; **3**, semimembranosus muscle; **4**, semitendinosus muscle; **5**, adductor magnus muscle; **6**, gracilis muscle; **7**, sartorius muscle; **8**, lateral head of the gastrocnemius muscle; **9**, medial head of the gastrocnemius muscle; **10**, common peroneal nerve; **11**, sural nerve; **12**, popliteal vein; **13**, popliteal artery; **14**, tibial nerve.

and nerves. The proximomedial border of the diamond is formed by the semimembranosus and semitendinosus muscles. With the knee in a slightly flexed position, the thin, round tendon of the semitendinosus muscle is easy to palpate. Medial and lateral to this tendon are the deeper parts of the semimembranosus muscle. At the proximolateral part of the diamond, the biceps tendon is found. This tendon is palpable together with the common peroneal nerve (lying medial to the tendon).

Under the tendons of the semimembranosus and the semitendinosus muscles is a bursa that can become irritated. In these instances, the patient experiences pain during contraction of these muscles; the tendons are pulled taut, compressing the painful bursa. A hernia of this bursa can be felt as a thick, round swelling in the fossa. This is also called a Baker cyst.*

The distal border of the popliteal fossa is more difficult to find on palpation because the origins of the gastrocnemius and the plantaris muscles lie deeper. Palpation can be simplified, however, by positioning the knee in slight flexion to relax the firm knee fasciae.

Systematic Palpation of the Popliteal Fossa

With the subject prone, the palpated knee is flexed slightly. The thin, round tendon of the semitendinosus muscle can be palpated in a medial direction in the back of the knee (Figure 8–10). This should be done by placing the index and middle fingers on either side of the tendon; alternating pressure is exerted as the tendon, musculotendinous junction, and proximal muscle belly are followed proximally (Figure 8–11). If this presents problems, the subject should be asked to keep the knee actively flexed. A gently performed palpation will allow the clinician to feel the muscle.

*Willem Morant Baker, British surgeon, 1839–1896.

the distal continuation of the adductor canal. Only during dissections and operations does it have a real diamond shape.

Palpation of structures in this space is difficult, but by precisely locating its borders the clinician can more easily find blood vessels

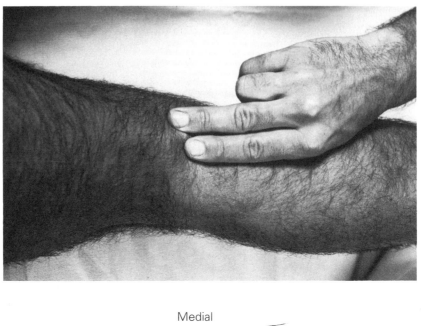

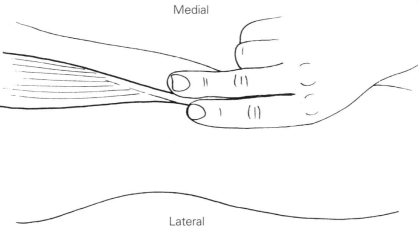

Figure 8–10 Palpation of the tendon of the semitendinosus muscle, left leg.

Directly medial to and deeper than the rolling tendon of the semitendinosus muscle, a flat, bandlike tendon can be felt. This is the wide tendon of the semimembranosus muscle (Figure 8–12). The tendon should be pal- pated distally as far as possible. The semi- membranosus can also be palpated in a proxi- mal direction by placing the middle finger in the groove between this muscle and the graci- lis muscle. Using the same technique as de-

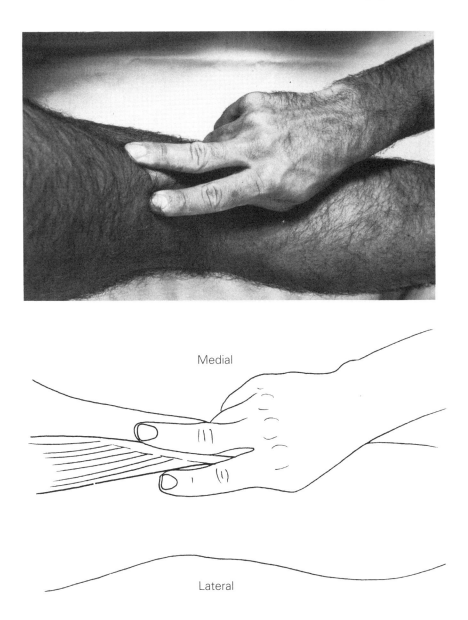

Figure 8–11 Palpation of the tendon of the semitendinosus muscle to proximal, left leg.

scribed for the semitendinosus muscle, a large part of the semimembranosus, medial to the semitendinosus muscle, can be easily palpated.

A small part of the semimembranosus muscle (roughly 2 cm) that lies lateral to the tendon of the semitendinosus muscle can be palpated deeply with the tips of the fingers

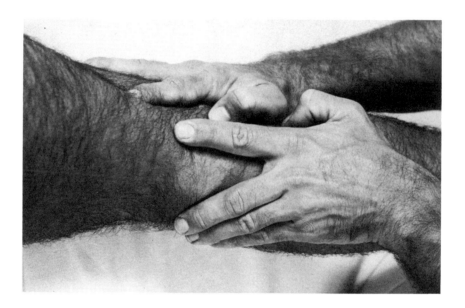

Medial

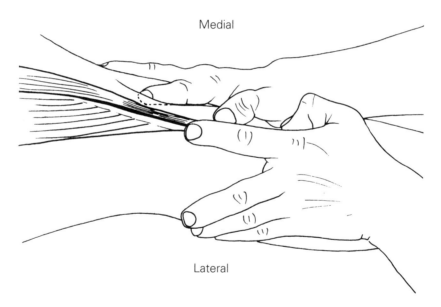

Lateral

Figure 8–12 Palpation of the semimembranosus muscle, left leg.

pointed in a medial direction (Figure 8–13). This is a difficult palpation. It is sometimes easier when there is a rupture of the fascia, which allows this part of the semimembranosus muscle to be more superficial. This can be seen as a normal anatomic variation in women and is easy to confuse with a Baker cyst.

After these muscles are marked, the thick tendon of the biceps femoris muscle can be followed from a point lateral to the fossa (Fig-

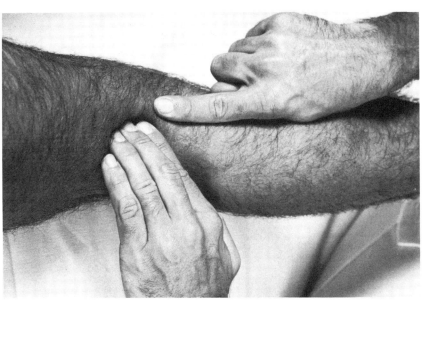

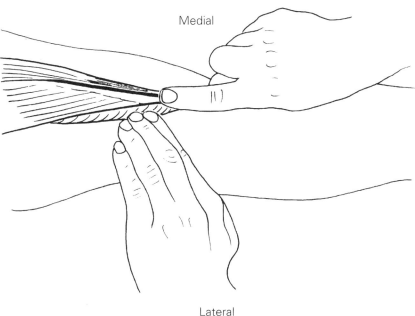

Medial

Lateral

Figure 8–13 Palpation of the semimembranosus muscle lateral to the tendon of the semitendinosus muscle, left leg.

ure 8–14). By placing the index and middle fingers on either side of the tendon and exerting alternating pressure, the clinician can fol-

low the tendon, musculotendinous junction, and proximal muscle belly proximally. The palpation can be continued until the ischial

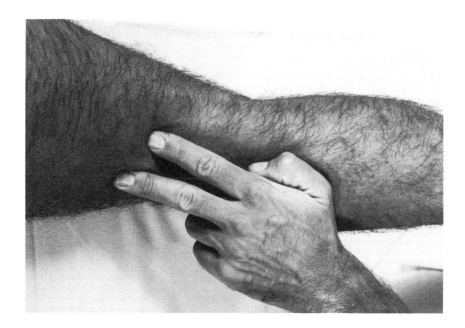

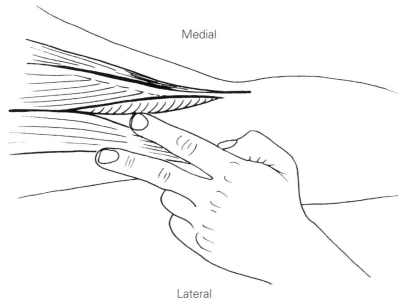

Medial

Lateral

Figure 8–14 Palpation of the biceps femoris muscle, left leg.

tubercle is reached. Using this method, the palpating fingers "walk" through the muscle grooves formed by the biceps and vastus lateralis muscles on one side and the semitendinosus and biceps muscles on the other side.

Gastrocnemius Muscle

The distal borders of the popliteal fossa are palpated by positioning the subject's knee in slight flexion together with active plantar

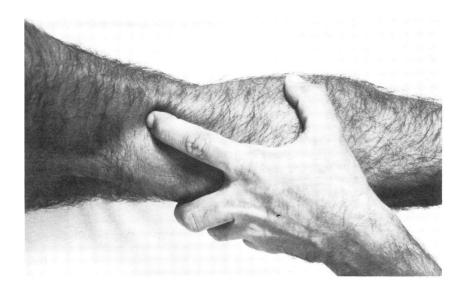

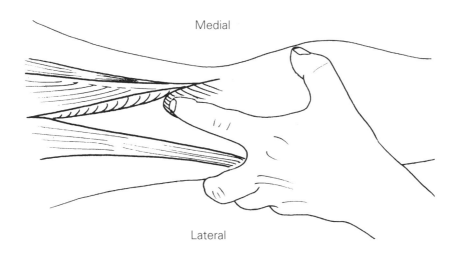

Figure 8–15 Palpation of the medial head of the gastrocnemius muscle, left leg.

flexion of the foot. The palpating finger is placed deeply and medial in the fossa to feel the medial head of the gastrocnemius muscle (Figures 8–9 and 8–15). This palpation can also be done transversely. Note that the palpation starts deeply and lateral to the tendon of the semitendinosus muscle, on the thigh proximal to the fold of the knee.

The same method is used to palpate the lateral head of the gastrocnemius muscle, but deep and medial to the tendon of the biceps muscle. The palpation should start more proximally than for the medial head.

In some people, medial to the lateral head of the gastrocnemius muscle, a muscle belly is visible and palpable. This is the plantaris muscle (Figure 8–16).

The common peroneal nerve is easy to locate, just medial to the tendon of the biceps muscle. For this palpation, the leg should be placed in a slightly flexed and internally rotated position in the hip and knee; the nerve is felt as a cordlike structure that rolls under the palpating finger (Figure 8–17).

Tibial Nerve

Central in the fossa, a thick, cordlike structure is palpable. This is the tibial nerve (Figure 8–9). The nerve is most easily palpable when the subject is supine, with the hip and knee in a 90° flexed position and the foot in maximal dorsal flexion.

Popliteal Artery and Vein

The popliteal vein is deep, directly medial, and not palpable—it covers the popliteal artery (Figure 8–9). During extension of the knee, the fascia is tight, and pulsations cannot be felt. With 90° knee flexion and the lower leg relaxed over the examination table, however, pulsations from the artery can be felt. If the artery still cannot be located, the subject should be put in a prone position with a flexed knee. The clinician supports the lower leg. When the subject is completely relaxed, the pulsations in the popliteal fossa can best be felt. Some subjects have to perform 10 deep knee bends before this technique is successful. A complete absence of pulsations from the dorsal

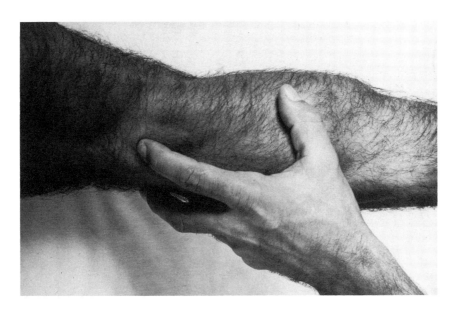

Figure 8–16 Palpation of the plantaris muscle, left leg.

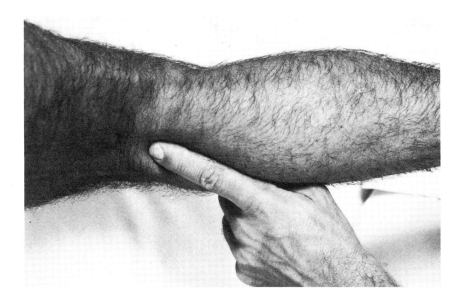

Figure 8–17 Palpation of the common peroneal nerve, left leg.

pedal artery, the posterior tibial artery, and the popliteal artery can be seen in subjects with intermittent claudication. This is a disorder seen primarily in men; it occurs when the arteries of the lower legs do not provide sufficient blood circulation to the muscles. Muscle function is impaired, sometimes causing a limp. The limp difficulty abates with rest, becoming intermittent, hence the term *intermittent claudication*.

Lesser Saphenous Vein

The lesser saphenous vein enters the back of the knee from distal, where, together with the medial cutaneous nerve, it runs between the heads of the gastrocnemius muscle. In addition to these vessels and nerves, the fossa is filled with fatty tissue and lymph nodes, which can swell in the presence of foot infections.

Chapter 9

Examination of the Knee

KNEE JOINT (ARTICULATIO GENUS)

- *Zero position:* The lower leg is in line with the thigh.
- *Maximal loose-packed position*

  1. Bony: Approximately 25° flexion of the knee.

  2. Ligamentous: Approximately 80° flexion of the knee.

- *Maximal close-packed position:* Maximal extension of the knee.
- *Capsular pattern:* Flexion is much more limited than extension. For instance, there is a 5° to 10° extension limitation compared with a 60° flexion limitation. The rotations are only limited in severe capsular limitations of motion (Figure 9–1).

PROXIMAL TIBIOFIBULAR JOINT (ARTICULATIO TIBIOFIBULARIS PROXIMALIS)

- *Maximal loose-packed position:* Approximately 10° flexion of the talocrural joint.
- *Maximal close-packed position:* Maximal extension of the talocrural joint.

OVERVIEW OF THE FUNCTIONAL EXAMINATION

Most articular and periarticular disorders of the knee cause local pain. In some cases, there is slight radiating pain either proximally or distally. Some lesions of the lumbar spine and of the hip can cause pain at the knee instead of pain at the level of the lesion. This misleading symptom is particularly seen in coxarthrosis cases. Pain at the anterior side of the knee can be referred from the hip or from the L2 or L3 nerve roots. Pain at the lateral side of the knee can be referred from the L4 or L5 nerve roots, and at the posterior aspect from the S1 or S2 nerve roots.

General Inspection

Useful information can be gathered as the patient enters the room. The examiner should take note of the general posture, facial expression, and any obvious limitation of motion. Particular attention should be focused on the patient's gait. The use of a cane, crutches, cast, or brace should also be noted.

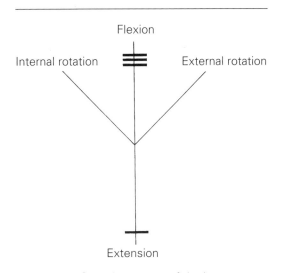

Figure 9–1 Capsular pattern of the knee.

166

History

Age

The age of the patient is particularly important when trauma is concerned. For example, a young adolescent is more likely to experience an apophyseal fracture as the result of forces on the knee than an adult. In an adult, trauma is more likely to lead to capsuloligamentous tears or ruptures. In adolescents there is a greater chance that these structures will remain intact.

Occupation, Hobby, Sport

General information about a patient's occupation, hobbies, and participation in sports is always useful in assessing the patient's overall state of health and risk factors that could cause problems. Specific information is necessary in the case of trauma caused by participation in any of these activities. Specific causes typically include accidents, overuse, and improper equipment or techniques, to name only a few. By determining the exact cause, the therapist can prescribe causal treatment, which is necessary regardless of other treatment, to prevent recurrence.

Chief Complaints

Depending on the type of pathology, complaints can consist of one or more of the following:

- pain
- swelling
- giving way of the knee
- locking of the joint
- loss of range of motion
- crepitation or popping sounds in the knee

Pain is experienced with almost every lesion of the knee and thus is nonspecific when one is trying to make a diagnosis. If pain occurs immediately after severe trauma and then disappears rather quickly afterward, however, this is usually an indication that a structure has been completely ruptured. Pain will return later as a result of the hemarthrosis. The location of the pain generally corresponds to the site of the lesion.

Diffuse swelling that occurs directly after trauma usually indicates the presence of a hemarthrosis. If swelling occurs several hours or days after the trauma, this usually indicates the presence of joint synovial effusion. Local swelling is usually caused by a bursitis or ganglion.

Giving way of the knee occurs with various disorders: instability, some meniscus lesions, loose bodies, and patellofemoral problems. The direction in which the knee gives way depends on the form of instability. In some patellofemoral problems, and in a mediopatellar plica syndrome, the patient sometimes has the feeling that the knee gives way, although in reality it does not.

Locking of the knee can occur as the result of the impingement of a meniscus or where loose bodies are involved. If only extension is limited, this usually indicates a meniscus lesion. Loose bodies can cause either an extension or a flexion limitation. Pseudolocking sometimes occurs as part of a mediopatellar plica syndrome.

Limitations of motion can have various causes. By means of the functional examination, the type of limitation can be determined.

Almost every knee crepitates or pops somewhat. As long as this is not painful, it is not clinically significant. Painful crepitation, popping, or clicking can occur in gonarthrosis and in some instances of meniscus lesions (clicking in particular).

Onset

Several key points regarding onset can aid in establishing the diagnosis. What was the patient doing when the symptoms started? Was there a trauma? Did the symptoms occur gradually or suddenly? It is of great diagnostic importance to determine as precisely as possible under what conditions the symptoms began.

If the symptoms occurred traumatically, what was the position of the knee, and what forces were acting on the joint? It is important to know the direction of either direct or indirect forces acting on the knee (at the time of the trauma) to determine the location and severity of the lesion.

After the trauma, could the patient use the knee normally? If the patient can use the knee normally after trauma, the lesion is usually not severe. The anatomic position of the knee plays an important role as well: After a valgus trauma, a patient with genu varum can often walk without difficulty. If the patient has genu valgum, however, the same lesion can cause significant problems in knee function.

Did the patient feel or hear a popping or tearing during the trauma? A loud pop often occurs in a meniscus tear and particularly in a total rupture of the anterior cruciate ligament. A tearing sound is usually caused by tears or ruptures of part of the capsuloligamentous complex.

Progression of Symptoms

Two important questions to ask the patient concern the symptoms: Has the location of pain changed or spread? Did the symptoms disappear only to come back again? If so, how often and under what circumstances does the pain recur? When the symptoms spread, some form of inflammation is usually present. In these instances, the presence of a tumor should always be ruled out. Recurrence is often seen in tendinitides, patellofemoral problems, and all disorders in which the causal treatment was ineffective, permitting the underlying causes to continue to exist.

Do the symptoms change on ascending or descending stairs or inclined surfaces? Lesions of the extensor mechanism usually cause more symptoms on ascending inclined surfaces or stairs. Lesions of the joint and an iliotibial tract friction syndrome usually cause the most pain on descending an incline or stairs.

Involvement of Other Joints

If the patient has complaints about other joints, systemic diseases such as rheumatoid arthritis, psoriasis, ankylosing spondylitis, and gout should be considered.

Medications

Administering mechanical therapy such as mobilization, manipulation, or transverse friction is contraindicated if the patient is taking anticoagulants. When the patient is on antihypertensive medication, exercise programs should be closely monitored (to ensure that the patient maintains proper breathing). If the patient is on nonsteroidal antiinflammatory medication and is getting relief from the symptoms, one should suspect pathology in which inflammation is involved. If the patient is on antidepressant medication, the symptoms being experienced may be complicated by psychologic factors.

Previous Treatment and Results

The question of previous treatment is important in planning a current treatment program. In general, a treatment that has already been applied and was not successful should not be repeated, unless there is doubt concerning whether the treatment was correctly performed.

Specific Inspection

Gait

As in the general inspection, the knee function is observed, and the examiner looks for differences between the affected and normal knees.

In Standing

The examiner gives special attention to the presence of a varus or valgus positioning of the knees, genu recurvatum, flexed position of the knee, patella alta, or internal or external rotation of the tibia. The position of the feet is examined. The position of the pelvis is assessed. The quadriceps angle (Q angle) is measured.

In Supine

Each side is compared for color and condition of the skin. The presence of swelling or scars is noted, both at the knee and in the lower leg or foot (refer also to Chapter 8).

Palpation

Before starting the functional tests, the examiner palpates the area for warmth. If there is visible swelling, consistency is assessed.

Functional Examination

Before the functional examination, the examiner determines whether the patient is experiencing symptoms at that specific moment. The examiner notes whether the symptoms change during or as a result of the test. The affected side is always compared with the nonaffected side. This means that both sides are tested, first the nonaffected side (to have an idea of what is normal) and then the affected side.

In the following description of the functional examination, the essential tests are printed in ***underlined bold italics***; these make up the basic functional examination. The other tests are conducted as required, depending on the findings in the basic functional examination.

In Standing

9.1 Palpation of the patellofemoral joint during flexion of the knee

In Supine

9.2 Patellar ballottement (maximal effusion)
9.3 Test for moderate effusion
9.4 Test for minimal effusion

Passive Motions.

9.5 Passive knee hyperextension
9.6 Passive knee extension, end-feel test
9.7 Passive knee flexion
9.8 Passive knee external rotation
9.9 Passive knee internal rotation
9.10 Passive varus test in slight knee flexion
9.11 Passive varus test in knee extension
9.12 Passive valgus test in slight knee flexion
9.13 Passive valgus test in knee extension
9.14 Gravity sign
9.15 Anterior drawer test in 80° flexion, without rotation
9.16 Anterior drawer test in 80° flexion and maximal external rotation
9.17 Anterior drawer test in 80° flexion and 50% internal rotation
9.18 Anterior drawer test in 80° flexion and maximal internal rotation
9.19 Posterior drawer test in 80° flexion
9.20 Posterior drawer test in 80° flexion and maximal external rotation
9.21 Posterior drawer test in 80° flexion and maximal internal rotation
9.22 Anterolateral drawer test in 90° flexion
9.23 Lateral shear test in 90° flexion
9.24 Medial shear test in 90° flexion
9.25 Lachman's test (anterior drawer test in slight flexion)
9.26 Pivot shift test
9.27 Modified McMurray's test
9.28 Steinmann's test
9.29 Medial shift of the patella
9.30 Lateral shift of the patella

9.31 Distal shift of the patella

9.32 Medial shift of the patella in about 30° knee flexion (Mital-Hayden test)

9.33 Pulling up the passively distally shifted patella

In Prone

Resisted tests.

9.34 Resisted knee extension

9.35 Resisted knee flexion

9.36 Resisted knee flexion with external rotation

9.37 Resisted knee flexion with internal rotation

Palpation

After the functional examination, the region is palpated again for warmth, swelling, and synovial thickening. If the palpation is negative for swelling or warmth before the functional examination but positive afterward, an articular problem is indicated. Based on the findings from the functional examination, the suspected structure is located and palpated for tenderness.

Accessory Examination in Limitations of Motion

If a limitation of motion in a noncapsular pattern has been found, the appropriate joint-specific translatory tests should be given to determine whether the limitation is indeed caused by the capsule.

If the patient's symptoms could not be elicited during the clinical examination, the next diagnostic phase is provocation of the symptoms. For instance, if a long-distance runner only experiences symptoms after 15 minutes of running, the functional examination will probably be negative. Thus the patient is instructed to run until the symptoms have arisen, and then the functional examination is repeated. Usually, the patient's pain can now be elicited. If a diagnosis still cannot be completed, further examination is necessary.

Other Examinations

If necessary, other examinations can also be performed either to confirm a diagnosis or to gain further information when a diagnosis cannot be reached based on the functional examination:

- imaging techniques (eg, conventional radiographs, computed tomography [CT], CT arthrography, magnetic resonance imaging, and ultrasonography)
- laboratory tests
- arthroscopy
- electromyography

DESCRIPTION OF THE FUNCTIONAL EXAMINATION

Note: In the clinic, a simpler procedure is used for the functional examination of the capsuloligamentous complex of the knee than would be used for a biomechanical examination. This more simplified procedure, however, is useful in a clinical setting, especially when it concerns the function of the cruciates, where the differences between the clinical and biomechanical procedures are extensive.

In Standing

9.1 Palpation of the Patellofemoral Joint during Flexion of the Knee

The patient stands on the affected leg, and the examiner sits or squats next to the patient. Using the entire surface of the palm, the examiner exerts slight pressure in a posterior direction against the patient's patella (initial position).

The patient is now asked to bend the knee slowly, if possible, to about 90°, with the foot on the floor and bearing the body weight (end position). Meanwhile, the examiner palpates for crepitation and locking of the patella. Crepitation or locking indicates patellofemoral chondropathy or patellofemoral arthrosis.

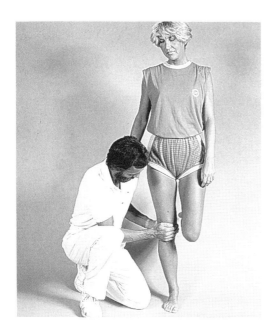

Test 9.1 Initial position.

Test 9.1 End position.

While standing on one foot, the patient is then asked to bend the knee again to approximately 90°, during which the examiner assesses the course of movement of the patella.

In patellar malalignment or pathologies of the corresponding femoral joint surface, movement of the patella can be disturbed. Lateralization of the patella can occur during flexion, particularly when the Q angle is too large. You will remember that the Q angle is the acute angle formed by the intersection of two imaginary lines: one that connects the anterior superior iliac spine with the middle of the patella, and one that connects the middle of the patella with the middle of the upper aspect of the tibial tuberosity.

In Supine

9.2 Patellar Ballottement (Maximal Effusion)

The patient is in a supine position on the examination table.

Using the contralateral hand, the examiner grasps the patient's thigh at the anterior aspect about 10 cm above the patella. The fingers are medial and the thumb lateral. The patient's knee is extended. With the ipsilateral hand, the examiner grasps the patient's lower leg about 5 cm distal to the patella. The fingers are medial and the thumb lateral (initial position).

The proximal hand exerts compression against the anterior, lateral, and medial aspects of the thigh and, without losing this pressure, slides distally. The distal hand exerts compression in a similar way and slides proximally. Using the index finger of the distal hand, the examiner now taps the patella against the femur (end position).

This test is positive when the patella can be tapped against the femur. This is possible when there is a significant synovial effusion or hemarthrosis in the knee joint.

Sometimes, this test can produce false-positive results. Generally when this is the

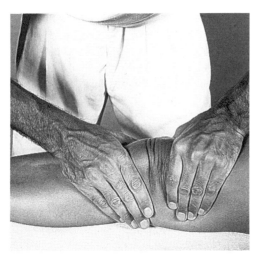

Test 9.2A Initial position.

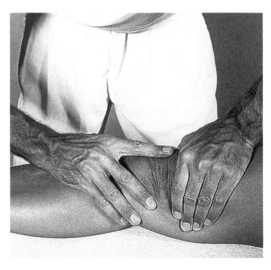

Test 9.2B End position.

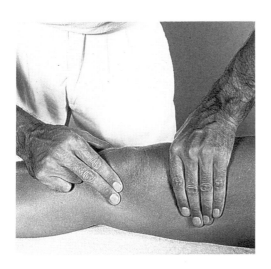

Test 9.3A Initial position.

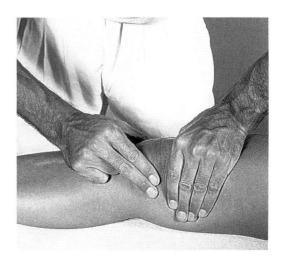

Test 9.3B End position.

case, the nonaffected side will test positive as well.

9.3 Test for Moderate Effusion

The patient is supine on the examination table.

Using the contralateral hand, the examiner grasps the patient's thigh at the anterior aspect about 10 cm above the patella. The fingers are medial and the thumb lateral. The patient's knee is extended. The examiner places the index and middle fingers of the ipsilateral hand at the level of the medial joint space and the thumb at the lateral joint space (initial position). Fingers and thumb exert slight pressure.

The proximal hand now slides distally, exerting moderate pressure, until the superior edge of the patella is reached (end position).

This test is positive when the thumb and fingers are pushed away from each other by the moderate amount of fluid in the joint.

9.4 Test for Minimal Effusion

The patient is supine on the examination table. Using the dorsal aspect of the fingers of the ipsilateral hand and applying moderate pressure, the examiner strokes from just distal to the medial joint space (initial position, medial side of the knee), over the medial side of the knee, to the midline at the anterior aspect of the thigh, about 10 cm proximal to the patella (end position, medial side of the knee). In so doing, the medial side of the patella is followed from its mediodistal edge to its medioproximal edge. This movement is

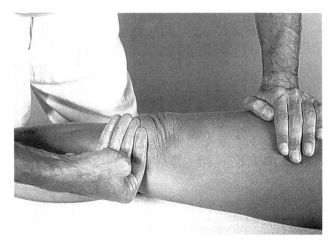

Test 9.4A Initial position, medial side of the knee.

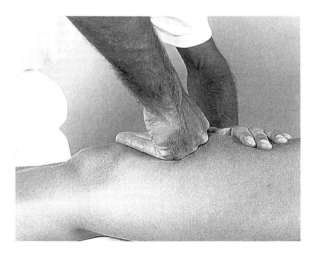

Test 9.4B End position, medial side of the knee.

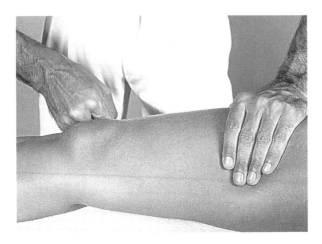

Test 9.4C Initial position, lateral side of the knee.

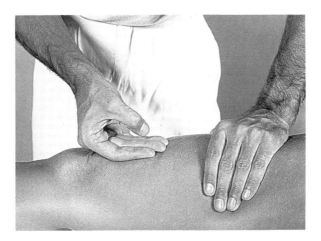

Test 9.4D End position, lateral side of the knee.

repeated two or three times. Directly afterward, the same movement is performed against the lateral aspect of the knee (initial and end positions, lateral side of the knee).

The test is positive when, at the end of the movement of the examiner's hand at the lateral side of the knee, the small indentation at the medial side of the knee temporarily fills with fluid. This indicates a slight synovial effusion in the knee.

Passive Motions

By means of passive movements, the amount of motion and the end-feel are determined. In diagnosing motion limitations, differentiation is made between capsular and noncapsular patterns. Limitations of motion in a capsular pattern indicate arthritis or arthrosis (osteoarthrosis). Motions that provoke symptoms are carefully noted.

9.5 Passive Knee Hyperextension

The patient is supine on the examination table. The examiner fixates the patient's thigh against the examination table by using the contralateral hand, placed just proximal to the patella. The other hand grasps the medial aspect of the lower leg, just proximal to the malleolus, and gently performs a hyperextension of the patient's knee.

Knee extension can be limited as a result of an articular disorder. Usually an arthritis or arthrosis (capsular pattern), a lesion of one of the menisci, or a loose body is involved.

9.6 Passive Knee Extension, End-Feel Test

The patient is supine on the examination table. To test the end-feel in passive knee extension, the examiner uses the contralateral hand to grasp the patient's knee from the lateral side. The other hand grasps the distal part of the lower leg from the medial side. The knee is now slightly flexed and then, with an

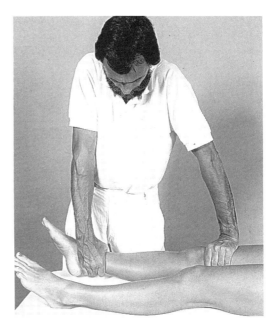

Test 9.6

abrupt movement, extended. This abrupt movement can be performed either by allowing the knee to fall into maximal extension or by simultaneously exerting slight posterior pressure with the thumb, which is positioned just proximal to the knee.

Under normal conditions, the end-feel is usually hard.

If, on the affected side, there is increased range of motion in extension and the end-feel in passive extension is softer compared with the nonaffected side, these conditions are usually the result of an overstretching or partial rupture of the posterior joint capsule or anterior cruciate ligament. In severe cases, the posterior cruciate ligament can also be affected.

9.7 Passive Knee Flexion

The patient is supine on the examination table. Using the ipsilateral hand, the examiner grasps the anterior aspect of the patient's lower leg, just proximal to the malleoli. The contralateral hand grasps the anterior aspect

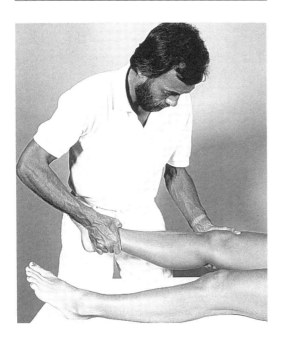

Test 9.5

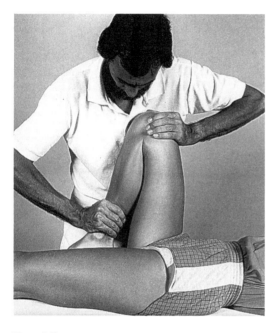

Test 9.7

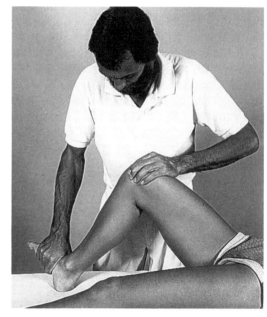

Test 9.8

of the patient's thigh, just above the patella. The patient's hip is flexed to about 90°. The distal hand flexes the knee while the proximal hand fixates the thigh. At the end of the range of motion, the examiner exerts slight overpressure.

The end-feel under normal conditions is usually soft.

A flexion limitation is usually the result of an articular lesion. Usually an arthritis or arthrosis (capsular pattern), a lesion of one of the menisci, or a loose body is involved.

9.8 Passive Knee External Rotation

The patient is supine on the examination table. Using the ipsilateral hand, the examiner grasps the dorsomedial aspect of the patient's foot and brings the ankle into maximal extension. The contralateral hand grasps the anterior aspect of the patient's thigh, just proximal to the patella, in such a way that the

index and middle fingers can palpate the medial joint space. The patient's knee is flexed to 90° and the hip to about 45°.

The distal hand performs an external rotation. During this movement, it is important to maintain maximal extension in the ankle. At the end of the range of motion, the examiner exerts slight overpressure.

Under normal conditions, the end-feel is firm.

The examiner notes whether pain is provoked or whether there is a hypermobility or hypomobility. Pain can be the result of a lesion of the medial meniscotibial ligament, medial meniscus, medial collateral ligament, or posteromedial capsuloligamentous complex. Hypermobility can be the result of a lesion of the posteromedial capsuloligamentous complex, often in combination with lesions of the medial collateral ligament and the anterior cruciate ligament. Hypomobility is seen only in severe articular disorders with significant capsular limitations of motion.

9.9 Passive Knee Internal Rotation

The patient is supine on the examination table. Using the ipsilateral hand, the examiner grasps the dorsomedial aspect of the patient's foot and brings the ankle into maximal extension. The contralateral hand grasps the anterior aspect of the patient's thigh, just proximal to the patella, in such a way that the index and middle fingers can palpate the medial joint space. The patient's knee is flexed to 90° and the hip to about 45°.

The distal hand performs an internal rotation. During this movement, it is important to maintain maximal extension in the ankle. At the end of the range of motion, the examiner exerts slight overpressure.

Under normal conditions, the end-feel is firm.

The examiner notes whether pain is provoked or whether there is hypermobility or hypomobility. Pain can be the result of a lesion of the lateral meniscotibial ligament, lateral meniscus, or posterolateral capsuloliga-

mentous complex. Hypermobility can be the result of a lesion of the posterolateral capsuloligamentous complex. Hypomobility is seen only in severe articular disorders with significant capsular limitations of motion.

The following accessory test can be performed when osteochondritis dissecans of the knee is suspected: The initial position of this test is the same as described above, except here the examiner flexes the patient's hip and knee to 90°. Axial compression is exerted in the knee by pushing proximally, in line with the tibia, with the distal hand. This time, the lower leg is held in internal rotation while the knee is slowly extended and axial compression is maintained. In many cases of osteochondritis dissecans, the patient experiences pain because the pressure on the medial cartilaginous surfaces increases significantly. This is brought about as a result of the cruciate ligaments, which intertwine with each other during the internal rotation. If the knee is then externally rotated, the pain disappears.

9.10 Passive Varus Test in Slight Knee Flexion

The patient is supine on the examination table. In acute cases of instability, the patient's thigh should rest on the examination table (initial position with acute instability). In more chronic lesions, the examiner, sitting on the examination table, can lift the patient's leg (initial position with chronic instability). The knee is held in slight flexion.

Using the contralateral hand, the examiner grasps the lateral side of the patient's lower leg, just proximal to the malleolus. The ipsilateral hand grasps the medial aspect of the patient's knee such that the thenar eminence is located proximal and the hypothenar eminence distal to the joint space.

During the varus test, the proximal and distal hands work simultaneously and with equal force. The distal hand moves the lower leg medially while the proximal hand moves the knee in a lateral direction. There is almost al-

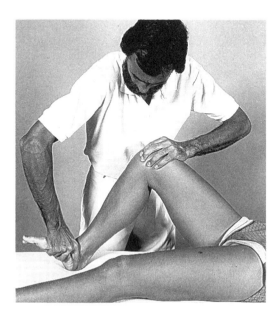

Test 9.9

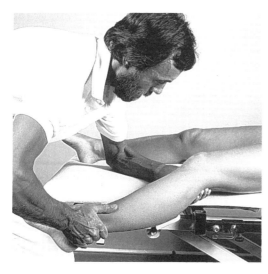

Test 9.10A Initial position with acute instability.

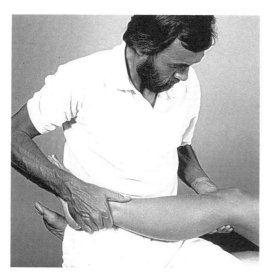

Test 9.10B Initial position with chronic instability.

ways some movement possible in varus. To be able to assess the amount of varus movement, the examiner has to repeat the motion several times. Then, at the end of the range of motion, the examiner exerts slight overpressure.

Under normal conditions, the end-feel is firm.

If this provokes pain, there is likely to be a sprain of the lateral collateral structures or the connections of these with the lateral meniscus. If hypermobility is a factor, the amount of increased motion determines the extent of the lesion (refer to the two sections on lateral instability in Chapter 10).

9.11 Passive Varus Test in Knee Extension

The varus test in extension of the knee is performed in the same manner as described for Test 9.10, except that now the knee is positioned in maximal normal extension. The position of normal extension is determined by the nonaffected side.

Under normal conditions, the end-feel is firm.

Although the lateral collateral structures are most taut in maximal knee extension, the posterolateral capsule is actually the primary varus stabilizer of the extended knee. Even if the lateral collateral structures were to be completely ruptured, no abnormal varus motion would occur in extension when the posterolateral capsule is intact.

If the normal extension position of the affected knee (compared with the nonaffected

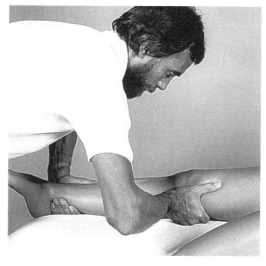

Test 9.11

side) demonstrates abnormal varus motion during this test, there is likely to be a lesion of the structures of the posterolateral capsule.

9.12 Passive Valgus Test in Slight Knee Flexion

The initial position of the patient and examiner is the same as for the varus test in slight flexion (Test 9.10), with the exception that the examiner's distal hand grasps the medial side of the patient's lower leg and the proximal hand grasps the lateral side of the patient's knee.

Normally, there is little or no valgus movement in the knee. In any case, it should be less than the amount of varus motion.

Under normal conditions, the end-feel is firm.

Pain without hypermobility is caused by an overstretch of the medial collateral structures or the connection of these structures with the medial meniscus. If hypermobility is a factor, the amount of excess motion determines the extent of the lesion (refer to the two sections on medial instability in Chapter 10).

9.13 Passive Valgus Test in Knee Extension

This test is performed in same manner as described in Test 9.12, but with the knee positioned in maximal normal extension. The position of normal extension is determined by the nonaffected side.

Under normal conditions, the end-feel is firm.

Valgus stability in extension is primarily influenced by the structures in the posteromedial corner of the capsule.

9.14 Gravity Sign

The patient is supine on the examination table. The examiner bends the hips and knees of the patient to 90°. Using the distal hand, the examiner supports the heels while the proximal hand stabilizes the thighs just proximal to the patella. The examiner assesses the contour of the tibial tuberosities.

If there is a (partial) rupture of the posterior cruciate ligament, the tibial tuberosity on the affected side will be less visible than on the nonaffected side. This is caused by an

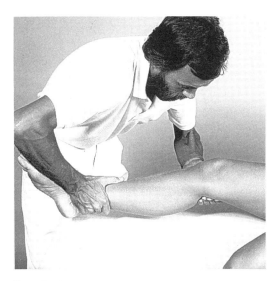

Test 9.12

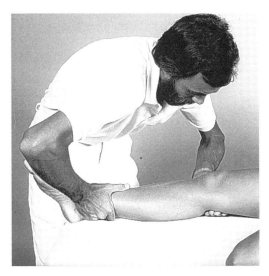

Test 9.13

Test 9.14

---

abnormal posterior translation motion resulting from a rupture of the posterior cruciate ligament. In cases of doubt, the patient can be asked to contract the hamstrings slightly by pushing the heels into the examiner's hands. This will usually result in an increase in the posterior translation of the tibia.

This maneuver is often performed as a quick test for integrity of the posterior cruciate ligament. If this test is negative, however, there still may be a lesion of the posterior cruciate ligament. The anterolateral drawer test in 90° flexion is the most reliable test for diagnosis of a posterior cruciate ligament (see Test 9.22).

9.15 Anterior Drawer Test in 80° Flexion without Rotation

The patient is supine on the examination table. The examiner grasps the lower leg of the patient just distal to the joint space of the knee. The patient's knee is flexed 80°, and the lower leg is not rotated. The examiner fixates the patient's leg by sitting on the foot. The examiner can place the thumbs either in the joint space or just distal to it to assess abnor-

mal mobility. The examiner tests the tension in the musculature. It is important that *all* muscles around the knee be relaxed; otherwise the translatory movement during the drawer test can be masked. With both hands, the examiner now pulls the lower leg forward in a slightly manipulative way.

This test is positive when an abnormal anterior movement of the tibia occurs compared with the other side. In this case, there is likely to be a lesion of the anterior cruciate ligament. This finding assumes that the gravity sign and anterolateral drawer test are negative.

9.16 Anterior Drawer Test in 80° Flexion and Maximal External Rotation

The initial positions of the patient and examiner are the same as in Test 9.15, with the exception that the lower leg is maximally externally rotated. For the performance, refer to Test 9.15.

The anterior cruciate ligament and the medial and posteromedial capsuloligamentous structures are tested in this position. If this test is positive, there is likely to be an anteromedial rotatory instability. Which specific medial and posteromedial structures are affected can be further differentiated by the valgus tests (Tests 9.12 and 9.13).

9.17 Anterior Drawer Test in 80° Flexion and 50% Internal Rotation

The initial positions of the patient and examiner are the same as in Test 9.15, with the exception that the lower leg is placed in 50% internal rotation. For the performance, refer to Test 9.15.

The anterior cruciate ligament and the (postero)lateral capsuloligamentous structures are tested in this position. If this test is positive, there is likely to be an anterolateral rotatory instability. The varus tests (Tests 9.10 and 9.11) allow for further determination as to which of the lateral and posterolateral structures are affected.

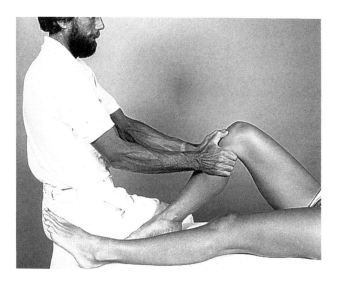

Test 9.15

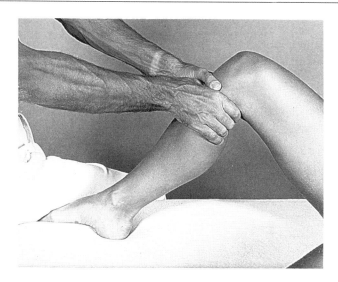

Test 9.16

9.18 Anterior Drawer Test in 80° Flexion and Maximal Internal Rotation

The initial positions of the patient and examiner are the same as in Test 9.15, with the exception that the lower leg is now at the maximal internally rotated position. Performance of this test is the same as described for Test 9.15.

When in maximal internal rotation, the posterior cruciate ligament can completely restrict anterior translation of the tibia. Thus for this test to demonstrate excessive anterior

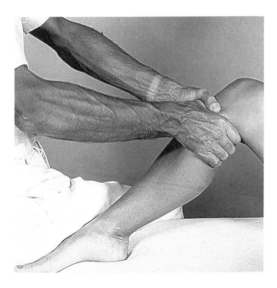

Test 9.17

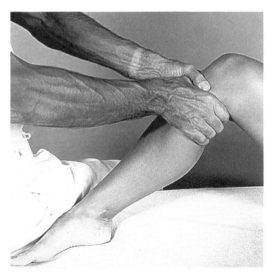

Test 9.18

translation, the posterior cruciate ligament, the anterior cruciate ligament, and the lateral or posterolateral capsuloligamentous structures have to be affected.

9.19 Posterior Drawer Test in 80° Flexion

The initial positions of the patient and examiner are the same as in Test 9.15, with the exception that the examiner holds the elbows in more flexion. When performing the test, the examiner now pushes the lower leg, with a slight manipulative movement, backward.

Through this movement, the posterior cruciate ligament, in particular, is tested. In many cases, the gravity sign (Test 9.14) is also positive. To confirm a lesion of the posterior cruciate ligament, however, the anterolateral drawer test (Test 9.22), *must* be positive.

9.20 Posterior Drawer Test in 80° Flexion and Maximal External Rotation

The initial positions of the patient and examiner are the same as in Test 9.19, with the exception that the lower leg is now at the maximall, externally rotated position. Perfor-

mance of this test is the same as described in Test 9.19.

This procedure tests the posterior cruciate ligament along with the posterolateral capsuloligamentous structures. If this test is positive, there is likely to be a posterolateral rotatory instability. The varus tests (Tests 9.10 and 9.11) are used to differentiate further which lateral and posterolateral structures are affected.

9.21 Posterior Drawer Test in 80° Flexion and Maximal Internal Rotation

The initial positions of the patient and examiner are the same as in Test 9.19, with the exception that the lower leg is now in a maximally internally rotated position. Performance of this test is the same as described for Test 9.19.

This procedure tests the posterior cruciate ligament along with the posteromedial capsuloligamentous structures. If this test is positive, there is likely to be a posteromedial rotatory instability. The valgus tests (Tests 9.12 and 9.13) are used to differentiate further which of the medial and posteromedial structures are affected.

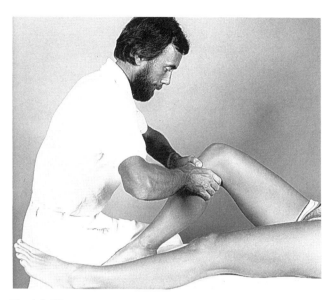

Test 9.19

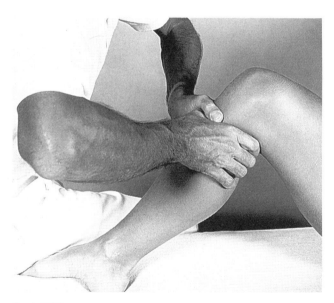

Test 9.20

9.22 Anterolateral Drawer Test in 90° Flexion

The patient is supine on the examination table. The patient's knee is flexed 90°, and the lower leg is not rotated.

Using the ipsilateral hand, the examiner grasps the posteromedial aspect of the lower leg of the patient just distal to the joint space. The other hand exerts counterpressure at the femur, against the anterolateral aspect, just proximal to the joint space (avoid pushing on

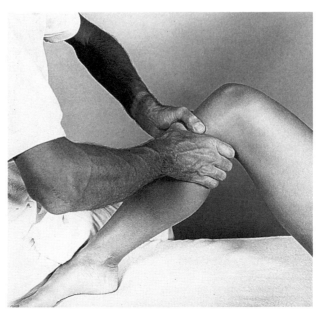

Test 9.21

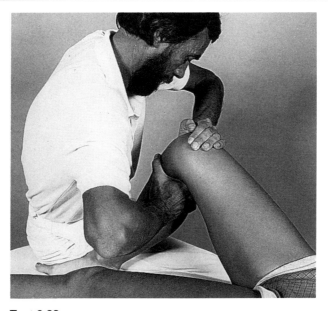

Test 9.22

the iliotibial band). The ipsilateral hand moves the tibia in an anterolateral direction in relation to the femur.

This test is positive when, in comparison with the nonaffected side, there is hypermobility. A positive test indicates the existence of a lesion of the posterior cruciate ligament. This test is pathognomonic for a lesion of the posterior cruciate ligament.

9.23 Lateral Shear Test in 90° Flexion

The patient is supine with the knee flexed to 90°, and the lower leg is not rotated.

Using the thenar and hypothenar eminences of the ipsilateral hand, the examiner grasps the medial aspect of the tibia just distal to the joint space. The thenar and hypothenar eminences of the contralateral hand are placed at the lateral aspect of the femur just proximal to the joint space. The examiner pushes the tibia in a lateral direction in relation to the femur.

This test is positive when the patient experiences pain. In most cases, a meniscus lesion (either medial or lateral) or a loose body is involved.

9.24 Medial Shear Test in 90° Flexion

The patient is supine with the knee flexed to 90°, and the lower leg is not rotated.

Using the thenar and hypothenar eminences of the contralateral hand, the examiner grasps the lateral aspect of the tibia just distal to the joint space. The thenar and hypothenar eminences of the ipsilateral hand are placed at the medial aspect of the femur just proximal to the joint space. The examiner pushes the tibia in a medial direction in relation to the femur.

This test is positive when the patient experiences pain. In most cases, a meniscus lesion (either medial or lateral) or a loose body is involved.

9.25 Lachman's Test (Anterior Drawer Test in Slight Flexion)

The patient is supine on the examination table. Using the ipsilateral hand, the examiner grasps the medial side of the patient's lower leg as proximally as possible. The other hand grasps the lateral side of the thigh just proximal to the patella. The examiner flexes the patient's knee to about 10° and, with the distal hand, moves the tibia anteriorly in relation to the fixated thigh (Lachman's test,

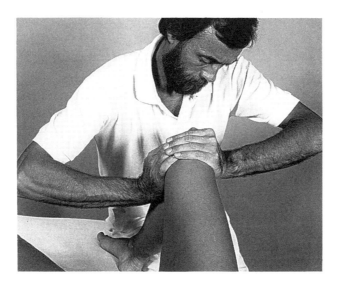

Test 9.23

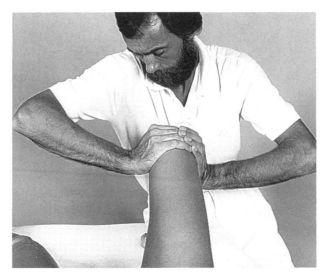

Test 9.24

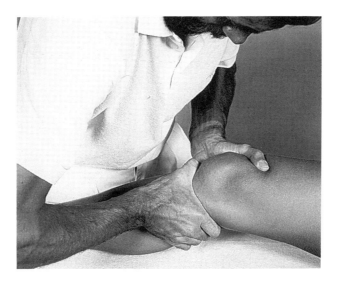

Test 9.25A Lachman's test, standard method.

standard method). Only a small amount of force is necessary to perform this test well.

The test is positive when the anterior translatory movement is greater than on the nonaffected side. In this instance, there is a lesion of the anterior cruciate ligament. This test has two advantages over the anterior drawer test in 90° knee flexion. First, all parts of the anterior cruciate ligament are more or less equally taut. Second, in acute lesions it is often impossible to position the knee in 90° flexion because of a hemarthrosis. If positive,

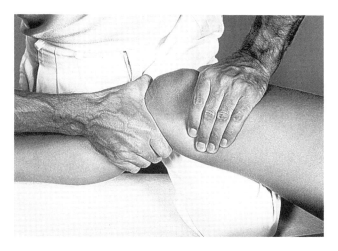

Test 9.25B Lachman's test, first alternative method.

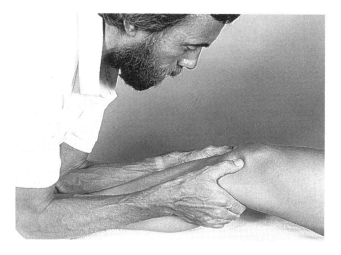

Test 9.25C Lachman's test, second alternative method.

this test is pathognomonic for a lesion of the anterior cruciate ligament.

An alternative performance of the Lachman test is particularly appropriate when the examiner's hands are too small to be able to grasp the patient's thigh adequately. The patient's thigh is fixated with the therapist's contralateral hand. The other hand now moves the tibia anteriorly in relation to the femur (Lachman's test, first alternative method).

In a second alternative performance of the Lachman test, the examiner grasps the patient's lower leg with both hands as proximally as possible. The tips of the thumbs are placed just proximal to the joint space on the femur, at either side of the patellar apex. With both forearms, the examiner fixates the patient's heel to the examination table. By pushing the thumbs and fingers toward each other and simultaneously ulnarly deviating the wrists, the examiner brings the tibia forward in relation to the femur (Lachman's test, second alternative method).

9.26 Pivot Shift Test

The patient is supine on the examination table with the legs straight.

Using the ipsilateral hand, the examiner grasps the patient's heel from the plantar aspect; the other hand is placed against the lateral side of the patient's lower leg just distal to the joint space. The examiner lifts the patient's straightened leg (initial position) and exerts axial compression (from the heel toward the hip). Then, while slightly flexing the knee and simultaneously internally rotating the lower leg, the examiner pushes the tibial plateau in an anteromedial direction with the contralateral hand (at about 30° and 45° flexion). In acute cases of instability in which there is severe pain, the test can be performed with the affected leg lying on the table (position with acute instability). This test can also be performed in the opposite sequence.

The test is positive when, between 30° and 45° of knee flexion, the lateral tibial plateau subluxates anteromedially and then spontaneously repositions with increasing flexion. In instances of positive test results, there is likely to be a lesion of the anterior cruciate ligament, often in combination with a lesion of part of the lateral or posterolateral capsuloligamentous complex. The varus tests (Tests 9.10 and 9.11) are used for further differentiation of affected structures at the lateral and anterolateral aspects of the knee.

9.27 Modified McMurray's Test

The McMurray test was originally developed to diagnose posterior horn lesions of the medial meniscus. By modifying this test, it is possible to diagnose other meniscus lesions as well.

The patient is supine on the examination table.

Using the ipsilateral hand, the examiner grasps the dorsum of the patient's foot in such a way that the thumb is lateral, the index and middle fingers are medial, and the ring and little fingers hold the medial edge of the foot.

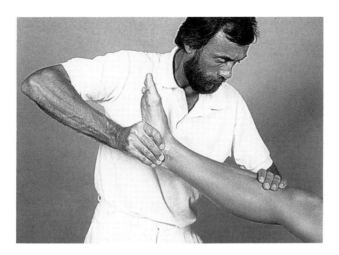

Test 9.26A Initial position.

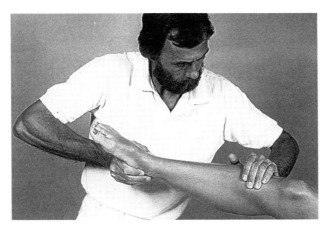

Test 9.26B At about 30° flexion.

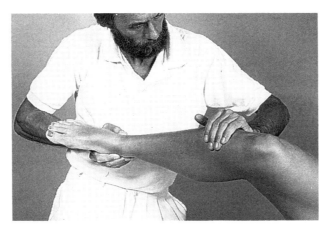

Test 9.26C At about 45° flexion.

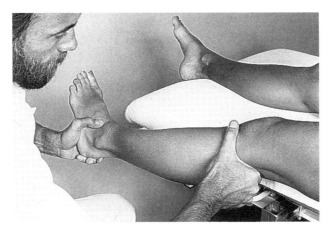

Test 9.26D Position with acute instability.

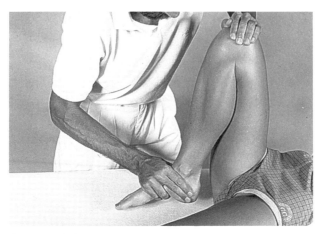

Test 9.27A Initial position.

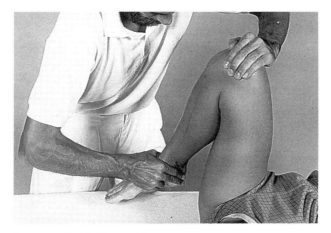

Test 9.27B Middle position.

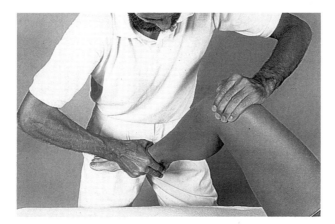

Test 9.27C End position.

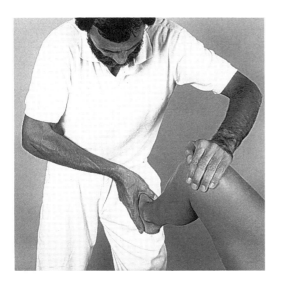

Test 9.27D Valgus–external rotation.

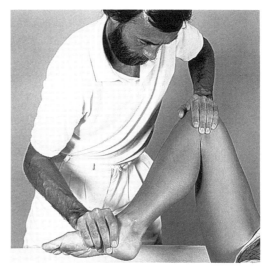

Test 9.27E Varus–external rotation.

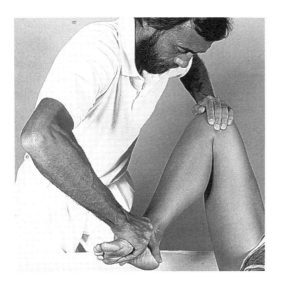

Test 9.27F Varus–internal rotation.

lower leg is slightly externally rotated. The knee is flexed as far as possible (depending on the amount of pain), after which the foot is brought into a valgus direction with simultaneous internal rotation of the lower leg (middle position). The examiner then rather quickly extends the knee to about 120°, and at the same time exerts valgus pressure on the knee with the proximal hand (end position).

This test is positive when a palpable or audible click is elicited that is also painful. The location of the pain determines the site of the lesion. It has long been known that, when this test is positive, it is not always the posterior horn of the medial meniscus that is affected. Not only can the lesion be elsewhere in the medial meniscus, but a lesion of the lateral meniscus can also provoke pain during this test. If this test is negative, there still may be a meniscus lesion.

One after the other, a similar maneuver can be repeated with valgus pressure and external rotation (valgus–external rotation), then with varus pressure and external rotation (varus–external rotation), and finally with varus pressure and internal rotation (varus–internal rotation).

The contralateral hand is placed against the lateral aspect of the patient's knee (initial position). By rotating the patient's lower leg several times, the examiner can assess whether the patient is fully relaxed.

The ipsilateral hand now moves the patient's foot in a varus direction while the

9.28 Steinmann's Test

Steinmann[10] formulated several different tests to diagnose meniscus lesions. The test described here is the most useful.

The patient is supine on the examination table.

Using the ipsilateral hand, the examiner grasps the patient's lower leg just proximal to the malleolus. The other hand grasps the lateral side of the patient's lower leg as proximally as possible and in such a way that the thumb can palpate the medial joint space. The knee is extended, and the part of the me-

dial meniscus between the patellar tendon and the medial collateral ligament is palpated (initial position). The consistency of the edge of the meniscus is assessed. Sometimes local swelling from a meniscal cyst or ganglion can be palpated. After the most painful site on the meniscus is located with the thumb, pressure against this spot is maintained while the knee is simultaneously flexed (end position). After several degrees the pain disappears, and the painful site can sometimes again be palpated more posteriorly in the joint space.

If the most painful site is found in the joint space at the level of the medial collateral liga-

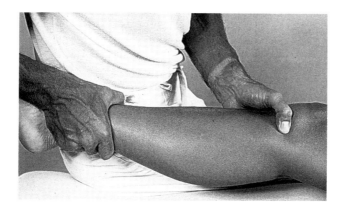

Test 9.28A Initial position.

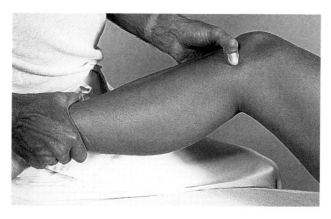

Test 9.28B End position.

ment, the test is less reliable. This is true because both the medial meniscus and the ligament move posteriorly during flexion.

9.29 Medial Shift of the Patella

The patient is supine with the knee extended.

The examiner places both thumbs together at the lateral aspect of the patella and pushes the patella medially.

In this test, the amount of motion and the end-feel are assessed. Often the patella is found to have less range of motion medially than laterally. Whether this condition is pathologic is best determined by comparing to the nonaffected side. This patellar movement is often limited after surgery and after immobilization.

9.30 Lateral Shift of the Patella

The patient is supine with the knee extended.

The examiner places the fingertips of both hands against the medial aspect of the patella and pushes the patella laterally.

The amount of motion and the end-feel are assessed. Usually the patella has more range of motion laterally than medially. Where there are instabilities of the patella, the lateral mobility is usually abnormally great. This pa-

tellar movement is also often limited after surgery and after immobilization.

9.31 Distal Shift of the Patella

The patient is supine with the knee extended.

With the thenar and hypothenar eminences placed against the base of the patient's patella, the examiner pushes the patella in a distal direction. As with Tests 9.29 and 9.30, the amount of motion and end-feel are assessed. The motion is usually limited in instances of patella alta (a high position of the patella), after surgery, and after immobilization.

9.32 Medial Shift of the Patella in About 30° Knee Flexion (Mital-Hayden Test)

The patient is supine on the examination table.

The examiner positions the patient's knee in about 30° flexion, supporting the patient's knee on either a towel roll or the examiner's own thigh, which rests on the table. The examiner places both thumbs together at the lateral aspect of the patella and pushes the patella medially.

If a painful click is elicited during this test, there is likely to be a symptomatic mediopa-

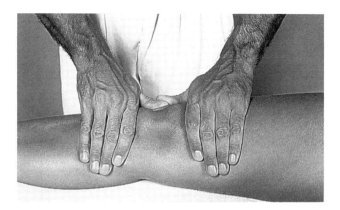

Test 9.29

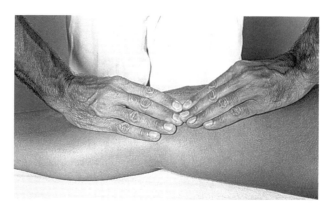

Test 9.30

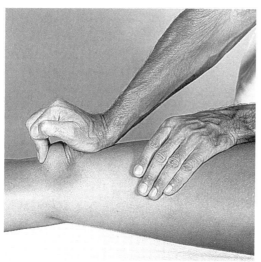

Test 9.31

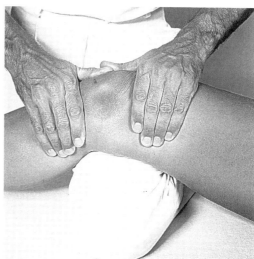

Test 9.32

tellar synovial plica. When this is the case, the passive external rotation test is also likely to be painful.

9.33 Pulling up the Passively Distally Shifted Patella

The patient is supine on the examination table.

The examiner positions the patient's knee in about 30° flexion and places the patient's leg on either a towel roll or the examiner's own thigh, which rests on the table. The examiner pushes the patient's patella in a distal direction. While continuing to exert pressure in a distal direction, the examiner instructs the patient to contract the quadriceps muscle.

If this test is painful, there is likely to be a symptomatic patellar chondromalacia. If this is the case, the patient will generally also have

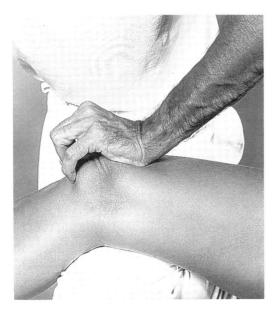

Test 9.33

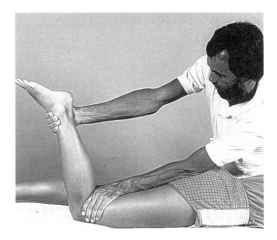

Test 9.34

a Q angle greater than 15°, and the patella will demonstrate abnormal lateral movement during the first 30° of flexion.

When the same test is performed with an extended knee, pain is almost always provoked, even when there are no patellofemoral problems. Therefore, this test variation is not clinically significant.

Resisted Tests

Contractile structures are evaluated through the use of isometric resisted tests. It is important to note weakness and the provocation of pain. At the knee joint, positive tests are usually indicative of an insertion tendopathy. It should be kept in mind, however, that the menisci are connected to these contractile structures and therefore could also be a source of pain during resisted tests.

9.34 Resisted Knee Extension

The patient is prone on the examination table.

Using the ipsilateral hand, the examiner grasps the medial aspect of the patient's lower leg just proximal to the malleolus. The other hand, which is placed at the back of the knee, fixes the thigh to the examination table. The examiner flexes the patient's knee to about 80° and instructs the patient to straighten the knee. At the same time, the examiner exerts isometric resistance. In so doing, the extensor mechanism is tested.

When this test provokes pain, there is likely to be an insertion tendopathy of the extensor mechanism. Through the connection of the extensor mechanism to the menisci, however, a painful test can also indicate a meniscus lesion.

9.35 Resisted Knee Flexion

The patient is prone on the examination table.

Using the ipsilateral hand, the examiner grasps the posterior aspect of the patient's lower leg just proximal to the malleolus. The other hand, which is placed at the back of the knee, fixes the thigh to the examination table. The examiner flexes the patient's knee to about 70° and instructs the patient to bend the knee. At the same time, the examiner ex-

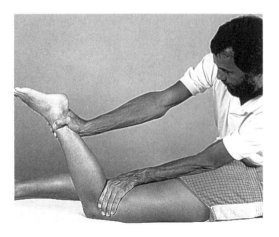

Test 9.35

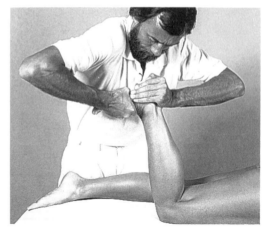

Test 9.36

erts isometric resistance. In so doing, the knee flexors are tested.

When this test provokes pain, further differentiation should be made by performing Tests 9.36 and 9.37. To differentiate between the internal rotating and external rotating flexors, resisted flexion of the knee can be combined with resisted internal rotation or resisted external rotation.

9.36 Resisted Knee Flexion with External Rotation

The patient is in a prone position.

The examiner flexes the patient's knee to about 80°. With the ipsilateral hand, the examiner grasps the lateral side of the patient's foot. The other hand is placed against the posterior aspect of the patient's heel. The patient is instructed to turn the foot outward and simultaneously bend the knee while the examiner exerts isometric resistance. In so doing, the biceps femoris muscle is tested.

A painful test can indicate a lesion of the biceps femoris muscle, where there are various predilection sites. A lesion of the lateral meniscus may also be indicated because of the connection of the tendon fibers of the biceps femoris with the lateral aspect of the lateral meniscus. Further differentiation can be

made through palpation and functional examination.

9.37 Resisted Knee Flexion with Internal Rotation

The patient is in a prone position.

The examiner flexes the patient's knee to about 80°. Using the ipsilateral hand, the ex-

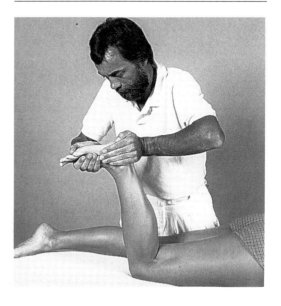

Test 9.37

aminer grasps the medial side of the patient's foot. The other hand is placed against the posterior aspect of the patient's heel. The patient is instructed to turn the foot inward and simultaneously bend the knee. At the same time, the examiner exerts isometric resistance.

Pain provoked at the medial side of the knee can indicate a lesion of the internal rotators and flexors of the knee, particularly the pes anserinus superficialis. It may also indi-

cate a lesion of the medial meniscus because of the connection of the tendon fibers of the semimembranosus with the posterior horn of the medial meniscus. Further differentiation can be made through palpation and functional examination. If the patient experiences lateral knee pain during this test, there is likely to be a lesion either of the popliteus muscle or of the posterior horn of the lateral meniscus at the site where it is connected to the popliteus.

Chapter 10

Pathology of the Knee

10.1 JOINT PATHOLOGY

PATHOLOGY WITH LIMITED MOTIONS IN A CAPSULAR PATTERN

ARTHRITIS

Traumatic Arthritis

Traumatic arthritis of the knee, in its purest form—that is, without complications such as meniscus or ligamentous lesions—is rare. Trauma to the knee in which no forced movement of the knee occurs can lead to a synovial reaction (Figure 10–1). Examples of such trauma include a fall, blow, or kick to the knee. Patients with gonarthrosis can incur a traumatic arthritis as the result of trauma or overuse. This condition is termed activated arthrosis.

Clinical Findings

Synovial effusion(swelling of the knee) usually occurs within 12 to 24 hours after the trauma. In gonarthrosis, a severe joint effusion can occur. Swelling that occurs more quickly indicates bleeding in the joint. Termed hemarthrosis, this is a sign of a severe lesion.

Functional Examination

The knee is warm to palpation. Under normal conditions, the temperature of the knee is slightly lower than that of the thigh and lower leg. As a result of the swelling, a capsular pattern of limited motions is found; the flexion limitation is much greater than the extension limitation.

After performing the functional examination, if the examiner is still unsure whether there is an associated lesion, further assessment using techniques such as radiologic examination or arthroscopy is indicated.

Treatment

The treatment depends on the severity of the swelling. In mild to moderate swelling, it is usually sufficient for the patient to wear an elastic sleeve and to decrease activities for a period of several days to 1 week. A severe joint effusion should be aspirated and then bandaged, using, for example, an Ace wrap. Activities should be limited for 1 week. After 1 week, the knee should be reexamined. Recurring effusion usually indicates that there is an associated lesion, requiring further examination.

A hemarthrosis should always be aspirated because blood in a joint can quickly lead to severe adhesions. After the aspiration, an arthroscopic evaluation should be made (Martens M. Personal communication. 1991) (Figure 10–2).

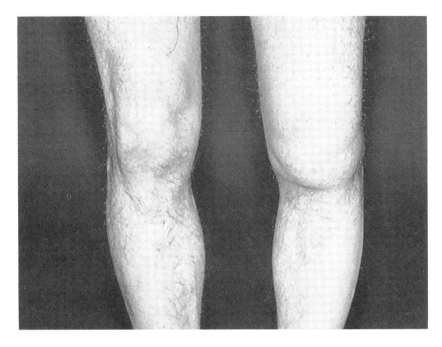

Figure 10–1 Clinical picture of traumatic arthritis of the left knee. This diffuse joint swelling is characteristically seen in cases of synovial effusion and hemarthrosis.

An intraarticular injection with a corticosteroid is effective for treating a painful persistent joint effusion in an activated arthrosis of the knee.

Nontraumatic Arthritis

There are many causes of a nontraumatic arthritis of the knee. Because of this, the patient's age, general health, and family history are of particular significance. For example, at a younger age, juvenile rheumatoid arthritis and ankylosing spondylitis are seen. In young adults, ankylosing spondylitis, Reiter's disease, and psoriatic arthritis are seen. In middle-age people, gout and rheumatoid arthritis are more commonly seen, and pseudogout is found in the elderly.

In nontraumatic arthritis, early recognition is important for the prognosis of the joint. After the inflammation stage, a destruction stage follows, in which, systematically, first the cartilage and then the bone become irreversibly damaged. After a period of time, a local osteoporosis occurs.

Clinical Findings

The knee is swollen, and, depending on the cause, the clinical stage, and the severity of the disorder, the effusion can vary from minimal to severe. The examiner should differentiate between a serous, serofibrinous, purulent, or hematic/bloody effusion. Serous effusion usually develops after trauma, in rheumatoid arthritides, and in arthritides that result from metabolic disturbances. Serofibrinous effusion is typically seen in chronic polyarthritis. It is a septic effusion resulting from a bacterial infection of the joint, in which the bacteria reached the joint either directly or indirectly (through the blood). A hematic effusion, or hemarthrosis, occurs traumatically. Usually the joint is also warm to palpation, but, as is true for the extent of swelling,

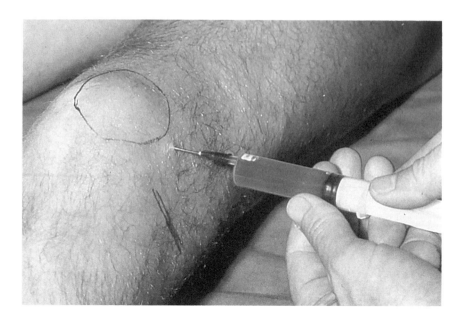

Figure 10–2 Aspiration of a hemarthrosis. Arthroscopic examination is recommended when the fluid aspirated from the knee is found to be hematic.

the temperature depends on the cause, stage, and severity of the disorder.

The patient complains of pain at rest that increases during movement. With systemic disorders in particular, the patient can also experience general malaise and fever. Atrophy of the musculature, particularly of the quadriceps muscle, quickly occurs as a result of inactivity.

The functional examination discloses limited motions in a capsular pattern. In most cases, blood and urine tests are necessary to determine the cause of the arthritis.

Treatment

Treatment depends on the cause but in most cases consists of systemic antiinflammatory medication. In some instances, an intraarticular injection with a corticosteroid is effective.

Even after the local arthritis has resolved, there is often a residual limitation of motion.

Treatment for this condition should be joint-specific mobilization. Strengthening exercises should be given for the (often severe) muscle atrophy.

ARTHROSIS (GONARTHROSIS)

Arthrosis of the knee can be primary or secondary. Primary arthrosis occurs without a prior incidence of abnormal loading of the joint. It is caused, for example, by a functional disturbance or an abnormal position of the knee or other joints of the lower extremity.

A secondary arthrosis occurs when there is disproportion between the load and loadability of the joint, resulting in mechanical damage of the joint. The most frequent causes of this disproportion include congenital or acquired aberrations in alignment, previous joint injuries, previous surgery, and long periods of immobilization. Therefore, after a total meniscectomy early degenerative changes almost always occur. After a lateral meniscectomy the clinical and radiologic changes are more severe than after a medial meniscectomy. Therefore, whenever possible, partial meniscectomies or meniscal repairs should be performed (refer also to "Meniscus Lesions," below).

In gonarthrosis patients, symptoms can sometimes suddenly increase. If pain is the only symptom, the cause could be a stress fracture of the tibia. If there is sudden, shooting pain followed by a paralyzed feeling in the leg, the cause is likely to be a loose body. In some cases, a varus deformity of the knee gradually develops (Figure 10–3).

Clinical Findings

The symptoms depend on the stage of the arthrosis and possible complications, such as loose bodies. The most significant complaints are crepitation during movement, stiffness at the beginning of activity, and pain at the beginning of activity. These symptoms decrease during activities in the course of the day. Later in the day, they appear again in the form of a feeling of fatigue.

Functional Examination

Findings in the functional examination include warmth and swelling of the joint, limita-

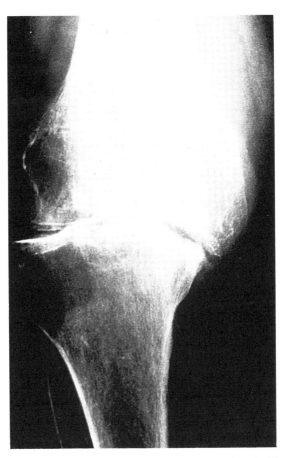

Figure 10–3 Conventional radiograph of a right knee with severe arthrosis. The joint space has almost disappeared, and the tibia is subluxated slightly laterally.

tion of motion in a capsular pattern with a hard end-feel, and, over the course of time, visible joint deformation.

Sometimes, a loose body can cloud the clinical picture of an arthrosis (Figure 10–4). The patient complains of suddenly occurring,

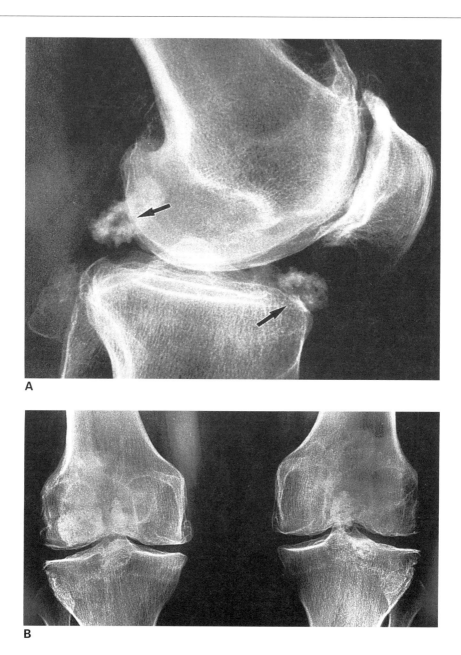

Figure 10–4 (A) Lateral conventional radiograph of an arthrotic right knee. Severe arthrotic changes and loose bodies are visible (arrows). **(B)** Anteroposterior conventional radiograph of both knees of the patient in **A**.

instantaneous, sharp, shooting pain, whereby normal weight bearing of the joint is impossible for a few seconds to minutes. The diagnosis of a loose body is often missed, however, and the patient is told that the knee has "degenerated."

Plain films show the various stages of the arthrosis.

Treatment

In the first instance, all the factors that further or aggravate the arthrotic process have to be considered. Treatment techniques vary from case to case and can range from a functional orthotic for the foot to an osteotomy of the femur or tibia.

In the early stage of arthrosis, movement therapy is indicated, particularly involving joint-specific mobilization and muscle stretching. Many patients react well to oral doses of nonsteroidal antiinflammatory medication, particularly in the early stages. Much

experimentation has been done, and will continue to be done, with substances that have an influence on cartilage metabolism. These experiments have not been successful, and at this point there is not much hope for the immediate future. In severe cases, intraarticular injections with a corticosteroid can significantly help relieve the symptoms for extensive periods of time. This is often a helpful treatment for patients for whom surgery is not yet indicated. In the end stages, surgery is performed, consisting of a partial or total joint replacement (Figure 10–5).

Most of the time, for patients with a loose body, a simple manipulation under traction is successful.

HEMARTHROSIS

Hemarthrosis in the knee is seen particularly in hemophiliac patients, in whom it is the most commonly affected joint. After an insignificant trauma, a large amount of intraarticu-

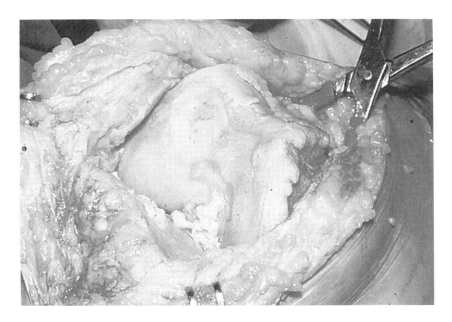

Figure 10–5 Operative view of a severely arthrotic joint. The femoral joint cartilage has almost completely disappeared, and large osteophytes are visible. In this case, a total joint replacement will be performed.

lar bleeding occurs. The chance for recurrent bleeding is great.

In the differential diagnosis, the examiner has to consider an acute infection in the joint. In the case of an infection, the swelling occurs more slowly than when bleeding is the cause.

Clinical Findings

Immediately after a mild trauma, a warm, tingling feeling is experienced in the joint; directly afterward there is a quick increase in pain. There is severe swelling in the joint. The knee is warm to palpation.

Functional Examination

The functional examination indicates limited motions in the capsular pattern.

Treatment

The knee should be aspirated and bandaged with an elastic wrap. In addition, the joint should be immobilized for several days. After 3 to 4 days, the knee should be carefully mobilized using both active and passive mobilization techniques.

PATHOLOGY WITH LIMITED MOTIONS IN A NONCAPSULAR PATTERN

OSTEOCHONDRITIS DISSECANS

Differentiation is made between juvenile osteochondritis dissecans (JOCD) and osteochondritis dissecans in adults (OCD). In young individuals, the disorder occurs before the closing of the distal femoral epiphysis (Figure 10–6) and in adults it occurs afterward. It involves a lesion of the subchondral bone. Later, it also includes a lesion of the joint surface cartilage, located at the lateral aspect of the medial femoral condyle. This disorder is seen four times more often in boys than in girls. The age group is between 15 and 25 years. Sometimes the patient is younger, but rarely younger than 10 years.

There is still some discussion regarding the etiology. It is assumed that trauma, both internal and external, plays an important role. In recent medical literature, ischemia and inflammation have been discarded as possible causes. The current popular theory relates to a multifactoral cause, in which trauma is the most important factor. It is conjectured that in the originally normal subchondral bone a fatigue fracture occurs. Bone scans in patients with JOCD demonstrate a typical healing process that has a course similar to that of skeletal fractures elsewhere.

As soon as the diagnosis of JOCD has been confirmed, the "race" begins between the healing process of the disorder and the closing of the femoral epiphysis. If the JOCD has not healed before the epiphyseal plate closes, it becomes an OCD; the race has been lost, and the prognosis is less favorable. The most important part of the treatment of JOCD is preventing gonarthrosis.

JOCD and OCD can occur not only in the knee joint but also in other joints at the same time. In many patients there is no genetic predisposition. There is an important subgroup of patients with a history of familial multiple JOCD and OCD, however. These disorders are associated with short people.

Four stages can be differentiated with the use of plain films and bone scan. In the first stage, the bone scan does not demonstrate any aberrations, but the defect is easily visible on the conventional radiograph as a slight concavity at the lateral aspect of the medial femoral condyle. In the second stage, the bone scan demonstrates activity around the lesion. In the third stage, the bone scan indi-

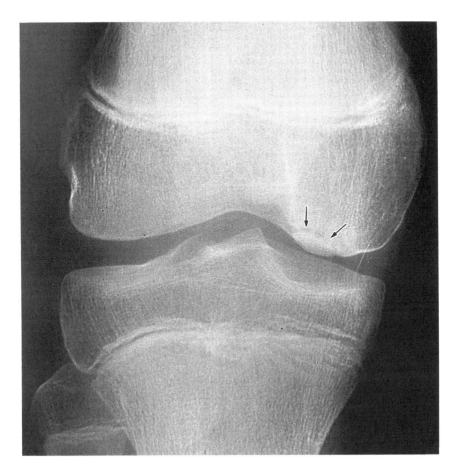

Figure 10–6 Anteroposterior conventional radiograph of a right knee demonstrating JOCD at the level of the medial femoral condyle. The sequestered segment is still in place (arrows).

cates an extension of the lesion to the entire medial femoral condyle. In the fourth stage, there is also spreading to the medial tibial plateau.

The use of a bone scan is important in determining the best therapy. The size of the lesion and the age of the patient are also important in this decision. Surgery is indicated for children older than 12 in whom there is a lesion larger than 1 cm and a dislodged fragment (loose body).

OCD of the knee is seen in the patella, but less frequently. The lesion can be found in any of the facets of the patella because there are no predisposition sites.

Clinical Findings

Symptoms vary widely, depending on the clinical stage of the disorder. Sometimes the patient experiences pain throughout the whole knee and sometimes only at the medial aspect. Some patients feel pain only during activities, and others can also have pain at rest. In many cases there is a chronic mild synovitis with intermittent slight joint effusion.

Functional Examination

Usually in the functional examination, a mild capsular pattern of limited motions is found. Often, pain can be provoked by bringing the knee from 90° flexion toward extension while maintaining internal rotation. If the leg is then externally rotated at the point where the patient's pain is provoked, the pain disappears. This relief of pain occurs because, on externally rotating the tibia, the cruciate ligaments are under less tension, and there is less pressure exerted against the affected site at the femoral condyle.

Sometimes there is patellofemoral crepitation when pressure is exerted against the patella and it is passively moved over the femur. In some cases, an acute hemarthrosis can occur after activity. In the presence of a loose body, an acute locking of the joint can occur; sometimes the flexion is limited, at other times the extension. The diagnosis is best confirmed by means of radiologic examination, particularly bone scan.

Patients with OCD of the patella complain of vague patellar pain that is of gradual onset. The pain increases with activity, particularly during loaded flexion movements, such as ascending and descending stairs. Sometimes there is intermittent swelling and a vague feeling of knee instability. Locking of the knee is caused by the presence of a loose body in the joint.

Treatment

JOCD.

The treatment of JOCD is primarily conservative. Activities should be significantly reduced. Bracing and the use of crutches are necessary to control the activities and reduce the symptoms. This period of immobilization should not last longer than 12 weeks. Early mobilization is important because otherwise the treatment will bring worse results than the disorder! If the symptoms have not resolved within 10 to 12 weeks and the bone scan does not demonstrate improvement, surgery is indicated.

If there is a loose body in the joint, surgery is always indicated. The same is true if epiphyseal closure is expected within 6 to 12 months after the diagnosis has been made. Surgery is also indicated when, after adequate conservative treatment, there are still residual symptoms or the bone scan demonstrates unsatisfactory healing.

OCD.

After closure of the femoral epiphysis, surgery is almost always indicated. Treatment of OCD of the patella is surgical in cases of persistent pain, loose bodies, and subchondral sclerosis (Figure 10–7).

LOOSE BODIES

Loose bodies in the knee joint can be idiopathic or have various known causes. The following are some of the known causes:

- OCD
- synovial (osteo)chondromatosis
- gonarthrosis
- meniscus lesion
- retropatellar chondropathy
- trauma

Figure 10–7 Surgical photograph showing a loosened osteochondral fragment in OCD.

Idiopathic

Occasionally a patient without underlying knee pathology is seen who complains of sudden, sharp, instantaneous pain in the knee, usually localized to the medial side. The pain has a paralyzing character, and the patient complains of the knee "giving way" without really falling. Because of this, the patient has an unstable feeling in the knee; certain activities (eg, ascending stairs) can become problematic.

Clinical Findings

The patient usually has a slightly swollen and warm knee.

Functional Examination

The functional examination can vary from case to case. Usually the functional examination demonstrates a limitation of motion that is *not* in a capsular pattern. For instance, there is a slight extension limitation with a pathologic end-feel, but the flexion is normal. The flexion can be limited and the extension normal.

In some patients, the passive varus test is painful. This is seen particularly in patients who have pain at the medial aspect of the knee. In such cases, the medial collateral ligament can be tender to palpation, without there being any suspicion of a ligamentous lesion. The ligament is irritated by the loose body. After the manipulative treatment, the local ligamentous pain usually resolves within a few days, and normal movement is restored. This phenomenon confirms that the cause of the tenderness at the medial collateral ligament was indeed the loose body.

Treatment

Treatment is primarily conservative. In most instances, a simple rotation manipulation under traction leads to complete recovery (refer to Chapter 11 for a detailed description of this manipulation). The loose body moves to the periphery of the joint, where it usually becomes encapsulated in the joint capsule. In cases where there is a recurrence after a manipulation, the treatment should be repeated several times. If the symptoms continue to return, however, arthroscopy is indicated.

Traumatic

Loose bodies can afflict patients with gonarthrosis, as well as patients with a normal knee joint, as the result of trauma. Such traumas usually produce a single cartilage fragment or a number of fragments.

Clinical Findings

The clinical symptoms are the same as described for an idiopathic loose body. In patients with gonarthrosis, the loose body is sometimes large. Irritation of the common peroneal nerve at the back of the knee sometimes occurs, causing characteristic sensory disturbances, particularly those affecting the first and second toes.

Treatment

As is the case with the idiopathic loose body, manipulative treatment is performed first. In recurrent problems, the diagnosis should be confirmed through either radiographs or arthroscopy and arthroscopically removed.

SYNOVIAL (OSTEO)CHONDROMATOSIS

Synovial osteochondromatosis is a disorder that is seldom seen (Figure 10–8). It involves a chondroid metaplasia of the synovial membrane that leads to the formation of multiple small bodies. These small bodies range from the size of a rice kernel to 1 cm. After a period of time, these synovial bodies calcify, a condition termed osteochondromatosis. Other predilection sites for this disorder are the joints in the elbow, hip, and, rarely, the shoulder.

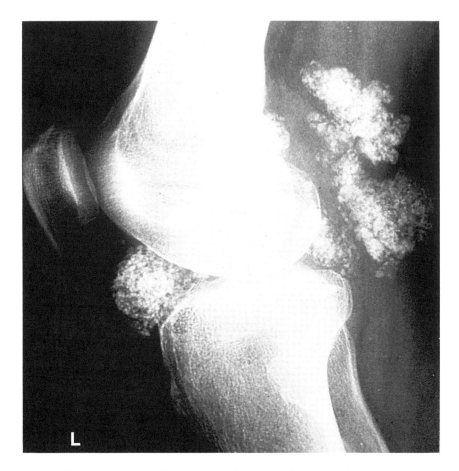

Figure 10–8 Lateral conventional radiograph of a left knee demonstrating significant intraarticular calcified osteochondral elements, typical of a synovial osteochondromatosis.

Clinical Findings

Often, the symptoms initially are activity related. Most patients have periods of intermittent painful effusion, during which the knee can be warm to palpation.

Functional Examination

Initially, there may be a minimal limitation of motion. If the bodies become loose from the synovial membrane, they "fall into the joint," causing it to lock. As long as the bodies have not calcified, the radiologic examination is normally negative (Figure 10–9). Double-contrast arthrography reveals the abnormal contour of the capsule. Arthroscopy, computed tomography (CT), and particularly magnetic resonance (MR) imaging will clearly disclose the aberration.

Treatment

The treatment should be surgery with an extensive synovectomy to prevent recurrence.

MENISCUS LESIONS

Meniscus lesions are frequently seen, with occurrences in the medial meniscus being more common than those in the lateral meniscus.

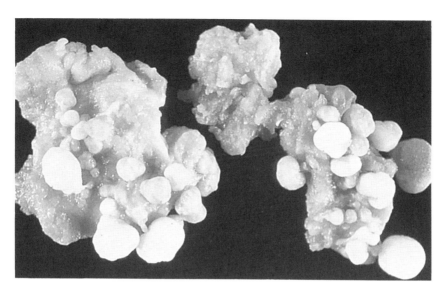

Figure 10–9 Resected synovial membrane in a patient with synovial chondromatosis showing the stemmed chondral elements. In this case, the radiograph was negative for loose bodies because calcification had not occurred.

Differentiation is made between longitudinal tears, which run parallel to the long axis of the meniscus, and transverse tears, which run perpendicular to the long axis of the meniscus (Figure 10–10). In addition, tears are classified according to the plane in which they are located. The cross-section of the meniscus has the form of a wedge with a small base. If the plane in which the tear is located runs parallel to this base, it is termed a vertical tear. If the plane is perpendicular to the base, it is termed a horizontal tear (Figure 10–11). If a large part or the entire length of the meniscus is torn, the central part can luxate toward the intercondylar fossa. This is the so-called bucket-handle tear (Figure 10–12).

If the attachment of the meniscus to the capsule is overstretched or torn (usually the meniscotibial or coronary ligament is involved), part of, or sometimes the entire, meniscus can become loose in the joint. Actually, this is more of a capsule lesion than a meniscus lesion. Combinations of the various tears are regularly seen (Figures 10–13 to 10–18).

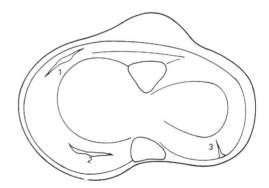

Figure 10–10 Longitudinal and transverse tears of the meniscus. **1**, Longitudinal tear in the anterior horn of the medial meniscus; **2**, longitudinal tear in the posterior horn of the medial meniscus; **3**, transverse tear in the posterior horn of the lateral meniscus.

Besides the above mentioned types of tears, there are also unusual lesions of the meniscus that are generally classified as meniscal sprains or meniscal fraying. Meniscoligamentous lesions are frequently seen, particularly in athletes.

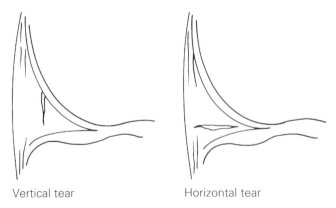

Vertical tear   Horizontal tear

Figure 10–11 Vertical and horizontal meniscus tears.

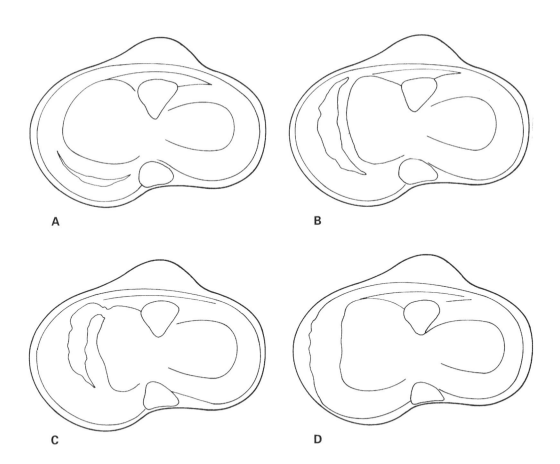

Figure 10–12 Examples of bucket-handle tears of the medial meniscus. (**A**) Bucket-handle tear in the posterior horn. (**B**) Complete bucket-handle tear. (**C**) Complete bucket-handle tear but torn from the anterior horn. (**D**) Peripheral bucket-handle tear (torn from the capsular collateral ligaments).

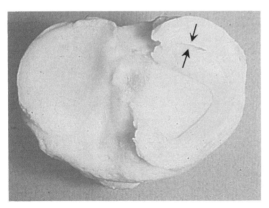

Figure 10–13 Posterior horn tear of the medial meniscus (arrows).

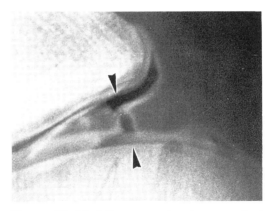

Figure 10–14 Arthrogram showing a vertical tear of the posterior horn of the medial meniscus (arrowheads).

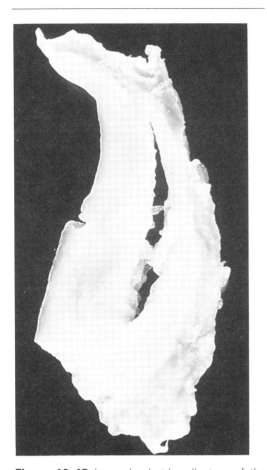

Figure 10–15 Large bucket-handle tear of the medial meniscus.

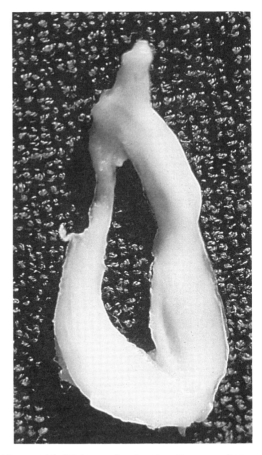

Figure 10–16 Large bucket-handle tear of the medial meniscus in which the torn piece (left) luxated medially, causing locking of the knee.

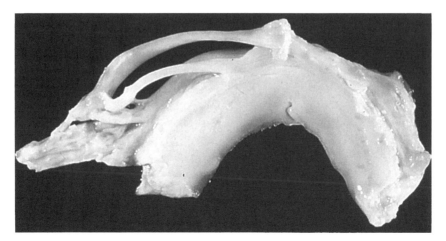

Figure 10–17 Multiple tears of the posterior horn of the medial meniscus. This patient had a well-established posterior horn tear and experienced recurring locking of the knee caused by repeated luxations of the torn part of the meniscus.

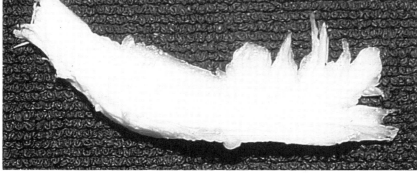

Figure 10–18 Degeneratively changed posterior horn of the medial meniscus with a longitudinal tear at the end of the resected piece.

Other disorders of the meniscus are the ganglion of the meniscus (Figure 10–19) and the discoid meniscus (Figures 10–20 to 10–22). The ganglion of the meniscus is a swelling consisting of a number of synovium-filled cavities. These cavities are separated by connective tissue septa. In general, these ganglia lie in the synovial membrane and are merged with the base of, usually, the lateral meniscus. The ganglion lies within the fibrous capsule.

Sometimes, however, a ganglion can push through the fibrous capsule and spread out underneath the superficial fascia. The ganglia of the lateral meniscus are usually connected to the middle segment of the meniscus and only occasionally to the anterior horn. This ganglion can become large and then usually pushes through the fibrous capsule. Often, in conjunction with a meniscal ganglion, there is also a tear of the meniscus. In the lateral me-

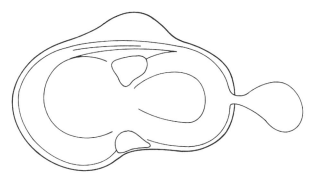

Figure 10–19 Ganglion of the lateral meniscus.

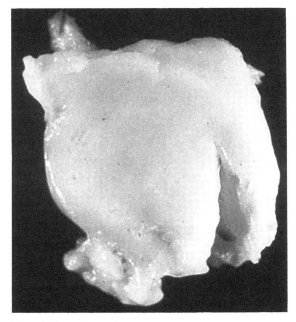

Figure 10–20 Resected discoid lateral meniscus.

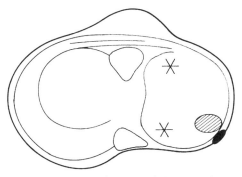

Figure 10–21 Discoid lateral meniscus with fixation of the anterior and posterior horns to the tibia (asterisks). Tears usually occur just anterior (shaded area) to the popliteus tendon (black area).

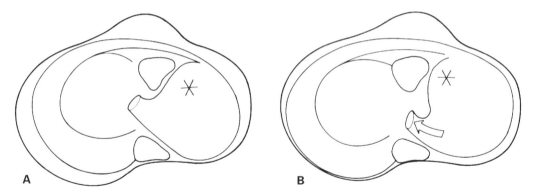

Figure 10–22 Two illustrations of a Wrisberg type discoid lateral meniscus. (**A**) During flexion of the knee, the meniscus is only fixated to the tibial plateau at the level of the anterior horn (asterisk). (**B**) During extension of the knee, the meniscus luxates (snapping knee) toward the intercondylar fossa because of the too-short Wrisberg ligament (arrow).

niscus, this is usually a transverse tear; in the medial meniscus, it is more often a longitudinal tear.

In the medical literature, there are several theories regarding the origin of ganglia. Some authors describe a degenerative etiology; others consider the ganglion a swelling. Large ganglia are particularly seen in younger patients, making the degenerative theory less likely.

In older knee patients, often during the clinical examination a "filled" medial or lateral joint space can be palpated, in which an irregular, somewhat crepitating surface can be felt. Cases such as these mostly involve degenerative changes in the outer edge of the meniscus.

The discoid meniscus is a congenital anomaly in which the entire meniscus or part of the meniscus is wider than normal, somewhat resembling a disk (Figure 10–20). This is seen much more often at the lateral side of the knee than at the medial side. Patients with a lateral discoid meniscus quite often have the so-called snapping knee syndrome. This syndrome occurs in discoid menisci having only one attachment at the posterior horn by way of the posterior meniscofemoral ligament, known as Wrisberg's ligament. The liga-

ment is too short to allow normal extension of the knee. Hypermobility of the posterior horn of the lateral discoid meniscus results in secondary hypertrophy (thickening) of the meniscus. This disorder is seen particularly in children between the ages of 6 and 18 years. An audible click is produced as the knee is bent and then straightened. On returning the leg to almost full extension, a palpable snap occurs. Pain is experienced at the lateral side of the joint. Usually a vertical tear occurs in the hypermobile posterior horn of the discoid meniscus (Figures 10–21 and 10–22). A lateral discoid meniscus that is well fixed to the tibia at the level of the posterior horn rarely causes complaints. In most cases, a lateral discoid meniscus is an incidental discovery made, for example, during arthroscopy. If a tear does occur in the lateral discoid meniscus, it usually occurs just anterior to the tendon of the popliteus muscle.

One of the problems in making a correct diagnosis after trauma is that it is difficult, without the functional examination, to determine whether there might also be a meniscus lesion. When analyzing the traumatic forces that occurred during trauma, it is rather easy to predict which capsuloligamentous structures are injured. In many instances, however, a meniscus lesion remains unpredictable. It is entirely possible for the menisci to remain intact even after trauma resulting in a severe ligamentous lesion. On the other hand, it is also possible for a severe meniscus lesion to occur as the result of insignificant trauma even though the capsuloligamentous complex remains entirely intact.

Often, patients with an anterior knee instability have a lesion, first, of the posterior horn of the medial meniscus and, later, of the posterior horn of the lateral meniscus. Frequently, in anterolateral rotatory instability, a lesion first occurs in the posterior horn of the lateral meniscus. These injuries occur when the anterior cruciate can no longer guide the roll–glide mechanism of the knee during activities. This leads to an abnormal amount of rolling of the femur in a posterior direction, and the posterior horn of the meniscus becomes crushed.

Clinical Findings

There are many so-called specific tests described for the menisci. Most of these tests, however, are not completely reliable. Rather than attempting specific tests, it is more important to be able to interpret correctly the findings from the standard functional examination of the knee. Knowledge of the anatomy and arthrokinematics involved is a prerequisite to proper interpretation.

The anterior horn of the medial meniscus is connected to the extensor mechanism, and the posterior horn is connected to the tendon fibers of the semimembranosus muscle. The anterior horn of the lateral meniscus is also connected to the extensor mechanism. The posterior horn of the lateral meniscus is also an important insertion site of the popliteus muscle.

Functional Examination

Often, in the acute stage of a meniscus tear, there is minimal to moderate synovial effusion or hemarthrosis, depending on whether the tear is in the avascular or vascular part of the meniscus. In the clinic, the examiner will find any number of tests to be painful for the patient. Positive findings vary from patient to patient and can include the following:

- locking of the knee in extension or flexion as a result of a bucket-handle tear
- painful passive extension due to impingement of the meniscus, a ganglion, or sometimes a cystic change in the anterior horn
- springy end-feel in passive extension, often as a result of a bucket-handle tear in the medial meniscus
- painful passive flexion due to impingement of a torn or completely loose posterior horn
- click during active flexion and extension in a discoid meniscus
- painful snap in the last degrees of extension in a discoid lateral meniscus
- painful passive external rotation in lesions of the medial meniscus or medial meniscotibial ligament
- painful passive internal rotation in lesions of the lateral meniscus or lateral meniscotibial ligament
- painful passive varus test in lesions of the medial or lateral meniscus (differentiation is determined by the location of the pain)
- painful passive valgus test in lesions of the medial or lateral meniscus (differentiation is determined by the location of the pain)
- painful lateral or medial shear test (differentiation is determined by the location of the pain)
- painful resisted extension, when there is an anterior horn lesion of the medial or lateral meniscus
- painful resisted flexion with external rotation, when there is a posterior horn lesion of the lateral meniscus
- painful resisted flexion with internal rotation (lateral pain, posterior horn of the

lateral meniscus via the insertion of the popliteus muscle; medial pain, posterior horn of the medial meniscus via the semimembranosus muscle insertion)

In many cases, confirmation of the diagnosis is possible through arthroscopy. Some lesions, however, are better diagnosed by means of the functional examination than by arthroscopy. This is particularly true for small meniscoligamentous lesions and small lesions on the outer surface of the menisci, which will cause pain during the resisted tests.

Treatment

The treatment is entirely dependent on the type of lesion and the severity of the patient's symptoms. Another significant factor to consider is whether the meniscus lesion is the only problem or is associated with another lesion, such as ligamentous instability.

Most solitary, small lesions in the vascularized part of the meniscus can be conservatively treated. This is particularly true for meniscoligamentous lesions. A sprain of the meniscotibial ligament (usually medial) responds well to transverse friction.

Surgery is indicated when the patient experiences locking of the joint, large tears in the avascular part of the meniscus, a large ganglion, or a symptomatic discoid meniscus. Tears that run from the vascularized part of the meniscus into the avascular part can be repaired with sutures. The same is true for tears that are only in the vascularized part of the meniscus. Arthrotomy or arthroscopy is the surgical procedure most used. Arthroscopy is preferred because there appears to be less chance for early arthrosis.

As previously stated, meniscus lesions often occur particularly in anterior instability of the knee. Sometimes, conservative treatment for an instability can ultimately lead to further damage to the rest of that meniscus or to the meniscus on the other side. These are usually lesions of the posterior horn. Therefore, reconstructive surgery for the anterior cruciate ligament is recommended to prevent further injury of the menisci and joint cartilage.

In cases of acute locking of the joint, typically accompanied by a severe limitation of extension resulting from a bucket-handle lesion of the medial meniscus, a repositioning manipulation is almost always successful. Immediately afterward, the patient can fully extend the knee again. Further treatment depends on recurrence of the symptoms.

In the typical vertical tear in the posterior horn of a lateral discoid meniscus, a total meniscectomy is the preferred treatment. In a tear of the discoid meniscus just anterior to the popliteus tendon, part of the disc is resected, and the peripheral part of the meniscus is left intact.

PLICA SYNDROME

In the early stages of embryologic development, the knee consists of three separate synovial covered chambers. Gradually, the separating walls disappear, and by the fourth month the actual knee cavity is formed. In a certain percentage of individuals (varying in the medical literature from 20% to 60%), residual "shelves" remain from one or more of these separating walls. Such a structure, now visible as a fold in the synovial membrane, is termed a plica. The infrapatellar plica is the plica most often present, followed by the suprapatellar plica, and the least present mediopatellar plica.

The infrapatellar plica, also called the mucous ligament, runs like a piece of tape from the medial surface of the lateral femoral condyle to the infrapatellar fat pad. Its form can vary considerably. Although this plica is most often present, it causes the fewest problems. Because of its course, the infrapatellar plica looks like the anterior cruciate ligament and has in the past been mistaken for this ligament.

If the suprapatellar plica is present in its entirety, it separates the suprapatellar bursa (or recess) from the joint cavity. Here, too, there are many anatomic variations. This structure rarely causes problems.

The mediopatellar plica, also termed Lino's shelf, can be classified into two types: complete and incomplete. The complete type is half-moon shaped with the convexity medial. It runs from the medial side of the suprapatellar plica, if present, or from the neighboring joint capsule to the infrapatellar fat pad. This plica can lie partly in the patellofemoral joint. In the incomplete type, the origin lies more distally. As mentioned earlier, the mediopatellar plica is the least often present but definitely causes the most problems (Figure 10–23).

Normally, a plica is thin, elastic, and asymptomatic. As a result of pathologic changes of the knee, such as chondromalacia, OCD, overuse (microtrauma), or trauma, a plica can become irritated causing an inflammatory reaction with thickening and fibrosing of the plica. A large or pathologically thickened mediopatellar plica can become pinched between the medial femoral condyle and the patella, causing pain at the medial side of the knee. Over time, a pathologically thickened

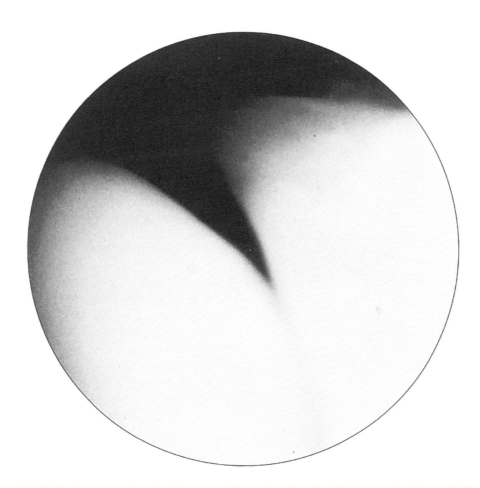

Figure 10–23 Arthroscopy showing a large mediopatellar plica (right) lying next to the medial femoral condyle (left).

plica can damage the cartilage of the patella or medial femoral condyle.

Clinical Findings

Patients, ranging in age from adolescent to adult, usually complain about pain at the medial side of the knee, particularly during activities such as ascending or descending stairs or biking. A classic symptom is pain at night that disappears when the patient straightens the knee. Many patients complain of an occasional feeling that the knee gives way. This is a complaint that is shared by patients with knee instability, retropatellar chondromalacia, and loose body conditions. Sitting for long periods increases the patient's pain, a complaint shared by patients with retropatellar chondromalacia. Sometimes, there is an audible snap during flexion and extension of the knee, a symptom shared by patients with meniscus lesions. Often, there is slight synovial effusion.

Functional Examination

In spite of the fact that these patients are usually active in sports, there is almost always slight atrophy of the quadriceps muscle. In the functional examination, there is sometimes a slight flexion or extension limitation of motion. During the movement of flexion to extension, pain can occur in the trajectory between 30° and 90°. This so-called painful arc occurs because the mediopatellar plica becomes pinched in the patellofemoral joint. Passive external rotation of the lower leg is usually painful, again as a result of impingement in the patellofemoral joint. Usually, the medial side of the patella and the medial femoral condyle are tender to palpation.

The Mital-Hayden test, in which the patella is pushed medially with the knee in 30° flexion, can be painful. Sometimes a click is also felt. The modified McMurray test can be positive because of the external rotation of the lower leg and the movement from extension into and out of flexion.

The hardened free edge of the mediopatellar plica can sometimes be palpated as a thin cord just distal to the patella, parallel to the patellar ligament. Care should be taken not to confuse this plica with the medial patellotibial retinaculum, which runs from the medial aspect of the patellar apex diagonally in a mediodistal direction to the tibia and is also easily palpable. When the examiner pushes the plica in a proximolateral direction with the thumb and simultaneously flexes and extends the patient's knee, the patient experiences specific pain, sometimes accompanied by a click.

The diagnosis is best confirmed through arthroscopy.

Treatment

Initial treatment is conservative, involving a decrease in appropriate activities, physical therapy modalities such as ultrasound or iontophoresis, and, if necessary, injection of the symptomatic plica with a corticosteroid.

Bicycle racers often develop the mediopatellar plica. This has been attributed to the foot being fixed in toe clips that do not allow for physiologic rotations when flexing and extending the knee. External rotation is hindered during extension and internal rotation during flexing. In these cases, part of the treatment consists of exchanging the toe clips for rotating foot plates.

When results with conservative therapy are unsuccessful or when problems are recurrent, surgery is indicated. The surgery can consist of arthroscopy or arthrotomy. The plica is either cut in three or four places from the free edge to its base to decrease the tension in the plica, or it is completely resected. If the possibility of recurrence is an issue, the latter procedure is preferred.

INTRAARTICULAR ADHESIONS

Intraarticular adhesions usually develop as the result of a trauma-induced hemarthrosis after which the knee was not aspirated, after an arthrotomy, and, much less often, after arthroscopy. A progressive but painless loss of motion in flexion is seen, even if the patient has received what might be considered adequate physical therapy. In the differential diagnosis, Pellegrini-Stieda syndrome should be considered.

Clinical Findings

The patient has little or no pain at rest. Active flexion and extension can be painful, however.

Functional Examination

The functional examination demonstrates a significant flexion limitation of motion, and the extension is (usually) normal. The rest of the functional examination is negative.

Treatment

At one time, treatment consisted of forced manipulation under anesthesia. Recently, this disorder has been treated through arthroscopy, during which the adhesions are cut and, if necessary, the frayed portions of the synovium are resected. Recurrence is rarely seen.

PELLEGRINI-STIEDA SYNDROME

Pellegrini-Stieda syndrome is a disorder in which there is a radiologically visible calcification at the level of the origin of the medial collateral ligament at the adductor tubercle. The cause is almost always traumatic, such as a valgus trauma of the knee or trauma with a valgus component. This syndrome can be classified into two types: calcification in the ligament itself (Figure 10–24) and calcification of the attachment of the ligament at the adductor tubercle (Figure 10–25). With the

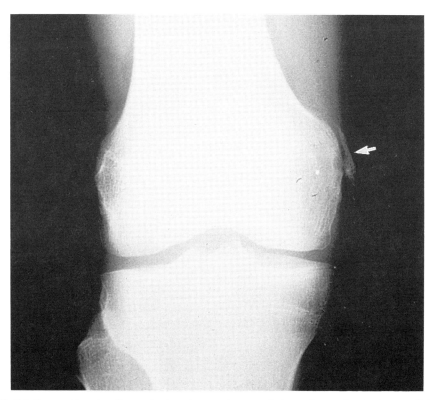

Figure 10–24 Conventional radiograph showing posttraumatic bone formation in the medial collateral ligament at the level of the adductor tubercle (arrow). This is characteristic of Pellegrini-Stieda syndrome type I.

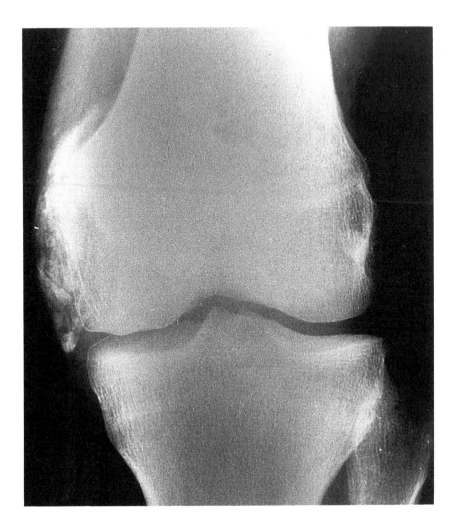

Figure 10–25 Conventional radiograph showing posttraumatic bone formation in the attachment of the medial collateral ligament at the adductor tubercle. This is characteristic of Pellegrini-Stieda syndrome type II.

first type, a calcium shadow is visible medial to the adductor tubercle; in the second type, the calcification is firmly attached to the adductor tubercle.

Clinical Findings

The patient complains of pain and tenderness at the level of the medial femoral condyle, particularly during knee flexion.

There is an increasing limitation of flexion. Sometimes, there is local warmth and redness.

Functional Examination

Usually, the functional examination reveals a severe limitation of motion in flexion and normal extension. Passive valgus in slight flexion is often painful.

Treatment

Generally, there is unassisted recovery in 6 to 12 months. Local physical therapy modalities are ineffective in the treatment of this disorder. The same is true for injections with local anesthetic or corticosteroids. Surgery will not help the recovery process either. Just trust in Providence and keep an eye on the calendar!

10.2   PATHOLOGY OF THE CAPSULOLIGAMENTOUS COMPLEX

Pathology of the capsuloligamentous complex of the knee can be divided into lesions with and lesions without resultant instability. Lesions without instability involve a contusion or sprain, which almost always responds well to conservative treatment. One exception is Pellegrini-Stieda syndrome, which can occur after valgus trauma or after trauma with a valgus component. Lesions with instability involve either a partial or a complete rupture and often require reconstructive surgery followed by functional rehabilitation. Both with and without instability, these lesions can be further classified as acute (newly acquired) and chronic (lingering) lesions.

In most cases, the patient's history provides a good indication of the specific lesion to be suspected. It is particularly important in planning the therapy to be able to reconstruct, as closely as possible, the onset and course of the trauma. Detailed knowledge of the anatomy, particularly of the dynamic and static stabilizers of the knee, is necessary for proper diagnosis and treatment, whether conservative or operative.

The stabilizers of the knee joint are classified into four functional units: the medial complex, the lateral complex, the posterior structures, and the anterior structures. Further differentiation is made between static and dynamic stabilizers (Figure 10–26).

The Medial Complex

- Static stabilizers
  1. Medial (tibial) collateral ligament
  2. Medial capsular ligament structures (meniscofemoral and meniscotibial ligaments)
  3. Posterior oblique ligament
  4. Posteromedial capsule (including the popliteal oblique ligament)
  5. Medial meniscus
  6. Contour of the medial femoral condyle and the tibial plateau
  7. Anterior and posterior cruciate ligaments
- Dynamic stabilizers
  1. Semimembranosus muscle
  2. Sartorius muscle
  3. Gracilis muscle
  4. Semitendinosus muscle
  5. Vastus medialis muscle
  6. Medial head of the gastrocnemius muscle

The Lateral Complex

- Static stabilizers
  1. Iliotibial tract
  2. Lateral (fibular) collateral ligament

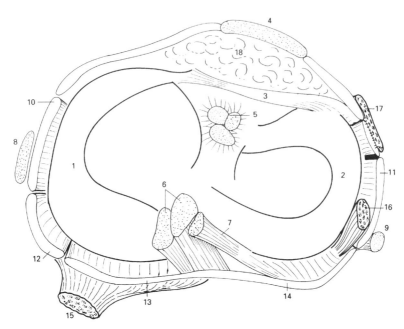

Figure 10–26 View of the right knee from above. **1**, Medial meniscus; **2**, lateral meniscus; **3**, transverse ligament of the knee; **4**, patellar ligament; **5**, anterior cruciate ligament; **6**, posterior cruciate ligament; **7**, posterior meniscofemoral ligament (Wrisberg's ligament); **8**, medial collateral ligament; **9**, lateral collateral ligament; **10**, medial capsuloligament; **11**, lateral capsuloligament; **12**, posteromedial collateral ligament (posterior oblique ligament); **13**, popliteal oblique ligament; **14**, popliteal arcuate ligament; **15**, semimembranosus muscle; **16**, popliteus muscle; **17**, iliotibial tract; **18**, infrapatellar fat pad.

---

3. Lateral capsular ligament (meniscofemoral and meniscotibial ligaments)
4. Posterolateral capsule (including the popliteal arcuate ligament)
5. Lateral meniscus
6. Anterior and posterior cruciate ligaments
- Dynamic stabilizers
  1. Biceps femoris muscle
  2. Popliteus muscle
  3. Vastus lateralis muscle
  4. Lateral head of the gastrocnemius muscle
  5. Iliotibial tract

The Posterior Structures

- Differentiation is not made between static and dynamic stabilizers

1. Posterior capsule
2. Popliteal arcuate ligament
3. Popliteal oblique ligament
4. Posterior oblique ligament
5. Popliteus muscle
6. Gastrocnemius muscle (lateral and medial heads)
7. Semimembranosus muscle
8. Biceps femoris muscle

The Anterior Structures

- Differentiation is not made between static and dynamic stabilizers; extensor mechanism:
  1. Medial: vastus medialis muscle, vastus medialis obliquus muscle, medial retinaculum

2. Anterior: rectus femoris muscle, vastus intermedius muscle, suprapatellar quadriceps tendon, patella, patellar ligament, infrapatellar fat pad

3. Lateral: vastus lateralis muscle, lateral retinaculum

CLASSIFICATION OF KNEE INSTABILITIES

UNIPLANAR INSTABILITY

Uniplanar instability is a condition where there is stability in one direction without the occurrence of a rotation. According to Hughston and colleagues,[11] in a uniplanar instability, the posterior cruciate ligament is *always* deficient. In orthopaedic literature, there are widely differing opinions about this. Differentiation is made between the following: medial instability, lateral instability, anterior instability, and posterior instability.

ROTATORY INSTABILITY

In rotatory instability, there is a shift of the tibia in relation to the femur around an axis of rotation. Hughston et al[11] describe the intact posterior cruciate ligament as the axis of rotation. This theory is not accepted by many authors, however. In the context of this book, the posterior cruciate ligament classification according to Hughston et al is not applied. Classically, differentiation has been made among the following: anteromedial rotatory instability, anterolateral rotatory instability, posteromedial rotatory instability, and posterolateral instability.

COMBINED ROTATORY INSTABILITY

Combined rotatory instabilities involve combinations of two or more forms of the rotatory instabilities. The most frequently seen combination is the anterolateral with anteromedial rotatory instability. The severest form of this is a dislocation of the knee. Further differentiation is commonly made according to the amount of instability (Figures 10–27 and 10–28). The following grading scale is used internationally:

- 1+ (+): a displacement (translation or "gapping") of less than 5 mm
- 2+ (++): a displacement between 5 and 10 mm
- 3+ (+++): a displacement of more than 10 mm

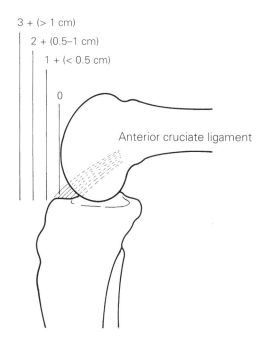

Figure 10–27 Schematic illustration of anterior instability.

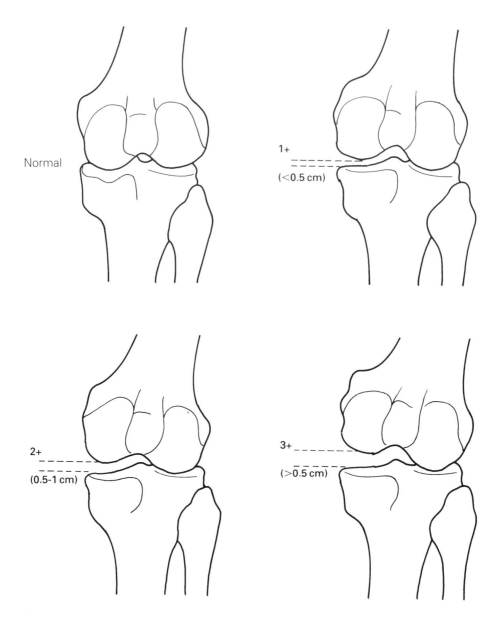

Figure 10–28 Schematic illustration of medial instability.

CAPSULOLIGAMENTOUS PATHOLOGY WITHOUT INSTABILITY

SPRAIN OF THE MEDIAL COLLATERAL LIGAMENT AND POSTERIOR OBLIQUE (OR POSTERIOR MEDIAL COLLATERAL) LIGAMENT

A sprain of the medial collateral ligament usually occurs as the result of a valgus–flexion–external rotation trauma, the so-called VFE trauma. It is less often the result of a pure valgus trauma. In principle, the ligament can be injured anywhere along its course. The most frequently affected sites are the origin, the adductor tubercle of the medial femoral condyle, and the level of the joint space. A lesion can also occur in the distal part of the ligament, underneath the pes anserinus superficialis. In this case, it is not always easy to differentiate among a ligament sprain, tendinitis of the pes anserinus, and a pes anserinus bursitis. A complication of a medial ligament sprain at the level of the origin is Pellegrini-Stieda syndrome.

Clinical Findings

The patient complains of pain at the medial side of the knee. If the posteromedial collateral ligament is affected at the level of the joint space, there is usually slight effusion in the knee. If only the extraarticular (superficial) medial collateral ligament is affected, there should not be any joint effusion. If there is only a sprain of the ligament, the knee does not usually feel warm to the touch.

Functional Examination

There can be a slight flexion limitation caused by a minimal amount of joint effusion. Passive external rotation can be painful. The passive valgus test in slight flexion is the most painful test. The passive valgus test in extension is negative. Palpation for the exact location of the lesion is important; the ligament is 8 to 12 cm long.

A chronic stage can occur, resulting from adhesion of the medial collateral ligament with the medial femoral condyle. If this is the case, the functional examination generally discloses a slight limitation in flexion or extension.

Treatment

Treatment in the acute stage is focused on decreasing pain and edema through the use of an elastic wrap or sleeve and physical therapy modalities. In the subacute stage, transverse friction can be performed to help prevent adhesions, maintain mobility, and decrease pain. Transverse friction is applied in both maximal flexion and maximal extension of the knee. After friction treatments, the knee should be carefully moved passively within the limits of pain. When improvement is such that this can be performed without pain, it should be done actively as well. Strengthening of the quadriceps muscle, particularly the vastus medialis obliquus and the vastus medialis, is important because with this lesion atrophy of these muscles occurs quickly.

In the chronic stage, the adhesions can be ruptured by means of a manipulation (refer to Chapter 11). This manipulation is only indicated in cases where there are very small limitations of motion. This manipulation is always preceded by transverse friction in maximal flexion and maximal extension of the knee. In stubborn cases, and only when the origin is affected, a dropwise injection of the lesion is indicated.

SPRAIN OF THE MEDIAL MENISCOTIBIAL (CORONARY) LIGAMENT

The medial meniscotibial ligament is part of the medial joint capsule and can be sprained in traumas that particularly involve external rotation of the lower leg. Differentiation should always be made between an uncomplicated sprain and a complicated sprain, in which there is also a lesion of the medial meniscus. Pain experienced even after a partial medial meniscectomy is often the result of an overstretch of the medial meniscotibial ligament.

Clinical Findings

The patient complains of pain at the medial side of the knee, at the level of the joint space. Sometimes there is slight joint effusion.

Functional Examination

Passive external rotation of the lower leg is the most painful test. Passive valgus can also be painful. The exact site of the lesion is located by means of palpation, performed in 90° knee flexion and maximal external rotation of the lower leg.

Treatment

The uncomplicated lesion of the medial meniscotibial ligament responds well to transverse friction. This is probably because of the good vascularization of this structure. In therapy-resistant cases, a local injection with corticosteroid is occasionally indicated.

SPRAIN OF THE LATERAL COLLATERAL LIGAMENT

The lateral collateral ligament is much less often affected than the medial collateral ligament. The ligament is extraarticular, and when it is sprained there is no resultant joint effusion. Sprains of this ligament occur as the result of varus trauma or of trauma with a varus component.

Clinical Findings

The patient complains of pain at the lateral side of the knee.

Functional Examination

The varus test in slight flexion is painful, and the varus test in extension is negative.

Palpation for the exact site of the lesion is best performed with the patient in the figure-4 position (refer to Chapter 8).

Treatment

Sprains of the lateral collateral ligament respond well to transverse friction. The friction is best performed with the patient in the figure-4 position.

SPRAIN OF THE LATERAL MENISCOTIBIAL (CORONARY) LIGAMENT

Solitary lesions of the lateral meniscotibial ligament, which is part of the lateral joint capsule, are rarely seen. Lesions of the lateral meniscus, iliotibial tract, and tendon of the popliteus should be considered part of the differential diagnosis. Lesions of this ligament are almost always in conjunction with a lesion of another part of the lateral capsuloligamentous complex and are the result of an internal rotation trauma or trauma with an internal rotation component.

Clinical Findings

Because a lesion of the lateral meniscotibial ligament almost always occurs in combination with a lesion of the lateral capsuloligamentous complex, a number of different tests can be painful.

Functional Examination

Passive internal rotation is specifically painful for the ligament. In some cases, the passive varus test in slight knee flexion can be mildly painful. Palpation with the lower leg in maximal internal rotation and the knee at 90° flexion will disclose the exact site of the lesion.

Treatment

As is the case with sprain of the medial meniscotibial ligament, transverse friction is the preferred treatment for a sprain of the lateral meniscotibial ligament.

CAPSULOLIGAMENTOUS PATHOLOGY WITH INSTABILITY

In all forms of acute instability, the knee is almost always swollen as a result of hemarthrosis or synovial effusion, which can be differentiated by knowing how quickly the swelling occurred. The knee can also be warm. In such cases, there are always limitations of motions in the capsular pattern, with flexion being much more limited than extension.

Note: A general consideration during conservative and postoperative treatment of capsuloligamentous structures is that, in every lesion of the capsuloligamentous complex, there is a disturbance in the proprioception of the joint. Therefore, it is important to pay special attention to proprioceptive training. This type of training can easily be incorporated into the muscle-strengthening program.

In all forms of anterior instability, the hamstrings should be exercised twice as intensively as the quadriceps. The opposite is true for all forms of posterior instability (for more details, refer to Chapter 11).

The appropriate laxity tests for the forms of knee instability described in this section are listed under "Clinical Findings" for each form.

MEDIAL INSTABILITY IN SLIGHT KNEE FLEXION

Medial instability in slight knee flexion involves an instability of the knee in the frontal plane in a valgus direction. Medial instability is caused by valgus trauma or trauma with a valgus component, usually a valgus–flexion–external rotation trauma.

Stability is tested in slight knee flexion. The following structures can be affected:

- 1+ Instability
  1. Medial meniscotibial ligament

  2. Medial collateral ligament (sprain or partial tear)
  3. Possibly the lateral meniscus
- 2+ Instability
  1. Medial meniscotibial ligament
  2. Medial collateral ligament
  3. Posterior oblique ligament
  4. Possibly the lateral meniscus
- 3+ Instability
  1. Medial meniscotibial ligament
  2. Medial collateral ligament
  3. Posterior oblique ligament
  4. Possibly the lateral meniscus
  5. Anterior or posterior cruciate ligament

The "unhappy triad" described by O'Donoghue[12] consists of lesions of the medial collateral ligament, anterior cruciate ligament, and medial meniscus. A medial meniscus lesion in this instance is, in fact, a capsular lesion. If there is a meniscus lesion in this injury, it is usually in the lateral meniscus.

Clinical Findings

- 1+ Instability
  1. Painful passive external rotation of the lower leg
  2. Painful passive valgus test in slight knee flexion
  3. Sometimes a positive McMurray or Steinmann test
- 2+ Instability
  1. The same positive tests as for 1+ instability
  2. Pain on the passive valgus test with the knee in extension
- 3+ Instability
  1. The same positive tests as for 2+ instability

2. Positive anterior drawer test or posterior drawer test in 80° knee flexion
3. Positive anterior drawer test in 80° knee flexion and maximal external rotation
4. Positive Lachman's test
5. If the posterior cruciate is affected:
   —Positive anterolateral drawer test in 90° flexion
   —Positive posterior drawer test in 80° flexion and maximal internal rotation

Treatment

Initially, treatment of a 1+ to 2+ instability is conservative and may include transverse friction, muscle strengthening, and proprioceptive exercises. In certain circumstances, for athletes as an example, surgery is indicated for a 2+ instability. In 3+ instability, the preferred treatment is surgical reconstruction. Afterward, the patient should undergo functional rehabilitation.

MEDIAL INSTABILITY IN KNEE EXTENSION

Medial instability in knee extension involves an instability of the knee in the frontal plane in a valgus direction. As is the case with medial instability in slight knee flexion, this instability is the result of valgus trauma or of trauma with a valgus component.

Stability is tested in knee extension. The following structures can be affected:

- 1+ Instability
  1. Posterior oblique ligament (posteromedial corner of the capsule)
  2. Possibly the medial meniscus
  3. Medial collateral ligament (sprain or partial tear)
- 2+ Instability
  1. The same as for 1+ instability
  2. Medial meniscotibial ligament

3. Anterior (and sometimes also posterior) cruciate ligament
- 3+ Instability
  1. The same as for 2+ instability
  2. Posterior cruciate ligament

Clinical Findings

- 1+ Instability
  1. Painful passive valgus test in knee extension
  2. Sometimes a positive McMurray or Steinmann test
- 2+ Instability
  1. The same positive tests as for 1+ instability
  2. Painful passive external rotation of the lower leg
  3. Positive passive valgus test in slight knee flexion
  4. Positive Lachman's test
  5. Positive anterior drawer test in 80° flexion
  6. Positive anterior drawer test in 80° flexion and maximal external rotation
  7. If the posterior cruciate ligament is affected, the anterolateral drawer test will also be positive
- 3+ Instability
  1. The same positive tests as for 2+ instability
  2. Positive tests for the posterior cruciate ligament

Treatment

Initially, treatment of a 1+ to 2+ instability is conservative and may include transverse friction, muscle strengthening, and proprioceptive exercises. In certain circumstances, for athletes as an example, surgery is indicated for a 2+ instability. In 3+ instability, the preferred treatment is surgical reconstruction. Afterward, the patient should undergo functional rehabilitation.

LATERAL INSTABILITY IN SLIGHT KNEE FLEXION

Lateral instability in slight knee flexion involves an instability of the knee in the frontal plane in a varus direction. A lateral instability of the knee is the result of varus trauma or trauma with a varus component, the most common being a varus–flexion–internal rotation trauma.

Stability is tested in slight flexion of the knee (some varus mobility in slight flexion of the knee is physiological). The following structures can be affected:

- 1+ Instability
  1. Lateral meniscotibial ligament
  2. Lateral collateral ligament (sprain or partial tear)
  3. Possibly the lateral meniscus
- 2+ Instability
  1. The same as for 1+ instability
  2. Iliotibial tract
  3. Possibly the anterior or posterior cruciate ligament
- 3+ Instability
  1. The same as for 2+ instability
  2. Lateral collateral ligament (complete tear)
  3. Popliteal arcuate ligament and the tendon of the popliteus muscle
  4. Anterior or posterior cruciate ligament

Clinical Findings

- 1+ Instability
  1. Painful passive internal rotation of the lower leg
  2. Painful passive varus test in slight knee flexion
  3. Sometimes a positive McMurray or Steinmann test
- 2+ Instability
  1. The same positive tests as for 1+ instability
  2. Positive tests for the anterior or posterior cruciate ligament
- 3+ Instability
  1. The same positive tests as for 2+ instability
  2. Positive tests for the anterior and posterior cruciate ligaments

Treatment

Initially, the treatment of a 1+ instability is conservative and may include transverse friction, muscle strengthening, and proprioceptive exercises. In 2+ and 3+ instabilities, the preferred treatment is surgical reconstruction. Afterward, the patient should undergo functional rehabilitation.

LATERAL INSTABILITY IN KNEE EXTENSION

Lateral instability in knee extension involves an instability of the knee in the frontal plane in a varus direction. This instability is also the result of varus trauma or of trauma with a varus component.

Stability is tested in knee extension. The following structures can be affected:

- 1+ Instability
  1. Popliteal arcuate ligament
  2. Lateral meniscotibial ligament
  3. Possibly the lateral meniscus
  4. Lateral collateral ligament (sprain or partial tear)
- 2+ Instability
  1. The same as for 1+ instability
  2. Lateral collateral ligament and the tendon of the popliteus muscle (complete rupture)
  3. Anterior or posterior cruciate ligament (frequent)
- 3+ Instability
  1. The same as for 2+ instability
  2. Anterior and posterior cruciate ligaments and iliotibial tract (complete tear)

Clinical Findings

- 1+ Instability
  1. Painful passive varus test with the knee in extension
  2. Painful passive internal rotation of the lower leg
  3. Sometimes, positive McMurray or Steinmann test
- 2+ Instability
  1. The same positive test as for 1+ instability
  2. Positive tests for the anterior or posterior cruciate ligament
- 3+ Instability
  1. The same positive tests as for 2+ instability
  2. Positive tests for the anterior and posterior cruciate ligaments

Treatment

As is the case with lateral instability in slight flexion of the knee, the treatment of a 1+ instability is conservative and may include transverse friction, muscle strengthening, and proprioceptive exercises. In 2+ and 3+ instabilities, the preferred treatment is surgical reconstruction. Afterward, the patient should undergo functional rehabilitation.

ANTERIOR INSTABILITY

Anterior instability involves a forward instability of the knee in the sagittal plane. An anterior instability can be the result of a hyperextension–internal rotation trauma or of trauma whereby a force acts against the posterior aspect of the lower leg. Usually, it involves a rotation trauma with a valgus or varus component. Immediately after the trauma, severe swelling of the knee often occurs, resulting from bleeding of the synovial membrane. If the anterior cruciate is completely torn, the patient often hears a pop.

The anterior stability of the knee is tested with the knee in 80° flexion as well as in slight flexion (Lachman's test). The lower leg is not rotated during these tests. When the anterior cruciate ligament is torn, an anterolateral rotatory instability often occurs because of the incongruence of the lateral joint surfaces of the tibia and femur. For this reason, the Martens test, which is a combination of the Lachman and pivot shift tests, should also be performed to differentiate a pure anterior instability from an anterolateral instability.

The following structures can be affected:

- 1+ Instability
  1. Anterior cruciate ligament
  2. Often the medial meniscus
- 2+ Instability
  1. The same as for 1+ instability
  2. Medial or lateral meniscotibial ligament (an associated lesion)
  3. Possibly the medial or lateral collateral ligament (associated lesion)
- 3+ Instability
  1. The same as for 2+ instability
  2. Posterior cruciate ligament
  3. Iliotibial tract (in the case of an associated lateral instability)

Clinical Findings

- 1+ Instability
  1. Positive passive hyperextension test
  2. Positive Lachman's test (pathognomonic)
  3. Possibly a positive anterior drawer test in 80° knee flexion
  4. Possibly a positive McMurray or Steinmann test
  5. Possibly a positive Martens test
- 2+ Instability
  1. The same positive tests as for 1+ instability
  2. Painful internal or external rotation of the lower leg

3. Possibly a positive passive valgus or varus test in slight knee flexion
- 3+ Instability
  1. The same positive test as for 2+ instability
  2. Positive tests for the posterior cruciate ligament

Treatment

Initial treatment of a 1+ to 2+ instability is conservative and may include transverse friction, muscle strengthening, and proprioceptive exercises. In 3+ instability, the preferred treatment is surgical reconstruction. Afterward, the patient should undergo functional rehabilitation.

POSTERIOR INSTABILITY

Posterior instability involves a backward instability of the knee in the sagittal plane (Figure 10–29). Solitary posterior instability can occur as the result of "dashboard trauma." (The dashboard trauma is typically the result of a motor vehicle accident in which an individual is thrown forward, hitting the dashboard with the proximal end of the tibia. This causes an enormous posterior translatory force on the knee with resultant rupture of the posterior cruciate ligament.) In most cases, however, the posterior instability is the result of rotation trauma with a valgus or varus component.

When there is a complete tear of the posterior cruciate ligament, a hematoma in the calf often occurs. This happens because the posterior capsule also tears, allowing blood to leak out of the joint.

Posterior instability is tested with the knee in 90° flexion. If this is not possible because of swelling, it can also be tested in about 60° flexion. The following structures can be affected:

- 1+ Instability
  1. Posterior cruciate ligament

- 2+ Instability
  1. Posterior cruciate ligament
  2. Posteromedial or posterolateral capsuloligamentous structures
- 3+ Instability
  1. The same as for 2+ instability
  2. Generally complete ruptures are involved

Clinical Findings

- 1+ Instability
  1. Positive anterolateral drawer test (pathognomonic)
  2. Positive posterior drawer test in 80° flexion
  3. In the presence of the gravity sign (Figure 10–30) there will also be a false-positive anterior drawer test in 80° knee flexion
- 2+ Instability
  1. The same positive tests as for 1+ instability
  2. Positive passive valgus or varus test in knee extension
  3. Positive posterior drawer test in 80° flexion and maximal internal or external rotation
- 3+ Instability
  1. The same as for 2+ instability
  2. Even more movement is noted

Treatment

Initially, treatment of a 1+ to 2+ instability is conservative and may include transverse friction, muscle strengthening, and proprioceptive exercises. In certain circumstances, for athletes as an example, surgery is indicated for a 2+ instability. In 3+ instability, the preferred treatment is surgical reconstruction. Afterward, the patient should undergo functional rehabilitation.

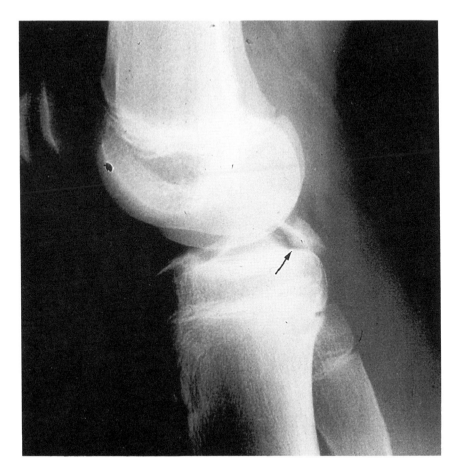

Figure 10–29 Conventional radiograph of a young patient with an avulsion fracture of the tibial plateau at the level of the tibial insertion of the posterior cruciate ligament (arrow).

ANTEROMEDIAL ROTATORY INSTABILITY

Anteromedial rotatory instability involves an instability of the knee in the sagittal plane (anterior subluxation of the medial tibial plateau) and in the transverse plane (external rotation of the tibia in relation to the femur). This form of instability is almost always caused by valgus trauma or valgus trauma with an external rotation component. Usually, an anterolateral rotatory instability occurs as well.

The following structures can be affected:

- 1+ Instability
  1. Medial meniscotibial ligament
  2. Possibly the posterior oblique ligament
  3. Possibly the medial meniscus
  4. Usually the anterior cruciate ligament
- 2+ Instability
  1. Same as for 1+ instability
  2. Posterior oblique ligament

Figure 10–30 Clinical picture showing a posterior subluxation of the right tibia, the so-called gravity sign, resulting from a rupture of the posterior cruciate ligament.

- 3+ Instability
  1. Same as for 2+ instability
  2. Medial collateral ligament
  3. Anterior cruciate ligament

Clinical Findings

- 1+ Instability
  1. Painful passive external rotation of the lower leg
  2. Positive anterior drawer test in 80° flexion and maximal external rotation
  3. Possibly a positive passive valgus test in extension
  4. Possibly a positive Lachman's test
- 2+ Instability
  1. The same positive tests as for 1+ instability
  2. Positive passive valgus test in extension
  3. Possibly a positive Lachman's test

- 3+ Instability
  1. The same positive tests as for 2+ instability
  2. Positive valgus test in slight knee flexion
  3. Positive Lachman's test

Treatment

A 1+ instability is almost always treated conservatively. A 2+ or 3+ instability is almost always treated surgically followed by functional rehabilitative treatment.

ANTEROLATERAL ROTATORY INSTABILITY

Anterolateral rotatory instability is a frequently encountered instability in the sagittal plane (anterior subluxation of the lateral tibial plateau) and in the transverse plane (internal rotation of the tibia in relation to the femur). This form of instability is caused by varus trauma, varus trauma with an internal rotation component, or any trauma in which the anterior cruciate ligament is ruptured.

It is difficult to determine a classification according to the sequence of affected structures in 1+, 2+, and 3+ instabilities. The anterior cruciate ligament is always completely torn. In addition, the lateral structures can be torn, usually involving the lateral or posterior part of the lateral meniscotibial ligament and the iliotibial tract. Sometimes, the anterior part of the meniscotibial ligament is also torn; in this instance, the patient's knee is tender to palpation just distal to the joint space at the level of the lateral aspect of the tibia.

Clinical Findings

The Lachman's test is positive. The passive varus test in extension can be positive, but in slight flexion it is almost always positive. The Martens test is positive and pathognomonic. The pivot shift test is sometimes positive (it is always positive when the patient is under general anesthesia). The anterior drawer test in 50% internal rotation is slightly positive. In maximal internal rotation it is negative as a result of the intact posterior cruciate ligament. On plain films, an avulsion fracture is sometimes visible at the level of the attachment of the capsule at the lateral aspect of the tibia.

Treatment

A 1+ instability is almost always treated conservatively. A 2+ instability is sometimes treated conservatively, and in other cases it is treated surgically. A 3+ instability is almost always treated surgically. Surgical procedures are always followed up with functional rehabilitative treatment.

POSTEROMEDIAL ROTATORY INSTABILITY

Posteromedial rotatory instability occurs in the sagittal plane (posterior subluxation of the medial tibial plateau) and in the transverse plane (internal rotation of the tibia in relation to the femur). Posteromedial rotatory instability is the result of an internal or external rotation trauma, in which the posterior cruciate ligament is also ruptured. A rare variation of this instability is when it is in combination with an anteromedial rotatory instability.

The posterior cruciate ligament and the posteromedial capsuloligamentous structures are always torn. It is difficult to determine a classification according to the sequence of affected structures in 1+, 2+, and 3+ instabilities.

Clinical Findings

Usually, the passive valgus test in extension, as well as in slight flexion, is positive. The anterolateral drawer test is positive. Sometimes, a posterior drawer test in 80° knee flexion and maximal internal rotation is positive.

Treatment

A 1+ or 2+ instability can almost always be successfully treated conservatively. In principle, a 3+ instability is treated surgically. Surgical procedures are always followed up with functional rehabilitative treatment.

POSTEROLATERAL ROTATORY INSTABILITY

Posterolateral rotatory instability is an instability in the sagittal plane (posterior subluxation of the lateral tibial plateau) and in the transverse plane (external rotation of the tibia in relation to the femur). This form of instability is seen more often than the just described posteromedial rotatory instability.

The affected structures include the posterolateral capsuloligamentous structures (the arcuate complex), the posterior cruciate ligament, and, in severe cases, the lateral collateral structures (superficial and deep). It is difficult to determine a classification according to the sequence of affected structures in 1+, 2+, and 3+ instabilities.

Clinical Findings

Usually, the passive varus test in extension, as well as in slight flexion, is positive. The anterolateral drawer test in 90° flexion is positive. The posterior drawer test in 80° knee flexion and maximal external rotation is positive, showing a significant increase in laxity in ruptures of the posterior cruciate ligament.

Treatment

A 1+ or 2+ instability can usually be successfully treated conservatively. In principle, a 3+ instability is treated surgically, followed by functional rehabilitative treatment.

10.3 PATHOLOGY OF THE PATELLOFEMORAL JOINT

SUBLUXATION OF THE PATELLA

Subluxation of the patella can occur traumatically, but this does not happen often. In most cases, there is a chronic lateral subluxation resulting from an incongruence between the form and position of the patella on one side and the patellar groove of the femur on the other side (patellar malalignment). In particular, patella alta (high position), a shallow patellofemoral groove, and dysplasia of the lateral femoral condyle can lead to dislocation or subluxation of the patella.

In 1941 and 1964, Wiberg[13] and Baumgartl[14] described the various types of patellas (Figure 10–31). The first two types are the most stable, with well-formed medial and lateral patellar facets. The other types are less stable and undergo uneven forces during activities, often resulting in lateral subluxation or dislocation.

When the knee is extended from a flexed position, the patella moves from its lateral and internally rotated position in a medial direction. Particularly in the last part of its trajectory (20° to 0°), the patella again moves laterally. It is usually just in this phase that the symptoms occur.

In patients with malalignment, an increased quadriceps angle (Q angle) is usually seen (Figure 10–32; the Q angle is the acute angle formed by two imaginary intersecting lines: one that connects the anterior superior iliac spine with the middle of the patella, and one that connects the middle of the patella with the middle of the upper aspect of the tibial tuberosity). In the medical literature, there is much disagreement as to the significance of the Q angle. Clinically, it has become less important in the last several years. The Q angle is neutralized when the knee is flexed farther than 30°. Thus the risk that the patella will subluxate or dislocate decreases when the knee is beyond 30° flexion.

Recent MR studies of patellar movement in healthy subjects and in patellar subluxations demonstrate that the greatest deviation in movement can occur between 10° and 0° knee flexion. In general, lateral movement of the patella is greater in women than in men. This is particularly obvious when the knee is moving into extension from a position of 20° flexion. This could explain why the subluxating patella is a disorder that is seen most often in women in the later stages of adolescence. Often, the subluxation occurs bilaterally. In many cases, the disorder is familial.

Subluxation of the patella is seen more often in cases of general hypermobility. If there is a patella alta (high position of the patella), the chance of subluxation increases with the height of the patella. This relationship exists because the high patella enters the groove too late during flexion of the knee or leaves the groove too early during extension.

Electromyographic studies have demonstrated that clear aberrations of the quadriceps muscle occur in conjunction with chronically subluxating patellas. Floyd et al[15] propose that there is a primary muscular defect in many cases that is the cause of this chronic subluxation.

When there is decreased strength of the quadriceps, full extension of the knee will not be achieved when running, resulting in a shortening of the hamstrings and leading to an increase in the extension of the ankle joint. A compensatory hyperpronation of the foot takes place, leaving the subject vulnerable to all the possible consequences (see the section on achillodynia in Chapter 17).

Isometric contraction of the quadriceps in an extended knee restricts the lateral tilting of the patella and moves the patella either medially or laterally; this varies among individuals. After a period of time, changes in pressure against the various patellar facets can

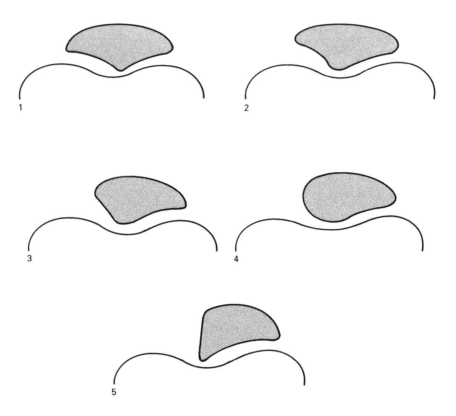

Figure 10–31 Form variations of the patella as described by Wiberg and Baumgartl. The medial facet becomes more and more vertical. Type 5 is termed the "hunter's cap" form.

---

damage the cartilage, causing patellar chondromalacia. Another common consequence of a chronic subluxating patella is an insertion tendopathy of part of the patellar insertions of the extensor mechanism. This can be supra- as well as infrapatellar and medio- or lateropatellar.

Acute dislocation of the patella is easy to differentiate from chronic subluxation. In acute dislocation, the patella does not reposition. The patient has severe pain and is unable to bend the knee (refer to the section, Dislocation of the Patella). In cases of chronic subluxation, the patella generally subluxates and immediately "goes back into place" (Figure 10–33). Habitual subluxation can result from an acute dislocation.

Differential Diagnosis

- Patellar chondromalacia (patients complain particularly of pain in more than 30° knee flexion)
- OCD of the patella (plain films confirm the diagnosis)
- Sinding-Larsen-Johansson disease (this is an aseptic bone necrosis of the apex of the patella)
- Prepatellar bursitis (there is local tenderness, and there may be swelling that fluctuates under the palpating fingers)
- Infrapatellar bursitis, superficial or deep (there is local tenderness, and there may be swelling that fluctuates under the palpating fingers)

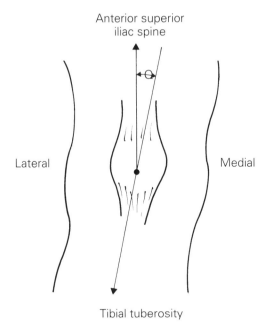

Figure 10–32 Q angle.

- Osgood-Schlatter disease (this is an aseptic bone necrosis of the tibial tuberosity; the patient complains of pain distal to the patella; plain films confirm the diagnosis)

- Patella (bi)partita (the patient complains of pain lateral or proximolateral to the patella; plain films are diagnostic)

- Fracture or pseudoarthrosis of the patella

- Various patellar insertion tendopathies (in particular, pain is provoked during resisted extension of the knee; palpation confirms the diagnosis)

- Inflammation of the infrapatellar fat pad, also termed Hoffitis (there is local tenderness)

- Patella alta (This is a condition of an unstable patella, in that the patella no longer lies in the corresponding femoral groove. On inspection, the so-called camel-back knee is noted. When looking at the knee from lateral, one normally sees only one convexity at the level of the patella. In patella alta, two convexities are visible: The first one is the patella, and the more distal one is the infrapatellar fat pad.)

- Meniscus lesion (keep in mind the attachment of the extensor mechanism to the menisci, which can result in provocation of pain during resisted testing)

Clinical Findings

The patient complains of pain at the medial or lateral side of the patella. If there is a supra- or infrapatellar insertion tendopathy, the patient will also complain of pain at the level of the base or apex of the patella. The pain occurs particularly in the last 20° of extension or in the first 20° of flexion. After 20° flexion, the pain decreases because the patella can no

Figure 10–33 Axial conventional radiograph of the patella in a patient showing obvious hypoplasia of the lateral facets (arrows) with shallow femoral grooves.

longer subluxate. If there is also chondromalacia of the patella, pain can occur in positions of more than 30° flexion.

On inspection, usually the Q angle is larger than 15°. Occasionally it is less than 15°. Often, the patella appears to be "looking" in a medial direction; this is the so-called squinting patella. A severe form is called kissing patellae.

The position of the hip, knee, and foot can alter the Q angle, leading to an abnormal movement pattern of the patella. The most frequent cause is femoral anteversion. This can be assessed by a simple test: The therapist grasps the ankles of the supine patient and rotates the patient's hips from a neutral position (with extended knees) internally and externally. In the case of femoral anteversion, the internal rotation is greater than the external rotation.

Another often seen cause of an altered Q angle is hyperpronation of the foot. This can also be easily determined by the presence of a greater amount of movement of the first metatarsal in relation to the second metatarsal in a plantar to dorsal direction. The normal movement excursion during this passive test is not more than 5 mm dorsally and 5 mm plantarly. If the amount of motion is greater, hyperpronation is indicated.

The active and passive movements of the patella are carefully assessed with the patient standing and lying down. Often, the patella has an abnormal range of motion in a lateral direction (Figure 10–34; for more details, refer to the "Clinical Findings" section under "Chondromalacia of the Patella," below).

Treatment

The treatment is primarily conservative. By the use of a special brace or taping, the abnormal lateral movement of the patella can be influenced but not actually corrected. Often, the connecting fibers between the patella and the iliotibial tract are too short, but they can be manually stretched (refer to Chapter 11). An insertion tendopathy can be treated with transverse friction. A shortened rectus femoris muscle can be stretched. Shortened hamstrings are treated with stretching exercises. The patient should perform all stretching exercises several times daily at home.

Muscle-strengthening exercises are also an important part of the treatment program. Emphasis should be placed on the vastus medialis obliquus, vastus medialis, and quadriceps muscles. These exercises can only be initiated when resisted knee extension is painless, however.

If the symptoms cannot be resolved by conservative therapy, surgery may be indicated. The results of many surgical procedures are not favorable. Thorough evaluation of patellar movement by means of CT or MR imaging should be done before the decision for surgery is made. This will help determine the exact structures at fault so that unnecessary or inappropriate procedures can be avoided.

DISLOCATION OF THE PATELLA

Dislocation of the patella is one of the more commonly seen disorders of the knee. Approximately one fourth of all patients with this problem visit the physician with the patella still in its dislocated position. The knee is held in flexion, and the patella is visible and palpable next to the lateral femoral condyle. Medial dislocations of the patella are rare. This disorder is seen more often in men than in women.

Usually the patients describe an incident when the patella slipped in and out of place. Although many patients can attribute the dislocation to an accident, it appears that most of the time there was an abrupt, unguarded flexion of the knee, in which the quadriceps were suddenly forced to contract eccentrically. In rare instances, the patella dislocates as the result of a laterally directed force against the medial aspect of the patella.

In a dysplastic patella, once the patella has dislocated it becomes more susceptible to recurrent dislocations with certain movements. This is termed a recurring patellar dislocation. The patella dislocates during normal

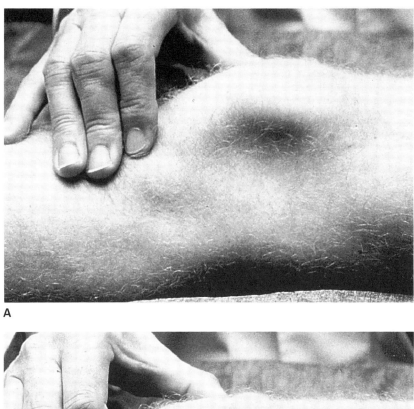

A

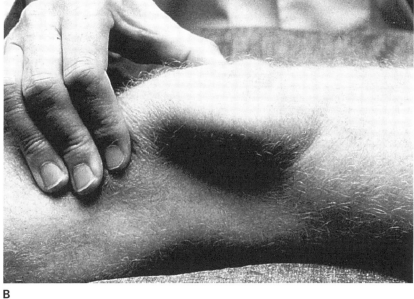

B

Figure 10–34 Patient with recurrent patellar subluxation (**A**) who has severe laxity of the patella in a lateral direction (**B**).

movement and spontaneously relocates. Often the patient has a congenital hypermobility of all the joints in combination with patellar dysplasia.

Predisposing factors for a dislocating patella include the following:

- patellofemoral dysplasia (refer to the section, Subluxation of the Patella, for the types of patella identified by Wiberg[13] and Baumgartl[14]

- patella alta (refer to the differential diagnosis section under Subluxation of the Patella)
- malalignment of the hip (femur), knee (tibia), or foot (pes plano valgus)
- hypermobility syndrome

Clinical Findings

The patient has severe pain during the dislocation and while the patella is still in the dislocated position. In most cases, an acute hemarthrosis occurs. There is tenderness to palpation at the level of the medial retinaculum, which is ruptured during the dislocation. The medial patellar facet can also be tender to palpation as the result of a subchondral lesion. The lateral femoral condyle is often tender to palpation as a result of osteochondral damage, which usually occurs during the spontaneous or improperly performed manual reduction.

The apprehension test, performed only when the patella is no longer dislocated, is positive. With the knee in 10° flexion, the examiner moves the patella laterally with both thumbs. In so doing, the patient experiences pain and does not allow further movement. In spite of a negative test, if a dislocation is still suspected, the patient is asked to flex the knee while the patella is pushed laterally. As a result of pain, the patient will abort the attempt to actively flex the knee. If this test is positive, the diagnosis of patellar dislocation is confirmed.

Radiologic examination, particularly a tangential patellar view, is important to detect the presence of osteochondral fractures. Arthroscopy is indicated when the diagnosis is not clear or when damage to the cartilage is suspected.

Treatment

In the case of an actual dislocation, the patella must be repositioned. This has to be done carefully because otherwise the chance for an osteochondral lesion of the femoral condyle is great. The flexed knee is supported by an assistant, and the patella is laterally fixated and lifted slightly. Then the knee is slowly extended. When the knee is almost extended, the patella glides automatically into place.

If there are complications, or when loose fragments are removed during arthroscopy, the knee should be treated as described under the section, Subluxation of the Patella. In this case, more attention is given to the patient's pain and swelling during the rehabilitation process.

CHONDROMALACIA OF THE PATELLA

Chondromalacia literally means softening of the cartilage; *chondropathy* is a term for pathology of the cartilage. The term *chondropathy* is best used for the clinical syndrome of anterior patellar knee pain until, by means of arthroscopy, arthrotomy, or microscopic examination, a diagnosis of chondromalacia of the patella can be confirmed (Figure 10–35).

Classification

The main classification of the various stages of chondromalacia is based on the first classifications of Aleman,[16] described in 1928. His classifications were further modified by such authors as Insall[17] and, finally, Bently.[18]

Stage 1: Localized softening of the cartilage, swelling and fibrillation or fissure formation in an area smaller than 0.5 cm

Stage 2: Fibrillation or fissure formation in an area of 0.5 to 1 cm

Stage 3: Fibrillation or fissure formation in an area of 1 to 2 cm

Stage 4: Fibrillation or fissure formation in an area larger than 2 cm or without visible subchondral bone

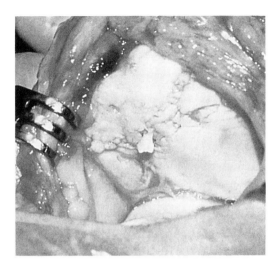

Figure 10–35 Surgical photograph showing severe signs of chondromalacia of the patella with fragmentation of the joint cartilage in a young basketball player.

Etiology

Most cases of chondromalacia of the patella are seen in adolescents. Almost all authors describe a traumatic etiology. Both acute and chronic traumas are considered. The following conditions are all considered primary causes of chronic microtrauma:

- incongruence in geometry between the patella and the corresponding femoral joint surface
- form variations of the patella (with subluxation of the patella as a result; Figure 10–36).
- osteochondral ridges
- hypo- and hyperpressure in the patellofemoral joint

In a prospective study, Insall[17] found an abnormal Q angle in 50%, and patella alta in 30%, of all patients who had undergone surgery for chondromalacia.

A consistent point of discussion is whether chondromalacia is the result of too much lateral hyperpressure or too little medial hypopressure. Some researchers conclude that in most of the cases the lateral side is affected, while the others indicate that it is the medial facet that is more often affected.

Using pressure-sensitive film, Huberti and Hayes[19] researched the contact pressure of the various patellar facets with the femur.

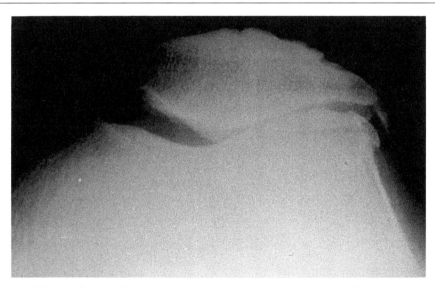

Figure 10–36 "Sunrise" view of the patella showing a combination of chondromalacia with a laterally subluxating patella.

This was done in 20°, 30°, 60°, 90°, and 120° knee flexion. If there is no abnormal Q angle, the pressure on the medial and lateral facets of the patella should be almost equal. The most pressure occurs in 90° knee flexion and is approximately 6.5 times the body weight (Figure 10–37). A 10° larger Q angle results in increased pressure of all the facets, and in 20° flexion there is 45% more pressure. A 10° smaller Q angle in some knees results in decreased pressure on part of the lateral facet; this decreased pressure was always coupled with an increase in pressure in another facet (50% more in 20° flexion). This means that the site of increased pressure in abnormal Q angles causes an unpredictable pattern of increased or decreased cartilage pressure elsewhere in the patella. These findings are significant when surgery that would alter the Q angle is being considered.

Pain in Chondromalacia of the Patella

Cartilage is not innervated. Thus there are many theories described in the medical literature about the occurrence of pain in chondromalacia of the patella. Some authors believe the joint capsule to be responsible for the pain, but biopsies have rarely found a synovitis.[17] Some authors state that the increased pressure of the innervated subchondral bone causes the pain. This, too, remains an open question as long as the discussion of hypo- and hyperpressure is unresolved.

It has been postulated that a painful and too-tight retinaculum is the cause of pain in chondromalacia. With age, the retinaculum also becomes more stiff and less elastic, which means that with increasing age more symptoms will arise. Just the opposite is the case, however.

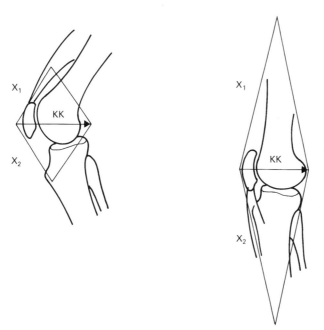

Figure 10–37 Schematic diagram of compression force (KK) in the knee. The compression force decreases when the knee is moved from flexion to extension.

Relationship with Arthrosis

There is also much disagreement in the medical literature regarding the relationship between patellar chondromalacia and arthrosis. Some believe that chondromalacia is a forewarning of arthrosis of the patellofemoral joint. We think that this is unlikely, however, because arthrosis of the patellofemoral joint is rarely seen in elderly people, whereas chondromalacia is seen often, particularly in young people. Patients with arthrosis of the patellofemoral joint seldom indicate that they had knee problems in their adolescence.[17,18]

Relationship with Instability/ Hypermobility

In many instances, chondromalacia occurs as the result of a long-standing posterior instability of the knee. Because in this condition the tibia "hangs" slightly posteriorly, more pressure is exerted on the patellar cartilage.

There is a strange phenomenon experienced by some young children who complain of pain, particularly at night, that is found to be the result of transient chondromalacia. In these cases, the functional examination is usually negative, but often such patients are found to have a hypermobility of the patella in a lateral direction. Generally, these children react well to children's aspirin, and after several months or more the symptoms disappear. This condition should be differentiated from (extremely rare) bone tumors, some of which also cause pain particularly at night.

Anterior knee pain is frequently seen in girls during puberty; this is the so-called young girl's knee syndrome. The cause is unknown, and the symptoms eventually disappear without treatment. This can sometimes take years, however. For this group of patients, surgery has devastating results. It is important to convince the parents of these patients that the problem will eventually disappear and that operative treatment usually only leads to further surgery.

Consequences of Chondromalacia of the Patella

The most frequent consequence of chondromalacia of the patella is an insertion tendopathy at one of the insertion sites of the extensor mechanism at the patella. This can be supra-, infra-, medio-, or lateropatellar.

Differential Diagnosis

Refer to the differential diagnosis section, Subluxation of the Patella.

Clinical Findings

The patient complains of pain at the level of the patella. Sometimes the pain is experienced behind the patella or around the patella, particularly superomedial and medial. In a number of cases, pain is also felt laterally. Prolonged sitting with the knee in 90° flexion is painful in many instances (termed "moviegoer's sign"). The same is true for lying with flexed knees. The pain disappears when the knee is straightened. Descending and ascending stairs can be painful.

If the pain is experienced mostly infrapatellar, there is likely to be an apexitis of the patella, also termed "jumper's knee." An apexitis of the patella can be a consequence of chondromalacia. This pain is often activity related but can also occur at rest.

Some patients complain of a "giving way" of the knee, which can occur with or without accompanying pain. Another frequently described symptom is the feeling as if the knee locks; this is not a true locking, however, and is thus termed pseudolocking.

Functional Examination

Slight synovial effusion of the knee can occur, especially after activities. If there is severe swelling that disappears after 1 day, there is likely to be cartilage damage not on the patella but in the femoral groove. In these cases, when the patient stands and the examiner exerts pressure against the patella, there is an obvious painful arc during active flexion. These patients respond well to arthroscopy (often better than with patellar cartilage damage).

Inspection while the patient is first standing, then walking, and finally in a supine position can bring many significant factors to light. Positioning of the hips, lower legs, and feet can reveal, for example, torsion of the femur, torsion of the lower leg, or a tendency to flat feet. These are but a few of the conditions that can influence the Q angle and, with it, the movement pattern of the patella. Frequently there is atrophy, particularly of the vastus medialis obliquus and vastus medialis muscles (it can often be determined, through the use of electromyography, that the strength of the quadriceps is diminished).

While standing on the affected leg, the patient is asked to flex the knee to 90° and to indicate whether pain is experienced. In most instances, pain is felt at about 30° flexion. Then the movement is repeated while the examiner palpates the knee. Painful crepitation is a particularly significant finding. In some cases, there is a painful arc. This is a result of a small local lesion either at the back of the patella or on the femoral condyle. An abrupt angular change in patellar trajectory usually indicates aberrations in the form of the patella or of the femoral gliding surface.

With the patient lying down, the course of patellar movement is assessed and compared with that observed in standing. Motion of the patella is then specifically tested: The patella is moved in distal, proximal, medial, and lateral directions. In patella alta (high position of the patella, which can be radiographically confirmed), the distal movement can be limited. In an abnormally large lateral joint facet of the patella, the medial motion of the patella can be limited, and the lateral movement is increased.

In about 30° flexion, the patella is pushed distally (Test 9.33 in the functional examination), and the patient is asked to contract the quadriceps. Normally, the patient is able to move the patella proximally against resistance from the examiner without pain. In many instances, however, this test is performed with the knee in full extension; in this case pain is almost always provoked, even in nonaffected knees! From different positions of flexion, resistance against extension is performed. In many cases, this test is painful. When muscle length is assessed, there may be a shortening of the rectus femoris muscle.

Treatment

Almost all authors are in agreement that treatment should initially be conservative. Based on the findings in the clinical examination, attempts should be made to correct static posture. For example, this can be achieved by means of a correcting orthotic for a flat foot, by which the patella no longer "squints" (Figure 10–38). If there are also problems with subluxation of the patella, the therapeutic measures discussed under "Subluxation of the Patella" (above) should be followed.

If resisted knee extension is painful, the most tender site is located by specific palpation. Transverse friction massage offers quick pain relief. The friction treatment in these cases should last for 10 to 15 minutes. Most patients with pain during resisted extension of the knee have a shortening of the rectus femoris muscle. This condition can be treated by the use of stretching exercises. The patient should perform these exercises several times a day at home.

After 6 months of conservative therapy if there is no improvement, arthroscopy is indicated. In the presence of a loose body in the joint, arthroscopy should be performed first, and followed by conservative rehabilitation.

PATELLA (BI)PARTITA

Patella (bi)partita is usually a coincidental finding on plain films (Figures 10–39 and 10–40). The lateral upper pole of the patella appears to be separate from the rest of the pa-

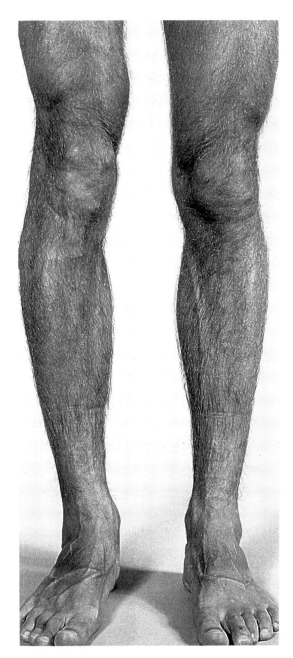

Figure 10–38 Clinical picture of a right-sided flat foot with "squinting" patella.

tella, but it is connected with fibrous tissue. In the same way, a patella tripartita can be found, in which the lateral upper pole of the patella consists of two parts connected by fi-

brous tissue. Even a patella multipartita is possible; in this instance, the medial upper pole usually also has a fibrous connection with the rest of the patella. Occasionally,

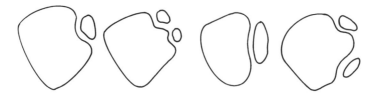

Figure 10–39 Various forms of patella bipartita and tripartita.

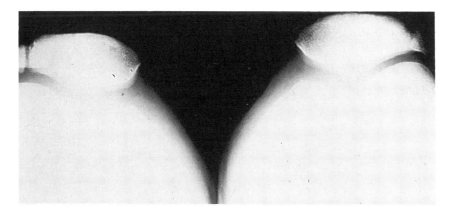

Figure 10–40 Axial conventional radiograph of the patellae. Patella bipartita is visible on the right (left on the film).

these anatomic variations can cause symptoms in athletes. In the case of patella (bi)partita, there is too much play between the different parts of the patella.

Stress fractures should be considered in the differential diagnosis. There can also be a pseudoarthrosis, which is usually lateral, because the lateral aspect of the patella is hypovascular or avascular.

Clinical Findings

Usually, the patient complains of pain at the proximolateral aspect of the patella. The functional examination is usually negative unless other disorders of the patella are present, such as chondromalacia, chronic subluxation, or an insertion tendopathy. There is significant local tenderness. After trauma, a fracture of the patella should be ruled out through radiologic examination.

Treatment

Treatment consists of an injection of local anesthetic. In stubborn cases, an injection with a corticosteroid can be given. In this instance, the patient should refrain from significant activity, particularly sports, for 2 weeks.

IRRITATION OF THE INFRAPATELLAR FAT PAD (HOFFITIS)

Hoffitis involves a painful swelling as the result of edema, hypertrophy, or fibrosis of the infrapatellar fat pad. This rare disorder usually occurs as a complication of other knee pathology, usually chondromalacia, or it can occur from direct trauma. In some cases, there appears to be no other underlying knee pathology, and there was no prior trauma; this is seen in women and is called the premenstrual fat pad syndrome. Too often, the infrapatellar fat pad is mistakenly held responsible for knee symptoms.

Clinical Findings

The patient complains of pain when ascending and descending stairs, when squatting, during twisting activities with the lower leg, and when hyperextending the knee.

Functional Examination

Initially, the functional examination is negative, and there is only tenderness on palpation of the swollen fat pad medial and lateral to the patellar ligament. Palpation is performed with the patient's knee in extension, and results are compared with palpation on the nonaffected side. In later stages, passive hyperextension is also painful.

Treatment

If the lesion occurred as the result of trauma, decreasing sports activities for several weeks is sufficient. The fat pad heals quickly because it is well vascularized. If the lesion is the result of another knee problem, the primary disorder should be treated first; usually, the Hoffitis disappears on its own. In severe cases of the premenstrual fat pad syndrome, the infrapatellar fat pad is surgically removed.

10.4 PATHOLOGY OF THE BURSAE

SUPERFICIAL AND DEEP INFRAPATELLAR BURSITIS

The superficial infrapatellar bursa lies between the patellar ligament and the skin; the deep infrapatellar bursa lies between the patellar ligament and the tibia. Inflammation of one of these bursae can occur as the result of chronic mechanical irritation (Figure 10–41) during such activities as kneeling; this disorder is sometimes called "nun's knee." It may also be caused by direct trauma. In the latter instance, there is usually some slight bleeding in the bursa.

Differential Diagnosis

- Infrapatellar insertion tendopathy
- Osgood-Schlatter disease
- Chondromalacia of the patella
- Sinding-Larsen-Johansson disease (juvenile osteochondrosis of the patellar apex)

Clinical Findings

The patient complains of pain at the anterior aspect of the knee, usually just distal to the patella. This pain occurs particularly during compression. In some cases, moderate to severe swelling is visible.

Functional Examination

The functional examination is usually negative; sometimes maximal passive flexion of the knee is painful. Resisted knee extension can also be painful if there is swelling of the deep infrapatellar bursa. If this is the case, resisted knee extension with the knee positioned in end-range flexion is much more painful than when performed with the knee in 20° to 30° flexion.

There is tenderness to palpation just distal to the patella. Palpation can be used to differentiate between a superficial infrapatellar and a deep infrapatellar bursitis. In a deep infrapatellar bursitis, palpation distal to the

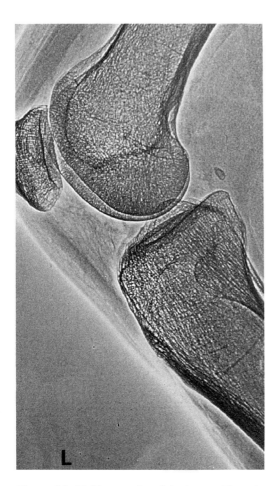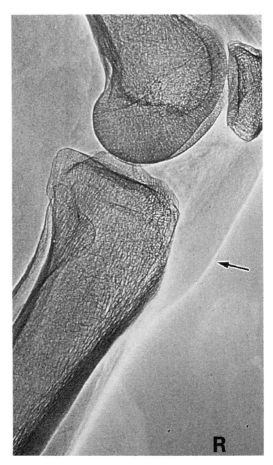

Figure 10–41 Xerography of the knees. There is a superficial infrapatellar bursitis on the right; the local swelling is visible (arrow).

patella (particularly over the patellar ligament) will be much more painful with the knee in extension than with the knee in maximal flexion.

Treatment

If there is obvious swelling, it should be aspirated. Injection with 2 mL of local anesthetic is the most effective therapy. This can be given immediately after the aspiration. In this instance, the knee should be wrapped to keep the swelling from recurring. If the results are unsatisfactory or there is recur-

rence, injection with a solution of local anesthetic and corticosteroid is indicated. If the bursitis continues to recur, surgical resection is indicated.

PREPATELLAR BURSITIS

The prepatellar bursa lies between the skin and the anterior aspect of the patella. Inflammation of this bursa can occur as a result of either acute or chronic trauma. Chronic irritation of the bursa can especially be caused by activities in which the individual is habitually

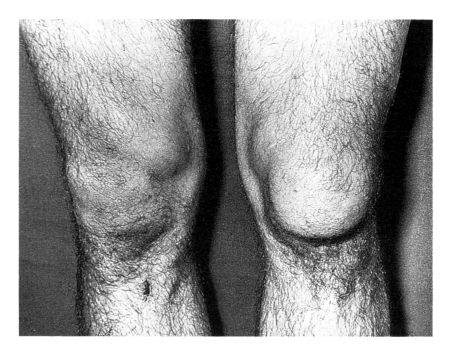

Figure 10–42 Clinical view of prepatellar bursitis of the left knee.

on hands and knees. This form of bursitis is often called "carpet-layer's knee."

Clinical Findings

The patient complains of pain at the anterior aspect of the knee, particularly during compression. Sometimes, there is a visible swelling on the patella (Figure 10–42); in this instance, the consistency of the swelling is fluctuating.

Functional Examination

The functional examination is usually negative, but in cases of swelling passive knee flexion can be painful.

Treatment

If there is obvious swelling, it should be aspirated. Injection with local anesthetic is the most effective therapy. This can be given immediately after the aspiration. In this instance, the knee should be wrapped to keep the swelling from recurring. If the results are unsatisfactory or there is recurrence, injection with a solution of local anesthetic and corticosteroid is indicated. If the bursitis continues to recur, surgical resection is indicated.

SUPERFICIAL PES ANSERINUS BURSITIS

At the level of the superficial pes anserinus, various bursae can become inflamed from chronic irritation. This can involve a bursa between the medial collateral ligament and superficial pes anserinus or, in principle, any of the bursae lying between the various tendons of the superficial pes anserinus. This form of bursitis is most often seen in swimmers and in long-distance runners who have recently taken up the sport.

Clinical Findings

The patient complains of pain at the anteromedial aspect of the knee just distal to the joint space. Sometimes, there is obvious swelling along with warmth and redness. In most cases, the swelling is only minimal with a mildly fluctuating consistency.

Functional Examination

The functional examination is almost always negative. Because of this, it is easy to differentiate between a tendinitis (where resisted tests provoke pain) and a bursitis of the superficial pes anserinus. In cases of doubt, a trial of transverse friction can be performed to the most painful site of the superficial pes anserinus. If the patient's pain increases, there is probably a bursitis in this region.

Treatment

If there is obvious swelling, it should be aspirated. Injection with local anesthetic is the most effective therapy. This can be given immediately after the aspiration. In this instance, the knee should be wrapped to keep the swelling from recurring. If the results are unsatisfactory or there is recurrence, injection with a solution of local anesthetic and corticosteroid is indicated. If the bursitis continues to recur, surgical resection is indicated.

MEDIAL COLLATERAL LIGAMENT BURSITIS

A medial collateral ligament bursa is a small bursa that lies under the medial collateral ligament. There are five possible locations for this bursa:

1. between the ligament and the joint capsule proximal to the medial meniscus, to which it is not connected, and reaching as far as the medial femoral epicondyle
2. between the ligament and the proximal part of the medial meniscus
3. between the ligament and the meniscus
4. just distal of the meniscus
5. between the ligament and the tibia

This lesion is often mistaken for a meniscus lesion or a lesion of the medial meniscotibial ligament. In a medial collateral bursitis, however, there is no trauma in the patient history, and usually the patient is older than 35 years.

Clinical Findings

The patient complains of pain at the medial aspect of the knee at the level of the joint space.

Functional Examination

The functional examination is negative; thus lesions of the medial meniscotibial and medial collateral ligaments are ruled out. There is tenderness to palpation at the level of the medial joint space or just proximal or distal to it.

Treatment

Injection with local anesthetic is the most effective therapy. If the results are unsatisfactory or there is recurrence, injection with a solution of local anesthetic and corticosteroid is indicated. In most patients, the symptoms disappear within 4 weeks. If the bursitis continues to recur, arthroscopy is indicated.

ILIOTIBIAL TRACT FRICTION SYNDROME

An iliotibial tract friction syndrome is a typical sports lesion, seen particularly in long-distance runners and bicycle racers. The cause is friction of the iliotibial tract over the prominent lateral femoral epicondyle. Friction occurring in this region can lead to either an irritation of the bursa between the iliotibial tract and the lateral femoral condyle or to a local tendinitis.

In long-distance runners, the disorder particularly occurs when training takes place in hilly or mountainous terrain. Especially during running downhill, the knee is held in slightly more flexion, during which the iliotibial tract has more intense contact with the lateral femoral epicondyle. Because of a varus position of the knee or the calcaneus, the iliotibial tract is placed on stretch, creating a predisposing condition to this syndrome. The same can occur by constantly running on one side of the road (which is usually slightly curved); on the left side of the road varus stress occurs at the left knee, on the right side of the road at the right knee.

In bicycle racers, the cause of the symptoms can usually be traced to incorrect adjustment for leg length in relation to the frame of the bike or the use of pedal devices that fix the shoe on the pedal, thereby inhibiting the normal rotation motion in the knee during flexion and extension.

Differential Diagnosis

- Sprain of the lateral collateral ligament
- Sprain of the lateral meniscotibial ligament
- Insertion tendopathy of the biceps femoris muscle
- Insertion tendopathy of the popliteus muscle

Clinical Findings

The patient complains of pain at the lateral side of the knee. Usually, the pain cannot be precisely located; in many cases there is radiating pain to just distal of the joint space. In severe cases, the pain is so sharp that the patient cannot walk normally. Running aggravates the pain; the longer the patient runs, the more the pain increases. At some point, further running is impossible. The pain increases when running downhill. Pain also increases when the length of the stride increases (during downhill running, the stride lengthens). In some patients, a local, sometimes crepitating, swelling is palpable.

Functional Examination

The basic functional examination is negative. Active or passive extension of the knee from 90° flexion, while the examiner exerts pressure against the lateral femoral epicondyle, is painful between about 40° and 30° flexion. This test can also be performed in standing (Figure 10–43). The patient affirms that this is the exact same pain as experienced during running or biking.

Treatment

In the acute stage it is impossible to perform sports activities, and rest is indicated until the patient is again able to run or bike without pain. Activities that place an abnormal load on the knee and training in hilly terrain should be avoided. In runners, sometimes it is helpful to shorten the length of stride. When running on the road, regularly changing from the left to the right side of the road is important.

If, in static posture, deviations of the knee or foot are discovered, an attempt can be made to influence this through orthotics. Usually a lateral wedge can be temporarily placed in the shoe to correct the varus position of the calcaneus or knee. When there is hyperpronation of one or both feet, special running shoes or functional orthotics are recommended. If a metal foot plate is used, bicycle racers are advised to remove it or to enlarge the groove so that during pedaling the knee can rotate. Toe clips are usually less of a problem, but these should also be adjusted or removed if they cause undue interference with normal motion in the knee.

In stubborn cases, an injection of corticosteroid can be given, if necessary mixed with local anesthetic. This injection also helps confirm the diagnosis because, in many instances, it is the only possible way to differentiate between a bursitis and a tendinitis. If the pain symptoms are caused by a bursitis, the physician will not feel resistance from the needle at the moment the patient experiences pain during the injection. When the tendon is the painful structure, the physician will feel a firm resistance as the needle contacts this structure. Sometimes, surgery is indicated.

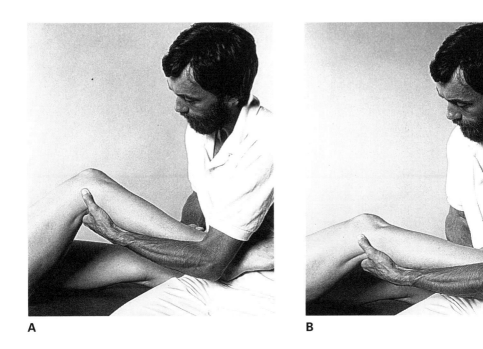

A   **B**

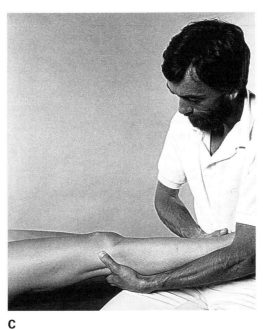

C

Figure 10–43 Positive tests in an iliotibial tract friction syndrome. (**A**) With the patient supine, the examiner places the knee in about 90° flexion. (**B**) The examiner slowly extends the patient's knee while exerting pressure against the lateral femoral epicondyle; the typical pain is provoked between 40° and 30° flexion. (**C**) At less than 30° flexion, the pain disappears again. Thus there is a painful arc during flexion. (**D** and **E**) This test also can be given with the patient standing.

D

E

BAKER CYST

Up to six different bursae are found at the posteromedial aspect of the knee. The two most clinically important are the bursa between the capsule and the medial head of the gastrocnemius, and the bursa between the medial head of the gastrocnemius and the tendon of the semimembranosus.

These and other bursae can not only be connected to each other, but also have contact with the knee joint. The latter case is termed a Baker cyst (Figure 10–44). Usually a Baker cyst is asymptomatic and is a coincidental finding during a rarely performed knee arthrogram (Figure 10–45).

In a synovial effusion of the knee, this cyst can fill up and eventually become painful. Sometimes the cyst becomes so large that it protrudes through the muscle fascia, partly ending up between the muscles of the calf. In rheumatoid arthritis, a Baker cyst can be-

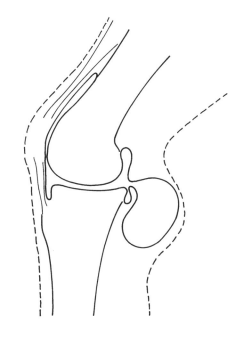

Figure 10–44 Baker cyst.

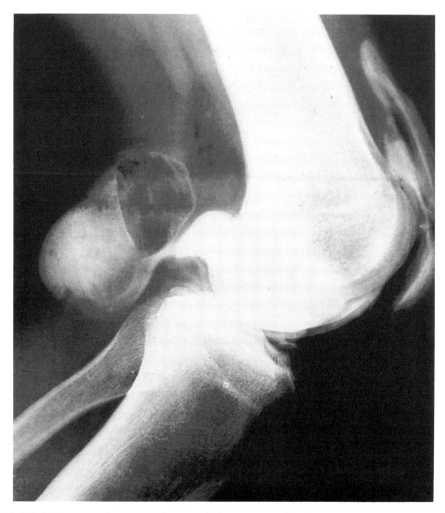

Figure 10–45 Arthrogram demonstrating an obvious connection between the posterior part of the joint cavity and the semimembranosus bursa. As a result, this cavity fills with air and radiopaque medium after an intraarticular injection.

come very large and lead to venous obstruction or a compression neuropathy of the tibial nerve. A Baker cyst can rupture in children as well as in adults. In children, this usually involves a pathologically altered Baker cyst caused by juvenile rheumatoid arthritis.

Differential Diagnosis

Particularly in men, and especially during resisted flexion of the knee, a swelling just proximal to the popliteal fossa can often be seen. This swelling is located just lateral to the tendon of the semitendinosus. By means of palpation, the examiner will find it to be the muscle belly of the semimembranosus. This swelling is not clinically significant, does not cause symptoms, and probably results from a local laxity of the fascia.

Clinical Findings

The patient complains of a painful and tight feeling at the back of the knee. In some cases, there is a visible, round swelling in the popliteal fossa. This swelling has an elastic feeling. Sometimes the swelling is the size of a tennis ball.

Functional Examination

The functional examination reveals a painful active flexion of the knee. Passive flexion is also painful and is slightly limited. Maximal extension of the knee can be painful as well. Clinical findings of an acute rupture of the Baker cyst are similar to those in a tear of the gastrocnemius muscle.

Treatment

Most cases of Baker cyst only lead to symptoms caused by effusion of the knee joint resulting from an articular disorder. In these cases, treatment should be primarily focused on the articular disorder. A primary symptomatic Baker cyst should be aspirated. If it continues to recur, surgical resection is indicated.

10.5 PATHOLOGY OF THE MUSCLE–TENDON UNIT

PARAPATELLAR INSERTION TENDOPATHY

A parapatellar insertion tendopathy is seen almost exclusively in athletes and is the result of primary or secondary overuse. Primary overuse is diagnosed as the cause of an insertion tendopathy when no other pathology of the knee can be found, such as a chronic lateral subluxation of the patella or chondromalacia of the patella. Secondary overuse is when the insertion tendopathy is the direct result of other knee pathologies. This disorder concerns an insertion tendopathy of part of the structures that attach to the medial and lateral aspect of the patella, the so-called quadriceps expansion. This quadriceps expansion includes various parts of the extensor mechanism and the joint capsule.

Clinical Findings

Patients most often complain of pain at the level of the medial upper pole of the patella even though, in principle, all other parts of the quadriceps expansion may be affected. Differentiation can be made among the classic clinical stages of tendinitis. Resisted extension of the knee is painful in stages 3 and 4; in stages 1 and 2, resisted extension is only painful when tested immediately after the patient performs the pain-provoking activity. Often, there is a shortening of the rectus femoris muscle. Palpation can determine the exact site of the lesion.

Treatment

Transverse friction and stretching exercises are usually effective in relieving the patient's symptoms. The patient should also do stretching exercises several times per day at home. When there is an underlying pathology, such as chronic lateral subluxation of the patella or chondromalacia of the patella, these disorders should also be treated.

SUPRAPATELLAR INSERTION TENDOPATHY

A suprapatellar insertion tendopathy is a typical sports lesion that is the result of overuse. It is seen much less often than the infrapatellar or parapatellar insertion tendopathies, however. Usually, this lesion is seen in athletes older than 40 years.

Differential Diagnosis

Particularly in boys between the ages of 9 and 12 years, radiographs should be taken. In this age group, the potential for a juvenile aseptic necrosis of the bone is of concern. Prepatellar bursitis should also be considered in the differential.

Clinical Findings

The patient complains of pain at the anterior aspect of the knee just proximal to the patella. As is the case with the other insertion tendopathies of the patella, differentiation among the four clinical stages can be made.

Functional Examination

Passive flexion of the knee can be painful. Resisted extension of the knee is painful in stages 3 and 4; in stages 1 and 2, resisted extension is only painful when tested immediately after the patient performs the pain-provoking activity. Often, there is a shortening of the rectus femoris muscle. The exact site of the lesion can be determined using palpation.

Treatment

Transverse friction and stretching exercises are usually effective in relieving the patient's symptoms. The patient should also do stretching exercises several times per day at home.

RUPTURE OF THE QUADRICEPS TENDON

The quadriceps tendon is the attachment of the rectus femoris muscle to the base of the patella. A rupture of the quadriceps tendon is rather rare, and when it does occur it is generally traumatic. It is seen more often in men than in women, with a ratio of 6:1. Ruptures of the quadriceps tendon occur mostly in individuals older than 40 years. This is in contrast to ruptures of the patellar ligament, which are mostly seen in individuals younger than 40. The severe bleeding and accompanying swelling frequently inhibit a correct diagnosis. If a rupture occurs without trauma or after insignificant trauma, the underlying cause is usu-

ally a gonarthritis resulting from gout, psoriasis, rheumatoid arthritis, or long-standing diabetes mellitus. The earlier the diagnosis is made, the better the prognosis.

Clinical Findings

At the moment of the trauma, acute pain is experienced, often in combination with a tearing sound. There is almost always a diffuse swelling at the anterior side of the knee as a result of the severe bleeding. The patella is usually displaced distally.

The patient cannot actively straighten the knee, and the passively straightened knee cannot be held in extension against gravity. If active extension is completely impossible, there is likely to be a rupture of the quadriceps tendon and the medial and lateral retinacula. In the acute stage, there is a palpable gap in the suprapatellar region. In a later stage, this gap can no longer be felt because of the bleeding and the formation of scar tissue. Radiologic examination should be used to determine whether there is a fracture of the patella.

Treatment

Treatment is always surgical.

INFRAPATELLAR INSERTION TENDOPATHY ("JUMPER'S KNEE," PATELLAR APEXITIS)

As is true with both the above described lesions, an infrapatellar insertion tendopathy is a typical sports injury that is seen particularly in runners and jumpers. Candidates for this malady, who range in age between 18 and 25 years, include not only high jumpers and long jumpers but also basketball and volleyball players. This disorder involves the insertion of the patellar ligament at the apex of the patella.

The lesion can be the result of both primary and secondary overuse (see "Parapatellar Insertion Tendopathy," above). In many cases, the patient has an underlying anterior knee instability, such as a hypermobile patella or hyperextension of the knee. Sometimes deviations in the static posture of the hip, knee, or foot can also be responsible for the symptoms. Various problems of the patellar ligament can arise after arthroscopy of the knee when the arthroscope is inserted through the ligament. In many instances, conservative treatment of these problems is ineffective, and surgery is the only alternative.

Differential Diagnosis

- Superficial infrapatellar bursitis
- Deep infrapatellar bursitis
- Sinding-Larsen-Johansson disease (aseptic bone necrosis of the patellar apex)
- Osgood-Schlatter disease (aseptic bone necrosis of the tibial tuberosity)

Clinical Findings

The patient complains of pain at the anterior side of the knee just distal to the patella. Sometimes a mild swelling is visible. This swelling can be differentiated from a superficial infrapatellar bursitis by palpation; on palpation, the swelling from the bursitis usually has a fluctuating consistency. Sometimes a hard nodule or cord can be felt in the middle of the tendon just distal to the patella. In such cases, conservative treatment is usually worthless. If there is no improvement after three trial treatments, surgery to remove the nodule is indicated (Figure 10–46).

Functional Examination

Passive knee flexion is sometimes painful. Resisted extension of the knee is painful in stages 3 and 4; in stages 1 and 2, resisted extension is only painful when tested immediately after the patient performs the pain-provoking activity. Often, there is a shortening of the rectus femoris muscle. By means of palpation, the exact site of the lesion can be determined.

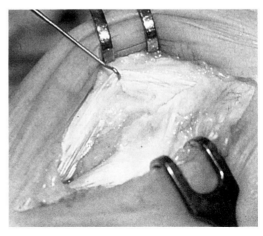

Figure 10–46 Surgical photograph of a patient with a therapy-resistant "jumper's knee." The patellar tendon is surgically split, and a nodular lesion at the level of the tendon insertion at the patellar apex can be seen.

mined. Ultrasound can give a good image of the lesion; scar tissue, inflamed tissue, and in many cases a nodule can be easily seen.

Treatment

If this lesion is the result of secondary overuse, the first priority is to treat the underlying pathology. If there are deviations in the static position of the hip, knee, or foot (eg, flat foot or difference in leg length), orthotics can be used to try to correct or influence the aberrations.

As is the case for the previously discussed insertion tendopathies, this lesion reacts well to transverse friction and stretching exercises. The patient should also do stretching exercises several times per day at home. Conservative treatment, however, is not always successful in treating long-standing problems (longer than 6 months). Surgery is then indicated. Postoperative immobilization is necessary for a period of at least 5 weeks. The patient can usually return to sports 4 months after surgery. Corticosteroid injections are contraindicated because of the risk of ruptures.

RUPTURE OF THE PATELLAR LIGAMENT

As is the case in rupture of the quadriceps tendon, rupture of the patellar ligament is seen more often in men than in women, with a ratio of 6:1. The patients are usually younger than 40 years. The rupture occurs traumatically. An avulsion fracture of the tibial tuberosity can occur in children with a severe form of Osgood-Schlatter disease.

Clinical Findings

The patient complains of severe pain at the moment of rupture. The patella is displaced proximally. As a result of severe bleeding, a diffuse swelling occurs.

Functional Examination

In the acute stage, there is a palpable gap distal to the patella. The patient cannot actively extend the knee.

Treatment

Treatment is always surgical.

LESIONS OF THE MUSCLE BELLIES OF THE QUADRICEPS FEMORIS AND HAMSTRINGS

Lesions of the muscle bellies of the quadriceps femoris and hamstrings are discussed in Chapter 4.

INSERTION TENDOPATHY OF THE SUPERFICIAL PES ANSERINUS

The superficial pes anserinus is the common insertion of the semitendinosus, gracilis, and sartorius. Insertion tendopathy of the superficial pes anserinus is seen particularly in long-distance runners and swimmers but is also seen as a complication in patients with gonarthrosis.

Differential Diagnosis

- Superficial pes anserinus bursitis
- Lesion of the medial collateral ligament

Clinical Findings

There is local pain and sometimes slight swelling. There is usually more swelling in patients with gonarthrosis. In some cases, there is a snapping of the tendon of the pes anserinus during movement of the knee.

Functional Examination

Resisted flexion of the knee is painful. There is an increase in the pain when simultaneously resisted internal rotation is introduced. In some cases, the resisted tests have to be repeated several times before pain is provoked. The passive valgus test is negative. Palpation is used to locate the exact site of the lesion and to differentiate between a tendinitis and a bursitis.

Treatment

Treatment consists of transverse friction, stretching of the hamstrings and adductors, and temporary cessation of pain-provoking activities. The patient should do stretching exercises several times per day at home. In cases where there is a painful snapping, surgery is indicated. In cases of gonarthrosis, quick results can be achieved using a local corticosteroid injection.

INSERTION TENDOPATHY OF THE SEMIMEMBRANOSUS MUSCLE

The various insertions of the semimembranosus muscle are collectively termed the pes anserinus profundus. An insertion tendopathy of the semimembranosus muscle is a typical sports injury that is particularly seen in sprinters and triathletes. It can occur as the result of primary overuse (ie, without an underlying pathology). It can also result from secondary overuse (a situation in which there is an underlying pathology), usually concerning a problem of the posterior horn of the medial meniscus or chondromalacia of the patella.

Differential Diagnosis

- Lesion of the posterior horn of the medial meniscus
- Tendinitis of a tendon of the superficial pes anserinus

Clinical Findings

The patient complains of pain in the posteromedial aspect of the knee, particularly during activities.

Functional Examination

Resisted knee flexion is painful; the pain increases with simultaneously performed resisted internal rotation. The site of the lesion can be precisely located by means of palpation. Usually the site of the lesion is the posteromedial corner of the knee just distal to the joint space.

Treatment

Transverse friction and stretching exercises can usually achieve a cure within a few weeks. The patient should do stretching exercises several times per day at home. If necessary, athletes should refrain from performing sports activities that provoke the pain.

INSERTION TENDOPATHY OF THE BICEPS FEMORIS MUSCLE

An insertion tendopathy of the biceps femoris muscle is also a typical sports lesion. This disorder is seen in bicycle racers, long-distance runners (especially when training on uneven terrain, such as a soft beach), and cross-country skiers. The insertion on the fibular head is the most often affected site. The insertion on the tibia is almost never affected. The attachment to the lateral meniscus, if one exists, is only occasionally affected. In some cases, there is a complete tear or an avulsion fracture of the fibular head.

Differential Diagnosis

- Lateral meniscus lesion
- Lesion of the popliteus

- Lesion of the iliotibial tract
- Lesion of the lateral collateral ligament

Clinical Findings

The patient complains of pain at the lateral side of the knee, particularly after activity.

Functional Examination

Resisted flexion of the knee is painful and increases with simultaneous resisted external rotation. The exact site of the lesion can be located by means of palpation. When there is a complete tear or an avulsion fracture of the fibular head, the resisted tests are extremely painful, and response to the resistance is slightly weak.

Treatment

Treatment consists of transverse friction and stretching exercises. The patient should do the stretching exercises several times per day at home. If the insertion at the lateral meniscus is affected, an injection with a few drops of corticosteroid can be given. A complete rupture or avulsion fracture is surgically treated.

LESIONS OF THE POPLITEUS MUSCLE

In lesions of the popliteus muscle, differentiation is made among tenosynovitis, insertion tendopathy, sprain of the muscle belly (in the popliteal fossa), and rupture.

Tenosynovitis and insertion tendopathy of the popliteus muscle are frequent causes of lateral knee pain. In many instances, the lesion is missed. These lesions are typical sports injuries and are particularly seen in patients who participate in martial arts, such as karate. A rupture occurs traumatically, usually through varus trauma, which contributes to lateral knee instability.

Differential Diagnosis

- Lesion of the lateral meniscus, specifically the attachment of the posterior horn of the lateral meniscus with the popliteus muscle

- Lesion of the iliotibial tract
- Lesion of the biceps femoris
- Lesion of the lateral capsuloligamentous structures

Clinical Findings

The patient complains of pain at the lateral aspect of the knee, particularly during activities where the knee is in 15° to 30° flexion. Walking uphill, walking up stairs, and sometimes just normal walking are painful. The knee pain can last 24 to 48 hours after the painful activity. Some patients have pain when sitting with the legs crossed.

Functional Examination

By using the stability tests, the examiner can determine whether there is a tear of the tendon and can assess the severity of the instability. Resisted flexion of the knee is painful at the lateral side of the knee when combined with resisted internal rotation. In some cases, passive hyperextension of the knee is painful. Passive external rotation of the knee can also be painful. Palpation in the figure-4 position leads to further differentiation. In an insertion tendopathy, the most tender site is just anterior to the lateral collateral ligament, close to the insertion at the lateral femoral epicondyle. In a tenosynovitis, the most painful site lies just posterior to the lateral collateral ligament. If the muscle belly is affected, the most tender site is the popliteal fossa.

Treatment

Transverse friction and stretching exercises lead to complete relief of pain within a few weeks. If necessary, the pain-provoking activities should be reduced or, in severe cases, temporarily stopped.

10.6 OTHER PATHOLOGIES

OSGOOD-SCHLATTER DISEASE (ADOLESCENT TIBIAL APOPHYSITIS)

Osgood-Schlatter disease is considered a traction apophysis that results from an abnormal position of the patella. This condition causes a deficiency in the vascularization of the tibial tuberosity.

Schoen and Marti[20] found that, if one were to imagine a line running through the underside of the patellar apex and the most distal part of the patellar articular joint surface and another line running over the articular joint surface of the patella, the angle formed by the juncture of these two lines is usually smaller in the affected knee than in the nonaffected knee (Figure 10–47). In patients with Osgood-Schlatter disease, the angle averages 33°; in the normal knee the angle is an average of 46°. The result is that the quadriceps muscle in the affected leg has to make a stronger contraction to achieve the same function as the muscle in the nonaffected leg. This increase in pulling force can be an etiologic factor in this traction apophysis.

Furthermore, in Osgood-Schlatter disease the patella is often found to be positioned too low (patella baja). Sometimes part of the tibial tuberosity loosens (Figure 10–48); occasionally, an avulsion fracture occurs. This disorder is seen mostly in boys between 10 and 15 years of age and causes pain only during sports activities or after trauma.

Differential Diagnosis

- Superficial infrapatellar bursitis
- Deep infrapatellar bursitis
- Apexitis of the patella

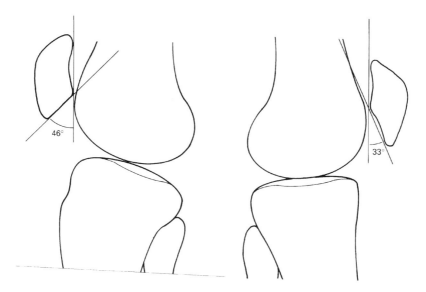

Figure 10–47 Schematic diagram of Osgood-Schlatter disease. The angle formed by a line running through the underside of the patellar apex and the most distal part of the patellar articular joint surface and another line running over the articular joint surface of the patella averages 33° in Osgood-Schlatter disease and 46° in normal knees.

Clinical Findings

The patient complains of local pain, and there is visible swelling at the tibial tuberosity (Figure 10–49).

Functional Examination

In some cases, passive knee flexion is painful. Usually after sports activities, resisted knee extension is painful. Many patients have significantly shortened hamstrings. On palpation, the lesion can be precisely located and differentiated from the following disorders:

- patellar chondromalacia (the patient's main complaint is pain, particularly with the knee in greater than 30° flexion)
- osteochondritis dissecans of the patella (plain films confirm the diagnosis)
- Sinding-Larsen-Johansson disease (aseptic bone necrosis of the apex of the patella)

- prepatellar bursitis (there is local tenderness, and swelling may be present that is fluctuating in consistency on palpation)
- superficial or deep infrapatellar bursitis (there is local tenderness, and swelling may be present that is fluctuating in consistency when palpated distal to the patella)
- patella (bi)partita (the patient complains of pain lateral or proximolateral to the patella; plain films are diagnostic)
- fracture or pseudoarthrosis of the patella (plain films are diagnostic)
- various patellar insertion tendopathies (the patient complains of pain particularly on resisted extension of the knee; palpation confirms the diagnosis)
- inflammation of the infrapatellar fat pad (Hoffitis; there is local tenderness)

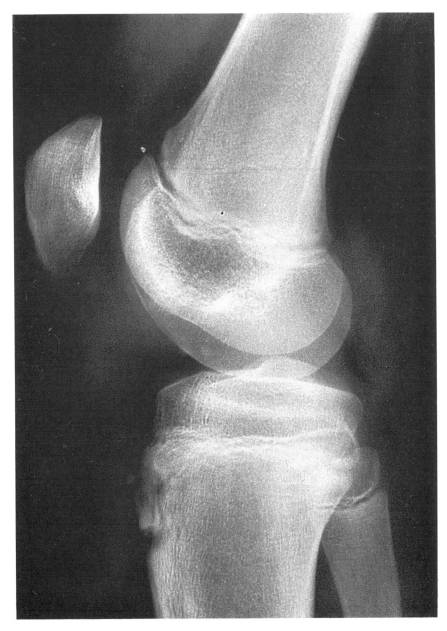

Figure 10–48 Conventional lateral radiograph of the right knee showing fragmentation of the tibial tuberosity, characteristic of Osgood-Schlatter disease.

- patella alta (In this instance, the patella is unstable in that it no longer lies in the corresponding femoral groove. On inspection, the so-called camelback knee is noted. When looking at the knee from lateral, one normally sees only one convexity at the level of the patella. In patella alta, two convexities are visible:

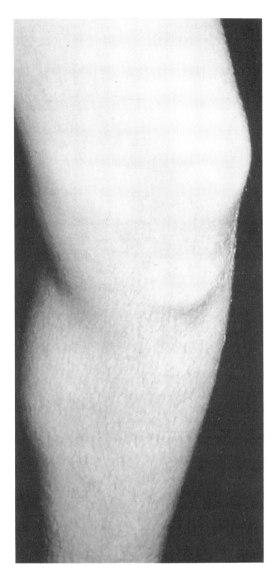

Figure 10–49 Clinical picture showing an obvious swelling at the level of the tibial tuberosity, characteristic of Osgood-Schlatter disease.

The first one is the patella, and the more distal one is the infrapatellar fat pad.)

- meniscus lesion (keep in mind the attachment of the extensor mechanism to the menisci; this can lead to provocation of pain during resisted knee extension)

Treatment

The patient should reduce the pain-provoking sports activities. The patient should be instructed in hamstring stretching exercises. The quadriceps should *not* be stretched. A reduction in pain-provoking activities combined with rehabilitative exercise should bring about complete recovery within about 2 years. In cases of severe avulsions of the tibial tuberosity or parts of the tibial tuberosity, surgery is indicated.

DISLOCATION OF THE PROXIMAL TIBIOFIBULAR JOINT

Dislocation of the proximal tibiofibular joint is an injury that is seldom seen. The dislocation can be superior, posterior, or anterior, with anterior being the most common. This lesion usually results from hyperflexion trauma, in which the foot is in extension and supination. This condition pulls the head of the fibula in a lateral and forward direction. Dislocations of the proximal tibiofibular joint are most often seen in skydivers. They are also seen in patients who participate in athletic events such as pole vaulting and as a result of motor vehicle accidents.

The symptomatology is similar to that experienced in a lateral meniscus dislocation. Early diagnosis in the acute stage is important for proper treatment, usually manual reduction.

Clinical Findings

The patient complains of acute lateral knee pain as the result of hyperflexion trauma. Weight bearing on the affected leg is impossible. A dislocation in a posterior direction is also possible as the result of an abruptly performed, forceful flexion of the knee from an extended position. Some patients complain of locking of the knee.

Functional Examination

There may be a slight limitation of knee extension. The dislocation can be seen on plain films.

Treatment

During the acute stage, manual reduction can be easily performed. After the reduction, the joint should be appropriately taped, and the patient should not put weight, or should put only partial weight, on the affected knee for several weeks. Flexion activities in particular should be avoided. If the disorder is not promptly diagnosed, manual reduction of the fibular head is impossible. In these instances, operative resection of the fibular head is the only solution.

POPLITEAL ARTERY COMPRESSION SYNDROME

Compression of the popliteal artery is seen particularly in young athletes. Compression of blood vessels usually occurs in anatomically narrow spaces in the body, such as in the thoracic outlet region. The primary cause of a compression of the poplitcal artery is muscle hypertrophy due to sports activities, anatomic variations in the immediate area of the artery, or variations in the course of the artery itself.

Classification

- *Type 1:* The popliteal artery deviates medially in the popliteal fossa, then runs under the tendon of the medial head of the gastrocnemius, and afterward runs distally between the femur and gastrocnemius tendon.
- *Type 1a:* The tendon of the medial head of the gastrocnemius attaches more proximally than normal at the femoral metaphysis. The further course of the popliteal artery is the same as described in type 1, but with less deviation medially.
- *Type 2:* The attachment of the medial head of the gastrocnemius lies more proximally and laterally. The popliteal artery, without changing its course, runs through the gastrocnemius tendon, causing it to be compressed when the muscle is contracted.
- *Type 2a:* The popliteal artery can become compressed by the more medial attachment of the plantaris muscle, under which it runs.

When the popliteal artery has an atypical course, muscle activity, particularly plantar flexion of the foot when the knee is extended, can lead to irritation and eventually spasm of the vessel wall. This can lead to damage of the intima with thrombosis as an end result. In the worst case, when there is a complete closure of the popliteal artery in the presence of insufficient collateral circulation, an acute ischemia of the lower leg can occur.

Clinical Findings

Intermittent claudication in young male athletes with otherwise healthy blood vessels is the most significant symptom. The pain in the lower leg occurs gradually and intermittently, or suddenly and acutely, during or after prolonged sports activities.

Functional Examination

The two following tests typically provoke the patient's symptoms: passive dorsiflexion of the ankle when the knee is extended, and resisted plantar flexion of the ankle with simultaneous resisted knee flexion. During these tests, the peripheral pulses of the dorsal pedal artery and posterior tibial artery are no longer palpable. Sometimes a stenosis can be heard in the popliteal artery.

Doppler sonography and angiography are necessary to rule out other blood vessel disorders. The angiography should be done with the knee in two positions: the neutral position and the provocation position. It should also be done bilaterally because congenital anomalies often occur on both sides. All three of the following criteria have to be positive to diagnose a popliteal artery compression syndrome:

1. medial deviation of the popliteal artery
2. closing of the middle segment of the popliteal artery
3. poststenotic dilation

Treatment

Treatment is always surgical. The deviation is bilateral in 25% of all cases, requiring surgery on both sides. The surgical procedure depends on the anatomic variation that is found and the amount of damage to the popliteal artery.

SOLEUS SYNDROME

The soleus syndrome is a separate form of popliteal artery compression. Hypertrophy of the soleus muscle, perhaps as the result of sports activities, causes the tendinous arch of the soleus muscle to compress not only the popliteal artery but also the vein and the tibial nerve.

Clinical Findings

The clinical findings are the same as in popliteal artery compression syndrome. The difference is that, in this syndrome, the popliteal vein and tibial nerve can also be compressed, causing symptoms of venous pooling and possibly paresthesia in the calf, heel, and sole of the foot. These symptoms are in addition to the intermittent claudication. The diagnosis is confirmed through angiography, phlebography, and electromyography.

Treatment

Treatment consists of surgery to resect the tissue responsible for compressing the neurovascular structures.

* * * *

For a quick overview of the common pathologies of the knee, refer to Appendix E, Algorithms for the Diagnosis and Treatment of the Lower Extremities.

Chapter 11

Treatment Techniques in Lesions of the Knee

Hemarthrosis and Effusion in the Knee Joint, or (Rheumatoid) Arthritis of the Knee Joint

Functional Examination

Capsular pattern: Flexion is more limited than extension.

ASPIRATION AND INTRAARTICULAR INJECTION

A hemarthrosis in the knee should always be aspirated. Effusion should be aspirated in severe cases or to do further laboratory analysis of the fluid. An intraarticular injection with a corticosteroid is sometimes indicated in cases of severe arthritis in rheumatic disorders when other medication therapies are unsuccessful or in cases of severe arthrosis of the knee joint.

Position of the Patient

The patient is supine on the treatment table. The knee rests in as much extension as possible. There is almost always a capsular pattern of limited motions and thus an extension limitation. If necessary, a pillow or roll is placed underneath the knee.

Position of the Physician

The physician sits next to the treatment table, at the patient's affected side. With the

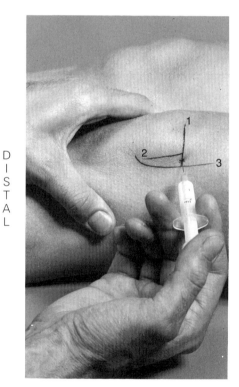

DISTAL

PROXIMAL

Figure 11–1 Intraarticular injection of the knee joint. **1**, Proximal edge of the patella; **2**, Lateral edge of the patella; **3**, Anterior edge of the iliotibial tract.

fingers, the physician pushes the patella laterally as far as possible.

Performance

The aspiration and injection are performed at the middle of a vertical line (**1** in Figure 11–1) between the horizontally running lateral edge of the patella (**2**) and iliotibial tract (**3**). The 3- to 5-cm long needle is inserted horizontally.

Note

If knee extension is limited more than 10°, the needle is inserted at the anterior aspect of the knee, in the indentation just lateral to the patellar ligament. The disadvantage to this technique is that the well-vascularized infrapatellar fat pad is punctured, increasing the chance for additional bleeding.

LOOSE BODY IN THE KNEE JOINT

Functional Examination

Either flexion or extension of the knee is both actively and passively limited.

MANIPULATION

Loose bodies in the knee joint can have various causes. For example, a meniscus fragment or loose pieces of bone or cartilage may be caused by arthrosis, patellofemoral arthrosis, or synovial chondromatosis.

Position of the Patient

The patient lies prone on the treatment table. The knee being treated is flexed to 80° and lies about 10 cm from the edge of the table.

Position of the Therapist

The position of the therapist depends on the direction of the manipulation. The following description concerns the external rotation manipulation.

The treatment table is adjusted to the level of the therapist's patella. If, for example, the patient's right knee is being treated, the therapist's left foot is placed on the treatment table, between the patient's knee and the edge of the table (Figure 11–2A). The patient's foot rests on the therapist's thigh. The therapist's other foot is placed against the foot support of the table, which is either an accessory piece or standard on some treatment tables.

With the right hand, the therapist grasps the patient's lower leg just above the malleoli; the other hand grasps the heel in such a way that the foot is held in maximal extension. This is simply done by placing the ulnar side of the forearm against the sole of the patient's foot.

Position of the Assistant

The assistant stands next to the treatment table at the side of the leg being treated. Without exerting pressure, the assistant places both hands against the distal part of the posterior aspect of the patient's thigh.

Performance

The therapist lifts the patient's knee slightly from the table, and the assistant exerts as much pressure as necessary against the patient's thigh to fix it to the table, still allowing for the patient to relax completely. In so doing, traction is applied to the knee joint. Then, the therapist lifts his or her left leg and shifts it slightly posteriorly without allowing it to touch the floor; the therapist is

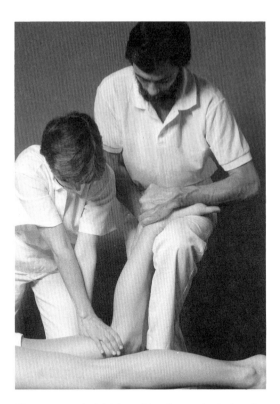

Figure 11–2A Initial position in manipulation for a limitation of motion in the knee joint based on a loose body.

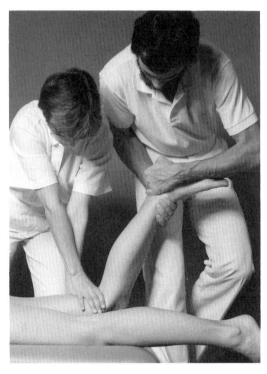

Figure 11–2B Lifting the patient's knee.

now standing only on the right leg (Figure 11–2B).

The patient's lower leg is now externally rotated under traction in a manipulative way (Figure 11–2C) The knee is then slowly rotated internally and brought slightly farther into extension (Figure 11–2D).

In this new position, the patient's lower leg is again externally rotated. At the same time, the therapist moves his or her left leg sideways, without placing the foot on the floor (Figure 11–2E). Using these techniques, the external rotation is repeated one to two more times. Just after the last external rotation (because the knee is nearly straight, the amount of rotation is minimal), the therapist's foot is placed back on the floor.

After the manipulation, the knee is reassessed. If the range of motion has increased, the pain is decreased, or the end-feel is changed for the better, the entire maneuver is repeated. If there is no immediate improvement after the manipulation, an internal rotation manipulation is performed, in which the knee is brought from an externally rotated position toward neutral. Manipulation into absolute internal rotation is not advised because the cruciate ligaments intertwine with each other, resulting in increased tension of these ligaments along with a decrease of space in the joint cavity.

The patient should be reexamined 1 week later. Additional manipulation may be needed. The appropriate manipulation can be repeated three to six times per treatment session, as long as there is improvement and the patient can relax. Sometimes, the patient obtains complete relief from symptoms after a single manipulation.

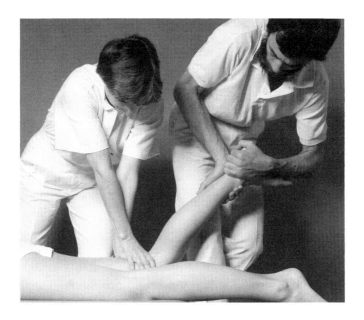

Figure 11–2C External rotation of the lower leg.

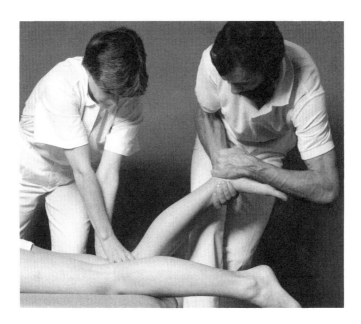

Figure 11–2D Internal rotation and slight extension of the knee.

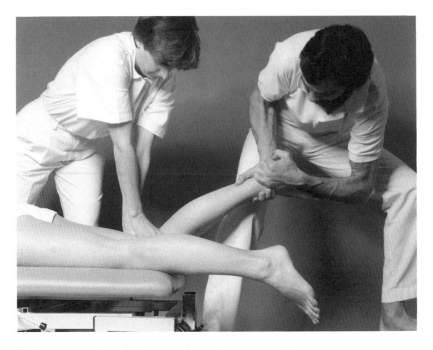

Figure 11–2E External rotation of the lower leg in the new position.

MENISCAL IMPINGEMENT WITH EXTENSION LIMITATION OF THE KNEE

Function Examination

Refer to Functional Examination in Meniscus Lesions section, Chapter 10.

REPOSITION MANIPULATION

If a patient has a sudden painful extension limitation of the knee with or without trauma and an abnormal end-feel during passive extension, there is a great possibility that the (usually medial) meniscus is torn. Sometimes this condition is in combination with other capsuloligamentous pathology. Often in these cases a bucket-handle lesion is involved; usually there is little swelling, and it is still possible to perform an assessment of the

capsuloligamentous structures. Although a bucket-handle lesion is usually treated surgically, especially in acute cases, a manipulative treatment can temporarily reposition the meniscus.

Position of the Patient

The patient is supine on the treatment table. Generally, because of the malpositioned meniscus, the patient automatically holds the knee in flexion.

Position of the Therapist

The therapist stands next to the treatment table at the patient's affected side. If, for example, the patient's right knee is being treated, the therapist grasps the patient's foot

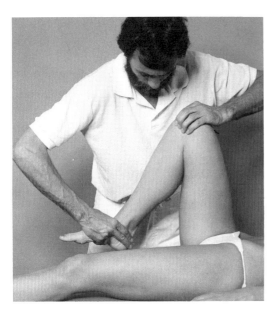

Figure 11–3 Initial position in a meniscus reposition manipulation.

with the right hand in such a way that extension (dorsiflexion) can be maintained. This can be achieved by one of the following positions:

1. The index and middle fingers are placed at the medial side of the foot, just distal to the medial malleolus. The ring and little fingers rest against the sole of the patient's foot, and the thumb lies against the dorsolateral aspect of the foot (Figure 11–3). To bring about an alternating external and internal rotation of the lower leg using this hand grip, the therapist does an alternating extension and flexion of the wrist.

2. The fingers are placed against the medial aspect of the patient's foot, and the thumb is at the lateral aspect (Figure 11–4). With this hand position, the alternating internal and external rotation of the lower leg occurs through an alternating pronation and supination of the therapist's forearm.

3. The therapist grasps the patient's heel with the thumb at the medial aspect and the fingers against the posterior aspect. The sole of the patient's foot rests against the volar aspect of the therapist's forearm (Figure 11–5). By internally and externally rotating the shoulder, the therapist induces an internal and external rotation of the patient's lower leg.

Performance

The following description is based on repositioning procedures for the right knee. The patient's knee is brought into the maximum possible flexion, and the therapist places the fingers of the left hand in the medial joint space. The patient's foot is grasped with the other hand, and alternating internal and external rotation motions are performed (Figures 11–3 to 11–6). At the same time, the knee is slightly extended. This maneuver is done in preparation for the manipulation, but sometimes it is sufficient to accomplish the reduction.

If the reduction does not occur, the therapist places the left hand against the lateral side of the patient's knee. Now, from a position of maximum flexion, the knee is brought into extension while undergoing alternating internal and external rotation (Figure 11–7). While doing this maneuver, the therapist must remain aware of the extension limitation and take care never to extend the knee farther than it can be actively straightened.

During this movement toward extension, the following procedures are executed:

1. Valgus pressure is applied; the hand at the knee pushes the knee medially, while the other hand pulls the foot in a distal and lateral direction (Figure 11–8).

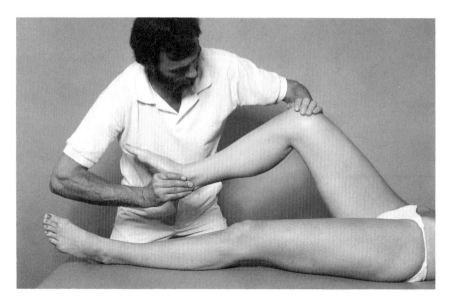

Figure 11–4 Rotations of the lower leg through pronation and supination of the therapist's forearm.

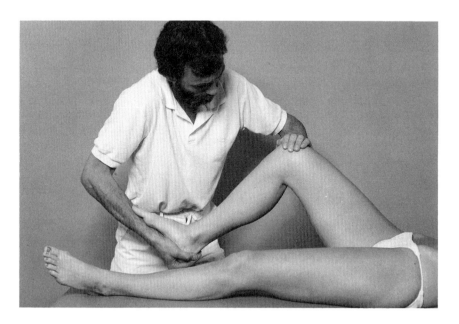

Figure 11–5 Rotations of the lower leg through internal and external rotation of the therapist's shoulder.

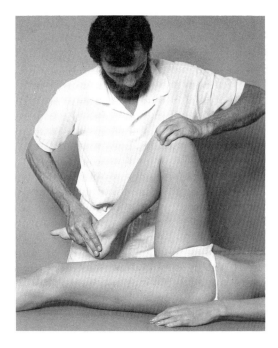

Figure 11–6 Preparation for the manipulation. The lower leg is alternately internally and externally rotated, while the fingers apply pressure against the medial joint space.

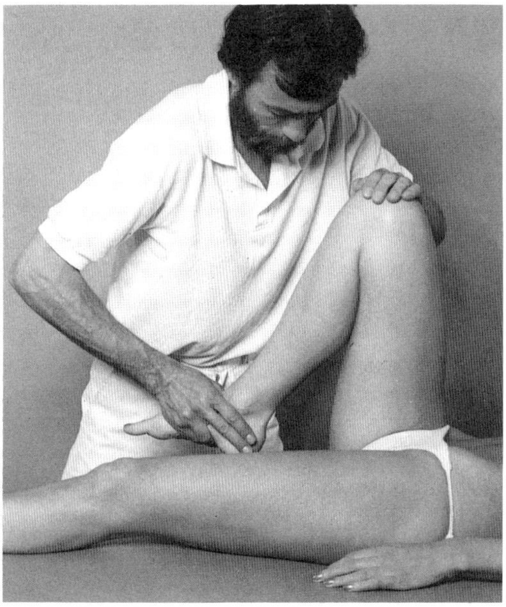

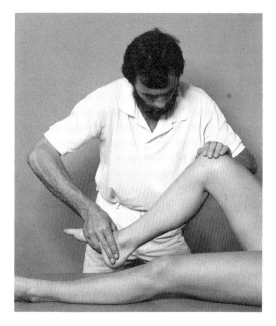

Figure 11–7 Internal rotation of the lower leg.

Figure 11–8 More extension, more valgus pressure, and external rotation of the lower leg.

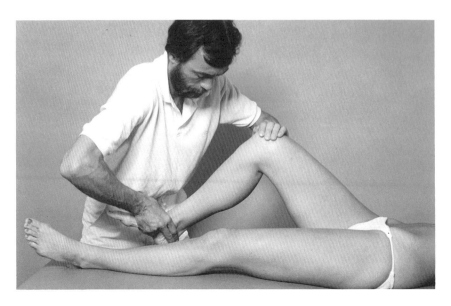

Figure 11–9 Shifting the body weight from the left leg to the right leg.

2. The forearm of the hand applying medial pressure at the knee remains perpendicular to the leg; to achieve this, the therapist shifts body weight from the left leg to the right leg while moving from flexion toward extension (Figure 11–9).

3. At the end of the movement, the therapist exerts maximal pressure, providing sufficient room in the medial joint cavity to prevent the knee from "shooting" into extension, an event that can be painful to the patient (Figure 11–10).

When this treatment is performed in a well-coordinated manner, the patient will not experience pain, and in acute cases reduction is almost always achieved.

After the manipulation, the knee is carefully retested. Manipulative reduction can occur during the first manipulation, but sometimes it takes two or more attempts. Usually, the therapist should stop the procedure if, after as many as six manipulations, successful reduction has still not been achieved.

In most cases, after successful treatment, passive external rotation remains painful. This is the result of a sprain of the medial meniscotibial ligament. These symptoms usually quickly disappear with a few treatments of transverse friction. In many cases, however, there is recurrence, particularly in athletes. Manipulation can be repeated, but surgery is usually indicated. Surgery is not indicated, however, for treatment of patients who experience a rare recurrence of a meniscus lesion caused by a minor rotation trauma if the individual is not active in sports and the manipulative reduction was easily achieved.

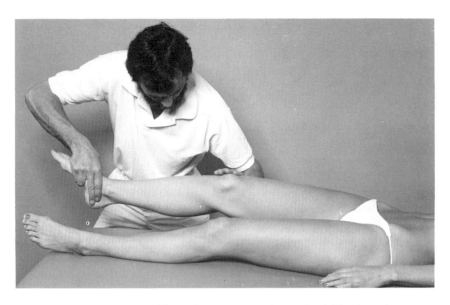

Figure 11–10 End of the maneuver. The valgus pressure is maximal. The knee is never completely extended!

SPRAIN OF THE MEDIAL OR LATERAL MENISCOTIBIAL (CORONARY) LIGAMENTS

Functional Examination

If only the meniscotibial ligaments are affected and there is no other capsuloligamentous pathology or meniscus lesion:

- medial meniscotibial ligament: passive external rotation of the lower leg is painful
- lateral meniscotibial ligament: passive internal rotation of the lower leg is painful

TRANSVERSE FRICTION OF THE MEDIAL MENISCOTIBIAL LIGAMENT

Posttraumatic overstretching, particularly of the medial meniscotibial ligament, is frequently seen with or without a meniscus le-

sion, after a meniscus luxation, or after a (partial) meniscectomy.

Position of the Patient

The patient is supine on the treatment table. The knee being treated is flexed 90°, and the lower leg is maximally (as far as the pain will allow) externally rotated.

Position of the Therapist

The therapist stands next to the treatment table at the patient's affected side, at the level of the lower leg. With either a sandbag or the knee (as pictured), the therapist fixes the patient's lower leg in maximum possible external rotation (Figure 11–11).

If, for example, the right knee is being treated, the therapist places the index finger of the right hand, reinforced by the middle

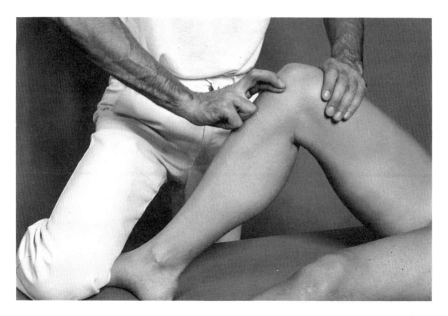

Figure 11–11 View from medial of the initial position in transverse friction of the medial meniscotibial ligament, pars anterior.

finger, just medial to the site of the lesion (to learn the location of this ligament, refer to Chapter 8). The thumb is placed against the lateral aspect of the lower leg, perpendicular and distal to the index finger (Figure 11–12). This initial position is used for a lesion of the medial meniscotibial ligament at a site anterior to the medial collateral ligament.

If the medial meniscotibial ligament posterior to the medial collateral ligament is being treated, the therapist places the tip of the index finger on the tibial plateau (in general, this site is difficult to locate) at an angle of 45° in relation to the horizontal (Figure 11–13). In this instance, the thumb is placed more proximally against the lateral side of the lower leg (Figure 11–14).

Performance

Regardless of the location of the lesion, the friction is performed in the same manner. During the friction phase, the therapist extends the wrist and slightly adducts the arm. The index and middle fingers remain slightly curved during the friction phase. In so doing, the fingers are moved over the lesion from medial to lateral or, when the posterior part of the ligament is affected, from posteromedial to anterolateral.

Duration

The transverse friction treatment should last about 15 minutes and be administered daily or at least three times per week. A total of 3 to 10 treatments is usually necessary to eliminate the symptoms completely.

Note

If the lateral meniscotibial ligament is affected, the same principles described above are applied, with the exception that the lower leg is now positioned in internal rotation. In this way, the anterior part of the lateral tibial plateau can function as a base for friction of the ligament. Isolated lesions are rare; usually other (postero)lateral structures are affected, and an anterolateral rotatory instability is involved.

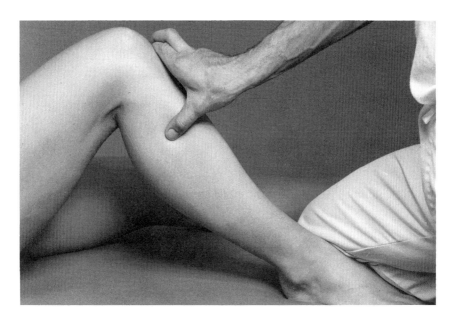

Figure 11–12 View from lateral of the position of the thumb in transverse friction of the medial meniscotibial ligament, pars anterior.

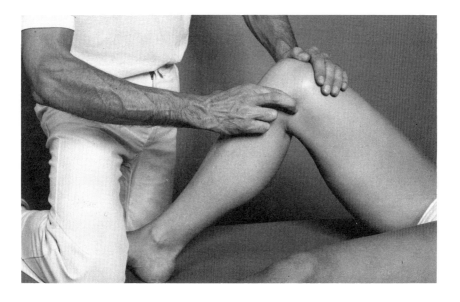

Figure 11–13 View from medial of the initial position in transverse friction of the medial meniscotibial ligament, pars posterior.

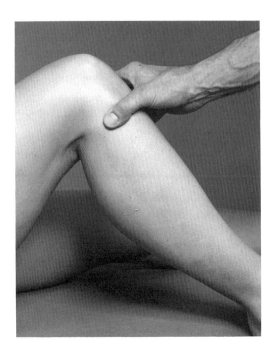

Figure 11–14 View from lateral of the position of the thumb in transverse friction of the medial meniscotibial ligament, pars posterior.

SPRAIN OF THE MEDIAL (TIBIAL) COLLATERAL LIGAMENT

Damage to the medial collateral ligament is usually caused by a valgus–flexion–external rotation trauma, such as might be sustained while playing soccer or skiing. Less frequently, it results from a pure valgus trauma. In most instances, damage to this ligament is not solitary. The trauma that caused the injury may have also caused other damage to the knee, such as lesions of the medial meniscotibial or meniscofemoral ligaments or the posteromedial capsule (in particular, the posterior oblique ligament). In severe cases, there may also be lesions of the lateral meniscus (more often than medial meniscus), anterior cruciate ligament, and sometimes even the posterior cruciate ligament (3+ instability). Treatment depends on the severity of the lesion.

Functional Examination

The valgus test in slight flexion is painful, but there is not an abnormal amount of valgus movement. In extension, the valgus test is negative (indicating stability through the posteromedial capsule).

In the acute stage, there is usually slight effusion with an accompanying (slight) capsular pattern of limited passive motions (ie, flexion is slightly limited and painful, and extension is not limited but painful).

TREATMENT

In the first 2 to 4 days, the acute stage, treatment consists of rest, analgesic measures (to include medication or physical therapy modalities), and, if necessary, modalities to decrease swelling.

In the subacute stage, treatment is focused on the prevention of adhesions by administration of limited and carefully performed transverse friction at the site of the sprain. The transverse friction treatments should last only a few minutes. After each daily treatment, the knee is gently moved within the limits of pain. As soon as normal movement without too much pain is possible, the patient can start an active rehabilitative exercise program. The gait pattern should be specifically observed, and if necessary gait training should be administered to ensure a quick return to the normal gait pattern.

Occasionally, in spite of the treatment described above, when the proximal part of the ligament is affected an increasing flexion limitation occurs while the extension range of motion remains normal. In this instance, the cause is likely to be a calcification at the level of the adductor tubercle, the so-called Pellegrini-Stieda disease. Radiologic examination confirms this diagnosis. In such cases, physical therapy should be discontinued. The symptoms and the calcification usually disappear gradually within several months to 2 years. In extreme cases, where there is severe pain, surgery is recommended.

The chronic stage occurs only in patients who did not receive treatment during the acute or subacute stage. A typical finding in this stage is local pain, particularly during or after activity. Usually, there is slight swelling in the knee. The pain and swelling are caused by adhesions between the ligament and its surroundings. Therapy consists of manipulative treatment of the (usually minimal) flexion or extension limitation of the knee. This type of manipulation is only performed for small limitations (a few degrees). If the limitation is greater than 3° to 5°, the knee is first mobilized with joint-specific techniques until the limitation is so small that a manipulation is indicated. The manipulation must only be performed when there is no effusion in the joint, however. The manipulation is preceded by 10 minutes of transverse friction with the knee in maximum possible extension and then 10 minutes in maximum possible flexion.

Transverse Friction

Position of the Patient

The patient is supine on the treatment table. The knee is extended as far as possible and supported by a small pillow or roll.

Position of the Therapist

The therapist sits or stands next to the treatment table at the patient's affected side, at the level of the knee. The therapist finds the most painful site by palpating the ligament from the adductor tubercle to just distal to the pes anserinus superficialis. If, for example, the right knee is affected, the tip of the right index finger is placed just medial to the lesion, with the thumb at the lateral aspect of the knee. The other hand fixes the thigh directly proximal to the patella (Figure 11–15A).

Performance

The index finger is reinforced by the middle finger, and by wrist extension the tip of the index finger is moved over the lesion from posteromedial to anterolateral (Figure 11–15B). After about 10 minutes of trans-

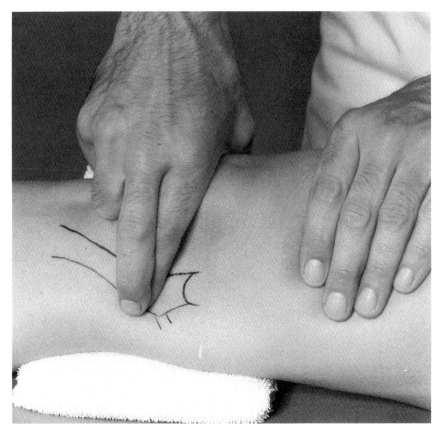

Figure 11–15A Initial position of the hand during transverse friction of the medial (tibial) collateral ligament in an extended knee.

verse friction with the knee extended, the knee is flexed as much as possible, and another 10 minutes of transverse friction is performed (Figure 11–16).

Extension Manipulation

Position of the Patient

The patient is supine on the treatment table with the affected knee as extended as possible. If necessary, a small roll is placed behind the knee.

Position of the Therapist

If, for example, the right knee is being treated, the therapist fixes the patient's thigh to the table by applying posterior pressure to the thigh just proximal to the patella. The thigh is brought into slight internal rotation. With the right hand, the therapist grasps the lower leg just proximal to the malleoli (Figure 11–17A).

Performance

The therapist now straightens both arms and, while extending the patient's knee, makes a quick but minimal right rotation of the trunk (Figure 11–17B). This exerts an external rotation force on the extended knee. This technique should only be performed one time per treatment session and, at the most, a total of three times. The patient should ac-

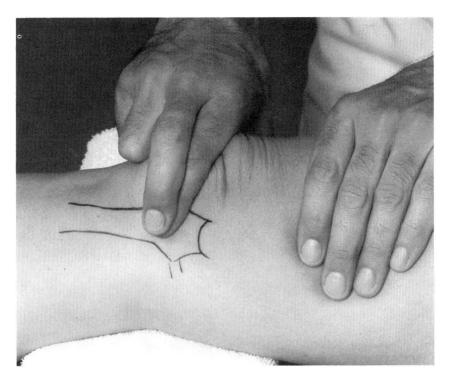

Figure 11–15B End position of the hand during transverse friction of the medial (tibial) collateral ligament. Note that the therapist's wrist is now extended.

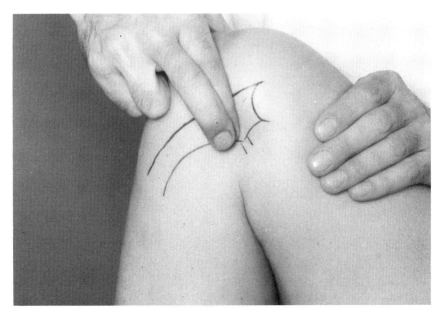

Figure 11–16 Transverse friction of the medial (tibial) collateral ligament with the knee in flexion.

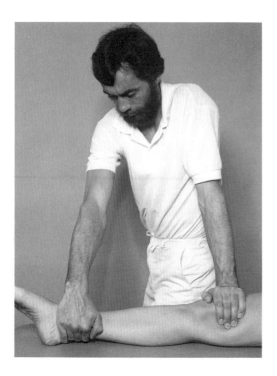

Figure 11–17A Extension manipulation of the knee: Initial position.

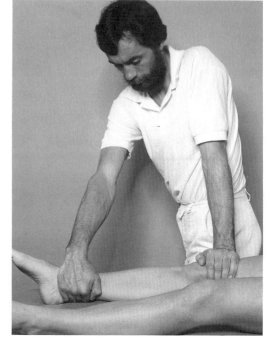

Figure 11–17B Extension manipulation of the knee: End position.

tively maintain the newly achieved range of motion by doing exercises several times daily.

Flexion Manipulation

Performance

With the right hand, in maximum possible flexion of the patient's knee, the therapist grasps the patient's lower leg just proximal to the malleoli. The other hand stabilizes the patient's thigh just proximal to the patella. The distal hand then initiates an instantaneous knee flexion while the already internally rotated lower leg is brought slightly farther into internal rotation (Figure 11–18). Usually a sound like tearing cloth is heard. In some cases, the patient experiences slight joint effusion, which disappears after a few days. As with the extension manipulation,

this technique should only be performed one time per treatment session, and, at the most, a total of three times. The patient should actively maintain the newly achieved range of motion by doing exercises several times daily.

Duration

In most chronic cases, only one to three treatments are necessary to achieve complete relief; afterward the patient can gradually increase the weight load on the knee. Sports activities can usually be started about 2 weeks after recovery.

Instability.

If the functional examination of the knee reveals a medial instability, the treatment depends on a number of factors. In partial tears of the medial collateral ligament, the treatment plan that was just described can be fol-

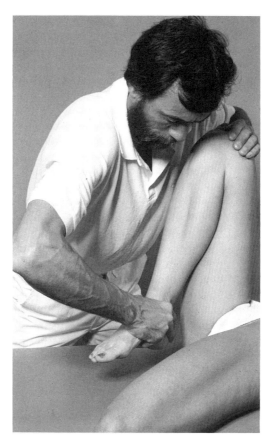

Figure 11–18 Flexion manipulation of the knee.

lowed. Strengthening exercises should be initiated as soon as possible after the pain and swelling have subsided. Especially in uniplanar instabilities, the results from functional rehabilitation are often better than those from surgical treatment.

SPRAIN OF THE LATERAL (FIBULAR) COLLATERAL LIGAMENT

Functional Examination

The varus test in slight knee flexion is painful (in slight flexion, normally more movement is possible in a varus direction than in a valgus direction). In knee extension no movement is possible, and no pain will be experienced as long as the posterolateral capsule is intact.

TRANSVERSE FRICTION

Compared with the medial collateral ligament, the lateral collateral ligament is much less often affected. A sprain or partial rupture of this ligament is usually caused by trauma with a varus component. As is the case with the medial collateral ligament, the treatment of a lateral collateral ligament depends on the severity of the lesion. In general, the same principles described in the treatment plan for the medial collateral ligament can be applied here.

Position of the Patient

The patient is supine on the treatment table with the affected knee in about 80° flexion. The lower leg rests on top of the other thigh just proximal to the patella (in the figure-4 position; refer to Chapter 8). In this position, the lateral collateral ligament is easily palpable from its origin at the lateral femoral epicondyle to its insertion at the fibular head (Figure 11–19).

Position of the Therapist

The therapist stands at thigh level next to the treatment table, on the patient's nonaf-fected side. The therapist locates the most tender site on the lateral collateral ligament. If, for example the left knee is affected, the tip of the right index finger is placed just postero-lateral to this spot. A thickening of the ligament can usually be felt just proximal to the fibular head; this is a part of the biceps femoris muscle, which at this point runs lateral to the ligament. The thumb exerts counterpressure at the medial side of the knee, and the other hand fixes the lower leg.

Performance

The index finger is reinforced by the middle finger. By extension of the wrist during the active phase of the transverse friction, the tip of the index finger is moved from posterolateral to anterolateral over the affected part of the ligament (Figure 11–20). The hand relaxes during wrist flexion. In contrast to the treatment of the medial collateral ligament, the extraarticular lateral collateral ligament is only treated in one position.

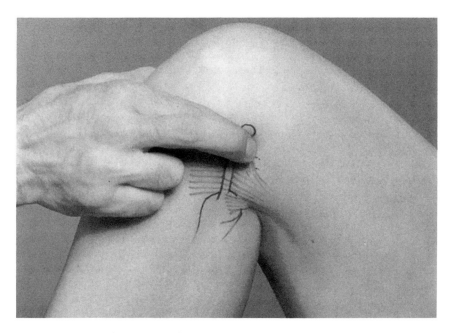

Figure 11–19 Localization of the lateral (fibular) collateral ligament.

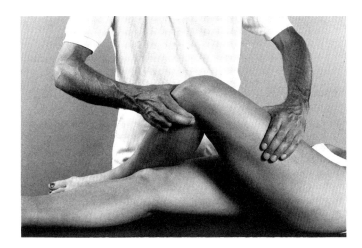

Figure 11–20 Initial position during transverse friction of the lateral (fibular) collateral ligament.

Duration

The transverse friction should be performed for 15 minutes daily for athletes and at least three times per week for others. Six to 12 treatments are usually necessary to achieve complete relief. In cases of instability, the same considerations mentioned in the treatment of the medial collateral ligament hold true.

INSTABILITY OF THE KNEE

General

Considerations in planning the appropriate treatment program for patients with a knee instability include:
- is the instability acute or chronic?
- severity of the instability (1+, 2+, 3+)
- patient's occupation
- patient's hobbies or sports
- motivation of the patient regarding the intensive rehabilitation programs (pre- and post-surgery) and conservative treatment)
- professional experience of the orthopaedic surgeon with the various conservative and surgical methods

BASIC (MUSCLE) REHABILITATION PROGRAM FOR KNEE INSTABILITY

Acute Stage in New Instability

The goals of the rehabilitation program are pain relief and resolution of swelling (eg, the use of ice, transcutaneous electrical nerve stimulation, high-voltage galvanic stimulation, or interferential current) and prevention of muscle atrophy (use of exercises featuring isometric contraction).

Isometric Exercises

During all isometric contractions, the patient should not hold his or her breath. Instead, the patient should concentrate on breathing in a relaxed manner.

- *Quadriceps:* The patient sits with the knee extended and pushes the back of the knee as forcefully as possible into the supporting surface. This position is held for 6 seconds, followed by 2 seconds of relaxation. The exercise is done in sets of 20 repetitions, 3 to 4 times per day.
- *Hamstrings:* Exercise for the hamstrings is more important than for the quadriceps whenever one is treating any type of instability in which the tibia can anteriorly translate or rotate or in injuries where the anterior cruciate ligament is ruptured. In the sitting position, the patient places the foot of the nonaffected extremity behind the ankle of the affected side in such a way that the affected knee is flexed 70°. The patient then contracts the hamstrings of the affected side while the nonaffected side exerts so much counterpressure that no movement occurs. This exercise is performed for 6 seconds, followed by 2 seconds of rest. In total, the exercise should be repeated 20 times, 3 to 4 times per day.

During the first week, this program should be performed with daily reassessment by the physical therapist. The circumference of the leg is measured at various levels: at the joint line and 10 cm and 20 cm proximal to the joint line. If there is an increase in joint effusion, the program is reduced accordingly. As the swelling decreases, the program can be advanced. The acute phase usually lasts from 1 to 3 weeks. In the second and third weeks, reassessment by the physical therapist is necessary three times per week.

This exercise program can also be followed after surgery. Because of pain, however, it is not possible for many patients to develop the required 60% of maximal muscle force necessary to prevent muscle atrophy. This muscle atrophy occurs quickly but can be somewhat slowed by the use of electric stimulation.

If the initiation of the isometric exercise program goes well, isotonic exercises can be started, often while the lesion is still in the acute stage.

Isotonic Exercises

- *Quadriceps (knee extension):* Isotonic exercises can be performed with elastic bands, but they are best done on a knee extension table, where the weight can be increased as the patient gains strength. While sitting, the patient slowly extends the knee from a starting position of 90° flexion to an ending position of 45° flexion. This maneuver restricts the forces working to pull the tibia forward. In other words, they are significantly less than if the knee were extended farther. This exercise is repeated 15 times, 3 to 4 times per day.
- *Hamstrings (knee flexion):* still in the sitting position, but now starting from extension, the knee is maximally flexed. Here, too, the resistance is increased as the patient is able to exert more force without provoking pain or causing swelling. This exercise is also repeated 15 times, 3 to 4 times per day.

The above program can be performed before surgery as well, with the following goals:

- The patient can learn to perform correctly the exercises that will be part of the postsurgical rehabilitation program.
- The muscles can be developed to optimal condition so that, after the operation, atrophy of the thigh muscles will occur more slowly and to a lesser extent.

Often there is no time to prepare the patient for surgery or for the postoperative program because in many cases a new instability is operated on in the acute stage.

After surgery, the isotonic program described above is followed with the understanding that there is a limitation of motion. Exercises are performed within the limits of pain and within the available range of motion. These exercises can best be performed within the established limitations of motion by use of a brace (eg, a Lenox-Hill brace).

Subacute Stage in New Instability and Old Instability

The goals of the rehabilitation program are to obtain equal or greater strength, endurance, and proprioceptive awareness of the affected knee in comparison to the nonaffected side. At the same time, full passive range of motion is achieved along with complete resolution of swelling and pain.

Isokinetic Exercises

Isokinetic exercises are performed after a specified amount of time or after certain goals have been met and constitute an important part of both conservative and postoperative rehabilitation programs. It is important to keep the postoperative immobilization period as short as possible. Movement helps prevent damage to the joint cartilage. In addition, ligaments heal better and faster under the influence of (restricted) movement. These movements should not exert an excess of force on the repaired structures, and it is recommended that movements be restricted to between 20° and 60° flexion (here, too, with the help of a Lenox-Hill brace). The isokinetic exercises are best done on a Cybex II or similar isokinetic machine. They can also be done without this type of machine, but the movements will not be as precise.

- *Hamstrings:* Only those patients who have not undergone surgery should start the program exercising flexion of the knee at a velocity of 120° per second for 20 repetitions. Depending on the patient's progress, the resistance and range of motion can be increased each day, and eventually the number of rep-

etitions is increased. Three to five sets of these repetitions should be performed at each therapy session.

- *Quadriceps:* As described for the hamstrings, the quadriceps can also be exercised isokinetically, again only by the patients who have not undergone surgery. In these exercises, knee extension is performed starting at a velocity of 90° per second. Quadriceps exercises are particularly important when the posterior cruciate ligament is ruptured or when excessive translation or rotation of the tibia occurs posteriorly. To restrict the tendency for the tibia to translate forward during the isokinetic quadriceps exercises, the resistance should not be applied at the level of the malleoli but rather more proximal on the lower leg.[20]

- *Quadriceps and hamstrings:* Exercises for both muscle groups consist of 10 repetitions at velocities of 180°, 240°, and 300° per second. Progression can follow the recommendations described for the hamstrings.

In addition, the muscles and muscle groups that can actively decrease the knee instability should be strengthened. For example, in an anteromedial rotatory instability, specific exercises for the flexors and internal rotators of the knee should be used along with exercises to strengthen the hamstrings and quadriceps. In the case of an anterolateral rotatory instability, more specific exercises for the flexors and external rotators of the knee should be used.

Isokinetic exercises should always be preceded by a thorough period of warming-up, using, for example, hot packs, massage, or isotonic exercises. After the exercises, ice can be applied for 10 to 15 minutes. Here, too, the exercise program must always be adjusted to fit the needs of the individual by accommodating such circumstances as pain or the presence of joint effusion. In addition, consideration has to be given to the mobility of the knee. If necessary, the therapist can apply careful joint-specific mobilization.

Isokinetic exercises can also be performed eccentrically; it has been shown that this leads to faster muscle strengthening (not to more muscle strengthening). Nonsurgical patients with more than 50% loss of strength need an average of eight sessions to restore strength; patients with less than a 50% loss need an average of six sessions.[21]

Patients with a solitary or associated lesion of the anterior cruciate ligament can participate in a considerably higher level of sports (and activities in general) when the strength of the hamstrings is greater than that of the quadriceps. The opposite is needed for patients with a posterior cruciate ligament lesion. Patients with lesions of the medial collateral ligament, for example, even in long-term follow-up, also react extremely well to muscle-strengthening exercise therapy.[22]

As soon as the mobility of the knee is normal, the muscle strength is optimal, and the muscle circumference is properly increased, loaded movements from activities of daily living can be initiated. Participation in activities must still be tempered by pain, swelling, and the feeling of instability (giving way of the knee). The types of movement that should be undertaken gradually include ascending and descending stairs, squats, jumping, biking, and generally motions that especially stress the knee joint. Later, full loading in specific training conditions is begun, and later still competition is initiated. The affected extremity eventually has to become stronger than the nonaffected extremity.

Studies[23] have indicated that, where speed is involved, the least harmful sports are those that have the fewest sudden starts, stops, or jumps. Unfavorable sports include soccer, volleyball, basketball, and racquet sports, with the exception of tennis. The reason why tennis is generally good exercise is unknown.

It is extremely important to discuss the rehabilitation program with the patient beforehand. If the patient is not sufficiently motivated, therapy will probably have disappointing results. The entire rehabilitation program lasts at least 6 months to a year. Even afterward, it is important to maintain strength and condition of the musculature, preferably through sports activities. Swimming, bicycling, and long distance running are some of the most suitable sports. Many other sports, particularly those involving body contact, increase the chances that degenerative changes will occur in the knee joint and that the instability will increase as a result of trauma.[24] In many cases, patients who engage in high-risk sports may benefit from the use of a derotation brace.[25]

PARAPATELLAR, SUPRAPATELLAR, AND INFRAPATELLAR INSERTION TENDOPATHIES

Functional Examination

Resisted knee extension is painful (usually only when tested immediately after the patient performs the pain-provoking activity). Sometimes stretch of the rectus femoris (extension of the hip combined with flexion of the knee) is painful. Differentiation between a parapatellar, suprapatellar, and infrapatellar tendopathy is made by palpation. For further clinical findings, refer to the section on the Pathology of the Patellofemoral Joint, Chapter 10.

A parapatellar, suprapatellar, or infrapatellar insertion tendopathy is often misdiagnosed as chondromalacia of the patella.

TRANSVERSE FRICTION FOR A PARAPATELLAR INSERTION TENDOPATHY

Position of the Patient

The patient is supine on the treatment table. The affected knee is extended.

Position of the Therapist

The therapist stands at knee level next to the treatment table. When the lesion is located at the medial side of the patella, the therapist stands at the patient's affected side. When the lesion is located at the lateral side of the patella, the therapist stands at the patient's nonaffected side.

If, for example, the medial aspect of the right knee is affected, the therapist uses the left thumb to push the patella medially and places the tip of the right middle finger just proximal to the lesion against the posteromedial edge of the patella. The nail of the middle finger "faces" posteriorly. The middle finger is reinforced by the index finger. The right thumb is placed on the left thumb and applies counterpressure (Figure 11–21A).

Performance

The active phase of the transverse friction is performed through an extension of the wrist. In so doing, the middle finger moves from proximomedial to distomedial over the site of the lesion (Figure 11–21B).

This treatment is performed in combination with stretching of the quadriceps. If necessary, strengthening of the vastus medialis and medialis obliquus, stretching of the iliotibial tract, and control of the patella through taping or bracing can also be added to the treatment program.

Duration

Depending on the severity of the symptoms, from 4 to 15 treatments are required to

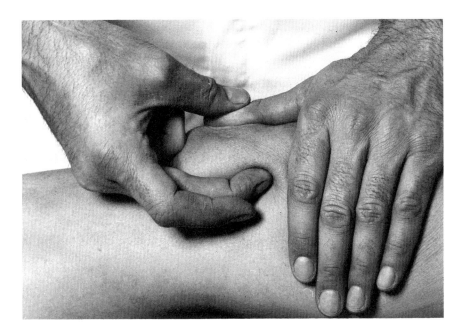

Figure 11–21A Initial position in transverse friction of medial parapatellar insertion tendopathy.

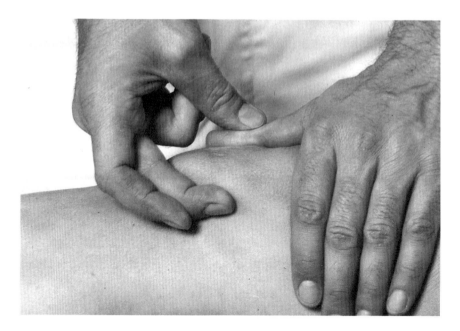

Figure 11–21B End position of transverse friction of medial parapatellar insertion tendopathy. The wrist is now extended.

obtain complete relief. The transverse friction is performed for 10 to 15 minutes. Many athletes should continue to wear the patellar tape or brace during their sports activities.

TRANSVERSE FRICTION FOR AN INFRAPATELLAR INSERTION TENDOPATHY (APEXITIS PATELLAE, "JUMPER'S KNEE")

Position of the Patient

The patient is supine on the treatment table with the affected knee extended.

Position of the Therapist

The therapist sits or stands at knee level next to the treatment table, at the patient's affected side. If, for example, the right knee is affected, the therapist places the web space of the left hand against the base of the patella in such a way that the thumb is lateral and the fingers medial. When pressure is exerted in a posterior direction, the apex of the patella tips upward, away from the tibia. The tip of the right middle finger is now placed just medial to the lesion; the nail of the middle finger is positioned vertically. The right thumb is placed behind the left thumb and applies counterpressure (Figure 11–22A).

Performance

The right middle finger, reinforced by the index finger, exerts pressure against the patella in a proximoposterior direction. During the active phase of the transverse friction, the wrist extends. In so doing, the middle finger is moved from medial to lateral over the lesion (Figure 11–22B).

As with parapatellar insertion tendopathy, transverse friction therapy is combined with other therapeutic measures, such as stretching of the rectus femoris muscle. Pain-provoking activities should be limited, depending on the severity of the lesion. For more detailed information, refer to the sections on the

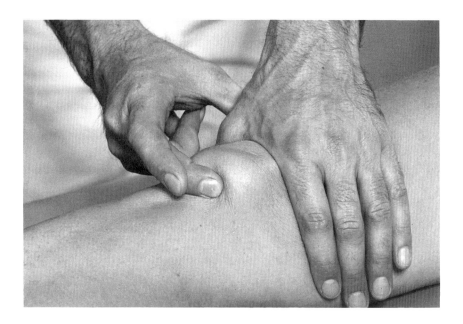

Figure 11–22A Initial position in transverse friction of infrapatellar insertion tendopathy.

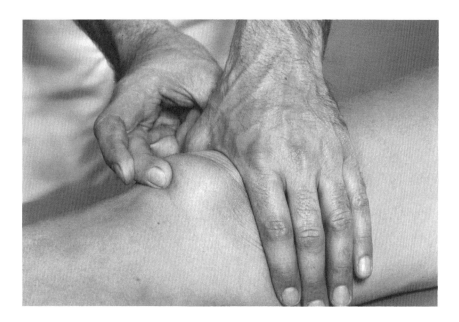

Figure 11–22B End position in transverse friction of infrapatellar insertion tendopathy. The wrist is extended.

"Pathology of the Patellofemoral Joint" and "Infrapatellar Insertion Tendopathy" in Chapter 10.

Note

Sometimes the most painful site is found not on the inferior aspect of the apex of the patella but on the anterior aspect. The hand position changes so that patella fixation with the left hand prevents the patella from moving medially or laterally: The thumb rests against the lateral side of the patella and the index finger at the medial side. Transverse friction is performed with the tip of the right index finger, during which the pressure is now exerted in a posterior direction (Figure 11–22C).

Duration

The number of treatments to achieve complete relief of symptoms varies from 6 to 15. Transverse friction should be performed for 10 to 15 minutes each session. If there is little to no improvement after 6 treatments, an injection with a corticosteroid is indicated.

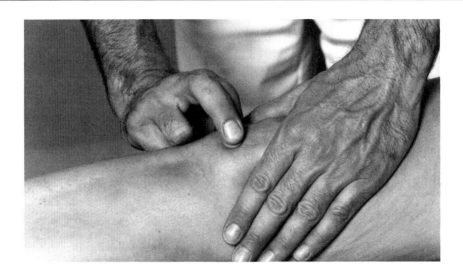

Figure 11–22C Transverse friction at the anterior aspect of the apex of the patella.

TRANSVERSE FRICTION FOR A SUPRAPATELLAR INSERTION TENDOPATHY

Functional Examination

Resisted knee extension is painful (usually only when tested immediately after the patient performs the pain-provoking activity).

Suprapatellar insertion tendopathy is a typical sports injury and is seen less often than infrapatellar insertion tendopathy.

Position of the Patient

The patient is supine on the treatment table. The affected knee is in slight flexion and supported by a small pillow or roll.

Position of the Therapist

The therapist sits or stands at lower leg level next to the treatment table, at the patient's affected side. If, for example, the right knee is being treated, the therapist places the web space of the right hand on the apex of the patella and pushes posteriorly so that the base of the patella is tipped forward. The tip of the left middle finger palpates the base of the patella from medial to lateral to locate the most tender spot. The nail of the middle finger should be held as vertically as possible. The thumb of this hand is placed against the dorsal side of the right thumb.

Performance

The middle finger is reinforced by the index finger, or these fingers can be transposed. Transverse friction is performed from medial to lateral over the site of the lesion. During the active phase the wrist is extended, and pressure is exerted in a distal direction (Figure 11–23).

As with parapatellar and infrapatellar insertion tendopathy, the friction treatment should be combined with stretching of the rectus femoris. In some cases, patellar taping or bracing can also be helpful.

Duration

Usually, depending on the severity of the symptoms, 6 to 10 treatments with transverse friction lasting 10 to 15 minutes each are sufficient to provide complete relief.

BRACING OR TAPING

The taping and bracing methods described below are appropriate in conjunction with the transverse friction treatment and stretching exercises and should be applied before sports activities.

Position of the Patient

The patient is supine on the treatment table with the affected knee in an extended position.

Position of the Therapist

The therapist sits or stands next to the patient's affected side.

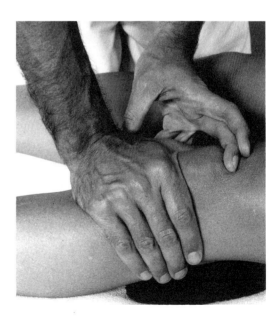

Figure 11–23 Transverse friction of suprapatellar insertion tendopathy.

Performance

A 6-cm wide elastic tape is first applied in a circular manner just distal to the apex of the patella. Then a strip of nonelastic tape, 2 cm wide, is placed over the patellar ligament in the same circular way (Figure 11–24).

Figure 11–25 shows an example of a brace that can be used to control the pa-tella. In patients with an increased quadri-ceps angle, the tendency of the patella to be pulled too far laterally is somewhat re-stricted by the bracing. Usually, minimal medially directed pressure is sufficient to achieve this restriction. Like the taping, this brace is most appropriate for use during sports activities.

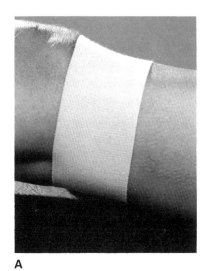

A

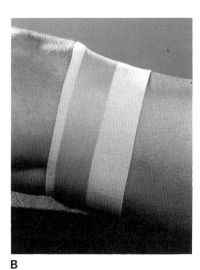

B

Figure 11–24 Taping method.

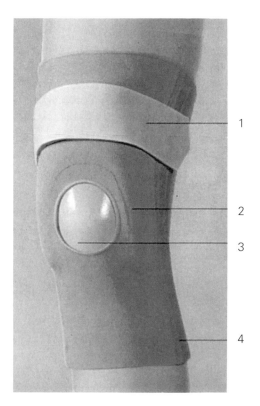

Figure 11–25 Brace for control of the patella. **1**, Adjustable strap with Velcro closure for extra compression; **2**, horseshoe-shaped felt pad in-side the brace at the medial aspect of the patella opening, which guarantees proper guiding of the patella; **3**, opening to avoid compression of the patella; **4**, interwoven flexible spiral springs.

SUBCUTANEOUS PREPATELLAR BURSITIS

Functional Examination

The functional examination is usually negative. Sometimes, passive knee flexion is mildly painful.

INJECTION

The subcutaneous prepatellar bursitis is usually caused by chronic compression. Such compression is typically found in occupations such as carpet or tile laying, or it can be the result of a systemic (rheumatic) disease.

Position of the Patient

The patient is supine on the treatment table with the affected knee extended.

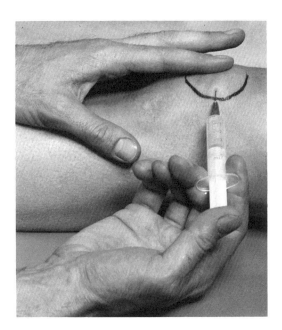

Figure 11–26 Injection of the subcutaneous prepatellar bursa.

Position of the Physician

The physician sits or stands next to the treatment table, at the patient's affected side.

Performance

From a lateral direction, a 5-cm needle is inserted horizontally between the patella and the skin. An obviously swollen bursa should first be aspirated and then injected. When the swelling is minimal, aspiration should still be attempted but is generally not successful. Local anesthetic is used, and it is injected in a fan-shaped manner as directed by the patient's pain and depending on the amount of resistance. When the needle passes through the wall of the bursa, the patient typically experiences pain. At this point, the needle is inserted farther until the pain is no longer felt. Some of the solution is then injected as the needle is withdrawn from this area. This method of inserting and injecting as the needle is withdrawn is repeated in all directions until the entire painful area of the bursa has been injected. If the needle enters a nonpainful area, no solution is injected (Figure 11–26).

The presence of a bursitis is usually confirmed when, during the process of insertion, the patient clearly feels pain and the physician feels minimal to no resistance. The amount of local anesthetic injected, 2 to 5 mL, depends on the size of the bursa.

Follow-Up

After 1 week, the results of the injection are evaluated. If the symptoms have decreased, the injection is repeated. If there has been no significant change, 1 to 2 mL of corticosteroid is injected. The number of injections necessary to achieve complete relief varies between one and six. If there is no improvement after three injections, surgical removal of the bursa should be considered.

SUPERFICIAL OR DEEP INFRAPATELLAR BURSITIS

Functional Examination

The functional examination is usually negative. In some cases, passive knee flexion is painful (usually in superficial infrapatellar bursitis), and sometimes resisted knee extension is also painful (usually in deep infrapatellar bursitis).

INJECTION

Causes of a superficial or deep infrapatellar bursitis can be chronic compression, Osgood-Schlatter's disease, muscular overuse, or rheumatic disease.

Position of the Patient

The patient is supine on the treatment table with the affected knee in approximately 30° flexion. The knee is supported by a pillow or small bolster.

Position of the Physician

The physician stands or sits next to the treatment table at the patient's affected side.

Performance

Superficial Infrapatellar Bursitis.
From a lateral direction, a 3-cm long needle is inserted between the patellar ligament and the skin (Figure 11–27). An obviously swollen bursa should first be aspirated and then injected. When the swelling is minimal, aspiration should still be attempted but is generally not successful. Local anesthetic is used, and it is injected in a fan-shaped manner as directed by the patient's pain and depending on the amount of resistance. When the needle passes through the wall of the bursa, the patient typically experiences pain. At this point, the needle is inserted farther until the pain is no longer felt. Some of the solution is then injected as the needle is withdrawn from this area. This method of inserting and injecting

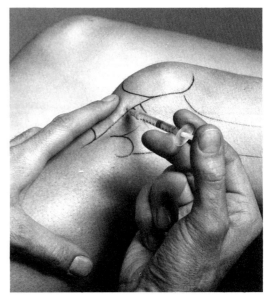

Figure 11–27 Injection of the superficial infrapatellar bursa.

as the needle is withdrawn is repeated in all directions until the entire painful area of the bursa has been injected. If the needle enters a nonpainful area, no solution is injected.

The presence of a bursitis is usually confirmed when, during the process of insertion, the patient clearly feels pain and the physician feels minimal to no resistance. The amount of local anesthetic injected, 2 to 5 mL, depends on the size of the bursa.

Deep Infrapatellar Bursitis. From a
lateral direction, a 3-cm needle is inserted between the tibia and patellar ligament (Figure 11–28). An obviously swollen bursa should first be aspirated and then injected. When the swelling is minimal, aspiration should still be attempted but is generally not successful. Local anesthetic is used, and it is injected in a fan-shaped manner as directed by the patient's pain and depending on the amount

of resistance. When the needle passes through the wall of the bursa, the patient typically experiences pain. At this point, the needle is inserted farther until the pain is no longer felt. Some of the solution is then injected as the needle is withdrawn from this area. This method of inserting and injecting as the needle is withdrawn is repeated in all directions until the entire painful area of the bursa has been injected. If the needle enters a nonpainful area, no solution is injected.

The presence of a bursitis is usually confirmed when, during the process of insertion, the patient clearly feels pain and the physi-cian feels minimal to no resistance. The amount of local anesthetic injected is usually 1 mL.

Follow-Up

After 1 week, the results of the injection are evaluated. If the symptoms have decreased, the injection is repeated. If there has been no significant change, 1 to 2 mL of corticosteroid are injected. The number of injections necessary to achieve complete relief of symptoms varies between one and three. If there is no improvement after three injections, surgical removal of the bursa should be considered.

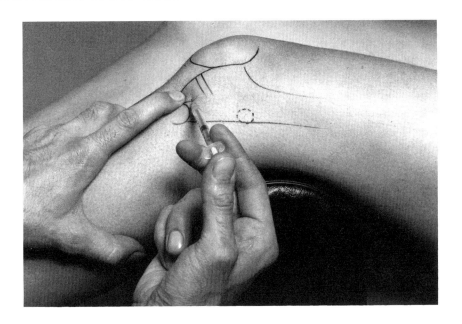

Figure 11–28 Injection of the deep infrapatellar bursa.

PES ANSERINUS SUPERFICIALIS BURSITIS

Functional Examination

The functional examination is usually negative.

INJECTION

Differentiation between a bursitis and an insertion tendopathy of the superficial pes

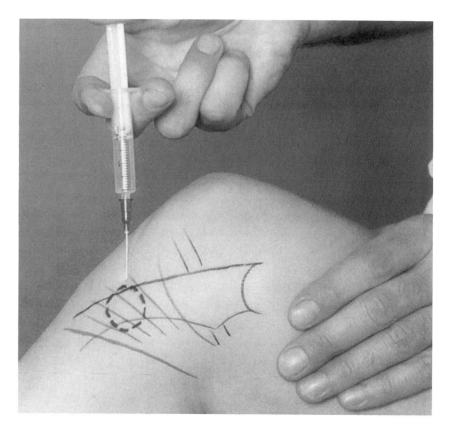

Figure 11–29 Injection of a bursitis at the level of the pes anserinus superficialis, for instance between the medial collateral ligament and the pes anserinus superficialis.

anserinus is often difficult. In the presence of a bursitis, there is usually only tenderness to palpation and sometimes local swelling that is fluctuating in consistency when palpated.

Position of the Patient

The patient is supine on the treatment table with the affected side as close as possible to the edge of the table and the knee in 90° flexion.

Position of the Physician

The physician stands next to the treatment table at the patient's affected side.

Performance

After careful localization of the bursitis, a 5-cm long needle is inserted almost vertically, parallel to the structures between which the bursa is located (Figure 11–29). An obviously swollen bursa should first be aspirated and then injected. When the swelling is minimal, aspiration should still be attempted but is generally not successful. Local anesthetic is used, and it is injected in a fan-shaped manner as directed by the patient's pain and depending on the amount of resistance. When the needle passes through the wall of the bursa, the patient typically experiences pain. At this point, the needle is inserted farther until the pain is no longer felt. Some of the solution is then injected as the needle is withdrawn from this area. This method of inserting and injecting as the needle is withdrawn is repeated in all directions until the entire painful area of the bursa has been injected. If the needle enters a nonpainful area, no solution is injected.

The presence of a bursitis is usually confirmed when, during the process of insertion, the patient clearly feels pain and the physician feels minimal to no resistance. The amount of local anesthetic injected is usually 1 to 2 mL.

Follow-Up

After 1 week, the results of the injection are evaluated. If the symptoms have decreased, the injection is repeated. If there has been no significant change, 1 to 2 mL of corticosteroid are injected. The number of injections necessary to achieve complete relief of symptoms varies between one and three. If there is no improvement after three injections, a thorough evaluation and subsequent correction of lower extremity alignment should be initiated.

INSERTION TENDOPATHY OF THE PES ANSERINUS SUPERFICIALIS

Functional Examination

Resisted knee flexion combined with resisted internal rotation of the lower leg is painful (particularly when performed repeatedly).

TRANSVERSE FRICTION

Unless the bursa is obviously swollen, it is not always easy to differentiate between a tendinitis of the pes anserinus superficialis and a bursitis. If the pain increases during the transverse friction treatment, there is likely to be a bursitis.

Position of the Patient

The patient is supine on the treatment table with the affected knee extended.

Position of the Therapist

The therapist stands or sits next to the treatment table, at the patient's affected side. If, for example, the right knee is being treated, the therapist places the left hand on the patient's thigh while, after careful palpation, the tip of the right index finger is placed just posterior to the site of the lesion.

Performance

During the active phase of the transverse friction, the wrist is extended, creating the motion by which the index finger, reinforced by the middle finger, is moved transversely over the lesion from posteromedial to anterolateral and slightly proximal (Figure 11–30).

Duration

Patients who are athletes should be seen daily and others at least three times per week for 2 to 4 weeks. Patients with gonarthrosis (osteoarthrosis of the knee) should receive transverse friction treatments two to three times per week in combination with joint-specific mobilization of the knee.

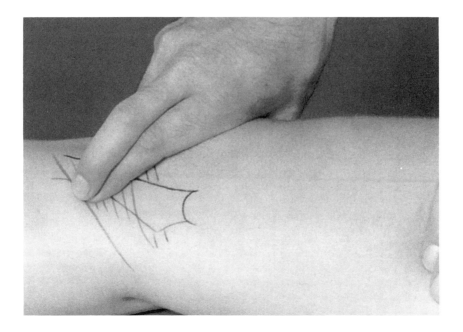

Figure 11–30 Transverse friction of the pes anserinus superficialis.

ILIOTIBIAL BAND FRICTION SYNDROME

Functional Examination

The basic functional examination is usually negative. Pressure against the lateral femoral epicondyle provokes pain when the knee is actively or passively flexed or extended between 30° and 40°.

INJECTION

The iliotibial band friction syndrome is a typical sports injury, seen particularly in long-distance runners and bicyclists. In most instances, it is not the tendon but rather the bursa between the tendon and the lateral femoral epicondyle that is affected.

Position of the Patient

The patient is supine on the treatment table with the knee positioned in 30° to 40° flexion. The knee is supported by a pillow or small bolster.

Position of the Physician

The physician stands or sits next to the treatment table at the patient's affected side.

Performance

The lateral femoral epicondyle is located; the simplest method is to put the leg in the figure-4 position and to follow the lateral collateral ligament to its proximal insertion. A 4-cm needle is inserted vertically between the iliotibial tract and the lateral femoral epicondyle (Figure 11–31). For the first injection, 1 mL of local anesthetic is injected. If, after 1 week, the symptoms have not significantly improved, 1 mL of corticosteroid is injected.

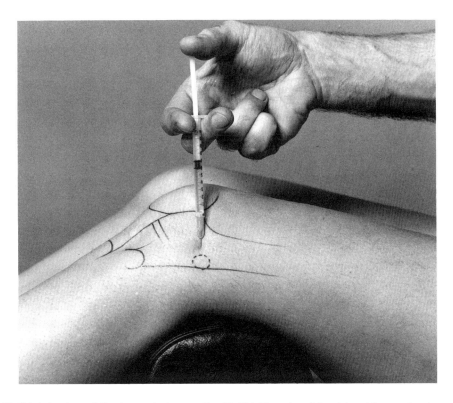

Figure 11–31 Injection of the bursa between the iliotibial band and the lateral femoral epicondyle.

Usually one to three injections are necessary to achieve complete relief of pain. In addition, the iliotibial tract is stretched. If necessary, the static position of the lower extremities is corrected by means of orthotics in the shoes. Athletes should temporarily reduce or stop activities that provoke their pain. For example, running on uneven terrain should be avoided, and the distance normally covered during running or biking should be reduced.

STRETCHING

Position of the Patient

The patient is supine on the treatment table with the affected leg in maximal adduction and the knee supported in slight flexion. The other leg is flexed at the hip and knee to the extent necessary to achieve maximal adduction of the affected leg. The trunk is maximally sidebent toward the nonaffected side.

Position of the Therapist

The therapist stands next to the treatment table at the patient's affected side. If, for example, the right iliotibial tract is being stretched, the therapist grasps the patient's lower leg with the right hand just above the ankle, bringing the entire leg as far as possible into adduction. The other hand grasps the patella with the thenar and hypothenar eminences lateral and the thumb and fingers medial.

Performance

The therapist slowly pushes the patella medially, making sure not to cause pain or muscle splinting (Figure 11–32). With this

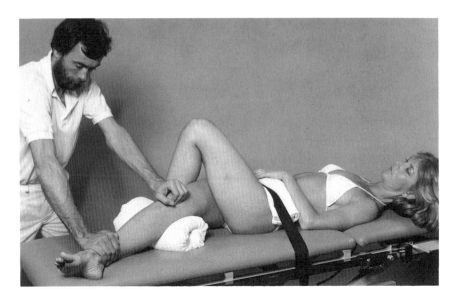

Figure 11–32 Stretching of the iliotibial tract, particularly the fibers to the patella.

technique, in particular the fibers of the iliotibial tract that insert at the patella are stretched. It is difficult to stretch these fibers of the iliotibial tract without the assistance of a therapist. Therefore, self-stretching exercises are not discussed.

INSERTION TENDOPATHY OF THE BICEPS FEMORIS MUSCLE

Functional Examination

Resisted flexion of the knee, especially when combined with resisted external rotation of the lower leg, is painful.

TRANSVERSE FRICTION

In almost all cases of this typical sports injury, the insertion of the biceps femoris at the head of the fibula is affected.

Position of the Patient

The patient is supine on the treatment table with the knee slightly flexed, supported by a small pillow or roll.

Position of the Therapist

The therapist sits or stands next to the treatment table at the patient's nonaffected side. If, for example, the left knee is affected, the therapist (after carefully palpating to locate the most tender spot) places the tip of the right index finger at the proximolateral aspect of the fibular head. The right thumb is positioned at the medial side of the lower leg, more distally than the index finger.

Performance

With the tip of the index finger reinforced by the middle finger, transverse friction is

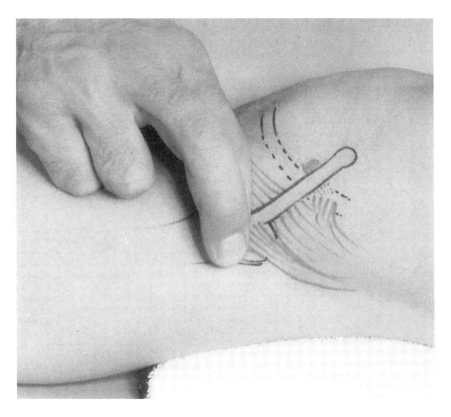

Figure 11–33 Transverse friction of the biceps femoris insertion at the head of the fibula.

applied over the lesion from posterolateral to anteromedial and slightly distal. The active phase of the transverse friction is performed by extending the wrist (Figure 11–33).

Duration

Depending on the stage of the insertion tendopathy, transverse friction treatment should be performed two to three times per week, lasting about 20 minutes each session. In the first or second stage of tendopathy, when pain is experienced after (or at the beginning of as well as after) the activity, 6 to 10 treatments are usually required to achieve complete relief. The patient should also perform self-stretching exercises regularly throughout the day (see the stretching exer-

cises in "Lesions of the Hamstrings" in Chapter 5).

In the third stage of a tendinitis, pain is constant but performance is not affected. In the fourth stage, pain is constant and performance is affected as well. The treatment of either of these stages includes temporary cessation of the symptom-provoking activities in addition to transverse friction. Usually 10 to 15 transverse friction treatments are required to achieve complete relief.

INJECTION

If there is minimal to no improvement after six sessions of transverse friction, an injection of the insertion of the biceps femoris is indicated.

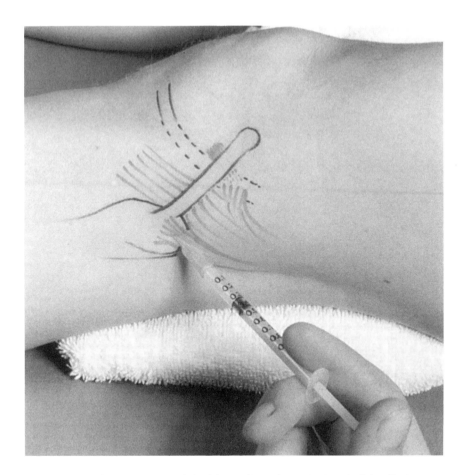

Figure 11–34 Injection of the insertion of the biceps femoris at the head of the fibula.

Position of the Patient

The patient is supine on the treatment table with the knee slightly flexed, supported by a small pillow or roll.

Position of the Physician

The physician stands at knee level or sits next to the treatment table at the patient's affected side.

Performance

The physician carefully locates the site of the lesion. A syringe is filled with 1 mL of corticosteroid. For this injection, a 3-cm needle is inserted almost horizontally in a medial and slightly distal direction (Figure 11–34). Directed by the patient's pain, the injection is made at the fibular head in a drop-wise fashion.

Follow-Up

The patient is advised to restrict activities with the affected knee for 3 to 4 days. In many cases, the patient experiences increased pain after the injection, which can last several days. After 1 week, the knee is reassessed. If the functional examination still provokes pain, a second injection is given. Usually two to four injections are required to achieve complete relief.

Note

Sometimes, during the palpation, tenderness cannot be elicited either at the fibular head or at the tibial insertion. When this is the situation, the fibers of the biceps femoris that insert at the lateral meniscus are involved, or there is a lesion of the lateral meniscus itself. In such cases, the diagnosis can be confirmed with an injection of a local anesthetic.

The knee is flexed 90°, and the injection is given in the joint space just posterior to the lateral collateral ligament (Figure 11–35).

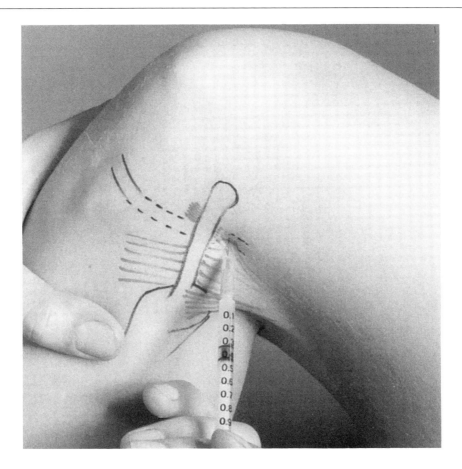

Figure 11–35 Injection of the biceps femoris fibers that insert at the posterior horn of the lateral meniscus.

INSERTION TENDOPATHY OF THE POPLITEUS MUSCLE

Functional Examination

Resisted flexion of the knee, particularly when combined with resisted internal rotation of the lower leg, is painful at the lateral side of the knee (usually only painful directly after the pain-provoking activity has been performed).

INJECTION

An insertion tendopathy of the popliteus muscle is a rarely seen lesion at the lateral aspect of the knee. Differentiation between an insertion tendopathy of the popliteus and a lesion of the posterior horn of the lateral meniscus is often difficult and, in many cases, is only possible by means of an injection with a local anesthetic.

Position of the Patient

The patient is supine on the treatment table with the knee slightly flexed, supported by a small pillow or roll.

Position of the Physician

The physician stands or sits next to the treatment table at the patient's affected side.

Performance

First, the physician locates the lateral collateral ligament by putting the patient's leg in the figure-4 position. Next, the lateral femoral epicondyle is located. In this position, the insertion of the popliteus muscle is found just distal to the lateral femoral epicondyle and anterior to the lateral collateral ligament.

A syringe is filled with 1 mL of local anesthetic, and a 2- to 3-cm needle is inserted perpendicular to the skin (Figure 11–36). The insertion is then injected in a drop-wise fashion, corresponding to where the patient experiences pain.

If, after the injection, the functional examination is negative, the diagnosis is confirmed. In some cases, this treatment will already have a therapeutic effect. If not, transverse friction can be tried, or the injection can be repeated with 0.5 mL of corticosteroid.

After injection with a corticosteroid, the patient is advised to limit knee-stressful activities for several days. The patient is seen again for follow-up after 1 week. If pain is still provoked during the follow-up functional examination, the injection can be repeated. No more than four injections at 1-week intervals should be administered.

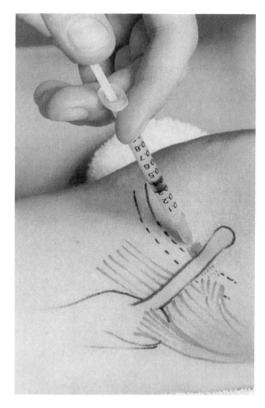

Figure 11–36 Injection of the insertion of the popliteus muscle.

COMPRESSION NEUROPATHY OF THE SAPHENOUS NERVE

Functional Examination

The functional examination of the knee is negative except when compression occurs through subluxation of the medial meniscus or is the result of trauma in which medial knee structures have been injured. For further clinical findings, refer to Chapters 10 and 12.

INJECTION

There are two possible sites of compression: at the medial side of the knee, location of the compression is determined by the site of most tenderness to palpation, and at the site where the saphenous nerve exits the subsartorial canal.

Position of the Patient

The patient is supine on the treatment table with the affected knee extended. The lower part of the other leg, with the knee flexed, hangs over the edge of the table.

Position of the Physician

The physician sits or stands next to the treatment table at the patient's nonaffected side.

Performance

A 2-mL syringe is filled with a local anesthetic (eg, 1% lidocaine). A 5-cm needle is inserted horizontally 5 to 7 cm proximal to the adductor tubercle at the site of most tenderness between the vastus medialis and sartorius muscles. The needle is pushed in until the patient feels a tingling sensation (an increase in symptoms) from the saphenous nerve. Then the needle is withdrawn slightly, and 2 mL of solution are slowly injected (Figure 11–37).

Follow-Up

There are no specific measures that the patient has to follow after this injection. After 1 week, the patient's condition should be reassessed. In instances of improvement, 1 mL of corticosteroid is injected to achieve more permanent results (when this disorder is treated, the problem almost always recurs when only a local anesthetic is used in the injections). Surgery is seldom indicated.

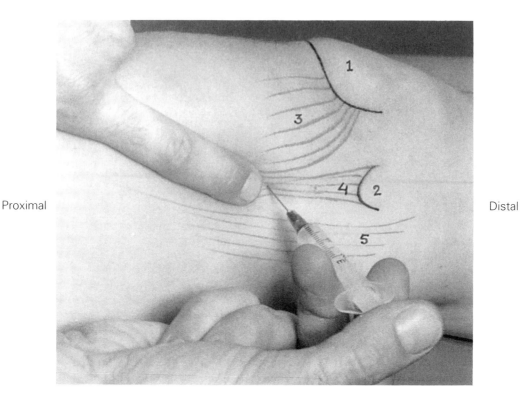

Proximal   Distal

Figure 11–37 Perineural injection of the saphenous nerve where the nerve exits the subsartorial canal. **1**, Patella; **2**, adductor tubercle; **3**, vastus medialis muscle; **4**, adductor magnus muscle; **5**, sartorius muscle.

COMPRESSION NEUROPATHY OF THE COMMON PERONEAL NERVE

Functional Examination

In severe cases, there is loss of strength of the extensors and evertors of the foot. For further clinical findings, refer to Chapters 10 and 12.

INJECTION

Differentiating compression of the common peroneal nerve from an L4 or L5 nerve root irritation, compression of the superficial peroneal nerve, or compression of the deep peroneal nerve is not always easy. Therefore, injection with a local anesthetic is always done before the diagnosis can be complete.

Position of the Patient

The patient is supine on the treatment table with the knee slightly flexed and the hip internally rotated.

Position of the Physician

The physician sits next to the treatment table at the patient's affected side.

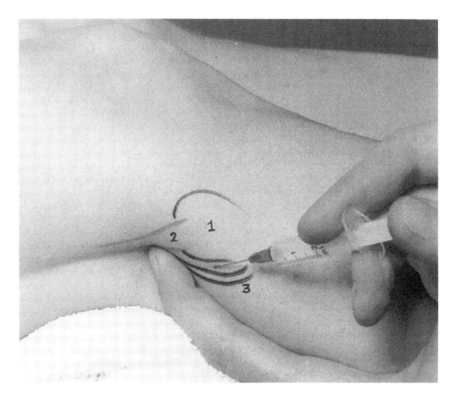

Figure 11–38 Perineural injection of the common peroneal nerve at the level of the neck of the fibula. **1**, Head of the fibula; **2**, biceps femoris muscle; **3**, common peroneal nerve.

Performance

A 2-mL syringe is filled with a local anesthetic (eg, 1% lidocaine). With the patient in the above described position, the nerve is easily palpated just medial to the tendon of the biceps femoris and can be followed from this point distally until symptoms are provoked by the manual pressure exerted on the nerve. At this site, 2 mL of local anesthetic are injected around the lesion with a 4-cm needle (Figure 11–38).

Follow-Up

There are no specific measures that the patient has to follow after this injection. After 1 week, the patient should be seen for reassessment. If the symptoms have improved, the injection is repeated. If there is no change in the symptoms but directly after the first injection they had decreased or disappeared, 1 mL of corticosteroid is injected. In some therapy-resistant cases, surgery is indicated.

Chapter 12

Peripheral Compression Neuropathies in the Knee Region

COMPRESSION NEUROPATHY OF THE SAPHENOUS NERVE

The saphenous nerve springs from the femoral nerve (L2 to L4). It is a cutaneous nerve and gives off branches at the medial aspect of the knee (Figure 12–1). Compression of the saphenous nerve usually occurs either at the site where the nerve leaves the subsartorial canal or on the medial side of the knee (Figure 12–2). There is a wide variety of causes of compression. These can include direct trauma, genu valgum (often in conjunction with obesity), medial meniscus subluxation, and complications resulting from a medial incision used in knee surgery. Indirect trauma, such as one that induces a knee instability (typically a valgus–flexion–external rotation trauma), can also damage the nerve.

Clinical Findings

The patient experiences pain at the medial aspect of the knee and lower leg, extending to the medial edge of the foot. Pain is chiefly provoked during activities in which the knee is flexed more than 60°, such as when climbing stairs.

Functional Examination

The examiner is usually unable to provoke the patient's symptoms during the functional examination, unless the underlying pathology is known. Palpation at the site of compression causes not only local but also radiating pain. Palpation for the saphenous nerve at the opening in the subsartorial canal is done at a site that is approximately the width of four fingers above the medial femoral condyle, between the vastus medialis and sartorius muscles.

Treatment

A perineural injection at the site of the compression with a solution of corticosteroid and local anesthetic is almost always effective. Surgery is rarely necessary.

COMPRESSION NEUROPATHY OF THE TIBIAL NERVE

The tibial nerve (L4 to S3) lies well protected in the popliteal fossa and is rarely pathologically compressed. The tibial nerve can be damaged from a dislocation of the knee. In this instance, however, the common peroneal nerve is much more often affected. Lesions of the tibial nerve are occasionally seen in tibia fractures. A compression of the tibial nerve can occur in young athletes as the result of a soleus syndrome.

Clinical Findings

The first symptom to appear in a compression neuropathy of the tibial nerve is a sensory disturbance at the sole of the foot. In later stages, sensory disturbances are experienced from midcalf to the heel. In severe lesions, motor deficit is experienced in all the foot and toe flexors, including the short muscles except for the extensor digitorum and extensor hallucis brevis. Even with total paralysis of the nerve, the patient is still able, albeit weakly, to actively plantar flex the foot by contracting the peroneus longus muscle.

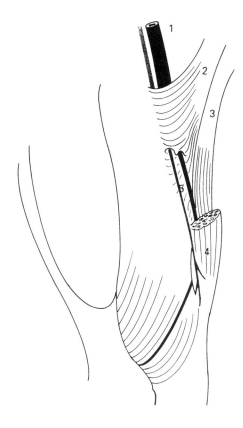

Figure 12–1 Saphenous nerve (anteromedial aspect of the right knee). **1**, Femoral artery; **2**, adductor magnus muscle; **3**, gracilis muscle; **4**, sartorius muscle; **5**, saphenous nerve.

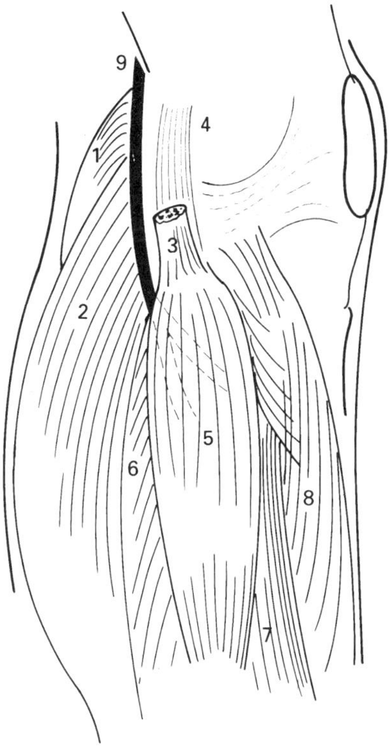

Figure 12–2 Common peroneal nerve (lateral side of the right knee). **1**, Plantaris muscle; **2**, gastrocnemius, lateral head; **3**, tendon of the biceps femoris muscle; **4**, lateral collateral ligament; **5**, peroneus longus muscle; **6**, soleus muscle; **7**, peroneus brevis muscle; **8**, tibialis anterior muscle; **9**, common peroneal nerve.

Treatment

The type of treatment varies according to the type and severity of the lesion. For instance, if the nerve has been damaged as the result of a fracture or dislocation of the knee, and if neurologic signs and symptoms of a tibial nerve lesion are still present after the fracture or dislocation has been surgically repaired, surgery is again indicated, but this time to release the entrapped nerve. In instances of a soleus syndrome, treatment consists of surgery to resect the tissue responsible for compressing the neurovascular structures.

COMPRESSION NEUROPATHY OF THE COMMON PERONEAL NERVE

Compression of the common peroneal nerve (L4 to S2) occurs most often at the level of the fibular neck (see Figure 12–2). The cause is generally traumatic. In an acute case, the cause is often direct or indirect trauma, such as an inversion trauma of the foot. In a chronic case, the disorder is often the result of repeated crawling with the foot in inversion, a common practice of gardeners. A loose body from the knee joint occasionally causes compression of this nerve.

Differential Diagnosis

- Compression neuropathy of the deep or superficial peroneal nerves, in which proximally radiating pain can also occur.
- Anterior tibial compartment syndrome.

Clinical Findings

Pain is experienced at the anterolateral aspect of the lower leg, the dorsum of the foot, and the first four toes. Sensory disturbances can be experienced in the form of hyperesthesia, hypoesthesia, or anesthesia. Loss of strength of the evertors and extensors (dorsiflexors) of the foot can occur.

Treatment

Treatment consists of decreasing the tension of the fasciae of the lower leg and peroneal muscles by means of orthotics with a lateral wedge. If necessary, an injection with a solution of corticosteroid and local anesthetic can be administered at the site of the compression. In recurrent cases, when conservative treatment is unsuccessful, surgical neurolysis is indicated.

PART II—KNEE REVIEW QUESTIONS

1. Name the localization and the various connections of the contractile structures surrounding the menisci.

2. Name the clinically most important flexors of the knee.

3. Give the definition of a plica.

4. What is the clinically most important plica in the knee, and where does it run?

5. In which knee position are both cruciate ligaments fully relaxed?

6. In which knee position are both collateral ligaments fully relaxed?

7. In which direction do the menisci move during flexion and extension?

8. Name the maximal loose-packed and the maximal close-packed positions of the knee.

9. Which arthritides of the knee are seen mostly in children?

10. In which disease does hemarthrosis of the knee frequently occur?

11. What is osteochondritis dissecans of the knee, and which types can be differentiated?

12. What is the most important goal in treatment of juvenile osteochondritis dissecans?

13. Name three causes of a loose body specific to the knee.

14. Name five different lesions of the menisci.

15. Define the "snapping knee" syndrome.

16. Define Pellegrini-Stieda disease.

17. What four types of uniplanar instabilities can be differentiated in the knee?

18. Which test is *always* positive with a sprain of the medial meniscotibial (coronary) ligament?

19. Which structures can be affected in a 1+ medial instability with the knee in slight flexion?

20. Which structures can be affected in a 1+ medial instability with the knee in extension?

21. Which structures can be affected in a 1+ anterior instability of the knee?

22. Which structures can be affected by a 2+ posterior instability of the knee?

23. Which type of rotatory instability of the knee is seen most often? In a 1+ instability, which structures are affected?

24. In which age group is chondromalacia of the patella most common, and what is the etiology?

25. Clinically, what is the greatest difference between subluxation of the patella and chondromalacia of the patella?

26. In which way can one best diagnose an iliotibial band syndrome?

27. Which tendon lesions of the knee joint are most frequently seen?

28. How can one best diagnose a compression neuropathy of the saphenous nerve?

29. Define Osgood-Schlatter disease.

30. In which direction does the proximal tibiofibular joint most frequently dislocate?

PART II—KNEE REVIEW ANSWERS

1. Anterior: both medially as well as laterally through the medial and lateral patellotibial ligaments (part of the extensor mechanism). Posterior: medially through a tendon from the semimembranosus muscle and laterally through the popliteus tendon. Lateral: through the biceps femoris tendon

2. Popliteus, biceps femoris, semimembranosus, semitendinosus, gracilis, and sartorius.

3. Synovial folds in the joint capsule that are residual from septa present in the embryologic stage of the joint.

4. Mediopatellar plica: It runs from the underside of the quadriceps insertion just proximal to the patella and over the cartilage of the medial femoral condyle to the infrapatellar fat pad.

5. The cruciates are never fully relaxed.

6. The collateral ligaments are never fully relaxed.

7. In general, during flexion they move backward and during extension they move forward.

8. Maximal loose-packed position: approximately 25° knee flexion. Maximal close-packed position: maximal extension of the knee.

9. Juvenile rheumatoid arthritis and ankylosing spondylitis.

10. Hemophilia.

11. A lesion of the subchondral bone and later also of the joint cartilage, localized in the lateral aspect of the medial femoral condyle. The cause has many factors; trauma is the most important factor. One differentiates between juvenile osteochondritis dissecans (in children) and osteochondritis disse-

cans in adults. In the first case, the lesion occurs before the closing of the distal femoral epiphysis, and in adults it occurs afterward.

12. Prevention of osteoarthrosis in the knee.

13. Gonarthrosis (osteoarthrosis), meniscus fragment, retropatellar chondropathy.

14. Longitudinal tear, transverse tear, meniscus fraying, ganglion, discoid meniscus.

15. The syndrome occurs when a lateral discoid meniscus is poorly attached to the posterior horn by the posterior meniscofemoral ligament (Wristberg's ligament). This ligament can be too short to allow normal extension of the knee. Therefore, hypermobility of the posterior horn of the flat meniscus occurs with resulting hypertrophy. During flexion and extension of the knee, an audible click occurs.

16. After trauma with a valgus component or a pure valgus trauma, a progressive flexion limitation occurs. On radiographs, one can see a calcification at the site of the origin of the medial collateral ligament (usually above, at, or just below the adductor tubercle).

17. Medial instability, lateral instability, anterior instability, posterior instability.

18. Passive external rotation of the tibia.

19. The media meniscotibial (coronary) ligament and possibly the medial meniscus.

20. The posterior oblique ligament (posteromedial corner of the capsule), the medial collateral ligament (sprain or

partial rupture), possibly the medial meniscus.

21. The anterior cruciate ligament, possibly the medial meniscus.

22. Posterior cruciate ligament, posteromedial and/or posterolateral capsuloligamentous structures.

23. Anterolateral rotatory instability. The anterior cruciate ligament, possibly the lateral meniscotibial (coronary) ligament (the lateral or the posterior part, sometimes the anterior part).

24. In adolescents; the etiology is traumatic.

25. With a subluxation of the patella, the problems usually occur in the first 30° of flexion; in patellar chondromalacia, the problems usually occur around 90° flexion.

26. With the patient in either standing or supine, the examiner exerts pressure on the lateral femoral epicondyle while the knee is slowly brought from an extended position into flexion. The patient indicates the most pain between 30° and 40° flexion.

27. Tendopathy of the extensor mechanism at its supra-, infra-, and parapatellar insertions. Insertion tendopathy of the pes anserinus superficialis and the biceps femoris.

28. The functional examination is usually negative. One exerts pressure on the hiatus at the level of the subsartorial canal, about 4 cm above the proximal aspect of the medial femoral condyle. This compression test is diagnostically significant when not only local but also radiating pain is provoked.

29. This concerns a traction apophysitis as a result of an abnormal position of the patella, which is usually seen in boys between 10 and 15 years of age.

30. Anteriorly.

REFERENCES

1. Wiberg G. Röntgenographic and anatomic studies on the femoral patellar joint with special reference to chondromalacia patellae. *Acta Orthop Scand.* 1941;12:319–410.

2. Last RJ. The popliteus muscle and the lateral meniscus—With a note on the attachment of the lateral meniscus. *J Bone Joint Surg Br.* 1950;32:93–99.

3. Jouanin T, Dupont JY, Pandlassan JP. The synovial folds of the knee joint: Anatomical study based on the dissection of 200 knee joints. *Anat Clin.* 1982;4:47–53.

4. Huson A. Biomechanische Probleme des Kniegelenks. *Orthopäde.* 1974; 3:119–126.

5. Menschik A. Mechanik des Kniegelenkes: Teil I. *Z Orthop.* 1974;112:481–495.

6. Menschik A. Mechanik des Kniegelenkes: Teil II. *Z Orthop.* 1975;113:388–400.

7. Kapandji IA. *Bewegingsleer, Deel 2: De onderste extremiteit.* Utrecht, Netherlands: Bohn, Scheltema & Holkema; 1982.

8. Frankel VJ, Nordin M, Snijders CJ. *Biomechanica van het Skeletsysteem: Grondslagen en Toepassingen.* Lochem, Holland: De Tijdstroom; 1984.

9. Morrison JB. The mechanics of the knee joint in relation to normal walking. *J Biomech.* 1970;3:51–58.

10. Steinmann

11. Hughston JC, Andrews JR, Cross MJ, Moshi A. Classification of knee ligament instabilities, Part I: The medial compartment and cruciate ligaments. *J Bone Joint Surg Am.* 1976;58:173–179.

12. O'Donoghue DH. Injuries to the ligaments of the knee. *Am J Orthop.* 1961;3:46–52.

13. Wiberg

14. Baumgartl F. *Das Kniegelenk, Erkrankungen, Verlezungen und ihre Behandlung mit Hinweisen für die Begutachtung.* Berlin-Göttingen-Heidelberg: Springer-Verlag; 1964.

15. Floyd A, Philips P, Khan MRH, et al. Recurrent dislocation of the patella: Histochemical and electromyo-

graphic evidence of primary muscle pathology. *J Bone Joint Surg Br.* 1987;69:790–793.

16. Aleman

17. Insall J. Current concepts review patellar pain. *J Bone Joint Surg Am.* 1982;64:147–151.

18. Bently G. Articular cartilage changes in chondromalacia patellae. *J Bone Joint Surg Br.* 1985;67:769–774.

19. Huberti HH, Hayes WD. Patellofemoral contact pressures: The influence of Q-angle and tendofemoral contact. *J Bone Joint Surg Am.* 1984;66:715–724.

20. Schoen JL, Marti RK. De diagnostiek van knieletsels. *Reuma Trauma.* 1989;13-1:12–15.

21. Chatrenet Y. Récupération de la force musculaire des fléchisseurs du genou par solliciations dynamiques excentriques. *Ann Kinésither.* 1982;9:319–329.

22. Indelicato PA. Non-operative treatment of complete tears of the medial collateral ligament of the knee. *J Bone Joint Surg Am.* 1983;65:323–329.

23. Giove TP. Non-operative treatment of the torn anterior cruciate ligament. *J Bone Joint Surg Am.* 1983;65:184–192.

24. Noyes FR. Intra-articular cruciate reconstruction, I and II. *Clin Orthop.* 1983;172:71–78.

25. Nicholas JA. Bracing the anterior cruciate ligament of deficient knee using the Lenox Hill derotation brace. *Clin Orthop.* 1983;172:137–143.

PART II—SUGGESTED READING

Abdon P, Bauer M. Incidence of meniscal lesions in children: Increase associated with diagnostic arthroscopy. *Acta Orthop Scand.* 1989;60:710–711.

Abson P. Meniscal lesions—With special reference to diagnostic procedures and childhood conditions. *Acta Orthop Scand.* 1990;61(Suppl 239):95.

Aglietti P, Insall JN, Buzzi R, Deschamps G. Idiopathic osteonecrosis of the knee. *J Bone Joint Surg Br.* 1983;65:588–597.

Alste HE, van Mankow H, Von Rheinbaben HM. Der alloplastische Ersatz des vorderen Kreuzbandes. *Prak Sport Traumatol Sportmed.* 1987;2:43–45.

Amirault JD, Cameron JC, MacIntosh DL, Marks P. Chronic anterior cruciate ligament deficiency. *J Bone Joint Surg Br.* 1988;70:622–624.

Amis AA, Kempson SA, Campbell JR, Miller JH. Anterior cruciate ligament replacement. *J Bone Joint Surg Br.* 1988;70:628–634.

Andrews JR. Posterolateral rotatory instability of the knee. *Phys Ther.* 1980;60:1637.

Andrews JR, Sanders R. A "mini-reconstruction" technique in treating anterolateral rotatory instability (ALRI). *Clin Orthop.* 1983;172:93–97.

Appel M, Hawe W, Gradinger R. Die Architektur des Kreuzbandaufbaus. *Prakt Sport Traumatol Sportmed.* 1989;1:19–23.

Arnoczky SP. Anatomy of the anterior cruciate ligament. *Clin Orthop.* 1983;12:19–26.

Arnoczky SP, Tarvin GB, Marshall JO. Anterior cruciate ligament replacement using patellar tendon. *J Bone Joint Surg Am.* 1982;64:217–224.

Baker CL, Hughston JC. Miyakawa patellectomy. *J Bone Joint Surg Am.* 1988;70:1489–1494.

Baker CL, Norwood LA, Hughston JC. Acute posterolateral rotatory instability of the knee. *J Bone Joint Surg Am.* 1983;65:614–618.

Bartlett EC. Arthroscopic repair and augmentation of the anterior cruciate ligament in cadaver knees. *Clin Orthop.* 1983;172:107–112.

Basmajian JV. *Muscles Alive.* Baltimore, Md: Williams & Wilkins; 1967.

Bassett F. Anterolateral rotatory instability of the knee. *Phys Ther.* 1980;60:1635.

Batten J, Menelaus MB. Fragmentation of the proximal pole of the patella: Another manifestation of the juvenile traction osteochondritis? *J Bone Joint Surg Br.* 1985;67:249–251.

Baudoin P. Artoscopie: De mechanische knie. *Tempo Med Ned.* 1981;11:20–23.

Beltran JE. Resection arthroplasty of the patella. *J Bone Joint Surg Br.* 1987;69:604–607.

Benedetto KP, Genelin A, Suckert K. Knieverletzungen im alpien Skisport. *Prakt Sport Traumatol Sportmed.* 1988;1:30–33.

Benedetto KP, Sperner G, Glötzer W. Der Kniegelenkhämarthros: Differentialdiagnostische Überlegungen zur Planung einer Operation. *Orthopäde.* 1990;19:69–76.

Bergman NR, Williams PF. Habitual dislocation of the patella in flexion. *J Bone Joint Surg Br.* 1988;70:415–419.

Bernett P, Hampl N, Hawe W. Kniegelenkerguß bei Kindern und Jugendlichen aus der Sicht des Sporttraumatologen. *Prakt Sport Traumatol Sportmed.* 1989;1:8–11.

Boersma JW. Monarthritis van de knie: Een leeftijdsrelatie in de differentiaaldiagnostiek. *Reuma Trauma.* 1989;13–1:29–30.

Bots RAA. Artroscopie van de knie. *Reuma Trauma.* 1989;13-1:44–46.

Bradley J, FitzPatrick D, Daniel D, Shercliff T, O'Connor J. Orientation of the cruciate ligament in the sagittal plane. *J Bone Joint Surg Br.* 1988;70:94–99.

Bray RX, Flanagan JP, Dandy DJ. Reconstruction for chronic anterior cruciate instability. *J Bone Joint Surg Br.* 1988;70:100–105.

Breederveld RS. Preventie van knieletsels. In: van Mourik JB, Patka P, eds. *Letsels van de Kie.* Haren, Netherlands: Symposiumcommissie Chirurgie Nederland; 1988, 284–290.

Brok AGMF. Chondropathia patellae en sportbeoefening. *Geneeskd Sport.* 1982;15:115–117.

Brok AGMF, Prakke PC. Operatief herstel van de meniscus bej sportmensen. *Geneeskd Sport.* 1989;22:63–65.

Broos PLO, Janssen LJM, Rommens P, et al. Fracturen van het tibiaplateau. In: van Mourik JB, Patka P, eds. *Letsels van de Kie.* Haren, Netherlands: Symposiumcommissie Chirurgie Nederland; 1988, 188–200.

Burbach T, Veraart BEEMJ. Beoordeling en behandeling van acute kniebandletsels. *Ned Tijdschr Geneeskd.* 1987;122:9–14.

Butler-Manual PA, Guy RL, Heatley FW, Nunan TO. Scintography in the assessment of anterior knee pain. *Acta Orthop Scand.* 1990;61:438–442.

Cabaud ME. Biomechanics of the anterior cruciate ligament. *Clin Orthop.* 1983;177:147.

Cahill B. Treatment of juvenile osteochondritis dissecans and osteochondritis dissecans of the knee. *Clin Sports Med.* 1985;4:367–383.

Casteleyn B. Traumatic hemarthrosis of the knee. *J Bone Joint Surg Br.* 1985;70:404–406.

Chapman JA. Popliteal artery damage in closed injuries of the knee. *J Bone Joint Surg Br.* 1985;67:420–423.

Chen SC, Ramanathan EBS. The treatment of patellar instability by lateral release. *J Bone Joint Surg Br.* 1984;66:344–348.

Cho KO. Reconstruction of the anterior cruciate ligament by semitendinosus tenodesis. *J Bone Joint Surg Am.* 1975;57:608–612.

Clain A, ed. *Hamilton Bailey's Demonstrations of Physical Signs in Clinical Surgery.* New York, NY: Wright & Sons; 1965.

Clancy WG. Anterior cruciate ligament functional instability: A static intra-articular and dynamic extra-articular procedure. *Clin Orthop.* 1983;172:102–107.

Clancy WG, Ray M, Zoltan DJ. Acute tears of the anterior cruciate ligament: Surgical versus conservative treatment. *J Bone Joint Surg Am.* 1988;70:1483–1488.

Clark CR, Ogden JA. Development of the menisci of the human knee joint: Morphological changes and their potential role in childhood meniscal injury. *J Bone Joint Surg Am.* 1983;64:538.

Cotta M. *Kurzgefaßtes Lehrbuch der Orthopädie.* Stuttgart, Germany: Thieme; 1978.

Coventry MB. Proximal tibial varus osteotomy for osteoarthritis of the lateral compartment of the knee. *J Bone Joint Surg Am.* 1987;69:32–38.

Crawford Adams J. *Outline of Orthopaedics.* 6th ed. London, England: Churchill Livingstone; 1967.

Cross MJ, Schmidt DR, Mackie IG. A no-touch test for the anterior cruciate ligament. *J Bone Joint Surg Am.* 1987;69:300.

Curl WW. Agility training following anterior cruciate ligament reconstruction. *Clin Orthop.* 1983;172:133–137.

Cyriax J. *Textbook of Orthopaedic Medicine.* 7th ed. London, England: Baillière Tindall; 1978; 1.

Dahhan P, Delepine G, Larde D. The femoropatellar joint. *Anat Clin.* 1981;3:23–39.

Dahlsted L. Anterior cruciate deficient knees: Arthrometry stabilization. *Acta Orthop Scand.* 1990;61(Suppl 235):82.

Daniel DM, Malcom LL, Losse G, et al. Instrumented measurement of anterior laxity of the knee. *J Bone Joint Surg Am.* 1985;67:720–726.

Daniel DM, Stone ML, Barnett PP, Sachs R. Use of the quadriceps active test to diagnose posterior cruciate ligament disruption and measure posterior laxity of the knee. *J Bone Joint Surg Am.* 1988;70:386–391.

Danzig L. Blood supply to the normal and abnormal menisci of the human knee. *Clin Orthop.* 1983;172:271–277.

David Sisk T. Knee injuries. In: Crewshas AH, ed. *Campbell's Operative Orthopaedics.* St Louis, Mo: Mosby; 1987;3:2283–2496.

De Haven KE. Arthroscopy in the diagnosis and management of the anterior cruciate deficient knee. *Clin Orthop.* 1983;172:52–57.

Denham RH. Dorsal defect of the patella. *J Bone Joint Surg Am.* 1984;66:116–120.

Den Hollander H. Behandeling van letsels van het collaterale bandapparaat van de knie. In: van Mourik JB, Patka P, eds. *Letsels van de Kie.* Haren, Netherlands: Symposiumcommissie Chirurgie Nederland; 1988:115–119.

Den Toom PJ, Schuurman MIM. Incidentie en epidemiologie. In: van Mourik JB, Patka P, eds. *Letsels van de Kie.* Haren, Netherlands: Symposium-commissie Chirurgie Nederland; 1988, 5–16.

Dersheid GL, Malone TR. Knee disorders. *Phys Ther.* 1980;60:1582.

Desai SS, Patel MR, Michelli LJ, et al. Osteochondritis dissecans of the patella. *J Bone Joint Surg Br.* 1987;69:320–423.

Dickhaut SC, Delee JC. The discoid lateral meniscus syndrome. *J Bone Joint Surg Am.* 1982;64:1068–1072.

Dimakopoulos P, Patel D. Partial extension of discoid meniscus: Arthroscopic operation of 10 patients. *Acta Orthop Scand.* 1989;60:40–41.

Driessen MJM. *Verse Kniebandletsels: Een prospectieve studie naar het effect van het herstel van de voorste kruisbanruptuur.* Amsterdam, Holland: Academic Dissertation; 1989.

Eikellar HR. *Arthroscopy of the Knee.* Groningen, Holland: Academic Dissertation; 1975.

Elias N. *Über den Prozeß der Zivilisation.* 5th ed. Baden-Baden, Germany: Suhrkamp; 1978.

El-Khoury GY, Usta HY, Berger RA. Meniscotibial (coronary) ligament tears. *Skeletal Radiol.* 1984;11:191–196.

Ellison AE. Knee lesions, II: Anterior instability. In: Jenkins DHR, ed. *Ligament Injuries and Their Treatment.* New York, NY: Chapman & Hall; 1985:145–157.

Elsaman M. Zugfestigkeiten und histologische Heilverläufe partiell durchtrennter Knieseitenbänder nach oder ohne Gipsruhigstellung. *Orthopäde.* 1975;6:267–269.

Engebretsen L, Lew WD, Lewis JL, et al. Anterolateral rotatory instability of the knee: Cadaver study of extraarticular patellar tendon transposition. *Acta Orthop Scand.* 1990;61:225–230.

Engebretsen L, Tegnander A. Poor short-term results of the nonoperated on, isolated anterior cruciate ligament tear. *Acta Orthop Scand.* 1990;61(Suppl 236):14.

Espley AJ, Wauch W. Regeneration of menisci after total knee replacement: A report of five cases. *J Bone Joint Surg Br.* 1981;63:387–390.

Ewald FC, Jacobs MA, Miegel RE, et al. Kinematic total knee replacement. *J Bone Joint Surg Am.* 1984;66:1032–1040.

Fahmy NRM, Williams EA, Noble J. Meniscal pathology and osteoarthritis of the knee. *J Bone Joint Surg Br.* 1983;65:24–28.

Fahrer H, Rentsch HU, Gerber NJ, et al. Knee effusion and reflex inhibition of the quadriceps. *J Bone Joint Surg Br.* 1988;70:635–638.

Falkenberg P, Nygaard H. Isolated anterior dislocation of the proximal tibiofibular joint. *J Bone Joint Surg Br.* 1983;54:310–312.

Farquharson-Roberts MA, Osborne AH. Partial rupture of the anterior cruciate ligament of the knee. *J Bone Joint Surg Br.* 1983;65:32–34.

Feagin JA. The anterior cruciate ligament deficient knee. *Clin Orthop.* 1983;172:2–3.

Feagin JA, Blake WP. Postoperative evaluation and result recording in the anterior cruciate ligament reconstructed knee. *Clin Orthop.* 1983;172:143–148.

Ferkel RD, Fox JM, Del Pizzo W, et al. Reconstruction of the anterior cruciate ligament using a torn meniscus. *J Bone Joint Surg Am.* 1988;70:715–723.

Fetto JF, Marshall JL. The natural history of diagnosis of anterior cruciate ligament insufficiency. *Clin Orthop.* 1980;147:29–39.

Flock K, Feller AM, Gradinger R, Hipp E. Differentialdiagnose lateraler Knieschmerz. *Prakt Sport Traumatol Sportmed.* 1990;3:12–19.

Fondren FB, Goldner JL, Bassett FH. Recurrent dislocation of the patella treated by the modified Roux-Goldthwait procedure: A prospective study of forty-seven knees. *J Bone Joint Surg Am.* 1985;67:993–1005.

Forte M. Das "scheinbare Meniskussyndrom" bei frontalem Fehlgleiten im Menisko-Tibialgelenk. *Man Med.* 1987;25:86–88.

Fowler PJ. The classification and early diagnosis of knee joint instability. *Clin Orthop.* 1980;149:15–22.

Fox JM. Extra-articular stabilization of the knee joint for anterior instability. *Clin Orthop.* 1980;147:56–62.

Freeman BL, Beaty JH, Haynes DB. The pes anserinus transfer: A long term follow up. *J Bone Joint Surg Am.* 1982;64:202–207.

Friden T, Zätterström R, Lindstrand A, Moritz U. Disability in anterior cruciate ligament insufficiency: An analysis of 19 untreated patients. *Acta Orthop Scand.* 1990;61:131–135.

Fried JA, Bergveld JA, Weiker G, Andrish JT. Anterior cruciate reconstruction using the Jones-Ellison procedure. *J Bone Joint Surg Am.* 1985;67:1029–1033.

Fujikawa K, Iseki F, Mikura Y. Partial resection of the discoid meniscus in the child's knee. *J Bone Joint Surg Br.* 1981;63:391–395.

Fulkerson JP. Anteromedialization of the tibial tuberosity for patellofemoral malalignment. *Clin Orthop.* 1983;177:176–181.

Funk FJ. Osteoarthritis of the knee following ligamentous injury. *Clin Orthop.* 1983;172:154–158.

Galway MR, MacIntosh DL. The lateral pivot shift: A symptom and sign of anterior cruciate ligament insufficiency. *Clin Orthop.* 1980;147:45–51.

Gardner E, Gray DJ, O'Rahilly R. *Anatomy.* Philadelphia, Pa: Saunders; 1975.

Gasco J, Del Pino JM, Gomar-Sancho F. Double patella: A case of duplication in the coronal plane. *J Bone Joint Surg Br.* 1987;69:602–603.

Gaston C, Gallay C. Kongenitale Kniegelenksluxation. *Krankengymnastik.* 1988;40:826–829.

Gerber C, Hoppeler H, Claassen H, et al. The lower extremity musculature in chronic symptomatic instability of the anterior cruciate ligament. *J Bone Joint Surg Am.* 1985;67:1034–1043.

Gerber C, Matter P. Biomechanical analysis of the knee after rupture of the anterior cruciate ligament and its primary repair. *J Bone Joint Surg Br.* 1983;65:391.

Gerding JC. *Instability of the Knee.* Groningen, Holland: Academic Dissertation; 1979.

Giladi M, Milgrom C, Simkin A, et al. Stress fractures and tibial bone width: A risk factor. *J Bone Joint Surg Br.* 1987;69:326–328.

Gollehon DL, Tozilli PA, Warren RF. The role of the posterolateral and cruciate ligaments in the stability of the human knee: A biomechanical study. *J Bone Joint Surg Am.* 1984;66:734–740.

Grace TG, Skipper BJ, Newberry JC, et al. Prophylactic knee braces and injury to the lower extremity. *J Bone Joint Surg Am.* 1988;70:422–427.

Grace TG, Sweeter ER, Nelson MA, et al. Isokinetic muscle imbalance and knee joint injuries: A prospective blind study. *J Bone Joint Surg Am.* 1984;66:734–740.

Gradinger R, Haller W, Allgayer B. Die MR-Tomographie zur Beurteilung des vorderen Kreuzbandersatzes. *Prakt Sport Traumatol Sportmed.* 1987;4:48–51.

Gradinger R, Paulsen J, Haller W. Der autologe Ersatz des vorderen Kreuzbandes mit freiem Patellarsehnentransplantat. *Prakt Sport Traumatol Sportmed.* 1987;2:29–31.

Gray H, Williams PL, Warwick R. *Gray's Anatomy.* 36th ed. London, England: Churchill Livingstone; 1980.

Grood ES, Suntay WJ, Noyes FR, Butler DL. Biomechanics of the knee extension exercise: Effect of cutting the anterior cruciate ligament. *J Bone Joint Surg Am.* 1984;66:725–734.

Güßbacher A, Graf J, Niethard FU. Probleme der Diagnose und Therapie chondraler und osteochondraler Frakturen im Berich des Kniegelenkes. *Prakt Sport Traumatol Sportmed.* 1987;2:46–48.

Haak A, Steendijk R, de Wijn IF. *De samenstelling van het menselijk lichaam.* Assen, Holland: Van Gorcum; 1968.

Hafferl A. *Lehrbuch der topographischen Anatomie des Menschen.* Berlin, Germany: Springer Verlag; 1957.

Haller W, Flock K. Neue Wege in der Rehabilitation nach Kniegelenksverletzungen durch isokinetische Trainingsgeräte. *Prakt Sport Traumatol Sportmed.* 1987;1:42–46.

Halperin N. Anterior cruciate ligament insufficiency syndrome. *Clin Orthop.* 1983;179:179.

Hamberg P, Gillquist J, Lysholm J. A comparison between arthroscopic meniscectomy and modified open meniscectomy: A prospective randomized study with emphasis on postoperative rehabilitation. *J Bone Joint Surg Br.* 1984;66:189–192.

Hamberg P, Gillquist J, Lysholm J. Suture of new and old peripheral meniscus tears. *J Bone Joint Surg Am.* 1983;65:193–197.

Hamilton WJ, Simon G, Hamilton SGI. *Surface and Radiological Anatomy.* 5th ed. London, England: Macmillan; 1976.

Hardaker WT. Diagnosis and treatment of the plica syndrome of the knee. *J Bone Joint Surg Am.* 1980;62:11–15.

Hastings DE. The non-operative management of collateral ligament injuries of the knee joint. *Clin Orthop.* 1980;147:22–29.

Hawe W, Dörr A, Bernett P. Sonographische Befunde am verletzten hinteren Kreuzband. *Prakt Sport Traumatol Sportmed.* 1989;1:29–31.

Hayashi LK, Yamaga H, Ida K, Miura T. Arthroscopic meniscectomy for discoid lateral meniscus in children. *J Bone Joint Surg Am.* 1988;70:1495–1499.

Healy EJ, Seybold WD. *A Synopsis of Clinical Anatomy.* Philadelphia, Pa: Saunders; 1969.

Hede A, Jensen DB, Blyme P, Sonne-Holm S. Epidemiology of meniscal lesions in the knee: 1215 open operations in Copenhagen 1982–1984. *Acta Orthop Scand.* 1990;61:435–437.

Heere LP. Letsels en aandoeningen van de knie ten gevolge van sport. In: van Mourik JB, Patka P, eds. *Letsels van de Kie.* Haren, Netherlands: Symposiumcommissie Chirurgie Nederland; 1988:87–100.

Heere LP. Slotverschijnselen van de knie. *Geneeskd Sport.* 1989;22:25.

Heerkens YF, Meijer OG. *Tractus-anatomie.* Amsterdam, Holland: Interfaculty Physical Education; 1980.

Heers H. Posttraumatishe Instabilitäten des Kniegelenks. *Krankengymnastik.* 1983; 9.

Heller L, Langman J. The meniscofemoral ligaments of the human knee. *J Bone Joint Surg Br.* 1964;46:307–313.

Henche HR. Die arthroskopische Meniskusresektion. *Orthopäde.* 1990;19:77–81.

Hermans GPH, Rondhuis G. Kniebandconstructies bij "late" instabiliteit: Operatie en revalidatie. *Geneeskd Sport.* 1982;15:100–106.

Hertel P. Rearthroskopien. *Orthopäde.* 1990;19:107–110.

Heß H. *Sportverletzungen am Kniegelenk: Therapie.* Presented at the Symposium on Sports Lesions of the Capsuloligamentous Complex of the Knee and Ankle. November 1984; Stuttgart, Germany.

Hewson GF. Drill guides for improving accuracy in anterior cruciate ligament repair and reconstruction. *Clin Orthop.* 1983;172:119–125.

Hey Groves EW. Operation for repair of the crucial ligaments. *Clin Orthop.* 1980;147:4–7.

Hill E. Das Problem "Patellofemoralgelenk." *Orthopäde.* 1990;19:90–96.

Hirschfeld P. Die Bedeutung der Anamnese in der Klinischen Basisuntersuchung des Kniegelenkes. *Krankengymnastik.* 1983;9:497–500.

Hirschfeld P. *Die Sportverletzung und ihre Behandlung, I. Das Knie.* München: Schwarzeck; 1976, 1

Hooper GJ, Walton DI. Reconstruction of the anterior cruciate ligament using the bone-block iliotibial tract transfer. *J Bone Joint Surg Am.* 1987;69:1150–1154.

Hoppenfeld S. *Physical Examination of the Spine and Extremities.* New York, NY: Appleton-Century-Crofts; 1976.

Hughston JC. Knee surgery: A philosophy. *Phys Ther.* 1980;60:1611–1980.

Hughston JC, Barrett GR. Acute anteromedial rotatory instability: Long term results of surgical repair. *J Bone Joint Surg Am.* 1983;65:145–153.

Hughston JC, Jacobson KE. Chronic posterolateral rotatory instability of the knee. *J Bone Joint Surg Am.* 1985;67:351–359.

Hughston JC, Norwood LA. The posterolateral drawer test and external rotational recurvatum test for posterolateral rotatory instability of the knee. *Clin Orthop.* 1980;147:82–88.

Hunter GA. Ligamentous injuries of the knee. *Clin Orthop.* 1980;147:2–4.

Huson A. Anatomie en kinesiologie van de knie. *Reuma Trauma.* 1985;13-1:6–8.

Hvid I, Anderson LI. The quadriceps angle and its relation to femoral torsion. *Acta Orthop Scand.* 1982;53:577–579.

Inoue M, Shino K, Hirose H, et al. Subluxation of the patella: Computed tomography analysis of patellofemoral congruence. *J Bone Joint Surg Am.* 1988;70:1331–1337.

Jackson AM, Hutton PAN. Injection induced contractures of the quadriceps in childhood: A comparison of proximal release of the distal quadricepsplasty. *J Bone Joint Surg Br.* 1985;67:97–102.

Jakob JP, Miniaci A. A compression pinning system for osteochondritis dissecans of the knee. *Acta Orthop Scand.* 1990;60:319–321.

Jakob RP, Stäubli HU, Deland JT. Grading the pivot shift: Objective tests with implications for treatment. *J Bone Joint Surg Br.* 1987;69:294–299.

James SL. Biomechanics of knee ligament reconstruction. *Clin Orthop.* 1980;146:90–101.

James SL. Knee ligament reconstruction. In: McCollister Evarts C, ed. *Surgery of the Musculoskeletal System.* New York, NY: Churchill Livingstone; 1983;3:7.31–7.111.

Janis JL, Mahl GF, Kagan J, Holt RR. *Personality, Dynamics, Development, and Assessment.* New York, NY: Harcourt, Brace and World, Inc; 1969.

Jensen DB, Hansen LB. Patellectomy for chondromalacia. *Acta Orthop Scand.* 1989;60:17–19.

Johnson D. Controlling anterior shear during isokinetic knee extension exercise. *J Orthop Sports Phys Ther.* 1982;4:23–31.

Johnson DP. Midline or parapatellar incision for knee arthroplasty. *J Bone Joint Surg Br.* 1988;70:656–658.

Johnson RJ. The anterior cruciate ligament problem. *Clin Orthop.* 1983;172:14–19.

Jokl P, Kaplan N, Stovell P, Keggi D. Non-operative treatment of severe injuries to the medial and anterior cruciate ligaments of the knee. *J Bone Joint Surg Am.* 1984;66:741–744.

Jones KG. Results of use of the central one-third of the patellar ligament to compensate for anterior cruciate ligament deficiency. *Clin Orthop.* 1980;147:39–45.

Jonsson H, Kärrholm J. Brace effects on the unstable knee in 21 cases: A roentgen stereophotogrammetric comparison of the three designs. *Acta Orthop Scand.* 1990;61:313–318.

Jonsson T. Management of the acute rupture of the anterior cruciate ligament. *Acta Orthop Scand.* 1990;61(Suppl 239):98.

Kaelin A, Hulin PH, Carlioz H. Congenital aplasia of the cruciate ligaments: A report of six cases. *J Bone Joint Surg Br.* 1986;68:827–828.

Kannus P, Järvinen M. Knee ligament injuries in adolescents. *J Bone Joint Surg Br.* 1988;70:772–776.

Kaplan EB. The iliotibial tract: Clinical and morphological significance. *J Bone Joint Surg Am.* 1958;40:817–832.

Kaplan EB. The patellofibular and short lateral ligaments of the knee joint. *J Bone Joint Surg Am.* 1961;43:169–179.

Kärrholm J, Selvik G, Elmqvist LG, et al. Three dimensional instability of the anterior cruciate deficient knee. *J Bone Joint Surg Br.* 1988;70:777–783.

Katz MM, Hungerford DS. Reflex sympathetic dystrophy affecting the knee. *J Bone Joint Surg Br.* 1987;69:797–806.

Kay SP, Gold RH, Bassett LW. Meniscal pneumatocoel: A case report of spontaneous, persistent intra-articular and juxta-articular gas. *J Bone Joint Surg Am.* 1985;67:1117–1119.

Kennedy JC. Application of prosthetics to anterior cruciate ligament reconstruction and repair. *Clin Orthop.* 1983;172:125–129.

Kennedy JC. *The Injured Adolescent Knee.* Baltimore, Md: Williams & Wilkins; 1979.

Kentsch A, Binnet MS, Lauber P, Müller W. Die Technik des vorderen Kreuzbandersatzes mit freiem Ligamentum patellae-Transplantat. *Prakt Sport Traumatol Sportmed.* 1987;2:32–35.

Kerlan RK, Glousmann RE. Tibial collateral ligament bursitis. *Am J Sports Med.* 1988;16:344–346.

King J. Knee lesions, VI: Peripheral reconstruction for anterior cruciate loss. In: Jenkins DHR, ed. *Ligament Injuries and Their Treatment.* New York, NY: Chapman & Hall; 1985:207–225.

Klasen HJ. Letsels van de proximale epifyse van de tibia. In: van Mourik JB, Patka P, eds. *Letsels van de Kie.* Haren, Netherlands: Symposiumcommissie Chirurgie Nederland; 1988:143–160.

Koch B. Hemophiliac knee: Rehabilitation techniques. *Arch Phys Med Rehabil.* 1982;36:379–382.

Kortelainen P, Jalovaara P. Arthrodesis of the knee with intramedullary nailing as a primary or secondary procedure. *Acta Orthop Scand.* 1990;61(Suppl 235):43.

Koskinen SK, Hurme M, Kujala UM, Kormano M. Effect of lateral release on patellar motion in chondromalacia: An MRI study of 11 knees. *Acta Orthop Scand.* 1990;61:311–312.

Krahl H. "Jumper's Knee": Ätiologie, Differential-diagnose und therapeutische Möglichkeiten. *Orthopäde.* 1980;9:193–197.

Krahl H. *Sportverletzungen am Kniegelenk: Diagnostik.* Presented at the Symposium on Sports Lesions of the Capsuloligamentous Complex of the Knee and Ankle; November 1984; Stuttgart, Germany.

Krompinger WJ, Fulkerson JP. Lateral retinacular release for intractable lateral retinacular pain. *Clin Orthop.* 1983;179:191.

Krueger P, Neumann A, Schweiberer L. Die arthroskopische Kreuzbandreinsertion und augmentation Indikation, operative Technik. *Orthopäde.* 1990;19:97–102.

Kujala UM, Oesterman K, Kormano M, et al. Patellar motion analyzed by magnetic resonance imaging. *Acta Orthop Scand.* 1989;60:13–16.

Lambert KL. Vascularized patellar tendon graft with rigid internal fixation for anterior cruciate ligament insufficiency. *Clin Orthop.* 1983;147:85–90.

Larson RL. Combined instabilities of the knee. *Clin Orthop.* 1980;147:68–76.

Larson RL. Physical examination in the diagnosis of rotatory instability. *Clin Orthop.* 1983;172:38–45.

Last RJ. Some anatomical details of the knee joint. *J Bone Joint Surg Br.* 1948;30:683–687.

Lemaire M, Miremad C. Les instabilités chroniques antérieures et internes du genou: Étude théorique, diagnostic clinique et radiologique. *Rev Chir Orthop.* 1983;69:3–16.

Levack B, Flannagan JP, Hobbs S. Results of surgical treatment of patellar fractures. *J Bone Joint Surg Br.* 1985;67:416–419.

Levy IM. The effect of medial meniscectomy on anterior-posterior motion of the knee. *J Bone Joint Surg Br.* 1982;64:883–888.

Leyshon RL, Channon GM, Channon GM, et al. Flexible carbon fibre in late ligamentous reconstruction for instability of the knee. *J Bone Joint Surg Br.* 1984;66:196–200.

Lieb FJ, Perry J. Quadriceps function. *J Bone Joint Surg Am.* 1971;53:749.

Lim TE. *Extra-articular reconstructie voor chronische anterolaterale rotatoire instabiliteit van de knie.* Amsterdam, Holland: Academic Dissertation; 1989.

Lloyd-Roberts GC, Jackson AM, Albert JS. Avulsion of the distal pole of the patella in cerebral palsy: A cause of deteriorating gait. *J Bone Joint Surg Br.* 1985;67:252–254.

Lohman AGM. *Vorm en beweging. Leerboek van het bewegingsapparaat van de mens.* 4th ed. Utrecht, Netherlands: Bohn, Scheltema & Holkema; 1977.

Losee RE. Concepts of the pivot shift. *Clin Orthop.* 1983;147:45–52.

Lynch MA. Knee joint surface changes: Long term follow-up of meniscus tear treatment in stable anterior cruciate ligament reconstructions. *Clin Orthop.* 1983;172:148–154.

Mac Eachern AG, Plewes JL. Bilateral simultaneous spontaneous rupture of the quadriceps tendons: Five case reports and a review of the literature. *J Bone Joint Surg Br.* 1984;66:81–83.

Mann RA, Hagy JL. The popliteus muscle. *J Bone Joint Surg Am.* 1977;59:924.

Markolf KL, Hochan A, Amstutz HC. Measurement of knee stiffness and laxity in patients with documented absence of the anterior cruciate ligament. *J Bone Joint Surg Am.* 1984;66:242–252.

Martens M, Wouters P, Burssens A, Mulier J. Patellar tendinitis: Pathology and results of treatment. *Acta Orthop Scand.* 1982;53:445.

Marti RK, Schoen JL. Fracturen van het distale femur. In: van Mourik JB, Patka P, eds. *Letsels van de Kie.* Haren, Netherlands: Symposiumcommissie Chirurgie Nederland; 1988, 171–187.

Mathies H. *Aktuelle Rheumaprobleme: Arthritis/Arthrose.* Basel, Switzerland: Geigy; 1988.

Mayfield GW. Popliteus tendon tenosynovitis. *Am J Sports Med.* 1977;5:31–36.

McCanial WJ, Dameron TB. The untreated anterior cruciate ligament rupture. *Clin Orthop.* 1983;172:158–164.

McCluskey G, Blackburn TA. Classification of knee ligament instabilities. *Phys Ther.* 1980;60:1575.

McConnel J. The management of chondromalacia patellae: A long term solution. *Aust J Physiother.* 1986;32:215–223.

McCoy GF, McCrea JD, Beverland DE, et al. Vibration arthrography as a diagnostic aid in diseases of the knee: A preliminary report. *J Bone Joint Surg Br.* 1987;69:288–293.

McLeod WD, Hunter S. Biomechanical analysis of the knee. *Phys Ther.* 1980;60:1561.

McMinn RMH, Hutching RT. *A Color Atlas of Human Anatomy.* London, England: Wolfe Medical; 1977.

Menke W, Schmitz B, Grimm J. Frühergebnisse der Kniegelenksalloarthroplastik be Patienten mit chronischer Polyarthritis unter besonderer Berücksichtigung der Kniegelenksfunktion. *Krankengymnastik.* 1988;40:830–832.

Merchant AC, Mercer RL. Lateral release of the patella: A preliminary report. *Clin Orthop.* 1974;103:40–45.

Michele AA, Nielsen PM. Tibiotalar torsion: Bioengineering paradigm. *Orthop Clin North Am.* 1976;7:929–946.

Mirovsky Y, Halperin N, Hendel D. Abduction-traction injury of the knee. *J Bone Joint Surg Br.* 1984;66:201–205.

Mitsou A, Vallianatos P, Piskopakis N, Nicolaou P. Cruciate ligament replacement using a meniscus. *J Bone Joint Surg Br.* 1988;70:784–786.

Möller H. Incarcerating mediopatellar synovial plica syndrome. *Acta Orthop Scand.* 1981;52:357–361.

More RC, Markolf KL. Measurement of stability of the knee and ligament force after implantation of a synthetic anterior cruciate ligament: In vitro measurement. *J Bone Joint Surg Am.* 1988;70:1020–1031.

Mott HW. Semitendinosus anatomic reconstruction for cruciate ligament insufficiency. *Clin Orthop.* 1983;172:90–93.

Muckle DS. Open meniscectomy: Enhanced recovery after synovial prostaglandin inhibition. *J Bone Joint Surg Br.* 1984;66:193–195.

Muhr G, Wagner M. *Kapsel-Band-Verletzungen des Kniegelenkes.* Berlin, Germany: Springer Verlag; 1981.

Müller W. *Das Knie: Form, Funktion und ligamentäre Wiederherstellungschirurgie.* Berlin: Springer Verlag; 1982.

Müller W. Das Kniegelenk des Fussballers: Seine Beanspruchung und seine Schäden. *Orthopäde.* 1974;3:193–200.

Müller W. Functional anatomy related to rotatory stability of the knee joint. In: Chapcal G, ed. *Injuries of the Ligaments and Their Repair.* Springer-Verlag: Germany; 1977:39–46.

Munzinger U. Die funktionelle Nachbehandlung des Kniegelenks nach Bandplastiken bei globaler vorderer Instabilität. *Krankengymnastik.* 1983; 9.

Murray MP, Jacobs PA, Gore DR, et al. Functional performance after tibial rotationplasty. *J Bone Joint Surg Am.* 1985;67:392–399.

Nakamura N, Ellis M, Seedhom BB. Advancement of the tibial tuberosity: A biomechanical study. *J Bone Joint Surg Br.* 1985;67:255–260.

Naver L, Aalber JR. Rupture of the quadriceps tendon following dislocation of the patella: Case report. *J Bone Joint Surg Am.* 1985;67:324–325.

Noble CA. Iliotibial band friction syndrome in runners. *Am J Sports Med.* 1980;8:232–234.

Norwood LA, Hughston JC. Combined anterolateral and anteromedial rotatory instability of the knee. *Clin Orthop.* 1980;147:62–68.

Noyes FR. Clinical biomechanics of the knee: Ligament restraints and functional stability. In: American Academy of Orthopedic Surgery, ed. *Symposium on the Athlete's Knee.* Edinburgh, Scotland: Churchill Livingstone; 1986: 308–318.

Noyes FR. Knee ligament tests: What do they really mean? *Phys Ther.* 1980;60:1578.

Noyes FR. Knee sprains and acute knee hemarthrosis. *Phys Ther.* 1980;60:1596.

Noyes FR, Grood ES, Butler DL, Males M. Clinical laxity test and functional stability of the knee: Biomechanical concepts. *Clin Orthop.* 1980;100:23–55.

Noyes FR, Grood ES, Suntay WJ. Three-dimensional motion analysis of clinical stress tests for anterior knee subluxations. *Acta Orthop Scand.* 1989;60:308–318.

Noyes FR, Mooar PA, Matthews DS, Butler DL. The symptomatic anterior cruciate deficient knee, parts I & II: The long term functional disability in athletically active individuals & the results of rehabilitation, active modification, and counseling on functional disability. *J Bone Joint Surg Am.* 1983;65:154–174.

Odensten M, Gillquist J. Functional anatomy of the anterior cruciate ligament and a rationale for reconstruction. *J Bone Joint Surg Am.* 1985;67:257–262.

O'Donoghue DH. Meniscectomy. *Phys Ther.* 1980;60:1617.

Oostvogel HJM. Fracturen van de eminentia intercondylaris bij het kind. In: van Mourik JB, Patka P, eds. *Letsels van de Kie.* Haren, Netherlands: Symposiumcommissie Chirurgie Nederland; 1988: 143–160.

Paar O. Meniskuserhaltende Eingriffe am Kniegelenk. *Sportverletz und Sportschaden.* 1988;2:16–19.

Pappas AM, Anas P, Toczylowski HM. Asymmetrical arrest of the proximal tibial physis and genu recurvatum deformity. *J Bone Joint Surg Am.* 1984;66:575–581.

Paterson FWN, Trickey EL. Meniscectomy for tears of the meniscus combined with rupture of the anterior cruciate ligament. *J Bone Joint Surg Br.* 1983;65:388.

Patka P. De toepassing van keramische implantaten bij impressiefracturen van het tibiaplateau. In: van Mourik JB, Patka P, eds. *Letsels van de Kie.* Haren, Netherlands: Symposiumcommissie Chirurgie Nederland; 1988:201–205.

Paulos L, Rusche K. Patellar malalignment: A treatment rationale. *Phys Ther.* 1980;60:1624–1632.

Pavlov H. The radiographic diagnosis of the anterior cruciate ligament deficient knee. *Clin Orthop.* 1983;172:57–65.

Pavlov H, Ghelman B, Vigorita VJ. *Atlas of Knee Menisci.* Norwalk, Conn: Appleton-Century-Crofts; 1983.

Pavlov H, Warren RF, Sherman MF, Cayea PD. The accuracy of double-contrast arthrographic evaluation of the anterior cruciate ligament: A retrospective review of one-hundred and sixty-three knees with surgical confirmation. *J Bone Joint Surg Br.* 1983;65:175–183.

Petri L, Müller EH. Das Patellarsehnensyndrom: Differentialdiagnose und Therapie. *Phys Ther.* 1988;9:586–597.

Pieper B, Rodammer G, Paulsen J, Flock K. Einsatzmöglichkeiten von Kniegelenkorthesen (Braces) im Sport. *Prakt Sport Traumatol Sportmed.* 1989;1:32–41.

Poelman PJIM, Hermans GPH, Blankevoort L. Mechanical behavior of the patellar tendon after removal of a graft for the anterior cruciate ligament. *Acta Orthop Scand.* 1990;61(Suppl 235):9.

Poliacu Prosé L. *De Functionele Stabiliteit van de Knie: Een experimentele en biomechanische analyse van de bijdrage van de ligamenten en spieren.* Brussels, Belgium: Academic Dissertation; 1985.

Prins APA. Hydrops van de Knie. *Reuma Trauma.* 1989;13-1:9–11.

Pun WK, Chow SP, Chan KC, Leong JCY. Effusions in the knee in elderly patients who were operated on for fracture of the hip. *J Bone Joint Surg Am.* 1988;70:117–118.

Raarikainen T, Väänänen K, Tamelander V. Effect of glycosaminoglycan polysulfate on chondromalacia patellae: A placebo controlled 1 year study. *Acta Orthop Scand.* 1990;61:443–448.

Rand JA, Chao EYS, Stauffer RN. Kinematic rotating-hinge total knee arthroplasty. *J Bone Joint Surg Am.* 1987;69:489–497.

Ray JM, Clancy WG, Lemon RA. Semimembranosus tendinitis: An overlooked cause of medial knee pain. *Am J Sports Med.* 1988;16:347–350.

Reider B, Marshall JL, Koslin B, et al. The anterior aspect of the knee joint. *J Bone Joint Surg Am.* 1981;63:351–356.

Reikerås O. Brace with a lateral pad for patellar pain: 2 year follow-up of 35 patients. *Acta Orthop Scand.* 1990;61:319–320.

Rijnks J. *Chondropathia Patellae.* Groningen, Holland: Academic Dissertation; 1976.

Ritter MA. *The Knee: A Guide to the Examination and Diagnosis of Ligament Injuries.* Springfield, Ill: Thomas; 1979.

Rodammer G, Lehner K, Träger J, Scheyerer M. Die Knorpelbeurteilung mit der Magnet-Resonanz-Tomographie (MRT). *Prakt Sport Traumatol Sportmed.* 1989;1:24–27.

Rolland JD, Bron R. Entorses graves du genou operées. *Ann Kinésithér.* 1982;9:99–116.

Rondhuis GB. Oefentherapie na kruisband operaties. *Nederlands Tijdschrift voor Fysiotherapie.* 1984;94:178–183.

Rondhuis GB. Revalidatie na (behandelde) kniebandletsels. *Reuma Trauma.* 1989;13:23–27.

Rosenberg TD, Paulos LE, Parker RD, et al. The forty-five degree posteroanterior flexion weight-bearing radiograph of the knee. *J Bone Joint Surg Am.* 1988;70:1479–1482.

Rosenberg TD, Paulos LE, Wnorowski DC, Gurley WD. Arthroskopische Chirurgie: Meniskusrefixation und Meniskusheilung. *Orthopäde.* 1990;19:82–89.

Ross AC, Chesterman PJ. Isolated avulsion of the tibial attachment of the posterior cruciate ligament in childhood. *J Bone Joint Surg Br.* 1986;68:747.

Rozendal RH. *Inleiding in de Kinesiologie van de Mens.* Culemborg: Stam Kemperman; 1968.

Rozing PM, De Jonge-Bok JM. Idiopathische osteonecrose van de mediale femurcondyl: Een zeldzame oorzaak van pijn in de knie bij de oudere patiënt. *Ned Tijdschr Geneeskd.* 1983;127:809–813.

Russe O, Gerhardt JJ, King PS. *An Atlas of Examination, Standard Measurements and Diagnosis in Orthopaedics and Traumatology.* Bern, Switzerland: Huber Verlag; 1972.

Sandber R, Balkfors B, Nilsson B, Westlin N. Operative versus non-operative treatment of recent injuries to the ligaments of the knee: A prospective randomized study. *J Bone Joint Surg Am.* 1987;69:1120–1126.

Satku K, Kumar VP, Pho RWH. Stress fractures of the tibia in osteoarthrosis of the knee. *J Bone Joint Surg Br.* 1987;69:309–311.

Savelberg HHCM, Kooloos JGM, Huiskes R, Kauer JMG. A functional analysis of the ligaments of the human wrist joint. *Acta Orthop Scand.* 1990;61(Supp 235):41.

Schoemaker SC. In vivo rotatory knee instability: Ligamentous and muscular contributions. *J Bone Joint Surg Am.* 1982;64:78–82.

Schulien P. Das instabile Kniegelenk: Die habituelle Patellaluxation und ihre Behandlung. *Phys Ther.* 1987;8:222–224.

Schulte LAM. *Tears and Cysts of the Menisci of the Knee Joint.* Utrecht, Netherlands: Academic Dissertation; 1987.

Schwarz B, Heisel J. Veraltete einfache und kombinierte Kniebinnenverletzungen. *Prakt Sport Traumatol Sportmed.* 1988;3:49–54.

Schwarz B, Heisel J. Vorgehen bei frischen Kniebinnenverletzungen. *Prakt Sport Traumatol Sportmed.* 1987;2:22–28.

Scott WN, Rubinstein M, Scuderi G. Results after knee replacement with a posterior cruciate substituting prosthesis. *J Bone Joint Surg Am.* 1988;70:1163–1173.

Scott WN, Schosheim PM. Intra-articular transfer of the iliotibial muscle-tendon unit. *Clin Orthop.* 1983;172:97–102.

Scuderi G, Cuomo F, Scott WN. Lateral release and proximal realignment for patellar subluxation and dislocation: A long term follow-up. *J Bone Joint Surg Am.* 1988;70:856–861.

Seebacher JR, Inglis AE. Marshall JL, Warren RF. The structure of the posterolateral aspect of the knee. *J Bone Joint Surg Am.* 1982;64:536–541.

Seedhom BB. Loadbearing function of the menisci. *Physiotherapy (London).* 1976;62:223.

Segantini P, Mona D. Diagnostik und Behandlung der akuten Kniegelenksverletzungen durch Arthroskopie. *Prakt Sport Traumatol Sportmed.* 1987;2:16–21

Shakespeare DT, Rigby HS. The bucket-handle tear of the meniscus. *J Bone Joint Surg Br.* 1983;65:383.

Shaw JA, Murray DG. The longitudinal axis of the knee and the role of the cruciate ligaments in controlling transverse rotation. *J Bone Joint Surg Am.* 1974;56:1603.

Shutte MJ, Dabezies EJ, Zimmy ML, Happel LT. Neural anatomy of the human anterior cruciate ligament. *J Bone Joint Surg Am.* 1987;69:243–247.

Singer KM, Henry J. Knee problems in children and adolescents. *Clin Sports Med.* 1985;4:385–397.

Siwek CW, Rao JP. Ruptures of the extensor mechanism of the knee joint. *J Bone Joint Surg Am.* 1981;63:932–937.

Sjölander P. A sensory role for the cruciate ligaments: Regulation of joint stability via reflexes onto the muscle-spindle system. *Acta Orthop Scand.* 1990;61(Suppl 235):99.

Slocum DB, Larson RL, James SL. Late reconstruction of ligamentous injuries of the medial compartment of the knee. *Clin Orthop.* 1974;100:23–55.

Snook GA. A short history of the anterior cruciate ligament and the treatment of tears. *Clin Orthop.* 1983;172:11–14.

Sobotta J, Becher PH. *Atlas of Human Anatomy.* 9th English ed. Berlin, Germany: Urban & Schwarzenberg; 1975;1–3.

Sperner GKP, Glötzer BW. Die Wertigkeit der Arthroskopie nach traumatischer Patellaluxation. *Sportverletzung und Sportschaden.* 1988;2:20–23.

Stahl T, Feldmeier C, Bernett P. Die Augmentationssplastik zur Behandlung von vordern Kreuzbandläsionen unk ihre spezielle Nachbehandlung. *Prakt Sport Traumatol Sportmed.* 1987;2:36–42.

Steadman JR. Rehabilitation of acute injuries of the anterior cruciate ligament. *Clin Orthop.* 1983;172:129–133.

Steinbrück K. *Vorschlag für Untersuchungstechniken am Kniegelenk.* Presented at the Symposium on Sports Lesions of the Capsuloligamentous Complex of the Knee and Ankle; November 1984; Stuttgart, Germany.

Steindler A. *Kinesiology of the Human Body under Normal and Pathological Conditions.* Springfield, Ill: Thomas; 1955.

Stibbe AB. Overbelastingssyndromen van de knie. *Reuma Trauma.* 1989;13-1:32–36.

Stoller DW. The effects of exercise, ice and ultrasonography on torsional laxity of the knee. *Clin Orthop.* 1983;174:172–180.

Styff J, Nakhostine M, Gershuni D. Prophylactic knee braces increase intramuscular pressure. *Acta Orthop Scand.* 1990;61(Suppl 239):239.

Sullivan D, Levy M, Sheskier S, et al. Medial restraints to anterior-posterior motion of the knee. *J Bone Joint Surg Am.* 1984;66:930–936.

Suman RK, Stother IG, Illingworth G. Diagnostic arthroscopy of the knee in children. *J Bone Joint Surg Br.* 1984;66:535–537.

Teitz CC, Hermanson BK, Kronmal RA, Diehr PH. Evaluation of the use of braces to prevent injury to the knee in collegiate football players. *J Bone Joint Surg Am.* 1987;69:2–8.

Tregonning RJA. Closed partial meniscectomy. *J Bone Joint Surg Br.* 1983;65:378.

Tremblay GR. The challenge of prosthetic cruciate ligament replacement. *Clin Orthop.* 1980;147:88–93.

Trickey EL. Injuries to the posterior cruciate ligament: Diagnosis and treatment of early injuries and reconstruction of late instability. *Clin Orthop.* 1980;147:76–82.

Turner MS, Smillie IS. The effect of tibial torsion on the pathology of the knee. *J Bone Joint Surg Br.* 1981;63:396–398.

Van der Korst JK. *Gewrichtsziekten.* Utrecht, Netherlands: Bohn, Scheltema & Holkema; 1980.

Van Dijk R, Bots RAA. Gehandelingsresultaten van de pivot-shift operatie volgens Macintosh. *Ned Tijdschr Geneeskd.* 1981;91:34–40.

van Mourik JB. De knieluxatie. In: van Mourik JB, Patka P, eds. *Letsels van de Kie.* Haren, Netherlands: Symposiumcommissie Chirurgie Nederland; 1988:206–220.

van Velzen JHA, Kemper HCG. Maximale momentwaarden, isokinetisch gemeten tijdens extensie en flexie van het kniegewricht bij jong volwassenen. *Geneeskd Sport.* 1988;21:59–66.

Veraart BEEMJ. Vrese kniebandletsels: Biomechanica en functionele anatomie in relatie tot letsels van het bandapparaat van de knie. *Ned Tijdschr Geneeskd.* 1978;89:15–19.

Verbeek HOF. Corpora aliena in het kniegewricht. *Ned Tijdschr Geneeskd.* 1978;122:1288–1290.

Verbiest B, Veraart BEEMJ. Het plicasyndroom van de knie. *Ned Tijdschr Geneeskd.* 1982;126:1214–1220.

Verdonk R. Medial plica synovialis or shelf syndrome of the knee. *Acta Orthop Belg.* 1982;48:463–467.

Vielpeau C. La rotule du jeune sportif. *Sci Sports.* 1986;1:65–73.

Vierhout PAM. Het meniscusletsel. In: van Mourik JB, Patka P, eds. *Letsels van de Kie.* Haren, Netherlands: Symposiumcommissie Chirurgie Nederland; 1988: 128–134.

Visuri T. Proximal dislocation of the patella with large osteochondral fragment: A report of 3 cases. *Acta Orthop Scand.* 1990;61(Suppl 235):73.

Von Lanz T, Wachsmuth W. *Praktische Anatomie: Bein und Statik.* Berlin, Germany: Springer Verlag; 1972.

Waldrop JI, Broussard TS. Disruption of the anterior cruciate ligament in a three-year-old child: A case report. *J Bone Joint Surg Am.* 1984;66:1113–1114.

Walsh WM. Anteromedial rotatory instability of the knee. *Phys Ther.* 1980;60:1633.

Warren RF. Primary repair of the anterior cruciate ligament. *Clin Orthop.* 1983;172:65–71.

Warren RF, Levy IM. Meniscal lesions associated with anterior cruciate ligament injury. *Clin Orthop.* 1983;172:32–38.

Weh L. Die überdehnte Kniescheibensehne beim Patellaspitzensyndrom. *Sportverletz Sportschaden.* 1988;2:26–34.

Welsh RP. Knee joint structure and function. *Clin Orthop.* 1980;147:7–15.

Wendt PP, Johnson RP. A study of quadriceps excursion, torque, and the effect of patellectomy on cadaver knee. *J Bone Joint Surg Br.* 1985;67:726–732.

Windhager R, Engel A. Zur operativen Behandlung des Morbus Osgood-Schlatter. *Z Orthop.* 1988;126:179–184.

Winkel D, Fisher S. *Schematisch handboek voor onderzoek en behandeling van weke delen aandoeningen van het bewegingsapparaat.* 6th ed. Delft, Netherlands: Nederlandse Akademie voor Orthopedische Geneeskunde; 1982.

Wismans JC. *A Three-Dimensional Mathematical Model of the Human Knee Joint.* Eindhoven, Holland: Academic Dissertation; 1982.

Yashuda K, Majima T. Intra-articular ganglion blocking extension of the knee: Brief report. *J Bone Joint Surg Br.* 1988;70:837.

Part III

The Ankle and Foot

Chapter 13

Functional Anatomy of the Ankle

Although the term *ankle* is often used merely to describe the junction between the lower leg and the foot, the ankle in fact encompasses an intricate joint complex. This complex includes the following joints:

- the talocrural joint (which is the actual "ankle joint")
- the subtalar joint
- the joints between the calcaneus and cuboid, (lateral), and between the talus and navicular joints (medial), also called the midtarsal joints

JOINT MORPHOLOGY

Bony and Capsuloligamentous Structures

Talocrural Joint (Articulatio Talocruralis)

The talocrural joint is formed by the distal end of the tibia (the medial malleolus) and the distal end of the fibula (the lateral malleolus) as well as the anterior inferior tibiofibular ligament on one side and the talus on the other side.

The part of the talus that articulates with the "fork" of the ankle, termed the talar trochlea, is convex in an anteroposterior direction and is concave in the frontal plane. The anterior part of the talus is wider than the posterior part. The talar joint surfaces with both malleoli are continuous with the hyaline cartilage from the trochlea.

The talocrural joint capsule is relatively thin both anteriorly and posteriorly but is reinforced by collateral ligaments at the sides. At the medial side, the collateral ligaments are difficult to differentiate from each other; they can be seen as a homogenous thickening of the capsule, which is termed, as a whole, the deltoid ligament (Figure 13–1). This ligament can be divided into a superficial and a deep layer. The deep layer is the anterior tibiotalar ligament. The superficial layer consists of three parts: the tibionavicular ligament (anterior), tibiocalcaneal ligament (middle), and posterior tibiotalar ligament (posterior).

At the lateral side, there are three separate capsular ligaments (Figure 13–2). The anterior talofibular ligament runs from the anterior edge of the lateral malleolus to the lateral side of the talar neck. The posterior talofibular ligament runs almost horizontally from the posterior side of the lateral malleolus to the lateral aspect of the posterior talar process (a slip from this ligament runs to the medial malleolus). The calcaneofibular ligament, which is the middle ligament, runs as a cord from the underside of the lateral malleolus in a plantar and posterior direction to its attachment to the calcaneal tuberosity. Of all the ankle and foot ligaments, the lateral collateral ligaments are the most frequently injured as a result of the often seen inversion trauma.

The anterior and posterior parts of the capsule are loosely constructed. This condition is

333

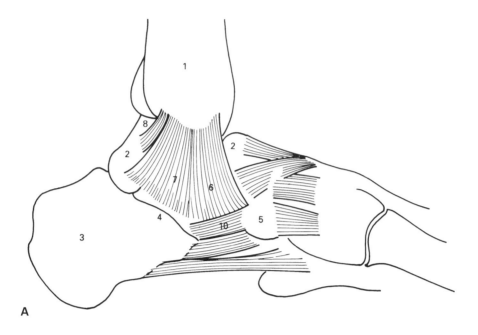

A

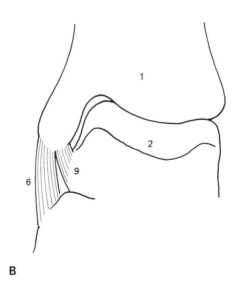

B

Figure 13–1 (**A**) Ligaments at the medial side of the left ankle and midtarsal joints. (**B**) Anterior view of the left deltoid ligament. **1**, Tibia; **2**, talus; **3**, calcaneus; **4**, sustentaculum tali; **5**, navicular tuberosity; **6**, anterior tibiotalar and tibionavicular ligaments; **7**, tibiocalcaneal ligament; **8**, posterior tibiotalar ligament; **9**, anterior tibiotalar ligament (deep part); **10**, plantar calcaneonavicular ligament.

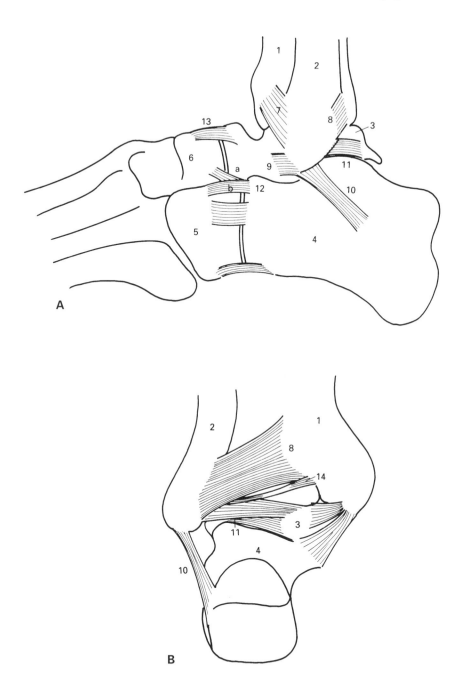

Figure 13–2 (**A**) Ligaments at the lateral side of the left ankle and midtarsal joints. (**B**), Posterior view of the left ankle. **1**, Tibia; **2**, fibula; **3**, posterior talar process; **4**, calcaneus; **5**, cuboid; **6**, navicular; **7**, anteroinferior tibiofibular ligament; **8**, posterior inferior tibiofibular ligament; **9**, anterior talofibular ligament; **10**, calcaneofibular ligament; **11**, posterior talofibular ligament; **12**, bifurcate ligament (**a**, calcaneonavicular ligament; **b**, calcaneocuboid ligament); **13**, talonavicular ligament; **14**, slip of the posterior talofibular ligament to the medial malleolus.

necessary to allow for the required amount of flexion (plantar flexion) and extension (dorsiflexion) in the ankle joint. During maximal flexion and extension, there is sufficient space between the talus and the tibia that the soft tissue—the capsule and fat pad at the posterior and anterior aspects of the joint— does not become compressed. As the result of a traumatic flexion or extension movement, this space can decrease, leading to painful compression. When plantar flexion is the cause of compression of the soft tissue, the condition is designated as posterior tibiotalar compression syndrome. When the condition is caused by an extension movement, it is called an anterior tibiotalar compression syndrome.

Talocalcaneal Joint (Articulatio Talocalcanea)

The talocalcaneal joint, also called the subtalar joint, consists of the anterior and posterior connections between the talus and calcaneus. Although both connections form a functional unity, the anterior part is morphologically considered as belonging to the talocalcaneonavicular joint.

The posterior talocalcaneal connection is formed by the plantarly located concave joint surface of the posterior part of the talus and the dorsally located convex joint surface of the posterior part of the calcaneus. The thin capsule is reinforced by a number of strong ligaments. Extra augmentation comes from the short, strong interosseous ligament. This ligament restricts valgus motion in the joint, so that movement in this direction is almost impossible.

Talocalcaneonavicular Joint (Articulatio Talocalcaneonavicularis)

The convex head of the talus has contact with the concave joint surface of the navicular. The lower aspect of the talar head also has contact with the middle and anterior facets of the calcaneus. The rather thin joint capsule is augmented by ligaments in several places. In addition, extra reinforcement is supplied by the talonavicular ligament, the plantar calcaneonavicular ("spring") ligament, and the calcaneonavicular part of the bifurcate ligament.

Calcaneocuboid and Talonavicular Joints (Articulationes Calcaneocuboidea/ Talonavicularis)

The calcaneocuboid and talonavicular joints form the so-called midtarsal joint. The line formed by their joint spaces is known as Chopart's exarticulation line. Here, too, the thin capsule is reinforced in various places by strong ligaments. The capsule is strengthened dorsally by the calcaneocuboid part of the bifurcate ligament and plantarly by the long plantar and plantar calcaneocuboid ligaments.

From the clinician's point of view, the midtarsal joints play an important role in regard to foot pathology. The other intertarsal joints are less clinically significant and thus are only identified:

- the cuneonavicular joint (between the three cuneiform bones and the navicular)
- the cuboideonavicular joint (between the cuboid and navicular)
- the small joints between each of the cuneiform bones and between the cuboid and lateral cuneiform (Figure 13–3)

Muscles, Tendons, and Ligaments

Considering the talocrural joint functionally and anatomically during movement, one can identify an infinite number of continually shifting axes. In clinical situations, however, motions in only one axis, flexion-extension, are usually significant. The muscles involved in these motions are listed in Table 13–1.

Movements   and   relationships   in   the

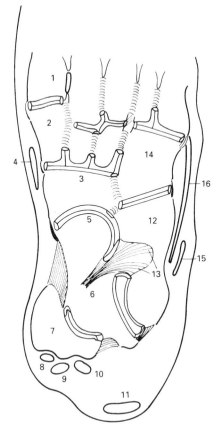

Figure 13–3 Transverse section through the right foot, from above. **1**, First metatarsal; **2**, medial cuneiform; **3**, navicular; **4**, tibialis anterior tendon; **5**, talar head; **6**, talus; **7**, medial malleolus; **8**, tibialis posterior tendon; **9**, flexor digitorum longus tendon; **10**, flexor hallucis longus tendon; **11**, Achilles tendon; **12**, calcaneus; **13**, interosseous talocalcaneal ligament; **14**, cuboid; **15**, peroneus longus tendon; **16**, peroneus brevis tendon.

subtalar and midtarsal joints are much more intricate. The movements in these joints are strongly coupled with each other. The combined movements that occur in these joints are inversion and eversion. Inversion is a combination of the following movements: flexion, adduction, and supination in the midtarsal joints with varus movement in the subtalar joint. Eversion is the opposite movement: extension, abduction, and pronation in the midtarsal joints and valgus movement in the subtalar joint.

The clinically important muscles that perform inversion are the posterior tibialis and triceps surae. The extensor digitorum muscle performs eversion. The clinically important peroneal muscles and the tibialis anterior muscle have the following combined function: The tibialis anterior muscle performs extension, adduction, and supination; and the peroneal muscles perform flexion, abduction, and pronation.

The common peroneal nerve runs between the two origins of the peroneus longus muscle, at the head of the fibula and the neck of the fibula, where it can become compressed. The peroneus brevis muscle originates at the distal two thirds of the fibula. The tendons from both muscles run together in one tendon sheath, posterior to the lateral malleolus, and are held in place by the peroneal retinaculum. The tendon of the peroneus longus runs plantar to the calcaneal peroneal trochlea and then farther diagonally over the plantar aspect of the foot to the base of the

Table 13–1 Muscles Involved in Flexion and Extension of the Talocrural Joint

Flexion	*Extension*

Gastrocnemius and soleus muscles, with contribution from:
   Plantaris muscle
   Tibialis posterior muscle
   Flexor digitorum longus muscle
   Peroneus longus and brevis muscles
	Tibialis anterior muscle, with contribution from:
	   Extensor digitorum longus muscle
	   Extensor hallucis longus muscle
	   Peroneus tertius muscle

first metatarsal and the medial cuneiform. The peroneus brevis runs dorsal to the peroneal trochlea and attaches to the tuberosity of the base of the fifth metatarsal (Figure 13–3).

The tibialis posterior tendon runs distally through the tarsal tunnel, over the posterior aspect of the medial malleolus to the plantar aspect of the navicular tuberosity. From there, tendon fibers fan out to all other tarsals and metatarsals, with most fibers going to the first metatarsal and medial cuneiform.

The crural fascia is continuous with the fascia lata of the thigh. It firmly envelops the muscles of the lower leg and is firmer at the front than at the back. A large part of the proximal attachment of the tibialis anterior muscle is to the crural fascia. The tibialis anterior, together with the extensor digitorum longus and extensor hallucis longus muscles

and the anterior tibial artery, lies in a compartment (Figure 13–4). This compartment is formed medially by the tibia, laterally by the anterior crural intermuscular septum and fibula, anteriorly by the crural fascia, and posteriorly by the interosseous membrane. Because of the rigid borders of the compartment, swelling of the muscle belly of the tibialis anterior can rather quickly lead to a disturbance in the circulation as a result of compression of the anterior tibial artery.

The tendon of the tibialis anterior muscle inserts at the medioplantar aspect of the first metatarsal and medial cuneiform.

The Achilles tendon is not a solitary structure; rather, it forms the attachment of the gastrocnemius and soleus muscles to the calcaneus. It is the thickest and strongest tendon in the human body. The fibers of the soleus

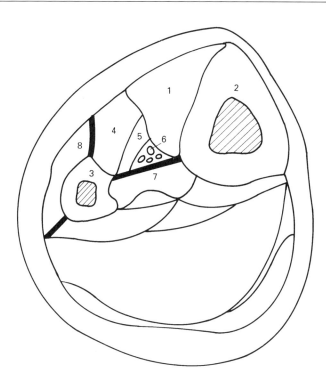

Figure 13–4 Anterior tibial compartment. **1**, Tibialis anterior muscle; **2**, tibia; **3**, fibula; **4**, extensor digitorum longus muscle; **5**, extensor hallucis longus muscle; **6**, anterior tibial artery; **7**, interosseous membrane; **8**, anterior crural intermuscular septum.

muscle run primarily in the medial part of the tendon, the site where the Achilles tendon is most often affected. The tendon inserts at the distal part of the calcaneal tuberosity. The fibers fan out medially and laterally. In addition, the tendon runs over the plantar aspect of the foot, finally becoming continuous with the plantar fascia. Because of this far distal attachment, the effectiveness of the triceps surae muscle is significantly increased. The tendon is separated from the bone by the subtendineal Achilles bursa at the level of the proximal part of the calcaneal tuberosity.

Other Structures

Superficial Peroneal Nerve

The superficial peroneal nerve is a continuation of the common peroneal nerve, which in turn is a branch of the sciatic nerve. The nerve runs between the peroneal muscles and the extensor digitorum longus. It innervates both peroneal muscles.

This nerve, at the level of the distal third of the lower leg, perforates the crural fascia and becomes more superficial in its course. Then it divides into medial, intermediate, and lateral branches. The medial branch runs over the front of the ankle and the dorsum of the foot to the first and second toes, where it innervates the skin. The intermediate branch (ramus intermedius) is superficial and visible in many people during inversion of the foot. This branch innervates the skin of the second through fifth toes and also supplies sensation (proprioception) to the lateral side of the ankle and midtarsal joints. In traumatic inversion, the nerve can be overstretched, which will affect proprioception in this area. The lateral branch is also known as the sural nerve, the nerve that runs at the lateral side of the Achilles tendon. It can easily become damaged during operations in this region.

Tibial Nerve

When one considers the tibial nerve, its anatomic relation in the tarsal tunnel is of particular significance. In the popliteal fossa, the nerve gives off branches to the knee joint and to the gastrocnemius, plantaris, soleus, and popliteus muscles. From there it runs distally between the soleus and deep flexor muscles.

When this nerve reaches the level of the medial malleolus, it runs in the tarsal tunnel, which is the space between the calcaneus and medial malleolus, covered by the flexor retinaculum (also termed the lacinate ligament). In the tarsal tunnel, the following structures run from anteromedial to posterolateral:

- tendon of the tibialis posterior muscle
- tendon of the flexor digitorum longus muscle
- posterior tibial vein and artery and tibial nerve
- tendon of the flexor hallucis longus muscle

At the level of the flexor retinaculum, a branch of the tibial nerve is given off to the skin over the medial aspect of the calcaneus. Just after emerging from the tarsal tunnel, the tibial nerve divides into the medial and lateral plantar nerves. These two branches run through two fibrous tunnels in the abductor hallucis muscle to the plantar aspect of the foot. As the height of the medial arch of the foot decreases (pes plano valgus), a (chronic) stretch of these branches can occur, causing paresthesia at the sole of the foot.

Posterior Process of the Talus

The posterior process of the talus, the most posterior part of the talus, has two tubercles: the pointed tip of the lateral tubercle and the more rounded medial tubercle. The tendon of the flexor hallucis longus muscle runs between these two tubercles. In many individuals, the lateral tubercle is abnormally large or is even separated from the posterior process of the talus. The latter instance is termed an os trigonum; this accessory bone is only connected to the talus by means of ligaments.

Pathologic changes are often seen in this region, particularly in people who have either an abnormally large lateral tubercle or an os trigonum. Symptoms can occur after plantar flexion trauma of the ankle, whereby the capsule becomes pinched between the lateral tubercle or os trigonum and the tibia; this lesion is called the posterior tibiotalar compression syndrome.

BIOMECHANICS

The following discussion, which classifies the various joint functions as though they were separate and distinct, should be considered theoretical. Later, in Chapter 14, it be-

comes clear that all joints of the foot are functionally and inseparably connected with each other.

Talocrural Joint

The movements of the ankle joint can be rather simply described as occurring almost exclusively around a transverse axis. The talus can also move to some degree around longitudinal and sagittal axes, but these movements are only clinically relevant in instances of instability.

The transverse axis is not purely transverse but rather runs from the lowest point of the medial malleolus to the lowest point of the lateral malleolus (Figure 13–5). The lowest

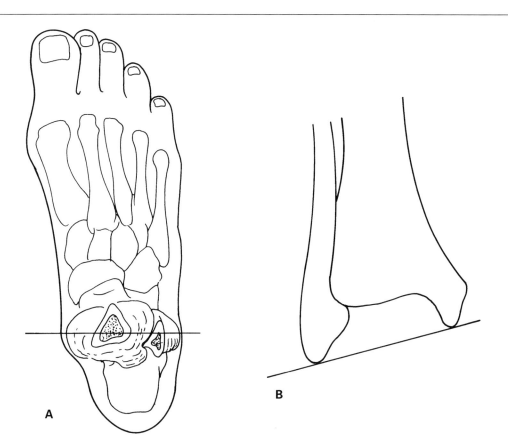

Figure 13–5 (**A**) Transverse axis through the talocrural joint, from above. (**B**) Transverse axis through the talocrural joint, from the front.

point of the lateral malleolus is located more distally and posteriorly than the lowest point of the medial malleolus.

The motions around this axis are plantar flexion and extension (also called dorsiflexion). The amount of motion varies among individuals and ranges from 10° to 20° in extension and 25° to 35° in plantar flexion.

Talocalcaneal Joint

The subtalar joint has long been considered a single-axis joint. In reality, however, during movement it is an extremely complex joint with a large number of constantly changing axes.[1]

Minimal roll-glide movements resulting in varus and valgus motions take place in this joint during foot motions.

Talonavicular and Calcaneocuboid Joints

Very complicated movements also occur in the midtarsal joints, around a large number of axes. Although morphologically the joint comes nowhere near qualifying as ball and socket, functionally it can be seen as one, an accommodation that greatly simplifies the clinical examination. The movements are mainly initiated from the subtalar joint. The movements are flexion and extension, abduction and adduction, and pronation and supination. The combination movements are called inversion (flexion, adduction, and supination) and eversion (extension, abduction, and pronation). The amount of motion varies significantly among individuals. Thus in the clinical examination, a comparison with the nonaffected side must always be made.

The subtalar joint also has an influence on where the axes lie and thereby on the amount of stability. During eversion, the axes of the calcaneocuboid joint and the talonavicular joint lie parallel to each other, causing the amount of motion to increase. During inversion, the axes of both joints make an angle of about 30° in relation to each other, causing a "locking" to occur and the foot to become more stable.[2]

Distal Tibiofibular Joint

For years, it was accepted that the fibula translated proximally during extension and distally during flexion. This finding, however, was determined in cadaver studies. In vivo studies have demonstrated that the fibula moves distally during the entire weight-bearing phase. Thus during walking, the "fork" of the ankle deepens, resulting in increased stability.

Chapter 14

Functional Anatomy of the Foot

For the purposes of discussion, the foot is addressed as being separate from the rest of the anatomy of the lower extremity. This classification is artificial and based entirely on anatomic distinctions. Functionally, no joint in the ankle or foot can move independently. In this discussion, the term *foot* refers to the bony and soft tissue structures found distal to the midtarsal joints.

JOINT MORPHOLOGY

Bony and Capsuloligamentous Structures

Tarsometatarsal Joints (Articulationes Tarsometatarseae)

The tarsometatarsal joints connect the five metatarsal bones with the cuneiform bones and the cuboid. The first joint is found between the first metatarsal and medial cuneiform bones. This joint has its own synovial cavity. The second metatarsal articulates with the intermediate cuneiform, and the third metatarsal articulates with the lateral cuneiform. The second and third joints share a common cavity. The fourth metatarsal articulates with both the lateral cuneiform and the cuboid, and the fifth metatarsal only articulates with the cuboid. The fourth and fifth joints also share a common cavity.

The capsules of the tarsometatarsal joints are reinforced by ligaments at their dorsal and plantar aspects. Additional reinforcement is provided by interosseous cuneiform and interosseous cuneometatarsal ligaments. These ligaments are strong and allow only limited translatory movements, which are ultimately initiated from the subtalar and the midtarsal joints and from the toes.

Intermetatarsal Joints (Articulationes Intermetatarseae)

The first and second metatarsals are not connected to each other by ligaments; sometimes a bursa is found here. Between the other metatarsals, there are ligamentous connections (the interosseous metatarsal ligaments). In addition, there are transverse ligamentous connections (the deep transverse metatarsal ligaments) just proximal to the metatarsophalangeal joints.

Normally, movement in these connections is rather minimal. Particularly in athletes who have hyperpronated, however, an abnormally large amount of motion is found between the first and second metatarsals.

Metatarsophalangeal Joints (Articulationes Metatarsophalangeae)

The joints between the metatarsals and the phalanges are ellipsoid joints. The flexion, extension, and in particular abduction and adduction motions are restricted by rather strong, cordlike collateral ligaments.

Proximal and Distal Interphalangeal Joints (Articulationes Interphalangeae Proximales/Distales Pedis)

The proximal and distal interphalangeal joints are hinge joints, formed by the head of the proximal phalanx and the socket of the adjacent distal phalanx. These joints also have collateral ligaments.

Muscles, Tendons, and Ligaments

The intrinsic muscles are arranged in four layers. Isolated activity of the foot muscles does not occur in most people except for the muscles of the great and little toes. In this sense, the muscles can be functionally divided into medial, lateral, and middle groups: the medial for the great toe and the lateral for the little toe, and the middle group formed by the interosseous and lumbrical muscles (the so-called short flexors).

The intrinsic muscles of the foot help maintain the transverse arch and have minimal to no effect on maintaining the longitudinal arches. These longitudinal arches, the lateral and medial, are supported mainly by ligaments, particularly by the long plantar ligament and the plantar aponeurosis.[3] In the non–weight-bearing foot, the position of the transverse arch is mostly maintained by the transverse head of the adductor hallucis muscle. Morton[4] and Collis and Jayson[5] propose that in the weight-bearing foot the heads of all the metatarsals contact the ground and are loaded.

The four layers of the intrinsic muscles, from superficial to deep, are as follows:

- first layer: flexor digitorum brevis, abductor digiti minimi, and abductor hallucis (with the tendon sheath of the long flexors)
- second layer: lumbricals
- third layer: flexor hallucis brevis, adductor hallucis, and flexor digiti minimi brevis

- fourth layer: dorsal and plantar interosseous muscles

At the dorsal aspect of the foot, the only intrinsic muscle is the extensor digitorum brevis. The part of the muscle belly with the tendon running to the great toe is sometimes separately named the extensor hallucis brevis muscle.

Table 14–1 lists the muscles involved in motions of the metatarsophalangeal joints.

Other Structures

Plantar Aponeurosis

The plantar aponeurosis is a strong collagenous structure lying superficially and consisting of fibers that run from the calcaneus to the phalanges. The central part is the thickest and superficially is connected to the skin. The deep layer is connected with the intrinsic muscles of the foot and the deep transverse metatarsal ligaments.

Through its connection with the phalanges, the plantar aponeurosis becomes taut during extension of the toes. In so doing, the medial longitudinal arch of the foot also becomes taut. This is a particularly important feature for running.

Interdigital Nerves

The two terminal branches of the tibial nerve are the lateral and medial plantar nerves. At the sole of the foot, these branches divide again into the interdigital nerves. Each interdigital nerve innervates skin between two adjacent toes. Seen from plantar, these branches run at a superficial level (compared with the deep transverse ligaments) between the metatarsal heads. When the toes are extended, these nerves are pulled taut over these ligaments, which function as pulleys.

BIOMECHANICS

Metatarsophalangeal Joints

The most important movements in the metatarsophalangeal joints are flexion and

Table 14–1 Muscles Involved in Motions of the Metatarsophalangeal Joints

Flexion	Extension	Abduction*	Adduction
Flexor digitorum brevis	Extensor digitorum	Interosseous muscle	Plantar interosseous
Lumbricals	longus	belonging to the	muscles
Interosseous muscles	Extensor digitorum	corresponding	
Assisted by flexor	brevis	metatarsal	
digitorum longus	Extensor hallucis		Of the great toe:
	longus		adductor hallucis
		Of the great toe:	
Of the great toe	(Extensor hallucis	abductor hallucis	
exclusively: flexor	brevis, one head of	Of the little toe:	
hallucis longus and	extensor digitorum	abductor digiti minimi	
brevis	brevis)		

*The axis of reference runs through the second toe.

extension. The axis around which these motions take place is not uniform (Figure 14–1). For the first two metatarsophalangeal joints, it is an axis that can be considered almost transverse. For the other three joints, the axis runs diagonally. This difference facilitates motions important for walking. Refer to the section on gait pattern for further information.

In the metatarsophalangeal joints, abduction and adduction also take place. The reference axis for these motions runs longitudinally through the second metatarsal (Figure 14–1). Active abduction is only possible in combination with extension, and adduction is only possible in combination with flexion.

Interphalangeal Joints

Actively, only flexion and extension motions are possible in the interphalangeal joints. Passively, they can also be moved around their longitudinal axis, and some translation is possible in all directions.

Arches of the Foot

The longitudinal arches of the foot include a medial and a lateral arch. The medial arch is formed by the calcaneus, talus, navicular, and the three medial metatarsals. The lateral arch consists of the calcaneus, cuboid, and the two lateral metatarsals. The primary function of the medial arch is dynamic, and that of the lateral one is load carrying.

The medial arch owes its stability to the construction of the bony structures and corresponding joints and to the plantar aponeurosis and the long plantar ligament. The plantar aponeurosis contributes to the stability mainly in a dynamic way. During extension of the toes, the metatarsal heads are used as a "windlass," around which the plantar aponeurosis is pulled taut. In this way, the medial arch is increased. Bojsen Möller[3] describes why this "windlass" mechanism works more effectively on the medial side than on the lateral side (Figure 14–2). There appears to be a significant difference in the radius of the metatarsal heads. The radius of the first metatarsal head (windlass) averages 15 mm, and that of the third metatarsal head is about 8 mm. One of the factors that determines the effectiveness of a windlass is the radius of the pulley: the greater the radius, the greater the effectiveness.

An indirect influence on the medial arch takes place as a result of motion in the lower leg. It appears that internal rotation of the tibia results in a heightening of the medial

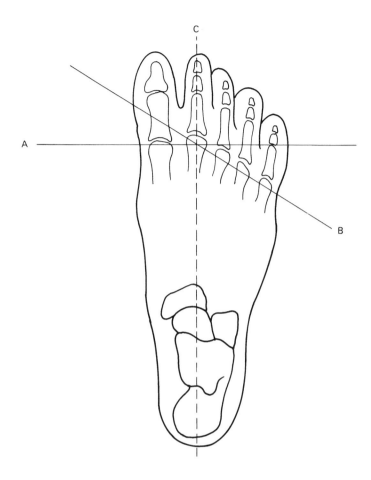

Figure 14–1 Flexion-extension axis through the metatarsophalangeal joints. **A**, Transverse axis; **B**, diagonal axis; **C**, axis of reference for abduction and adduction.

arch. The heightening and stabilizing of the longitudinal arches is of great importance in the distribution of weight during walking and running.

Gait Pattern

It is not easy to describe the phases of the gait pattern because, as mentioned earlier, different activities often take place simultaneously and motions in one joint are often initiated by motions in another joint.

As a starting point for the analysis of the gait pattern we will use the data from Mann.[6]

Figure 14–3 depicts not only the behavior of the joints but also the activity of the various muscle groups.

Except for minor variations, most authors describe the parts of each step in percentages. There is a further general division in two phases, known as the stance phase and the swing phase. Each of these phases is again divided. The gait cycle is defined as what happens between the first foot contact and the moment that the same foot again contacts the ground. During normal walking, the stance phase is about 62% of the cycle, and the swing phase is about 38%. During the first 12% of

Figure 14–2 "Windlass" function of the metatarsal heads.

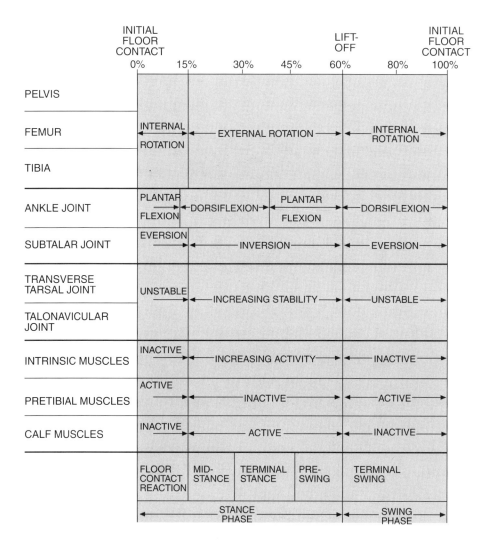

Figure 14–3 Schematic representation of the complete walking cycle; the rotations in the various joints as well as the activity from the lower leg and foot muscles are indicated. *Source:* Reprinted with permission from RA. Mann. *Atlas of Orthotics,* copyright© 1985, Mosby-YearBook.

the stance phase, there is double foot contact with the ground. During the second part of the stance phase (38%), there is contact with one foot, and during the last 12%, there is again double foot contact.

In the walking cycle, motions in the ankle joints are particularly important (Figure 14–4). Motions in the other bony connections are initiated from these joints. There are two plantar flexion peaks: at initial heel contact and at lift-off. Extension (or dorsiflexion) takes place during the phase when the foot is flat on the ground. In the subtalar joint, the range of motion is small. Mann[7] registered an amount of maximally 4° valgus in the midstance phase and approximately 4° during toe-off. In instances of flat foot, sometimes up to 11° of valgus motion occurs during heel contact. Also, to compensate for limitations of motion in the talocrural joint, hypermobility can occur in the subtalar joint. During the stance phase, the varus motion in the subtalar joint gradually increases; in so

doing, the midtarsal joints are stabilized. During the initial floor contact, there is a valgus position in the subtalar joint, whereby the midtarsal joints are much more flexible. This is important for absorbing the forces exerted on the foot during this phase. In the metatarsophalangeal joints, there is no flexion motion during normal walking. The interphalangeal joints are continuously held in almost maximal flexion, however.

During walking, the vertical force during heel contact is greater than the body weight. The same peak load is also present before toe-off. During the first peak force, the extensors are primarily active; during the second peak force, the intrinsic muscles of the foot and the flexors are primarily active (see Figure 14–3). During walking, the vertical force shifts from the heel, in a slightly convex line, to the lateral edge of the foot. Research by Bojsen Möller[3] indicates that this line shifts more medially during running. Pronation of the foot increases with an increase in velocity, whereby

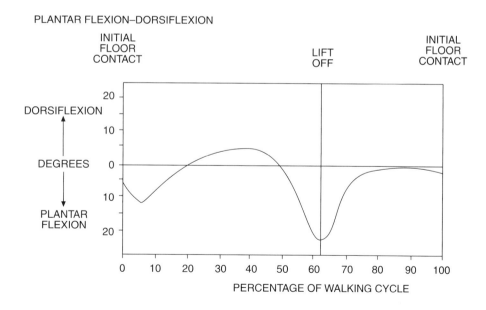

Figure 14–4 Range of motion of the ankle joint during normal walking. *Source:* Reprinted with permission from RA. Mann. *Atlas of Orthotics,* copyright© 1985, Mosby-YearBook.

the stance phase takes place more at the medial part of the foot.

Closing Consideration

Many questions concerning the biomechanics of the foot remain unanswered. The goal of this chapter is not to present exhaustive information but rather to provide an idea of how complicated the functions of the foot and ankle are. For further study, refer to the suggested reading at the end of Part III.

Chapter 15

Surface Anatomy of the Lower Leg, Ankle, and Foot

15.1 SURFACE ANATOMY OF THE LOWER LEG

Initial Position

The starting position is for the patient to sit for examination of the front part of the leg and to assume a prone or standing position for examination of the back part of the leg.

TIBIA

The sharp anterior edge of the tibia can be inspected and palpated from the tibial tuberosity to the level of the medial malleolus (Figure 15–1). Medial from this edge is the easily palpable medial surface of the tibia. It is advisable to mark the medial malleolus in this phase of the surface anatomy evaluation. Clinicians who have difficulty differentiating between the borders of the medial malleolus and the medial aspect of the talus should practice this first (see "Surface Anatomy of the Ankle and Foot").

The tibia should be thoroughly examined and felt for possible tender spots and areas of thickening. Subperiostal bleeding, such as that caused by a kick in the shins, results in extreme pain. Tumors of the bone are mainly seen in young people, and stress fractures are usually caused by sports.

FIBULA

Just distal to the fibular head, a small part of the fibula is still palpable. Farther down, the fibula is covered with muscles and is only indirectly palpable. Ten centimeters to 20 cm proximal to the lateral malleolus, the fibula is again easily palpable. During this study of surface anatomy, it is advisable to mark the lateral malleolus.

ANTERIOR TIBIAL COMPARTMENT

The anterior tibial compartment is located between the tibia and the fibula (Figure 15–1). Along with the extensor muscles, the anterior tibial artery and the deep peroneal nerve are also located in this compartment. These latter two structures are not palpable at this location but may be palpated at the foot. The best way to evaluate these muscles is from their insertions on the dorsum of the foot.

Tibialis Anterior Muscle

The insertion of the tibialis anterior muscle is easily visible at the level of the medial cuneiform bone and the base of the first metatarsal. The muscle is most easy to see when the foot is brought into supination and extension (dorsiflexion) without extension of the toes. This motion can also be used to evaluate the function of the muscle.

The palpation starts from distal using the alternating finger method. The edge of the tibialis anterior muscle that lies along the medial border of the tibia is easy to locate. It takes some practice, however, to locate the lateral edge next to the extensor digitorum longus muscle. To aid in identification and location, the patient should be asked to extend and flex the toes. The extensor digitorum longus contracts during toe extension.

Extensor Hallucis Longus Muscle

The insertion of the extensor hallucis longus muscle at the big toe is clearly visible (Figure 15–1). The muscle is even more visible when the big toe is extended.

Palpation should start from distal using the alternating finger method. Proximal to the extensor retinaculum, the muscle disappears in the fork between the tibialis anterior muscle and the extensor digitorum longus muscle.

Extensor Digitorum Longus Muscle

The insertion of the extensor digitorum longus muscle from the second to the fifth toes is easily visible (Figures 15–1 and 15–2). This muscle is more pronounced when the toes are extended and the foot is pronated. Quite often, the muscle has an extra lateral insertion at the lateral edge of the foot and not at the toes. This tendon is then called the peroneal tertius muscle and is an often seen anatomic variation.

Palpation of the extensor digitorum longus muscle is performed with the alternating finger method from distal. The common tendon of the extensor digitorum longus muscle runs under the extensor retinaculum and lateral to the extensor hallucis longus muscle, which in turn runs lateral to the tibialis anterior muscle. Farther proximally, the border between the extensor digitorum and tibialis anterior muscles is difficult to discern (refer to the section on the tibialis anterior). In locating the border with the peroneal muscles, the patient can be asked to alternately flex and extend the foot. During plantar flexion, the peroneal muscles contract. During extension,

the extensor digitorum longus muscle contracts. If the clinician encounters difficulty, the peroneus longus muscle can be located and marked first (refer to the section on the peroneus longus muscle, below).

PERONEAL COMPARTMENT

The superficial peroneal nerve, which runs through the peroneal compartment, is normally palpable on the dorsum of the foot (see "Systematic Palpation of the Dorsum of the Foot"). The sural nerve can sometimes be palpated behind the lateral malleolus. The peroneal muscles can best be palpated from proximal (Figure 15–2). Differentiation at the level of the malleolus can be difficult. Distal to the malleolus, both tendons are clearly visible when the foot is actively brought into pronation.

Peroneus Longus Muscle

The peroneus longus muscle is palpated starting from the head of the fibula. A finger is placed at both sides of the fibular head. Using the alternating finger technique, palpation is performed to distal. This muscle is more easily palpated when the foot is pronated and plantar flexed, although in this position specific differentiation between the peroneus longus and peroneus brevis muscles is not possible. The tendon of the peroneus longus muscle runs superficially, for the most part, behind the lateral malleolus.

The peroneus longus and brevis muscles can slip over the lateral malleolus in people who do not have a peroneal retinaculum. This can also occur in children with a pes calcaneovalgus.

During pronation of the foot, the peroneus longus tendon can be seen to dive under other soft tissue at the lateral side of the foot. This muscle inserts on the plantar aspect of the medial edge of the foot, at the medial cuneiform bone and the first metatarsal bone. The peroneus longus muscle and the tibialis anterior muscle "grasp" the foot like a stirrup.

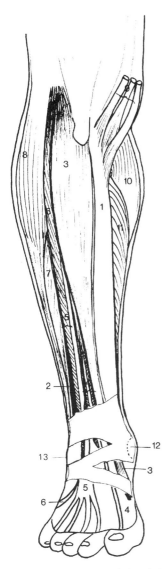

Figure 15–1 Front side of the right leg. **1**, Tibia (medial side); **2**, fibula; **3**, tibialis anterior muscle; **4**, extensor hallucis longus muscle; **5**, extensor digitorum longus muscle; **6**, peroneus tertius muscle; **7**, peroneus brevis muscle; **8**, peroneus longus muscle; **9**, pes anserinus superficialis; **10**, gastrocnemius muscle; **11**, soleus muscle; **12**, medial malleolus; **13**, lateral malleolus.

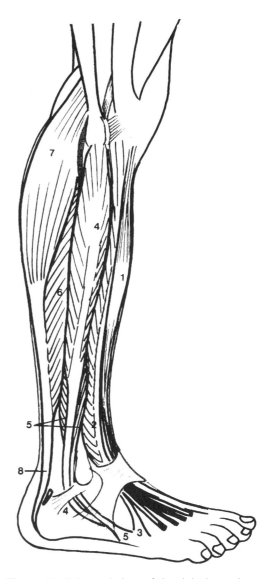

Figure 15–2 Lateral view of the right lower leg. **1**, Tibialis anterior muscle; **2**, extensor digitorum longus muscle; **3**, peroneus tertius muscle; **4**, peroneus longus muscle; **5**, peroneus brevis muscle; **6**, soleus muscle; **7**, gastrocnemius muscle; **8**, Achilles tendon.

Peroneus Brevis Muscle

The peroneus brevis muscle originates more distal to the peroneus longus muscle and lies deeper. Palpation of this muscle is difficult because of the tight crural fascia. Behind the lateral malleolus, the tendon normally is partially covered by the tendon of the peroneus longus muscle. Occasionally the tendon of the peroneus brevis muscle runs superficially, however. This can be determined by following the tendon of the peroneus brevis muscle from distal to proximal. On the lateral edge of the foot, the tendon runs superficially to its insertion at the tuberosity of the fifth metatarsal bone. This insertion is easily visible and palpable.

SUPERFICIAL FLEXORS

Palpation of the origin of both heads of the gastrocnemius muscle is described in Chapter 8. The superficial plantar flexor muscles are responsible for plantar flexion and inversion of the foot.

Gastrocnemius Muscle

In an extended position of the knee, two vertically running grooves are visible in the popliteal fossa, proximal to the transverse fold of the knee. After palpating the origins of the gastrocnemius muscle, the palpating fingers of both hands are placed in these grooves. By palpating deeply in a distal direction, the clinician can identify and locate the medial and lateral borders of the heads of the gastrocnemius muscle (Figures 15–2 and 15–3). The muscle edges can be followed to their junction with the Achilles tendon. If difficulties are encountered during this palpation, the exact border of the muscle can be found by bringing the foot actively into plantar flexion and inversion; the palpating finger is placed along the expected border of the muscle, and the finger is then pushed longitudinally along the edge of the muscle. At the same time, a sideways palpation (against the edge of the muscle) with the finger is also possible.

To find the exact site of the musculotendinous junction, the deeply palpating finger can be placed on the tendon and moved proximally. During this difficult palpation, the clinician will find that the medial head of the gastrocnemius extends farther distally than the lateral head.

Deep palpation of the muscle in the presence of a deep vein inflammation can produce sharp pain. Forceful extension of the foot with an extended knee increases the pain even more.

Soleus Muscle

The soleus muscle is palpable on both sides of the gastrocnemius muscle. This muscle is easily visible in muscular people when they stand on their toes. By placing the fingers on each side of the muscle, and sliding distally with alternating pressure, the clinician can follow the proximal parts of the soleus muscle. The muscle belly of the soleus is located distal to the gastrocnemius muscle. With one finger placed longitudinally alongside the border of the soleus muscle, and by gently pushing the finger distally, the clinician can feel both sides of the distal part of the soleus. Asking the patient to alternately plantar flex and extend the foot makes the palpation easier.

Achilles Tendon

The Achilles tendon comprises the tendons of the soleus muscle and the gastrocnemius muscle's medial and lateral heads (Figure 15–3). The thin and unpalpable tendon of the plantaris muscle runs medial to, and is not part of, the Achilles tendon. Even when the Achilles tendon has been totally ruptured, this tendon is almost always completely intact. The Achilles tendon is normally quite visible and easily palpable over its entire length (5 to 7 cm).

In Achilles tendon injuries, the tendon should be palpated on both sides, anteriorly, posteriorly, and at its insertion. Palpation should be done thoroughly because the affected site of this tendon is usually localized to a very small area. When palpating for the most painful site in Achilles tendon problems, palpating transverse to the fibers is most ef-

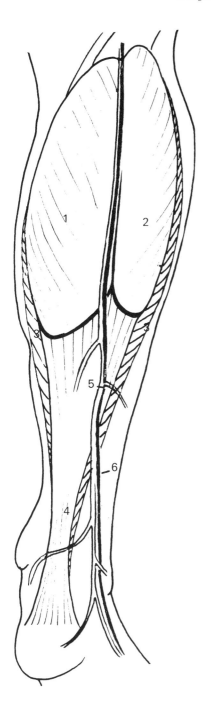

fective. Often, palpation along the length of the tendon does not provoke pain.

Palpation of the medial and lateral edges of the tendon can be performed with a transverse movement between the thumb and index finger. The entire tendon, from just proximal to the calcaneus to the musculotendinous junction, can be evaluated with this technique; the foot is kept in extension, which keeps the tendon stretched (Figure 15–4).

Palpation of the anteromedial or anterolateral aspects of the tendon (quite often forgotten, but quite often injured) should be performed with the tip of the middle finger and a supination motion of the forearm. To make the anterior aspect of the tendon more accessible, the thumb of the other hand gently pushes the Achilles tendon medially or laterally, toward the side being palpated. The ankle is positioned in plantar flexion, which relaxes the tendon (Figure 15–5).

If the site of the lesion is the anterodistal aspect of the tendon, at the level of the proximal calcaneus, the palpation cannot be per-

Figure 15–3 Dorsal view of the right lower leg. **1**, Gastrocnemius muscle (medial head); **2**, gastrocnemius muscle (lateral head); **3**, soleus muscle; **4**, Achilles tendon; **5**, lesser saphenous vein; **6**, medial sural cutaneous nerve.

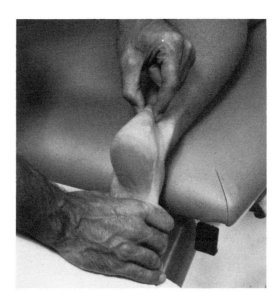

Figure 15–4 Palpation of the medial and lateral sides of the right Achilles tendon.

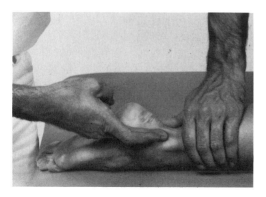

Figure 15–5 Palpation of the anterolateral aspect of the right Achilles tendon.

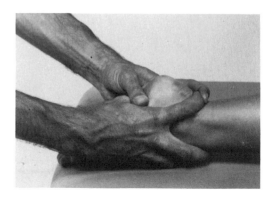

Figure 15–6 Indirect palpation of the antero-distal aspect of the right Achilles tendon at the level of the proximal calcaneus.

formed as mentioned above; the lesion can only be reached indirectly. In this case, the foot is kept in plantar flexion, and the relaxed tendon is pressed against the calcaneus with both index fingers while a transverse motion is made (Figure 15–6). It should be noted that also during this technique the subtendinous Achilles bursa becomes compressed. Injection with a local anesthetic into the bursa can help determine whether it is the bursa or the anterodistal aspect of the tendon that is causing the pain.

The posterior aspect of the tendon is rarely affected. With the ankle positioned in extension, this site can be palpated with the tip of the thumb or index finger.

The tenoosseous insertion of the Achilles tendon is located at the distal half of the calcaneal tuberosity. At its insertion, the tendon fans out in medial and lateral directions. During this palpation, the ankle is again brought into extension, and, with the tip of the thumb, the entire insertion can be palpated transverse to the running of the fibers. Here, too, a bursa (the subcutaneous calcaneal bursa) can be inflamed.

Disorders of the Achilles tendon are most often the result of small, biomechanical changes, such as aberrations in the position of the foot, knee, or hip. Treatment should concentrate not only on alleviation of the symptoms but also on alleviation of the primary cause of the symptoms.

DEEP FLEXORS

Normally, the deep flexors of the lower leg are not palpable. During their examination, the clinician should keep two points in mind. First, their topography at the level of their origins is different from that of their insertions: The flexor digitorum longus muscle has the most medial origin (and the most lateral insertion), the tibialis posterior muscle has its origin in the middle (and has the most medial insertion), and the flexor hallucis longus muscle has the most lateral origin (and its insertion is in the middle). Second, distally in the lower leg topographic differences occur on two levels: Proximal to the medial malleolus, the flexor digitorum and the tibialis posterior muscles cross each other (posterior to the medial malleolus, the tibialis posterior is the most medial tendon); distal to the medial malleolus, the tendons of the flexor digitorum longus and the flexor hallucis longus muscles cross each other, after which the digitorum disappears underneath other soft tissue structures.

Tibialis Posterior Muscle

The tendon of the tibialis posterior muscle is visible and palpable at the level of the medial malleolus. Of all the longitudinally running structures in this area, the tendon of the tibialis posterior is the most medial and is easily visible when the foot is in a plantar flexed and supinated position.

Flexor Hallucis Longus Muscle

Distal and medial to the tendon of the tibialis posterior muscle, the crossing of the flexor digitorum longus and flexor hallucis longus tendons can be felt on deep palpation. At the level of the crossing, differentiation between these tendons cannot be made. Distal to this site, a small part of the flexor hallucis longus tendon is still palpable.

Posterior Tibial Artery

Behind the medial malleolus, pulsations of the posterior tibial artery can be felt. Too much or too little pressure will prevent this palpation. If there is poor circulation in the leg, the posterior tibial artery will not be palpable. Sometimes, however, the pulsations cannot be felt even in healthy, young people. Not much time should be spent on the posterior tibial artery when there are other signs of poor circulation.

Tibial Nerve

The tibial nerve, lying deep behind the medial malleolus, usually cannot be palpated. In instances when palpation is possible, the nerve will be felt as a rolling cord underneath the finger.

Greater and Lesser Saphenous Veins

In some people, the lesser saphenous vein is visible in the middle of the gastrocnemius muscle. During a gentle transverse palpation, the vein can be felt rolling underneath the palpating finger. The vein enters the lower leg behind the lateral malleolus and ends in the popliteal vein (see Figure 15–3). Normally, the greater saphenous vein enters the lower leg in front of the medial malleolus and runs proximally to the knee area. The patient should be examined for a varicose condition.

15.2 SURFACE ANATOMY OF THE ANKLE AND FOOT

Palpation of specific structures of the ankle and foot is not easy. Foot disorders are seen frequently, so that it is important for the clinician to feel comfortable with the examination of the foot. When practicing surface anatomy, the clinician should use a skin marker to outline important structures. Quite often it is difficult to localize precisely a particular structure, especially in regard to the ligaments. Therefore, it is recommended that the clinician first locate specific, reliable structures as orientation points before beginning systematic palpation of a certain area. To find the joint lines, passive motions can sometimes be used; passive motions that "gap" the two joint partners are often most helpful.

IMPORTANT PALPABLE STRUCTURES IN THE ANKLE AND FOOT

The following orientation points and palpable structures are discussed in detail in the remainder of this chapter.

- **Medial orientation points**
    1. Medial malleolus

2. Sustentaculum tali

3. Navicular tuberosity

4. First tarsometatarsal joint

- **Systematic palpation of the medial aspect of the foot**
  1. Hallux (great toe)
  2. First metatarsal
  3. Medial cuneiform
  4. Navicular
  5. Talus
  6. Calcaneus
  7. Plantar calcaneonavicular ligament
  8. Deltoid ligament
  9. Medial retinaculum

- **Lateral orientation points**
  1. Lateral malleolus
  2. Peroneal trochlea
  3. Lateral part of the talar head
  4. Tuberosity of the fifth metatarsal

- **Systematic palpation of the lateral aspect of the foot**
  1. Little toe
  2. Fifth metatarsal
  3. Tarsal sinus
  4. Cuboid
  5. Talus
  6. Calcaneus
  7. Abductor digiti minimi muscle
  8. Peroneal muscles
  9. Lateral ankle ligaments
  10. Lateral retinaculum

- **Orientation points at the dorsum of the foot**
  1. Lisfranc's line
  2. Chopart's line

- **Systematic palpation of the dorsum of the foot**
  1. Metatarsals
  2. Cuneiform bones
  3. Navicular
  4. Talus

5. Cuboid

6. Extensor digitorum brevis muscle

7. Extensor hallucis brevis muscle

8. Dorsal retinaculum

9. Inferior extensor retinaculum

10. Dorsal pedal artery

11. Superficial peroneal nerve

12. Deep peroneal nerve

13. Saphenous nerve

14. Greater saphenous vein

- **Plantar aspect of the ankle and foot**
  1. Calcaneal tuberosity
  2. Heads of the metatarsals
  3. Sesamoid bones of the flexor hallucis longus muscle
  4. Plantar aponeurosis

MEDIAL ORIENTATION POINTS

Initial Position

The starting position is with the patient sitting on the examination table and the clinician sitting on a stool at a lower level.

Medial Malleolus

The medial border of the medial malleolus should be palpated and marked (Figure 15–7). Distal to the malleolus, a small piece of the talus is palpable. During alternating passive extension and plantar flexion, movements between both bones can be felt.

Sustentaculum Tali

Distal to the small part of talus described above is the sustentaculum tali (Figure15–7). This bony prominence is a plateau formed by the calcaneus and bears the medial part of the talus. The name *sustentaculum tali* means "carrier of the talus." The sustentaculum can be felt as a knob roughly 1 cm distal to the rounded tip of the medial malleolus. Usually, one can easily palpate the prominence of this bony structure both in a plantar to dorsal direction and in a posterior to distal direction. At the dorsal edge of the sustentaculum tali, the joint line with the talus is located. This joint line can be felt during alternating pronation and supination movements of the foot; this moves the calcaneus in relation to the talus.

If there is difficulty locating the sustentaculum tali, the clinician should first find the tendon of the tibialis posterior muscle. The sustentaculum is normally located just distal to this tendon, perpendicular to the rounded tip of the malleolus. The sustentaculum tali is the only medially prominent part of the calcaneus.

Navicular Tuberosity

When the palpating finger moves distally (toward the toes) from the sustentaculum tali, the tuberosity of the navicular is usually the first bony prominence that is met after the sustentaculum (Figure15–7). When an individual has flat feet, however, the talar head can sometimes be the most prominent structure, which can cause confusion. Use of the tendon of the tibialis posterior muscle provides another way to locate the tuberosity. Activity of the tibialis posterior muscle is generated by resisting plantar flexion, adduction, and supination of the foot. The tendon can be followed to its insertion on the plantar aspect of the navicular tuberosity. If one is still not sure of the location, with the foot in the neutral position the index finger is placed between the anterior aspect of the medial malleolus and the tendon of the tibialis anterior. Upon moving the index finger in a plantar direction, it comes against a bony prominence: the navicular tuberosity.

The talonavicular joint space lies directly proximal to the navicular tuberosity. To palpate the joint space and to find in which direction it runs, place the index finger between the medial malleolus and the navicular tuber-

osity with the fingertip pointing toward the heel. By performing passive adduction of the forefoot, the navicular can be felt to "slide over" the index finger while the head of the talus moves more laterally.

First Tarsometatarsal Joint

To locate the first tarsometatarsal or medial cuneiform–first metatarsal joint, the finger is placed against the middle of the medial side of the first metatarsal and slides lightly over the skin in a distal to proximal direction. A slight prominence (the base of the metatarsal) will be felt; the finger will then "fall" into a small V, which is the joint space. Sometimes this prominence and subsequent V can be felt better by palpating more along the dorsomedial aspect or the plantar-medial aspect of the bone. The location of the joint line can be confirmed by inducing activity of the tibialis anterior with the foot in the neutral position. The joint space lies directly in line with the running of the tendon (Figures 15–7 to 15–9). The joint line should be marked as a point of reference.

SYSTEMATIC PALPATION OF THE MEDIAL ASPECT OF THE FOOT

Hallux (Great Toe)

The joint line of the first metatarsophalangeal joint is palpable approximately 1 cm proximal and medial to the web space between the first and second toes (Figure 15–9). Another way of locating the joint line of the first metatarsophalangeal joint is by giving a gentle pull on the great toe. This opens up the joint space, making it more easy to see and palpate. The clinician should try to palpate the joint line as far as possible plantarly.

In cases where the first phalanx of the great toe is in an abnormal position, the first metatarsophalangeal joint is badly deformed. The push-off phase of the gait pattern puts tre-

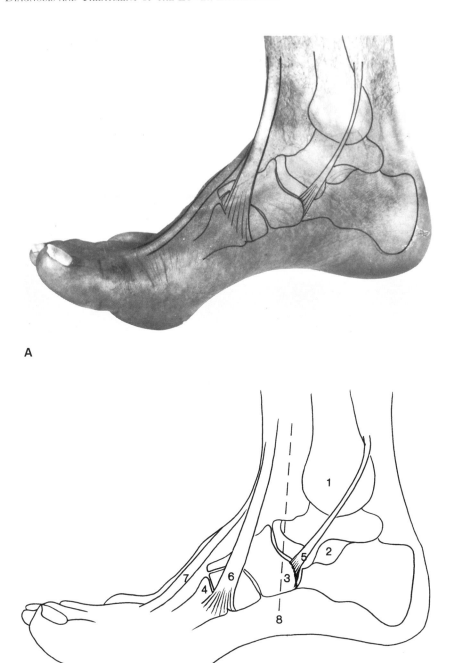

Figure 15–7 (**A** and **B**) Medial orientation points of the right foot. **1**, Medial malleolus; **2**, sustentaculum tali; **3**, tuberosity of the navicular bone; **4**, first tarsometatarsal joint; **5**, tibialis posterior muscle; **6**, tibialis anterior muscle; **7**, extensor hallucis longus muscle; **8**, line between the medial malleolus (anterior aspect) and the tibialis anterior tendon (this is an imaginary line to help locate the joint between the talus and navicular).

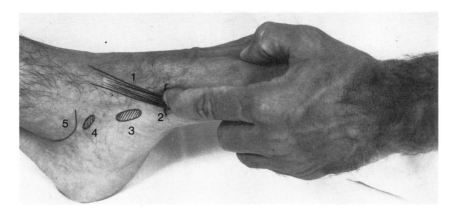

Figure 15–8 Palpation of the joint line between the medial cuneiform and the first metatarsal of the left foot. **1**, Tendon of the tibialis anterior muscle; **2**, joint line between the medial cuneiform and the first metatarsal; **3**, navicular tuberosity; **4**, sustentaculum tali; **5**, medial malleolus.

mendous loads on this joint. Abnormal loading can lead to pain and, in later stages, often causes bone deformations. The great toe can be inspected to determine whether its position is abnormal. The clinician should also be alert to possible growth disorders of the nail or other conditions that can interfere with the normal gait, such as extra callus formation on the skin.

First Metatarsal

The proximal and distal borders of the first metatarsal are discussed above (see the sections on the first tarsometatarsal joint and hallux). In cases of hallux valgus, the head of the first metatarsal stands out in the medial direction and is sensitive to pressure and loading. As a form of protection for this prominent area, a bursa can develop. With time, however, as a result of irritation from rubbing against the shoe, this bursa can become symptomatic (red and swollen). The abductor hallucis muscle can be felt directly medioplantar to the first metatarsal (Figure 15–9).

To comprehend better the form of the medial arch of the foot, a line can be drawn connecting the lower medial part of the first metatarsal, the medial cuneiform, the navicular, and the calcaneus.

Medial Cuneiform

The distal border of the medial cuneiform is discussed above (see the section on the first tarsometatarsal joint). The proximal border—the joint between the navicular and the medial cuneiform—is located just proximal to the midpoint of an imaginary line connecting the navicular tuberosity to the first tarsometatarsal joint (Figure 15–9). By palpation in this area, the V-shaped indentation of the navicular–medial cuneiform joint space can usually be felt. Movement in this joint is minimal during inversion and eversion and thus is not helpful in confirming the joint line. If the clinician is not sure but would still like to mark the joint, a dotted line can be used; this will indicate that it is a projection instead of a confirmed location.

Navicular

As already mentioned, there are three ways to locate the navicular tuberosity (Figure 15–9):

1. It is generally the most prominent bony structure on the medial side of the foot,

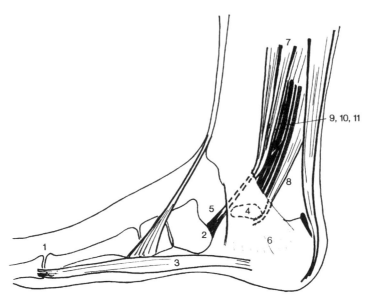

Figure 15–9 Medial view of the right foot. **1**, First metatarsophalangeal joint; **2**, navicular tuberosity; **3**, abductor hallucis muscle; **4**, sustentaculum tali; **5**, tibialis posterior muscle; **6**, flexor retinaculum; **7**, flexor digitorum longus muscle; **8**, flexor hallucis longus muscle; **9**, posterior tibial vein; **10**, posterior tibial artery; **11**, tibial nerve.

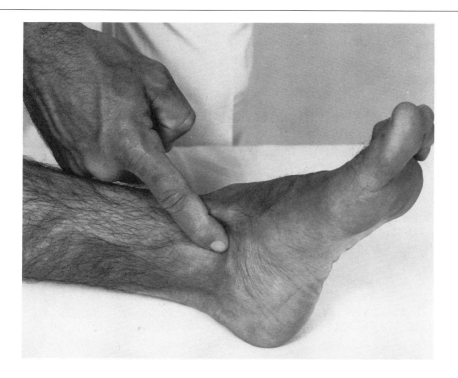

Figure 15–10 Palpation of the talonavicular joint of the left foot.

although when an individual has flat feet the talar head can sometimes be the most prominent structure.

2. Generate activity of the tibialis posterior muscle by resisted plantar flexion, adduction, and supination. Follow the tendon to its insertion on the plantar aspect of the navicular tuberosity.

3. With the foot in the neutral position, place the index finger directly between the anterior aspect of the medial malleolus and the tendon of the tibialis anterior. Upon moving the index finger in a plantar direction, it comes against bone: the navicular tuberosity.

The talonavicular joint space lies directly proximal to the navicular tuberosity. The best way to find this joint is to place the foot in the middle position between extension and plantar flexion and place the palpating finger between the tendon of the tibialis anterior muscle and medial malleolus. By moving the palpating finger distally while alternating inversion and eversion are performed, the talonavicular joint space can be felt (Figure 15–10). This joint should be marked at the medial side of the foot. Continued palpation in a plantar direction will lead to the plantar calcaneonavicular ligament.

Talus

By palpating between the sustentaculum tali and the navicular tuberosity just proximal to the talonavicular joint line, another bony convexity can be felt, particularly with the forefoot held in eversion. This is the medial part of the talar head (Figure 15–11). Palpating farther plantarly, the inferior calcaneonavicular ligament is reached; the head of the talus rests on this ligament.

By palpating just posterior and superior to the sustentaculum tali, the medial tubercle of the posterior process of the talus can be located. It becomes prominent in eversion of the foot and almost disappears in inversion.

The borders of this tubercle can be marked to the place where the talus disappears under the malleolus.

Calcaneus

Because all the bony orientation points on the medial side of the foot and ankle have been outlined with a skin marker, the medial aspect of the calcaneus can now be easily palpated (Figure 15–11). The lower and upper edges should be marked. The lower edge can be palpated easily at the calcaneal tuberosity but only with difficulty distally because of the presence of the "spring" ligament, the inferior calcaneonavicular ligament. The upper edge of the calcaneus is located behind the medial tubercle of the talus.

Plantar Calcaneonavicular Ligament

The calcaneus and the navicular are connected to each other not by a joint but rather by several ligaments: the plantar calcaneonavicular ligament (the "spring" ligament) and the calcaneonavicular part of the bifurcate ligament (discussed later).

The spring ligament is palpable between the front edge of the sustentaculum tali and the navicular tuberosity. Sometimes the ligament is felt as a round cord and sometimes as a more diffuse layer of collagen tissue. In the latter case, the border between the talus and the calcaneus is difficult to locate. The plantar calcaneonavicular ligament forms a sideways V with the tendon of the tibialis posterior, where the tendon runs from the medial malleolus and the navicular. The tendon forms the upper leg of the sideways V and the ligament the lower leg of the V; the apex of the V is at the navicular tuberosity.

Deltoid Ligament

The deltoid ligament is not palpable because it is covered by tendons and a retinaculum (Figure 15–11). Because several bony orientation points have been located, however, the course of the ligaments can be easily determined. The anterior tibiotalar ligament (running from the anterior edge of the medial malleolus to the talus) is covered by the tibionavicular ligament (which runs from the anterior edge of the medial malleolus to the navicular). The tibiocalcaneal ligament runs from the distal tip of the medial malleolus to the sustentaculum tali. Although not palpable, the posterior tibiotalar ligament runs between the medial tubercle of the talar posterior process and the medial malleolus.

Medial Retinaculum

The medial (or flexor) retinaculum fans out from the medial malleolus to the heel (Figure 15–10). The presence of the retinaculum can be confirmed by palpation. Palpation should be performed distal to the medial malleolus, where the retinaculum will feel slightly elastic. The posterior aspect of the retinaculum is generally easier to palpate using the following technique: Bring the finger forward and downward between the Achilles tendon and the malleolus while the foot is placed in eversion.

Between the flexor retinaculum (lying superficially) and the posterior tibiotalar ligament, several structures run. This entire region is termed the tarsal tunnel. In sequence, from anterior to posterior, the following structures are located under the medial (or flexor) retinaculum:

- tibialis posterior muscle
- flexor digitorum longus muscle
- tibialis posterior artery and vein
- tibial nerve
- flexor hallucis longus muscle

For palpation of these structures, see "Surface Anatomy of the Lower Leg."

LATERAL ORIENTATION POINTS

Initial Position

The starting position is for the patient to sit on the examination table with the clinician sitting on a stool at a lower level.

Lateral Malleolus

The borders of the lateral malleolus should be marked (Figure 15–12). This malleolus is more pointed and extends farther distally than the medial malleolus. In traumatic inversions, the lateral ligaments are damaged, and swelling around and under the lateral malleolus is clearly visible.

Peroneal Trochlea

Approximately 1 cm plantar and 1 cm distal to the tip of the malleolus one can palpate a bony prominence (of variable size) on the calcaneus; this is called the peroneal trochlea. This structure separates the peroneus brevis and the peroneus longus tendons as they diverge to reach their respective insertions (Figure 15–12). This bony point should be marked.

Lateral Part of the Talar Head

Above the peroneal trochlea and anterior to the lateral malleolus, the finger can be placed in a deep space; this is the tarsal sinus. When pressure is exerted with the palpating finger in a medial direction, a bony prominence can be felt. This palpation is only possible when the foot position is alternated between inversion and eversion. During every inversion, the process comes against the palpating finger. This is the lateral part of the head of the talus (Figure 15–12). Once identified, the process should be marked.

Tuberosity of the Fifth Metatarsal

The tuberosity of the fifth metatarsal is found by following the peroneus brevis muscle to its insertion (Figures 15–12 and 15–13). Another method is to follow the lateral side of the foot, sliding the palpating finger distally from the calcaneus. At the level of the cuboid, the finger slides over an obvious bony prominence: the proximal edge of the fifth metatarsal tuberosity. As the finger trav-

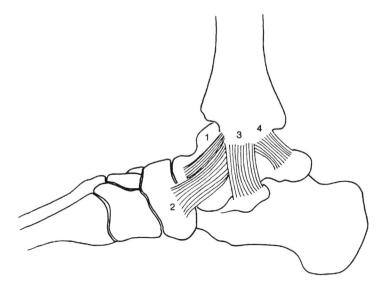

Figure 15–11 Medial ligaments of the right foot, which together make up the deltoid ligament. **1**, Anterior tibiotalar ligament; **2**, tibionavicular ligament; **3**, tibiocalcaneal ligament; **4**, posterior tibiotalar ligament.

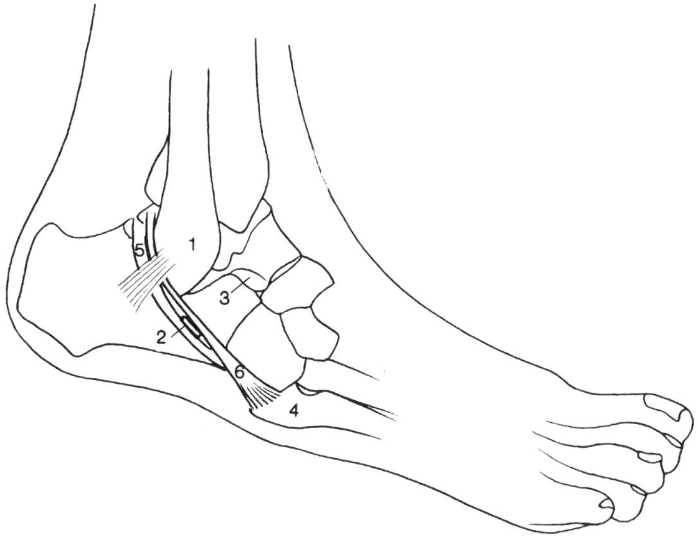

Figure 15–12 Lateral orientation points of the right foot. **1**, Lateral malleolus; **2**, peroneal trochlea; **3**, lateral part of the talar head; **4**, fifth metatarsal tuberosity; **5**, peroneus longus muscle; **6**, peroneus brevis muscle.

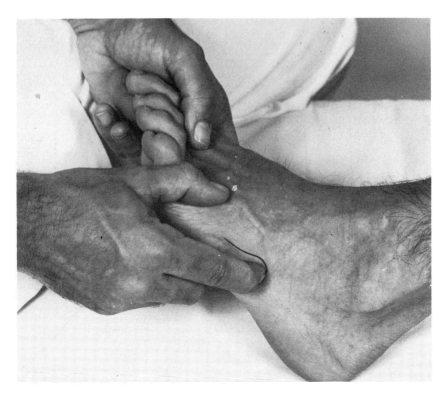

Figure 15–13 Palpation of the fifth metatarsal tuberosity of the left foot.

els more distally, the entire tuberosity can be felt. A third possibility of locating the tuberosity is by placing the palpating finger on the middle of what is obviously the fifth metatarsal and moving it proximally until it comes to a thickening; this is the base of the fifth metatarsal. The knob on top of this thickening is the tuberosity.

SYSTEMATIC PALPATION OF THE LATERAL ASPECT OF THE FOOT

Little Toe

The little toe can be deformed as a result of wearing tight shoes. The clinician should look for abnormal color, nail conditions, and callus formation.

The fifth metatarsophalangeal joint can easily be found with the little toe in flexion. By following the fifth metatarsal proximally, the finger reaches this joint line (Figure 15–14). On the lateral side of this joint is a bursa that can become irritated from pressure. In a chronic inflammation, periostal calcification can occur.

Fifth Metatarsal

Palpation of the fifth metatarsal is generally not difficult. Medioplantar to the fifth metatarsal, the abductor digit minimi muscle can be felt (Figure 15–14). To gain an idea of the position of the lateral arch of the foot, an imaginary line can be drawn describing the inferolateral part of the fifth metatarsal, the cuboid, and the calcaneus.

Tarsal Sinus

By superficial inspection, the tarsal sinus is visible as a concave space lying between the lateral tendon of the extensor digitorum lon-

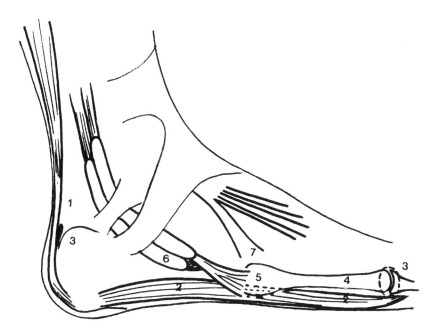

Figure 15–14 Lateral side of the right foot. **1**, Achilles tendon; **2**, abductor digiti minimi muscle; **3**, bursa; **4**, fifth metatarsal bone; **5**, insertion of the peroneus brevis muscle; **6**, peroneus longus muscle; **7**, peroneus tertius muscle.

gus muscle and the anterior aspect of the lateral malleolus. The origin of the short extensor digitorum muscle is at the level of the tarsal sinus.

Cuboid

When outlining the borders of the cuboid bone, first mark the easily palpable plantolateral edge of the cuboid and the calcaneus. The plantolateral edge of the cuboid is felt as a notch just proximal and mainly dorsal to the tuberosity of the fifth metatarsal.

To find the distal border of the cuboid, a slightly distally concave line should be drawn connecting the tuberosity of the fifth metatarsal with the mark indicating the first tarsometatarsal joint line on the medial aspect of the foot (see "Systematic Palpation of the Medial Aspect of the Foot"). By palpating along this line while performing dorsoplantar translatory movements with the fifth and

fourth metatarsals (fix the cuboid), the location of the exact joint space can be determined. In older people, the joint may be difficult to palpate. In those cases, a dotted line should be used for marking to indicate that it is a tentative location (Figure 15–12).

Palpation of the proximal border of the cuboid, the calcaneocuboid joint line, is difficult but important for orientation to the lateral side of the foot. Begin by applying pressure with the palpating finger plantarly against the bone in the area of the tarsal sinus. This is the dorsolateral aspect of the calcaneus. From here, palpate distally along the dorsolateral aspect of the calcaneus. At one point, a sharp edge can be felt. This is the upper edge of the trumpet-formed distal end of the calcaneus. With the foot in the neutral position, a line can be drawn from the tip of this "trumpet" perpendicular to the sole of the foot (Figure 15–15). By positioning the foot in inversion, an obvious bony step is felt when palpation is performed in a distal to proximal direction transversely over the line. This is the end of the "trumpet," or the calcaneocuboid joint line.

A helpful hint in orientation for the examiner locating the calcaneocuboid joint line at the lateral side of the foot is that it is located at approximately mid–muscle belly of the extensor digitorum brevis. (The extensor digitorum brevis has a small, somewhat rounded, and often prominent muscle belly that is usually slightly purple in color. It is often mistaken by both patients and clinicians as a swelling on the side of the foot.)

The clinician should attempt to draw the entire lateral joint line. In those cases where the palpation cannot be done with 100% accuracy, a dotted line should be drawn.

Talus

The lateral parts of the talus are not always easy to palpate (see "Orientation Points at the Dorsum of the Foot," below). The lateral part of the talar head, however, is easily palpable in virtually everyone. Beginning the palpation in the tarsal sinus, the palpating finger exerts pressure medially. Upon contacting bone, the finger has reached the neck of the talus. From here, while alternating passive inversion and eversion of the foot is performed, the finger is now moved in a distal direction. During inversion, an obvious bony prominence can be felt that almost disappears in eversion. This is the lateral part of the talar head.

Calcaneus

The lateral part of the calcaneal tuberosity and the plantolateral edge of the calcaneus are generally easy to palpate. In people in whom a small piece of the talus is palpable under the malleolus, the border with the calcaneus should be felt. On exerting pressure plantarly with the finger in the tarsal sinus, the dorsal aspect of the calcaneus can be felt. This is the upper edge of the trumpet-shaped

distal prominence of the calcaneus. From this site, on palpating farther distally, the calcaneocuboid joint is found (Figure 15–15).

Abductor Digiti Minimi Muscle

The abductor digiti minimi muscle is palpable not only at the level of the fifth metatarsal but also between the lower edge of the calcaneal tuberosity and the tuberosity of the fifth metatarsal (Figure 15–14).

Peroneal Muscles

By asking the patient to resist against plantar flexion, abduction, and pronation, one can follow the peroneal tendons as they travel in one tendon sheath behind the lateral malleolus and then separate at the peroneal trochlea on the lateral aspect of the calcaneus. The peroneus brevis can be followed to its insertion on the tuberosity of the fifth metatarsal, and the longus can be palpated at the peroneal trochlea just before it runs plantarly to its insertion at the first cuneiform and first metatarsal bones.

Lateral Ankle Ligaments

For the most part, the lateral ankle ligaments are difficult to palpate as solitary structures (Figure 15–16). Because several bony orientation points have been located, however, the course of the ligaments can be easily determined. The anterior talofibular ligament can be found deep in the tarsal sinus. To gain a general outline of the ligament, the foot is held in the neutral position. The index finger, positioned parallel to the sole of the foot, can slide over the lateral side of the foot in a plantar to dorsal direction until it contacts the distal tip of the lateral malleolus. A line should be drawn directly above the index finger; this indicates the lower border of the ligament. By palpating approximately 1 cm upward from this border against the most anterior aspect of the lateral malleolus, one can feel where the

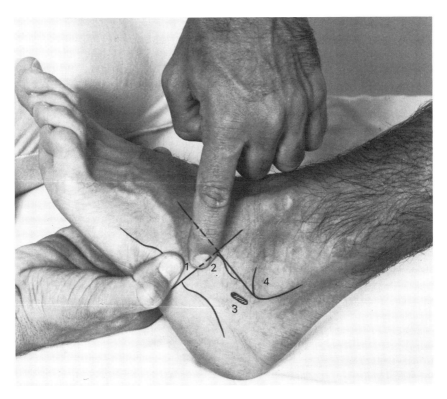

Figure 15–15 Palpation of the calcaneocuboid joint line of the left foot. **1**, Calcaneocuboid joint line; **2**, trumpet form of the distal end of the calcaneus; **3**, peroneal trochlea; **4**, lateral malleolus.

ligament inserts on the fibula. To find the insertion on the talar neck, the fingers should remain in the area of the most anterior aspect of the malleolus while the other hand performs passive inversion of the foot. It can be noticed that a bony edge comes out against the palpating finger. This bony edge is the junction between the lateral facet of the talus (the talar part of the talofibular joint surface) and the proximal part of the talar neck. On palpating slightly more distally just over this edge, a concavity is encountered that is the neck of the talus (with palpation even farther distally, one comes up against another bony prominence: the head of the talus). The anterior talofibular ligament inserts at the beginning of the talar neck directly distal to the bony edge just palpated. It should be noted that the ligament is quite short, only 0.5 to 1.0 cm long.

The calcaneofibular ligament is palpable only at its insertion on the tip of the lateral malleolus. This is because it is covered by the peroneal tendons, which in turn are covered by the lateral retinaculum. The foot should be positioned in plantar flexion to bring the peroneal tendons away from the tip of the malleolus. Palpation then takes place directly in front of the tendons at the tip of the lateral malleolus. Sometimes one can feel the ligament becoming taut at this point by bringing the calcaneus into varus.

The posterior talofibular ligament is usually not palpable; it runs from the lateral malleolus to the lateral tubercle of the posterior talar process. Where possible, it can be reached by placing a finger in the space between the Achilles tendon and the lateral malleolus.

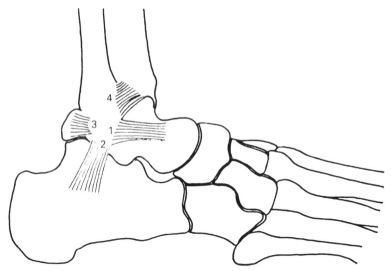

Figure 15–16 Lateral ligaments of the right foot. **1**, Anterior talofibular ligament; **2**, calcaneofibular ligament; **3**, posterior talofibular ligament; **4**, anterior inferior tibiofibular ligament.

Lateral Retinaculum

The tendons of the peroneal muscles are kept in place by a lateral retinaculum behind and under the lateral malleolus (Figure 15–14). The best way to test this retinaculum is to evaluate whether the tendons of the peroneal muscles stay in place during dorsiflexion.

ORIENTATION POINTS AT THE DORSUM OF THE FOOT

Initial Position

The starting position is with the patient sitting on the examination table and the clinician sitting on a stool at a lower level.

Lisfranc's Line

Lisfranc's line* should be drawn between the tuberosity of the fifth metatarsal and the first tarsometatarsal joint (Figure 15–17). A dotted line is recommended.

_____

*Jacques Lisfranc, French surgeon, 1790–1847.

Chopart's Line

Using a dotted line, Chopart's line† should be drawn from the top of the medial part of the talonavicular joint to the top of the calcaneocuboid joint (Figure 15–17).

SYSTEMATIC PALPATION OF THE DORSUM OF THE FOOT

Metatarsals

First, the form and position of the toes should be inspected. Attention should be given to the skin and the nails, and the toes should be palpated. Next, all the metatarsals are palpated; pain caused by pressure can have different causes. A local swelling in the region of the metatarsals may indicate a fracture caused by overloading.

The joints between the metatarsals and the tarsal bones are quite often difficult to pal-

_____

†François Chopart, French surgeon (Paris), 1743–1795.

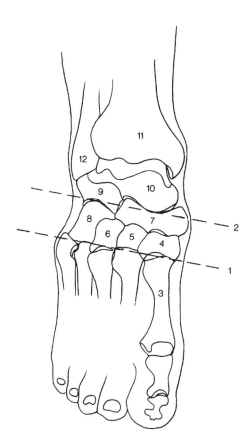

Figure 15–17 Dorsal orientation lines of the right foot. **1**, Lisfranc's line; **2**, Chopart's line; **3**, first metatarsal bone; **4**, medial cuneiform bone; **5**, intermediate cuneiform bone; **6**, lateral cuneiform bone; **7**, navicular bone; **8**, cuboid bone; **9**, calcaneus and tarsal sinus; **10**, talus; **11**, tibia; **12**, fibula.

pate, as are the intermetatarsal joints. The first and the fifth tarsometatarsal joints have already been identified and located; further orientation is done with Lisfranc's line. Quite often there is still some locational ambiguity, even when the forefoot is passively moved in alternating supination and pronation. The clinician should realize that it is always better not to draw any line (except the dotted orientation line) if the identification or location is less than certain.

Cuneiform Bones

The joints between the individual cuneiform bones are difficult to palpate with 100% accuracy because they are too thickly covered with collagen structures. Quite often, it is possible to locate the joint between the cuboid and the lateral cuneiform by palpating during alternating passive inversion and eversion of the forefoot. In general, the cuboid-lateral cuneiform joint lies under the distal two-thirds of a line connecting the most distolateral point of the lateral part of the talar head to the proximal point of the intertarsal joint between the third and fourth metatarsals.

From the previously located navicular–medial cuneiform joint (see "Systematic Palpation of the Medial Aspect of the Foot," above), the distal border of the navicular can be palpated to its lateral end. If the palpation is performed accurately, the border can be indicated with a skin marker.

Navicular

Quite often, the proximal border of the navicular bone can only be partially palpated because of the covering tendons. The technique is to start from the already located joint line of the talonavicular joint (see "Systematic Palpation of the Medial Aspect of the Foot," above) and palpate in the direction of the tarsal sinus. Alternating passive inversion and eversion of the foot helps the examiner differentiate between the distal border of the talar head and the proximal border of the navicular; the talar head moves opposite the motion, and the navicular moves in the same direction as the motion. The lateral border, where the navicular meets the cuboid, is not accessible to palpation because it lies underneath the extensor digitorum brevis muscle. To gain a general idea of where the navicular meets the cuboid, the previously drawn line representing the cuboid lateral cuneiform joint (described in the "Cuneiform Bones" section) should be divided into three equal parts. Then a line is drawn to connect the point between the proximal and middle thirds of this line to the already drawn navicular–medial cuneiform joint line (on the medial aspect of the foot). It should be noted that the navicular is more narrow laterally.

Talus

Palpation of the various parts of the talus has already been described because the talus can be felt from every aspect of the foot. The proximal border of the talus, where the talar trochlea meets the tibia, can best be palpated with the ankle and toes in passive extension; this relaxes the tendons running in this area. It is best to begin the palpation at the anterior edge of the medial malleolus. From there, the distal edge of the tibia can be palpated farther anteriorly to where it meets the fibula.

Directly distal from the anterodistal edge of the tibia, one finds a bony structure that can easily be held from medial and lateral between thumb and index finger. This is the neck of the talus. The neck of the talus can be followed distally while the clinician makes slight passive movements of the foot alternately into inversion and eversion. It will be noticed that on eversion a bony prominence is felt medially and on inversion a bony prominence is felt laterally. This is the head of the talus; on the lateral side it extends slightly more distally than on the medial side.

Cuboid

The palpable borders of the cuboid are already located (refer to "Systematic Palpation of the Lateral Aspect of the Foot," above).

Extensor Digitorum Brevis Muscle

The extensor digitorum brevis muscle originates at the level of the tarsal sinus and runs over the calcaneocuboid joint (Figure 15–18). The origin is covered with the tendons of the extensor digitorum longus muscle, but the muscle belly of the brevis muscle is easily visible and palpable. Actively alternately extending and flexing the toes will make palpation simpler. The muscle belly should not be confused with thickenings of the joint capsule.

Extensor Hallucis Brevis Muscle

The extensor hallucis brevis is the most medial part of the muscle mass that is palpated during the evaluation of the extensor digitorum brevis (Figure 15–18). The tendon is normally palpable on the dorsum of the foot.

Dorsal Retinaculum

The superior extensor retinaculum is located distal on the front side of the lower leg; it is not discussed further (Figure 15–18).

Inferior Extensor Retinaculum

The Y-shaped inferior extensor retinaculum is palpable during active extension of the foot (Figure 15–19). The palpation should start in the tarsal sinus, where the retinaculum can be felt as a wide collagen band. The superior part of the retinaculum is especially easy to palpate between the tendons of the extensor digitorum longus muscle and the tibialis anterior muscle.

Dorsal Pedal Artery

The pulsations of the dorsal pedal artery can be felt when the finger is placed between the first and second metatarsal bones and is moved in a proximal direction until the pulsations are felt. The location of the artery is variable and requires some searching (Figure 15–19). Too much or too little pressure will defeat efforts to feel the pulse.

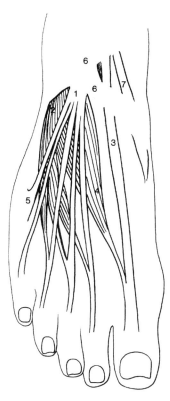

Figure 15–18 Muscles of the dorsum of the right foot. **1**, Extensor digitorum longus muscle; **2**, extensor digitorum brevis muscle; **3**, extensor hallucis longus muscle; **4**, extensor hallucis brevis muscle; **5**, peroneus tertius muscle; **6**, inferior extensor retinaculum; **7**, tibialis anterior muscle.

Superficial Peroneal Nerve

The superficial peroneal nerve exits the peroneal compartment distal in the lower leg and is palpable as a rolling cord anterior to the lateral malleolus. The dorsal intermediate cutaneous branch runs lateral and closer to the malleolus. When two cords are felt, the most medial is the superficial peroneal nerve. Most of the palpable nerve branches on the dorsum of the foot belong to the superficial peroneal nerve.

Deep Peroneal Nerve

The deep peroneal nerve reaches the dorsum of the foot roughly at the level of the first tarsometatarsal joint and lateral to the base of the first metatarsal (Figure 15–20). The nerve is palpable at this spot.

Saphenous Nerve

The saphenous nerve runs parallel with the greater saphenous vein on the medial edge of the foot (Figure 15–21). Care must be exercised during injections of the deltoid ligament so that this nerve is not penetrated.

Greater Saphenous Vein

The greater saphenous vein starts on the back of the foot at the level of the first meta-

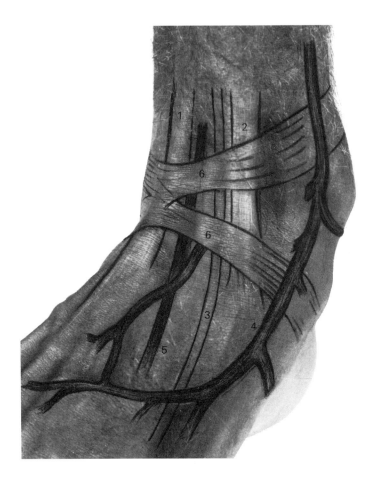

Figure 15–19 Palpation points of the dorsum of the right foot. **1**, Tendon of the extensor digitorum longus muscle; **2**, tendon of the tibialis anterior muscle; **3**, tendon of the extensor hallucis longus muscle; **4**, greater saphenous vein; **5**, dorsal pedal artery; **6**, two diverging parts of the inferior extensor retinaculum to medial.

tarsal and runs proximally (Figures 15–19 and 15–21). Even though the exact location is variable, it will be consistently in the vicinity of the medial malleolus. The best way to see the vein is to bring the foot into extension and pronation.

Figure 15–20 Nerves of the dorsum of the right foot. **1**, Superficial peroneal nerve; **2**, deep peroneal nerve.

PLANTAR ASPECT OF THE ANKLE AND FOOT

Initial Position

The starting position is with the patient prone or standing with the lower leg in a flexed position.

Calcaneal Tuberosity

The plantar part of the calcaneal tuberosity is palpable through the plantar aponeurosis.

Heads of the Metatarsals

The heads of the metatarsals are palpable plantarly from the phalanges of the toes.

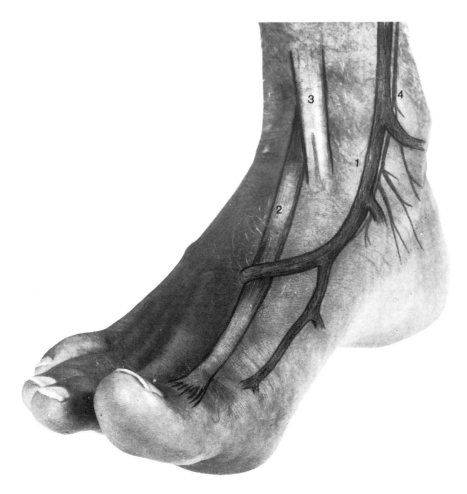

Figure 15–21 Structures on the medial side of the right foot. **1**, Projection of the greater saphenous vein just anterior to the medial malleolus; **2**, tendon of the extensor hallucis longus muscle; **3**, tendon of the tibialis anterior muscle; **4**, saphenous nerve.

Pressure-induced pain at the level of the heads of the metatarsals is seen in a number of disorders with the common name *metatarsalgia* (refer to Chapter 17).

Sesamoid Bones of the Flexor Hallucis Longus Muscle

Quite often, there are two sesamoid bones at the level of the head of the first metatarsal.

These can be felt in the tendon of the flexor hallucis longus muscle. During inflammations, they are sensitive to pressure.

Plantar Aponeurosis

The biggest part of the palpable plantar aspect of the foot is covered by the plantar aponeurosis, a wide, firmly elastic structure. Weakening of this aponeurosis can cause the arch of the foot to flatten.

Chapter 16

Examination of the Ankle and Foot

TALOCRURAL JOINT (ARTICULATIO TALOCRURALIS)

- *Zero position:* The lateral side of the foot makes an angle of 90° with the longitudinal axis of the lower leg. A perpendicular line from the anterior superior iliac spine runs through the middle of the patella to the second toe.
- *Maximal loose-packed position:* About 10° plantar flexion in the talocrural joint and the midposition between inversion and eversion of the foot.
- *Maximal close-packed position:* Maximal extension (or dorsiflexion).
- *Capsular pattern:* Plantar flexion is more limited than extension (dorsiflexion) (Figure 16–1).

SUBTALAR JOINT (ARTICULATIO TALOCALCANEONAVICULARIS)

- *Zero position:* See Talocrural Joint.
- *Maximal loose-packed position:* See Talocrural Joint.
- *Maximal close-packed position:* Maximal inversion.

Extension

Flexion

Figure 16–1 Capsular pattern of the talocrural joint.

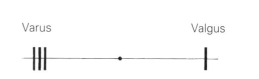

Varus   Valgus

Figure 16–2 Capsular pattern of the subtalar joint.

- *Capsular pattern:* Varus is more limited than valgus (Figure 16–2).

MIDTARSAL JOINTS (ARTICULATIONES CALCANEOCUBOIDEA/ TALONAVICULARIS), INTERTARSAL AND TARSOMETATARSAL JOINTS (ARTICULATIONES INTERTARSEAE/ TARSOMETATARSEAE), AND INTERTARSAL JOINTS (ARTICULATIONES INTERMETATARSEAE)

- *Zero position:* See Talocrural Joint.

- *Maximal loose-packed position:* See Talocrural Joint.

- *Maximal close-packed position:* Maximal inversion.

- *Capsular pattern:* For the midtarsal joints, inversion (flexion-adduction-supination) is more limited than extension (Figure 16–3).

FIRST METATARSOPHALANGEAL JOINT (ARTICULATIO METATARSOPHALANGEA HALLUCIS)

- *Zero position:* The longitudinal axis through the first metatarsal and the proximal phalanx are in line with each other.

- *Maximal loose-packed position:* Approximately 10° extension.

- *Maximal close-packed position:* Maximal extension.

- *Capsular pattern:* Extension is more limited than flexion (Figure 16–4).

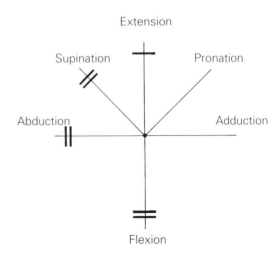

Figure 16–3 Capsular pattern of the midtarsal joints.

SECOND THROUGH FIFTH METATARSOPHALANGEAL JOINTS (ARTICULATIONES METATARSOPHALANGEAE II–V) AND INTERPHALANGEAL JOINTS (ARTICULATIONES INTERPHALANGEAE PROXIMALES/ DISTALES)

- *Zero position:* The longitudinal axis through the metatarsal and the corresponding articulating proximal phalanx are in line with each other.
- *Maximal loose-packed position:* Slight flexion.
- *Maximal close-packed position:* Maximal extension.
- *Capsular pattern:* Extension is either equally limited as or slightly more limited than flexion.

OVERVIEW OF THE FUNCTIONAL EXAMINATION

Most disorders of the lower leg, ankle, and foot cause local pain. Radiation of pain is usually minimal, except when pain is caused by

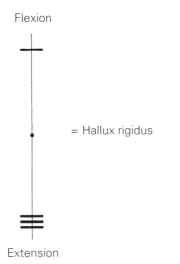

Flexion

= Hallux rigidus

Extension

Figure 16–4 Capsular pattern of the first metatarsophalangeal joint.

compression neuropathies, which can cause pain or paresthesia to radiate not only distally but also proximally. Furthermore, it should be kept in mind that pain from the lumbar spine, sacroiliac joint, and hip can radiate into the leg. Disorders from the hip can radiate pain in the L3 dermatome. Symptoms of problems originating in the lumbar spine and sacroiliac joint can be manifested in the following regions:

- L3 dermatome, to the anterior aspect of the lower leg
- L4 and L5 dermatomes, to the lateral aspect of the lower leg
- S1 and S2 dermatomes, to the posterior aspect of the lower leg

General Inspection

The clinician can begin to gather useful data as soon as the patient enters the examination area. The patient's general posture, facial expression, and any obvious limitation of motion should be noted. Particular attention should be given to the patient's gait and to whether the patient moves with the as-

sistance of a cane or crutches or wears a cast or brace.

History

Age

Age is an important diagnostic factor because some disorders are seen exclusively in certain age groups. For example, heel pain in children and in adults can be immediately differentiated. Heel pain in children is almost always the result of a calcaneal apophysitis or of a posterior calcaneal subcutaneous bursitis. In adults, heel pain is usually the result of an Achilles tendon lesion, a local bursitis, or a compression neuropathy. Achilles tendon lesions in children are almost never seen.

Occupation, Hobby, and Sport

To set a course for effective causal treatment, the clinician requires detailed information about the patient's occupation and hobbies. For example, an athlete can get an overuse problem as the result of inadequate footwear, soccer players often have different lesions than long-distance runners, and so on.

Chief Complaints

Depending on the type of pathology, complaints can consist of one or more of the following:

- *Pain.* Pain usually has a local cause. The possibility of referred pain should always be considered. In such cases, movements of the foot will not affect the patient's pain.
- *Paresthesia.* Paresthesia is usually caused by irritation of a nerve structure. In the foot, the cause can be local. Pathology in the lumbar spine, however, can also result in a feeling of paresthesia in the foot (or feet).
- *Feeling of warmth or coldness in the foot.* An abnormally warm foot can indicate local inflammation but can also

originate from a tumor in the pelvis or lumbar region. An abnormally cold foot usually indicates a vascular problem.

- *Swelling, either local or in the entire lower leg and foot.* Local swelling can be caused by trauma and then usually indicates a hematoma or hemarthrosis. Nontraumatic local swelling can be caused by a ganglion or can be the result of an arthritis. If there is swelling of the entire foot or lower leg (edema), the cause is usually vascular.

- *Locking of the joint.* Locking is often an indication of a loose body. The most usual causes of a loose body in the ankle are trauma or osteochondritis dissecans.

- *Loss of range of motion.* Limitations of motion can have various causes. The type of limitation can be determined by means of the functional examination.

Onset and Duration

If there is a nontraumatic onset, the symptoms usually arise gradually, as is the case in most tendinitides and arthritides. An acute onset is likely to occur in instances of an Achilles tendon rupture.

If the onset is traumatic, there are several key points concerning the trauma that can aid in establishing the diagnosis:

- *Details of the trauma.* The type of trauma provides significant information about the type of lesion. For instance, in an inversion trauma the lateral capsuloligamentous structures are affected, and in an eversion trauma the medial capsuloligamentous structures are affected.

- *The location of the pain immediately after the trauma.* The location of the pain directly after the trauma also helps indicate the site of the lesion.

- *Swelling immediately after the trauma or later.* Immediate swelling after the trauma is almost always caused by bleeding. A gradual occurrence of

swelling is usually the result of synovial effusion.

- *Loss of function immediately after the trauma or later.* An immediate loss of function usually involves a more severe lesion than when the loss of function occurs later.

- *Giving way of the ankle, with or without pain.* Painful giving way of the ankle is usually the result of either a loose body or an instability. A painless giving way of the ankle is most often the result of chronic instability.

Involvement of Other Joints

If the patient has complaints about other joints, systemic diseases such as rheumatoid arthritis, psoriasis, ankylosing spondylitis, or gout should be considered.

Medications

Administering mechanical therapy such as mobilization, manipulation, or transverse friction is contraindicated if the patient is taking anticoagulants. When the patient is on antihypertensive medication, exercise programs should be closely monitored (to ensure that the patient maintains proper breathing). If the patient is on nonsteroidal antiinflammatory medication and is getting relief from the symptoms, one should suspect pathology in which inflammation is involved. If the patient is on antidepressant medication, the symptoms being experienced may be complicated by psychologic factors.

Previous Treatment and Results

The history of previous treatment is important to plan the current treatment program properly. In general, a treatment that has already been applied and was not successful should not be repeated, unless there is doubt concerning whether the treatment was performed correctly.

Previous Surgery

The question of prior surgery can be of importance when the operation was for a malignant pathology. In that instance, the possibility of metastases should be thoroughly assessed.

Specific Inspection

Refer also to Chapter 15.

In Standing

With the patient standing, the examiner notes the position of the feet (eg, whether there is a flat foot or high arch). Varus or valgus positioning of the calcaneus is observed. Attention is given to the position of the midfoot, forefoot, and toes. The Achilles tendons are compared for symmetry. Inspection of the position of the knees, legs, hips, and pelvis is also important.

Each side is compared for color, condition of the skin, and (local) swelling. The presence of atrophy or scars is also noted. Changes in the skin, such as glistening, shining, flaking, callus formation, pigmentation, spots, or abnormal hair growth, are observed. The area on and around the nails should be examined for aberrations. Various systemic disorders, such as psoriasis and Reiter's disease, can be recognized by changes in the nails.

In Supine

With the patient in a supine position, the examiner notes whether the abnormalities seen in standing are still present in lying. Again, the region is inspected for diffuse or local swelling, atrophy, and changes in color.

Inspection of the Shoes

The shoes are inspected for wear and tear, flexibility, profile of the sole, and quality of the heel counter.

Palpation before the Functional Examination

Before starting the functional tests, the examiner palpates the area for warmth. If there is visible swelling, its consistency is assessed; differentiation is made between hard, firm, and soft or fluctuating swelling. If necessary, palpation can be used to assess pulses in the posterior tibial artery (which can be palpated one finger width distal and posterior to the medial malleolus) and the dorsal pedal artery (which can be palpated between the first and second metatarsals; this artery is absent in 10% to 15% of individuals). Pulses on the affected side are always compared with those on the nonaffected side.

Functional Examination

Before the functional examination, the examiner determines whether the patient is experiencing symptoms at that specific moment. Through testing, the examiner notes whether the symptoms change. Again, the affected side is always compared with the nonaffected side. This means that both sides are identically tested, first the nonaffected side (to have an idea of what is normal) and then the affected side.

In the following description of the functional examination, the essential tests are printed in ***bold italics and underlined;*** these represent the ***basic functional examination***. The other tests are performed additionally, depending on the findings from the basic functional examination.

In Standing

16.1 *Unilateral toe raise*
16.2 *Maximal extension of the ankles with flexed knees*

In Supine

Active Motions.

16.3 Active ankle extension with extended knees
16.4 Active ankle extension with slightly flexed knees
16.5 Active plantar flexion of the ankles
16.6 Active inversion of the feet

Passive Motions.

16. 7 Passive extension of the ankle with extended knees

16.8 Passive extension of the ankle with slightly flexed knees

16.9 Passive extension of the ankle, actively reinforced, with slightly flexed knees

16.10 Passive plantar flexion of the ankle

16.11 Passive varus test of the subtalar joint

16.12 Passive valgus test of the subtalar joint

16.13 Passive extension of the midtarsal joints

16.14 Passive flexion of the midtarsal joints

16.15 Passive abduction of the midtarsal joints

16.16 Passive adduction of the midtarsal joints

16.17 Passive pronation of the midtarsal joints

16.18 Passive supination of the midtarsal joints

16.19 Passive inversion of the foot

16.20 Passive adduction and supination of the foot from 10° plantar flexion

16.21 Passive adduction and supination of the foot from maximal extension

16.22 Passive abduction and pronation from maximal plantar flexion

16.23 Passive abduction and pronation of the foot from 10° plantar flexion

16.24 Passive eversion of the foot

16.25 Anterior drawer test

16.26 Anterior drawer test

16.27 Anterior drawer test for the medial structures

16.28 Varus click test

16.29 Passive mediolateral talus test

16.30 Passive plantar-dorsal test of the first metatarsal

16.31 Passive extension of the great toe

16.32 Passive flexion of the great toe

Resisted Tests.

16.33 Resisted inversion of the foot

16.34 Resisted extension-adduction-supination of the foot

16.35 Resisted eversion of the foot

16.36 Resisted flexion-abduction-pronation of the foot

Palpation after the Functional Examination

After the functional examination, the region is palpated again for warmth, swelling, and synovial thickening. Based on the findings from the functional examination, the suspected affected structure is located and palpated for tenderness.

Accessory Examination in Limitations of Motion

If a limitation of motion in a noncapsular pattern has been found, the appropriate joint-specific translatory tests should be performed to determine whether the limitation is indeed caused by the capsule.

If the patient's symptoms could not be elicited during the clinical examination, the next diagnostic phase is provocation of the symptoms. For instance, if a long-distance runner only experiences symptoms after 15 minutes of running, the functional examination will probably be negative. Thus the patient is instructed to run until the symptoms occur, and then the functional examination is repeated. Usually, the patient's pain can now be elicited. If a diagnosis still cannot be determined, further examination is necessary (see below).

Other Examinations

If necessary, other examinations can also be performed either to confirm a diagnosis or to gain further information when a diagnosis cannot be reached based on the functional examination. These include imaging techniques (such as conventional radiographs, computed tomography [CT], CT arthrography, magnetic resonance imaging, and ultra-sonography), laboratory tests, arthroscopy, and electromyography.

DESCRIPTION OF THE FUNCTIONAL EXAMINATION

- *Active motions:* Active motions are assessed to determine the amount of motion and course of movement. Provocation of pain is, of course, also important to note. In instances of limited movement, it should be determined whether the limitation is in a capsular or noncapsular pattern. This, however, can only be assessed based on limitations experienced during the passive movements.

- *Passive motions:* The quality of motion demonstrated during the passive evaluation is compared with active motion. In limitations of motion, distinction is made between capsular and noncapsular patterns. Limitations of motion in a capsular pattern indicate arthritis or arthrosis (osteoarthrosis). It is also important to determine and correctly interpret the end-feel and pain provocation.

- *Resisted tests:* By performance of isometric resisted tests, contractile structures can be evaluated. It is important to note weakness and pain provocation. Lesions of the contractile structures around the ankle and foot usually involve insertion tendopathies. Disorders of the various tendon sheaths are diagnosed by means of the passive tests, whereby these structures are brought into a stretch to test for pain.

In Standing

16.1 Unilateral Toe Raise

The patient stands on the toes of one foot; the examiner helps the patient maintain balance by lightly holding the patient's hands.

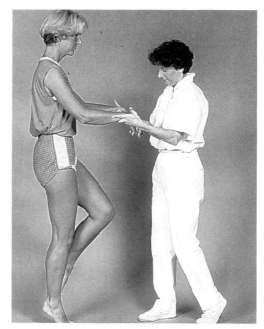

A

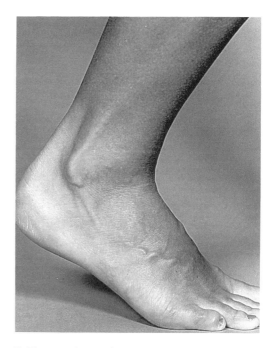

B The tendons of the peroneal muscles are quite visible.

Test 16.1

The patient is instructed to repeat this maneuver 10 times on each side.

This test is particularly performed to assess the plantar flexors of the ankle, but the amount of active plantar flexion in the ankle can also be noted. The most important plantar flexors are the triceps surae muscle, peroneal muscles, and tibialis posterior muscle.

In an Achilles tendon disorder, this test is often initially negative. In this instance, the pain-provoking activity has to be performed first. After provocation; this test is usually positive.

16.2 Maximal Extension of the Ankles with Flexed Knees

From a standing position, the patient slowly bends the knees and tries to keep contact with the heels on the floor as long as possible.

This test assesses the maximal amount of motion in ankle extension. The range of motion in standing is compared with the range of motion in supine (Tests 16.7 to 16.9).

Often, the amount of talocrural extension noted in standing is less than that noted in supine. This can be seen in instances of cartilage damage and anterior instability. In an instability, the ligaments can no longer hold the joint in its normal position during weight bearing. Because the joint surface of the tibia is declined in a posterolateral direction, this load on the talocrural joint, combined with the inefficiency of the ligaments, results in an excessive gliding of the tibia (and fibula) on the talus in a posteroinferior direction. Thus the two joint partners (tibia/fibula and talus), being malaligned, reach their end position much earlier during the extension motion. Without the load on the talocrural joint in the supine position, malalignment of the joint partners is minimal to nonexistent, and the range of motion during extension appears to be normal.

In Supine

16.3 Active Ankle Extension with Extended Knees

The patient lies supine and pulls the feet up as far as possible, keeping the knees straight. Directly afterward, the same test is repeated with slightly flexed knees.

16.4 Active Ankle Extension with Slightly Flexed Knees

The patient lies supine and pulls the feet up as far as possible, keeping the knees straight.

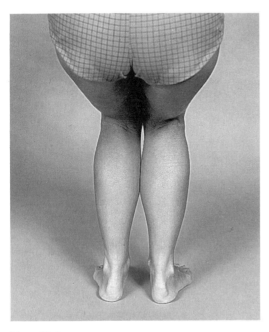

Test 16.2

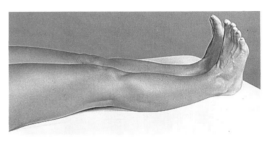

Test 16.3

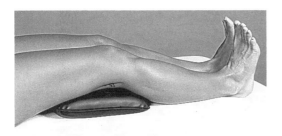

Test 16.4

Test 16.5

Directly afterward, the same test is repeated with slightly flexed knees.

With the knees in flexion, there is a larger range of motion of the talocrural joint in extension than with the knees straight because the Achilles tendon restricts maximal extension. If there is no difference in the amount of motion with extended versus flexed knees, the cause usually can be found in the talocrural joint.

In a capsular pattern of limited motions in the talocrural joint, the flexion is usually more limited than the extension.

16.5 Active Plantar Flexion of the Ankles

The patient is supine and flexes both ankles in the plantar direction as far as possible.

A slight limitation can usually be seen as a small concavity at the level of the talus in-stead of the normally seen convexity. In addition to the talocrural joint, the other tarsal and midtarsal joints are also tested at this time.

16.6 Active Inversion of the Feet

The examiner fixes the thighs of the supine patient just proximal to the knees, so that the legs are not rotated. The heels lie about 30 cm apart. The patient is now asked to bring the great toes toward each other.

This inversion motion tests the mobility of the talocrural, subtalar, midtarsal, and other tarsal joints. In addition, the anterolateral part of the capsuloligamentous complex is tightened.

After an inversion trauma, this test can be painful. In addition, the invertors of the foot (the triceps surae and tibialis posterior) are tested. The other invertors are rarely affected.

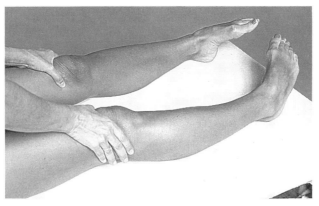

Test 16.6

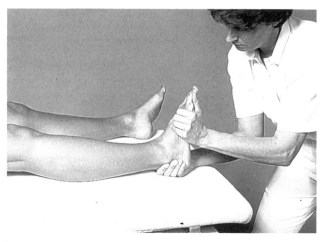

Test 16.7

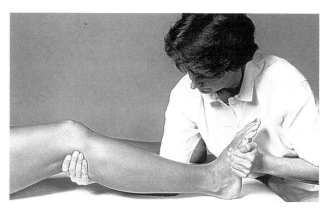

Test 16.8

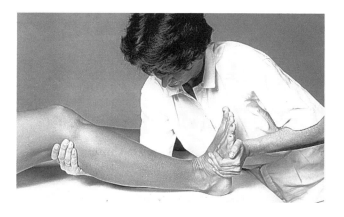

Test 16.9

16.7 Passive Extension of the Ankle with Extended Knees

For the description, see Test 16.9.

16.8 Passive Extension of the Ankle with Slightly Flexed Knees

For the description, see Test 16.9.

16.9 Passive Extension of the Ankle, Actively Reinforced, with Slightly Flexed Knees

The patient is supine on the treatment table. The examiner grasps the patient's heel with the ipsilateral hand. The other hand grasps the plantar aspect of the patient's foot from the lateral side. The patient's knee is extended.

The examiner brings the patient's ankle passively into the most maximal extension possible (Test 16.7). This motion is restricted by the Achilles tendon. Then, the examiner shifts the ipsilateral hand to the popliteal fossa of the patient's knee and, in so doing, slightly flexes the knee without losing the extension in the ankle (Test 16.8). Normally, the examiner will notice that extension in the talocrural joint increases by several degrees. In this position, the end-feel is still difficult to determine. The patient is now asked to actively pull the foot up; the extension range of motion usually increases even further, and the examiner exerts overpressure to test the end-feel (Test 16.9). The end-feel is normally hard.

Limitation in the extension motion can be caused by either a capsular lesion, or an anterior tibiotalar compression syndrome.

16.10 Passive Plantar Flexion of the Ankle

The patient is supine on the examination table. With the ipsilateral hand, the examiner grasps the medial aspect of the patient's heel. The other hand is placed on the dorsum of the midfoot. Both hands bring the patient's foot into maximal plantar flexion; the hand at the midfoot moves in a distal direction, and the ipsilateral hand moves the heel in a proximal direction.

This passive motion is first performed slowly to determine the amount of motion. To determine the end-feel, the examiner brings the foot a few degrees away from end-range plantar flexion and makes an abrupt manipulative movement with the foot into the full end range of plantar flexion. The end-feel is normally hard.

This motion is limited and painful when there is a capsular lesion of the talocrural joint. Plantar flexion is slightly limited and extremely painful in the presence of a posterior tibiotalar compression syndrome.

16.11 Passive Varus Test of the Subtalar Joint

The patient is supine on the examination table. The examiner places the patient's foot against the sternum. The patient's knee is flexed, and the talocrural joint is in maximal extension. With the ipsilateral hand, the examiner grasps the medial aspect of the patient's lower leg. The other hand grasps the lateral aspect of the heel. In instances when the therapist has difficulty controlling the patient's leg, an alternative is to grasp the patient's distal thigh with the ipsilateral hand. Slight axial compression of the knee is established with this hand, so that the knee can be better stabilized.

The contralateral hand now makes a varus motion of the calcaneus (the distal part of the heel is brought angularly in a medial direction). At the end of the motion, the examiner exerts overpressure to determine the end-feel.

This tests the varus mobility of the subtalar joint. Limitations of the varus motion in the subtalar joint are classified as a capsular pattern.

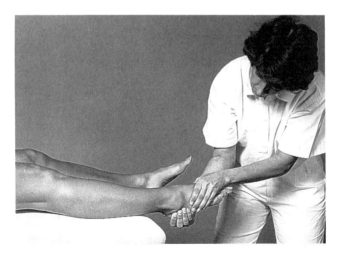

Test 16.10

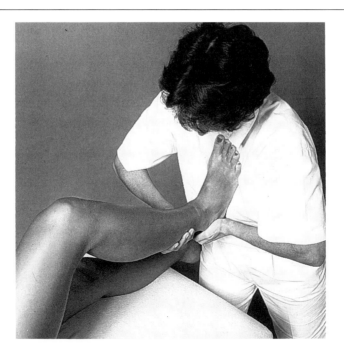

Test 16.11 Initial position.

16.12 Passive Valgus Test of the Subtalar Joint

The patient is supine on the examination table. The calcaneus is moved in a valgus direction in the same way as described for Test 16.11, except that for this test the examiner's ipsilateral hand grasps the medial aspect of the patient's heel, and the other hand grasps the lateral aspect of the lower leg or knee (if the alternative hand position is used).

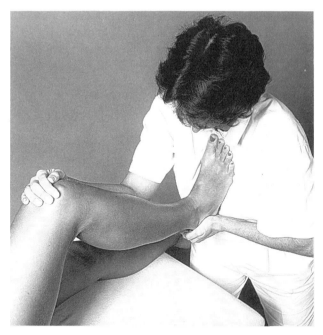

Test 16.11 Alternative hand position.

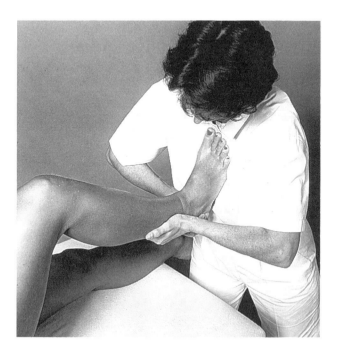

Test 16.12

Because the talocrural joint is in a maximally close-packed position during this test and Test 16.11, varus and valgus motions are hardly possible. The assessment of these tests requires considerable experience. Assessing the end-feel is critical to a diagnosis of limited motion.

16.13 Passive Extension of the Midtarsal Joints

The patient is supine with the knees extended. The examiner grasps the patient's heel with the ipsilateral hand. The other hand grasps the forefoot. By means of traction on the heel, both the talocrural and the subtalar joints are stabilized. The hand grasping the forefoot is the testing hand. The first test (Test 16.13) is extension of the midtarsal joints. The range of motion varies among individuals. The end-feel is normally hard.

The motions being examined at the midtarsal joints are performed with very little force. Although there is accompanying minimal movement of the intertarsal and tarsometatarsal joints, most of the movement takes place in the midtarsal joints. By evaluating the motion with the testing hand placed at the distal part of the forefoot, minimal differences can be easily determined. With the testing hand placed just distal to the midtarsal joints, assessing the range of motion and end-feel is almost impossible.

Without changing hand placement, the examiner can induce plantar flexion of the midtarsal joints (Test 16.14). Here, too, the range of motion varies significantly among individuals. The end-feel is normally hard.

Now, by shifting the testing hand to grasp the forefoot from its plantar aspect (thumb medial and fingers lateral), abduction and adduction of the midtarsal joints can be tested (Tests 16.15 and 16.16). The end-feel is normally hard.

By shifting the testing hand to grasp the midfoot from its dorsal aspect (thumb medial and fingers lateral), the midtarsal joints can be placed in pronation and supination (Tests 16.17 and 16.18). Because there is a significant amount of movement of the intertarsal and tarsometatarsal joints during pronation and supination of the foot, movement here can mask a limitation of motion in the midtarsal joints. Thus, unlike the previous tests for the midtarsal joints, when examining pronation and supination of the midtarsal joints the testing hand must be placed just distal to the corresponding joint lines. The end-feel is normally firm.

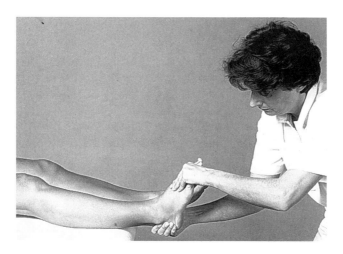

Test 16.13

Lesions of the midtarsal joints are frequently seen. These lesions particularly involve limitations of motion after a period of immobilization, for instance after inversion trauma or cast immobilization after a fracture. Limitations of motion in a capsular pattern are characterized by the greatest degree of limitation in inversion (flexion, adduction, and supination) and a lesser degree of limitation in extension. Abduction and pronation are the least limited motions.

During the supination and adduction motions of the midtarsal joints, the calcaneocuboid ligament is stretched. After inversion trauma, this ligament is often affected, causing these tests to provoke pain.

16.14 Passive Flexion of the Midtarsal Joints

Refer to the description under Test 16.13.

16.15 Passive Abduction of the Midtarsal Joints

Refer to the description under Test 16.13.

16.16 Passive Adduction of the Midtarsal Joints

Refer to the description under Test 16.13.

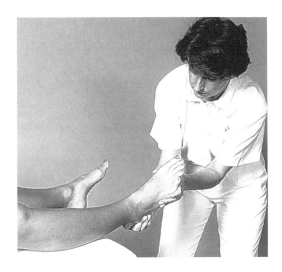

Test 16.15

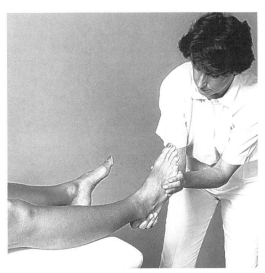

Test 16.16

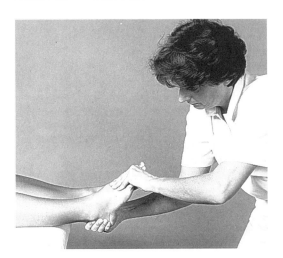

Test 16.14

16.17 Passive Pronation of the Midtarsal Joints

Refer to the description under Test 16.13.

16.18 Passive Supination of the Midtarsal Joints

Refer to the description under Test 16.13.

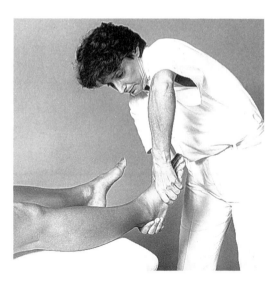

Test 16.17

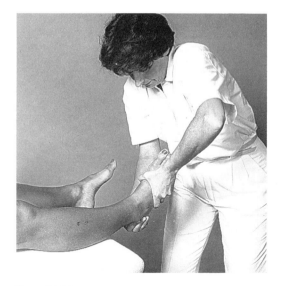

Test 16.18

16.19 Passive Inversion of the Foot

The patient is supine with the knees extended. With the ipsilateral hand, the examiner grasps the patient's heel from the medial

aspect. The other hand, coming from lateral, grasps the dorsum of the patient's foot. Both hands now bring the foot successively into plantar flexion, adduction, and supination. At the same time, the calcaneus is brought into varus.

In this test, the anterior talofibular ligament is stretched. After inversion trauma, this ligament is the most frequently affected, and in this case the test will be painful. Also, the calcaneocuboid ligament and the tendon sheath, in particular, of the extensor digitorum longus muscle are tested.

16.20 Passive Adduction and Supination of the Foot from 10° Plantar Flexion

The patient is supine with the knees extended. With the ipsilateral hand, the examiner grasps the patient's heel from the medial aspect. The other hand, coming from lateral, grasps the dorsum of the patient's foot. From a position of 10° plantar flexion, both hands now bring the foot into adduction and supination. At the same time, the calcaneus is brought into varus.

The structure best assessed by this test is the calcaneocuboid ligament.

16.21 Passive Adduction and Supination of the Foot from Maximal Extension

The patient is supine with the knees extended. With the ipsilateral hand, the examiner grasps the patient's heel from the medial aspect. The other hand, coming from lateral, grasps the dorsum of the patient's foot. From a position of maximal extension, both hands now bring the foot into adduction and supination. At the same time, the calcaneus is brought into varus.

The primary effect of this test is to stretch the posterior talofibular ligament and particularly to stretch the tendon sheath of the peroneal muscles.

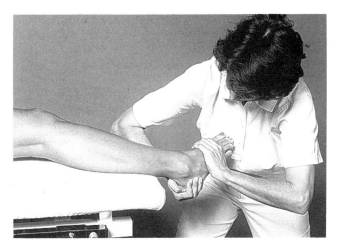

Test 16.19

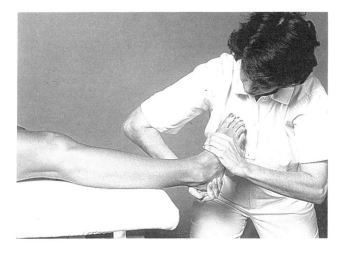

Test 16.20

16.22 Passive Abduction and Pronation from Maximal Plantar Flexion

The patient is supine with the knees extended. With the ipsilateral hand, the examiner grasps the patient's heel from the lateral aspect. The other hand, coming from medial, grasps the dorsum of the patient's foot. Both hands now bring the foot successively into plantar flexion, abduction, and pronation. At the same time, the calcaneus is brought into valgus.

In this way, the anterior part of the medial capsuloligamentous complex (the deltoid ligament) is tested. The ligaments primarily

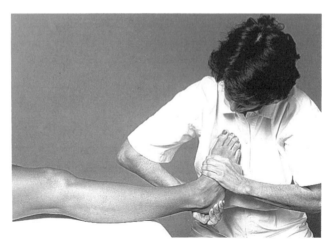

Test 16.21

affected are the anterior tibiotalar ligament and the tibionavicular ligament. The tibialis anterior muscle is also stretched.

16.23 Passive Abduction and Pronation of the Foot from 10° Plantar Flexion

The patient is supine with the knees extended. With the ipsilateral hand, the examiner grasps the patient's heel from the lateral aspect. The other hand, coming from medial, grasps the dorsum of the patient's foot. From a position of 10° plantar flexion, both hands now bring the foot into abduction and pronation. At the same time, the calcaneus is brought into valgus.

In this way, the tibiocalcaneal ligament (the middle part of the deltoid ligament) is tested.

16.24 Passive Eversion of the Foot

The patient is supine with the knees extended. With the ipsilateral hand, the examiner grasps the patient's heel from the lateral aspect. The other hand, coming from medial, grasps the dorsum of the patient's foot. From a position of maximal extension, both hands

now bring the foot into abduction and pronation. At the same time, the calcaneus is brought into valgus.

In this way, the posterior tibiotalar ligament (the posterior part of the deltoid ligament) is tested. The tibialis posterior muscle is also stretched.

16.25 Anterior Drawer Test

The patient is supine with the tested knee flexed to about 60°. With the ipsilateral hand, the examiner grasps the patient's lower leg just proximal to the malleoli in such a way that the fingers are on the lateral aspect. The other hand grasps the foot at the level of the talus in such a way that the thumb is at the medial side, the index and middle fingers are just distal to the lateral malleolus, and the ring and little fingers grasp the lateral edge of the foot.

The ankle is positioned in about 10° plantar flexion. The proximal hand is the testing hand; the distal hand fixes the talus and calcaneus against the examination table. The proximal hand moves the tibia dorsally, in line with the examiner's forearm, which makes a 90° angle to the patient's lower leg (Test 16.25). Although the tibia is moved dorsally

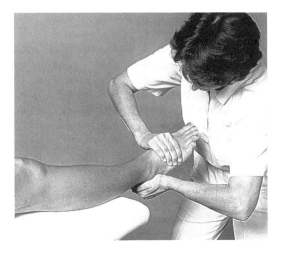

Test 16.22

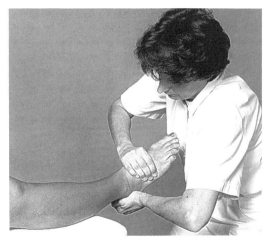

Test 16.23

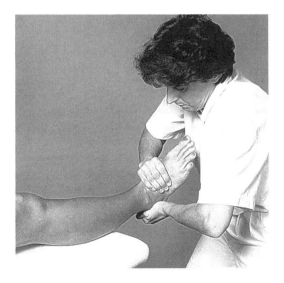

Test 16.24

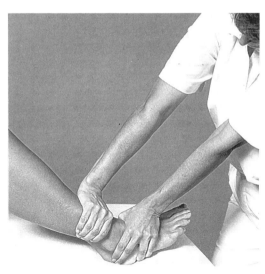

Test 16.25 Anterior drawer test in approximately 10° plantar flexion

here, the drawer test is in an anterior direction. The "drawer" is always termed according to the direction of the translatory movement of the distal bone.

In this test, the anterior ligaments, specifically the anterior talofibular, anterior

tibiotalar, and tibionavicular ligaments, are tested.

In the same manner but in more extension (Test 16.26A) and then in more plantar flexion (Test 16.26B), the anterior drawer test is repeated. In more ankle extension, the anterior drawer test will demonstrate increased motion because the ligaments are less taut. In contrast, in more plantar flexion the anterior drawer test will demonstrate decreased motion because the ligaments are more taut. If the drawer test still demonstrates increased mobility in this latter position, there is likely to be a total rupture of the ligaments being assessed.

There are two ways in which the capsuloligamentous lesions at the medial and lateral side of the ankle can be differentiated from each other. The lateral side can be more specifically tested, while pushing the lower leg dorsally, by adding a simultaneous passive external rotation of the tibia to the dorsal movement. This brings the anterior talofibular ligament under even more tension while the anterior tibiotalar and tibionavicular ligaments relax slightly. In a rupture of this ligament, the translation noted during the drawer test will increase even more.

Another way to make the differentiation is to change the position of both hands, so that the fingers are now placed at the medial side of the patient's lower leg and foot. By performing the drawer test and simultaneously passively internally rotating the lower leg, the medial structures are more specifically tested (test 16.27).

16.26 Anterior Drawer Test

For the description of the anterior drawer test in more extension and more plantar flexion of the ankle, see Test 16.25.

16.27 Anterior Drawer Test for the Medial Structures

For the description, see Test 16.25.

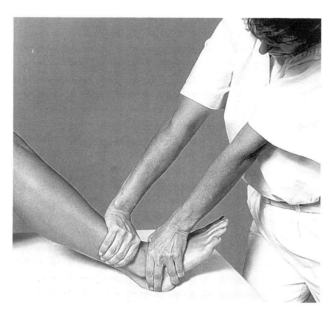

Test 16.26A Anterior drawer test in more extension of the ankle.

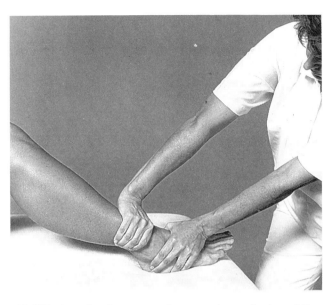

Test 16.26B Anterior drawer test in more plantar flexion of the ankle.

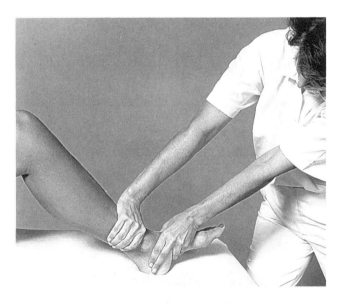

Test 16.27 Anterior drawer test for the medial structures.

16.28 Varus Click Test

The patient is supine on the examination table. With the ipsilateral hand, the examiner grasps the medial aspect of the patient's lower leg just proximal to the malleolus. The other hand grasps the lateral aspect of the patient's heel. The foot is positioned in its

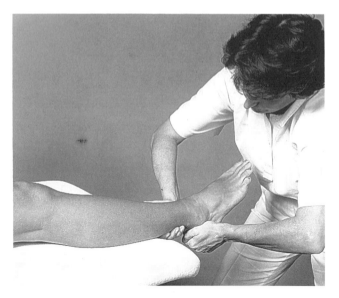

Test 16.28A Initial position.

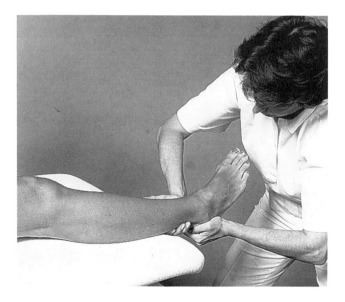

Test 16.28B End position in maximal varus position.

resting position (maximal loose-packed position), and the knee is extended. In a manipulative way, the examiner moves the calcaneus in a varus direction and back again. The examiner brings about this movement by quickly adducting and then again abducting the arm. If the examiner feels a click in the patient's joint (usually during the return movement), the maneuver is repeated, but now with the ankle positioned in extension.

The test is positive when a click can still be elicited with the ankle positioned in extension. This indicates a rupture of the calcaneofibular ligament. Because hypermobility is often noted during this test, comparison with the nonaffected side is (as always) important. Occasionally, this test is positive as the result of a rupture of the anterior inferior tibiofibular ligament of the syndesmosis. Differentiation can be made by performing Test 16.29.

16.29 Passive Mediolateral Talus Test

The patient is supine on the examination table. The examiner sits on the examination table, at the foot. The patient's knee is flexed, the lower leg rests on the examiner's lap, and the foot is positioned in its resting position (maximal loose-packed position). Without exerting force, the examiner grasps the patient's lower leg with the ipsilateral hand, just proximal to the malleoli, in such a way that the fingers are lateral and the thumb is medial. The other hand grasps the dorsal aspect of the talus.

With the distal hand, the talus is now gently moved within the "fork" of the ankle in alternating translatory medial and lateral directions. When moving the talus laterally, the fingers of the proximal hand keep the fibula from moving laterally. When moving medially, the thumb keeps the tibia from moving medially. If the examiner feels a click in the patient's joint, the maneuver is repeated, but now with the ankle positioned in extension.

The test is positive when a click can still be elicited with the ankle positioned in extension. This is the result of a partial or total rupture of the anterior inferior tibiofibular ligament and indicates an instability of the syndesmosis.

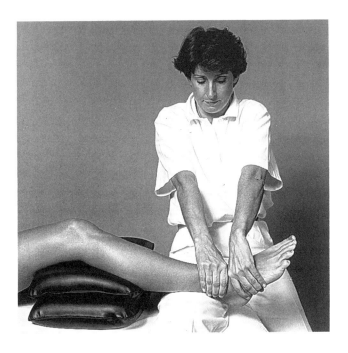

Test 16.29

16.30 Passive Plantar-Dorsal Test of the First Metatarsal

The patient is supine on the examination table. With the fingers of the ipsilateral hand, the examiner grasps the first metatarsal from the medial side. The fingers of the other hand grasp the second metatarsal from the lateral side. The first metatarsal is now moved in a plantar and dorsal direction in relation to the fixed second metatarsal.

The range of motion should not be greater than 1 cm. A larger amount of motion indicates hypermobility as the result of hyperpronation during walking or running.

16.31 Passive Extension of the Great Toe

The patient is supine on the examination table. With the fingers of the ipsilateral hand, the examiner grasps the first metatarsal from the medial side. The thumb of the other hand is placed against the plantar aspect of the

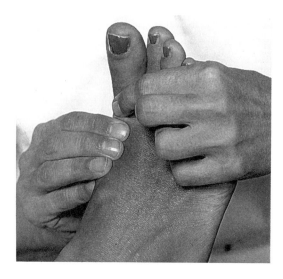

Test 16.31

proximal phalanx of the great toe, and the index finger is placed at the dorsum of this toe. The great toe is passively extended maximally.

The motion can be limited or painful as the result of a capsular lesion, usually hallux rigidus. Occasionally, there is an arthritis of this joint as the result of gout or other causes. The capsular pattern of limited motions in the first metatarsophalangeal joint results in a greater limitation of extension than flexion.

16.32 Passive Flexion of the Great Toe

The patient is supine on the examination table. With the fingers of the ipsilateral hand, the examiner grasps the first metatarsal from the medial side. The other hand grasps the proximal phalanx, also from the medial side, in such a way that the fingers are dorsal and the thumb is plantar. The great toe is passively maximally flexed.

The motion can be limited or painful as the result of a capsular lesion, usually hallux rigidus. Occasionally, there is an arthritis of this joint as the result of gout or other causes. The capsular pattern of limited motions in the

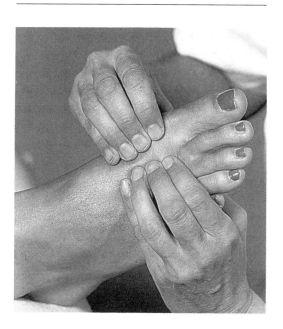

Test 16.30

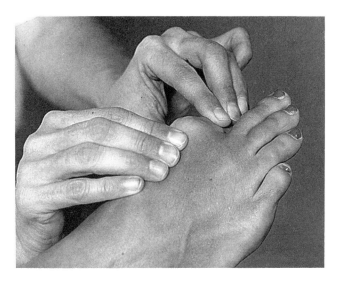

Test 16.32

first metatarsophalangeal joint results in a greater limitation of extension than flexion.

16.33 Resisted Inversion of the Foot

The patient is supine on the examination table. With the ipsilateral hand, the examiner grasps the medioplantar aspect of the patient's forefoot. The other hand grasps the patient's heel at the lateral side; the arm is positioned parallel and in line with the ipsilateral forearm. In this position, both forearms form a diagonal that makes an angle of about 45° to the lower leg, running from proximolateral to distomedial.

The patient is now instructed to move the foot in the direction of the examiner's ipsilateral elbow. At the same time, the examiner exerts isometric resistance.

In this way, the foot invertors are tested. If this test is painful, there is usually a lesion of the tibialis posterior. If only the tendon sheath is affected, this test will probably be negative, but passive eversion will be positive as a result of the stretch on the sheath (see Test 16.24).

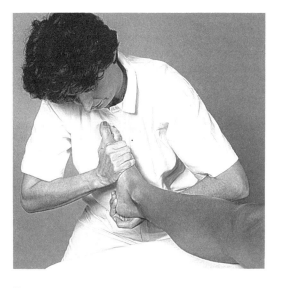

Test 16.33

16.34 Resisted Extension-Adduction-Supination of the Foot

The patient is supine on the examination table. With the ipsilateral hand, the examiner

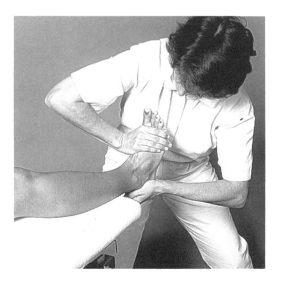

Test 16.34

grasps the medioplantar aspect of the patient's forefoot. The other hand grasps the patient's heel at the lateral side with the arm positioned parallel and in line with the ipsilateral forearm. In this position, both forearms form a diagonal that makes an angle of about 45° to the lower leg, running from proximomedial to distolateral.

The patient is now instructed to move the foot in the direction of the examiner's ipsilateral elbow. At the same time, the examiner exerts isometric resistance.

In this way, the muscles that simultaneously extend, adduct, and supinate the foot are tested. If this test is painful, there is usually a lesion of the tibialis anterior muscle. If only the tendon sheath is affected, this test will probably be negative, but passive plantar flexion, abduction, and pronation will be positive as a result of the stretch on the sheath (see Test 16.22).

By exerting resistance more distally against the great toe, the examiner can test the extensor hallucis longus more specifically. If the tendon sheath of this muscle is affected, this test will probably be negative. In the case of a tenosynovitis, performing Test

16.22 with simultaneous passive flexion of the great toe will provoke the most pain.

16.35 Resisted Eversion of the Foot

The patient is supine on the examination table. With the ipsilateral hand, the examiner grasps the medial aspect of the patient's heel. The other hand grasps the dorsum of the patient's forefoot at the lateral side; the arm is positioned parallel and in line with the ipsilateral forearm. In this position, both forearms form a diagonal running from proximolateral to distomedial, making an angle of about 45° to the lower leg.

The patient is now instructed to move the foot in the direction of the examiner's contralateral elbow. At the same time, the examiner exerts isometric resistance.

In this way, the foot evertors are tested. The foot evertors are seldom affected, but if this test is painful there is likely to be a lesion of the extensor digitorum longus. If only the tendon sheath is affected, this test will probably be negative, but passive inversion will be painful as a result of the stretch on the sheath (see Test 16.19). The extensor digitorum longus

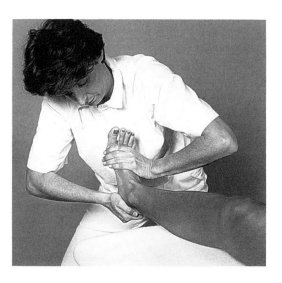

Test 16.35

can be even more specifically tested by shifting the hand and exerting resistance farther distally over the dorsum of the toes. In addition, the tendon sheath of the extensor digitorum can be brought under an even greater stretch by performing Test 16.19 with simultaneous flexion of the second to fifth toes.

16.36 Resisted Flexion-Abduction-Pronation of the Foot

The patient is supine on the examination table. With the ipsilateral hand, the examiner grasps the medial aspect of the patient's heel. The other hand grasps the dorsum of the patient's forefoot at the lateral side; the arm is positioned parallel and in line with the ipsilateral forearm. In this position, both forearms form a diagonal running from proximomedial to distolateral, making an angle of about 45° to the lower leg.

The patient is now instructed to move the foot in the direction of the examiner's contralateral elbow. At the same time, the examiner exerts isometric resistance.

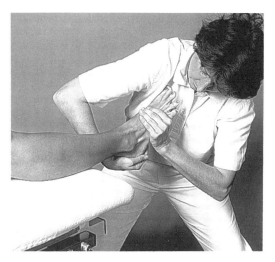

Test 16.36

In this way, the peroneal muscles in particular are tested. If only the tendon sheath is affected, this test will probably be negative, but the passive stretch of maximal extension, adduction, and supination will be painful (see Test 16.21).

Chapter 17

Pathology of the Ankle and Foot

17.1 TALOCRURAL JOINT PATHOLOGY

PATHOLOGY WITH LIMITED MOTIONS IN A CAPSULAR PATTERN

ARTHRITIS

Traumatic Arthritis

An inversion trauma of the foot is the most frequent cause of traumatic arthritis of the talocrural joint. Along with a primary lesion of the capsuloligamentous complex, there is a synovial reaction in the talocrural joint as a result of the trauma. This leads to pain, swelling, and limited motions. A solitary traumatic arthritis, without accompanying injury to bony or capsuloligamentous structures, is rarely seen.

Traumatic arthritis of the talocrural or subtalar joints should be strongly suspected in most cases if, months after the inversion trauma, the patient still experiences symptoms of pain and swelling after activities. After surgery on the talocrural joint (arthrotomy or arthroscopy), symptoms can also be experienced for a long time. This is especially true after activities and is the result of chronic irritation of the joint capsule.

Another form of traumatic arthritis is the activated arthrosis, an affliction of patients with arthrosis of the talocrural joint, who experience symptoms during and after activi-

ties. In most of these cases, there is also swelling of the ankle.

Clinical Findings

Usually, the most significant symptom is pain, characteristically occurring during weight-bearing activities. In some cases, however, swelling is the main complaint.

Functional Examination

There is a capsular pattern of painfully limited motions in which plantar flexion is usually slightly more limited than extension. In an activated arthrosis, the end-feel in both flexion and extension is hard.

Because a traumatic arthritis usually occurs in combination with another lesion, the entire functional examination should be performed. Various other tests can also be positive, depending on the accompanying lesions.

Treatment

Treatment is primarily directed toward maintaining or improving the mobility. By means of joint-specific mobilization techniques, a limitation of motion can be alleviated or prevented. Of course, other problems occurring with the traumatic arthritis should also be appropriately treated.

A traumatic arthritis after surgery of the talocrural joint should be treated with relatively prolonged rest. In other words, the patient can perform normal weight-bearing activities but should not participate in sports. Immobilization with a cast is always contraindicated.

Nontraumatic Arthritis

Because the talocrural joint is a synovial joint, in principle every collagenous disease or other systemic disease in which arthritides occur can also cause an arthritis in the talocrural joint. Even so, nontraumatic arthritides of the talocrural joint are rarely encountered. For instance, rheumatoid arthritis of the talocrural joint is rare, even though the other foot joints are quite frequently affected in rheumatoid arthritis. In rheumatoid arthritis, the foot is more often affected than the hand.

Clinical Findings

The patient complains of pain, swelling, and limitations of motion. Increased temperature of the skin around the talocrural joint, along with diffuse swelling, is usually found during palpation.

Functional Examination

A capsular pattern of painfully limited motions is found in the functional examination; plantar flexion is slightly more limited than extension. The end-feel of these passive motions is somewhat harder than normal.

Treatment

Treatment depends on the cause of the arthritis. When specific medication does not provide satisfactory results, in noninfectious arthritides good results can be expected from an intraarticular corticosteroid injection.

ARTHROSIS (OSTEOARTHRITIS)

Arthrosis of the talocrural joint is almost always a secondary condition. In other words, it is the result of a previously experienced disorder (eg, arthritis) or trauma (eg, a fracture of the talus, tibia, or fibula). Loose bodies and an activated arthrosis (traumatic arthritis) are the most frequent subsequent conditions resulting from an arthrosis in the talocrural joint.

Clinical Findings

Initially, the patient complains only of stiffness, followed by pain. Usually, there is crepitation in the joint during movement; in some cases, a slight to moderate effusion is present.

Functional Examination

There is a capsular pattern of limited motions and a harder end-feel in both flexion and extension.

Treatment

As a first step, an attempt should be made to improve joint mobility through joint-specific mobilization. The patient should maintain any newly gained mobility with a home exercise program.

In the early stage of arthrosis of the talocrural joint, a bilateral heel lift can offer immediate pain relief because the end-range extension is not reached. If the mobilization brings about an improvement in the extension function, the heel lifts should be removed. A shock-absorbing inlay of viscoelastic material is recommended and can provide further pain relief. These can be worn in conjunction with the heel lifts and should cover the entire bottom of the inside of the shoe. In the second stage of arthrosis, it is often necessary to prescribe medication to treat the symptoms. In cases of severe pain and limitations of motion, arthrodesic or endoprosthetic surgery may be indicated.

PATHOLOGY WITH LIMITED MOTIONS IN A NONCAPSULAR PATTERN

LOOSE BODY

Loose bodies can occur as the result of trauma, osteochondritis dissecans of the talus, or arthrosis; in some cases, the condition is idiopathic. Because arthroscopic evaluation and treatment of the talocrural joint have become more common, loose bodies have been found to be much more prevalent than previously thought.

Clinical Findings

The complaint pattern is classic. The patient complains of suddenly occurring, sharp pain during weight-bearing activity. Usually the patient is momentarily unable to place any weight on that leg, resulting in the inability to take the next step. Because this sharp, shooting, momentarily paralyzing pain occurs at the most unexpected moments, the patient can become anxious. Descending stairs and crossing busy streets can become frightening experiences.

During palpation, sometimes a slight effusion can be felt. Occasionally there is a slight increase in temperature of the skin around the joint.

Functional Examination

A painful limitation of flexion or extension is usually found. In many instances, however, the functional examination is completely negative. If the loose body is a complication of an arthrosis, both flexion and extension can be limited. The typically hard end-feel expected in an arthrosis, however, is more springy in one of the two motions.

Treatment

The treatment depends on the cause. Osteochondritis dissecans of the talus should be treated surgically. A loose body with a traumatic etiology in many cases can be treated manipulatively. If, for instance, the loose body is the result of a broken-off osteophyte or fragment of cartilage in an arthrotic joint, manipulation should be tried before arthroscopy is considered.

By means of quick movements under traction, the loose body can be shifted to a position where it does not lie directly between the two joint surfaces. Usually, when a loose body lies in such a favorable position, it ultimately becomes encapsulated.

If the symptoms continue to recur after repeated manipulations, arthroscopic treatment is indicated.

OSTEOCHONDRITIS DISSECANS OF THE TALUS

Osteochondritis dissecans is an aseptic bone necrosis that usually occurs in the medial aspect of the talar trochlea (Figure 17–1). The disorder is seen particularly in adolescents and occurs equally in boys and girls. Because of the location of the necrosis, some authors propose that an inversion trauma may be responsible for this disorder. There is often no clear traumatic event in the patient history, however. Because osteochondritis dissecans is often seen on both sides, the nonsymptomatic foot should always be evaluated radiologically as well.

Clinical Findings

In some cases, the disorder has a symptomless course and is a coincidental finding on a radiograph taken for some other reason. The patient complains of local pain that is initially intermittent and later gradually progresses to the point that it is almost constant. The symptoms occur particularly during and after vigorous weight-bearing activities. Some pa-

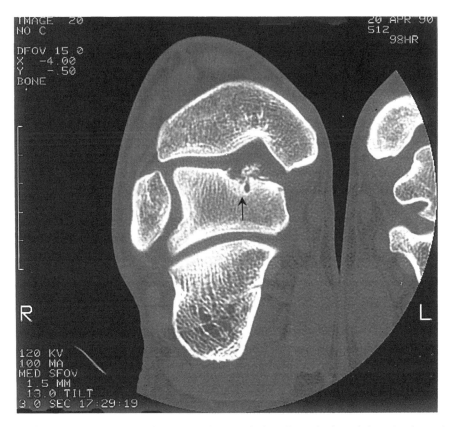

Figure 17–1 Computed tomogram demonstrating an obvious bone lesion of the talus (arrow), characteristic of osteochondritis dissecans.

tients are no longer able to walk normally. In some cases, swelling of the joint occurs, which can spontaneously disappear and regularly recur.

Functional Examination

In the functional examination, sometimes there is a limitation of motion. This will be the case when the necrotic area loosens from its site and becomes a dissecate in the joint. When this happens, there is usually a noncapsular limitation of motion in extension. In the early stages of this disorder (before the necrotic tissue loosens), a mild capsular pattern of limited motions can be found; it is usually accompanied by mild joint effusion and will be seen especially after the patient partici-

pates in vigorous activities. This is one of the first signs that there is pathology in the joint.

On palpation, there is tenderness at the anterior aspect of the joint. Sometimes there is a painful point at the medial side of the talus when the foot is positioned in plantar flexion. The diagnosis is confirmed radiographically.

Treatment

The younger the patient, the greater the chance of a good recovery with conservative treatment, without the danger of early arthrotic changes in the joint. When conservative treatment is unsuccessful (as determined radiographically), surgery is indicated. As long as the epiphyseal plates have not yet closed, however, surgery is contraindicated.

OSTEOCHONDRAL FRACTURE OF THE TALUS

Osteochondral fractures of the talus are located medially more often than laterally. Medial fractures are often larger and more severe than lateral ones. Usually, the talar trochlea or talar neck is involved (Figures 17–2 and 17–3). The cause of an osteochondral fracture is often traumatic, usually a severe inversion trauma. The fractured fragment can dislocate and cause severe symptoms of impingement (refer to "Loose Body," above). Osteonecrosis is a dangerous complication of such fractures; the result is almost always deformation of the joint with severe arthrotic changes.

Clinical Findings

Pain and severe limitation of motion, particularly extension, are the primary complaints. In the acute stage, weight bearing is absolutely impossible. Radiologic examination via conventional radiography, conventional tomography, or computed tomography confirms the diagnosis.

Treatment

In most instances, surgery is indicated.

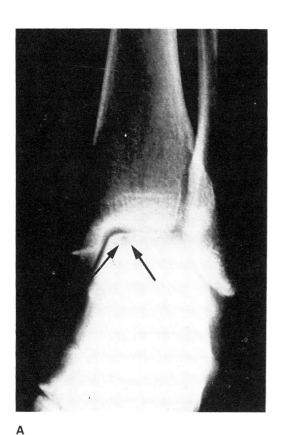
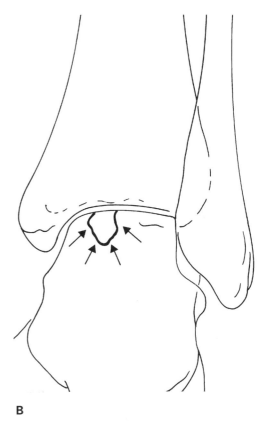

A   B

Figure 17–2 Osteochondral fracture of the talus. (**A**) Conventional radiograph demonstrating an osteochondral lesion at the medial side of the talus (arrows). (**B**) Schematic diagram.

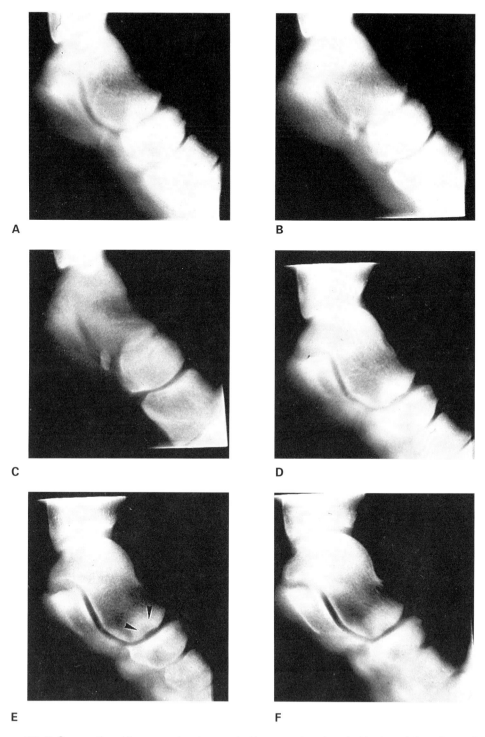

A

B

C

D

E

F

Figure 17–3 Conventional tomography demonstrating an osteochondral lesion of the talus at the level of the talonavicular joint (arrowheads in **E**) in an active high jumper.

ANTERIOR TIBIOTALAR COMPRESSION SYNDROME

Anterior tibiotalar compression syndrome is seen particularly in soccer players and ballet dancers. This is usually the result of an eversion trauma of the talocrural joint or of repeated forced extension of the talocrural joint, causing the compression to occur between the anterior lower edge of the tibia and the anterior side of the talar neck. Initially, there is pain as a result of capsular impingement and pinching at the site of the fat pad lying in that area. In cases of chronic forced extension, local exostoses can develop on the tibia and talar neck (Figure 17–4). In some cases, tibiotalar contact occurs between the anterior edge of the medial malleolus and the medial side of the talus. Exostoses can form here as well. This disorder is seen in all age groups and tends to occur in feet with high arches and limited subtalar mobility.

Clinical Findings

Initially, the patient complains of diffuse, later sharp, pain localized to the anterior side of the ankle. Ballet dancers complain in particular of pain during movements when the knees are bent or slightly bent with the back held straight (plié) and when landing after a jump.

The patient complains of limited extension of the talocrural joint and in many cases is performing stretching exercises to improve the range of motion. This results in an increase in the symptoms. Because of the stretching exercises, the pain can spread to the posterior side of the joint as a result of too much stretch on the posterior capsule. Thus the patient tends to exercise even more intensively, thinking that stretching is also needed for the Achilles tendon. When these exercises are performed with a flexed knee (taking the tension off the gastrocnemius and thereby allowing for increased extension in

the talocrural joint), the symptoms are provoked even more.

Functional Examination

The most positive finding is painful and limited talocrural joint extension. The pain is typically localized at the anterior aspect of the joint, but sometimes it is also at the medial or posterior aspect. Passive flexion is mildly painful, but there is minimal or no limitation of movement. There is local tenderness. Sometimes large exostoses are palpable at the anteroinferior edge of the tibia and at the neck of the talus. Plain films confirm the diagnosis. Bony contact between the tibia and the talus is visible when the talocrural joint is positioned in maximal extension.

Treatment

The treatment of a one-time extension trauma is much simpler than the treatment of problems caused by chronic forced extension. In the first instance, bilateral heel lifts are worn temporarily to prevent maximal extension. The painful soft tissue can be injected with a mixture of local anesthetic and corticosteroid. In the second instance, heel lifts, extension-restricting taping, and an injection can be beneficial when exostoses are not yet visible on plain films. If there are visible exostoses, however, surgery is indicated.

POSTERIOR TIBIOTALAR COMPRESSION SYNDROME

Posterior tibiotalar compression syndrome is a problem for people with an abnormally large lateral tubercle of the posterior process of the talus or for people who have an os trigonum (Figure 17–5). In some cases, the cause is an osteophyte on the upper aspect of the calcaneus. Compression can occur between the posteroinferior edge of the tibia and the lateral tubercle of the talus (or an os trigonum) as the result of flexion trauma or of chronic forced flexion of the talocrural joint

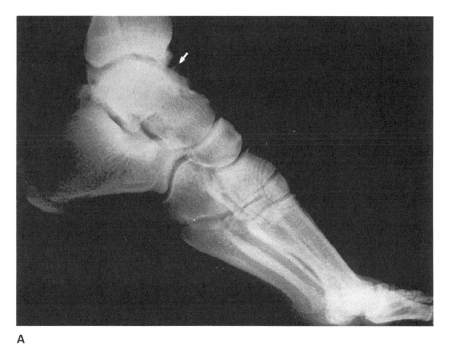

A

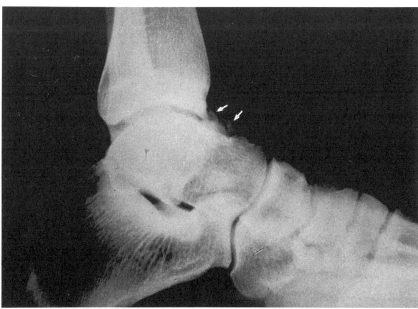

B

Figure 17–4 Lateral conventional radiographs in plantar flexion (**A**) and dorsal extension (**B**) revealing osteophytes at the level of the talar neck and anteroinferior edge of the tibia (arrows), characteristic of anterior tibiotalar compression syndrome.

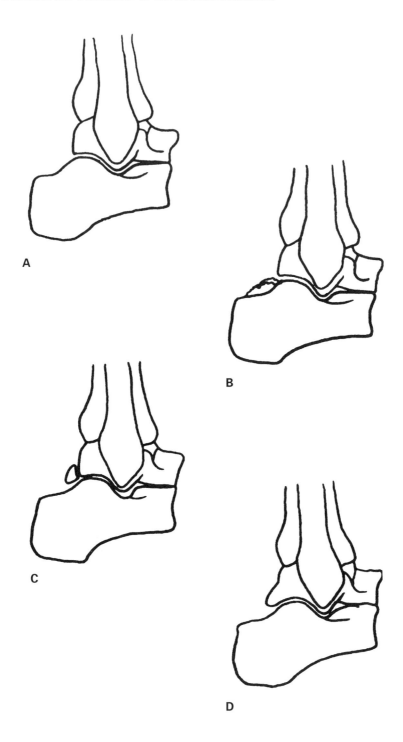

Figure 17–5 Various causes of posterior tibiotalar compression syndrome. (**A**) Normal anatomy. (**B**) Prominent calcaneus. (**C**) Os trigonum. (**D**) Enlarged lateral tubercle of the posterior process of the talus.

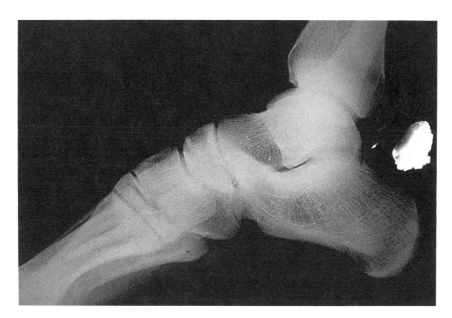

Figure 17–6 Lateral conventional radiograph demonstrating os trigonum. Because it became the cause of symptoms in this patient and was resistant to conservative treatment, it was surgically removed. The resected piece of bone, placed on the X-ray plate, is shown at actual size.

(Figure 17–6). Pain is caused by a pinching of the capsule and the local fat pad between the two bony structures. The most frequently seen flexion trauma is an inversion trauma of the foot, in which plantar flexion of the talocrural joint is a significant component. Ballet dancers, in particular those who do not have enough plantar flexion in the talocrural joint to dance on-point (on the tips of their toes), repeatedly try to force the foot into plantar flexion (Figure 17–7). This practice creates a chronic posterior tibiotalar compression syndrome.

Differential Diagnosis

- Tenosynovitis of the flexor hallucis longus
- Lesion of the subtalar joint

Clinical Findings

The patient complains of pain at the posterior aspect of the ankle, but the Achilles tendon is not tender to palpation.

Functional Examination

Passive flexion of the ankle is extremely painful. Maximal passive extension can also be mildly painful as a result of a stretch on the irritated posterior capsule and fat pad. The site of the lesion lies too deep to elicit tenderness clearly on palpation. Plain films reveal the compression when taken with the talocrural in a position of maximal plantar flexion. In cases of doubt, a bone scan can offer further information (Figure 17–8).

Treatment

When the lesion is caused by a one-time hyperflexion trauma, temporarily restricting the flexion by means of taping or bracing and administering a local injection with a solution of anesthetic and corticosteroid usually completely relieve the symptoms (Figure 17–9). In cases of chronic compression, typically experienced by athletes such as soccer players and ballet dancers, surgery is usually the only possible way to relieve the symptoms.

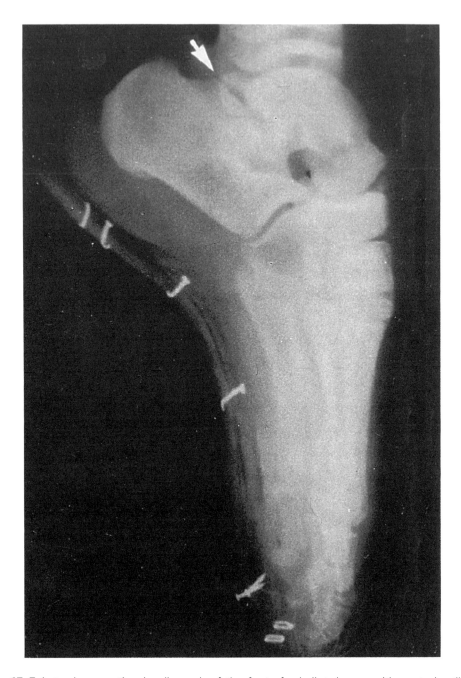

Figure 17–7 Lateral conventional radiograph of the foot of a ballet dancer with posterior tibiotalar compression syndrome (arrow). The radiograph was made with the ballet shoes on and with the patient in on-point position (ie, on the tips of her toes).

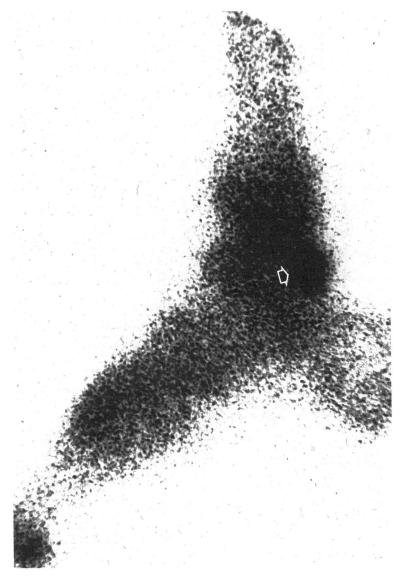

Figure 17–8 Bone scan demonstrating hyperactivity at the level of the posterior side of the ankle (arrow) in a patient with symptomatic os trigonum.

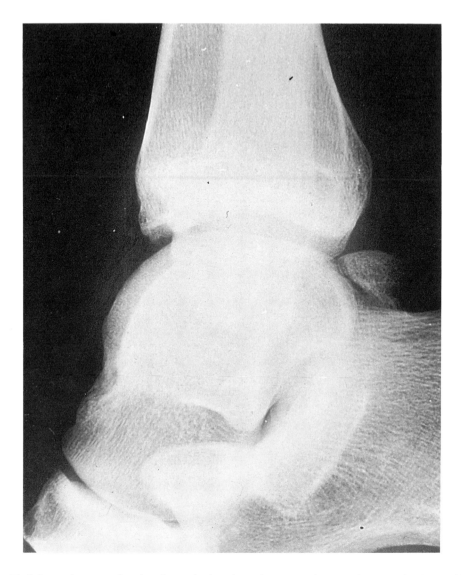

Figure 17–9 Lateral conventional radiograph showing a large os trigonum in a tennis player. After an inversion trauma, symptoms arose. Pain resolved with conservative treatment.

17.2   SUBTALAR JOINT PATHOLOGY

PATHOLOGY WITH LIMITED MOTIONS IN A CAPSULAR PATTERN

ARTHRITIS

Traumatic Arthritis

Traumatic arthritis of the subtalar joint is frequently seen as the result of inversion-varus trauma of the foot. The subtalar joint consists of the talocalcaneal and talocalcaneonavicular joints and is best called the subtalar complex. This complex provides both extra flexibility and stability in a mediolateral direction. Traumatic arthritis of the subtalar complex causes a painful limitation in varus motion. After inversion trauma, the symptoms from the injured capsuloligamentous structures usually demand the most attention. Because of this, traumatic arthritis of the subtalar complex is often missed, and in many instances there is accompanying traumatic arthritis of the midtarsal joints.

Clinical Findings

The patient complains of difficulty with "push-off" during ambulation, with pain in the medial, and sometimes also lateral, heel region. Often there is an increase in local pain and warmth after weight-bearing activities.

Functional Examination

The functional examination indicates a painful and limited passive varus test. Often, the passive valgus test is also painful.

Treatment

Manual traction, joint-specific mobilization, and shock-absorbing inlays in the shoes usually lead to complete recovery. In cases of swelling of the subtalar complex, and when the above therapy is unsuccessful in relieving symptoms, an intraarticular injection with corticosteroid is indicated. (For the exact procedure for the injection, refer to "Traumatic Arthritis of the Subtalar Joint" in Chapter 18.)

Nontraumatic Arthritis

As is the case with the midtarsal joints, the subtalar complex is often affected in patients with rheumatoid arthritis. Although in principle every systemic disease in which arthritides can occur can affect the subtalar complex, this is rarely seen. A monarthritis from the subtalar complex can be caused by an infection. Rheumatoid arthritis often leads to a progressive valgus deformity of the hindfoot, consisting of a flattening of the medial longitudinal arch, particularly in patients with hypermobile feet.

Clinical Findings

The patient complains of medial heel pain, or of pain at the anterolateral side of the lateral malleolus, at the level of the tarsal sinus. The pain is worse during movement than at rest. The calcaneus is positioned in valgus, and the medial longitudinal arch is usually absent.

Functional Examination

Frequently, varus motion is severely limited and painful. Passive valgus is also painful.

Treatment

Treatment depends on the cause of the disorder. Medication is usually the treatment in cases of arthritides that are the result of a systemic disease. If medication does not provide sufficient relief of symptoms, an intra-articular injection of the subtalar joint is indicated. The results are usually dramatic but, in most cases, only temporary.

In cases of valgus deformation and loss of the medial longitudinal arch, the use of orthotics is indicated. Special orthopaedic shoes should be worn when deformation is severe.

ARTHROSIS (OSTEOARTHROSIS)

Arthrosis of the subtalar complex is almost always secondary. In other words, it is the result of previous trauma, usually involving a fracture of the talus or calcaneus. Arthrosis of the subtalar complex can also occur as the result of previously experienced arthritis or as an adjunct to a congenital abnormality, such as clubfoot.

Clinical Findings

The patient complains of activity-related pain, usually localized at the medial heel region or at the level of the tarsal sinus.

Functional Examination

Varus motion is significantly limited and has a harder than normal end-feel. The passive valgus test is painful and also has a harder than normal end-feel.

Treatment

Manual traction and joint-specific mobilization can be successful, particularly in the early stages. Shock-absorbing inlays in the shoes are recommended. In severe cases, surgical arthrodesis is indicated.

SPASTIC (PERONEAL) FLAT FOOT SYNDROME

In many cases, spastic flat foot syndrome is idiopathic. Sometimes, it is the result of a synovitis of the subtalar complex secondary to various underlying causes. The most often seen underlying causes include the following:

- fibrous or osseous coalition of the talus with the calcaneus, usually concerning a

medial facet and only rarely the anterior or posterior facet
- fibrous or osseous coalition of the calcaneus with the navicular (Figure 17–10)
- fibrous or osseous coalition of the talus with the navicular
- arthrosis, sometimes as the result of a severe flat foot or clubfoot
- after fractures and dislocations (calcaneus and talus)
- rheumatoid arthritis and other collagenous and systemic diseases
- reflex sympathetic dystrophy
- tumors or infections (rare)

The disorder is seen particularly in middle-age, overweight women. The underlying cause is usually a beginning arthrosis of the subtalar joint. In adolescents, the cause is almost always a fibrous or osseous coalition of two or more tarsal bony structures. This condition is seen particularly in boys between 12 and 16 years of age. Besides the subtalar complex, the midtarsal joints are also affected. In this disorder, spasms of the peroneal muscles and extensor digitorum longus occur secondarily. After about 2 years, a painless fixation of the foot in a valgus-pronation-abduction position occurs. This is then termed a contractured flat foot.

Differential Diagnosis

- Neurologic spastic flat foot (this condition is seen particularly in patients with a cerebral paralysis; these patients do not have pain, however, and the spasm occurs gradually during a slowly induced passive inversion of the foot)

Clinical Findings

In the beginning (stage 1), the patient has slight pain during activities. The pain is often felt at the level of the tarsal sinus and is sometimes also experienced at the posteromedial aspect of the foot, just posterior and inferior to the medial malleolus. Often, the patient

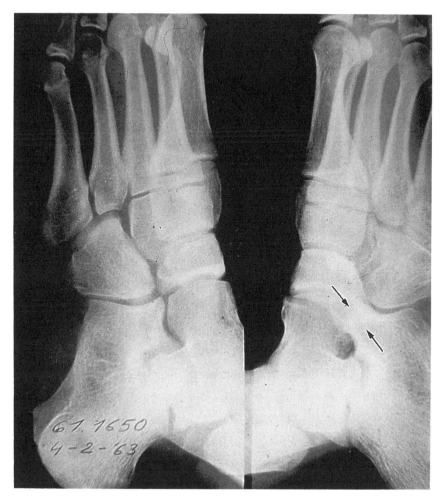

Figure 17–10 Oblique conventional radiograph showing a synostosis between the navicular and calcaneus in the right foot (arrows).

limps slightly. Patients in the middle-age group who have the disorder as a result of being overweight usually have pain, particularly in the midfoot, during activities.

Functional Examination

In the early stage, passive motion in inversion of the foot and varus of the subtalar complex can be performed, but muscle spasm is noted when the end-feel is tested. Later (stage 2), the foot is fixed in a valgus-pronation-abduction position. Spasm of the peroneal and extensor digitorum longus muscles prevents the examiner from performing a passive inversion-varus motion. Muscle function can be temporarily inhibited by means of a peroneal nerve block (with local anesthetic), and motions can be performed to a limited degree. In the end stage of this disorder, movement of the subtalar complex and midtarsal joints is impossible even when the muscle function is inhibited by a peroneal nerve block.

During the functional examination, middle-age patients who have the disorder as a result of being overweight will demonstrate a capsular pattern of painful limited motions of the midtarsal joints (inversion is more limited than extension).

Treatment

In the first stage, joint-specific mobilization of the subtalar complex and midtarsal joints is sometimes successful. The patient should reduce weight-bearing activities as much as possible. A wedge-shaped inlay, 3 to 5 mm thick, should be placed under the medial half of the heel. This holds the calcaneus in a more varus position, bringing the midtarsal joints into a slight supination-adduction position.

In the second stage, during a temporary block of the common peroneal nerve, the lower leg should be casted after the calcaneus is brought into a varus position. After 6 weeks, the cast is removed; subsequent treatment consists of those recommendations described for stage 1. This disorder is one of the few instances where the use of a cast may be indicated.

If there is not an osseous coalition, in stage 3 mobilization under anesthesia is recommended. If mobility is regained, initially the joints should be passively and actively mobilized on a daily basis. Subsequent treatment consists of those recommendations described for stage 1. If improvement cannot be obtained with this therapy, arthrodesis is indicated.

PATHOLOGY WITH LIMITED MOTIONS IN A NONCAPSULAR PATTERN

LIMITATION OF MOTION AFTER IMMOBILIZATION

After immobilization in a cast, limitations of motion exist primarily in the subtalar complex. Immobilization with a cast should be avoided as much as possible; if indicated, use of a cast should be kept to a minimum.

Clinical Findings

The painful limitation of motion of the subtalar complex results in an abnormal pattern of motion, leading to compensatory symptoms from other joints (often the knee). The limitation of motion depends on the position in which the calcaneus was immobilized.

Treatment

Treatment consists of passive and active mobilization of the subtalar complex.

LOOSE BODY

Loose bodies in the subtalar joint usually result from trauma. Sometimes they are seen in patients with an arthrosis of the joint. In many cases, however, the cause is unknown. The loose body is usually a cartilage fragment.

Clinical Findings

The patient complains of suddenly occurring, short-lasting, sharp, shooting pain in the heel region during weight-bearing activities. After the onset of the pain, further weight bearing is impossible for a short time. The pain often goes away after the patient wiggles the foot a few times, after which the patient can bear weight on that foot again. Sometimes a temporary, painful fixation of the calcaneus in a valgus position occurs.

Functional Examination

Either varus or valgus motion can be limited (noncapsular pattern). In instances when the calcaneus is fixed in a valgus position, varus motion is limited, and muscle spasm is noted when the end-feel is tested.

Treatment

Manipulation under traction is successful in many cases. Arthroscopic treatment is indicated when conservative treatment is unsatisfactory or with continued recurrence.

17.3 MIDTARSAL JOINT PATHOLOGY

ARTHRITIS

Traumatic Arthritis

As is the case in traumatic arthritis of the subtalar complex, arthritis of the midtarsal joint is usually the result of an inversion trauma of the foot. Because the symptoms from the injured capsuloligamentous complex mask the symptoms from the traumatic arthritis of the midtarsal joint, the disorder is often missed. Thus the signs and symptoms from this disorder are often seen residually after inversion trauma.

Clinical Findings

The pain is experienced at the level of the muscle belly of the extensor digitorum brevis and sometimes radiates medially. In some cases, the pain can also begin medially as a result of the compression that occurred during the forced inversion of the foot. Slight local swelling is visible in some patients.

Functional Examination

Passive motions are painfully limited in a capsular pattern; inversion (ie, plantar flexion, adduction, and supination) is more limited and painful than extension. Passive abduction and pronation are usually not limited, with minimal to no pain.

Treatment

The limitation of motion can almost always be alleviated through joint-specific mobilization. It is seldom necessary for the patient to perform specific active exercises at home because, through normal walking, this newly gained motion is easily maintained. Patients with primarily sedentary occupations are encouraged to take a daily walk.

Nontraumatic Arthritis

The most often seen nontraumatic arthritis of the midtarsal joints is rheumatoid arthritis. As is the case with the subtalar complex, the midtarsal joints are often affected in patients with rheumatoid arthritis. This disorder leads to severe valgus deformity in the subtalar complex and flattening of the medial longitudinal arch. The more mobile the patient's foot previously was, the more severe the deformation. In some cases, the disorder leads to total tarsal ankylosis. In many cases, one or more of the following disorders accompany the nontraumatic arthritis:

- tenosynovitis of the peroneal or tibialis posterior tendon sheaths
- posterior subcutaneous calcaneal bursitis
- plantar fasciitis
- achillodynia, or plantar nodules at the level of the calcaneus
- nodules in the tendons, causing a "trigger" phenomenon

Clinical Findings

In addition to heel pain, the patient will feel local pain, particularly at the level of the joint spaces of the midtarsal joints. This heel pain occurs because rheumatoid arthritis of the midtarsal joints almost always occurs in conjunction with arthritis in the subtalar complex. The patient has more pain during movement than at rest. In most cases, there is a valgus position of the calcaneus and a flattened medial arch.

Functional Examination

Severe limitations are noted in the capsular pattern; inversion (ie, plantar flexion, adduction, and supination) is more limited and painful than extension. Passive abduction and pronation are usually not limited. This is true for all forms of midtarsal joint arthritis.

Treatment

The therapy depends on the cause of the disorder. In most cases, the patient reacts well to medication, particularly in cases of rheumatoid arthritis. Often, it is necessary to make adjustments to the shoes to relieve pressure against the most painful areas. Furthermore, it is important to decrease weight bearing for a long period of time but still keep the joints moving. The patient is told to wear soft shoes with low heels and plenty of room for the forefoot. Corrective orthotics that also have a shock-absorbing function are usually beneficial. The position of the calcaneus can be corrected with the same orthotics when the medial side of the heel is about 0.5 cm higher than the lateral side. In severe cases, adaptive orthopaedic shoes are recommended.

Patients with rheumatoid arthritis react well to local injections of corticosteroid in the affected joints, tendon sheath, or bursae. These injections can usually be given without a risk of side effects. When the arthritis is no longer active, the residual limitations of motions can be partly or completely alleviated by means of joint-specific mobilization. In severe cases, surgery may be necessary. The surgical procedure can vary from a synovectomy to an arthrodesis.

ARTHROSIS

As is the case with the talocrural and subtalar joints, arthrosis of the midtarsal joints is almost always a secondary condition, for instance the result of a fracture or after an aseptic necrosis of the navicular (Köhler's disease).

Clinical Findings

Unless the arthrosis is extremely severe, there are usually minimal symptoms. Initially, there is only stiffness. Pain and crepitation are experienced later. Sometimes osteophytes are visible and palpable on the dorsum of the foot at the level of the joint spaces.

Functional Examination

Passive motions are limited in a capsular pattern. Conventional radiographs confirm the diagnosis.

Treatment

In the early stage, excellent results can be expected from joint-specific mobilization techniques. A functionally rigid orthotic is recommended to restrict mobility of the midtarsal joints during weight bearing.

SPASTIC (PERONEAL) FLAT FOOT SYNDROME

Spastic flat foot syndrome is described in "Subtalar Joint Pathology." In most cases, a disorder of the midtarsal joints is also present.

PATHOLOGY WITH LIMITED MOTIONS IN A NONCAPSULAR PATTERN

LIMITATION OF MOTION AFTER IMMOBILIZATION

Limitations of motion are often severe after immobilization in a cast.

Clinical Findings

The patient complains of the inability to ambulate with a normal stance phase. In many cases, this leads to complaints of local pain or symptoms in the more proximal joints, such as the knee or hip (sometimes these are joints on the contralateral side).

Functional Examination

All motions of the midtarsal joints are limited.

Treatment

Treatment consists of passive range of motion and joint-specific mobilization, which is later reinforced through active mobilization.

KÖHLER'S BONE DISEASE

Köhler's bone disease is an aseptic bone necrosis of unknown cause. Trauma may play an important role; it can be a one-time trauma or chronic repetitive microtrauma. Avascular necrosis of the navicular was first described by Köhler in 1908. In 1920 he described another disorder of the head of the second metatarsal. Aseptic bone necrosis of the second metatarsal is called Köhler's second disease.

These disorders are seen particularly in children between the ages of 3 and 8 years. Boys are affected more often than girls by a ratio of 6:1. In about 30% of the cases, Köhler's bone disease occurs in both feet at the same time.

Clinical Findings

As a result of, or even in the absence of, trauma, the child complains of pain at the medial side of the foot. An antalgic gait pattern develops that is initially intermittent and rather quickly progresses to a constant limp. The patient can precisely point out the location of pain. Sometimes there is local swelling of the soft tissue. The pain is caused by a synovitis of the talonavicular joint.

Functional Examination

The functional examination is usually negative, but forced movement in the midtarsal joints can provoke the pain symptoms. Radiographs confirm the clinical diagnosis (Figure 17–11).

Treatment

The treatment is primarily conservative. Possible position aberrations of the foot should be corrected by means of functional orthotics. Adequate support for the medial longitudinal arch is equally important. Use of a walking cast for 4 to 6 weeks is recommended when the child has severe pain. The lesion should be examined radiologically every 3 months. Generally the healing process takes 9 to 12 months. The use of a medial orthotic after complete recovery depends on whether there are residual aberrations in the position of the foot.

ACCESSORY OS NAVICULAR SYNDROME

Accessory os navicular syndrome is a disorder involving the frequently occurring accessory bone medial to the navicular. There are two types. Type 1 is a sesamoid bone in the tendon of the posterior tibialis muscle, also called os tibiale externum. Type 2 is a true accessory bony growth center that has not joined with the navicular but instead has formed a synchondrosis. Type 2 is often the cause of symptoms. Usually, but not always, the patients are adolescents, with 80% being girls.

Differential Diagnosis

- Avulsion fracture (particularly in athletes; Figure 17–12)
- Osteochondral lesion (also mostly in athletes; Figure 17–13)

Clinical Findings

With or without prior trauma, the patient complains of pain at the medial side of the foot. Posttraumatically, the pain occurs or increases as a result of activity, particularly participation in sports. The patient is able to locate the precise site of the painful lesion. Swelling is visible, and on

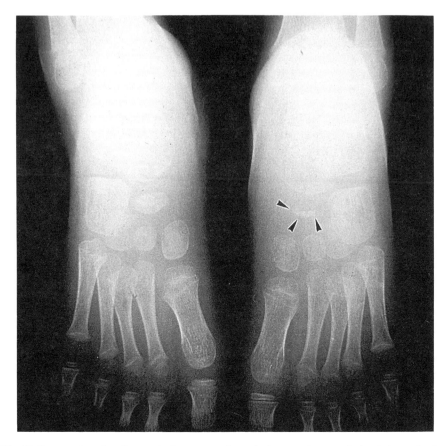

Figure 17–11 Conventional radiograph demonstrating obvious collapse of the left navicular (arrowheads). This is a characteristic radiologic finding in Köhler's bone disease.

palpation there is evidence of an abnormally formed navicular.

Functional Examination

Resisted inversion of the foot (contraction of the posterior tibialis muscle) is painful. Passive eversion of the foot is also painful because of the stretch on the tibialis posterior. There is local tenderness to palpation. On radiologic examination, the sesamoid bone will be seen to have a triangular or heart-shaped form, in contrast to the round or oval form of a normal os tibiale externum. In-creased activity will be visible on the bone scan.

Treatment

Treatment is primarily conservative. The almost always present pronation position of the foot is corrected by means of functional orthotics. Sometimes a local injection of corticosteroid helps relieve the symptoms. When conservative treatment is unsuccessful, the accessory bone, the synchondrosis, and the adjacent edge of the navicular bone may be surgically excised.

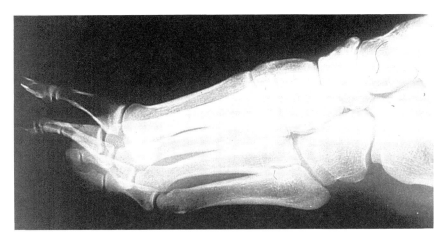

Figure 17–12 Lateral conventional radiograph demonstrating an old avulsion lesion at the level of the navicular bone in a basketball player.

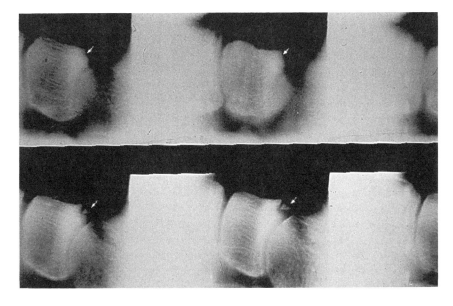

Figure 17–13 Tomographic examination demonstrating an osteochondral lesion at the level of the navicular bone in an athlete (arrows). This lesion causes recurrent symptoms during sports activities.

17.4   PATHOLOGY OF THE OTHER JOINTS

ARTHRITIS OF THE CUNEIFORM–FIRST METATARSAL JOINT

In the cuneiform–first metatarsal joint, the most common arthritides result from rheumatoid arthritis and gout. Other forms of arthritis are rare.

Clinical Findings

The patient complains of local pain, which is worse with movement than at rest. Tight-fitting shoes cannot be tolerated because of pain. In many cases, there is local swelling and redness.

Functional Examination

Translatory movements in the joint are limited and painful.

Treatment

The preferred treatment is primarily medication. If improvement cannot be achieved with medication, an intraarticular injection with corticosteroid is usually effective.

ARTHROSIS OF THE CUNEIFORM–FIRST METATARSAL JOINT

Arthrosis of the cuneiform–first metatarsal joint is seen in young people and is the result of a prior osteochondrosis, which is often bilateral. At the level of the joint, an osteophyte develops on the dorsum of the foot. Over time, motion becomes more limited, finally ending in fixation of the joint. This fixation results in a painful forefoot (metatarsalgia); the pain is located either at the level of the first metatarsophalangeal joint or at the sesamoid–first metatarsal joint.

Clinical Findings

The patient complains of local pain, particularly during activities and especially when tight-fitting shoes are worn. Local swelling is caused by an osteophyte, which is easily palpable.

Functional Examination

There is a significant limitation of the translatory joint motions in the cuneiform–first metatarsal joint.

Treatment

Wearing shoes with an open instep and a high heel unloads the joint. An intraarticular injection with corticosteroid is recommended when more conservative treatment fails. Surgery is only occasionally indicated.

LOOSE BODY OF THE CUNEIFORM–FIRST METATARSAL JOINT

A loose body of the cuneiform–first metatarsal joint is seldom seen but usually consists of a fragment of cartilage in the joint. It occurs particularly in athletes.

Clinical Findings

While the individual is running, an instantaneous pain is experienced in the forefoot, which disappears several seconds later. A residual, dull pain can remain for several hours, however.

Functional Examination

The functional examination is usually negative.

Treatment

Manipulative treatment is usually effective. If this is not the case, arthroscopy is indicated.

HALLUX VALGUS

Hallux valgus is seen particularly in women and can be the result of the following:

- pes planovalgus (flat foot)
- metatarsus primus varus (angulation of the first metatarsal toward the midline of the body)
- rheumatoid arthritis
- bad footwear (where the front of the shoe is too pointed).

When the great toe is in a valgus position (pointing laterally), the extensor hallucis longus tendon gradual shifts in a lateral direction. In so doing, the valgus position of the toe increases even more. The result is an overstretching of the medial collateral ligament of the first metatarsophalangeal joint. An osteophyte forms at the level of the attachment of the ligament at the head of the first metatarsal. Pressure of the shoe causes a local bursa ultimately to develop. This bursa becomes painfully irritated over the course of time (Figure 17–14). In extreme cases, necrosis of the skin can result from the pressure of the shoe (Figure 17–15). As a secondary condition to the hallux valgus, an arthrosis of the first metatarsophalangeal joint occurs.

Clinical Findings

The patient complains of local pain, which is primarily the result of a bursitis.

Functional Examination

If the joint is not yet arthrotic, only a limitation of medial abduction of the great toe is seen. Arthrosis causes a capsular pattern of limited motions.

Treatment

Initially, treatment is conservative; tight shoes should be avoided, and a small toe spreader should be placed between the first and second toes. If necessary, other adaptations of the shoe can be made to correct for an insufficient medial longitudinal or transverse arch. Specific mobilization of the joint, particularly in the early stages of the disorder, can lead to satisfactory results.

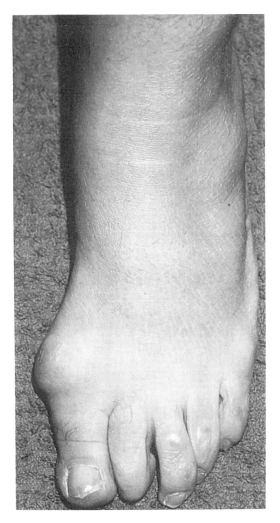

Figure 17–14 Clinical picture showing beginning hallux valgus with a bursitis.

HALLUX RIGIDUS

Hallux rigidus (stiff great toe) is characterized by limitations of motion in the first metatarsophalangeal joint (Figure 17–16). The disorder can occur early, in adolescence. This disorder, particularly in young men, is seen bilaterally and can lead to an early arthrosis of the joint. Hallux rigidus in older age groups is usually the result of an arthrosis. Often, large osteophytes occur on the dorsal side of the

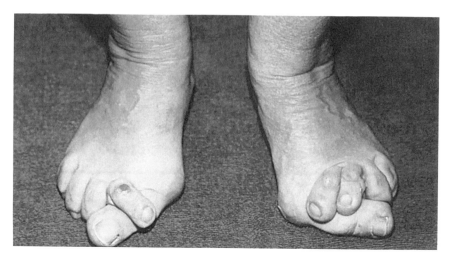

Figure 17–15 Clinical picture showing severe bilateral hallux valgus.

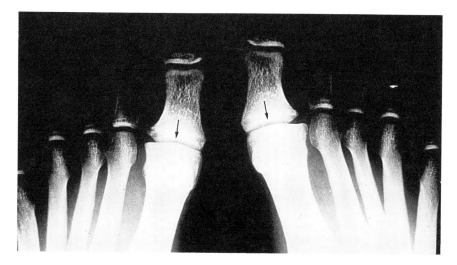

Figure 17–16 Anteroposterior conventional radiograph demonstrating a narrowing of the joint space of both first metatarsophalangeal joints (arrows) in a patient with bilateral hallux rigidus.

joint (Figure 17–17). As a result of pressure from the shoes, small bursae develop over these osteophytes, which can eventually become painfully irritated.

Clinical Findings

The patient complains of pain, particularly during the stance phase of walking. The pain is experienced locally. There is local swelling as a result of the osteophytes and, in later stages, from the bursitides.

Functional Examination

There is a significant capsular pattern of painfully limited motions; extension of the great toe is much more limited than flexion.

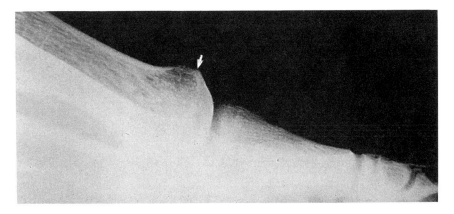

Figure 17–17 Lateral conventional radiograph of the first metatarsophalangeal joint showing a dorsal osteophyte (arrow). This is a typical finding in hallux rigidus.

Treatment

The treatment of a hallux rigidus depends on the age of the patient. In young people, joint-specific mobilization and a rocker bottom under the shoe can lead to good results. In therapy resistant cases, surgery to remove the osteophytes and bursae is indicated. In older patients, an intraarticular injection is often effective. One week after the injection, joint-specific mobilization should be initiated. Surgical treatment is more often indicated in older patients than in younger patients.

SESAMOIDITIS

Sesamoiditis is an irritation of the small joint formed by the medial sesamoid bone in the tendon of the flexor hallucis longus muscle and the plantar side of the head of the first metatarsal. This lesion occurs as a result of overuse or direct trauma, perhaps during sports. In the latter instance, there can even be a fracture of the sesamoid bone.

Differential Diagnosis

- Sesamoid fracture
- Sesamoid osteochondrosis

Clinical Findings

The patient complains of pain at the medioplantar side of the foot during weight bearing.

Functional Examination

Passive extension of the great toe is usually painful. Resisted flexion of the great toe is also painful. Radiologic examination confirms the diagnosis in most cases. In cases of doubt, a bone scan is indicated (Figure 17–18).

Treatment

Initially, treatment is conservative and consists of an inlay in the shoe with a cut-out at the level of the sesamoid bone. In stubborn cases, an intraarticular injection with corticosteroid can be given. Removal of the sesamoid bone is occasionally necessary.

HYPERMOBILE SECOND THROUGH FIFTH METATARSOPHALANGEAL JOINTS

With chronic, repetitive overstretching of the plantar ligaments, such as in the presence of a splay foot (flattened transverse arch),

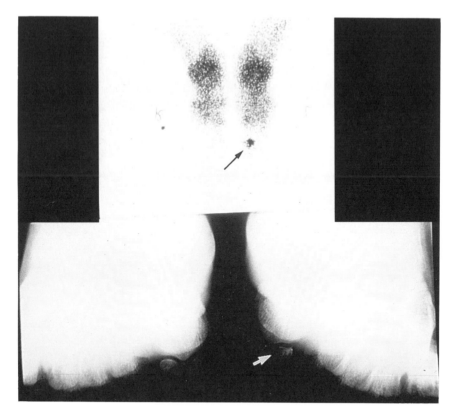

Figure 17–18 Bone scan clearly indicating a "hot spot" at the level of the sesamoid bone under the head of the first metatarsal.

hypermobility of the metatarsophalangeal joints can occur. This can lead to painful subluxation of these joints during weight-bearing activities. A splay foot can occur as a result of overuse of the (usually hypermobile) forefoot, for example by persons wearing heels that are too high or by ballet dancers who dance on demipoint. Splay foot can also develop as a complication arising from a pes equinus condition.

Clinical Findings

Pain is experienced in the forefoot, particularly during the stance phase of ambulation.

Functional Examination

Passive extension of the metatarsophalangeal joint(s) is the most painful motion.

The toes can be manually dislocated in relation to the metatarsals.

Treatment

The treatment is primarily conservative by means of functional corrective orthotics for the forefoot and, if necessary, a rocker bottom under the shoe. For athletes and ballet dancers, taping the forefoot often provides significant pain relief. Surgical treatment is sometimes necessary.

KÖHLER'S SECOND DISEASE

Although this aseptic bone necrosis was first described by Freiber in 1914, this disorder is generally named after Köhler, who further described the lesion in 1920. This disease is usually seen in women, occasionally in men, and particularly in adolescence (although it can also be seen in older age groups). Köhler's second disease is usually located in the head of the second metatarsal (Figure 17–19), but it can also be found in the head of the third or first metatarsals. In some cases, two metatarsal heads are affected. Sometimes it occurs in both feet at the same time. As is the case with the other aseptic bone necroses, the etiology is not completely known. It is possible that microtrauma, resulting, for example, from excessive running, may contribute to the cause.

Clinical Findings

The patient complains of pain at the plantar aspect of the affected metatarsal, particularly during activities. The pain decreases at rest.

Functional Examination

The mobility of the affected joint may be limited, but there is always pain at the end-ranges of motion. The site of the lesion can be precisely located through palpation. Radiologic examination confirms the diagnosis. In many cases, small loose bodies are visible.

Treatment

Treatment is usually conservative. Patients with severe pain should refrain from painful activities and use crutches during ambulation. As soon as the acute symptoms have decreased, a functional orthotic is prescribed to support the heads of the metatarsals. This orthotic should be made in such a way that direct pressure on the affected region of the foot is prevented. It is important that the patient wear shoes with low heels to place as minimal a load as possible on the metatarsal heads. Prolonged walking, running, and other sports activities should be avoided. In most cases, the disorder heals completely in 2 to 3 years.

Conservative therapy is not always successful, and in these instances there are various operative procedures that can be performed. In cases of loose bodies, surgery is usually required.

SESAMOID OSTEOCHONDROSIS

Osteochondrosis of the sesamoid bones in the tendons of the flexor hallucis longus and

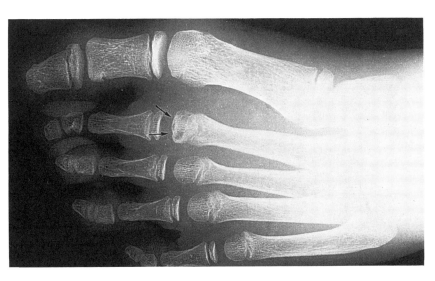

Figure 17–19 Anteroposterior conventional radiograph demonstrating an aberration at the level of the head of the second metatarsal (arrows). This aberration is characteristic of Köhler's second disease.

brevis is commonly seen. This disorder occurs particularly in children and adolescents and is usually the result of direct trauma. Generally the trauma involves an accident in which the ankle is in flexion and the toes are forced into maximal extension. Sesamoid osteochondrosis can also occur in adolescent and young adult athletes as the result of overuse. The disorder can be differentiated from the previously described sesamoiditis and fracture of the sesamoid bones by means of radiographic examination (Figure 17–20).

Clinical Findings

The pain is localized to the plantar aspect of the first metatarsal head and is only experienced during weight-bearing activities. The patient is unable to stand on tip-toe.

Functional Examination

Passive extension of the great toe is painful; sometimes there is an increase in pain when the ankle is simultaneously extended. Plain films will disclose typical bony changes.

Treatment

The treatment is conservative and consists of placing an inlay in the shoe that elevates the first metatarsal in such a way that direct pressure is no longer exerted against the sesamoid bones. If this therapeutic measure does not effectively relieve the pain, crutches should be used temporarily. Occasionally, an affected sesamoid bone has to be surgically removed.

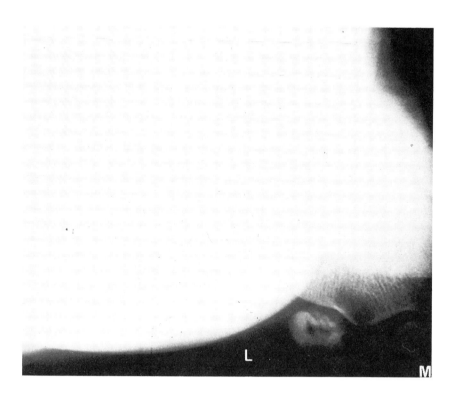

Figure 17–20 Axial conventional radiograph showing obvious changes at the level of the lateral sesamoid underneath the great toe. This is a case of an overuse lesion sustained by an athlete.

CALCANEAL APOPHYSITIS (SEVER'S DISEASE)

At one time, pain experienced by children in the region of the posterior calcaneus was assumed to be an osteochondrosis of the calcaneal apophysis at the level of the insertion site of the Achilles tendon. From recent radiographic studies, however, it appears that asymmetric development of the calcaneal apophysis with an increase in density often does not correlate with the clinical symptoms. Thus these findings of increased density in the calcaneal apophysis may actually have to be interpreted as normal observations (Figure 17–21). Symptoms therefore are usually the result of a soft tissue irritation, most often involving the posterior subcutaneous calcaneal bursa and less often the subtendineal Achilles bursa. This disorder is seen in children between 7 and 12 years of age, most frequently in 8- to 9-year-olds. The disorder is more frequently seen in boys than in girls, particularly in heavy-set, active boys.

Differential Diagnosis

- Avulsion fracture of the calcaneal apophysis (Figure 17–22)
- Insertion tendopathy of the Achilles tendon
- Subtendinous Achilles bursitis

Clinical Findings

Pain is experienced in the heel, particularly after activities; if the pain is already present, it increases after activities. The patient is no longer able to bear weight normally on the foot and thus is forced to limp. Swelling and redness sometimes occur.

Functional Examination

The functional examination is usually negative. In some cases, there is a slight limitation of ankle extension caused by a shortening of the triceps surae muscle. Palpation of the calcaneal tuberosity induces tenderness, particularly at the level of the Achilles tendon insertion.

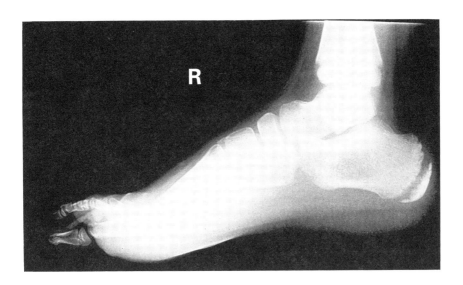

Figure 17–21 Lateral conventional radiograph demonstrating increased density at the level of the posterior apophysis of the calcaneus with an irregular growth plate. This aberration usually has no clinical significance.

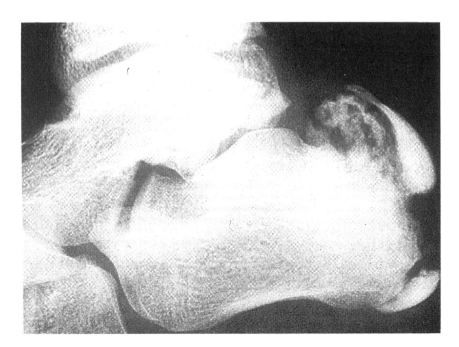

Figure 17–22 Conventional radiograph showing an avulsion fracture of the calcaneal apophysis in a young athlete (sprinter).

Treatment

Treatment is conservative. In severe cases, when there is significant pain, a reduction of activities and use of a heel lift (maximally 2 cm) are necessary. Sometimes, the heel counter in the shoe is too hard, and another type of shoe (with a softer and lower heel back) is recommended. The heel lift used to decrease pain acts to shorten the already short triceps surae muscle. Therefore, careful stretching exercises should be used to increase gradually the length of the muscle. After the muscle has lengthened, the patient is weaned from wearing the heel lift by decreasing the height of the heel lift by 5 to 10 mm at weekly intervals.

MARCH FRACTURE

Although the march fracture does not belong to the category of joint pathology, this stress fracture is described here because it is often incorrectly diagnosed to be a soft tissue problem. The disorder, also known as Deutschländer's disease, usually occurs in individuals between 18 and 30 years of age after vigorous physical activity. Individuals in the military often sustain this stress fracture. It is usually located in the neck of the second metatarsal and, less frequently, in the third or fourth metatarsal (Figure 17–23). This lesion is also seen, although less often, in patients in the middle-age group; the traumatic factor cannot always be determined, but these people are usually found to have an insufficiency of the first metacarpal (such as in a splay foot).

Clinical Findings

The patient complains of severe but alternating pain in the forefoot during weight

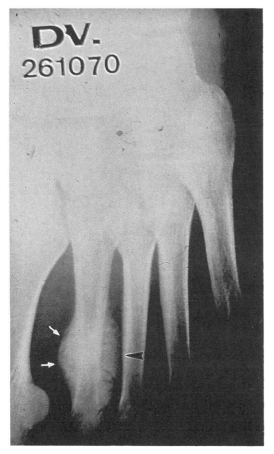

A

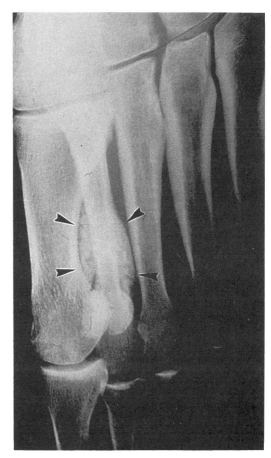

B

Figure 17–23 Anteroposterior radiographs showing an obvious callus formation at the level of the diaphysis of the second metatarsal (arrows and arrowheads). This is the typical radiographic appearance of the so-called march fracture.

bearing. The normal stance phase during ambulation is impossible, and the patient is forced to limp. There is local redness, swelling, and warmth.

Functional Examination

The functional examination is often negative. In some cases, besides pain on axial compression through the metatarsal, there is also local tenderness to palpation. The typical changes will first be demonstrated on plain films 2 weeks after the symptoms have occurred.

Treatment

Treatment is conservative and, in the acute phase, consists of medication or physical therapeutic pain-relieving measures, together with several days of rest. After the acute phase, the foot can be taped so that the affected metatarsal is unloaded. Because this disorder almost always concerns patients with a splay foot, it is important that the patient receive functional orthotics and continue to wear them even after complete recovery to prevent recurrent problems. In the absence of treatment, the symptoms will generally resolve after about 6 weeks. Even then, orthotics are still necessary.

Residual pain can often be the result of overuse of the interosseous muscles. These muscles react well to treatments of trans-verse friction. Four to six treatments of trans-verse friction (about 15 minutes each) are usually sufficient. Intensive muscle-strength-ening exercises for the intrinsic muscles of the foot are recommended.

17.5   PATHOLOGY OF THE CAPSULOLIGAMENTOUS COMPLEX

INVERSION-VARUS TRAUMA

The inversion-varus trauma, also called in-version trauma or supination trauma, is the most often seen trauma in the ankle and foot region. The trauma occurs in a combination of the following motions:

- flexion in the talocrural joint
- varus in the subtalar complex
- flexion, supination, and adduction of the midtarsal and distal joints

In almost all cases, there is a sprain or partial rupture of the capsuloligamentous complex of the ankle and, less often, of the midfoot. In addition, there are many complications re-sulting from this trauma (see "Complica-tions," below, for descriptions of those that are most commonly seen).

In determining which structures have been injured by the trauma and to what extent, it is important to analyze not only the position in which the trauma occurred but also the time it took for swelling to appear. Swelling that occurs immediately (within 2 hours of the trauma) indicates a hemarthrosis. If the swelling occurs much later (12 to 24 hours after the trauma), there is effusion or extraarticular swelling.

Grades

The severity of the lesion can be classified in the following grades:

- *Grade 1:* Sprain of the anterolateral structures, such as the anterior talofibular and calcaneofibular liga-ments
- *Grade 2:* Total rupture of the anterior talofibular ligament and sprain or partial tear of the calcaneofibular ligament
- *Grade 3:* Total rupture of the anterior talofibular and calcaneofibular liga-ments, and sprain or partial tear of the posterior talofibular ligament (in severe cases, the anterior inferior tibiofibular ligament can also rupture, thus affecting the tibiofibular syndesmosis)

Clinical Stages

The clinical stages are described as acute, subacute, and chronic. The acute stage usu-ally includes the first 3 days after the trauma. The subacute stage begins on the third or fourth day after the trauma, depending on the severity. The chronic stage is seen only in occasional, untreated cases. This usually oc-curs when the patient has experienced an inversion trauma months earlier; the patient can perform normal daily activities with minimal to no symptoms, but the "old pain," sometimes accompanied by slight swelling, occurs after vigorous activities, such as soccer, tennis, or jogging.

Complications

Lesion of the Calcaneocuboid and Calcaneonavicular Ligaments (Bifurcate Ligament). This lesion can occur as a result of forced supination and adduction of the midtarsal joints during the inversion trauma.

Lesion of the Cuboid–Fifth Metatarsal Ligament. This lesion can occur as the result of forced adduction of the midfoot and forefoot during the inversion trauma.

Lesion of the Anterior Part of the Medial Capsuloligamentous Complex. This lesion can occur as the result of forced plantar flexion of the ankle during the inversion trauma.

Lesion of the Peroneal Tendons. A lesion of the peroneal tendons is seen frequently. The usual cause is an overstretching of the tendon sheath of the peroneal muscles and sometimes of the tendons themselves. The superior peroneal retinaculum also can rupture, resulting in a dislocation of the peroneal tendons (Figure 17–24). This leads to the so-called "snapping ankle."

Another severe complication is an avulsion fracture of the tuberosity of the fifth metatarsal, the attachment site of the peroneus brevis muscle. An avulsion fracture of the tuberosity of the fifth metatarsal is characterized by severe local swelling, tenderness, and limping. Shortly after the trauma, there is discoloration (ecchymosis) resulting from the hematoma.

Lesion of the Tendon Sheaths or Tendons of the Extensor Digitorum Longus or Extensor Hallucis Longus. A lesion of the tendons or tendon sheaths of the extensor digitorum longus or extensor hallucis longus is not a frequently seen complication of the typical inversion trauma. When plantar flexion is the major component of the trauma (with minimal varus, adduction, and supination components), these structures are more likely to get injured.

Fractures. Fractures resulting from an inversion trauma are frequently seen. Usually they involve avulsion or traction lesions and sometimes impact or compression lesions (Figures 17–25 and 17–26).

Tarsal Sinus Syndrome. In tarsal sinus syndrome, the patient complains of a feeling of instability when walking and pain at the level of the tarsal sinus. This syndrome describes a chronic irritation of sensory nerve branches in the tarsal sinus, leading to disturbed proprioception and dysfunction of the peroneal muscles.

The functional examination, including the stability tests, is often negative. There is severe tenderness in the lateral opening of the tarsal sinus. The conventional radiograph does not reflect any abnormalities, but an arthrogram of the subtalar complex points to the presence of specific aberrations in the synovial recess. Injection of the tarsal sinus with a local anesthetic will confirm the diagnosis when the symptoms immediately, but only temporarily, disappear.

The treatment consists of weekly injections with a local anesthetic (2 mL of 1% lidocaine). Usually three to six injections are necessary to achieve complete pain relief. If this is not successful, a corticosteroid can be injected. Occasionally, surgery is needed to excise tissue from the lateral half of the tarsal sinus. In addition to being an integral part of the conservative treatment, muscle-strengthening exercises for the peroneal muscles and proprioceptive training are necessary before and after surgical treatment.

Posterior Tibiotalar Compression Syndrome. The posterior tibiotalar compression syndrome frequently occurs in individuals

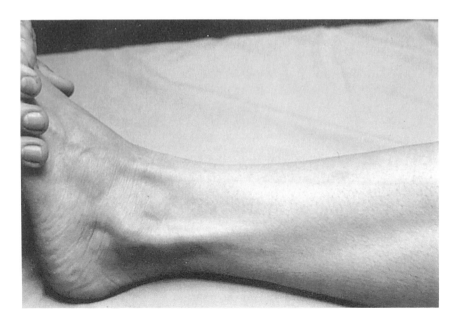

Figure 17–24 Clinical view of prominent peroneal tendons as the result of subluxation of the lateral malleolus during resisted eversion of the foot.

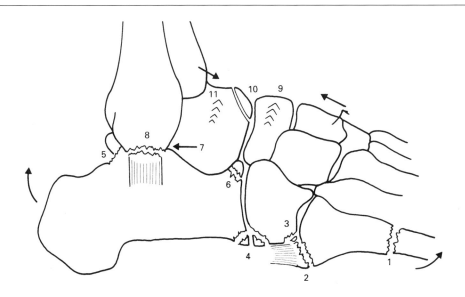

Figure 17–25 Possible complications in inversion trauma of the foot. Avulsion and traction lesions: **1**, Fracture of the diaphysis of the fifth metatarsal; **2**, fracture of the base of the fifth metatarsal; **3**, capsule tear and avulsion fracture of the cuboid; **4**, capsule tear and avulsion fracture of the calcaneus and cuboid; **5**, capsule tear (subtalar joint) and avulsion fracture of the calcaneus; **6**, fracture of the anterior process of the calcaneus; **7**, fracture of the lateral process of the talus; **8**, avulsion fracture of the lateral malleolus. Impact and compression lesions: **9**, Impression fracture of the navicular; **10**, shear and impression fracture of the talar head; **11**, impression fracture of the talar neck. *Source:* Data from Winkel D, Husan A, eds. *Voetenwerk*. Alphen aan den Rijn; Samson/Statlew; 1985.

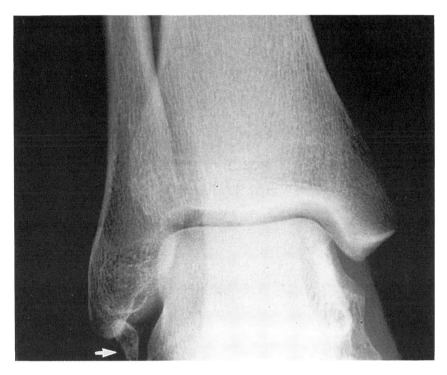

Figure 17–26 Anteroposterior conventional radiograph of the ankle joint disclosing a loose fragment as the result of an old fracture of the lateral malleolus. This fragment caused symptoms of impingement in a soccer player and was surgically removed.

with os trigonum or an abnormally large lateral tubercle of the posterior process of the talus (see the section on posterior tibiotalar compression syndrome for a more detailed description of this disorder).

Compression Neuropathies. Compression neuropathies resulting from inversion trauma are caused by an overstretch of the common peroneal, superficial peroneal, or deep peroneal nerve (refer to Chapter 19 for more information about these disorders).

Lesion of the Extensor Digitorum Brevis. The muscle belly of the extensor digitorum brevis lies just distal to the tarsal sinus, at the anterolateral side of the foot. After inversion trauma, the foot is often swollen at this site. Even after all the other symptoms have subsided, the patient often notices a blue-colored swelling at the level of the

muscle belly. Several days, or even weeks, after treatment, patients may occasionally complain that the foot is still swollen at a specific place. The examiner merely needs to compare the affected foot with the other foot to reassure the patient that what may appear to be swelling is just the muscle belly of the extensor digitorum brevis and is normal!

Clinical Findings

During and immediately after the trauma, the patient usually experiences severe pain on the anterior and lateral side of the ankle and foot. Running is almost impossible. Depending on the severity of the trauma, there can be immediate swelling, which is caused by bleeding.

Functional Examination

Passive extension of the ankle (talocrural joint) is painful and limited. The limited extension range of motion will be the result of traumatic arthritis, from either a hemarthrosis or joint effusion. Extraarticular bleeding can also cause limited extension. In severe cases, the anterior inferior tibiofibular ligament is affected. In this instance, pain during passive extension can be caused by the stretch of the sprained or partially torn ligament, and it may be caused as well by hypermobility (in spite of swelling) resulting from a complete rupture. Such pain will occur because, during extension of the ankle, the tibia and fibula are pushed apart by the talus.

In chronic cases, even when extension appears to be normal during the functional examination with the patient supine, it can still be limited in the standing position. This can be observed when the patient slowly flexes the knees and tries to keep the heels on the ground; the heel on the affected side lifts from the ground first (Figure 17–27). This phenomenon can be seen in instances of instability in the talocrural joint after inversion trauma. If the necessary support is not provided to the torn capsuloligamentous structures during rehabilitation (via bracing or taping), the lateral ligaments heal in a lengthened position. Thus, in standing, the load placed on the declined joint surfaces will result in a posterior and inferior slipping of the tibia and fibula on the talus. The ligaments are no longer effective in holding the talocrural joint partners in an aligned position, the kinematics in the joint are disturbed, and the end of the motion is reached too early. In supine, without the body weight on the joint, there is no subsequent backward slipping; the joint partners remain in alignment, and extension range of motion is normal.

Passive flexion of the ankle (talocrural joint) is painful and limited as a result of the swelling (which causes traumatic arthritis). It will also be painful because of the stretch on the affected anterior talofibular ligament and possibly on the anterior tibiotalar ligament or tendons of the extensor digitorum longus and extensor hallucis longus.

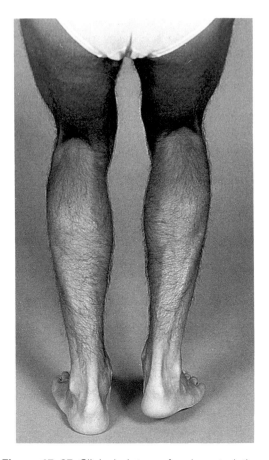

Figure 17–27 Clinical picture of a characteristic finding in chronic (traumatic) arthritis of the talocrural joint; in weight-bearing extension of the ankles, as knee flexion increases, the heel of the affected side lifts from the ground first. This finding is compared with the passive extension range of motion in supine.

Passive varus motion of the calcaneus, when performed in 10° plantar flexion, is painful as a result of the stretch on the affected calcaneofibular ligament. Passive varus of the calcaneus will also be painful and limited when there is traumatic arthritis of the subtalar complex; in this instance, the pain is usually experienced at the posteromedial aspect of the ankle.

Passive adduction of the midtarsal joints will be painful, especially when the calcaneocuboid and cuboid–fifth metatarsal ligaments are affected. Passive adduction will also be painful and limited when there is traumatic arthritis in the midtarsal joints. This latter condition will be accompanied by painful and limited plantar flexion and supination of the midtarsal joints (in a capsular pattern).

Passive supination of the midtarsal joints will be painful, particularly when the calcaneocuboid and bifurcate ligaments are affected. When there is traumatic arthritis in the midtarsal joints, passive supination will also be painful and limited, together with painful and limited (capsular pattern) plantar flexion and adduction of the midtarsal joints.

Passive inversion of the foot is painful because stretch is placed on all the anterolateral soft tissue structures, including the anterior talofibular, calcaneocuboid, bifurcate, and cuboid–fifth metatarsal ligaments. In addition, the extensor digitorum longus and extensor hallucis longus are stretched and, if so affected, can be painful. As a result of compression, pain can also be experienced on the medial side.

The resisted eversion test, used for the extensor digitorum longus and brevis and the extensor hallucis longus, will be painful when these contractile structures are affected (if the tendon sheaths of the extensor digitorum longus or extensor hallucis longus are affected, more pain will be provoked when these structures are stretched). The resisted flexion, abduction, and pronation test assesses the peroneal muscles. When the tendons of these muscles are affected, this resisted test will provoke pain. Much more often, however, the tendon sheath is the affected structure. In general, unless the lesion is severe, resisted tests have minimal effect on tendon sheaths; tendon sheaths provoke pain when placed under a stretch. Thus when the tendon sheath of the peroneal muscles is affected, the passive test (extension, adduction, and supination) will provoke significantly more pain than the resisted test.

On palpation, the site of the lesion can be located precisely. As an example, the anterior talofibular ligament is palpated at its origin at the anteroinferior aspect of the lateral malleolus, along its course, and at its insertion on the talus. The affected site of the calcaneofibular ligament can usually be palpated at the most distal point of the lateral malleolus. When affected, the peroneal tendons (and tendon sheath) can be painful to palpation over their entire course from behind the lateral malleolus to the insertion of the peroneus brevis at the tuberosity of the fifth metatarsal.

Where there is a grade 1 lesion, the stability tests will be negative in terms of abnormally increased motion. These tests can provoke pain, however. Where there is a grade 2 lesion, the anterior drawer test will disclose anterolateral instability, that is, an increase in translatory motion compared with the nonaffected side (Figure 17–28). Where there is a grade 3 lesion, both the anterior drawer test and the talar tilt test are positive (as demonstrated on plain films) for increased motion (Figure 17–29). In severe cases, the passive mediolateral talus test will also demonstrate hypermobility, caused by a rupture of the anterior inferior tibiofibular ligament.

Fractures will often cause pain when axial pressure is exerted. If that is the case, or if there is minimal or no improvement after 3 days of conservative treatment (pain-relieving and swelling-reducing modalities), plain films should be obtained.

Treatment

Arguments over whether operative or functional treatment is preferred are never ending. Grade 1 pathology falls outside the scope of this discussion; treatment here is always functional. Results from both functionally and surgically treated patients are usually quite good. Patients who receive functional treatment after surgery, rather than immobilization in a cast, score better in follow-up assessment. It is well known that the costs and

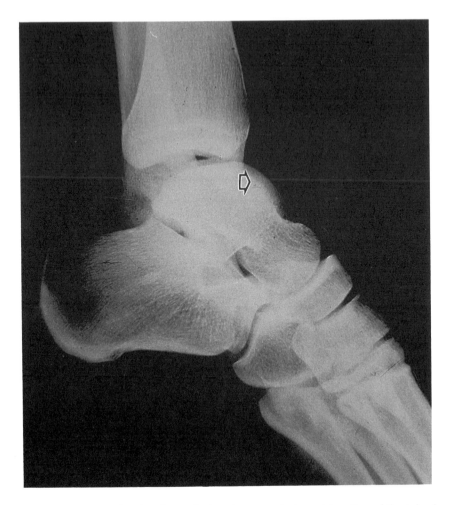

Figure 17–28 Lateral conventional radiograph showing an anterior subluxation of the talus in a patient who experienced a severe inversion trauma. The subluxation is visible as an increased distance between the posterior edge of the talus and the posterior edge of the tibia (arrow).

time lost at work are much lower for the functionally treated patients than for the surgically treated individuals.

Grade 1 Lesions. In the acute stage (the first 3 days after the trauma), therapeutic measures are taken to decrease the pain and swelling. Such measures can include cryotherapy, pulsed athermic high-frequency electric stimulation, and effleurage. Directly after these treatments, an elastic wrap or bandage should be placed around the foot and ankle. The patient should be taught the wrapping technique so that the bandaging can be redone at home if it becomes too tight or too loose.

When the ankle and foot have been wrapped, the patient should be given gait training to emphasize normal weight bearing and stance phase during ambulation. This functional training is important. Often, a patient who goes into physical therapy with a

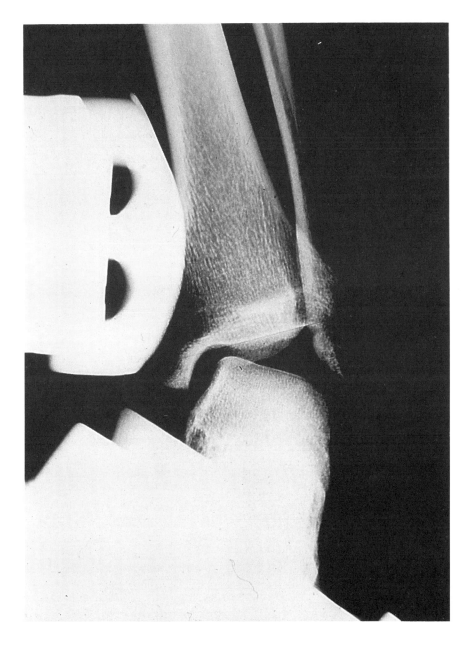

Figure 17–29 Anteroposterior conventional radiograph (the so-called talar tilt view) depicting severe laxity of the lateral collateral ankle structures with a tilting of the talus in a varus direction.

noticeable limp is able to leave with an almost normal gait pattern.

From the third or fourth day on, when swelling and pain have significantly de-creased, the subacute stage begins. Treat-ment should now include local transverse friction, initially lasting no longer than 2 to 4 minutes. This therapy is followed by muscle-strengthening exercises of the peroneal muscles and proprioceptive training. After the treatment, the affected limb should be taped or braced for functional support, with the patient being instructed in how to adjust the brace or wrap for proper fit.

By far, the greatest percentage of patients experience a complete resolution of symptoms within 7 to 10 days after the trauma. At this point, the patient can gradually return to sports activities with the support of a stabilizing brace or taping.

In some untreated cases, a chronic stage can occur. In this stage, the patient experiences symptoms only after activities. The functional examination should be performed immediately after these pain-provoking activities, when passive inversion is then painful at the level of the anterior talofibular ligament. Also, the motion is usually limited slightly as the result of adhesions on the anterior talofibular ligament.

These adhesions can be manipulatively ruptured. Manipulations of this type, however, should only be performed by a therapist experienced with this type of treatment. Before the manipulation, the therapist should treat the affected part with approximately 10 minutes of transverse friction to gain local mobilization and to provide pain relief. After the manipulation, the patient is taught an exercise program to maintain the newly gained mobility. Here, too, strengthening exercises and coordination training for the peroneal muscles are important.

Unfortunately, there are still many patients who are treated with cast immobilization even though there is not a fracture. As a result, after immobilization many patients have moderately to severely limited motions in the subtalar or midtarsal joints. Normal motions of the various joints should be restored as quickly as possible by means of joint-specific mobilization. The patient should engage in a home exercise program to maintain the improved mobility.

Note: In regard to ligamentous injuries, we now consider immobilization by means of casting to be obsolete. After immobilization, the cartilage function is always deficient, a condition that can last for up to 1 year, making the cartilage more vulnerable to every form of trauma. Thus the chance of arthrotic changes of the talocrural or subtalar complex is much greater in athletes who have been immobilized with a cast than in those who have been treated functionally.

Grade 2 and Grade 3 Lesions. When there is local swelling (a lateral "egg"), the joint should be aspirated. Blood in the joint is eventually reabsorbed but may adversely affect the joint cartilage and can cause intraarticular adhesions (in instances of intraarticular lesions, the patient often also complains of pain at the medial side of the ankle).

When the decision for conservative therapy is made, the patient should not put weight on the foot for the first 10 days. Therapeutic measures, as described for grade 1, should be applied to decrease pain and swelling. It is important that the patient keep moving the injured ankle and foot, but this must be done without placing weight on the affected extremity. Appropriate exercises to maintain motion should be done not only with therapist assistance but also on a repetitive basis by the patient at home.

If there is no significant improvement after 10 to 14 days, radiographs should be repeated. In many cases, a chondral fracture (usually of the talus) only becomes visible after that period of time. Further treatment should progress as described for the grade 1 lesion.

VALGUS TRAUMA

A valgus trauma is seen much less frequently than an inversion trauma. It is observed most often in people with a valgus-pronation-abduction position of the foot. The result of such a trauma is almost always a sprain of part of the deltoid ligament, which consists of the anterior tibiotalar, tibionavicular, tibiocalcaneal, and posterior tibiotalar ligaments. Because the deltoid ligament is extremely strong, ruptures seldom occur. There is a greater likelihood of an avulsion fracture of either the medial malleolus or the talus.

Chronic lesions occur as a result of the valgus position of the calcaneus when the medial longitudinal arch of the foot is not sufficiently supported. Such lesions are often seen together with lesions of the tendon or tendon sheath of the tibialis posterior. These problems are frequently seen in patients who fence or engage in long-distance running.

Clinical Findings

The patient complains of pain at the anteromedial side of the ankle. When bearing weight, there is usually a marked valgus position of the calcaneus with a collapsed medial longitudinal arch.

Functional Examination

Simultaneous passive flexion, abduction, and pronation, in combination with valgus movement of the calcaneus, is the most painful test. If the posterior tibiotalar ligament is affected (rare), the pain is particularly acute during passive valgus motion of the calcaneus, when the ankle is in 90° extension. When the same motion is repeated in maximal extension of the ankle, the pain disappears.

Treatment

Transverse friction is effective for all parts of the deltoid ligament. It is important that the patient wear good functional orthotics. Otherwise, the symptoms will only be decreased temporarily. If there is still a painful site in the ligament, it usually responds well to an injection of corticosteroid. If the insertion, tendon, or tendon sheath of the posterior tibialis muscle is also affected, excellent results can be expected from the use of transverse friction.

MIDTARSAL OVERUSE

Every deviation in position or form of the ankle or foot can lead to an overuse of one or more midtarsal ligaments. For example, when the medial longitudinal arch has given out, the plantar calcaneonavicular ligament, or so-called "spring" ligament, can cause significant symptoms.

Clinical Findings

The patient complains of pain at the medial side of the foot during weight-bearing activities.

Functional Examination

There is marked hypermobility of extension and flexion of the midtarsal joints. Forced passive pronation and supination of the midtarsal joints are painful. The plantar calcaneonavicular ligament is usually extremely tender to palpation.

Treatment

All types of local treatment are usually effective in decreasing the symptoms, but a functional orthotic has been found to be the best causal treatment. Many patients benefit from a slight heel lift, so that the forefoot goes into slightly less extension during weight-bearing activities. In stubborn cases, transverse friction or local corticosteroid injection is indicated.

17.6   PATHOLOGY OF THE MUSCLE-TENDON UNIT

ACHILLODYNIA

Achillodynia is an inflammatory and degenerative aberration in and around the Achilles tendon that can eventually lead to a partial rupture. Achillodynia is an overuse problem that is seen particularly in sprinters or athletes who run as part of their training program. In about 65% of all cases of achillodynia, the lesion is unilateral. When nonathletes complain of pain at the Achilles tendon, the cause is likely to be a systemic disorder, such as ankylosing spondylitis or Reiter's disease.

The causes of achillodynia can be divided into endogenous and exogenous factors. Endogenous factors concern influences from the body itself; exogenous factors are outside influences acting on the body. The presence of several of these predisposing factors increases the chance that achillodynia will occur.

Endogenous Factors

There are several key endogenous factors that can lead to achillodynia:

- diminished vascularization in the region 3 to 6 cm above the insertion
- disturbed biomechanics of the lower extremity; one of the most common causes is hyperpronation of the foot during the gait cycle
- left-right asymmetry of the hips, knees, lower legs, or feet
- hypermobility of the subtalar complex, for instance resulting from inversion-varus trauma of the foot
- minimal external tibial torsion
- high-arched foot
- hallux rigidus or other aberrations in the region of the first metatarsal, when too

much of the stance phase occurs on the lateral edge of the foot
- limited internal rotation of the hip

Some of the more common factors are discussed in detail below.

Hyperpronation. While running, the individual lands on the lateral side of the heel, after which the calcaneus goes into valgus in the subtalar joint and the midtarsal joints pronate and abduct. The term *hyperpronation* is used when these motions last too long during the stance phase. When this occurs, the triceps surae sustains an eccentric supinatory activity for a longer than normal period of time, which leads to an abnormal stretch of the medial side of the Achilles tendon. In addition, the tibia is internally rotated for an abnormally long period during the stance phase, and as the knee extends it is then abruptly rotated externally; thus abnormal torsion forces are exerted on the Achilles tendon. In the hypovascular zone of the Achilles tendon, these torsion forces cause the already small amount of blood found in this area to be pushed out. This phenomenon is known as the "wringing out" phenomenon and is comparable to the "wringing out" phenomenon of the supraspinatus tendon of the shoulder. Diminished vascularization can lead to early degenerative changes in the tendon. In many cases, this process does not generate any complaints. The Achilles tendon can spontaneously rupture, however. Most patients with an Achilles tendon rupture never experience symptoms preceding the rupture.

Because of the hyperpronation, the foot reaches the supination position too late. It is necessary to reach this position at the proper moment to stabilize the foot during toe-off. Thus not only is increased activity required from the stabilizing muscles, to include the triceps surae, but also movement occurs in the subtalar complex during toe-off. The tendon of the peroneus longus is no longer able to fix the medial arch of the foot during toe-off, which again leads to an even greater increase in the mobility of the subtalar complex.

The most frequent causes of hyperpronation are the following:

- forefoot varus
- forefoot valgus (here, hyperpronation is the result of compensatory supination in the subtalar and midtarsal joints)
- hypermobility of the medial longitudinal arch of the foot
- varus of the calcaneus
- limited extension in the talocrural joint, with a resultant compensatory valgus motion in the subtalar joint
- tibia vara
- too much internal femoral torsion; this leads to an adducted position of the foot, which is compensated for by hyperpronation
- shortening of the hamstrings and the iliopsoas, leading to an increase in the extension of the talocrural joint (although it is usually not completely possible, this is compensated for by hyperpronation of the foot)
- leg length difference (hyperpronation occurs in the longer extremity, caused by adduction in the hip; in the subtalar joint, a functional varus takes place)
- laxity of the lateral capsuloligamentous complex of the ankle

Pronation Gait. In a pronation gait, the heel-strike and the entire stance phase take place over the medial side of the foot sole (refer to "Biomechanics" in Chapter 14).

Causes of the pronation gait include the following:

- too much external rotation of the femur and tibia

- calcaneus valgus
- tibia valgum

Consequences of a pronation gait for the Achilles tendon can include the following:

- The foot lands in pronation. There is no shock-absorbing valgus-pronation movement of the subtalar and midtarsal joints. This can lead to overuse of the Achilles tendon.
- By landing in pronation, an extra stretch occurs on the medial side of the Achilles tendon.
- Because the foot remains in pronation for the entire stance phase, it never reaches the stable supination position. This leads to movement in the subtalar complex during toe-off, which again leads to stretch of the medial aspect of the Achilles tendon.

Supination Gait. In a supination gait, the foot lands on the lateral side, but the subsequent shock-absorbing pronation movement does not take place. The entire stance phase occurs over the lateral edge of the foot. When the heel leaves the ground, the foot rotates on the head of the fifth metatarsal, bringing the weight over to the medial side of the foot. Toe-off takes place with excessive load on the medial side of the great toe.

Causes of the supination gait include the following:

- forefoot valgus or plantar flexion of the first metatarsal (when these two deviations are not sufficiently compensated for through inversion of the forefoot, the rest of the compensation takes place in the subtalar complex)
- excessive movement in the valgus-pronation direction of the subtalar and midtarsal joints
- leg length difference (the foot of the shorter leg supinates)

The consequences of a supination gait for the Achilles tendon can include the following:

- overuse due to lack of shock absorption
- abnormal stretch of the medial side of the Achilles tendon at the end of toe-off due to the sudden valgus-abduction movement of the hindfoot during the rotation on the head of the fifth metatarsal

Exogenous Factors

The two key exogenous factors that can lead to achillodynia are footwear and running or walking surfaces.

Footwear. Shoes that are insufficiently adapted to the walking or running surface or to the manner of running can lead to problems. For instance, an absent or deficient varus wedge in the shoes of an individual who hyperpronates or has a pronation gait can lead to Achilles tendon injuries. A shoe sole that is too stiff allows for only minimal pronation and supination and can also limit extension of the ankle. If the sole of the shoe is too limp, or if the material of the insole is too hard, too soft, or too thin, shock absorption is diminished, causing the foot muscles to disperse all the forces. A heel counter that is not stiff enough does not give the calcaneus enough stability.

Walking or Running Surface. When an individual changes to a different running or walking surface, it should be done gradually to prevent overuse of the muscles. This is true particularly for unaccustomed running on hard, soft, or uneven ground. A habit of always walking on the same side of the street should be avoided because most streets are slightly curved. The foot on the street side is in constant pronation, and the foot on the curb side is constantly in a position of supination.

Differential Diagnosis

- Total rupture of the Achilles tendon (when there is a complete rupture, the patient experiences acute, severe pain at the level of the Achilles tendon; often, a "pop" is heard or felt, and walking is impossible)
- Partial rupture of the Achilles tendon (a partial rupture is seen particularly in older people; as in a total rupture, acutely severe pain occurs as the result of a seemingly insignificant trauma, but here the patient can walk with difficulty)
- Posterior subcutaneous calcaneal bursitis with pain at the level of the calcaneal tuberosity (this can be seen in patients, particularly those older than 50 years, with ankylosing spondylitis [Figure 17–30] or gout)
- Subtendinous Achilles bursitis (Figure 17–31); passive plantar flexion of the ankle is the most painful motion)
- Sever's disease (calcaneal apophysitis), usually involving a posterior subcutaneous calcaneal bursitis (occasionally, an avulsion fracture of the calcaneal apophysis is seen; this diagnosis can be confirmed by means of radiologic examination)
- Lumbar pathology (which sometimes causes pain only in the heel region [S1 and S2 nerve roots])

Clinical Findings

Usually the patient is able to self-diagnose the pain in the Achilles tendon region. Sports-specific history is important in addition to the patient's general history. Detailed information should be gathered regarding predisposing factors. Complaints will vary according to the stage of the lesion.

Acute Stage. In the acute stage, the classic signs and symptoms of inflammation are found: swelling, redness, warmth, and pain (Figure 17–32). The symptoms will have been present for less than 2 weeks. The pain is located 3 to 6 cm proximal to the calcaneus and is experienced after activities or at the beginning of activities.

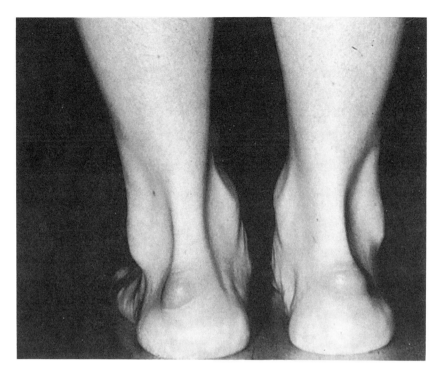

Figure 17–30 Clinical photograph showing Haglund's exostoses, often seen in ankylosing spondylitis, with irritation of the skin, the subcutaneous tissue, and the subcutaneous culcaaeal bursa (the left is worse than the right). The swelling and discoloration at the lateral side of the heel is typical of a Haglund exostosis.

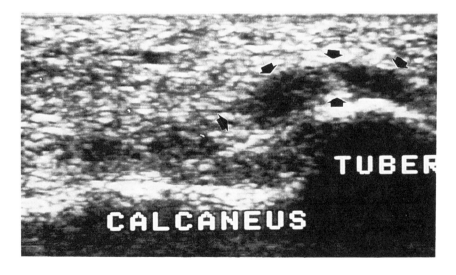

Figure 17–31 Ultrasonography clearly indicating a subtendinous Achilles bursitis (arrows) in a marathon runner. This disorder causes pain during and after sports activities.

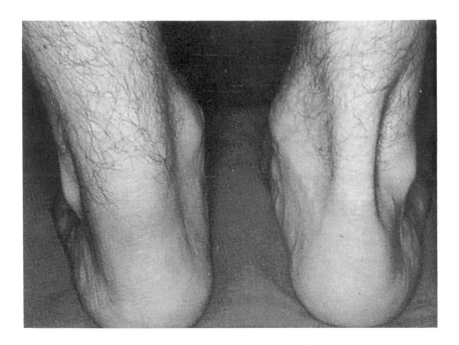

Figure 17–32 Clinical photograph of severe achillodynia in the left ankle.

Subacute Stage. In the subacute stage, the disorder will have been present for 3 to 6 weeks. The contour of the Achilles tendon is less visible. Often, crepitation is felt during active plantar flexion and dorsal extension of the ankle. The pain occurs at the beginning of the activity and increases according to the activity being performed.

Chronic Stage. In the chronic stage, the disorder will have been present for 6 weeks or longer. There is also pain at rest.

Functional Examination

The functional examination is often negative, except when performed directly after the pain-provoking activity. In this instance, resisted plantar flexion of the ankle (toe raises) is painful. In some cases, passive extension is also painful because of the stretch on the painful structures.

During the biomechanical examination, in addition to the talocrural joint, the other joints of the foot as well as the knee and hip joints should be evaluated. In the inspection during movement, which may be done with help of a video camera, the patient is viewed from behind while walking or running. The examiner should look for the following:

- A slight varus position of the subtalar joint before heel-strike is normal. Too much varus can result in hyperpronation, however. A valgus position indicates a pronation gait.

- During heel-strike, attention should be paid to how much valgus occurs in the subtalar joint. If there is more than 10°, hyperpronation is indicated. If the subtalar joint moves into the neutral position or stays in varus, a supination gait is indicated.

- In toe-off, the varus position of the subtalar joint is normal. Valgus in this joint points to an instability of the foot during toe-off; this is seen in both the hyperpronation and the pronation gait.

The shoes should also be examined. Findings such as wear and tear of the shoe sole, giving out of the insole, tears in the shoe, and the position of the heel counter can help confirm findings from the functional examination.

By means of palpation, the exact site of the lesion is determined (for the specific method of palpation, refer to Chapter 15). The tendon can be affected at the following sites:

- teno-osseous
- anterodistal, just proximal to the calcaneal tuberosity (in this instance, passive plantar flexion of the ankle is also painful in the functional examination)
- anteromedial (frequently seen)
- anterolateral (seldom seen)
- medial (most frequently seen)
- lateral (frequently seen)
- posterior (seldom seen)

Treatment

As a first step, treatment is always conservative. Causal therapy is the most important treatment and is structured to eliminate the sources of the overuse. In most cases, orthotics and adaptations to the shoes are recommended. In cases of hyperpronation as the result of an internal rotation of the tibia or femur or limited ankle extension, an orthotic with a medial wedge under the calcaneus is sufficient. In hyperpronation as the result of forefoot varus, an orthotic that offers support under the first metatarsal and the first metatarsophalangeal joint should be used. In instances of minimal hyperpronation, soft material should be used; in extensive hyperpronation, hard material should be used.

For the pronation gait, an orthotic should be placed in the shoe that forces the subtalar joint into supination at heel-strike. The result

of this is a stretch facilitation of the peroneus longus muscle, so that the foot pronates. This pronation is possible because the first metatarsal is unaffected by the orthotic. In the supination gait, the wedge is placed at the lateral side of the shoe. This forces the subtalar joint into valgus during heel-strike.

Limited extension of the foot or ankle joints should be treated with joint-specific mobilization. If the hypomobility lies in the subtalar and midtarsal joints, as is often the case, the appropriate joint-specific mobilization is performed. Muscle shortening is treated with stretching exercises. These exercises should be performed several times each day by the patient. Muscles most often needing stretching exercises include the triceps surae, hamstrings, and iliopsoas. A leg length difference should be corrected by means of a lift under the entire sole of the shoe.

Along with the causal therapy, local treatment is also recommended. Transverse friction is usually effective, and the pain generally disappears completely within a few weeks. Depending on the severity of the symptoms, it may be necessary to reduce or suspend temporarily the pain-provoking sports activities. Two weeks after resolution of the symptoms, the intensity of training can be increased, or, if the athlete completely stopped the sport, gradual training can be reinstituted. Training on unusually hard or soft surfaces should be avoided. Generally speaking, the athlete can be back to previous levels of sports after 4 weeks.

The following measures can help prevent recurrence:

- Stretching exercises should be performed daily, immediately after the patient gets up in the morning and before and after training.
- The transition between time off from the sport (to allow for the healing process) and returning to training should always be done gradually. This is also true for activities at the beginning and the end of

each training period; good warming-up and cooling-down procedures, lasting at least 15 minutes, are essential.

- The transition between diverse running surfaces should also be gradual. For instance, after a period of training on grass, the patient should avoid a sudden change to training on an artificial surface.

- The athletic shoes should have good shock-absorbing properties. The sole should not be too hard, there should be adequate space for the Achilles tendon, and there should be a stiff, stable heel-counter.

- Correcting performance when alternating among various running distances is important, especially during endurance training. The comparatively low tempo in endurance running makes it possible for the runner to strive for a full stance. The heel-strike is of great significance. Effective shock absorption combined with correct timing of the landing moment ensures a relatively full exertion of the calf muscles; thus the Achilles tendon is minimally loaded.

If, in spite of all the above mentioned measures, the Achilles tendon problem remains, surgery is indicated (Figure 17–33). Injections in and around the Achilles tendon are always contraindicated.

RUPTURE OF THE ACHILLES TENDON

In cases of rupture, acute, severe pain is felt at the Achilles tendon during sports. Usually, the patient hears or feels a "pop" or "snap" and is unable to bear weight on that foot (Figure 17–34). The rupture is the result of degenerative changes in the hypovascular zone of the Achilles tendon caused by various factors described under "Achillodynia" (above). Ruptures can also be caused by injections with a corticosteroid in and along the tendon.

This lesion is seen more often in men than in women, usually between the ages of 30 and 40 years.

Clinical Findings

In the acute phase, the patient is unable to perform a toe raise on the affected foot, and trying to do so is painful. There is a palpable gap in the middle of the Achilles tendon. After a few hours, the gap can no longer be palpated because it has filled with swelling.

Functional Examination

Passive and active extension of the ankle is painful. In a supine position, active plantar flexion is possible because the plantaris muscle is still intact and acts in conjunction with the peroneal muscles, tibialis posterior, and long toe flexors, which also assist in plantar flexion.

Simmonds' (also called Thompson's) test is positive. In this test, the patient lies prone with the feet over the edge of the table. The examiner squeezes the thickest part of the calf; normally the ankle flexes in a plantar direction. This movement does not occur if the Achilles tendon is completely ruptured (Figure 17–35).

The amount of motion in ankle extension is the same whether the knee is extended or flexed. Normally, extension increases by several degrees when the knee is slightly bent, which relaxes the gastrocnemius muscle.

Treatment

Treatment of a total rupture entails either surgery or conservative treatment (cast immobilization). With the use of conservative treatment, hospitalization is not required, and there are usually fewer residual symptoms. This form of treatment is only successful, however, if it can be administered within the first 24 hours of the rupture. Because tendons treated with immobilization have a greater incidence of rerupturing than those that have undergone surgical repair, and because the recovery time after surgery is

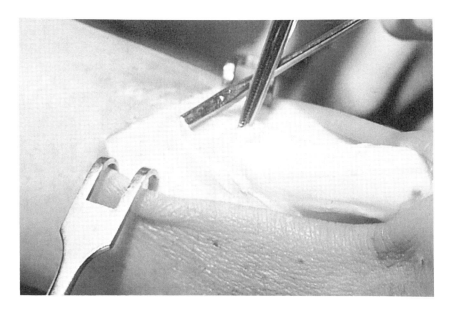

Figure 17–33 Photograph taken during surgery demonstrating a gel layer around (and adhering to) the Achilles tendon. This indicates a peritendinitis. The tendon itself did not show signs of tendinitis.

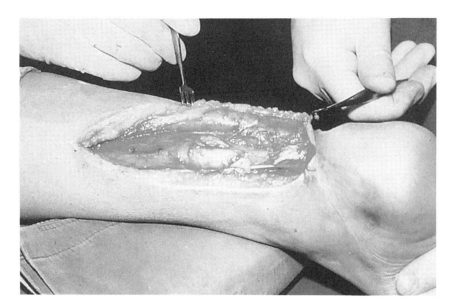

Figure 17–34 Photograph taken during surgery to repair a complete rupture of the Achilles tendon. The tendon of the plantaris is still intact.

shorter, the choice for surgery is usually made. After surgery and after cast immobilization, specific mobilization of the ankle and foot joints is indicated. The Achilles tendon should also be gradually stretched to a functionally normal length.

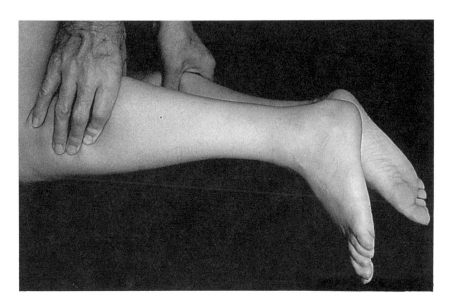

Figure 17–35 Positive Thompson's test on the left.

PARTIAL RUPTURE OF THE ACHILLES TENDON

A partial rupture of the Achilles tendon is commonly seen in middle-age and older individuals. As the result of an often insignificant trauma, acute pain occurs at the Achilles tendon. The pain is located in the hypovascular region, 3 to 6 cm above the calcaneus.

Clinical Findings

The patient can walk again, although with difficulty, within several minutes after onset. A localized area of thickness is visible on the Achilles tendon, usually on the medial side.

Functional Examination

Resisted plantar flexion of the ankle (toe raise) is the most painful test. Passive ankle extension is painful because of the stretch on the affected structure. Simmonds' (or Thompson's) test is negative.

Treatment

Treatment of a partial rupture of the Achilles tendon is almost always conservative. Transverse friction and careful stretching usually lead to a quick and full recovery. The patient should wear bilateral heel lifts for approximately 2 weeks. When the lesion does not respond to conservative care, surgery is sometimes necessary to remove necrotic tissue within or around the tendon.

PARTIAL RUPTURE OF THE GASTROCNEMIUS MUSCLE

A partial rupture of the gastrocnemius muscle usually occurs about 5 cm proximal to the musculotendinous junction. The medial head is affected more often than the lateral head. This lesion is most often seen in individuals older than 30 years, and it usually occurs during sports. The most significant cause is insufficient warm-up before the activity.

Clinical Findings

The patient experiences a sudden, severe, lashlike pain in the calf during the activity. Running becomes hardly possible.

Functional Examination

Resisted plantar flexion of the ankle is painful and weak, depending on the severity of the rupture. Both active and passive extension of the ankle can be moderately to significantly limited because of the painful stretch of the affected muscle. The site of the lesion is extremely tender to palpation. In severe cases, during the acute stage, a gap can be palpated. Sometimes, a hematoma is palpable and even visible in the subacute stage.

Treatment

In acute cases, the hematoma is aspirated, and afterward the leg is wrapped with an elastic bandage. The patient should perform home exercises of actively contracting the muscle from a position that does not stretch the muscle.

For the first days, the patient should avoid putting weight on the affected leg. Afterward, gentle transverse friction can be given on a daily basis, gradually increasing from 2 to 3 minutes at the outset to about 15 minutes. After the fourth day, conservative stretching exercises can be initiated. The amount of weight bearing can be gradually increased while the patient continues to use the bilateral heel lifts. Later in the recovery period, the height of the lifts is gradually reduced. Load on the muscles can be considerably decreased by using a specific procedure to tape the calf (see Chapter 18). After 10 to 14 days, the patient can gradually resume normal activities, to include sports. At the same time, the patient is weaned from the heel lifts.

TRICEPS SURAE SHORTENING IN CHILDREN

The etiology of triceps surae shortening in children is unknown. A slight form of spasticity may be involved in some cases.

Clinical Findings

The patient is unable to place the foot on the ground normally. The child tries to force this, however, and in so doing the leg is brought into external rotation with the foot in valgus, abduction, and pronation. With time, an overload of the midtarsal ligaments occurs and eventually causes hypermobility of the midtarsal joints.

Functional Examination

There is a limitation of both active and passive extension of the ankle.

Treatment

The treatment can take from several months to 1 year. The soleus and gastrocnemius muscles must be stretched. Until the muscles attain the correct length, a heel lift of 1.5 to 2.5 cm is worn to prevent midtarsal hypermobility. Heel lifts should be placed bilaterally. If the results from conservative therapy are unsatisfactory, surgical lengthening of the Achilles tendon is indicated.

LESIONS OF THE TIBIALIS POSTERIOR MUSCLE

Shin Splints

The term *shin splints* is a collective term for a number of overuse lesions that are manifested in the middle and lower thirds of the tibia. We restrict the meaning of this term to include only the so-called tibialis posterior syndrome. This disorder usually develops in runners from a single cause or combination of causes, including:

- inadequate training at the beginning of a running season
- changes in the type of running surface
- changes in footwear and the use of inappropriate shoes
- too rapid progression through the training program
- abnormal biomechanical factors

Tibialis Posterior Syndrome

Tibialis posterior syndrome describes an insertion tendopathy at the level of the middle and distal thirds of the tibia. The forces that act on the tibialis posterior muscle during running are not well dispersed through the matrix and thus exert more stress on the collagen fibers. Small tears appear that lead to an inflammatory reaction of the surrounding tissue. If a patient with this disorder continues to run, a periostitis can occur as a result of the constant forces.

The causes of the tibialis posterior syndrome can be divided into endogenous and exogenous factors. The presence of several of these predisposing factors increases the chance that this syndrome will occur. In addition, such factors as physical conditioning, general posture, nutrition, body weight, and coordination can also influence the onset and severity of this disorder.

Endogenous Factors

Hyperpronation of the Foot during Running. This is the most common cause of tibialis posterior syndrome. Because pronation puts the joints of the foot in a less stable position, a great deal of muscle activity is required to control this motion, and shock-absorption functions are shifted to the heel-strike. The tibialis posterior is one of the most important stabilizers of the ankle and foot. Every time the foot contacts the ground, this pronation occurs, exerting a significant pulling or traction force on the tibialis posterior muscle. When hyperpronation is combined with the great force at heel-strike, a slight laxity can be induced in the ligaments at the medial side of the foot and ankle. This condition can alter the movement pattern of the joints, so that the tibialis posterior, in struggling to prevent too much pronation, becomes overloaded. In excessive pronation, the flexor digitorum longus can also be affected.

Failure To Attain the Close-Packed Supination Position during Toe-off. If the foot does not attain the close-packed supination position during toe-off, more activity of the supinator muscles is required to stabilize the foot. Because of the increased forces that occur, the tibialis posterior muscle can be easily overloaded. There are a number of factors that can have a causative influence on an inability to achieve the close-packed position:

- As a result of the increased velocity of motions in running, the stance phase of the foot occurs in a much shorter period of time; it is possible that there is simply not enough time for the foot to attain the supination position.
- When a runner has a short stride, and thus increased adduction in the hips, it is much more difficult to supinate maximally.
- In some instances, the foot lands in an already supinated position.

Unstable Medial Arch. When there is an unstable medial arch, the tibialis posterior is overloaded because more force must be exerted to hold the arch in position. When the extension of the metatarsophalangeal joints is limited, the plantar fascia is not sufficiently wound up around the heads of the metatarsals. As a result, the medial arch stays collapsed and unstable.

Changes in Other Joints. Changes in other joints, forcing the tibialis posterior muscle to function over an altered trajectory, can also result in an overuse condition. Such changes, for instance, would be a limitation of ankle extension, limited hip or knee extension, a varus position of the knee, increased external rotation of the hip or knee, or a leg length difference.

Exogenous Factors

Footwear. A sole that is too stiff with insufficient torsion properties can restrict the midfoot and forefoot pronation and supination, as well as the extension of the metatarsophalangeal joints. A sole that is too floppy is often disadvantageous for shock absorption, so that, instead of the shoes, the muscles have to assimilate most of the forces. At the same time, there is less control over the pronation motion of the foot. An insole that is too soft, too thin, or too hard decreases the shock absorption of the shoe. A floppy heel counter does not offer enough stability to the calcaneous, thus making it easier for a valgus position to occur, which takes the foot into more pronation. Too much pronation occurs when a varus wedge is absent or when this wedge is made from material that is too soft or too thin.

Wear and tear of the shoes can also be significant. In runners with increased pronation, the medial side wears out, which allows the foot to stand in even more pronation. Shoes that are too tight can cause inactivity and even atrophy of the intrinsic foot flexors, so that the extrinsic foot muscles have to take over the function of maintaining the medial longitudinal arch. Shoes that are too wide decrease stability of the foot, which also leads to excessive load on the musculature.

Walking or Running Surface. When the walking or running surface is changed, a habituation period follows that often leads to an altered gait pattern, which in turn can lead to overuse of the musculature. A hard surface does not deform during walking or running. The forces acting upon the body at heel-strike are rather great, and the muscles have to exert more force to absorb the shock during ground contact. In walking or running on a soft surface, the deformation that takes place is sometimes too great, and thus the muscles become fatigued by the loss of energy. The same holds true for walking on uneven ground: The pronation motion of the foot is more difficult to control.

Habitual running on the same side of the street results in constant pronation of the foot on the curb side. Habitual running in the same direction on a running track gives the feet, specifically the inside foot, less opportunity to reach supination.

Differential Diagnosis

- Stress fracture (As a result of muscle fatigue, the bone undergoes repeated, rhythmic, submaximal resistance. When running, the individual experiences a searing pain, particularly during eccentric contraction of the muscles. The pain is precisely localized to one spot on the tibia, which is also tender to palpation. Differentiation between a stress fracture and the tibialis posterior syndrome is determined by means of radiologic examination [Figure 17–36]. For early diagnosis, a bone scan is indicated.)
- Tenomyosynovitis of the tibialis anterior muscle (in this case, the pain is located more at the anterior aspect of the tibia)

Clinical Findings

The patient complains of a sharp, shooting pain in the middle and lower thirds of the medial edge of the tibia. The pain increases with activities such as running. In addition to the patient's general history, specific information about the patient's participation in sports is also important to determine possible causal factors for the disorder. During the inspection, particular attention is paid to detect abnormalities in the positioning of the feet, the position of the calcanei, the medial longitudinal arches, and the lower legs, knees, and hips. As is the case with achillodynia, inspection during movement is made from behind the patient. It is important to note the amount of pronation of the foot, the stance phase of the foot, the amount of external rotation of the lower leg and thigh, any possible decrease in motion in one of the joints, and the stride.

Functional Examination

Not only the feet but also the knees and the hips are evaluated. Resisted inversion of the foot can be painful. Passive eversion of the foot can also be painful because of the stretch forces on the affected tibialis posterior. By means of palpation, the most painful site can

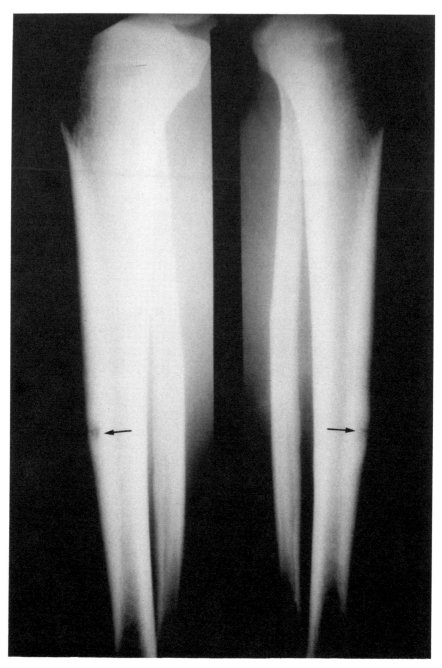

Figure 17–36 Conventional radiographs (two different views of the same lesion) disclosing a stress fracture in the diaphysis of the tibia (arrows).

be located at the posterior aspect of the medial edge of the tibia. Generally, the painful area is 7 to 10 cm long. In some cases, the examiner can palpate minimal swelling. The radiologic examination sometimes demonstrates a thickened cortex of the tibia. On bone scan, increased activity of the bone tissue is sometimes visible (Figure 17–37).

Treatment

Treatment is both causal and local. The causal treatment, of course, depends on the findings from the patient history, inspection, and functional examination. All of the aberrations found in this way should be corrected as much as possible by means of orthotics and

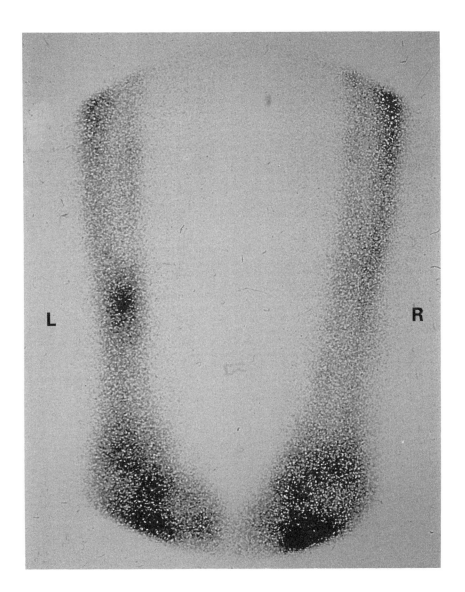

Figure 17–37 Bone scan depicting a "hot spot" in the diaphysis of the tibia, characteristic of a beginning stress (fatigue) fracture.

adaptations to the shoes. The most commonly used adaptations and orthotics for tibialis posterior syndrome include the following:

- increasing the height of the medial arch to prevent increased pronation and to support the medial arch
- stabilizing the calcaneus to prevent excessive movement of the subtalar complex
- a rocker bottom on the shoe to make the stance phase possible in hypomobile metatarsophalangeal joints
- a lift, either in or under the shoe, to even out a leg length difference.

If the cause of the problem lies in the shoe itself, it should be either adapted accordingly or replaced with a more appropriate shoe.

In many instances, the treatment is restricted to giving advice, such as recommending that the runner change sides of the street at regular intervals, change the running surface, or change directions on the running track. Local therapy consists of transverse friction, cryotherapy, and cautious stretching of the tibialis posterior muscle. Such treatment should always be done in combination with muscle-strengthening exercises for the plantar flexors and supinators, when such exercises can be done without pain. In stubborn cases, an injection with a local anesthetic or corticosteroid can be given in a dropwise manner. Surgery is indicated only in severe cases. To prevent recurrence, it is important that the athlete gradually increase training activities and adhere to advice received during the treatment period.

Tenosynovitis

Almost all disorders of the tibialis posterior muscle are caused in the same way as the previously described tibialis posterior syndrome. A tenosynovitis of the tibialis posterior muscle is an inflammation of the tendon sheath either just posterior or just distal to the medial malleolus.

Clinical Findings

The patient complains of pain and local swelling at the medial side of the ankle and foot (Figure 17–38).

Functional Examination

Resisted inversion of the foot can be painful in severe cases. Passive eversion of the foot is almost always the most painful test because the tendon sheath is stretched. The site of lesion can be precisely located by palpation.

Treatment

For causal treatment, refer to "Tibialis Posterior Syndrome," above. Local therapy consists of transverse friction and, in stubborn cases, injection of a corticosteroid between the tendon and tendon sheath. Occasionally, conservative treatment is unsuccessful, and surgery is indicated (Figure 17–39).

Insertion Tendopathy

An insertion tendopathy is a typical sports-induced lesion with the same causes as described in the discussion of tibialis posterior syndrome.

Clinical Findings

The patient complains of pain and local swelling at the medial side of the foot.

Functional Examination

Resisted inversion of the foot is the most painful test. Passive eversion of the foot can be painful because of the stretch forces on the affected insertion. Palpation can be used to determine the exact site of the lesion at the plantar aspect of the navicular tuberosity.

Treatment

For a discussion of causal treatment, refer to "Tibialis Posterior Syndrome." Local therapy consists of transverse friction and, in stubborn cases, injection of a corticosteroid between the tendon and tendon sheath. Occasionally, conservative treatment is unsuccessful, and surgery is indicated.

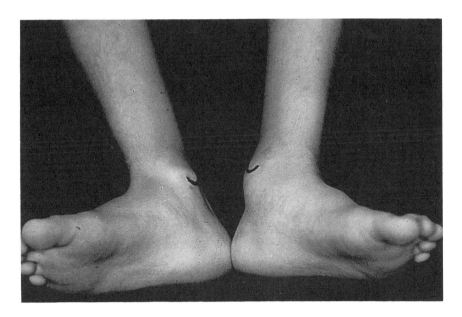

Figure 17–38 Clinical photograph of swelling underneath the left medial malleolus, caused by a chronic tenosynovitis of the tibialis posterior muscle.

Rupture

A rupture of the tendon of the tibialis posterior muscle is seen particularly in middle-age patients who have a pes plano valgus. This rupture can occur spontaneously, without the patient ever having experienced previous problems.

Clinical Findings

Although the rupture occurs spontaneously, the symptoms appear gradually. The symptoms are rarely severe, even though the patient has a significant loss of strength in inversion of the foot. There is a markedly collapsed medial arch on the affected side, and the region of the tibialis posterior tendon is obviously swollen.

Treatment

Conservative treatment by means of an orthotic is rarely effective. Surgery is usually the preferred treatment, and postoperatively the position of the foot should be corrected using orthotics. These procedures usually lead to complete recovery.

PLANTAR FASCIITIS

Plantar fasciitis is a disorder frequently seen in runners. It consists of an insertion tendopathy of the plantar fascia (plantar aponeurosis) at the medioplantar aspect of the calcaneus (Figure 17–40). A so-called heel spur will be visible in plain films when the condition has been left untreated for an extended period. As a complication, sometimes a stress fracture of the calcaneus occurs. This condition is characterized by diffuse pain under the heel and slight swelling of the soft tissue at both the lateral and the medial side of the calcaneus. Plain films confirm the diagnosis only 3 to 6 weeks after the onset of the symptoms.

Plantar fasciitis can be the result of biomechanical endogenous factors or of exogenous factors, such as footwear and running surface. The two endogenous factors are flat foot and high-arched foot (pes cavus). The flat foot is the most common cause of the disorder. When the foot is loaded, the medial longitudinal arch collapses, and the plantar fascia is stretched. During walking or running, the

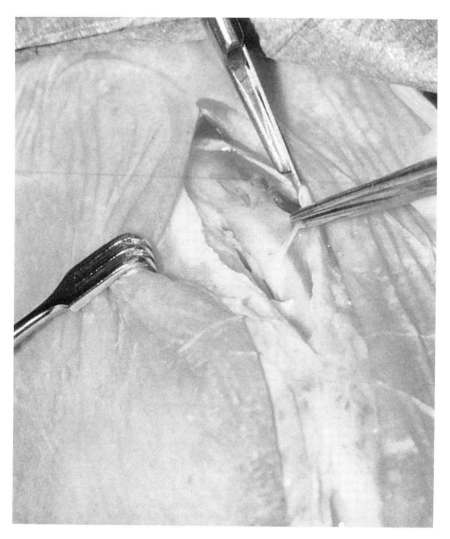

Figure 17–39 Photograph taken during surgery depicting a severe tenosynovitis around the tendon of the tibialis posterior, just plantar to the medial malleolus. Note the inflammatory coating around the tendon accompanied by an outpouring of fluid.

fascia comes under even more stretch forces during toe-off. Hyperpronation can further increase the stretch on the plantar fascia. In the high-arched foot, the fascia is shortened and as a result can come under too much stretch.

With regard to the exogenous factors, footwear plays a particularly important role. A sole that is too flexible increases pronation. A heel counter that is too soft provides insuffi-

cient stability to the calcaneus, allowing it to remain in a valgus position and again causing too much pronation of the foot. Inefficient shock absorption of the sole can also lead to plantar fasciitis. A too hard surface, particularly in combination with an inefficient shock-absorbing sole, is another contributing factor to plantar fasciitis.

When this disorder is seen bilaterally, it can be the result of a systemic disease, such as

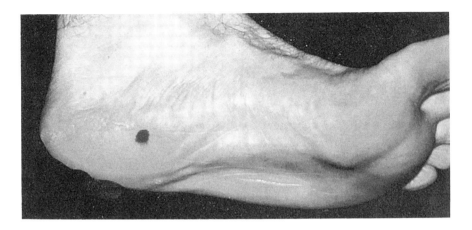

Figure 17–40 Typical location of pain in plantar fasciitis.

rheumatoid arthritis, ankylosing spondylitis, or Reiter's disease.

Differential Diagnosis

- *Calcaneodynia:* With aging, degenerative changes of the fat pad that lies between the plantar aspect of the calcaneus and the skin occurs (lipoatrophy). The loss of function of this fat pad can eventually lead to a contusion of the posteroplantar part of the calcaneus. Finally, microfractures or periostial irritation can follow. Initially, the patient only complains of local pain while walking or running; later, the pain is also experienced at rest. The functional examination is negative. There is severe tenderness to palpation at the site of the lesion. Treatment consists of making use of a heel cup of soft, shock-absorbing material, possibly with a cut-out at the site of the most tender point. A standard viscoelastic heel cup is sufficient in most cases.
- *Infracalcaneal bursitis:* Infracalcaneal bursitis is found between the inferior calcaneal tubercle and the plantar fascia. Differentiation between this bursitis and the plantar fasciitis is almost always only possible by means of an injection with a local anesthetic.
- *Compression neuropathy of the medial and lateral plantar nerves:* A compression neuropathy of the medial or lateral plantar nerves is seen particularly in individuals with flat feet and in runners with hyperpronation. As a result of the pronation, these nerves, which lie at the medial side of the calcaneus, are stretched. The patient complains of burning local and radiating pain.
- *Tarsal tunnel syndrome:* Tarsal tunnel syndrome is a compression neuropathy of the tibial nerve in the tarsal tunnel. As in the compression neuropathy described above, this syndrome can also occur as the result of a collapsed medial arch or a valgus position of the calcaneus. Most often it is the result of a fracture of either the medial malleolus or the calcaneus.

Clinical Findings

The patient's symptoms can be classified according to the clinical stages of an insertion tendopathy. As is the case with achillodynia and tibialis posterior syndrome, sport-specific history is of great importance in determining causal factors.

Functional Examination

Resisted toe flexion can be painful because the intrinsic toe flexors are connected to the insertion of the plantar fascia. Toe raises can be painful. There is tenderness to palpation at the medioplantar side of the calcaneus. A heel spur may be visible on plain films (Figure 17–41).

Treatment

As a first step, treatment is causal. An orthotic to support the medial arch, shock-absorbing inlays, a more stable heel counter, and wedges in the shoes are all treatments to be considered. In addition, the patient should reduce participation in sports activities at least to a level of acceptable pain tolerance. As the symptoms decrease, the activities can be gradually increased. Causal treatment usually leads to quick recovery. In stubborn cases, a local injection of corticosteroid can be given. After this injection, the patient should not put weight on the affected foot for 1 week.

LESIONS OF THE TIBIALIS ANTERIOR MUSCLE

In lesions of the tibialis anterior muscle, differentiation is made among tendinitis, tenosynovitis, and tenomyosynovitis.

Tendinitis

Tendinitis of the tibialis anterior muscle can be located anywhere in the tendon. The cause is usually overuse, often the result of uphill running, skating, or cross-country skiing. If this lesion goes untreated, the symptoms can last for months.

Clinical Findings

The patient complains of pain at the anterior side of the ankle and foot. Often there is visible swelling.

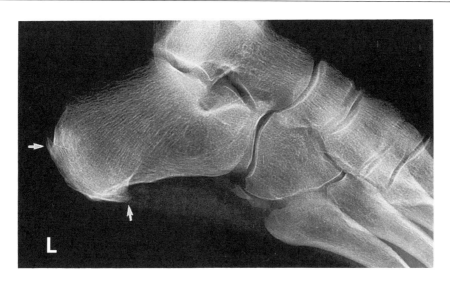

Figure 17–41 Lateral conventional radiograph of the foot of a long-distance runner. The classic heel spur (plantar arrow) can be seen, as can a traction osteophyte (posterior arrow) at the level of the insertion of the Achilles tendon.

Functional Examination

Resisted extension of the ankle, combined with supination and adduction of the foot, is painful. Often, passive plantar flexion, in combination with abduction and pronation of the foot, is painful because of stretch forces on the affected structure. Using palpation techniques, the examiner can precisely locate the site of the lesion.

Treatment

Transverse friction is effective in this lesion.

Tenosynovitis

Tenosynovitis of the tibialis anterior usually is caused by either indirect or direct trauma or as the result of microtrauma, such as irritation from poorly fitting footwear. If this lesion goes untreated, the symptoms can last for months.

Clinical Findings

The patient complains of pain at the anterior side of the ankle and foot. Often, there is visible swelling longitudinally along the tendon.

Functional Examination

Resisted extension of the ankle, combined with supination and adduction of the foot, is usually *not* painful. Passive plantar flexion in combination with abduction and pronation of the foot is the most painful test. Crepitation is sometimes palpable. The site of the lesion can be precisely located through palpation.

Treatment

Transverse friction is effective.

Tenomyosynovitis

Tenomyosynovitis of the tibialis anterior is a typical overuse lesion that is particularly seen in skaters and cross-country skiers. Sometimes, it is also seen in long-distance runners, particularly those who do a significant amount of uphill running.

Clinical Findings

The patient complains of local pain at the anterior side of the lower leg at the level of the musculotendinous junction. There is obvious local crepitation during active movements of the foot.

Functional Examination

Resisted extension of the ankle, combined with supination and adduction of the foot, is painful. Passive plantar flexion in combination with abduction and pronation of the foot is the most painful test. Using palpation, the examiner can precisely locate the site of the lesion.

Treatment

Complete resolution of the symptoms can usually be achieved in 2 to 4 weeks by combining transverse friction with a reduction of the pain-provoking activities during the period of treatment.

LESIONS OF THE PERONEAL MUSCLES

Tenosynovitis

Tenosynovitis of the peroneal muscles is a complication that is frequently seen as the result of inversion trauma of the foot.

Clinical Findings

The patient complains of pain at the lateral side of the ankle. Sometimes there is visible local swelling along the course of the peroneal tendons.

Functional Examination

Passive extension, supination, and adduction represent the most painful test, resulting from stretch forces on the affected tendon sheath. In severe cases, resisted plantar flexion of the ankle combined with abduction and pronation of the foot are painful. By the use of palpation, the exact site of the lesion can be located. This can vary from just behind the lateral malleolus to the base of the fifth metatarsal.

Treatment

The preferred treatment is transverse friction. Generally, the patient achieves complete relief of symptoms after about six 15-minute treatments. In therapy-resistant cases, which are rare, a local injection of corticosteroid can be given between the tendon and the tendon sheath.

Insertion Tendopathy of the Peroneus Brevis Muscle

Insertion tendopathy of the peroneus brevis muscle is an overuse lesion that is particularly seen in sprinters.

Clinical Findings

The patient complains of pain at the lateral edge of the foot.

Functional Examination

Resisted plantar flexion of the ankle combined with pronation and abduction of the foot are painful. Palpation reveals a tenderness at the tuberosity of the fifth metatarsal.

Treatment

In almost all cases, transverse friction is effective. In the third and fourth clinical stages of this insertion tendopathy, pain-provoking sports activities should be restricted.

Dislocation of the Peroneal Tendons

Dislocation of the peroneal tendons occurs as the result of inversion trauma of the foot in which the superior peroneal retinaculum ruptures. The tendons dislocate anteriorly, resulting in what is sometimes referred to as a "snapping ankle." Longitudinal tears sometimes develop in the tendon because of the repeated rubbing over the lateral malleolus (Figure 17–42).

Clinical Findings

The patient complains of pain posterior to the lateral malleolus, which is felt when walking. The dislocation occurs during active extension of the ankle in combination with pronation of the foot. In approximately 50% of all cases, a small piece of bone will be visible on conventional radiographs, indicating an avulsion of the retinaculum.

Treatment

Surgery is always indicated. Untreated patients are likely to develop a permanent "snapping ankle" with the feeling of instability.

TENOSYNOVITIDES OF THE FOOT

Tenosynovitis of the Extensor Hallucis Longus

In some cases, tenosynovitis of the extensor hallucis longus is the result of inversion trauma of the foot. Occasionally, it is caused by chronic irritation from ill-fitting shoes. In middle-age individuals, irritation of the tendon and tendon sheath can occur as the result of an osteophyte at the dorsal aspect of the navicular at the level of the talonavicular joint.

Clinical Findings

The patient complains of pain at the anteromedial side of the instep that increases with resisted extension of the great toe, passive flexion of the great toe (with the ankle and foot also in plantar flexion), or both. Crepitation is sometimes noted.

Treatment

Transverse friction is effective when the lesion is the result of inversion trauma. If the

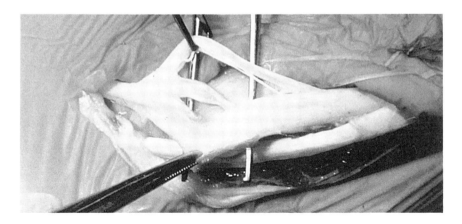

Figure 17–42 Photograph taken during surgery showing a severe lesion of the peroneus brevis tendon; the tendon is torn longitudinally. This lesion is typically found in patients with recurrent dislocation of the peroneal tendons.

lesion occurs because of an osteophyte of the navicular bone, surgical removal of the osteophyte is the only possible treatment.

Tenosynovitis of the Extensor Digitorum Longus

Tenosynovitis of the extensor digitorum longus, which is seldom seen, may be the result of inversion or plantar flexion trauma of the foot. It may also be caused by overuse, for example from hiking a long distance.

Clinical Findings

The patient complains of pain at the anterior aspect of the ankle and the instep.

Functional Examination

Passive inversion of the foot is painful, particularly when the toes are passively flexed. In severe cases, resisted eversion of the foot combined with resisted extension of the toes is also painful. Sometimes there is crepitation.

Treatment

In most cases, only a few treatments of transverse friction are necessary to achieve complete recovery.

Tenosynovitis (Stenosans) of the Flexor Hallucis Longus

Tenosynovitis of the flexor hallucis longus is seen rather frequently in ballet dancers. The irritation, or stenosis, is found at the posterior side of the talus, where the tendon runs between the medial and lateral tubercles of the posterior process of the talus. A second location for the lesion is at the base of the great toe between the two sesamoid bones.

Differential Diagnosis

- Posterior tibiotalar compression syndrome
- Subtendineal Achilles bursitis
- Tendinitis or tenosynovitis of the tibialis posterior or the flexor digitorum longus muscles (extremely rare)

Clinical Findings

The patient complains of pain and swelling behind the medial malleolus. The pain occurs particularly while jumping and during pliés (leaps that are executed while the knees are bent with the back held straight). Sometimes there is palpable and even audible crepitation.

Functional Examination

Resisted flexion of the great toe is painful. Passive extension of the great toe is also painful. A so-called functional hallux rigidus occurs. When the ankle and foot are held in plantar flexion, the great toe can be completely extended, but when the ankle and foot are in extension, the extension of the great toe is significantly limited (because of pain). When the lesion is located between the sesamoid bones at the base of the great toe, the patient, when walking, will experience pain at this site. Palpation will disclose a local tenderness. In this instance, the patient cannot perform active flexion of the interphalangeal joint of the great toe when the metatarsophalangeal joint is held in neutral position.

Treatment

Transverse friction, cautious stretching, and reducing the pain-provoking activities usually result in a quick recovery. In many cases, however, symptoms that still remain can be treated with several injections of a local anesthetic. In stubborn cases, corticosteroid injections are indicated. Surgery is sometimes needed to treat therapy-resistant cases.

17.7   COMPARTMENT SYNDROMES

Compartment syndromes are caused by the disturbed functioning of muscles, nerves, and blood vessels within a tightly enclosed space as the result of increased pressure. An increase of the arterial blood supply (and, through that, the muscle volume) impedes the venous flow, causing a vicious cycle to occur.

In the lower leg, four different compartment syndromes are identified (Figure 17–43):

1. *Anterior compartment syndrome:* The following structures are involved: deep peroneal nerve, tibialis anterior muscle, and extensor digitorum longus muscle.

2. *Lateral compartment syndrome:* This syndrome involves the superficial peroneal nerve and the peroneal muscles.

3. *Superficial posterior compartment syndrome:* This syndrome involves the gastrocnemius and soleus muscles.

4. *Deep posterior compartment syndrome:* This syndrome involves the tibialis nerve and the posterior tibialis and flexor digitorum longus muscles.

Clinical Findings

The patient complains of increasing pain in the affected compartment during activity, such as running, with a decrease in strength in the affected muscles. Sometimes there is paresthesia in the affected nerve's cutaneous area of innervation.

Functional Examination

In the functional examination, there is pain and loss of strength when the affected muscles are tested against resistance.

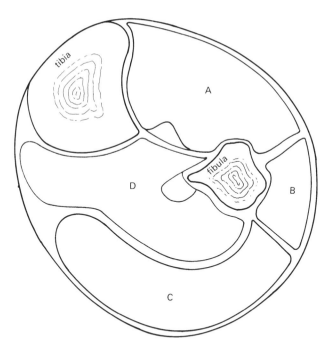

Figure 17–43 The four compartments of the lower leg. **A**, Anterior compartment; **B**, lateral compartment; **C**, superficial posterior compartment; **D**, deep posterior compartment.

Treatment

Conservative therapeutic measures are tried to diminish the symptoms, one of the most important being to decrease the causal sports activity. If conservative treatment does not result in improvement, a surgical fasciotomy is indicated. Surgery is critical when the symptoms do not spontaneously decrease with rest. In these cases, muscle necrosis can develop if surgery is not performed in time.

17.8   OTHER PATHOLOGY

GANGLION

A ganglion can occur at several different places in the foot. It can come from a tendon sheath or from out of a joint capsule (Figure 17–44). A frequently seen location is between the heads of two metatarsals, which causes them to splay.

Clinical Findings

In most cases, the patient does not have any pain unless the ganglion is so large that it causes chronic compression in the shoe. The ganglion is visible and can sometimes feel hard to the touch. When the ganglion is located between two metatarsal heads, an obvious local splaying of the metatarsals can be seen when the patient stands.

Treatment

In some cases, the ganglion disappears for either a short or a long period of time after it has been aspirated and then injected with a corticosteroid. In most cases, however, gan-

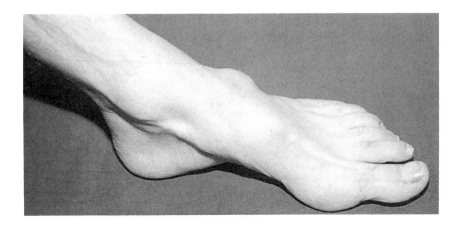

Figure 17–44 Clinical photograph of a ganglion coming from the tendon sheath of the extensor digitorum longus. This ganglion was successfully eliminated after three sessions of aspiration and the injection of 0.2 mL of triamcinolone acetonide (10 mg/mL).

glions recur. Therefore, surgery is indicated in patients for whom a ganglion may cause significant problems.

PLANTAR FIBROMATOSIS (DUPUYTREN'S CONTRACTURE)

About one third of all patients with plantar fibromatosis (a cordlike or nodular growth of collagenous fibers) also have Dupuytren's contracture in the hand. Most patients have a slightly sensitive nodule on the sole of the foot at the level of the flexor hallucis longus tendon (Figure 17–45), just proximal to the head of the first metatarsal. Sometimes, two or three slightly larger nodules occur more proximal at the sole of the foot. These nodules are firmly connected to the medial edge of the plantar fascia. Contractures, such as those seen in the hand, seldom occur in the foot.

Clinical Findings

Because the nodules are located at a place where relatively little weight bearing occurs,

there is usually minimal pain. The nodules are palpable and usually easily seen.

Treatment

A soft inlay for the shoe is recommended when the patient complains of pain. In general, the best treatment is just to reassure the patient by providing a thorough explanation of the disorder. Surgery is rarely necessary.

SUBTENDINOUS ACHILLES BURSITIS

Subtendinous Achilles bursitis is an inflammation of the bursa between the proximal part of the calcaneal tuberosity and the Achilles tendon. This lesion usually occurs as the result of chronic irritation, for instance a thickening of the Achilles tendon or a Haglund exostosis (see Figure 17–30).

Clinical Findings

The patient complains of pain at the posterior aspect of the ankle, increasing at end-range plantar flexion of the ankle.

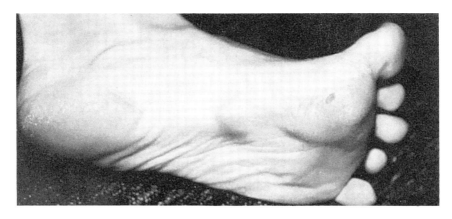

Figure 17–45 Clinical photograph of a nodule in the flexor hallucis longus tendon, characteristic of plantar fibromatosis.

Functional Examination

Sometimes toe raises are painful. The best way to differentiate this lesion from an Achilles tendon problem is by means of an injection of a local anesthetic.

Treatment

The treatment consists of an injection (after aspiration) of a local anesthetic. In instances of recurrence, an injection of corticosteroid can be given.

SUBCUTANEOUS CALCANEAL BURSITIS

The subcutaneous calcaneal bursa lies between the Achilles tendon and the skin and can become irritated through pressure from footwear. An excessively hard or high heel counter is usually involved. A Haglund exostosis can also be a possible cause of a subcutaneous calcaneal bursitis (see Figure 17–30). Often, after a period of time, thickening and hardening of the skin occur. Sometimes this is called the "winter heel" syndrome.

Clinical Findings

The patient complains of pain at the posterior aspect of the heel when walking or running. Often there is visible swelling and redness.

Functional Examination

Although the functional examination is negative, there is some local tenderness to palpation.

Treatment

The patient should wear shoes or boots with a soft heel counter. If necessary, the bursa can be injected with a local anesthetic.

* * *

For an overview of the common pathologies of the ankle and foot, refer to Appendix B, Algorithms for the Diagnosis and Treatment of the Lower Extremeties

17.9   ORTHESIOLOGY

A functional orthotic is a mechanical assistive device that is used to get the foot to function as physiologically correctly as possible.[8] A functional orthotic should never support the medial arch; rather, it should correct the abnormal (hyper)mobility of the foot. Either supple or hard materials can be used.

FUNCTIONAL SUPPLE ORTHOTICS

The making of these orthotics is based on measurements taken during the biomechanical foot examination and conclusions reached during a walking or running analysis. Such orthotics are best made by a podiatrist. As a working plan, the footprint of the patient is made with the help of a podograph. The orthotic should consist primarily of two elements: a supinating or pronating element, which particularly influences the function of the subtalar complex, and an element that is placed under the head of the first metatarsal to influence the function of the first metatarsal.

FUNCTIONAL RIGID ORTHOTICS

Functional rigid orthotics are made based on a cast of the foot, in which the correction principle is derived from the measurement results of the biomechanical examination and the conclusions of the walking analysis. The essential aim of these orthotics is to restrict abnormal pronation. Body weight is an important factor in the choice of material thickness.

Chapter 18

Treatment Techniques in Lesions of the Ankle and Foot

COMPRESSION NEUROPATHY OF THE SUPERFICIAL PERONEAL NERVE

Functional Examination

Passive inversion of the foot is sometimes painful. The remaining parts of the functional examination of the foot and knee are negative. For other clinical findings, refer to Chapter 19.

INJECTION

When there has not been an obvious inversion trauma of the foot before the onset of the symptoms, differentiation between a compression neuropathy of the superficial peroneal nerve and an L5 nerve root irritation is not always easy. A perineural injection of the superficial peroneal nerve can help confirm the diagnosis.

Position of the Patient

The patient either sits or lies supine on the treatment table.

Position of the Physician

The physician sits or stands next to the treatment table, at the patient's affected side.

Performance

The physician carefully brings the foot into the most maximal inversion possible. In most cases, the intermediate ramus of the superficial peroneal nerve becomes visible and is almost always palpable. The intermediate ramus is now followed proximally to the point where the nerve disappears under the deep fascia of the lower leg. Pressure on this point usually evokes the typical symptoms of the patient.

A syringe is filled with 1 mL of a local anesthetic (eg, 1% lidocaine). From distally, a 3-cm long needle is inserted parallel to the nerve (Figure 18–1). When the patient's symptoms are provoked, the needle is slightly withdrawn, and the local anesthetic is injected. If the symptoms disappear, the injection is repeated 1 week later with 1 mL of a corticosteroid.

Results from the injections are usually good. Surgery is needed only in rare instances.

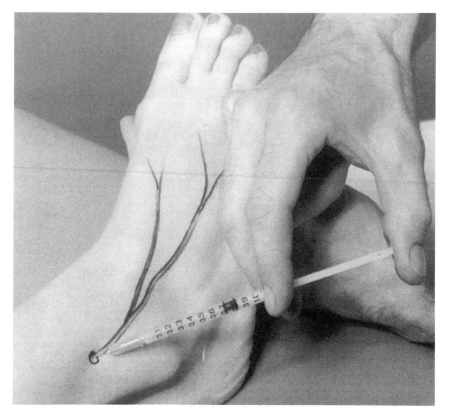

Figure 18–1 Perineural injection of the superficial peroneal nerve at the level of the compression site.

COMPRESSION NEUROPATHY OF THE DEEP PERONEAL NERVE

Functional Examination

Passive plantar flexion of the foot combined with passive flexion of the toes is often painful (as a result of the exertion of stretch forces on the nerve). In severe cases, there is a loss of strength in toe extension, resulting from a deficit of the extensor digitorum brevis. For other clinical findings, refer to Chapter 19.

INJECTION

Compression of the deep peroneal nerve usually occurs at the level of the base of the first metatarsal, where the nerve penetrates the deep fascia of the foot.

Position of the Patient

The patient sits or lies supine on the treatment table.

Position of the Physician

The physician sits or stands at the foot of the treatment table.

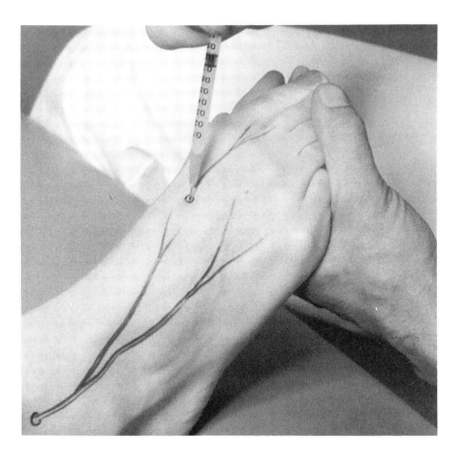

Figure 18–2 Perineural injection of the deep peroneal nerve at the level of the base of the first metatarsal.

Performance

The physician holds the foot and the toes in slight plantar flexion with one hand; the other hand locates the exact site of the compression.

A syringe is filled with 1 mL of local anesthetic (eg, 1% lidocaine), and a 3-cm long needle is inserted at an angle of about 70° in relation to the great toe (Figure 18–2). The needle is pushed in until there is an increase in the symptoms from the nerve. Then the needle is withdrawn slightly, and the solution is slowly injected.

If the symptoms decrease or completely disappear right after the injection, the injection is repeated 1 week later with 1 mL of a corticosteroid. If necessary, this injection can be repeated several times at 2-week intervals. If the symptoms continually recur, surgery is indicated.

TRAUMATIC ARTHRITIS OF THE TALOCRURAL JOINT

Functional Examination

There is a capsular pattern of painfully limited motions of the talocrural joint. Plantar flexion is usually slightly more limited than extension.

INTRAARTICULAR INJECTION

An intraarticular injection with a corticosteroid is only indicated when conservative measures, such as physical therapy and medication, do not provide the desired results.

Position of the Patient

The patient is supine on the treatment table with the foot in approximately 10° plantar flexion.

Position of the Physician

The physician sits or stands next to the foot of the treatment table. With one hand, the physician holds the patient's foot in 10° plantar flexion; the injection is given with the other hand.

Performance

The physician locates the joint space between the tibia and talus and between the tendons of the extensor digitorum longus and the tibialis anterior. Two milliliters of a corticosteroid is injected with a 3-cm needle, inserted vertically (Figure 18–3).

If a stubborn traumatic arthritis or a traumatized arthrosis is concerned, the injection almost always results in a cure. In rare instances, when the arthritis originates from one of the rheumatic diseases, several injections can be given at 3- to 6-month intervals.

Follow-Up

After the injection, the patient should keep weight off the affected leg for 3 days.

LOOSE BODY IN THE TALOCRURAL JOINT

Functional Examination

The functional examination of the foot is usually negative. Sometimes extension or plantar flexion of the ankle can be painful or limited.

MANIPULATION

Position of the Patient

The patient is supine on the treatment table, with the affected foot positioned just over the edge. The distal part of the lower leg is supported by a small pillow or towel roll.

Position of the Therapist

The therapist stands at the foot of the treatment table. If the left foot is affected, the therapist grasps the patient's heel from medial with the left hand, bracing this hand against the edge of the table. The right hand grasps the midfoot from the lateral aspect; the little finger is at the level of the talar neck.

Position of the Assistant

The assistant stands next to the treatment table, at the patient's affected side. The assistant grasps the patient's lower leg just distal to the knee and fixes it against the treatment table.

Two mobilization belts can be used when an assistant is not available. One belt is placed at the groin to prevent the patient from sliding distally. The other belt fixates the lower leg to prevent the knee from flexing.

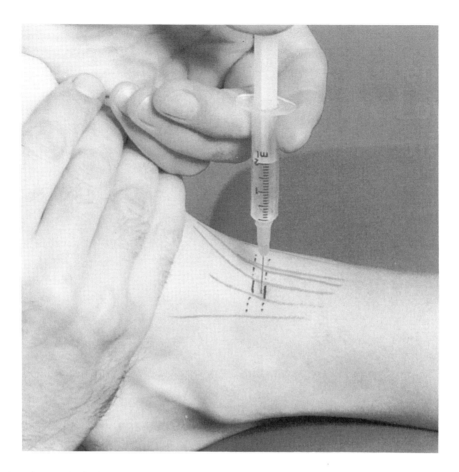

Figure 18–3 Intraarticular injection of the talocrural joint.

Performance

The therapist stands with one leg in front of the other and shifts the body weight backward. In so doing, the talocrural joint is placed in traction. As a first step, the therapist positions the patient's foot into a position of eversion. From here, the therapist makes as large a circumduction movement as possible with the patient's foot, moving from eversion toward inversion (in so doing, the therapist avoids reaching the end-range inversion position). The hand grasping the heel allows only slight motion; the other hand performs most of the movement. This circumduction movement, from eversion toward inversion, is performed quickly (manipulatively), after which the foot, which is still under traction, is brought slowly back to the initial position (Figure 18–4). This maneuver is repeated two to four times.

If the functional examination was negative before the treatment, the patient should decide during the next several days whether the treatment was effective. If the functional examination was positive, the painful and restricted movements are retested after

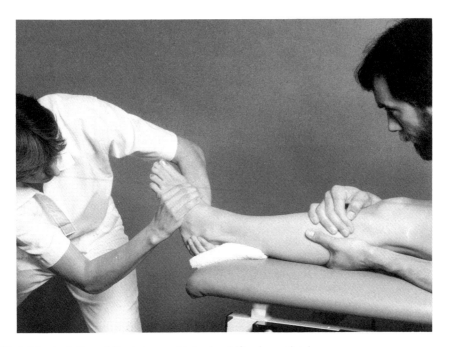

Figure 18–4 Manipulation of the talocrural joint to shift a loose body.

the manipulation. If the treatment provided improvement, the same maneuver can be repeated several times. If there is no change in the findings, the manipulation can be performed in an eversion direction.

In most cases, one to three treatments are necessary to achieve complete relief of the symptoms. If the treatment is ineffective and the symptoms are severe, the loose body may have to be removed surgically.

ANTERIOR TIBIOTALAR COMPRESSION SYNDROME

Functional Examination

Passive extension of the ankle is painful and sometimes limited. Passive plantar flexion of the ankle can be painful (as a result of the exertion of stretch forces on the affected soft tissue structures). For other clinical findings, refer to Chapter 17.

INJECTION

Although not always successful as a treatment for this syndrome, an injection should be tried before surgery is contemplated. Ap-

propriate surgery would include removal of the exostoses and affected soft tissue structures at the anterodistal aspect of the tibia and at the talar neck.

Position of the Patient

The patient is supine on the treatment table.

Position of the Physician

The physician sits or stands next to the foot of the treatment table. One hand holds the patient's foot in slight plantar flexion; the other hand gives the injection.

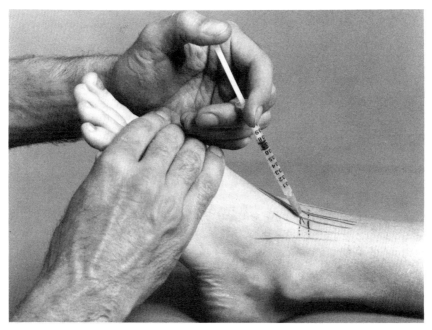

A

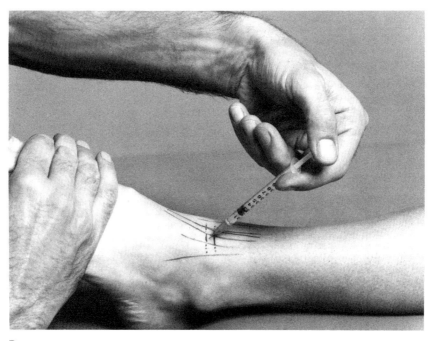

B

Figure 18–5 (**A**) Injection of the irritated soft tissue structures at the anterodistal aspect of the tibia in anterior tibiotalar compression syndrome. (**B**) Injection of the irritated soft tissue structures at the talar neck.

Performance

The physician locates the site of most tenderness. A Mantoux syringe with a 3-cm needle is filled with 1 mL of corticosteroid. Both the anterodistal aspect of the tibia and the neck of the talus are injected in a dropwise fashion, directed by the patient's pain (Figure 18–5).

Follow-Up

The patient should not put weight on the affected leg for 3 days after the injection. Usually, a second injection is necessary after 10 to 14 days. If the treatment has minimal or no effect, surgical exostectomy is the only alternative treatment.

POSTERIOR TIBIOTALAR COMPRESSION SYNDROME

Functional Examination

Passive plantar flexion of the ankle is the most painful test. Passive extension of the ankle is usually somewhat painful (as a result of the exertion of stretch forces on the irritated soft tissue structures).

INJECTION

Compression of the soft tissue structures between the talus and tibia at the posterior side of the ankle can occur when the lateral tubercle of the posterior process of the talus is abnormally large or when there is an os trigonum. This condition may be the result of plantar flexion trauma (usually inversion trauma) and is sometimes seen in dancers who dance on point. In some cases, an injection with a corticosteroid is indicated (refer to Chapter 17 for more specific information about this disorder).

Position of the Patient

The patient is prone on the treatment table, with the affected foot hanging just over the edge.

Position of the Physician

The physician stands or sits next to the foot of the treatment table. One hand holds the patient's foot in 0° so that the distance between talus and tibia at the posterior aspect is somewhat widened and the soft tissue is brought under slight tension.

Performance

A 2-mL syringe is filled with 1 mL of corticosteroid and 1 mL of local anesthetic. A 5-cm needle is inserted almost vertically, lateral to the Achilles tendon, at a point approximately 2 cm proximal to the distal point of the lateral malleolus. After the needle is pushed in 3 to 4 cm, the affected tissue is usually reached.

Guided by where the patient feels pain, the posterodistal edge of the tibia (proximal) and the lateral process of the talus (distal) are injected in a dropwise fashion (Figure 18–6). The joint capsule and the fatty tissue, in particular, are responsible for the symptoms.

Follow-Up

The patient should not put weight on the affected leg for 3 days after the injection. Afterward, the ankle can be taped to restrict maximal plantar flexion. Two weeks later, if there is significant improvement, a second injection can be given. Surgery is recommended in instances of recurrence.

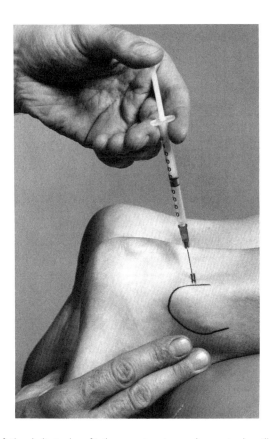

Figure 18–6 Injection of the irritated soft tissue structures in posterior tibiotalar compression syndrome.

TRAUMATIC ARTHRITIS OF THE SUBTALAR JOINT

Functional Examination

There is a capsular pattern of painful limited motions of the subtalar joint; varus movement is much more limited and painful than valgus.

INTRAARTICULAR INJECTION

An intraarticular injection in the subtalar joint is rarely indicated. Although it can offer relief lasting from months to years for patients with rheumatoid arthritis of this joint, it is only given when relief cannot be obtained from oral medication. Other disorders that may benefit from this injection include subacute traumatic arthritis and subacute arthritis in adults (refer to Chapter 17 for more specific information about these disorders).

Position of the Patient

The patient lies either supine or in sidelying with the affected side on the treatment table. In the first position, the knee is flexed and the hip is abducted and externally rotated so that the foot is supported flat on the table. In the second position, the patient lies in such a way that the medial side of the

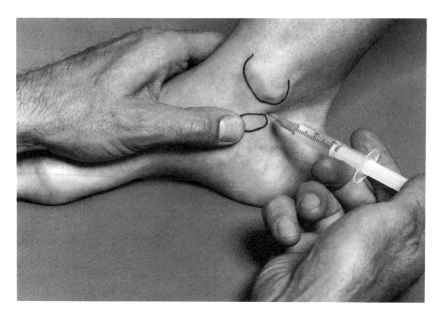

A

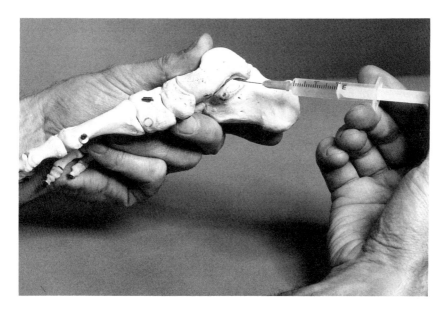

B

Figure 18–7 (**A**) Intraarticular injection in the anterior part of the subtalar joint. (**B**) Skeletal model of the intraarticular injection in the anterior part of the subtalar joint.

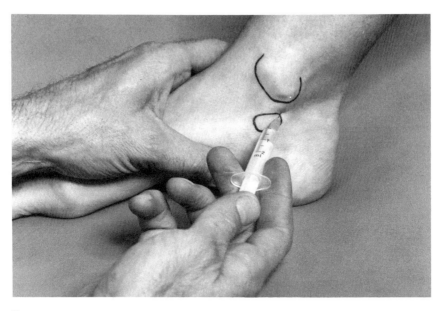

C

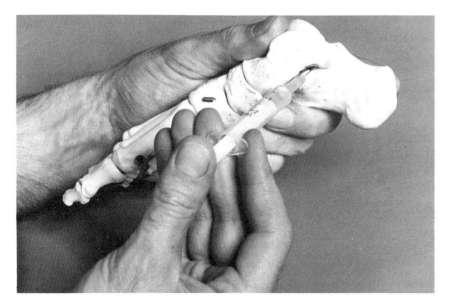

D

Figure 18–7 (C) Intraarticular injection in the posterior part of the subtalar joint. **(D)** Skeletal model of the intraarticular injection in the posterior part of the subtalar joint.

foot is up and the lateral side of the foot is flat against the table.

Position of the Physician

The physician stands or sits next to the treatment table, facing the medial side of the foot. The foot is usually in a valgus position because of the capsular pattern of limitations. The physician supports the foot in this position and gives the injection from medial.

Performance

First, the proximal edge of the sustentaculum tali is located. A 2-mL syringe is filled with a corticosteroid, and a 2-cm long needle is inserted horizontally just above the sustentaculum tali in the direction of the tarsal sinus at the lateral side of the foot. If the needle contacts bone after about 1 cm, the direction of the needle is slightly changed so that it can

be pushed farther in without resistance. The tip of the needle now lies in the anterior part of the subtalar joint, and here 1 mL of solution is injected (Figure 18–7, A and B).

The needle is now withdrawn to a point just underneath the skin and is reinserted at a 45° angle more posterior, where the posterior part of the subtalar joint is injected (Figure 18-7, C and D).

Follow-Up

The patient should not put weight on the affected leg for at least 3 days. Usually, the pain disappears after several days, but the limitation of motion usually remains for quite some time. This limitation can be treated with joint-specific mobilization. If the pain has not completely disappeared after 2 weeks, a second injection should be given.

HYPERMOBILITY OF THE SUBTALAR JOINT

TAPING OR BRACING

Hypermobility of the subtalar joint especially occurs as the result of inversion trauma. If this hypermobility is not corrected, achillodynia, shin splints, or plantar fasciitis can occur, particularly after vigorous sports activities (such as those requiring running and jumping). The following description emphasizes how, in particular, the varus movement of the calcaneus can be restricted.

Position of the Patient

The patient is supine on the treatment table, with the foot and the distal half of the lower leg extended over the edge.

Position of the Therapist

The therapist sits or stands at the foot of the treatment table, facing the patient's affected foot. With one hand, the therapist

holds the patient's foot in 0° extension. The other hand applies the tape.

Performance

First, the elastic foundation is applied as described in "Inversion (or Varus) Trauma" (Figure 18–8A). Next, the therapist applies two strips of nonelastic tape, beginning at the medial malleolus, to bring the calcaneus into the proper position, being careful not to overcorrect (Figure 18–8B). These fixation strips cross over each other at the lateral malleolus and run proximally about 20 cm farther. The tape construction is ended with the same taping technique as described in "Inversion (or Varus) Trauma" (Figure 18–8C).

When the main problem in the subtalar complex is an abnormal valgus position or valgus tipping of the calcaneus, the ankle can be taped in a similar manner, but the strips are applied opposite to the description above.

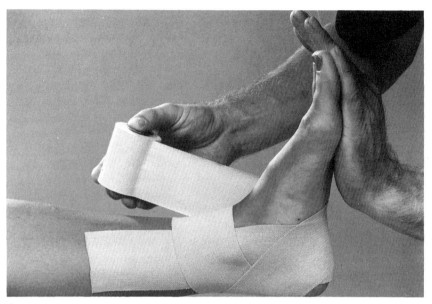

A

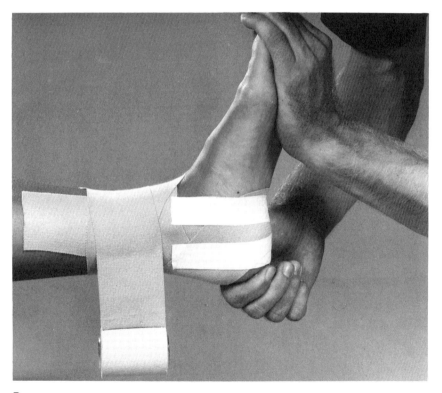

B

Figure 18–8 Tape application for varus hypermobility of the subtalar joint. (**A**) Application of the elastic foundation. (**B**) Tape to bring the calcaneus into proper position.

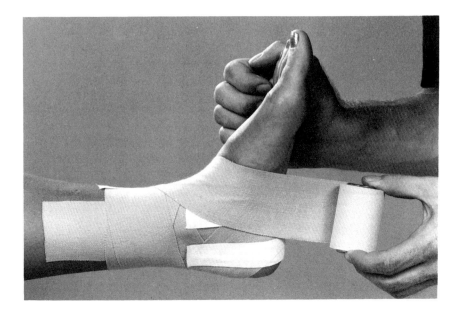

Figure 18–8 **(C)** Completion of taping.

Taping before sports activities should continue for several weeks after symptoms have disappeared. This treatment is generally combined with a corrective orthotic that is either supportive or shock absorbing, depending on the severity of the lesion.

LOOSE BODY IN THE SUBTALAR JOINT

Functional Examination

The examination is usually negative. Sometimes varus motion is significantly limited and painful with a muscle spasm as an end-feel.

MANIPULATION

A loose body (usually cartilage) can cause intense, shooting pain, particularly in patients with arthrosis of the subtalar joint but sometimes also in patients without an obvious disorder. The intense pain makes weight bearing on that foot momentarily impossible.

Position of the Patient

The patient is in a prone position on the treatment table with the foot hanging just over the edge. The distal part of the lower leg rests on a small pillow or towel roll.

Position of the Therapist

The therapist stands at the foot of the treatment table, facing the patient's affected foot. With both hands, the therapist grasps the patient's heel: The thumbs cross over the upper edge of the calcaneal tuberosity, the fingers lie at the dorsum of the midfoot, and the

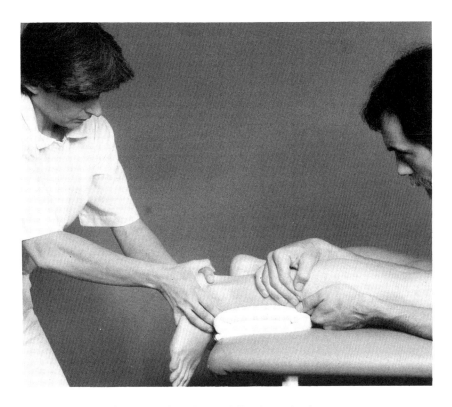

Figure 18–9 Manipulation of the subtalar joint to shift a loose body.

little fingers are at the plantar surface of the foot (if possible). The therapist shifts the body weight backward and, in so doing, applies as much traction as possible on the subtalar joint.

Position of the Assistant

The assistant stands next to the treatment table, at the patient's affected side. With both hands, the assistant fixes the patient's lower leg against the treatment table.

Performance

While maintaining traction on the subtalar joint, the therapist pronates both forearms as much as possible. This brings the patient's foot into extension, thus putting the talocrural joint in its maximal close-packed position. The therapist now extends one wrist while simultaneously flexing the other wrist. By quickly alternating both wrists in opposite motions, the therapist induces varus and valgus motions under traction in the subtalar joint. This maneuver is repeated three to six times in rapid succession (Figure 18–9).

If the patient's joint is locked in a valgus position, this technique is almost always successful, and varus motion is immediately restored. It is more difficult to shift the loose body to the extent that it no longer causes painful impingement in the joint. The manipulation should be repeated every 2 to 3 days until the patient no longer has complaints.

SPRAIN OF THE PLANTAR CALCANEONAVICULAR LIGAMENT

Functional Examination

Usually there is hypermobility of the midtarsal joints in extension and plantar flexion. Passive pronation and supination of the midtarsal joints are painful. The plantar calcaneonavicular ligament is tender to palpation.

TRANSVERSE FRICTION

The plantar calcaneonavicular ligament is particularly overloaded in every form or position aberration of the foot in which the calcaneus moves into valgus. In addition to correcting the primary aberration, local transverse friction can provide quick relief of the symptoms.

Position of the Patient

The patient is supine on the treatment table with the leg extended or with the distal part of the lower leg resting on the therapist's thigh and a roll under the knee.

Position of the Therapist

The therapist sits next to the foot of the treatment table, facing the lateral side of the affected foot, or sits on the end of the table with the distal part of the patient's lower leg resting on the lap (Figure 18–10).

With the ipsilateral hand, the therapist holds the patient's foot in about 0° extension, slight abduction, and slight pronation. In so doing, the plantar calcaneonavicular ligament is slightly stretched. The other hand locates

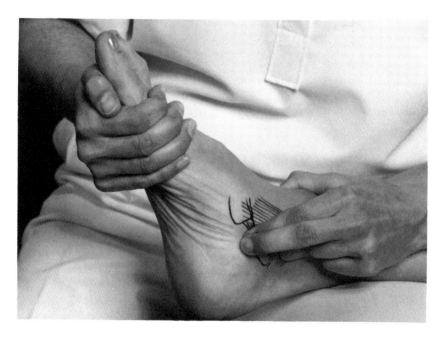

Figure 18–10 Transverse friction of the plantar calcaneonavicular ligament.

the sustentaculum tali and the navicular tuberosity. The ligament runs plantarly between these two bony prominences.

Palpating Performance

With the tip of the palpating index finger, the therapist locates the most tender site. The thumb applies counterpressure from lateral, at the level of the tarsal sinus. The index finger is reinforced by the middle finger and

moves from plantar to dorsal over the ligament during the active phase of the transverse friction. The friction movement is brought about through wrist extension.

Duration

If the position of the foot is corrected by orthotics, only a few treatments of 10 to 15 minutes of transverse friction are normally needed to achieve complete pain relief.

RHEUMATOID ARTHRITIS OF THE FIRST CUNEOMETATARSAL JOINT

Functional Examination

All passive motions of the midfoot can be painful at the end of the range of motion.

INTRAARTICULAR INJECTION

An intraarticular injection is indicated in cases of stubborn traumatic arthritis. This treatment, however, is most often used for cases of rheumatoid arthritis and gout when oral medication does not provide sufficient pain relief.

Position of the Patient

The patient is supine on the treatment table with the foot in the resting (maximal loose-packed) position. The nonaffected side is flexed so that the affected foot can be easily reached.

Position of the Physician

The physician sits or stands next to the treatment table at the patient's nonaffected side, facing the medial side of the affected foot.

Performance

First, the joint space between the medial cuneiform and first metatarsal is precisely located (refer to Chapter 15). A 2-mL syringe is half filled with a corticosteroid. A thin, 2-cm needle is inserted horizontally. After about 1 cm, the tip of the needle is intraarticular, and the solution is injected (Figure 18–11).

Follow-Up

A single injection is usually all that is needed for traumatic arthritis. In rheumatic arthritides, the injection can be repeated at 3- to 6-month intervals. Surgery is the alternative to injection treatment.

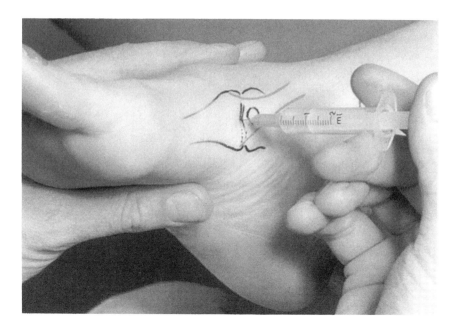

Figure 18–11 Intraarticular injection of the first cuneometatarsal joint.

RHEUMATOID ARTHRITIS OF THE FIRST METATARSOPHALANGEAL JOINT

Functional Examination

There is a capsular limitation of motion; extension of the great toe is more limited than plantar flexion, with pain at the end of each motion.

INTRAARTICULAR INJECTION

An intraarticular injection with a corticosteroid is indicated, and effective, in cases of rheumatoid arthritis, traumatic arthritis, and traumatized arthrosis.

Position of the Patient

The patient is supine on the treatment table with the knee flexed far enough to allow the affected foot to rest completely on the table.

Position of the Physician

With one hand, the physician grasps the proximal phalanx of the great toe and pulls so that traction occurs in the metatarsophalangeal joint. The other hand locates the joint space, which is now widened by the traction. The joint space should be accurately marked.

Performance

A 2-mL syringe is half filled with a corticosteroid, and a 2-cm needle is inserted almost vertically between the first metatarsal and the first proximal phalanx. After the tip of the

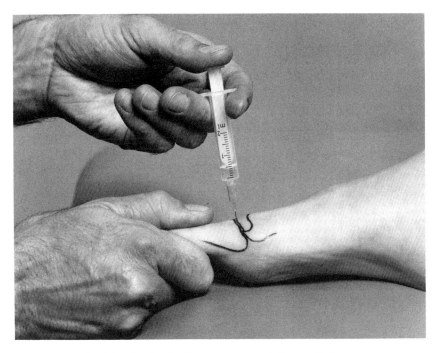

Figure 18–12 Intraarticular injection in the first metatarsophalangeal joint.

needle is intraarticular, the solution is injected. Traction is applied to the joint during the entire injection (Figure 18–12).

Follow-Up

The patient is instructed to load the joint as little as possible for the next 3 days. Particularly in cases of traumatic arthritis, the patient has complete relief of pain within 24 hours.

Note

When there are similar indications, the other metatarsophalangeal joints can be injected in the same way.

SESAMOIDITIS

Functional Examination

Passive extension of the great toe is usually painful. Resisted plantar flexion of the great toe is painful.

INTRAARTICULAR INJECTION

An injection in the joint between the head of the first metatarsal (plantar aspect) and the medial sesamoid bone, which lies in the tendon of the flexor hallucis longus, may be beneficial when an orthotic does not provide effective relief. The cause of a sesamoiditis in this region is traumatic, and the condition can be either acute or chronic.

Position of the Patient

The patient is supine on the treatment table with the foot in the resting (maximally loose-packed) position.

Position of the Physician

The physician sits or stands next to the foot of the treatment table. One hand brings the great toe into slight flexion, which relaxes the tendon of the flexor hallucis longus, allowing for more room between the medial sesamoid bone and the head of the first metatarsal. The other hand locates the medial sesamoid bone and precisely marks its position.

Performance

A Mantoux syringe is half filled (0.5 mL) with a corticosteroid. From a proximal ap-proach, a 2-cm needle is inserted in a plantar-medial direction between the medial sesamoid bone and the first metatarsal. After about 1 cm, the tip of the needle lies in the joint, and the solution is injected (Figure 18–13).

Follow-Up

The patient is advised to keep weight off the foot for 1 week. This treatment is usually effective. After 2 weeks, a second injection is sometimes necessary to achieve complete pain relief.

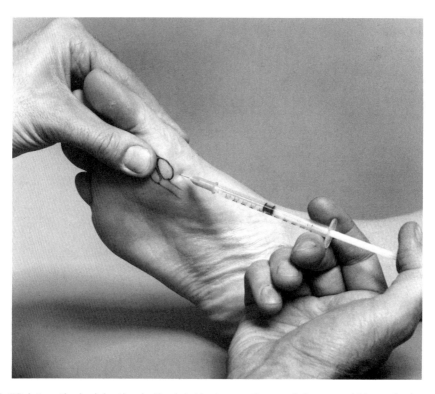

Figure 18–13 Intraarticular injection in the joint between the medial sesamoid bone in the tendon of the flexor hallucis longus and the head of the first metatarsal.

INVERSION (OR VARUS) TRAUMA: GENERAL PRINCIPLES

There is little agreement in the medical literature as to the appropriate treatment after inversion trauma. In spite of the diversity of recommended treatment methods, the results are often the same.

Ankle sprains are common injuries. The classic trauma consists of plantar flexion of the talocrural joint combined with varus motion in the subtalar joint and flexion supination-adduction of the midtarsal joints. This primarily results in an overstretch or rupture of the lateral capsuloligamentous complex of the talocrural joint. Usually, the first structure to be injured is the anterior talofibular ligament, followed by the calcaneofibular ligament. In only 3% of all cases, the posterior talofibular ligament is affected (refer to "Inversion-Varus Trauma" in Chapter 17 for further details).

It is important to analyze not only the position in which the trauma occurred but also the time it took for swelling to appear. Swelling that occurs immediately (within 2 hours of the trauma) indicates a hemarthrosis. If the swelling occurs much later (12 to 24 hours after the trauma), there is effusion or extraarticular swelling.

Functional Examination

In spite of pain and swelling, the functional examination can usually be performed in the acute phase (the phase during which the pain increases). During the examination, stability is tested. Although many stability tests are described in the orthopaedic literature, it appears that in the acute phase only the anterior drawer test can be performed reliably. In the chronic stage, on the other hand, several different stability tests can be performed. If the patient's history and functional examination indicate the presence of an instability, the patient should be referred for specialized testing, to include a thorough radiologic evaluation (refer to "Inversion-Varus Trauma" in Chapter 17 for further details).

Treatment

The presence of a hemarthrosis indicates a partial rupture of the capsuloligamentous complex with or without fractures. In fractures, surgical refixation or immobilization by means of casting is indicated. If there is only hemarthrosis, the joint should be aspirated and then immobilized with a bandage. After several days, the functional examination is repeated.

Directly after inversion trauma, an inflammation in the injured region develops. The duration and intensity of this inflammation phase depend on the amount of tissue damage (it can last up to 4 days). If there are no signs of instability, therapy in the acute stage is aimed at diminishing pain and swelling by means of the following:

- application of ice (three to five times per day for approximately 15 minutes)
- gentle compression by means of taping
- physical therapy electrical stimulation modalities
- effleurage techniques (to include lymph drainage)

Treatment should be administered daily.

In the subacute stage (second to third day), the pain no longer increases. When the affected structures (ligaments or tendons) are treated with transverse friction, there is a decrease in pain. The patient may experience mild discomfort during the treatment or no pain at all. On the third to fourth day after the trauma, collagen synthesis (fibroblast phase) occurs in the injured region. From here on, it is important to prevent the formation of adhesions. Along with transverse friction (for pain relief), active movements should be performed. These movements should be in non–weight bearing and remain within the painless range. By moving the foot within the painless range of motion, slight tension is placed on the affected structures (ligaments, tendons, and tendon sheaths), resulting in a better orientation of the collagen fibers. At home, the patient should also perform gentle range of motion exercises in non–weight bearing several times per day, staying within the limits of pain. In addition, it is important to emphasize the restoration of the normal gait pattern as soon as possible.

If there is a combined lesion, such as an injury to the tendons as well as the ligaments, progression toward full weight bearing should be more conservative. Weight bearing should be gradually increased only after the functional tests indicating lesions of the peroneal tendons are no longer painful. If, after 5 days, there is still severe pain, swelling, and loss of function, additional specific examinations, such as arthrography, should be undertaken. In these instances, there may be more significant lesions, such as capsuloligamentous ruptures or compression (impact) fractures (refer to "Inversion-Varus Trauma" in Chapter 17 for further details).

As the swelling decreases, the affected structures can be more easily reached. The transverse friction can be performed longer, up to 15 minutes, and with more pressure. As a result, the influence on the reparative process of the collagen connective tissue increases, shortening recovery time. In the subacute stage, treatment should be given two to three times per week. Treatment can also be enhanced by taping the ankle.

If the patient is not offered functional treatment, the injury reaches the chronic stage. In this stage there are adhesion formations. Treatment is now directed toward breaking up the adhesions by means of a manipulation. Manipulation is only considered when there is a solitary ligamentous lesion with a residual, minimal limitation of motion (often, only the end-feel is harder). Because the manipulation can be painful, it is preceded by approximately 10 minutes of transverse friction. The functional tests should be repeated after the transverse friction and before the manipulation; sometimes, transverse friction alone is sufficient to resolve the usually minimal limitation of motion. If transverse friction suffices, manipulation is no longer indicated. After the transverse friction and, if necessary, manipulation, it is important for the patient to maintain the newly gained range of motion by performing active exercises within the limits of pain.

INVERSION TRAUMA: SPRAIN OF THE ANTERIOR TALOFIBULAR LIGAMENT

TRANSVERSE FRICTION

The anterior talofibular ligament can be affected at different sites. The following are predilection sites:

- origin of the ligament at the lateral malleolus
- the ligament itself
- insertion of the ligament on the talus

Origin of the Ligament at the Lateral Malleolus

Position of the Patient

The patient is supine on the treatment table with the knee slightly flexed and supported by a roll. The distal part of the lower leg rests on the therapist's thigh.

Position of the Therapist

The therapist sits either on or next to the foot of the table. If, for example, the left foot is being treated, the therapist grasps the patient's forefoot with the right hand and holds the foot in the neutral position. The index finger of the other hand palpates for the most painful site at the origin of the ligament.

Performance

The left index finger, reinforced by the middle finger, is placed just posterior to the lesion against the anterodistal aspect of the lateral malleolus. The left thumb is placed at the medial aspect of the lower leg, just above the medial malleolus, and exerts counterpressure (Figure 18–14). During the active phase of the transverse friction (through extension of the wrist), the index finger moves from posterior to anterior over the lesion. Pressure is exerted in a proximomedial direction (Figure 18–15).

Duration

Transverse friction is applied for different lengths of time and with different amounts of pressure, depending on the stage of recovery. Refer to "Inversion Varus Trauma" in Chapter 17 for this discussion.

Anterior Talofibular Ligament in Its Course

Position of the Patient

The patient is supine on the treatment table, with the knee slightly flexed and supported by a roll. The distal part of the lower leg rests on the therapist's thigh.

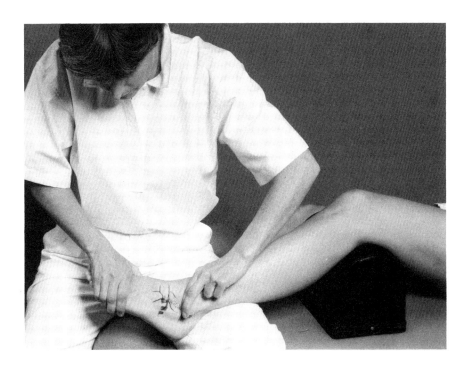

Figure 18–14 Transverse friction of the origin of the anterior talofibular ligament at the lateral malleolus: Initial position.

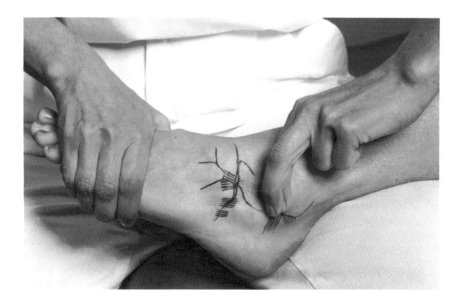

Figure 18–15 Transverse friction of the origin of the anterior talofibular ligament at the anterodistal aspect of the lateral malleolus: Ending position.

Position of the Therapist

The therapist sits either on or next to the foot of the table. If, for example, the left foot is being treated, the therapist grasps the patient's forefoot with the right hand and holds the foot in the resting position or in slight, but painless, inversion. The index finger of the other hand palpates for the most painful site along the course of the ligament.

Performance

The left index finger, reinforced by the middle finger, is placed just plantar to the lesion. The left thumb is placed at the medial aspect of the ankle, just opposite the index finger, and exerts counterpressure. By extension of the wrist during the active phase of the transverse friction, the index finger moves from plantar to dorsal over the ligament. Pressure is exerted in a medial direction (Figure 18–16).

Insertion of the Anterior Talofibular Ligament on the Talus

Position of the Patient

The patient is supine on the treatment table, with the knee slightly flexed and supported by a roll. The distal part of the lower leg rests on the therapist's thigh.

Position of the Therapist

The therapist sits either on or next to the foot of the table. If, for example, the left foot is being treated, the therapist grasps the patient's forefoot with the right hand and holds the foot in the resting position or in slight, but painless, inversion. The index finger of the other hand palpates for the most painful site at the insertion of the ligament.

Performance

The left index finger, reinforced by the middle finger, is placed just plantar to the le-

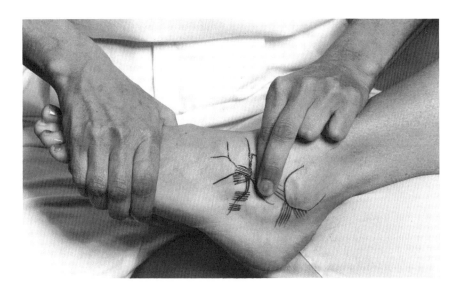

Figure 18–16 Transverse friction of the anterior talofibular ligament in its course.

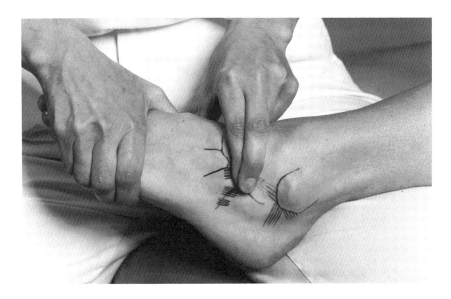

Figure 18–17 Transverse friction of the insertion of the anterior talofibular ligament on the talus.

sion. The left thumb is placed at the medial aspect of the ankle, slightly distal to the index finger, and exerts counterpressure. Through extension of the wrist during the active phase of the transverse friction, the index finger moves from plantar to dorsal and slightly distal over the lesion. Pressure is exerted in a mediodistal direction (Figure 18–17).

INJECTION

If transverse friction at the origin or insertion of the anterior talofibular ligament, combined with partial immobilization through a brace or taping, is ineffective in providing pain relief, a local injection with a corticosteroid is indicated.

Position of the Patient

The patient is supine on the treatment table.

Position of the Physician

The physician sits or stands next to the foot of the treatment table, facing the affected foot. With one hand, the physician positions the foot in slight inversion.

Performance

A Mantoux syringe is filled with 0.5 mL of corticosteroid. The origin of the ligament is injected at the anterodistal aspect of the lateral malleolus. A 2-cm needle is used, and the injection is done in dropwise fashion guided by the patient's pain (Figure 18–18).

Follow-Up

The patient should not put weight on the affected leg for 3 days after the injection. After 2 weeks, the functional examination is repeated. A second injection is seldom indicated. One month after the injection, the patient can resume sports.

INVERSION TRAUMA: SPRAIN OF THE CALCANEOFIBULAR LIGAMENT

TRANSVERSE FRICTION

The calcaneofibular ligament is almost always affected at its insertion on the lateral malleolus.

Position of the Patient

The patient is supine on the treatment table, with the knee slightly flexed and supported by a roll. The distal part of the lower leg rests on the therapist's thigh.

Position of the Therapist

The therapist sits either on or next to the foot of the treatment table. If, for example, the left foot is being treated, the therapist grasps the patient's forefoot with the right hand and holds the foot in slight plantar flexion and pronation. In this position, the origin of the calcaneofibular ligament can best be reached.

Performance

The left index finger, reinforced by the middle finger, is placed just posterior to the origin of the ligament. The left thumb is placed at the medial side of the lower leg, above the medial malleolus, and exerts counterpressure. Through extension of the wrist during the active phase of the transverse friction, the index finger is moved from posterolateral to anteromedial over the lesion. Pressure is exerted in a proximomedial direction (Figure 18–19).

Duration

Transverse friction is performed for different lengths of time and with different

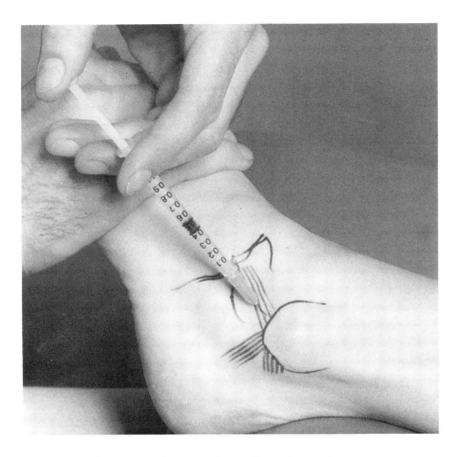

Figure 18–18 Injection of the origin of the anterior talofibular ligament.

amounts of pressure, depending on the stage of recovery. Refer to Chapter 17, the inversion-varus trauma section, for this discussion.

INJECTION

If transverse friction at the origin of the calcaneofibular ligament, combined with partial immobilization through a brace or taping, is ineffective in providing pain relief, a local injection with a corticosteroid is indicated.

Position of the Patient

The patient is supine on the treatment table.

Position of the Physician

The physician sits or stands next to the foot of the treatment table, facing the affected foot. With one hand, the physician positions the foot in slight plantar flexion, supination, and adduction.

Performance

A Mantoux syringe with a 2-cm long needle is filled with 0.5 mL of corticosteroid. The needle is inserted from lateral and plantar at the level of the origin of the ligament at the most distal aspect of the lateral malleolus. The lesion is injected using the dropwise technique as directed by the patient's pain (Figure 18–20).

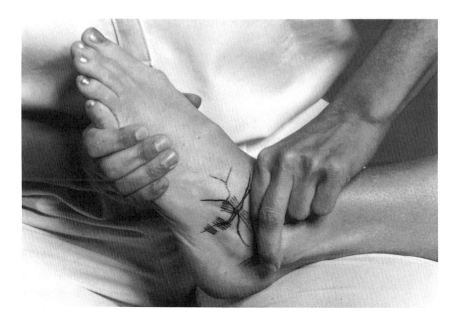

Figure 18–19 Transverse friction of the origin of the calcaneofibular ligament at the lateral malleolus.

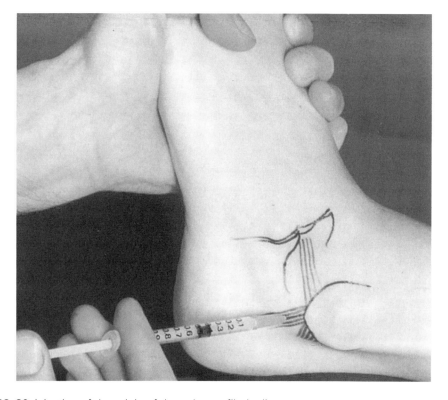

Figure 18–20 Injection of the origin of the calcaneofibular ligament.

Follow-Up

The patient should not put load on the affected leg for 3 days after the injection. After 2 weeks, the functional examination is repeated. As is the case with the anterior talofibular ligament, a second injection is seldom indicated. One month after the injection, the patient can resume sports.

INVERSION TRAUMA: SPRAIN OF THE CALCANEOCUBOID LIGAMENT

TRANSVERSE FRICTION

In some cases, a lesion of the ligaments between the calcaneus and cuboid occurs as a result of inversion trauma of the foot in conjunction with a sprain of the anterior talofibular and calcaneofibular ligaments. Usually, the middle and superior ligaments are affected (the superior ligament is part of the bifurcate ligament).

Position of the Patient

The patient is supine on the treatment table, with the knee slightly flexed and supported by a roll. The distal part of the lower leg rests on the therapist's thigh.

Position of the Therapist

The therapist sits either on or next to the foot of the treatment table. If, for example, the left foot is being treated, the therapist grasps the patient's forefoot with the right hand and holds the foot in slight inversion.

Performance

Through palpation, the lesion is located; in most cases, it lies at the level of the calcaneocuboid joint space. The left index finger, reinforced by the middle finger, is placed just plantar to the affected ligament. The thumb gives counterpressure at the medial side of the foot as the index finger performs the transverse friction from plantar-lateral to dorsomedial over the lesion. As described for the other lateral ligaments, the wrist extends during the active phase of the transverse friction (Figure 18–21).

Duration

Transverse friction is performed for different lengths of time and with different amounts of pressure, depending on the stage of recovery. Refer to Chapter 17, the inversion-varus trauma section, for this discussion.

MANIPULATION

Manipulative treatment of the lateral collateral capsuloligamentous complex and of the calcaneocuboid ligament is only indicated in the chronic stage, which in some cases occurs after inversion trauma. Transverse friction of the affected structures should always be performed before this manipulative treatment.

Position of the Patient

The patient is supine on the treatment table.

Position of the Therapist

The therapist stands next to the end of the treatment table, facing the affected foot. If, for example, the right side is to be treated, the therapist grasps the mid- and forefoot of the patient with the left hand; the other hand, approaching from the medial aspect, grasps the calcaneus.

Performance

The therapist's left hand brings the patient's foot into the greatest inversion possible; at the same time, the other hand brings the patient's calcaneus into varus. While the .

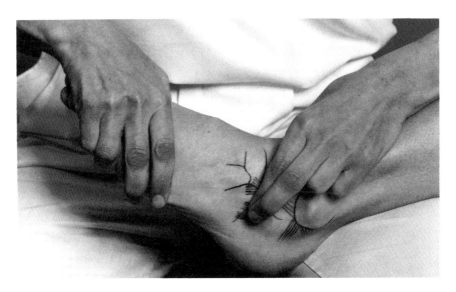

Figure 18–21 Transverse friction of the middle calcaneocuboid ligament.

calcaneus is held in maximal varus, the therapist brings the rest of the foot into slightly more inversion (plantar flexion, adduction, and supination). This is done by means of a quick and slight adduction movement with the right shoulder (Figure 18–22). In many cases, a sound of "tearing cloth" is heard. This maneuver is usually performed only once. A second manipulation is rarely necessary.

It is important for the patient to maintain the regained range of motion through appropriate exercise

Taping

In the last several years, it has been emphasized that the sooner a lesion of the musculoskeletal system is allowed to move, the faster and better the healing will be. This is especially true for injuries to the capsuloligamentous complex. The affected structures should move only within certain limits, however. Painful motions should be prevented as much as possible. The use of taping techniques to immobilize partially the affected member is an ideal way to permit reha-

bilitative activity within safe limits. After inversion trauma, taping can be an ideal alternative to immobilization in a cast or surgery.

The tape construction described in this section is easy to apply and allows the patient to walk normally. The tape bandage effectively prevents supination and varus movement of the foot, thus providing protection for the injured lateral ligaments. Taping can be done as soon as most of the swelling goes down and is repeated two to three times per week in conjunction with transverse friction therapy. A 6- or 8-cm wide elastic tape is used, depending on the size of the foot. The 6-cm width can be used for women and for men with a shoe size of 10 or smaller.

Position of the Patient

The patient is supine on the treatment table, with the foot and distal half of the lower leg hanging over the edge.

Position of the Therapist

The therapist sits or stands at the foot of the table, facing the patient's affected foot.

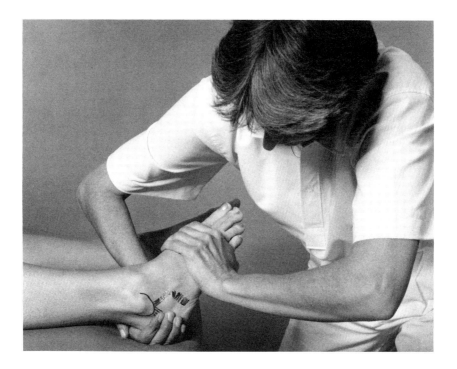

Figure 18–22 Manipulation of the lateral ligaments of the ankle in the chronic stage after a sprain.

With one hand, the therapist holds the patient's foot in 0° of extension. The patient should not actively hold the foot in this position because the foot extensors over the dorsum of the foot contract and become more prominent, leading to a less stable tape construction.

The taping is begun on the medial side of the lower leg, about 20 cm proximal to the medial malleolus (Figure 18–23A). From there, the tape is pulled along the lower leg to the medial edge of the foot, then underneath the foot to the lateral side and obliquely back-

ward to the Achilles tendon (Figure 18–23B).

The tape is now brought around behind the Achilles tendon. In so doing, the elasticity of the tape is pulled out, and a circle is then made around the lower leg just above the malleoli (Figure 18–23, C and D). Once again, at the Achilles tendon the tape is brought farther medially over the calcaneus, just under (plantar to) the medial malleolus, to the medial edge of the foot (Figure 18–23E).

From the medial edge of the foot, a circular loop is made over the midfoot (the elasticity is pulled out of the tape) until the lateral edge of

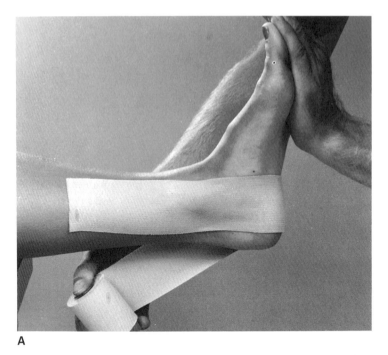

A

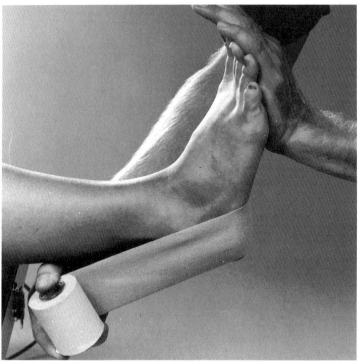

B

Figure 18–23 Foundation taping for inversion trauma of the left ankle. (**A**) Beginning of the foundation tape, medial view. (**B**) Lateral view of **A**.

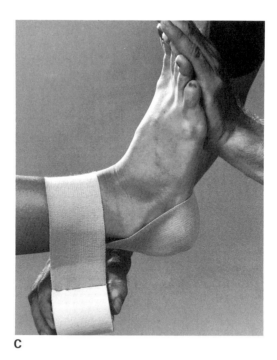

C

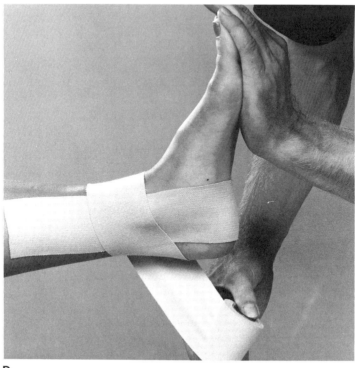

D

Figure 18–23 (**C**) Bringing the tape around behind the Achilles tendon, lateral view. (**D**) Medial view of **C**.

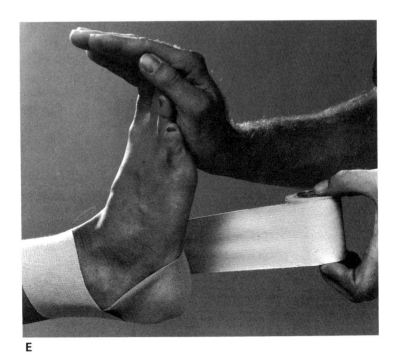

E

Figure 18–23 (**E**) Bringing the tape farther medially over the calcaneus, lateral view.

the foot is again reached (Figure 18–23F). From the lateral edge of the foot, the tape is brought in a proximal and medial direction to a point just proximal to the medial malleolus (Figure 18–23, G and H). During this movement, the elasticity is again pulled out of the tape. The foundation taping is then finished with a circular loop around the lower leg above the malleoli, slightly above the first circular loop (Figure 18–23I).

After the foundation tape, 2-cm wide elastic tape is applied to restrict the motions that occur during inversion trauma. The first tape starts on the medial side, just anterior to the medial malleolus, and goes straight down to the medial edge of the foot, underneath the foot, over the lateral malleolus, and to a point about 20 cm proximal to the lateral malleolus but on the anterior aspect of the lower leg. A second strip also begins medially, but just posterior to the medial malleolus, and runs parallel to the first strip to the lateral side of

the foot, passes over the lateral malleolus where it crosses the first strip, and ends at a point about 20 cm above the lateral malleolus but more at the posterior aspect of the lower leg (Figure 18–24A). These two stabilization strips limit the varus movement of the calcaneus.

The calcaneus, however, has to be fixed in the midposition, and this is accomplished with two more strips of tape. From the lateral side of the ankle, as previously described but now in reverse, two strips are pulled medially to cross over each other at the medial malleolus (Figure 18–24B). These strips are pulled less taut than the first two, because in our opinion, the function should now be more a facilitating one than a stabilizing one.

The next two strips begin at the middle of the sole of the foot, between the big toe and little toe, at an angle of 45° in relation to the transverse arch. The first strip runs proximally over the base of the fifth metatarsal,

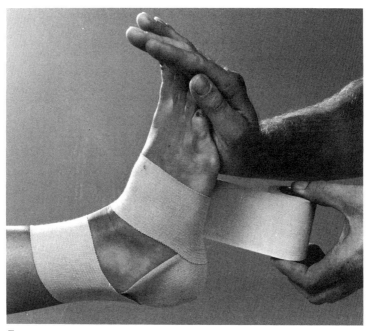

F

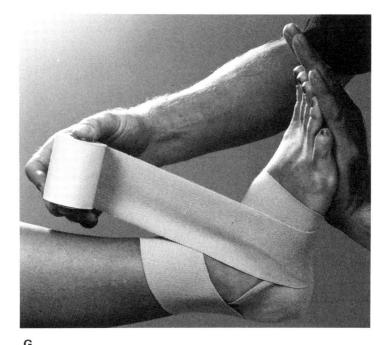

G

Figure 18–23 (**F**) Making a circular loop over the midfoot, lateral view. (**G**) Bringing the tape just proximal to the medial malleolus, lateral view.

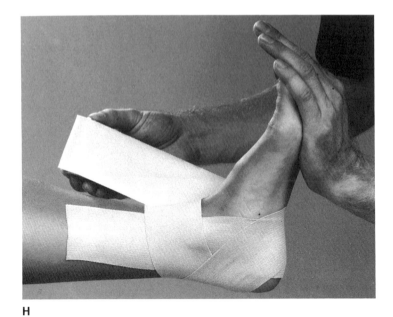

H

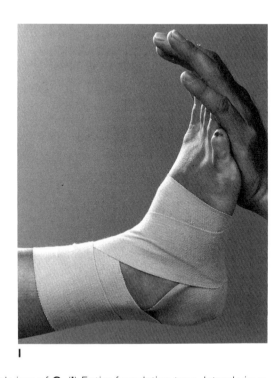

I

Figure 18–23 (**H**) Medial view of **G**. (**I**) Entire foundation tape, lateral view.

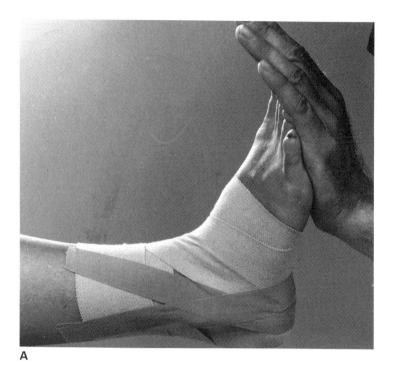

A

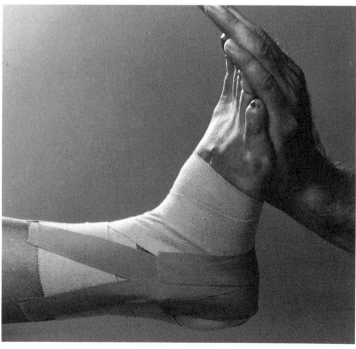

B

Figure 18–24 Stabilization taping for inversion trauma. (**A**) First two stabilization strips, lateral view. (**B**) Second two stabilization strips, lateral view.

anterior to the lateral malleolus, and ends on the circular loop of tape at the lower leg. Another strip of tape is applied following the same course and overlapping the first strip by two thirds (Figure 18–24C; be careful to avoid overcorrection).

The next two strips originate from the same point as the previous two strips but make a 90° angle to these strips on the sole of the foot. They then run to the medial edge of the foot, anterior to the medial malleolus, and end on the circular loop of tape at the lower leg.

Once the stabilization taping has been applied, the construction is finished with simple taping as reinforcement. The reinforcement tape begins at the medial side (see Figure 18–23A), but now, upon reaching the lateral edge of the foot, two circular loops are made around the midfoot. When again at the lateral edge of the foot, the tape is brought in a proximal direction (Figure 18–25A).

At this moment, the tape is pulled taut and then is pulled over the talus to a point just proximal to the medial malleolus. Here the taping is finished with one or two circular loops around the lower leg at the level of and just proximal to the first circular loops from the foundation construction (Figure 18–25, B and C).

After finishing the taping, the therapist now assesses, both actively and passively, the stability of the construction. If the stability is not sufficient, the entire taping construction must be repeated. Additionally, the gait pattern is evaluated, and the appropriate instructions are given to correct any deviations. The proper gait pattern, without substitution movements and deviations, is extremely important for proprioceptive and physiologic recovery. Weight bearing on the affected extremity should be gradually increased during the course of the first week after the trauma. The taping construction should be regularly removed before transverse friction treatment and reapplied after appropriate care is given to the skin.

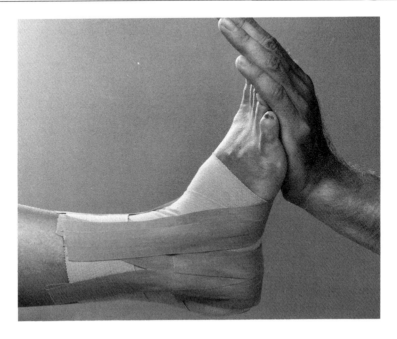

Figure 18–24 (**C**) Two strips running from the sole of the foot to the anterolateral aspect of the lower leg, lateral view.

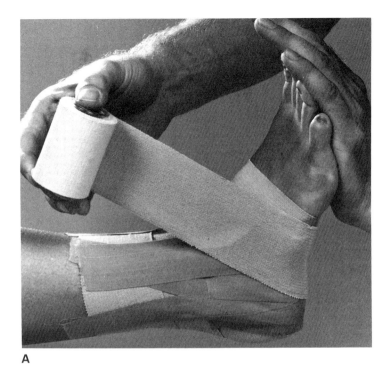

A

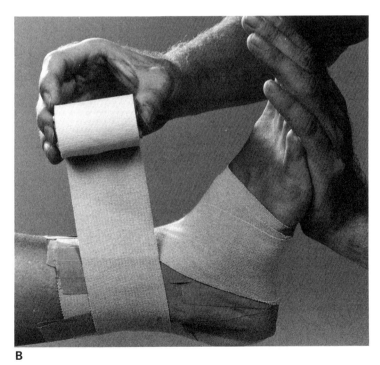

B

Figure 18–25 Reinforcement taping for inversion trauma of the left ankle. (**A**) Beginning of the reinforcement tape, lateral view. (**B**) Last loop around the lower leg, lateral view.

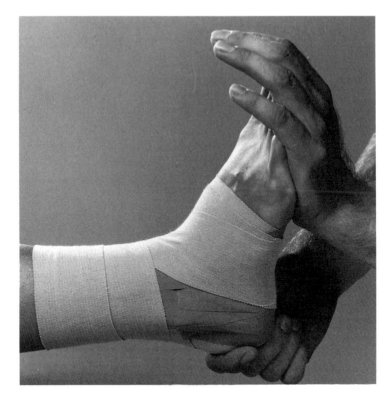

Figure 18–25 **(C)** Finished construction, lateral view.

TARSAL SINUS SYNDROME

Functional Examination

The functional examination is often negative. There is tenderness to palpation of the tarsal sinus. The patient history is typical: a feeling of instability without objective findings.

INJECTION

In almost all cases, an injection with a corticosteroid is effective, regardless of the duration of the symptoms.

Position of the Patient

The patient is supine on the treatment table.

Position of the Physician

The physician sits next to the treatment table, at the patient's affected side, and locates the tarsal sinus. The tarsal sinus is located between the lateral malleolus and the muscle belly of the extensor digitorum brevis.

Performance

A 5-mL syringe is filled with 2 mL of corticosteroid and 3 mL of local anesthetic. A 5-cm long needle is used for the injection. The tarsal sinus is explored with the needle, and a few drops of solution are injected at every site where the patient's pain is provoked. The long needle is needed because the lesion can lie superficially but extend deeply (Figure 18–26).

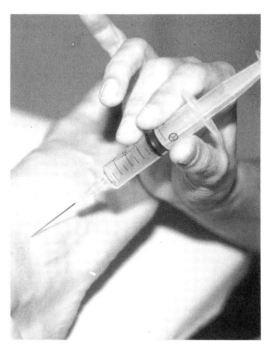

Figure 18–26 Injection of the tarsal sinus.

Follow-Up

The patient is instructed to restrict activities as much as possible for the next 3 days.

After 2 weeks, the patient is seen again for follow-up. If necessary, a second injection can be given.

SPRAIN OF THE DELTOID LIGAMENT (MEDIAL ANKLE SPRAIN): GENERAL PRINCIPLES

The deltoid ligament comprises four parts: the anterior and posterior tibiotalar ligaments, the tibionavicular ligament, and the tibiocalcaneal ligament. A medial ankle sprain can therefore affect any or all of these structures.

Functional Examination

The anterior tibiotalar and tibionavicular ligaments are painful on passive plantar flexion–abduction–pronation of the foot with the calcaneus held in valgus. The tibiocalcaneal ligament is painful on passive abduction-pronation with the foot in 10° plantar flexion, whereby the calcaneus is held in valgus. The posterior tibiotalar ligament is painful on valgus stress of the calcaneus, whereby the ankle is held in almost maximal extension and the midfoot is held in pronation and abduction; this is a rarely seen lesion and is not discussed further.

MEDIAL ANKLE SPRAIN: ANTERIOR TIBIOTALAR AND TIBIONAVICULAR LIGAMENTS

TRANSVERSE FRICTION

Lesions of the deltoid ligament can be caused by acute trauma (usually in plantar flexion–abduction–pronation), or they can occur through chronic overloading, such as in pes plano valgus (flat foot). In the latter case, corrective orthotics are recommended. In almost all cases, the origin of the ligaments at the medial malleolus is affected.

Position of the Patient

The patient is supine on the treatment table with the knee positioned in slight flexion, supported by a roll. The distal part of the lower leg rests in the therapist's lap.

Position of the Therapist

The therapist sits either on or next to the end of the treatment table. If, for example, the right foot is being treated, the therapist

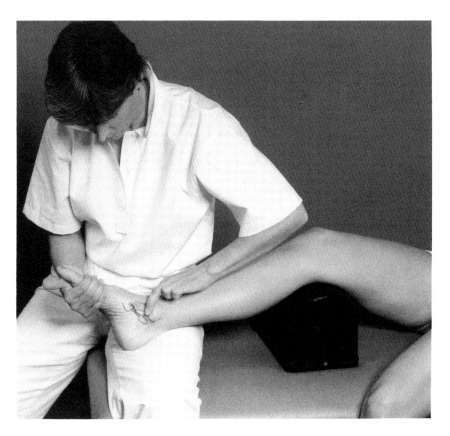

Figure 18–27 Transverse friction of the anterior part of the deltoid ligament, the origin of the anterior tibiotalar and tibionavicular ligaments: Initial position.

grasps the patient's forefoot from the medial aspect with the right hand and brings it into plantar flexion, abduction, and pronation.

Performance

The left index finger, reinforced by the middle finger, is placed just plantar to the lesion against the anterodistal aspect of the medial malleolus, at the origin of the ligaments (Figure 18–27). The active phase of the transverse friction is performed by extending the wrist, which moves the index finger from plantar to dorsal over the ligament. Pressure is exerted in a proximal direction (Figure 18–28).

Duration

Transverse friction should be performed for 10 to 15 minutes three times per week.

INJECTION

Although Cyriax[9] reported that transverse friction is not an effective treatment for this lesion, it has been used successfully on numerous occasions. If there is still no improvement after six treatments, however, injection of the origin of the ligament is indicated.

Position of the Patient

The patient is supine on the treatment table.

Position of the Physician

The physician sits or stands next to the foot of the treatment table, facing the affected foot. With one hand, the physician positions the foot in plantar flexion, abduction, and pronation.

Performance

A Mantoux syringe is filled with a local anesthetic. With a 2-cm needle, the origin of the ligament at the anterodistal aspect of the medial malleolus is injected in dropwise fashion, directed by where the patient feels pain (Figure 18–29).

Follow-Up

Because the patient has been injected with only a local anesthetic, he or she is advised to restrict activities only for 1 day, the day of the injection. The patient should be seen again after 1 week. If the symptoms have de-

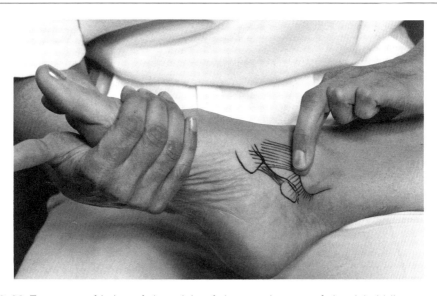

Figure 18–28 Transverse friction of the origin of the anterior part of the deltoid ligament: Ending position.

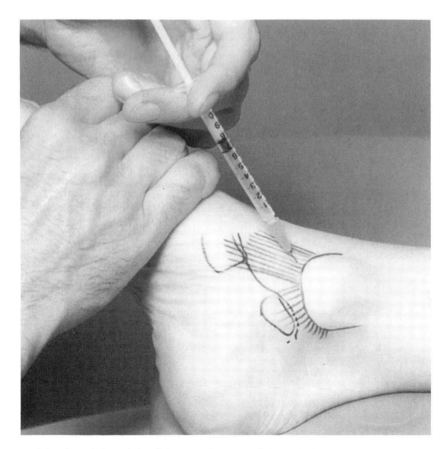

Figure 18–29 Injection of the origin of the anterior part of the deltoid ligament.

creased, a second injection is given. If injection had no effect, however, it is repeated, but this time with 0.5 mL of a corticosteroid. The patient should not put weight on the affected leg for 3 days after the corticosteroid injection. After 2 weeks, the functional examination is repeated. A second injection with corticosteroid is seldom indicated. One month after this injection, the patient can return to normal activities, including sports.

MEDIAL ANKLE SPRAIN: TIBIOCALCANEAL LIGAMENT

TRANSVERSE FRICTION

Position of the Patient

The patient is supine on the treatment table with the knee positioned in slight flexion, supported by a roll. The distal part of the lower leg rests in the therapist's lap.

Position of the Therapist

The therapist sits either on or next to the end of the treatment table. If, for example, the right foot is being treated, the therapist grasps the patient's forefoot from the medial aspect with the right hand and brings it into 10° plantar flexion, abduction, and pronation.

Performance

The left index finger, reinforced by the middle finger, is placed just posterior to the lesion against the most distal aspect of the medial malleolus, at the origin of the ligament. The active phase of the transverse friction is performed by extending the wrist, which moves the index finger from posterior to anterior over the ligament. Pressure is exerted in a proximal direction (Figure 18–30).

Duration

Transverse friction treatments should be given three times a week and last for 10 to 15 minutes.

INJECTION

Position of the Patient

The patient is supine on the treatment table.

Position of the Physician

The physician sits or stands next to the end of the treatment table, facing the affected foot. With one hand, the physician positions the foot in 10° plantar flexion, abduction, and pronation.

Performance

A Mantoux syringe is filled with a local anesthetic. With a 2-cm long needle, the origin of the ligament at the distal aspect of the medial malleolus is injected in dropwise fashion, guided by the patient's pain (Figure 18–31).

Follow-Up

Because the patient has been injected with only a local anesthetic, he or she is advised to restrict activities only for 1 day, the day of the injection. The patient should be seen again after 1 week. If the symptoms have de-

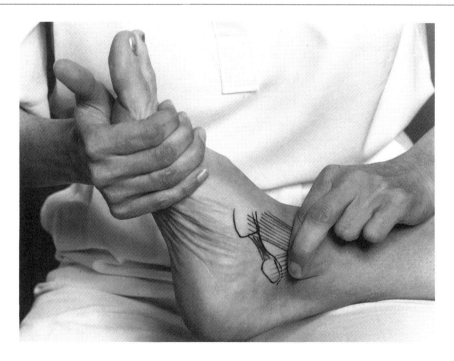

Figure 18–30 Transverse friction of the origin of the tibiocalcaneal ligament.

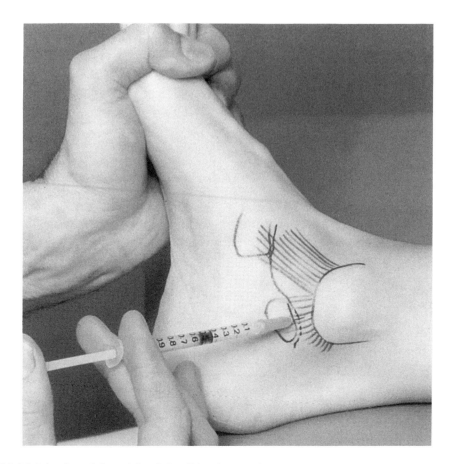

Figure 18–31 Injection of the origin of the tibiocalcaneal ligament.

creased, a second injection is given. If the injection had no effect, however, it is repeated, but this time with 0.5 mL of a corticosteroid. The patient should not put weight on the affected leg for 3 days after the corticosteroid injection. After 2 weeks, the functional examination is repeated. A second injection with corticosteroid is seldom indicated. One month after this injection, the patient can return to normal activities, including sports.

PARTIAL TEAR OF THE GASTROCNEMIUS-SOLEUS

Functional Examination

Dorsal extension of the ankle is both actively and passively painful and limited. Resisted plantar flexion of the ankle is painful.

TAPING

In the acute and subacute stages (ie, the first week) after a partial tear of the gastrocnemius-soleus, taping can be applied in conjunction with transverse friction treatment.

Position of the Patient

The patient stands on the treatment table, which is brought to its lowest level. If the treatment table is not adjustable, the patient stands on the floor. A roll of tape about 2 inches wide is placed under the heel of the affected extremity (Figure 18–32A).

Position of the Therapist

The therapist stands or sits obliquely behind the patient's affected side.

Performance

The tape is applied with the muscle bellies in a relaxed position. With a 6- to 8-cm wide elastic tape, the therapist begins from medial with a circular loop around the lower leg and then pulls the tape in a proximolateral direction, so that it is positioned just underneath the lesion (upper diagonal strip in Figure 18–32B). Then a circular loop is made around the lower leg just distal to the patellar ligament, after which the tape is brought distal and lateral, again positioned just underneath the lesion. With a 2-cm wide nonelastic tape, overlapping crosses are applied over the entire

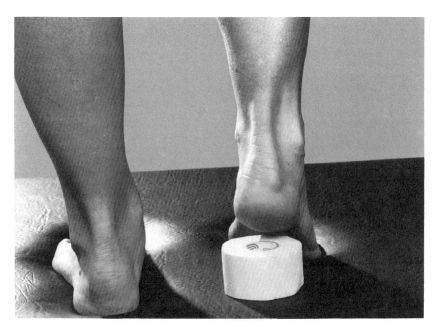

Figure 18–32 Taping for a partial tear of the gastrocnemius-soleus. (**A**) Initial position.

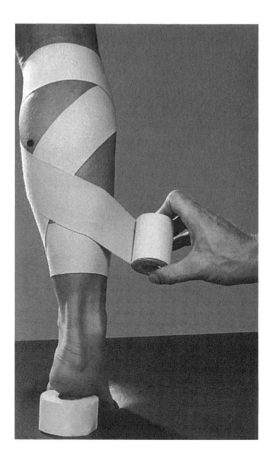

Figure 18–32 (B) Application of the first layer of elastic tape. The black dot indicates the site of the lesion.

surface of the proximodistally running elastic strips (Figure 18–32, C–E). Finally, this construction is covered from distal to proximal with elastic tape, which is applied in an oblique, spiraled manner. The tension in the tape should decrease with each passage around the lower leg from distal to proximal (Figure 18–32, F and G).

When performing transverse friction massage, the therapist only has to remove the upper layers of the elastic covering tape to reach the site of the lesion.

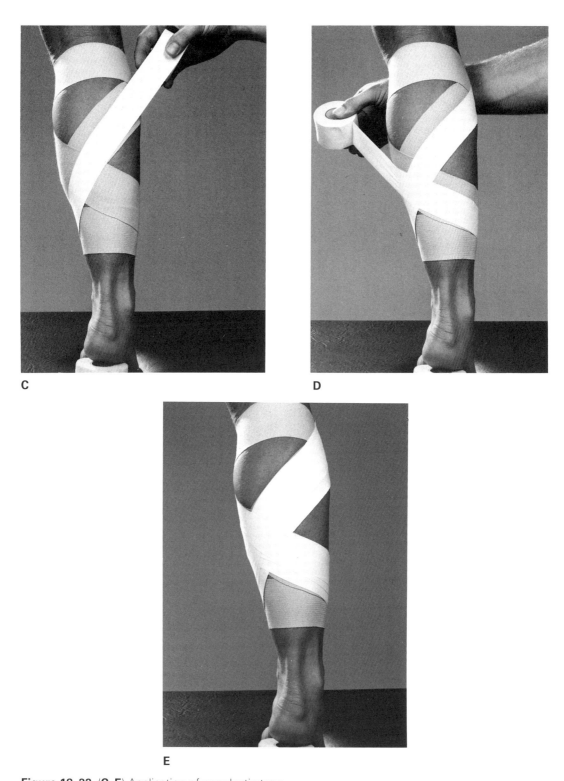

C

D

E

Figure 18–32 (**C–E**) Application of nonelastic tape.

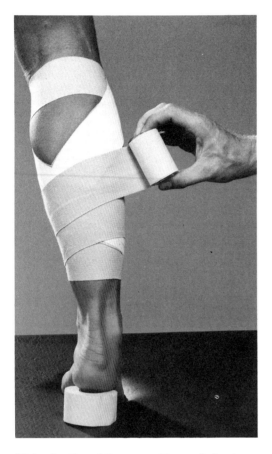
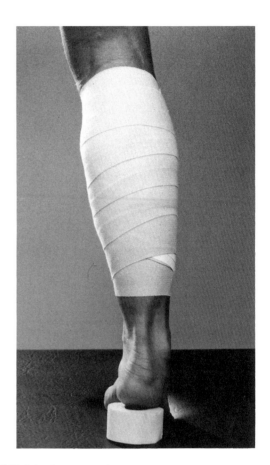

(**F**) Application of the second layer of elastic tape. (**G**) Finished construction.

PARTIAL TEAR OF THE CALF MUSCLES AND ACHILLODYNIA

STRETCHING OF THE CALF MUSCLES

Stretching the calf muscles is indicated during recovery from a partial rupture of the gastrocnemius-soleus and in all clinical stages of achillodynia (refer to Chapter 17 for more detailed information about these lesions). Because a significant amount of force must be exerted, it is simpler and much more effective for the patient to perform self-stretching ex-

ercises than to have the therapist attempt to stretch these muscles.

Gastrocnemius Muscle

Position of the Patient

The patient stands with the leg being stretched placed as far back as possible but with the heel still flat on the ground. The patient leans with the hands against a wall or on the back of a chair for support (Figure 18–33). The trunk is in line with the posterior leg. The anterior leg is positioned in hip and knee flexion to such a degree that the muscles remain relaxed.

Performance

The patient now shifts the body weight forward over the anterior leg to the point where a stretch is felt in the calf. The stretch is performed slowly and carefully, with care taken to avoid pain provocation and muscle splinting. The patient should continue to keep the trunk in line with the posterior leg so as not to allow a kyphosis. This stretch should be performed several times each day, especially first thing in the morning just after getting out of bed and before and after sports activities.

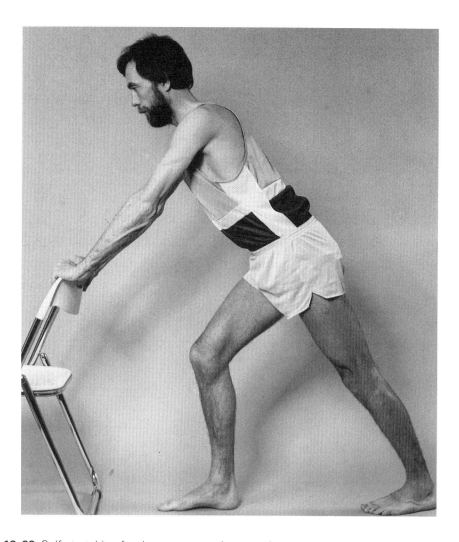

Figure 18–33 Self-stretching for the gastrocnemius muscle.

Soleus Muscle

Performance

After the gastrocnemius muscle is stretched, the soleus muscle can be stretched by maintaining the initial position described above and bending the knee of the posterior leg. Again, the heel has to remain flat on the ground, and the trunk has to remain parallel to the lower leg (Figure 18–34). This stretch, too, should be performed several times each day, especially first thing in the morning just after getting out of bed and before and after sports activities.

Figure 18–34 Self-stretching for the soleus muscle.

ACHILLODYNIA (PERITENDINITIS OF THE ACHILLES TENDON)

Functional Examination

Resisted plantar flexion of the ankle is painful. Passive plantar flexion of the ankle is painful when the anterior aspect of the tendon is affected just proximal to the calcaneus.

TRANSVERSE FRICTION

Treatment for achillodynia is primarily causal. In other words, the primary cause for the lesion should be determined and an attempt made to treat this. Several examples are:

- abnormal position or form of the foot (treatment consists of correcting the position by means of a functional orthotic)
- for athletes, use of inappropriate shoes (eg, with too little shock absorption or insufficient heel stability)
- also for athletes, training on surfaces that are too hard or too soft or to which they are unaccustomed (often a change in the training surface is important; for example, there are significant differences in forces exerted on the foot when running on a street, a track, or a beach or in the woods)

To obtain faster recovery, in addition to eliminating the causes this lesion can be treated locally with transverse friction and with stretching. In some instances, depending on the stage of tendinitis, the pain-provoking activities have to be reduced temporarily or even stopped.

Peritendinitis of the Medial or Lateral Part of the Achilles Tendon

Position of the Patient

The patient is prone on the treatment table with the affected foot hanging just over the edge of the table.

Position of the Therapist

The therapist sits next to the end of the treatment table, facing the medial or lateral side of the affected foot. With one hand, or with the knee, the therapist brings the patient's foot into extension. In so doing, the tendon and the peritendon are stretched, but not to the point where it becomes painful. After locating the most painful site at either the medial or lateral side (or both) of the Achilles tendon, the therapist grasps that part of the tendon between thumb and index finger, trying to get as anterior as possible. The thumb and index finger are held in a position that forms an O.

Performance

The thumb and index finger exert just enough pressure on the tendon that the mild pain that occurs can be easily tolerated. By now moving the hand in a posterior direction and taking the skin around the Achilles tendon with the movement from anterior to posterior, the therapist applies friction transversely to the fibers of the Achilles tendon (Figure 18–35). In the relaxation phase, the tendon is not released; instead, slight pressure is maintained to move, again with the skin, in an anterior direction in relation to the tendon.

An alternative technique is to let the thumb stay in one position and to move only the index finger transversely over the medial or lateral aspect of the tendon from anterior to posterior (not illustrated). This movement is brought about by extending the wrist.

Duration

Generally, 6 to 15 transverse friction treatments of about 15 minutes' duration, performed either daily or a minimum of three times a week, are required to achieve complete relief. This schedule holds true regard-

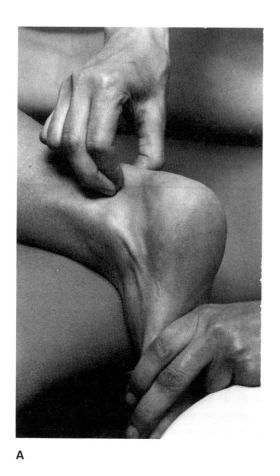
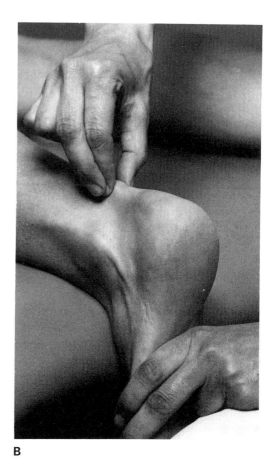

A   **B**

Figure 18–35 Transverse friction of the medial and lateral side of the Achilles tendon. **(A)** Initial position. **(B)** Final position.

less of the location of the lesion. As already mentioned, the cause of the lesion should also be determined and eliminated whenever possible.

Peritendinitis of the Medial or Lateral Anterior Part of the Achilles Tendon

Often, the anterior part of the Achilles tendon is affected, usually at the medial side. This is a predilection site for which local treatment is absolutely necessary. Here, causal therapy alone is insufficient.

Position of the Patient

The patient is prone on the treatment table. The foot rests in plantar flexion on the table,

and a small pillow or roll is placed under the distal part of the lower leg.

Position of the Therapist

The therapist sits next to the end of the treatment table, facing the sole of the patient's foot. With the thumb, the Achilles tendon is pushed from lateral to medial to treat the anterior aspect at the medial side (Figure 18–36). Just the opposite (medial to lateral) motion is induced to treat the anterior aspect at the lateral side (Figure 18–37).

The middle finger of the other hand is placed against the underside of the Achilles tendon. The ring and little fingers are flexed, the index finger reinforces the middle finger,

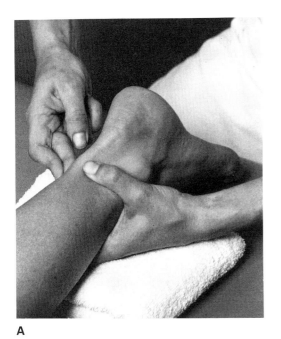
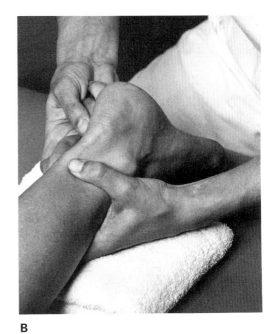

A   B

Figure 18–36 Transverse friction of the medial anterior aspect of the Achilles tendon. (**A**) Initial position. (**B**) Final position.

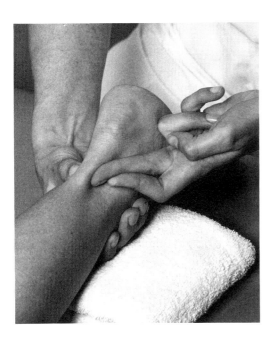

Figure 18–37 Transverse friction of the lateral anterior aspect of the Achilles tendon.

and the forearm is positioned in the neutral position or in slight pronation.

Performance

By maximal supination of the therapist's forearm, the middle finger moves transversely over the anterior aspect of the Achilles tendon. It is important first to take the skin slightly anterior with the middle finger so that, during the active phase of the transverse friction, not too much of the skin is pulled, which eventually will cause a blister.

Duration

Generally, 6 to 15 transverse friction treatments of about 15 minutes' duration, performed either daily or a minimum of three times a week, are required to achieve complete relief. This schedule holds true regardless of the location of the lesion. As already mentioned, the cause of the lesion should also be determined and eliminated whenever possible.

Peritendinitis of the Anterior Part of the Achilles Tendon Just Proximal to the Calcaneus

Of all the predilection sites in achillodynia, this region is the least often affected. It, too, however, is a predilection site in which local treatment is absolutely necessary; causal therapy alone is unsatisfactory.

Position of the Patient

The patient is prone on the treatment table, with the foot resting in plantar flexion and a small pillow or roll placed under the distal part of the lower leg.

Position of the Therapist

The therapist sits next to the foot of the treatment table, facing the plantar aspect of the patient's foot. The index finger is placed on the posterior aspect of the Achilles tendon, over the proximal third of the calcaneus, just medial to the site of the lesion. Usually, the most tender site is located somewhat medially. The other index finger is placed on top of the first index finger; the other fingers are flexed, and the thumbs, one on top of the other, give counterpressure at the plantar aspect of the foot.

Performance

The index fingers exert pressure in an anterodistal direction, so that the Achilles tendon is pushed against the posterior aspect of the proximal third of the calcaneus. By now bringing the wrist of the lateral arm into extension and of the medial arm into flexion, the index fingers are moved from medial to lateral over the lesion (Figure 18–38).

Note

If this treatment does not bring quick relief from pain, there is likely to be a subtendineal bursitis of the Achilles tendon.

Duration

Generally, 6 to 15 transverse friction treatments of about 15 minutes' duration, per-

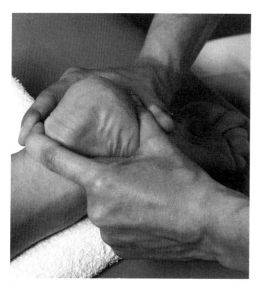
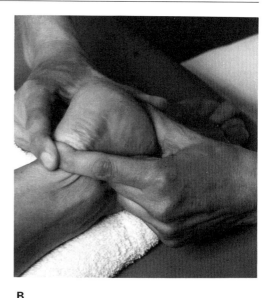

A   **B**

Figure 18–38 Transverse friction of the anterior part of the Achilles tendon at the proximal third of the calcaneal tuberosity. (**A**) Initial position. (**B**) Final position.

formed either daily or a minimum of three times a week, are required to achieve complete relief. This schedule holds true regardless of the location of the lesion. As already mentioned, the cause of the lesion should also be determined and eliminated whenever possible.

Insertion Tendopathy of the Achilles Tendon

The insertion of the Achilles tendon is located at the distal half to two thirds of the calcaneal tuberosity and extends underneath the heel.

Position of the Patient

The patient is prone on the treatment table with the affected foot hanging just over the edge of the table.

Position of the Therapist

The therapist sits next to the foot of the treatment table, facing the medial or lateral side of the foot being treated. With one hand, or with the knee, the therapist brings the patient's foot into extension. In so doing, the tendon and its insertion are stretched, but not to the point where it becomes painful. The most painful site at the insertion is located by using the thumb to palpate transversely over the course of the fibers.

Performance

The transverse friction can be performed with either the thumb or the fingers. The thumb is placed at the site of the lesion and moved from lateral to medial over the lesion by supination of the forearm during the active phase (Figure 18–39). Of course, the transverse friction can also be done from medial to lateral using the thumb of the other hand.

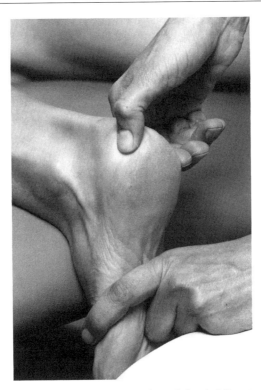

Figure 18–39 Transverse friction of part of the insertion of the Achilles tendon.

Note

If this treatment does not bring quick relief of pain, there is likely to be a subtendineal bursitis of the Achilles tendon.

Duration

Generally, 6 to 15 transverse friction treat- ments of about 15 minutes' duration, performed either daily or a minimum of three times a week, are required to achieve complete relief. This schedule holds true regardless of the location of the lesion. As already mentioned, the cause of the lesion should also be determined and eliminated whenever possible.

SUBTENDINOUS BURSITIS OF THE ACHILLES TENDON

Functional Examination

Passive plantar flexion of the ankle is painful (caused by compression of the bursa).

INJECTION

Differentiation between subtendinous bursitis and anterodistal peritendinitis of the Achilles tendon (at the level of the proximal third of the posterior aspect of the calcaneus) is only possible by means of a local anesthetic or through transverse friction. In the presence of bursitis, the pain will not disappear during the transverse friction treatment; chances are, it will increase. The pain will disappear upon injection of subtendinous bursitis with a local anesthetic, if it is indeed the structure that is affected.

Position of the Patient

The patient is prone on the treatment table with the foot hanging just over the edge.

Position of the Physician

The physician sits next to the end of the treatment table, facing the lateral side of the affected foot. With one hand, the physician holds the patient's foot in slight extension.

Performance

This bursa is seldom swollen to the point where aspiration is possible; however, the physician should always attempt to aspirate it before injecting. With a Mantoux syringe and a 3- to 4-cm needle, the bursa between the Achilles tendon and the calcaneus is injected from lateral, with the needle being held almost horizontally (Figure 18–40). From 0.5 to 1.0 mL of local anesthetic is injected in a fanshaped manner directed by where the patient feels pain. When the needle passes through the wall of the bursa, the patient typically experiences pain. At this point, the needle is inserted farther until the pain is no longer felt. The solution is then injected as the needle is withdrawn from this area. This method is repeated in all directions until the entire painful area of the bursa has been injected. If the needle enters a nonpainful area, no solution is injected.

Follow-Up

If the pain has not decreased after 1 week, the injection can be repeated using a corticosteroid. A third injection is rarely needed.

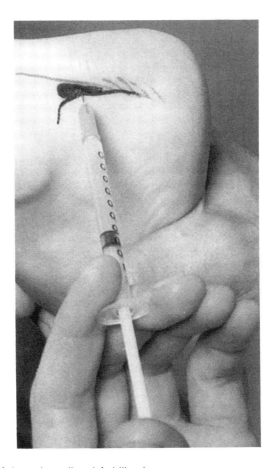

Figure 18–40 Injection of the subtendineal Achilles bursa.

POSTERIOR SUBCUTANEOUS CALCANEAL BURSITIS

Functional Examination

The functional examination is usually negative, but in severe cases passive extension of the foot can be painful. In some cases, when palpated, the swelling has a fluctuating consistency.

INJECTION

Differentiation between posterior subcutaneous calcaneal bursitis and insertion tendopathy of the Achilles tendon is only possible through transverse friction or by means of an injection with a local anesthetic. In the presence of bursitis, the pain will not disappear during the transverse friction treatment; chances are, it will increase. The pain will disappear upon injection of posterior subcutaneous bursitis with a local anesthetic, if it is indeed the structure that is affected. The cause of posterior subcutaneous calcaneal bursitis is usually shoes with heel counters that are too hard.

Position of the Patient

The patient is prone on the treatment table. The affected foot is positioned in slight plantar flexion on the table. The lower leg is supported distally with a small pillow or roll.

Position of the Physician

The physician sits next to the treatment table, facing the lateral side of the affected foot.

Performance

A Mantoux or 2-mL syringe, depending on the amount of swelling, is filled with a local anesthetic. A 2- to 3-cm needle should be used. If the bursa is swollen and has a fluctuating consistency when palpated, the physician should first attempt to aspirate it. Then, with the same needle inserted between the calcaneus and the skin, the bursa is injected in a fan-shaped manner as directed by the patient's pain (Figure 18–41). When the needle passes through the wall of the bursa, the patient typically experiences pain. At this point, the needle is inserted farther until the pain is no longer felt. The solution is then injected as the needle is withdrawn from this area. This method is repeated in all directions until the entire painful area of the bursa has been injected.

The presence of bursitis is usually confirmed if the patient clearly feels pain and the physician feels minimal to no resistance during the injection.

Follow-Up

If the pain has not decreased after 1 week, the injection can be repeated with a corticosteroid. Usually one to three injections are necessary to achieve complete relief of pain. In persistent cases, surgical removal of the bursa may be necessary.

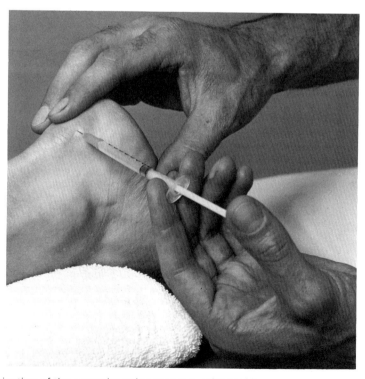

Figure 18–41 Injection of the posterior subcutaneous calcaneal bursa.

TENOSYNOVITIS OF THE TIBIALIS POSTERIOR MUSCLE

Functional Examination

Passive eversion of the foot is painful. In severe cases, resisted inversion of the foot can be painful.

TRANSVERSE FRICTION

Tenosynovitis of the tibialis posterior muscle almost always occurs as the result of chronic overload in people with pes plano valgus (flat foot). In addition to local treatment with transverse friction, the use of functional orthotics is indicated.

Position of the Patient

The patient is supine on the treatment table with the distal part of the lower leg resting on the therapist's thigh. The knee is positioned in slight flexion, supported by a pillow or roll.

Position of the Therapist

The therapist sits next to or on the end of the treatment table. If, for example, the right foot is being treated, the therapist grasps the patient's forefoot from the medial aspect with the right hand and, without provoking pain or muscle splinting, brings the foot into as much eversion as possible. The left index and middle fingers are placed just posterior to the lesion, with the thumb directly opposite at the lateral side of the ankle.

Performance

By extending the left wrist, the therapist moves the index and middle fingers transversely over the lesion from posterior to anterior (Figure 18–42). At the same time, the thumb exerts counterpressure.

Note

Depending on the extent of the lesion, transverse friction can also be performed with one finger. The index finger is usually used, reinforced by the middle finger. The tenosynovitis can be located proximal to, at the level of, or distal to the medial malleolus.

Duration

A schedule of 15 to 20 minutes of transverse friction two to three times per week for 2 to 4 weeks is usually sufficient to achieve complete relief of pain. If the transverse friction does not provide satisfactory results, an injection between the tendon and tendon sheath is indicated.

INJECTION

An injection between the tibialis posterior tendon and its sheath is indicated only when the transverse friction treatment fails. This treatment is only effective when the position of the foot has first been corrected with functional orthotics.

Position of the Patient

The patient is supine on the treatment table.

Position of the Physician

The physician sits or stands at the end of the treatment table, facing the affected foot. With one hand, the physician holds the patient's foot in slight eversion.

Performance

Because it is difficult in this initial position to palpate the tendon, the tendon should be marked before the injection is given. A Mantoux syringe is filled with 1 mL of corticosteroid. The 2-cm needle is inserted from distal until the resistance of the tendon is felt. The needle is then slightly withdrawn and directed proximally, almost parallel to the tendon. No resistance should

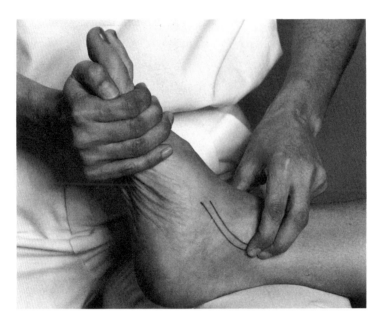

Figure 18–42 Transverse friction of the (tendon) sheath of the tibialis posterior muscle at the level of the medial malleolus.

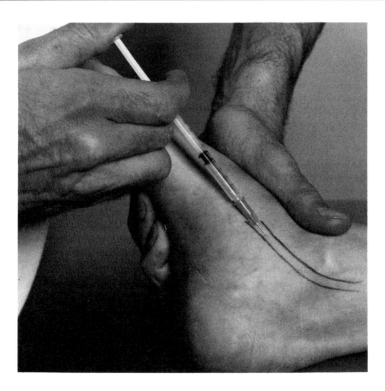

Figure 18–43 Injection between the tendon and tendon sheath of the tibialis posterior muscle.

be felt as the needle is pushed farther proximally (Figure 18–43). Next, a small amount of solution is injected. If a swelling along the tendon is observed, the needle is correctly located. While the needle is slowly withdrawn, all or part of the remaining solution is injected.

Follow-Up

The patient should not put weight on the foot for 3 days after the injection. After 10 to 14 days, the patient is seen again, and the foot is reassessed. Rarely are more than two injections needed to achieve complete pain relief.

INSERTION TENDOPATHY OF THE TIBIALIS POSTERIOR MUSCLE

Functional Examination

Passive eversion of the foot can be painful (as a result of the exertion of stretch forces on the affected muscle insertion). Resisted inversion of the foot is painful

TRANSVERSE FRICTION

Although the tibialis posterior muscle has a number of insertions, the insertion at the navicular tuberosity is the one most often affected.

Position of the Patient

The patient is supine on the treatment table with the distal part of the lower leg resting on the therapist's thigh. The knee is positioned in slight flexion, supported by a pillow or roll.

Position of the Therapist

The therapist sits next to or on the end of the treatment table. If, for example, the right foot is being treated, the therapist grasps the patient's forefoot from the medial aspect with the right hand, holding it in slight plantar flexion and supination so that the insertion site can be easily reached. The left index finger, reinforced by the middle finger, is placed at the plantar aspect of the navicular tuberosity. The thumb is placed on the lateral side of the

foot, opposite and slightly distal to the index finger.

Performance

Transverse friction of the insertion of the tibialis posterior muscle is performed through

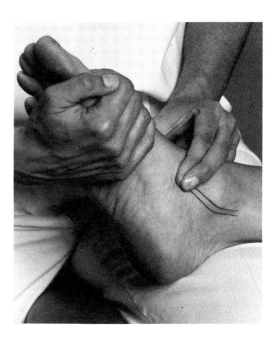

Figure 18–44 Transverse friction of the insertion of the tibialis posterior muscle at the navicular tuberosity.

an extension of the therapist's wrist. In so doing, the index finger is moved from plantar to dorsal over the lesion (Figure 18–44). Pressure is exerted in a lateral and slightly distal direction.

Note

If necessary, functional orthotics are used in addition to the transverse friction treatments.

Duration

Daily (especially for athletes) or three times weekly treatments of about 20 minutes usually lead to complete recovery within 2 to 3 weeks.

TENOMYOSYNOVITIS OF THE TIBIALIS ANTERIOR MUSCLE

Functional Examination

Passive plantar flexion, pronation, and abduction of the foot are painful. In severe cases, accompanied by significant crepitation, resisted extension, supination, and adduction of the foot are also painful.

TRANSVERSE FRICTION

Tenomyosynovitis of the tibialis anterior muscle is an overuse syndrome located at the level of the musculotendinous junction of the tibialis anterior.

Position of the Patient

The patient is supine on the treatment table with the distal part of the lower leg resting on the therapist's thigh. The knee is positioned in slight flexion, supported by a pillow or roll.

Position of the Therapist

The therapist sits next to or on the end of the treatment table. If, for example, the right foot is being treated, the therapist grasps the patient's forefoot from the dorsomedial aspect with the right hand, holding it in as much plantar flexion, pronation, and abduction as possible, without provoking pain or muscle splinting. The index, middle, and ring fingers of the other hand are placed just posterior to the lesion. The thumb gives counterpressure at the lateral side of the ankle.

Performance

During the active phase of the transverse friction, the fingers are moved from posteromedial to anterolateral over the lesion. This movement is brought about by making a large extension motion with the wrist while slightly adducting the arm (Figure 18–45). During this active phase, pressure is exerted in a lateral direction.

Duration

Treatments lasting 15 minutes should be given three times a week. In addition, pain-provoking activities should be avoided. Usually in 2 to 4 weeks, the symptoms have completely disappeared.

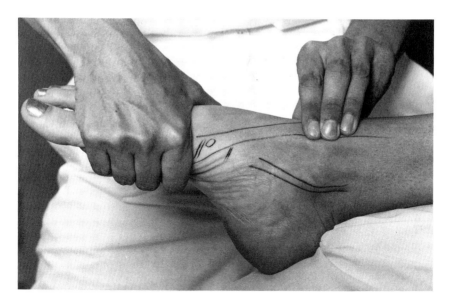

Figure 18–45 Transverse friction of the musculotendinous junction of the tibialis anterior muscle.

TENOSYNOVITIS OF THE TIBIALIS ANTERIOR MUSCLE

TRANSVERSE FRICTION

In transverse friction of tibialis anterior tenosynovitis, the position of the patient and therapist, as well as the performance, are the same as for the tenomyosynovitis. The only exception is that the lesion is located more distally.

INSERTION TENDOPATHY OF THE TIBIALIS ANTERIOR MUSCLE

Functional Examination

Passive plantar flexion, pronation, and abduction of the foot can be painful (as a result of the exertion of stretch forces on the affected structure). Resisted extension, supination, and adduction of the foot are painful.

TRANSVERSE FRICTION

Position of the Patient

The patient is supine on the treatment table with the knee slightly flexed and supported by a pillow or roll.

Position of the Therapist

The therapist sits next to the end of the treatment table, facing the lateral side of the foot. If, for example, the right foot is being treated, the therapist grasps the patient's forefoot from the dorsomedial aspect with the right hand and holds it in painless plantar flexion, pronation, and abduction. With the left index finger, the site of the lesion is located at the medial cuneiform or base of the first metatarsal. The thumb gives counterpressure at the dorsolateral side of the forefoot.

Performance

By extension of the wrist, the index finger, which is reinforced by the middle finger, is moved from plantar-medial to dorsolateral transversely over the lesion (Figure 18–46). During this active phase, pressure is exerted in a dorsolateral direction.

Duration

Three to 4 weeks of transverse friction, performed three times per week for about 15 minutes, are usually required to achieve complete pain relief. In addition to the transverse friction, stretching exercises should be performed.

STRETCHING

Stretching of the tibialis anterior is usually initiated after transverse friction treatment.

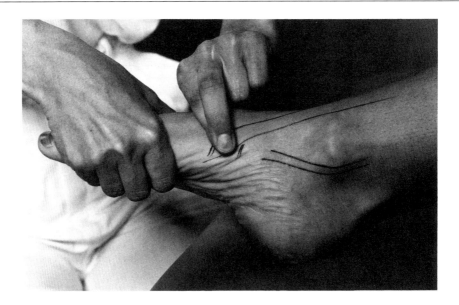

Figure 18–46 Transverse friction of the insertion of the tibialis anterior muscle.

Position of the Patient

The patient is supine on the treatment table with the heel just at the edge.

Position of the Therapist

The therapist sits next to the edge of the treatment table, facing the foot being treated. If, for example, the left foot is being treated, the therapist grasps the patient's forefoot from the dorsomedial aspect with the left hand. The right hand grasps the patient's heel from the lateral aspect.

Performance

Slowly, without causing pain or muscle splinting, the therapist brings the foot into plantar flexion, abduction, and pronation while the heel is moved into a valgus direction (Figure 18–47).

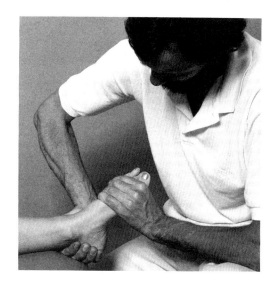

Figure 18–47 Stretching of the tibialis anterior muscle.

TENOSYNOVITIS OF THE PERONEAL MUSCLES

Functional Examination

Passive extension, supination, and adduction of the foot are painful. In severe cases, resisted plantar flexion, pronation, and abduction of the foot are painful.

TRANSVERSE FRICTION

After an inversion trauma or as a result of overuse, a tenosynovitis of the peroneal muscles can occur. The location can vary from just proximal of the lateral malleolus to just distal of the peroneal trochlea.

Tenosynovitis of the Peroneal Muscles Proximal to the Lateral Malleolus

Position of the Patient

The patient is supine on the treatment table, with the distal part of the lower leg resting on the therapist's thigh. The knee is positioned in slight flexion, supported by a pillow or roll.

Position of the Therapist

The therapist sits next to or on the end of the treatment table. If, for example, the left foot is being treated, the therapist grasps the patient's forefoot from the lateral aspect with the right hand, holding it in slight painless extension, supination, and adduction. The lesion is located using the index and middle fingers of the other hand, and the fingers are placed just posterior to the site. The left thumb gives counterpressure at the medial side of the ankle, just proximal to or on the medial malleolus.

Performance

By extension of the wrist during the active phase of the transverse friction, the fingers are moved from posterior to anterior over the affected structure (Figure 18–48). During the active phase of the transverse friction, pressure is exerted in a medial direction.

Duration

The duration of treatment varies. The transverse friction should be performed for about 20 minutes three times per week. It can, however, take from 1 to 4 weeks to reach full recovery. If there is no improvement after six sessions of transverse friction, an injection between the tendon and tendon sheath is indicated.

Tenosynovitis of the Peroneal Muscles at the Level of the Lateral Malleolus

Position of the Patient

The patient is supine on the treatment table.

Position of the Therapist

The therapist sits next to the end of the treatment table, facing the foot being treated. If, for example, the left foot is affected, the therapist grasps the patient's forefoot from the plantar aspect with the left hand, holding it in slight plantar flexion, supination, and adduction. The right middle finger is placed just posterior to the most tender site at the lateral malleolus. The index finger reinforces the middle finger, and the thumb, ring finger, and little finger are held in a flexed position.

Performance

By maximal supination of the forearm during the active phase of the transverse friction, the middle finger is moved from posterior to anterior transversely over the lesion (Figure 18–49).

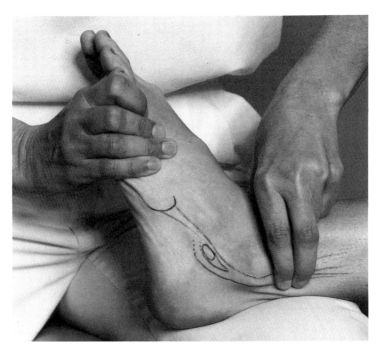

Figure 18–48 Transverse friction of the tendon sheath of the peroneal muscles just proximal to the lateral malleolus.

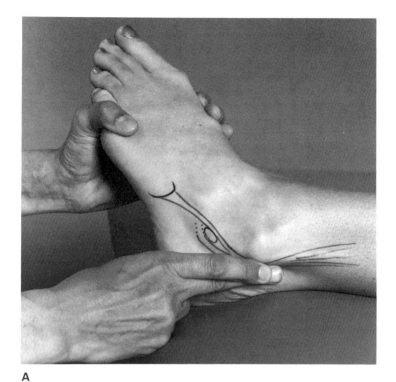

A

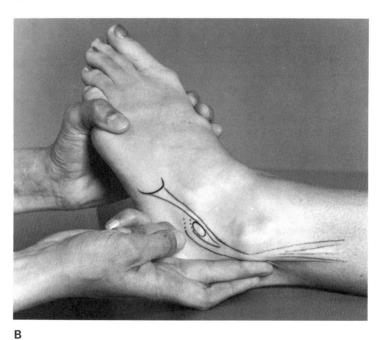

B

Figure 18–49 Transverse friction of the (tendon) sheath of the peroneal muscles at the level of the lateral malleolus. (**A**) Initial position. (**B**) Final position.

Duration

The duration of treatment varies. The transverse friction should be performed for about 20 minutes three times per week. It can take from 1 to 4 weeks to reach full recovery. If there is no improvement after six sessions of transverse friction, an injection between the tendon and tendon sheath is indicated.

INJECTION

An injection with a corticosteroid between the tendon and tendon sheath is indicated after at least six treatments of transverse friction have been tried with unsatisfactory results.

Position of the Patient

The patient is supine on the treatment table.

Position of the Physician

The physician sits or stands next to the end of the treatment table, facing the affected foot. With one hand, the physician holds the patient's foot in slight extension, supination, and adduction.

Performance

A Mantoux syringe is filled with 1 mL of corticosteroid. A 2-cm long, thin needle is inserted just distal to the lesion at an angle of 30° in relation to the tendon. It is pushed in until the resistance of the tendon is felt. The needle is then slightly withdrawn and positioned proximally, almost parallel to the tendon (Figure 18–50). No resistance should be felt as the needle is pushed farther proximally. Next, a small amount of solution is injected. If a swelling along the tendon is observed, the tip of the needle is correctly located. While the needle is slowly withdrawn, the rest of the solution is injected.

Follow-Up

The patient should not put weight on the foot for at least 3 days after the injection. After 10 to 14 days, the patient is seen again, and the foot is reassessed. It is rare when more than two injections are needed to achieve complete pain relief.

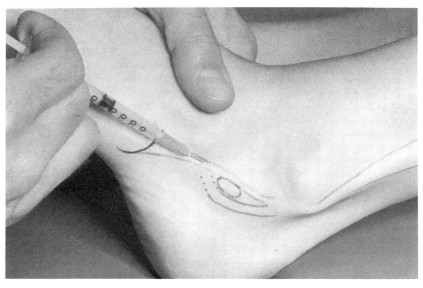

Figure 18–50 Injection between the tendon and tendon sheath of the peroneus brevis muscle just distal to the peroneal trochlea.

INSERTION TENDOPATHY OF THE PERONEUS BREVIS MUSCLE

Functional Examination

Passive extension, supination, and adduction of the foot are sometimes mildly painful (as a result of stretch forces on the affected structure). Resisted plantar flexion, pronation, and abduction of the foot are painful.

TRANSVERSE FRICTION

A lesion of the insertion of the peroneus brevis, at the tuberosity of the fifth metatarsal, is usually the result of overuse.

Position of the Patient

The patient is supine on the treatment table with the distal part of the lower leg resting on the therapist's thigh. The knee is positioned in slight flexion, supported by a pillow or roll.

Position of the Therapist

The therapist sits next to or on the end of the treatment table. If, for example, the left foot is affected, the therapist grasps the patient's forefoot from the medial aspect with the left hand and holds it in slight plantar flexion, pronation, and abduction. The right index finger, reinforced by the middle finger, is placed just plantar to the lesion. The thumb gives counterpressure at the medial side of the foot at the level of the first metatarsophalangeal joint.

Performance

By extension of the wrist during the active phase of the transverse friction, the index finger is moved from plantar to dorsal over the lesion (Figure 18–51). At the same time, pressure is exerted in a mediodistal direction.

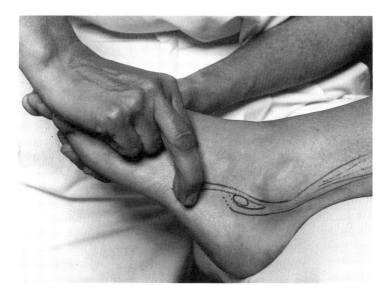

Figure 18–51 Transverse friction of the insertion of the peroneus brevis.

Duration

Usually four to six treatments of 15 minutes' duration are needed to provide complete pain relief. If, after six treatments, results are unsatisfactory, injection with a corticosteroid is indicated.

INJECTION

An injection at the level of the insertion of the peroneus brevis muscle is indicated when transverse friction has failed to achieve satisfactory results.

Position of the Patient

The patient is supine on the treatment table.

Position of the Physician

The physician sits or stands next to the end of the treatment table, facing the affected foot. With one hand, the physician holds the patient's foot in slight plantar flexion, pronation, and abduction.

Performance

A Mantoux syringe is filled with 1 mL of corticosteroid. From a proximal approach, a 2-cm long needle is inserted in a distal and medial direction at an angle of 40° to the lateral side of the foot (Figure 18–52). The site of the lesion is injected in a dropwise fashion, as directed by the patient's pain.

Follow-Up

The patient should not weight bear on the foot for 1 week after the injection. If a corticosteroid is used, usually only one injection is needed for full recovery. Sports activities are restarted 3 weeks later.

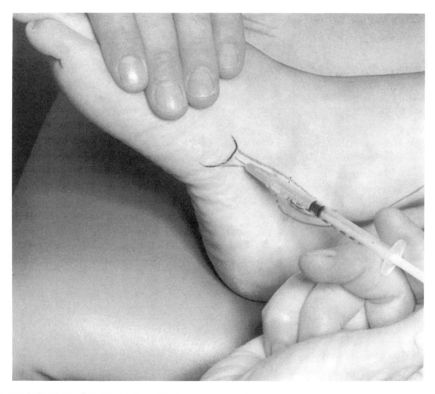

Figure 18–52 Injection of the insertion of the peroneus brevis.

TENOSYNOVITIS OF THE FLEXOR HALLUCIS LONGUS

Functional Examination

Passive extension of the great toe with the foot in extension is painful. In severe cases, accompanied by significant crepitation, resisted plantar flexion of the great toe is painful, especially when performed with the ankle in extension. For more detailed information, refer to Chapter 17.

TRANSVERSE FRICTION

Tenosynovitis of the flexor hallucis longus is particularly seen in gymnasts and ballet dancers.

Position of the Patient

The patient is supine on the treatment table.

Position of the Therapist

The therapist sits next to the end of the treatment table, facing the affected foot. If,

for example, the right foot is affected, the therapist grasps the patient's forefoot from the medioplantar aspect with the right hand, holding the foot in slight extension while the thumb holds the great toe in extension. The left index finger locates the lesion, just posterior to the sustentaculum tali. The left index finger, reinforced by the middle finger, is placed just posterior to the site of the lesion. The left thumb gives counterpressure at the level of the tarsal sinus on the lateral side of the ankle.

Performance

By extension of the wrist during the active phase of the transverse friction, the index finger is moved from posterior to anterior over the lesion (Figure 18–53). At the same time, pressure is exerted in a lateral direction.

Duration

The duration of treatment varies considerably. In some cases, only 3 treatments are

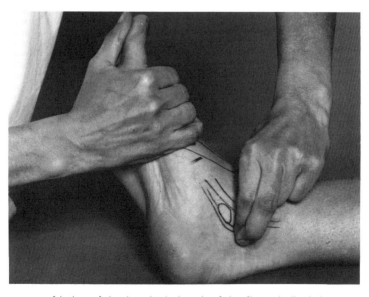

Figure 18–53 Transverse friction of the (tendon) sheath of the flexor hallucis longus.

needed. Other cases require as many as 10 to 15 sessions. Each treatment of transverse friction should last 10 to 15 minutes. If there is no significant improvement after 6 treatments, an injection between the tendon and tendon sheath is indicated.

INJECTION

An injection between the tendon and tendon sheath of the flexor hallucis longus is indicated when transverse friction has failed to achieve satisfactory results.

Position of the Patient

The patient is supine on the treatment table.

Position of the Physician

The physician sits or stands next to the end of the treatment table, facing the affected foot. With one hand, the physician holds the patient's leg in slight external rotation and the foot in slight extension.

Performance

A Mantoux syringe is filled with a local anesthetic (if there is no crepitation) or a corticosteroid (when there is crepitation). Just posterior to the sustentaculum tali, a 3-cm needle is inserted in a proximal direction until the resistance of the flexor hallucis longus tendon is felt. The needle is then slightly withdrawn, redirected almost parallel to the tendon, and pushed in again (Figure 18–54). As

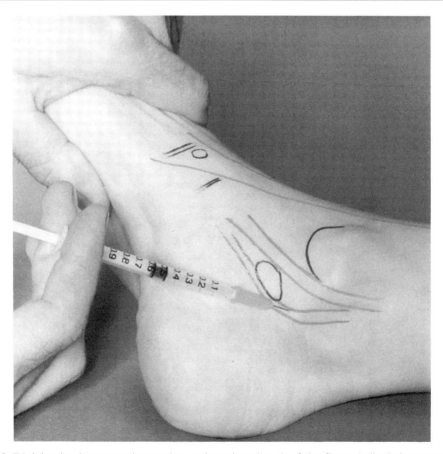

Figure 18–54 Injection between the tendon and tendon sheath of the flexor hallucis longus muscle.

long as there is no resistance against the needle, the tip lies between the tendon and tendon sheath. A small amount of solution is now injected. If there is an obvious longitudinal swelling along the tendon, the needle is correctly positioned, and the remainder of the solution is injected as the needle is slowly withdrawn.

Follow-Up

If a corticosteroid was used for the injection, the patient should not put weight on that foot for at least 3 days. If a local anesthetic was used, activities only have to be restricted for 1 day. Usually one to three injections are needed to achieve complete pain relief. In persistent cases, surgery may be indicated.

PLANTAR FASCIITIS

Functional Examination

The functional examination almost never provokes the patient's pain.

INJECTION

Plantar fasciitis is an overuse syndrome and is located at the mediodistoplantar aspect of the calcaneus. Here, the patient has localized tenderness to palpation.

Position of the Patient

The patient is supine on the treatment table.

Position of the Physician

The physician sits or stands next to the end of the treatment table, facing the affected foot. With one hand, the physician holds the patient's foot in extension.

Performance

Because the thick skin under the heel is difficult to disinfect, a point is chosen slightly more distal and medial, where the skin is thinner. A 2-mL syringe is filled with a corticosteroid, and a 5-cm long, thin needle is inserted in a posterior direction until the resistance of the fascia is felt, after which the bone of the calcaneus is contacted. Corresponding to the patient's pain, the site of the lesion is injected in a dropwise fashion (Figure 18–55).

Follow-Up

The patient should not put weight on the injected foot for at least 3 days after the injection. Afterward, a viscoelastic insole especially made for plantar fasciitis should be worn. After 1 week, the patient should begin stretching exercises for the calf muscles and Achilles tendon to stretch the fibers that connect the Achilles tendon to the plantar fascia. One injection is usually sufficient to achieve full recovery.

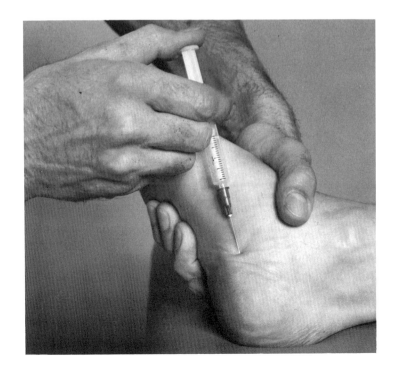

Figure 18–55 Injection of the origin of the plantar fascia at the calcaneus.

Chapter 19

Peripheral Compression Neuropathies in the Foot Region

COMPRESSION NEUROPATHY OF THE SUPERFICIAL PERONEAL NERVE

Compression neuropathies of the superficial peroneal nerve (L4 to S2) generally occur in the distal third of the lower leg at the lateral aspect, where the nerve goes through an opening in the deep fascia. Beyond this point, the nerve is only cutaneous (Figure 19–1). A compression neuropathy is usually caused by inversion or plantar flexion trauma of the foot.

Differential Diagnosis

- All lumbar and sacroiliac disorders that can cause pain in the L5 dermatome

Clinical Findings

The patient complains of burning superficial pain at the laterodistal aspect of the lower leg, the entire dorsum of the foot, and the first four toes. At a later stage, hypoesthesia and eventually anesthesia can occur.

Functional Examination

Passive inversion of the foot is painful. Palpation at the site of compression provokes pain that radiates in a distal direction.

Treatment

In many instances, the lesion heals after one to three perineural corticosteroid injections. A laterally wedged orthotic decreases the tension of the fascia at the laterodistal part of the lower leg. Surgical remedies may be pursued whenever conservative measures fail.

COMPRESSION NEUROPATHY OF THE DEEP PERONEAL NERVE

There are two predisposition sites in a compression neuropathy of the deep peroneal nerve: just distal to the inferior extensor retinaculum, and at the level of the base of the first metatarsal, where the nerve runs from underneath the tendon of the extensor hallucis brevis muscle to pierce the deep fascia (Figure 19–1). In the first instance, the cause of compression can be the wearing of shoes or boots that lace too high or too tightly. Edema, fractures, or inversion trauma can also damage the nerve. The nerve is vulnerable to direct trauma at the level of the base of the first metatarsal because of its rather unprotected course over the dorsum of the foot. The most common cause of a lesion at this site, however, is inversion trauma of the foot, whereby the nerve is overstretched.

Clinical Findings

Symptoms depend on the location of the compression (ie, whether the medial or lateral branch is affected). If the medial branch is affected, the patient experiences pain in the great toe and second toe. If the lateral branch is compressed, the patient complains of vaguely local-

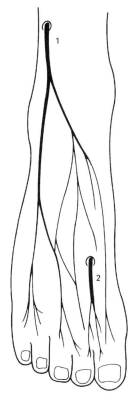

Figure 19–1 Superficial (**1**) and deep (**2**) peroneal nerves.

ized pain in the midfoot region. The pain often radiates proximally in the peroneal region, which makes locating the lesion difficult. In severe cases, weakness of the extensor digitorum is experienced.

Treatment

Initial treatment is conservative. After the site of compression is first confirmed by means of an injection with a local anesthetic, a perineural injection with corticosteroid can be given. Surgery may be indicated when conservative treatment is unsuccessful.

TARSAL TUNNEL SYNDROME

Tarsal tunnel syndrome involves both motor and sensory fibers of the tibial nerve (L4

to S3), which become compressed in the tarsal tunnel, underneath the flexor retinaculum at the medial side of the ankle (Figure 19–2). The cause is usually a fracture of the medial malleolus or the calcaneus. In most cases, the compression is brought about by posttraumatic edema. In some cases, an extreme valgus position of the calcaneus and a sagging medial arch can lead to compression.

Differential Diagnosis

- Lumbar and sacroiliac disorders that can cause pain in the L4 to S2 dermatomes
- Compression neuropathy of the plantar pedal nerves (in this instance, the heel is not painful)

Clinical Findings

The patient experiences burning pain in the heel alone or in conjunction with pain at the sole of the foot and the toes. In severe

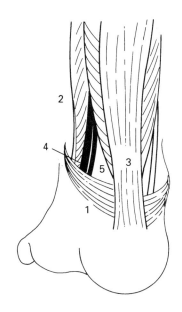

Figure 19–2 Tarsal tunnel (posteromedial aspect of the right foot). **1**, Flexor retinaculum; **2**, flexor digitorum longus muscle; **3**, Achilles tendon; **4**, posterior tibial artery; **5**, tibial nerve.

cases only, there may be a deficit of the intrinsic muscles of the foot, involving mostly the flexors of the metatarsophalangeal joints.

Functional Examination

Passive valgus of the calcaneus is sometimes painful. Local pressure provokes radiating pain at the level of the tarsal tunnel.

Treatment

If necessary, orthotics may be used to correct the weight-bearing position of the foot. Injection of a corticosteroid in the tarsal tunnel rarely resolves the symptoms. In chronic cases, surgical treatment is indicated.

COMPRESSION NEUROPATHY OF THE MEDIAL AND LATERAL PLANTAR NERVES

The medial plantar nerve is a sensory and motor nerve that primarily innervates the muscles that function to flex the toes. The lateral plantar nerve is also a sensory and motor nerve that innervates the other intrinsic muscles of the foot, such as the lumbricals and interossei. Both nerves spring from the tibial nerve and run through two fibrous openings in the abductor hallucis muscle at the medial side of the calcaneus (Figure 19–3). The cause of this lesion is usually either forced eversion or acute or chronic overstretching of the medial arch of the foot, such as in hyperpronation of the foot during running.

Differential Diagnosis

- Plantar fasciitis
- Tarsal tunnel syndrome
- Compression neuropathy of the pedal interdigital nerves

Clinical Findings

The patient complains of burning pain in the sole of the foot or toes. Depending on

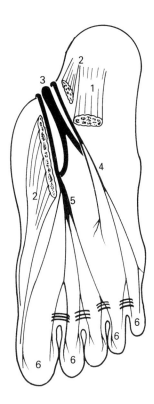

Figure 19–3 Nerves at the plantar aspect of the right foot. **1**, Flexor digitorum brevis muscle; **2**, abductor hallucis muscle; **3**, posterior tibial artery; **4**, lateral plantar nerve; **5**, medial plantar nerve; **6**, pedal digital nerves.

which branch is affected, the pain is felt more medially or laterally. If there are also sensory disturbances in the heel, the cause is more proximally located and usually results from tarsal tunnel syndrome.

Functional Examination

Passive inversion of the foot can be painful. There is severe tenderness to palpation at the site of compression.

Treatment

If necessary, an orthotic can be used to position the foot correctly. If the result is unsatisfactory, surgical measures are indicated. Left untreated, deficits of the intrinsic muscles can occur.

COMPRESSION NEUROPATHY OF THE PEDAL DIGITAL NERVES AND MORTON'S NEURALGIA

This compression neuropathy occurs between the heads of the metatarsals, under the metatarsal ligament. The disorder is called Morton's neuralgia when the pedal digital nerve between the heads of the third and fourth metatarsals is compressed. The cause is acute or chronic hyperextension of the metatarsophalangeal joints, which may be incurred in activities such as walking on high heels or rising up on the toes while in a squatting position. This lesion is often seen in conjunction with hallux valgus or other painful disorders of the big toe. The patient tends to place increased pressure on the other metatarsophalangeal joints so that the load can be taken off the first metatarsophalangeal joint.

Clinical Findings

Most of the time, pain is experienced in the lateral aspect of the third toe and the medial aspect of the fourth toe. Initially, symptoms are only felt during walking, but later pain is felt at rest, particularly at night. Pain often radiates proximally in the foot, especially when the lesion is located between the second and third metatarsals.

Functional Examination

Passive hyperextension of the metatarsophalangeal joints is painful. During palpation, severe tenderness is found between the heads of the metatarsals at the site of the compression neuropathy.

Treatment

Treatment consists of placing support under the heads of the metatarsals and correcting the position of the foot using orthotics. If conservative treatment is unsuccessful, the nerve may be surgically removed.

PART III—ANKLE AND FOOT REVIEW QUESTIONS

1. What is the maximal close-packed position of the ankle?

2. What is the maximal loose-packed position in the ankle?

3. What is the capsular pattern of the midtarsal joint?

4. List the different parts of the deltoid ligament.

5. What are the components of eversion in the foot?

6. What is the predilection site of osteochondritis dissecans of the talus? What is the predilection site of an osteochondral talus fracture?

7. Describe the clinical findings in anterior tibiotalar compression syndrome.

8. What are two causes of a significant inversion limitation of motion in the foot?

9. What is Köhler's bone disease?

10. Which motion is most limited in hallux rigidus? Which motion is most limited in hallux valgus?

11. Which structure is affected when the anterior drawer test of the ankle is painful but not hypermobile? What sort of lesion does this concern?

12. Which ligament, in particular, is tested during eversion of the foot with an extended knee?

13. List six possible complications in inversion trauma of the foot.

14. Why is stretching particularly of the soleus muscle so important in achillodynia?

15. What is the predilection site of an Achilles tendon rupture?

16. Which structures are compromised in anterior compartment syndrome?

17. What is the most painful test in tibialis posterior tenosynovitis?

18. What are the different lesions of the tibialis anterior muscle? List the predilection sites for each lesion.

19. What is a functional hallux rigidus?

20. Which test(s) is (are) usually positive during the functional examination of a patient with plantar fasciitis?

21. Where does the march fracture usually occur?

22. Define calcaneoapophysitis.

23. What is the most painful test in peroneal tenosynovitis?

24. How can one differentiate subtendinous Achilles bursitis from achillodynia?

25. What is plantar fibromatosis?

26. Where is a ganglion in the metatarsus usually seen?

27. Where can one best palpate the dorsal pedal artery?

28. Which branch of the peroneal nerve runs most superficially over the dorsum of the foot?

29. By which commonly seen form variation of the foot does a painful irritation of the plantar calcaneonavicular ligament occur?

30. Which motion is the most limited in arthritis of the subtalar joint?

PART III—ANKLE AND FOOT REVIEW ANSWERS

1. Maximal dorsiflexion.

2. Approximately 10° plantar flexion in the talocrural joint and the midposition between maximal inversion and eversion of the foot.

3. Inversion (plantar flexion–adduction–supination) is more limited than dorsiflexion.

4. Anterior tibiotalar ligament, tibionavicular ligament, tibiocalcaneal ligament, posterior tibiotalar ligament.

5. Dorsiflexion, abduction, and pronation with the calcaneus in valgus.

6. In osteochondritis dissecans, the lateral side of the talus is affected. In osteochondral fracture, the medial side of the talus is affected.

7. Pain at the anterior aspect of the ankle, painful passive dorsiflexion, local tenderness and sometimes swelling at the level of the neck of the talus and the anteroinferior aspect of the tibia.

8. Congenital fusion between two tarsal bones; it usually involves the talus and calcaneus or the calcaneus and navicular. Arthritis of the subtalar joint with a secondary spasm of the peroneal muscles and the extensor digitorum longus muscle.

9. Aseptic necrosis of the navicular bone in children between the ages of 3 and 8 years.

10. Extension in hallux rigidus. Adduction in hallux valgus.

11. Sprain of the anterior talofibular ligament or the anterior tibiotalar ligament. Grade 1 lesion.

12. Posterior tibiotalar ligament.

13. Dislocation of the peroneal tendons, strain of the peroneal tendons and/or tendon sheaths, tarsal sinus syndrome, avulsion fracture of the lateral malleo-lus, avulsion fracture of the base of the fifth metatarsal, impression fracture of the medial side of the neck of the talus.

14. The medial side of the Achilles tendon is the most frequently affected. At the level of the Achilles tendon, the soleus muscle fibers run predominantly medially.

15. The hypovascular zone, 2 to 6 cm proximal to the calcaneus.

16. Deep peroneal nerve, tibialis anterior muscle, extensor digitorum longus muscle.

17. Passive eversion of the foot (stretch).

18. Tendinitis, which can be localized anywhere in the tendon; tenosynovitis, at the level of the dorsum of the foot; tenomyosynovitis, at the level of the musculotendinous junction.

19. As a result of tendovaginitis stenosans, the great toe cannot be extended when the foot is positioned in dorsal extension. On the other hand, the great toe is able to extend when the foot is in other positions.

20. The functional examination is usually negative! Palpation is the only positive finding.

21. The neck of the second or third metatarsal.

22. Irritation of the soft tissue at the level of the calcaneal tuberosity as a result of compression (shoes). In less recent literature, the lesion is described as aseptic bone necrosis.

23. Passive dorsal extension, adduction, and supination of the foot (stretch).

24. When there is no clear fluctuation, one can differentiate by performing transverse friction (a decrease in pain occurs with achillodynia, whereas an increase in pain occurs with bursitis) or

by injecting a local anesthetic into the bursa.

25. The pathology concerns nodules that are connected to the medial aspect of the plantar fascia at the level of the flexor hallucis longus tendon just proximal to the head of the first metatarsal.

26. Between the heads of two metatarsal bones.

27. Between the heads of the second and third metatarsals.

28. Superficial peroneal nerve, intermediate ramus.

29. Pes plano valgus.

30. Varus motion.

PART III—REFERENCES

1. Langelaan EJ van. De bewegingen van de tarsale beenderen. In: Huson A, Winkel D, eds. *Voetenwerk.* Alphen aan den Rijn, Holland: Samsom/Stafleu;1985.

2. Mann RA, Inman VT. Phasic activity of intrinsic muscles of the foot. *J Bone Joint Surg Am.* 1964;46:469–478.

3. Bojsen Möller F. Calcaneocuboid joint and stability of the longitudinal arch of the foot at high and low gear push off. *J Anat.* 1979;129:165–176.

4. Morton DJ. *The Human Foot, Its Evolution, Physiology and Functional Disorders.* New York, NY: Columbia University Press; 1935.

5. Collis WJMF, Jayson MIV. Measurement of pedal pressures: An illustration of a method. *Ann Rheum Dis.* 1972;31:215–220.

6. Mann RA. Biomechanics of the foot. In: American Academy of Orthopaedic Surgeons, ed. *Atlas of Orthotics.* St Louis, Mo: Mosby; 1975:XX–XX.

7. Mann RA. Biomechanics. In: Jahss MH, ed. *Disorders of the Foot, I.* Philadelphia, Pa: Saunders; 1982.

8. Smekens J. *Podologische en biomechanische aspecten van het menselijk voortbewegings apparaat.* Brussels, Belgium: Independent University of Brussels Laboratory for Biomechanics and Biometry.

9. Cyriax J. *Textbook of Orthopaedic Medicine.* 7th ed. London, England: Baillière Tindall; 1978; 1.

PART III—SUGGESTED READING

Acker JH, Drez D. Nonoperative treatment of stress fractures of the proximal shaft of the fifth metatarsal (Jones' fracture). *Foot Ankle.* 1986;7:152–155.

Aldea PA, Shaw WW. Management of acute lower extremity nerve injuries. *Foot Ankle.* 1986;7:82–94.

Alexander IJ, Johnson DA, Berquist TH. Magnetic resonance imaging in the diagnosis of disruption of the posterior tibial tendon. *Foot Ankle.* 1987;8:144–147.

Alfred RJ, Jacobs R. Occult foreign bodies of the foot. *Foot Ankle.* 1984;4:209–211.

Allen MJ, Barnes MR. Exercise pain in the lower leg: Chronic compartment syndrome and medial tibial syndrome. *J Bone Joint Surg Br.* 1986;68:818–823.

Alvarez R, Haddad RJ, Gould N, Trevino S. The simple bunion: Anatomy at the metatarsophalangeal joint of the great toe. *Foot Ankle.* 1984;4:229–240.

Amis AA, Campbell JR, Miller JH. Strength of carbon and polyester fibre tendon replacements: Variation after operation in rabbits. *J Bone Joint Surg Br.* 1985;67:829–834.

Amis J, Jennings L, Graham D, Graham CE. Painful heel syndrome: Radiographic and treatment assessment. *Foot Ankle.* 1988;9:91–99.

Andrews JR, Previte WJ, Carson WG. Arthroscopy of the ankle: Technique and normal anatomy. *Foot Ankle.* 1985;6:29–33.

Aradi AJ, Wong J, Walsh M. The dimple sign of a ruptured lateral ligament of the ankle: Brief report. *J Bone Joint Surg Br.* 1988;70:327.

Aronson J, Nunley J, Frankovitch K. Lateral talocalcaneal angle in assessment of subtalar valgus: Follow-up of seventy Grice-Green arthrodeses. *Foot Ankle.* 1983;4:56–63.

Atar D, Grant AD, Lehmen WB. Trile arthrodesis. *Foot Ankle.* 1990;11:45–46.

Attarian DE, McCrackin HJ, DeVito HJ, et al. Biomechanical characteristics of human ankle ligaments. *Foot Ankle.* 1985;6:54–58.

Baird RA, Jackson ST. Fractures of the distal part of the fibula with associated disruption of the deltoid ligament: Treatment without repair of the deltoid ligament. *J Bone Joint Surg Am.* 1987;69:1346–1352.

Barbari SG, Brevig K, Egge T. Reconstruction of the lateral ligamentous structures of the ankle with a modified Watson-Jones procedure. *Foot Ankle.* 1987;7:362–368.

Battista AF, Battista R. The anatomy and physiology of the peripheral nerve. *Foot Ankle.* 1986;7:65–70.

Bauer M, Bengnér-Johnell O, Redlund-Johnell I. Supination-eversion fractures of the ankle joint: Changes in incidence over 30 years. *Foot Ankle.* 1987;8:26–28.

Baxter DE, Thigpen CM. Heel pain: Operative results. *Foot Ankle.* 1984;5:16–25.

Bejjani FJ, Halpern N, Pio A, et al. Musculoskeletal demands on flamenco dancers: A clinical and biomechanical study. *Foot Ankle.* 1988;8:254–263.

Bejjani FJ, Jahss MH. Ledouble's study of muscle variations of the human body, part II: Muscle variations of the foot. *Foot Ankle.* 1986;6:157–176.

Bell S. Repeat compartment decompression with partial fasciectomy. *J Bone Joint Surg Br.* 1986;68:815–817.

Berg D van den, Vogels M. Preventie! Noodzaak bij hardloopblessures. 'S Gravenhage: Haagse Hogeschool, Afdeling Fysiotherapie.

Bernstein SM, Berstein BH, Isaacson J. Scleroderma of the foot: Orthopaedic treatment. *Foot Ankle.* 1983;4:33–38.

Berry JL, Thaeler-Oberdoerster DA, Greenwald AS. Subchondral pathways to the superior surface of the human talus. *Foot Ankle.* 1986;7:2–9.

Bhansali RM, Bhansali RR. Accessory abductor hallucis causing entrapment of the posterior tibial nerve. *J Bone Joint Surg Br.* 1987;69:479–480.

Birkeland S, Mølster A, Hordvik M. Should syndesmosis screws be removed? *Acta Orthop Scand.* 1990;61(Suppl 239).

Boldingh EJK, Hermans J, Pijkeren T van, Wijkmans DW. De invloed van een tapis roulant op het looppatroon. *Ned Tijdschr Geneeskd.* 1984;94:234–237.

Bolton-Maggs BG, Sudlow RA, Freeman MAR. Total ankle arthroplasty: A long-term review of the London hospital experience. *J Bone Joint Surg Br.* 1985;67:785–790.

Boni M, Nenazzo F, Castelli C. Physiopathology of the tendon diseases in sports. *Sports Med Track Field Athlet.* 1985;28:29–34.

Bordelon RL. Subcalcaneal pain: A method of evaluation and plan for treatment. *Clin Orthop.* 1983;177:49–53.

Bracey SR. The effects of podiatric orthoses. Br *Osteopathol J.* 1983;15:135–137.

Bracey SR. The sporting foot. *Br Osteopathol J.* 1982;14:108–112.

Breederveld RS. Traumatische luxatie van de peroneus pezen. *Geneesknd Sport.* 1981;14:132–134.

Brodsky AE, Khalil MA. Talar compression syndrome. *Foot Ankle.* 1987;7:338–344.

Brody DM. Running injuries. *Clin Symp.* 1980;32-4:1–36.

Brunet JA, Wiley JJ. The late results of tarsometatarsal joint injuries. *J Bone Joint Surg Br.* 1987;69:437–440.

Bultsra SK, Neve WC. Resultaten van operatieve behandeling van laterale enkelbandlaesies. *Geneesknd Sport.* 1987;20:105–106.

Carden DG, Noble J, Chalmers J, et al. Rupture of the calcaneal tendon: The early and late management. *J Bone Joint Surg Br.* 1987;69:416–419.

Carl A, Ross S, Evanski P, Waugh T. Hypermobility in hallux valgus. *Foot Ankle.* 1988;8:264–270.

Cass JR, Morrey BF, Chao EYS. Three-dimensional kinematics of ankle instability following serial sectioning of lateral collateral ligaments. *Foot Ankle.* 1984;5:142–149.

Cavanagh PP. The biomechanics of lower extremity action in distance running. *Foot Ankle.* 1987;7:197–217.

Cavanagh PR, Andrew GC, Kram R, et al. An approach to biomechanical profiling of elite distance runners. *Int J Sports Biomech.* 1985;1:36–62.

Cetti R. Conservative treatment of injury to the fibular ligaments of the ankle. *Br J Med.* 1982;16:47–52.

Chang JW, Griffiths H, Chan DPK. A new radiological technique for the forefoot. *Foot Ankle.* 1984;5:77–83.

Clain A, ed. *Hamilton Bailey's Demonstrations of Physical Signs in Clinical Surgery.* Bristol, England: Wiley; 1965.

Clement DB, Taunton JE, Smart GW. Achilles tendinitis and peritendinitis: Etiology and treatment. *Am J Sports Med.* 1984;12:179–184.

Cofield RJ, Morrison MJ, Beaubout JW. Diabetic neuroarthropathy in the foot: Patient characteristics and patterns of radiographic change. *Foot Ankle.* 1983;4:15–22.

Colville MR, Colville JM, Manoli A. Posteromedial dislocation of the ankle without fracture. *J Bone Joint Surg Am.* 1987;69:706–710.

Condon SM, Hutton RS. Soleus muscle electromyographic activity and ankle dorsiflexion range of motion during four stretching procedures. *Phys Ther.* 1987;67:24–30.

Coughlin MJ. Crossover second toe deformity. *Foot Ankle.* 1987;8:29–39.

Cowell HR. The management of club foot. *J Bone Joint Surg Am.* 1985;67:991–992.

Crawford Adams J. *Outline of Orthopaedics.* 6th ed. London, England: Churchill Livingstone; 1967.

Dall G. Dynamic assessment of the load distribution on the plantar surface of the foot using the University of Capetown walkway and its clinical application. *Foot Ankle.* 1984;4:286–291.

DeRosa GP, Ahfeld SK. Congenital vertical talus: The Riley experience. *Foot Ankle.* 1984;5:118–124.

D'Hooghe M, Brys J. Biomechanische oorzaken van achillespees tendinitis en therapeutische benadering. In: *Congresboek. De Vijfde Sportgenesskundige Dagen van het AZ St Jan Brugge.* Brugge: Academisch Ziekenhuis St Jan; 1986:127–143.

Dooley BJ, Kudelka P, Menelaus MB. Subcutaneous rupture of the tendon of the tibialis anterior. *J Bone Joint Surg Br.* 1980;62:471–472.

Doxey GE. Calcaneal pain: A review of various disorders. *J Orthop Sports Phys Ther.* 1987;9:25–32.

Dyer CD. Visco-elastic insoles in long distance walking. *Br Osteopathol J.* 1983;15:79–82.

Edwards GS, DeLee JC. Ankle diastasis without fracture. *Foot Ankle.* 1984;4:305–312.

Ekstrand J, Tropp H. The incidence of ankle sprains in soccer. *Foot Ankle.* 1990;11:41–44.

Elftman H. The transverse tarsal joint and its control. *Clin Orthop.* 1960;16:14–47.

Elias N. *Über den Prozeß der Zivilisation.* 5th ed. Baden-Baden, Germany: Suhrkamp; 1978.

Evans GA, Hardcastle P, Frenyo AD. Acute rupture of the lateral ligament of the ankle. *J Bone Joint Surg Br.* 1984;66:209–212.

Falkenberg P, Nygaard H. Isolated anterior dislocation of the proximal tibiofibular joint. *J Bone Joint Surg Br.* 1983;65:310–311.

Fiévez AWFM, Biemen P van. Tenosynovitis van de flexor hallucis longus bij balletdansers: Sport-medische Praktijk. *Ned Tijdschr Geneeskd.* 1987;97:79–83.

Flick AB, Gould N. Osteochondritis dissecans of the talus (transchondral fractures of the talus): Review of the literature and new surgical approach for medial dome lesions. *Foot Ankle.* 1985;5:165–185.

Floyd DW, Heckman JD, Rockwood CA Jr. Tendon lacerations in the foot. *Foot Ankle.* 1983;4:8–14.

Freeman MAR. Treatment of ruptures of the lateral ligament of the ankle. *J Bone Joint Surg Br.* 1965;47:661–668.

Gardner E, Gray DJ, O'Rahilly R. *Anatomy.* Philadelphia, Pa: Saunders; 1975.

Gend J van, Vloedmans J. Hardloopschoenen en hun betekenis in de blessureprevenie. *Ned Tijdschr Geneeskd.* 1986;96:33–42.

Gessini L, Jandolo B, Pietrangeli A. The anterior tarsal syndrome: Report of four cases. *J Bone Joint Surg Am.* 1984;66:786–787.

Ghali NN, Abberton MJ, Silk FF. The management of metatarsus adductus et supinatus. *J Bone Joint Surg Br.* 1984;66:376–380.

Glasgow M, Jackson A, Jamieson AM. Instability of the ankle after injury to the lateral ligament. *J Bone Joint Surg Br.* 1980;62:196–200.

Glass MK, Karno ML, Sella EJ, Zeleznik R. An office based orthotic system in the treatment of the arthritic foot. *Foot Ankle.* 1982;3:37–40.

Graff KH, Krahl H. Überlastungschäden im Fußbereich beim Leichtathleten. *Lehre Leichtathlet.* 1984;3:81–87.

Graff KH, Krahl H, Kirschberger R. Streßfrakturen des Os Naviculare Pedis. *Z Orthop.* 1986;124:228–237.

Graham CE. Painful heel syndrome: Rationale of diagnosis and treatment. *Foot Ankle.* 1983;3:261–266.

Graham CE, Graham DM. Morton's neuroma: A microscopic evaluation. *Foot Ankle.* 1984;5:150–152.

Graswinckel JDCH, Koning J. Fibula- of enkelfractuur? *Ned Tijdschr Geneeskd.* 1978;122:2010–2013.

Gray H, Williams PL, Warwick R. *Gray's Anatomy.* 36th Ed. London, England: Churchill Livingstone; 1980.

Griffiths JD, Menelaus MB. Symptomatic ossicles of the lateral malleolus in children. *J Bone Joint Surg Br.* 1987;69:317–319.

Guiloff RJ, Scadding JW, Klenerman L. Morton's metatarsalgia: Clinical, electrophysiological and histological observations. *J Bone Joint Surg Br.* 1984;66:586–591.

Güngör T. A test for ankle instability: Brief report. *J Bone Joint Surg Br.* 1988;70:487.

Haak A, Steendijk R, de Wijn IF. *De samenstelling van het menselijk lichaam.* Assen: Van Gorcum; 1968.

Hafferl A. *Lehrbuch der topographischen Anatomie des Menschen.* Berlin, Germany: Springer Verlag; 1957.

Hamblen DL. Can the ankle joint be replaced? *J Bone Joint Surg Br.* 1985;67:689–690.

Hamilton WG. Sprained ankles in ballet dancers. *Foot Ankle.* 1982;3:99–102.

Hamilton WG. Stenosing tenosynovitis of the flexor hallucis longus tendon and posterior impingement upon the os trigonum in ballet dancers. *Foot Ankle.* 1982;3:74–80.

Hamilton WJ, Simon G, Hamilton SGI. *Surface and Radiological Anatomy.* 5th ed. London, England: Macmillan; 1976.

Hardaker WT Jr, Margello S, Goldner JL. Foot and ankle injuries in theatrical dancers. *Foot Ankle.* 1985;6:59–69.

Hardy AE. Assessment of foot movement. *J Bone Joint Surg Br.* 1987;69:838–839.

Harper MC. Deltoid ligament: An anatomical evaluation of function. *Foot Ankle.* 1987;8:19–22.

Hattrup SJ, Johnson KA. A review of ruptures of the Achilles tendon. *Foot Ankle.* 1985;6:34–38.

Hattrup SJ, Wood MB. Delayed neural reconstruction in the lower extremity: Results of interfascicular nerve grafting. *Foot Ankle.* 1986;7:105–109.

Hawkins RB. Arthroscopic treatment of sports-related anterior osteophytes in the ankle. *Foot Ankle.* 1988;9:87–90.

Healy EJ, Seybold WD. *A Synopsis of Clinical Anatomy.* Philadelphia, Pa: Saunders; 1969.

Heerkens YF, Meijer OG. *Tractus-anatomie.* Amsterdam, Holland: Interfaculty Physical Education. Amsterdam; 1980.

Helal B, Gibb P. Freiberg's disease: A suggested pattern of management. *Foot Ankle.* 1987;8:94–102.

Helming P, Fruensgaard S, Riss J, Støvring JO. Conservatively treated rupture of the Achilles tendon. *Acta Orthop Scand.* 1990;61(Suppl 239).

Hempfling H. Arthroskopie zur Diagnostiek der Instabilität am oberen Sprunggelenk (Bei unklaren klinischen und röntgenologischen Befunden). *Klinikarzt.* 1983;12:171–178.

Henderson J. Training to run marathons. *Runners World.* February 1978:74–78.

Herschel H, Van Meel PJ. Metatarsalgie. *Ned Tijdschr Geneesknd.* 1982;126:2056–2061.

Hocutt JE. Cryotherapy in ankle sprains. *Am J Sports Med.* 1982;10.

Hoppenfeld S. *Physical Examination of the Spine and Extremities.* New York, NY: Appleton-Century-Crofts; 1976.

Howard CB, Winston I, Bell W, et al. Late repair of the calcaneal tendon with carbon fibre. *J Bone Joint Surg Br.* 1984;66:206–208.

Howse AJG. Posterior block of the ankle joint in dancers. *Foot Ankle.* 1982;3:81–84.

Hynes RA, Romash MM. Bilateral symmetrical synchondrosis of navicular first cuneiform joint presenting as a lytic lesion. *Foot Ankle.* 1987;8:164–168.

Idema WL, Jansen BRH. Heilspoor bij lange afstandlopers. *Geneesknd Sport.* 1988;21:21–23.

Incavo SJ, Alvarez RG, Trevino SG. Occurrence of the plantaris tendon in patients sustaining subcutaneous rupture of the Achilles tendon. *Foot Ankle.* 1987;8:110–111.

Ippolito E, Ricciardi-Pollini PT. Invasive retrocalcaneal bursitis: A report of three cases. *Foot Ankle.* 1984;4:204–208.

Jahss MH. Shoes and shoe modifications. In: American Academy of Orthopaedic Surgeons, ed. *Atlas of Orthotics.* St Louis, Mo: Mosby; 1975:267–278.

Jahss MH. Spontaneous rupture of the tibialis posterior tendon: Clinical findings, tenographic studies, and a new technique of repair. *Foot Ankle.* 1982;3:158–166.

James S. Achilles tendon injuries. In: *Congresboek. De Vijfde Sportgenesskundige Dagen van het AZ St Jan Brugge.* Brugge: Academisch Ziekenhuis St. Jan; 1986:127–143.

James SL, Bates BT, Osternig LR. Injuries to runners. *Am J Sports Med.* 1978;6:40–45.

Janis JL, Mahl GF, Kagan J, Holt RR. *Personality, Dynamics, Development, and Assessment.* New York, NY: Harcourt, Brace & World; 1969.

Johnson EE, Markolf KL. The contribution of the anterior talofibular ligament to ankle laxity. *J Bone Joint Surg Am.* 1983;65:81–88.

Johnson KA. Tibialis posterior tendon rupture. *Clin Orthop.* 1983;177: 140–147.

Johnson KA, Spiegl PV. Extensor hallucis longus transfer for hallux varus deformity. *J Bone Joint Surg Am.* 1984;66:681–686.

Johnson KA, Stom DE. Tibialis posterior tendon dysfunction. *Clin Orthop.* 1989;239:196–206.

Johnson JE, Johnson KA. Dowel arthrodesis for degenerative arthritis of the tarsometatarsal (Lisfranc) joints. *Foot Ankle.* 1986;6:243–253.

Jones JR, Klenerman L. A study of the communicating branch between the medial and lateral plantar nerves. *Foot Ankle.* 1984;4:313–315.

Jørgensen U. Shock absorption of the heel pad is correlated with the anatomical structure. *Acta Orthop Scand.* 1990;61(Suppl 239).

Karlsson J, Bergsten T, Lansinger O, Peterson L. Lateral instability of the ankle treated by the Evans procedure: A long-term clinical and radiological follow-up. *J Bone Joint Surg Br.* 1988;70:476–480.

Karlsson J, Bergsten T, Lansinger O, Peterson L. Reconstruction of the lateral ligaments of the ankle for chronic lateral instability. *J Bone Joint Surg Am.* 1988;70:581–588.

Karlsson J, Lansinger O, Fraxen E. Nonsurgical treatment of chronic lateral insufficiency of the ankle joint. *Acta Orthop Scand.* 1990;61(Suppl 239).

Kay DB. The sprained ankle: Current therapy. *Foot Ankle.* 1985;6:22–28.

Kenzora JE. Symptomatic incisional neuromas on the dorsum of the foot. *Foot Ankle.* 1984;5:2–11.

Kernohan J, Dakin PK, Helal B. Dolorous calcification of the lateral sesamoid bursa of the great toe. *Foot Ankle.* 1984;5:45–46.

Kjærsgaard-Andersen P, Wethelund JO, Helmig P, Søballe K. The stabilizing effect of the ligamentous structures in the sinus and canalis tarsi on movements in the hindfoot: An experimental study. *Am J Sports Med.* 1988;16:512.

Kjærsgaard-Andersen P, Wethelund JO, Nielsen S. Lateral talocalcaneal instability following section of the calcaneofibular ligament: A kinesiologic study. *Foot Ankle.* 1987;7:355–361.

Kleiger B. Anterior tibiotalar impingement syndromes in dancers. *Foot Ankle.* 1983;3:69–73.

Kleinman M, Gross AE. Achilles tendon rupture following steroid injection. *J Bone Joint Surg Am.* 1983;65:1345–1347.

Kliman ME, Freiberg A. Ganglia of the foot and ankle. *Foot Ankle.* 1982;3:45–46.

Klos TVS, Tromperaars AJWM, Van Oppen RAM. Non-surgical treatment of complete ruptures of the Achilles tendon. *Acta Orthop Scand.* 1990;61(Suppl 239).

Koebke J. Der Fuß—eine fundtionell-anatomische Analyse, Teil 2. *Phys Ther.* 1988;9:662–668.

Konradsen L, Ravn JB. Ankle instability caused by prolonged peroneal reaction time. *Acta Orthop Scand.* 1990;61:388–390.

Konradsen L, Sommer H. Ankle instability caused by peroneal tendon rupture: A case report. *Acta Orthop Scand.* 1989;60:723–724.

Kosmahl EM, Kosmahl HE. Painful plantar heel, plantar fasciitis, and calcaneal spur: Etiology and treatment. *J Orthop Sports Phys Ther.* 1987;9:17–23.

Larsen E. Longitudinal rupture of the peroneus brevis tendon. *J Bone Joint Surg Br.* 1987;69:340–341.

Larsen E, Aru A. Synovitis in chronically unstable ankles. *Acta Orthop Scand.* 1989;60:340–344.

Lawson JP, Ogden JA, Sella E, Barwick KW. The painful accessory navicular. *Skeletal Radiol.* 1984;12:250–262.

Leach RE, Dilorio E, Harney RA. Pathologic hindfoot conditions in the athlete. *Clin Orthop.* 1983;177:116–121.

Leach RE, Seavey MS, Salter DK. Results of surgery in athletes with plantar fasciitis. *Foot Ankle.* 1986;7:156–161.

Leeds HC, Ehrlich MG. Instability of the distal tibiofibular syndesmosis after bimalleolar and trimalleolar ankle fractures. *J Bone Joint Surg Am.* 1984;66:490–503.

Leung PC, Hung LK, Leung KS. Use of the medial plantar flap in soft tissue replacement around the heel region. *Foot Ankle.* 1988;8:327–330.

Lillich JS, Baxter DE. Common forefoot problems in runners. *Foot Ankle.* 1986;7:145–151.

Löfström B. Zenuwblokkade in de enkelstreek. *Temp Med Ned.* 1981;10:47–57.

Löfvenverg R, Kärrholm J, Selvik G. Fibular mobility in chronic lateral instability of the ankle. *Foot Ankle.* 1990;11:22–29.

Löfvenverg R, Kärrholm J, Selvik G, et al. Chronic lateral instability of the ankle: Roentgen stereophotogrammetry of talar position. *Acta Orthop Scand.* 1989;60:34–39.

Lohman AGM. *Vorm en beweging. Leerboek van het bewegingsapparaat van de mens.* 4th ed. Utrecht, Netherlands: Bohn, Scheltema & Holkema; 1977.

London RT. Chronic intractable benign pain syndrome (CIBPS). *Foot Ankle.* 1986;7:133–137.

Lowdon A, Bader DL, Mowat AG. The effect of heel pads on the treatment of Achilles tendinitis: A double blind trial. *Am J Sports Med.* 1984;12:431–435.

Lusskin R. Orthopaedic aspects of chronic pain. *Foot Ankle.* 1986;7:138–141.

Lusskin R, Battista A. Evaluation and therapy after injury to peripheral nerves. *Foot Ankle.* 1986;7:71–81.

Lusskin R, Battista A, Lenzo S, Price A. Surgical management of late post-traumatic and ischemic neuropathies involving the lower extremities: Classification and results of therapy. *Foot Ankle.* 1986;7:95–104.

Maclellan GE, Vyvyan B. Management of pain beneath the heel and achilles tendinitis with visco-elastic heel inserts. *Br J Sports Med.* 1981;15:117–121.

Mann RA, Baxter DE, Lutter LD. Running symposium. *Foot Ankle.* 1981;1:190–224.

Mann RA, Mizel MS. Monarticular nontraumatic synovitis of the metatarsophalangeal joint: A new diagnosis? *Foot Ankle.* 1985;6:18–21.

Mann RA, Thompson FM. Rupture of the posterior tibial tendon causing flat foot: Surgical treatment. *J Bone Joint Surg Am.* 1985;67:556–561.

Maurice HD, Newman JH, Watt I. Bone scanning of the foot for unexplained pain. *J Bone Joint Surg Br.* 1987;69:448–452.

McCarroll JR, Schrader JW, Shelbourne KD, et al. Meniscoid lesions of the ankle in soccer players. *Am J Sports Med.* 1987;15:255–257.

McCullough CJ, Burge PA. Rotary stability of the load-bearing ankle: An experimental study. *J Bone Joint Surg Br.* 1980;62:460–464.

McDermott AGP. Monitoring dynamic anterior compartment pressures during exercise. *Am J Sports Med.* 1982;10:83–90.

McMinn RMH, Hutching RT. *A Color Atlas of Human Anatomy.* London, England: Wolfe Medical; 1977.

Melsert AC. Peritendinitis achillae. *Nederlands Tijdschrift voor Fysiotherapie.* 1980;6:202–208.

Meyer JM, Garcia J, Hoffmeyer P, Fritschy D. The subtalar sprain: A roentgenographic study. *Clin Orthop.* 1988;226:169–173.

Michel P, Segesser B, Feinstein R, Jenoure P. Chronische Achillessehnenbeschwerden: Prophylaktische

Maßnahmen im Training und beim Wettkampf. *Phys Ther.* 1987;8:20–23.

Milgrom C, Giladi M, Stein M, et al. Stress fractures in military recruits: A prospective study showing an unusually high incidence. *J Bone Joint Surg Br.* 1985;67:732–735.

Mitchell GP, Gibson JMC. Excision of calcaneo-navicular bar for painful spasmodic flat foot. *J Bone Joint Surg.* 1967;49:281–287.

Moppes FI, Van den Hoogenband CR, Greep JM. Adhesive capsulitis of the ankle (frozen ankle). *Arch Orthop Trauma Surg.* 1979;94:313–315.

Morgan CD, Henke JA, Bailey RW, Kaufer H. Long-term results of tibiotalar arthrodesis. *J Bone Joint Surg Am.* 1985;67:546–550.

Morgan RC Jr, Crawford AH. Surgical management of tarsal coalition in adolescent athletes. *Foot Ankle.* 1986;7:183–193.

Morgante D, Pathria M, Sartoris DJ, Resnick D. Subtalar and intertarsal joint involvement in hemophilia and juvenile chronic arthritis: Frequency and diagnostic significance of radiographic abnormalities. *Foot Ankle.* 1988;9:45–48.

Mosier KM, Asher M. Tarsal coalitions and peroneal spastic flat foot: A review. *J Bone Joint Surg Am.* 1984;66:977–984.

Mubarak SJ. The medial tibial stress syndrome. *Am J Sports Med.* 1982;10.

Murray MP, Drought AB, Kory RC. Walking patterns in normal men. *J Bone Joint Surg Am.* 1964;46:335–360.

Myerson MS. Experimental decompression of the fascial compartments of the foot: The basis for fasciotomy in acute compartment syndromes. *Foot Ankle.* 1988;8:308–314.

Nada A. Rupture of the calcaneal tendon: Treatment by external fixation. *J Bone Joint Surg Br.* 1985;67:449–453.

Nicholas JA, Marino M. The relationship of injuries of the leg, foot and ankle to proximal thigh strength in athletes. *Foot Ankle.* 1987;7:218–228.

Nigg BM. Belastung des menschlichen Bewegungsapparats bei ausgewählten Bewegungen im Kunstturnen. *Leistungssport.* 1981;11:93–100.

Nigg BM. Biomechanische Überlegungen zur Belastung des Bewegungsapparates: Die Belastungstoleranz des Bewegungsapparates, 3. *Heidelb Orthop Symp.* 1979:44–54.

Nigg BM, Luethi S. Bewegungsanalysen beim Laufschuh. *Sportwissenschaft.* 1980;10:309–320.

Nilsson S. Overuse injuries of the knee in runners: Injury mechanism and treatment. *Sports Med Track Field Athlet.* 1985;17:39–44.

Nistor L. Surgical and non-surgical treatment of Achilles tendon rupture. *J Bone Joint Surg.* 1981;63:394–399.

Nkele C, Aindow J, Grant L. Study of pressure of the normal anterior tibial compartment in different age groups using the slit-catheter method. *J Bone Joint Surg Am.* 1988;70:98–101.

Norfolk DF, Burton AK. Achilles tendinitis: A reasoned approach. *Br Osteopathol J.* 1983;15:61–64.

O'Brien T. The needle test for complete rupture of the Achilles tendon. *J Bone Joint Surg Am.* 1984;66:1099–1011.

Olney BW, Asher MA. Excision of symptomatic coalition of the middle facet of the talocalcaneal joint. *J Bone Joint Surg Am.* 1987;69:539–544.

Oppenheim W, Smith C, Christie W. Congenital vertical talus. *Foot Ankle.* 1985;5:198–204.

Parisien JS. Arthroscopy of the posterior subtalar joint: A preliminary report. *Foot Ankle.* 1986;6:219–224.

Parsch D. Sportverletzungen am Sprunggelenk. Spezielle Probleme beim Kind. Presented at the Symposium on Sports Lesions of the Capsuloligamentous Complex of the Knee and Ankle; November 1984; Stuttgart, Germany.

Pas CAGM van de. Acute en chronische dislocaties van de peroneus pezen. *Ned Tijdschr Geneesknd.* 1976;86:1–17.

Perry CR, Ritterbusch JK Jr, Burdge RE. Isolated avulsion of the tibial origin of the anterior tibiofibular ligament. *Foot Ankle.* 1986;6:260–264.

Perry J. Anatomy and biomechanics of the hindfoot. *Clin Orthop.* 1983;177:9–15.

Perry J, Ireland ML, Gronley J, Hoffer MM. Predictive value of manual muscle testing and gait analysis in normal ankles by dynamic electromyography. *Foot Ankle.* 1986;6:254–259.

Pförringer W. Sportberletzungen am Sprunggelenk. *Diagnostik.* Presented at the Symposium on Sports Lesions of the Capsuloligamentous Complex of the Knee and Ankle; November 1984; Stuttgart, Germany.

Pöll RG, Duijfjes F. The treatment of recurrent dislocation of the peroneal tendons. *J Bone Joint Surg Br.* 1984;66:98–100.

Powel JH, Whipple TL. Osteochondritis dissecans of the talus. *Foot Ankle.* 1986;6:309–310.

Pozo JL, Jackson AM. A rerouting operation for dislocation of peroneal tendons: Operative technique and case report. *Foot Ankle.* 1984;5:42–44.

Purnell ML, Drummond DS, Engber WD, Breed AL. Congenital dislocation of the peroneal tendons in the calcaneovalgus foot. *J Bone Joint Surg Br.* 1983;65:316–319.

Quiles M, Requena F, Gomez L, Garcia-Sancho L. Functional anatomy of the medial collateral ligament of the ankle joint. *Foot Ankle.* 1983;4:73–82.

Quirk R. Talar compression syndrome in dancers. *Foot Ankle.* 1982;3:65–68.

Ray S, Goldberg VM. Surgical treatment of the accessory navicular. *Clin Orthop.* 1983;177:61–66.

Renström P, Wertz M, Incavo S, et al. Strain in the lateral ligaments of the ankle. 1988;9:59–63.

Ricciardi-Pollini PT, Ippolito E, et al. Congenital club foot: Results of treatment of 54 cases. *Foot Ankle.* 1984;5:107–117.

Richardson EG. Injuries to the hallucal sesamoids in the athlete. *Foot Ankle.* 1987;7:229–244.

Rijt AJ van der, Evans GA. The long-term results of Watson-Jones tenodesis. *J Bone Joint Surg Br.* 1984;66:371–375.

Rorabeck CH. The treatment of compartment syndromes of the leg. *J Bone Joint Surg Br.* 1984;66:93–97.

Rorabeck CH, Bourne RB, Fowler PJ. The surgical treatment of exertional compartment syndrome in athletes. *J Bone Joint Surg Am.* 1983;65:1245–1251.

Rose GK, Welton EA, Marshall T. The diagnosis of flat foot in the child. *J Bone Joint Surg Br.* 1985;67:71–78.

Rosenberg ZS, Cheung Y, Jahss MH. Computed tomography scan and magnetic resonance imaging of ankle tendons: An overview. *Foot Ankle.* 1988;8:297–307.

Rosenkranz L, Cataletto MM. Metatarsalgia caused by an increase in circulating platelets: A case report. *Foot Ankle.* 1984;4:216–217.

Rossi WA. The high incidence of mismated feet in the population. *Foot Ankle.* 1983;4:105–112.

Roycroft S, Mantgani AB. Treatment of inversion injuries of the ankle by early active management. *Physiotherapy.* 1983;69:355–356.

Russe O, Gerhardt JJ, King PS. *An Atlas of Examination, Standard Measurements and Diagnosis in Orthopaedics and Traumatology.* Bern, Switzerland: Hans Huber Verlag; 1972.

Sande HBA van de. Wat te doen bij fikse distorsie van de laterale enkelbanden na een sprong bij volleyballen: (Röntgenfoto: geen fraktuur) Heeft direkte behandeling door de fysiotherapeut voordelen? *Vademecum.* 1983;1:26.

Sarrafian SJ. Functional characteristics of the foot and plantar aponeurosis under tibiotalar loading. *Foot Ankle.* 1987;8:4–18.

Satku K. Painful heel syndrome—an unusual cause: Case report. *J Bone Joint Surg Am.* 1987;66:607–609.

Schmidt DM, Romash MM. A traumatic avascular necrosis of the head of the talus: A case report. *Foot Ankle.* 1988;8:208–211.

Schoonbeek I van, Gheluwe B van, Deporte E. Wrijving bij tennis: De invloed van de tennisschoen, het speloppervlak en de voetstand. *Geneesknd Sport.* 1987;20:128–133.

Schreiber A, Differding P, Zollinger H. Talus partitus: A case report. *J Bone Joint Surg Br.* 1985;67:430–431.

Scranton PE. Treatment of symptomatic talocalcaneal coalition. *J Bone Joint Surg Am.* 1987;69:533–538.

Scranton PE. Use of internal compression in arthrodesis of the ankle. *J Bone Joint Surg Am.* 1985;67:550–555.

Scranton PE Jr, Shitesel JP, Farewell V. Cybex evaluation of the relationship between anterior and posterior compartment lower leg muscles. *Foot Ankle.* 1985;6:85–89.

Seale KS, Lange TA, Monson D, Hackbarth DA. Soft tissue tumors of the foot and ankle. *Foot Ankle.* 1988;9:19–27.

Segesser B. Sportverletzungen am Sprunggelenk. Therapie. Presented at the Symposium on Sports Lesions of the Capsuloligamentous Complex of the Knee and Ankle; November 1984; Stuttgart, Germany.

Segesser B, Nigg BM. Insertionstendinosen am Schienbein, Achillodynie und Überlastungsfolgen am Fuß—Ätiologie, Biomechanik, therapeutische Möglichkeiten. *Orthopäde.* 1980;9:207–214.

Seitz WH Jr, Grantham SA. The Jones' fracture in the nonathlete. *Foot Ankle.* 1985;6:97–100.

Sella EJ, Lawson JP. Biomechanics of the accessory navicular synchondrosis. *Foot Ankle.* 1987;8:156–163.

Shields CL, Redix L, Brewster CE. Acute tears of the medial head of the gastrocnemius. *Foot Ankle.* 1985;5:186–190.

Siegler S, Block J, Schneck CD. Mechanical characteristics of the collateral ligaments of the human ankle joint. *Foot Ankle.* 1988;8:234–242.

Silver RL, DeLaGarza J, Rang M. The myth of muscle balance: A study of relative strengths and excursions of normal muscles about the foot and ankle. *J Bone Joint Surg Br.* 1985;67:432–437.

Simons GW. Complete subtalar release in club feet, part I: A preliminary report. *J Bone Joint Surg Am.* 1985;67:1044–1055.

Simons GW. Complete subtalar release in club feet, part II: Comparison with less extensive procedures. *J Bone Joint Surg Am.* 1985;67:1056–1065.

Skraba JS, Greenwald AS. The role of the interosseous membrane on tibiofibular weightbearing. *Foot Ankle.* 1984;4:301–304.

Smart GW, Taunton JE, Clement DB. Achilles tendon disorders in runners: A review. *Med Sci Sports Exerc.* 1980;12:231–243.

Smith P III, Coker TP. Osteochondrosis dissecans occurring in the knee and ankle of the same patient. *Foot Ankle.* 1985;6:83–84.

Snel JG. Schokabsorberend vermogen van loopschoenen tijdens daadwerkelijk lopen. *Geneesknd Sport.* 1988;21:168–171.

Snijders CJ, Snijder JGN, Philippens MMGM. Biomechanics of hallux valgus and splay foot. *Foot Ankle.* 1986;7:26–39.

Sobotta J, Becher PH. *Atlas of Human Anatomy.* 9th English ed. Berlin, Germany: Urban & Schwarzenberg; 1975; 1–3.

Spiegl PV, Cullivan WT, Reiman HM, Johnson KA. Neurilemmoma of the lower extremity. *Foot Ankle.* 1986;6:194–198.

Staheli LT, Chew DE, Corbett M. The longitudinal arch: A survey of eight hundred and eighty-two feet in normal children and adults. *J Bone Joint Surg Am.* 1987;69:426–428.

Stauffer RN, Chao EYS, Brewster RC. Force and motion analysis of the normal, diseased and prosthetic ankle joint. *Clin Orthop.* 1977;127:189–196.

Steininger K. Das Sprunggelenk—eine Schwachstelle des menschlichen Bewegungsapparates. Prophylaktische Möglichkeiten und Tips zur funktionellen Nachbehandlung. *Phys Ther.* 1985;6:76–85.

Steininger K. Ursachen der Achillessehnenbeschwerden im Sport und prophylaktische Möglichkeiten. *Phys Ther.* 1985;6:523–531.

Stevens A, Rosselle A, Michels U, et al. A polyelectromyographical study of the lower extremity at sprain. *Electromyogr Clin Neurophysiol.* 1973;13:75–84.

Stibbe O. Chronisch spierlogesyndroom verreweg het meest frequent. *Maandbl NVVF.* 1985;11:11–18.

Stibbe O. Het spierlogesyndroom. *Arts Beweging.* 1986;5:3–5.

Stoller SM, Hekmat F, Kleiger B. A comparative study of the frequency of anterior impingement exostoses of the ankle in dancers and non-dancers. *Foot Ankle.* 1984;4:201–203.

St Pierre RK, Rosen J, Whitesides TE, et al. The tensile strength of the anterior talofibular ligament. *Foot Ankle.* 1983;4:83–85.

Taillard W, Meyer JM, Garcia J, Blanc Y. The sinus tarsi syndrome. *Int Orthop.* 1981;5:117–130.

Teitz CC, Harrington RM, Wiley H. Pressures on the foot in pointe shoes. *Foot Ankle.* 1985;5:216–221.

Ting AJ, Tarr RR, Sarmiento A, et al. The role of subtalar motion and ankle contact pressure changes from angular deformities of the tibia. *Foot Ankle.* 1987;7:290–299.

Tomino AJ. Behandelingsresultaten van conservatief behandelde bandletsels van het enkelgewricht. *Ned Tijdschr voor Fysiother.* 1982;20:21–24.

Turco VJ, Spinella AJ. Achilles tendon ruptures: Peroneus brevis transfer. *Foot Ankle.* 1987;7:253–259.

Vasavada PR, Vries DF de, Nishiyama Y. Plantar fasciitis: Early blood pool images in diagnosis of inflammatory process. *Foot Ankle.* 1984;5:74–76.

Viladot A, Lorenzo JC, Salazar J, Rodrequez A. The subtalar joint: Embryology and morphology. *Foot Ankle.* 1984;5:54–66.

Vink P. Is er een asymmetrie tijdens gewoon lopen. *Ned Tijdschr Fysiother.* 1984;94:238–239.

Visser JD. Achillespessruptuur. *Ned Tijdschr Geneesknd.* 1980;124:1340–1342.

Von Lambrecht R, Wagemann W, Fröhlich P. Beitrag zum Tibialis anterior-Syndrom. *Orthop Traumatol.* 1982;29:521–525.

Von Schnittker FJ, May E. Flake fractures der Talusrolle als Sportverletzung. *Dtsch Z Sportmed.* 1984;10:346–356.

Wagner KS, Tarr RR, Resnick C, Sarmiento A. The effect of simulated tibial deformities on the ankle joint during the gait cycle. *Foot Ankle.* 1984;5:131–141.

Walker AP, Ghali NN, Sild FF. Congenital vertical talus: The results of staged operative reduction. *J Bone Joint Surg Br.* 67:117–121.

Wallensten R. Results of fasciotomy in patients with medial tibial syndrome or chronic anterior compartment syndrome. *J Bone Joint Surg Am.* 1983;65:1252–1255.

Ward WG, Clippinger FW. Proximal medial longitudinal arch incision for plantar fascia release. *Foot Ankle.* 1987;8:152–155.

Werken C van der, Marti RK. Rupturen van de achilespees. *Ned Tijdschr Geneesknd.* 1982;126:2129–2132.

Williams PL, Smibert JG, Cox R, et al. Imaging study of the painful heel syndrome. *Foot Ankle.* 1987;7:345–349.

Winkel D, Fisher S. *Schematisch handboek voor onderzoek en behandeling van weke delen aandoeningen van het bewegingsapparaat.* 6th ed. Delft, Netherlands: Nederlandse Akademie voor Orthopedische Geneeskunde; 1982.

Winkel D, Huson A, eds. *Voetenwerk.* Alphen aan den Rijn; Samsom/Stafleu; 1985.

Wischhöfer E. Sportverletzungen am Sprunggelenk. Presented at the Symposium on Sports Lesions of the Capsuloligamentous Complex of the Knee and Ankle; November 1984; Stuttgart, Germany.

Wroble RR, Nepola JV, Malvitz TA. Ankle dislocation without fracture. *Foot Ankle.* 1988;9:64–74.

Young MC, Fornasier VL, Cameron HU. Osteochondral disruption of the second metatarsal: A variant of Freiberg's infraction? *Foot Ankle.* 1987;8:103–109.

Zinman C, Wolfson N, Reis ND. Osteochondritis dissecans of the dome of the talus: Computed tomography scanning in diagnosis and follow-up. *J Bone Joint Surg Am.* 1988;70:1017–1019.

Zwipp H, Tscherne H, Hoffmann R, Thermann H. Riß der Knöchelbände: Operative oder konservative Behandlung. *Dtsch Ärztebl.* 1988;85:2019–2022.

Zypen E van der, Tischendorf F. Die Topographie der Faszienlogen: Eine anatomische Studie zum Compartment-Syndrom der Extremitäten. *Phys Ther.* 1987;8:275–283.

Appendix A

Schematic Topography of the Lower Extremity Nerves and Blood Vessels

INNERVATION OF THE LOWER EXTREMITY

Innervation of the lower extremities is supplied by the ventral rami of the L1 to S3 spinal nerves. These rami join together to make up the lumbosacral plexus, with the lumbar plexus forming the cranial part and the sacral plexus forming the caudal part.

Most of the lumbar plexus, together with the psoas major muscle, runs caudally, innervating both this muscle and the quadratus lumborum. Nerves run from the lumbar plexus to the abdominal muscles and the region of the external sex organs. The iliohypogastric nerve runs in the abdominal wall over the iliac crest, supplying cutaneous innervation in the region of the gluteus medius. The ilioinguinal nerve runs below the iliohypogastric nerve and sends a branch to the scrotum or labia majora. The genitofemoral nerve divides into a genital ramus and a femoral ramus. The genital ramus runs through the inguinal canal and innervates a medial part of the groin and the sex organs. The femoral ramus runs through the lacuna vasorum and innervates the skin at the lateral part of the groin.

The lateral femoral cutaneous nerve is an important nerve arising from the lumbar plexus. It runs over the iliacus muscle and then either penetrates or runs underneath the inguinal ligament. This nerve innervates the skin at the lateral side of the thigh, where in some instances it can be palpated along its entire length.

After leaving the lumbar plexus, the obturator nerve dives for a short distance into the lesser pelvis and then runs through the obturator canal to the anterior side of the upper leg. It enters the thigh between the origins of the adductor muscles, which it innervates. Because it lies so deeply, it is difficult to palpate. Its small cutaneous branch, which innervates the part of the skin above the knee at the medial aspect of the thigh, is also difficult to palpate.

From the standpoint of surface anatomy, of all the nerves coming from the lumbar plexus, the femoral nerve is the most significant. It runs along the medial edge of the psoas muscle distally and exits the pelvis in the lacuna musculorum, where it is palpable just lateral to the femoral artery. In the pelvis, it innervates the iliacus muscle and also gives off several cutaneous branches. In the thigh, it innervates the quadriceps femoris and sartorius muscles. These motor branches and the small cutaneous branches from the femoral nerve cannot be palpated. A deeper sensory branch, the saphenous nerve, runs together with the artery in the adductor canal. The nerve then separates from the artery; whereas the artery runs posteriorly through the adductor hiatus, the nerve penetrates the fascia anteriorly, where it runs past the medial aspect of the knee. From here, it accompanies the greater saphenous vein in the lower leg.

The sacral plexus lies directly in front of the sacroiliac joints. Pathologic processes that take up space in this region can lead to diffuse and serious disturbances in the innervation of the legs. All the nerves from the sacral plexus run through the back wall of the lesser pelvis, through which they exit. The superior gluteal nerve exits directly above the piriformis muscle and innervates the abductor muscles. Paresis of this nerve leads to the so-called Trendelenburg* sign.

The inferior gluteal nerve exits the pelvis below the piriformis muscle and then innervates the gluteus maximus muscle. Patients with a paresis of this nerve can no longer get into the squatting position. The posterior femoral cutaneous nerve also exits the pelvis below the piriformis muscle and runs farther under the gluteus maximus. This nerve, which is not palpable, supplies the skin of the buttocks and perineum.

The sciatic nerve is by far the thickest nerve in the human body. After either penetrating or coming from below the piriformis muscle, it runs distally. It is palpable at the crossing point of the distal border of the gluteus maximus muscle and the lateral border of the biceps femoris muscle. Farther distally, it courses underneath the biceps femoris muscle to the back of the knee, where it divides into the common peroneal and tibial nerves. The precise level of this division is interindividually variable.

The common peroneal nerve is easily palpable at the medial side of the tendon of the biceps femoris muscle. In the popliteal fossa, this nerve gives off a branch (the lateral sural cutaneous nerve) that supplies sensory innervation to the lateral side of the lower leg. At the level of the fibular head, the common peroneal nerve divides into the deep and su-

perficial peroneal nerves. The deep peroneal nerve runs distally, deep within the extensor compartment. The superficial peroneal nerve innervates the peroneal muscles, becomes superficial at the distal end of the lower leg, and then runs farther to the dorsum of the foot, where it can be palpated. The deep peroneal nerve innervates the skin at the dorsum of the foot between the first and second metatarsals, where it can sometimes be palpated.

At the back of the knee, the tibial nerve gives off branches to the superficial flexors of the foot. Also in this region, a sensory branch divides from the tibial nerve. It innervates the posterior and lateral aspects of the lower leg and continues on as the lateral dorsal cutaneous nerve. The lateral dorsal cutaneous nerve can be palpated at the level of the lateral malleolus. The tibial nerve itself runs in the deep posterior compartment. Often, it can be palpated behind the medial malleolus. It divides into two terminal branches, the medial and lateral plantar nerves, which innervate the sole of the foot.

Sciatic Nerve (Figure A–1)

Derivation

From the nerve roots L4 to S3.

Course

The sciatic nerve exits the pelvis through the infrapiriformis foramen. Occasionally, it penetrates the piriformis muscle. It passes medial to the midpoint of a straight line between the greater trochanter and the ischial tuberosity and then runs to the tip of the popliteal fossa. In the thigh it divides into the tibial and common peroneal nerves. Unlike the popliteal artery and vein, the tibial nerve stays superficial in the popliteal fossa. The distal course of the tibial nerve is projected along an imaginary line from the midpoint of the popliteal fossa to a point between the Achilles tendon and the medial malleolus. It passes deeply behind the medial malleolus and then divides into the me-

---

*Friedrich Trendelenburg, 1844–1924, surgeon in Rostock, Bonn, and Leipzig, Germany.

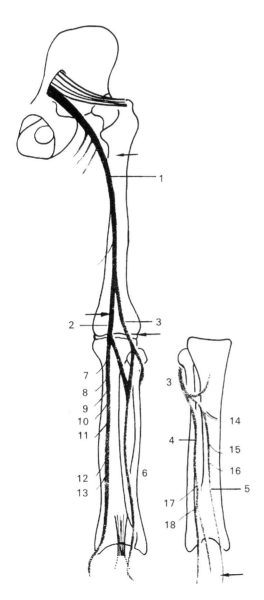

Figure A–1 Distribution of the sciatic nerve, right leg. Arrows indicate palpation sites. **1**, Sciatic nerve; **2**, tibial nerve; **3**, common peroneal nerve; **4**, superficial peroneal nerve; **5**, deep peroneal nerve; **6**, sural nerve. Innervation: **7**, gastrocnemius muscle; **8**, popliteus muscle; **9**, plantaris muscle; **10**, soleus muscle; **11**, tibialis posterior muscle; **12**, flexor digitorum longus muscle; **13**, flexor hallucis longus muscle; **14**, tibialis anterior muscle; **15**, extensor digitorum longus muscle; **16**, extensor hallucis longus muscle; **17**, peroneus longus muscle; **18**, peroneus brevis muscle.

dial and lateral plantar nerves. The common peroneal nerve runs laterally in the popliteal fossa. It follows the inner edge of the biceps femoris tendon; then, under the protection of the peroneus longus muscle, it takes a spiral course anteriorly from behind the fibular head. Having reached the peroneus longus muscle, it divides into a superficial and a deep branch. The superficial peroneal nerve, which primarily serves a sensory function, runs between the fibula and the peroneus longus muscle to the dorsum of the foot. The deep peroneal nerve, which primarily serves a motor function, runs deeply in the anterior tibial compartment. There it meets the tibialis anterior muscle from lateral, and together they run to the dorsum of the foot. Finally, the deep peroneal nerve divides into medial and lateral branches. The medial sural cutaneous nerve is a branch of the tibial nerve. It joins together with the peroneal communicating ramus to become the sural nerve, where it then runs behind the lateral malleolus.

Palpation

The exiting site can also be found at the midpoint of an imaginary line drawn between the midpoint of the edge of the sacrum and the proximal end of the greater trochanter. The sciatic nerve is palpable at the crossing point of the lateral edge of the biceps femoris muscle and the distal edge of the gluteus maximus muscle. The common peroneal nerve can be felt medial to the biceps femoris tendon in the popliteal fossa and behind the head of the fibula. Several branches of the superficial peroneal nerve can be palpated at the dorsum of the foot. The tibial nerve can be felt in the middle of the popliteal fossa.

Lesions

Deficits of the common peroneal nerve are seen relatively often in patients with occupations that require prolonged periods of kneeling. As the result of the inversion trauma of the foot, especially in conditions when there are fibrous soft tissue cords, the nerve can become overstretched between the head of the fibula and the peroneus longus muscle. This is also true for the superficial peroneal nerve at its exiting site through the crural fascia. The deep peroneal nerve runs underneath the tendon of the extensor hallucis brevis at the dorsum of the foot, where lesions can also occur as the result of inversion trauma.

Injuries to the tibial nerve most often occur in the tarsal tunnel, the region behind the medial malleolus and under the flexor retinaculum. Terminal branches of the tibial nerve, the medial and lateral plantar nerves, run through two connective tissue openings in the abductor hallucis muscle. Overstretching as the result of eversion trauma can lead to burning pain in the sole of the foot. Farther distally, these nerves divide into the common plantar digital nerves that run plantar to the toes and supply sensory cutaneous innervation. During their course, the nerves pass ligaments that connect the metatarsal heads to each other. Hyperextension of the metacarpophalangeal joints can lead to an overstretch of these nerve branches because of increased tension in these ligaments. The most frequent form of such a compression neuropathy is Morton's* neuralgia between the third and fourth metatarsals.

Femoral Nerve (Figure A–2)

Derivation

From the nerve roots L2 to L4.

Course

In a dissected pelvis, the femoral nerve is easily recognizable in its course lateral to the psoas major muscle. Together with the iliop-

---

*Thomas G. Morton, 1853–1903, American surgeon, Philadelphia, Pennsylvania.

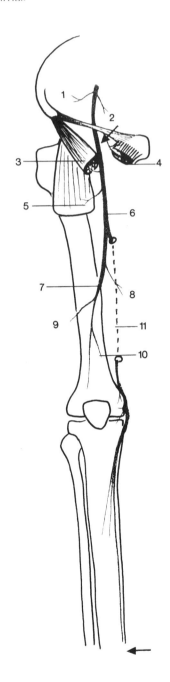

Figure A–2 Innervation of the femoral nerve, right leg. Arrows indicate palpation sites. **1**, Iliacus muscle; **2**, psoas major muscle; **3**, sartorius muscle; **4**, pectineus muscle; **5**, rectus femoris muscle; **6**, femoral nerve; **7**, primarily motor branch; **8**, vastus medialis muscle; **9**, vastus lateralis muscle; **10**, vastus intermedius muscle; **11**, adductor canal.

soas muscle, it runs beneath the inguinal ligament in the so-called lacuna musculorum. Here, it is separated from the femoral artery and nerve, which run through the lacuna vasculorum. Finally, the femoral nerve branches into various motor and sensory nerves. Its largest cutaneous branch is the saphenous nerve, which, together with the femoral artery, runs through the adductor canal. After leaving the adductor canal, the saphenous nerve runs between the tendons of the sartorius and gracilis muscles. In the lower leg, it accompanies the greater saphenous artery.

Palpation

The femoral nerve is palpable, but only for a short distance. To perform this palpation, the pulsations of the femoral artery must first be found at a site halfway between the anterior superior iliac spine and the pubic tubercle. The nerve can be felt just lateral to the artery. The saphenous nerve is sometimes palpable distal in the lower leg, just next to the greater saphenous vein.

Lesions

The femoral nerve is rarely injured. Occasionally, direct trauma can occur, for instance from sports injuries (eg, a kick in the groin) or traumatic hyperextension of the hip. Other causes of pathology include pelvic tumors, a psoas abscess (tuberculosis), and fractures of the pelvis or femur. Diabetes mellitus can also cause impairments of the femoral nerve.

The saphenous nerve becomes superficial at the level of the medial femoral condyle, where it emerges through the aponeurotic covering, and then gives off a branch to the patella (the infrapatellar ramus). Disorders of the knee joint, such as meniscus lesions and osteophytes, can result in a pinching of this ramus and a subsequent lesion.

ARTERIES OF THE LOWER EXTREMITY

Deep in the abdomen, at the level of the umbilicus, the aorta divides into the common iliac arteries. Both arteries run distally in front of the sacroiliac joints. At each side, an internal iliac artery arises, entering the lesser pelvis to supply the organs in this region. From the internal iliac artery, the obturator artery arises; together with the obturator nerve, it runs in the adductor canal. These structures lie too deep to palpate. The superior and inferior gluteal arteries also originate in the lesser pelvis and run, together with the similarly named nerves and veins, to the buttock region, which they vascularize. The pudendal artery runs anteriorly under the pelvic floor to vascularize the external sex organs.

The external iliac artery runs as a second branch of the common iliac artery along the edge of the lesser pelvis to the lacuna vasorum. There, it gives off branches to the abdominal wall and the sex organs. In the lacuna vasorum it becomes the femoral artery and can be easily palpated just underneath the inguinal ligament. A branch from the femoral artery, the deep femoral artery (not palpable), vascularizes the ventral thigh; several side branches penetrate the adductor magnus muscle to reach the posterior side of the thigh. The main trunk of the femoral artery runs farther distally through the adductor canal and the adductor hiatus, where it is called the popliteal artery. Here it can be palpated at the back of the knee. The popliteal artery provides blood to the knee by way of numerous side branches that anastomose with each other.

Below the knee, a large branch of the popliteal artery, termed the anterior tibial artery, penetrates the interosseous membrane of the lower leg and runs farther distally in the anterior tibial compartment. Palpation is possible at its distal end, where it becomes the dorsal pedal artery.

A second large branch of the popliteal artery, the posterior tibial artery, runs distally in the deep posterior compartment. Its pulsations can be felt behind the medial malleolus. From there the artery divides again into the medial and lateral plantar arteries.

Below the knee, the posterior tibial artery gives off a branch, the peroneal artery. This artery supplies the peroneal compartment and the region of the lateral malleolus.

Femoral Artery (Figure A–3)

Course

The course of the femoral artery can be projected in the following way: Imagine a line between the anterior superior iliac spine and the pubic tubercle. The midpoint of this line is the so-called midinguinal point. From this point, with the hip in slight external rotation and flexion, imagine a line from the midinguinal point to the adductor tubercle. The proximal two thirds of this line corresponds to the approximate course of the femoral artery. Part of the way through the adductor canal, it exits via the adductor hiatus (the opening between the two insertions of the adductor magnus muscle) to enter the popliteal fossa, where it is then called the popliteal artery. Covered by the popliteal vein and tibial nerve, the artery runs deeply at the back of the knee and, at the level of the distal edge of the popliteus muscle, divides into the posterior and anterior tibial arteries. The anterior tibial artery courses forward and reaches the anterior tibial compartment through an opening in the interosseous membrane of the lower leg. It remains deep in its distal course until it becomes superficial at the level of the ankle, between the tibialis anterior and extensor hallucis longus tendons. It ends at the dorsum of the foot as the dorsal pedal artery. The posterior tibial artery at first lies deeply underneath the soleus muscle, but it becomes superficial at the distal end of the lower leg. It runs behind the medial malleolus, where it lies between the tendons of the flexor digitorum longus and flexor hallucis longus. Distal to the ankle, the posterior tibial artery divides into the medial and lateral plantar arteries.

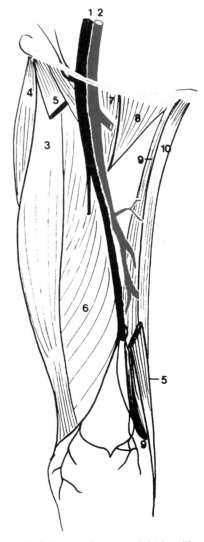

Figure A–3 Femoral artery, right leg (the femoral nerve, the adductor longus muscle, and the sartorius muscle are removed). **1**, Femoral artery; **2**, femoral vein; **3**, rectus femoris muscle; **4**, tensor fasciae latae muscle; **5**, sartorius muscle; **6**, vastus medialis muscle; **7**, iliopsoas muscle; **8**, pectineus muscle; **9**, adductor magnus muscle; **10**, gracilis muscle.

Palpation

After it passes underneath the inguinal ligament, the femoral artery can be palpated superficially in the medial femoral triangle for a distance of about 10 cm. Here, its pulsations can be easily felt. The popliteal artery is only palpable when the fascia of the knee is relaxed with the knee flexed. The dorsal pedal pulse can be felt by placing a finger in the groove between the first and second metatarsals and sliding it proximally. Behind the medial malleolus, the posterior tibial artery can be palpated.

Lesions

The femoral artery can be injured in its superficial course in the medial femoral triangle.

VEINS OF THE LOWER EXTREMITY

All the important smaller arteries are accompanied by two similarly named deep veins. All the larger arteries (proximal to the popliteal artery) are accompanied by one similarly named deep vein. The popliteal vein lies somewhat more superficial and lateral to the popliteal artery. In the thigh, the femoral vein lies medial to the femoral artery.

In the lower extremity, two important cutaneous veins are recognizable, with significant interindividual variance. The greater saphenous vein begins at the medial side of the foot and courses in front of the medial malleolus as it runs proximally to a position behind the medial femoral condyle, finally ending up at the saphenous hiatus. The lesser saphenous vein begins at the lateral side of the foot, runs behind the lateral malleolus, and then runs proximally over the calf, where it empties into the popliteal vein.

Greater Saphenous Vein (Figure A–4)

Derivation

From the dorsomedial venous network of the foot.

Course

The greater saphenous vein begins at the medial side of the foot. It runs in front of the

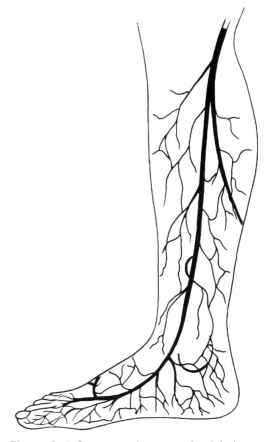

Figure A–4 Greater saphenous vein, right leg.

medial malleolus and then courses farther proximally to a position behind the medial femoral condyle. About 2 cm distal to the inguinal ligament, it empties into the femoral vein (which lies just medial to the femoral artery).

Palpation

Saphenous is derived from an arabic word meaning "hidden." Nevertheless, the greater saphenous vein is actually easy to palpate at the foot and lower leg. Its course in front of the medial malleolus is consistent.

Lesions

Varicose veins.

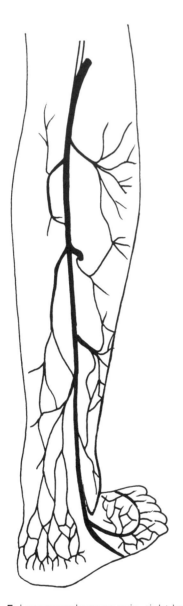

Lesser Saphenous Vein (Figure A–5)

Derivation

From the dorsolateral venous network of the foot.

Course

The lesser saphenous vein begins behind the lateral malleolus and then runs proximally between both heads of the gastrocnemius muscle to the popliteal fossa. There, it ends at the popliteal vein.

Palpation

The vein can be routinely palpated distal to the lateral malleolus and occasionally between the heads of the gastrocnemius.

Lesions

Varicose veins.

Figure A–5 Lesser saphenous vein, right leg.

Appendix B

Diagnosis and Treatment of Algorithms for the Lower Extremities

Symbols and Indications

$\bar{\underline{}}$ Possibilities mentioned are of equal rank; one can make a choice from the available data

1
2 Graded order of ranking; information is listed in order of importance or preference
3

$\downarrow \bar{\underline{}}$ Listed according to the passage of time

$\triangleright$ Indicates the sequence

$\longrightarrow$ In all probability, the following occurs

$\dashrightarrow$ It could possibly lead to the following

$\pm$ Approximately

LEGEND

Pain

     ○ = Sometimes painful

     ● = Painful

   ● ● = Most painful test

  ( ) = eg, ● (●) Signifies pain, and sometimes the most painful test

Limitation of Motion

     ○ = Sometimes (minimal) limitation of motion

     ● = Minimal limitation of motion

   ● ● = Moderate limitation of motion

 ● ● ● = Severe limitation of motion

  ( ) = eg, ● ● (●) Signifies moderate to severe limitation of motion

Muscle weakness

     ○ = Sometimes (minimal) weakness

     ● = Moderate weakness

   ● ● = Severe weakness

     □ = Hypermobility or instability

     ! = Test not performed

     + = Positive, but without pain, limitation of motion, weakness, or hypermobility

     ★ = Muscle tightness

  ( ) = Sometimes, eg, (+) signifies "sometimes positive"; (★) signifies "sometimes muscle tightness"

DIAGRAM FOR BASIC ORTHOPAEDIC EXAMINATION

I. Gemeral Inspection

II. General Inspection	Family General Specific

III Specific inspection

IV Palpation	Local swelling Local temperature

Before beginning the functional examination, ask the patient what he/she feels "at this moment" (at rest). During the functional examination, note whether the patient reports any change with each movement or test.

V Functional Examination	Active movements (patient) Passive movements (examiner) Isometric resisted tests (patient and examiner)

VI Palpation	Local swelling Local temperature Pain (palpation of the affected structure, which is indicated by the functional examination)

VII Accessory examinations (when indicated)	Laboratory analysis X-ray examination Other imaging tests (eg, MRI) Neurological examination Vascular tests

General Inspection and History

Specific Inspection

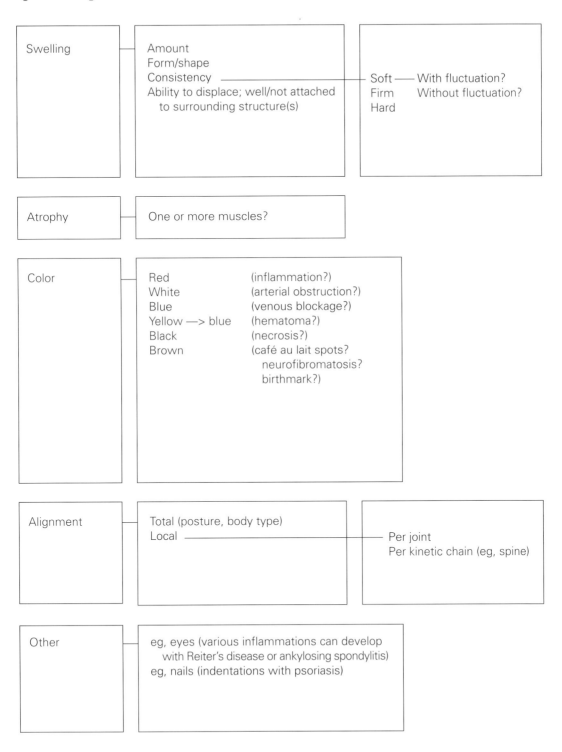

Functional Examination

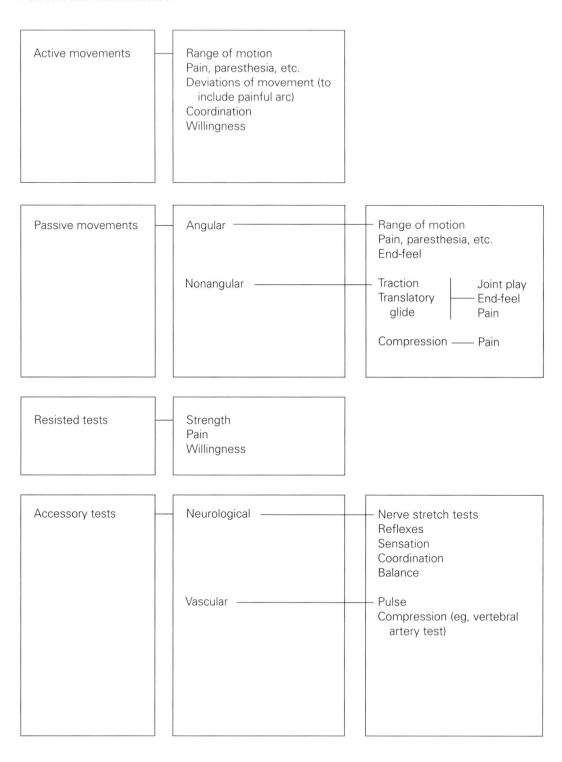

DIAGRAM FOR BASIC FUNCTIONAL EXAMINATION FINDINGS 1

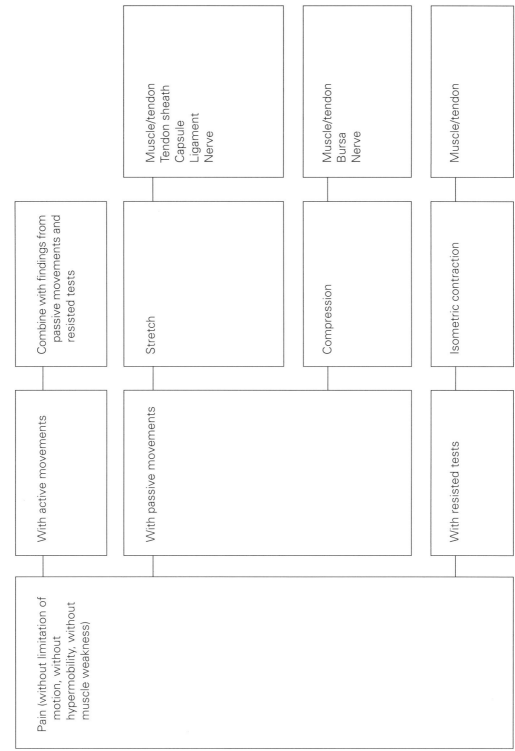

Pain (without limitation of motion, without hypermobility, without muscle weakness)

With active movements → Combine with findings from passive movements and resisted tests

With passive movements → Stretch → Muscle/tendon · Tendon sheath · Capsule · Ligament · Nerve

Compression → Muscle/tendon · Bursa · Nerve

With resisted tests → Isometric contraction → Muscle/tendon

DIAGRAM FOR BASIC FUNCTIONAL EXAMINATION FINDINGS 2

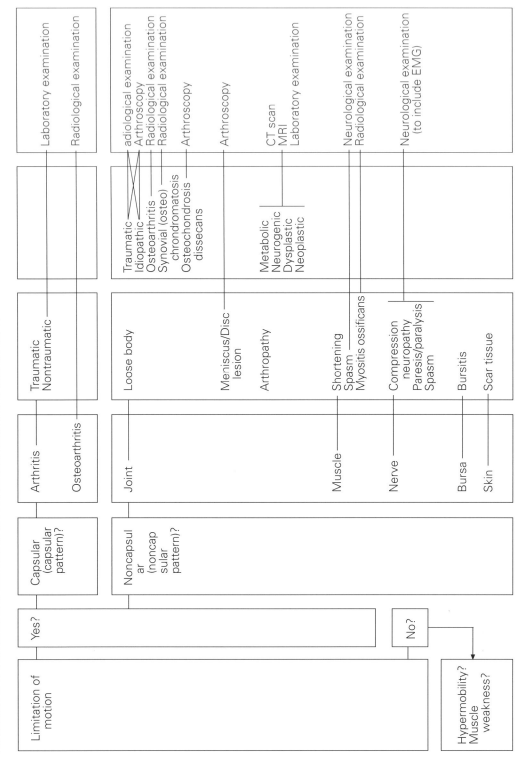

DIAGRAM FOR BASIC FUNCTIONAL EXAMINATION FINDINGS 3

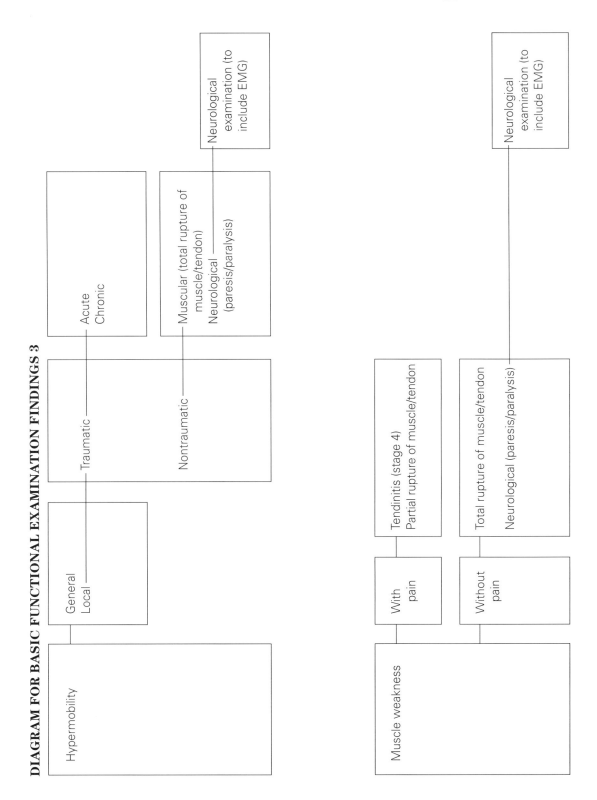

DIAGRAM FOR BASIC TREATMENT

Primary prevention	1 Information
	   • General
	     —posture
	     —body mechanics
	     —nutrition
	   • Work specific
	   • Sport specific
	2 Working conditions adapted to the working activities (ergonomics)
	3 Sport conditions
	   • Surface
	   • Equipment
	     —eg, shoes, racquet, etc.
	   • Clothes
	   • Warm-up/cool down
	   • Taping

Secondary prevention (= treatment)	1 Causal treatment
	   • see Primary prevention, 1, 2, 3
	2 Local treatment
	   • eg, transverse friction, ultrasound, cryotherapy
	   • mobilization (manipulation)
	   • stretching
	   • muscle strengthening
	   • injection
	   • taping
	   • stabilization
	3 General treatment
	   • limitation of activities
	   • general conditioning
	   • medication

Tertiary prevention	Prevent profession of the lesion by means of the measures listed under Secondary prevention

LOCAL TREATMENT

Lesion	Physical therapist	Physician	Patient
Joint and ligamentous lesions	Specific mobilization and/or manipulation of movement limitations Stabilization exercise program and taping or bracing of hypermobilities or instabilities Transverse friction massage for ligament sprains and small partial ruptures Modalities	Aspiration Intra-articular injection Infiltration (of ligament insertions)	Active exercises after mobilization/manipulation Eventually transverse friction massage Muscle-strengthening exercises
Musculotendinous lesions	Transverse friction massage Stretching Muscle-strengthening exercises Modalities	Infiltration (tendon insertion, musculotendinous junction, muscle belly) Injection (tenosynovitis, tenovaginitis)	Stretching exercises Muscle-strengthening exercises Eventually, when possible, transverse friction massage
Bursitis	Correction of local articular and/or muscular disturbances	Aspiration Infiltration	Maintain mobility after joint mobilization/manipulation and/or muscle stretching
Compression neuropathy	Correction of eventual muscle shortening by means of muscle stretching	Perineural infiltration	Stretching exercises

DIAGRAM FOR BASIC TREATMENT OF TENDINITIS

1 Causal (when possible)

2 Local
- Mobilization (to prevent or diminish adhesions)
  - In a transverse direction by means of transverse friction massage
  - In a lengthwise direction by means of stretching
- Muscle strengthening (initiated when resisted tests are negative)

3 General
- Limitation of specific activities that load the tendon
- General circulation-stimulating measures
- (If needed) medications (nonsteroidal anti-inflammatory drugs [NSAIDs]

When results are unsatisfactory
- All specific tendon-loading activities are stopped
- Infiltration with a local anesthetic (only the tendon insertion)
- (If needed) infiltration of a corticosteroid

Appendix C

Algorithms for Diagnosis and Treatment of the Lower Extremity—General

ZERO POSITION, MAXIMAL LOOSE-PACKED POSITION, AND MAXIMAL CLOSE-PACKED POSITION—LOWER EXTREMITY

Joint	Zero Position	Maximal Loose-Packed Position	Maximal close-Packed Position
Hip (art. coxae)	The upper leg is in line with the trunk. A straight line from the anterior superior iliac spine to the middle of the patella makes a right angle with the line that connects the inferior aspects of both anterior superior iliac spines.	±30° flexion, 30° abduction, and slight external rotation	Maximal extension, internal rotation, and adduction (ligamentous) Maximal extension, external rotation and abduction (bony)
Knee (art. genu)	The lower leg is in line with the upper leg.	±25° flexion	Maximal extension
Lower leg (crus) Consists of: Proximal tibiofibular joint Tibiofibular syndesmosis Art. tibiofibularis distalis		±10° plantar flexion in the talocrural joint	Maximal extension (dorsiflexion) in the talocrural joint
Ankle (art. talocrural)	The lateral side of the foot makes an angle of 90° with the longitudinal axis of the lower leg. The straight line from the anterior superior iliac spine through the middle of the patella goes to the second toe.	±10° plantar flexion in the talocrural joint and the middle point between maximal inversion and eversion of the foot	Maximal extension (dorsiflexion)
Tarsus and metatarsus	See ankle	See ankle	Maximal inversion
Toes Consist of: Metatarsophalangeal joints	The longitudinal axis through the metatarsal bone and its articulating phalanx are in line with each other.	±10° extension	Maximal extension
Interphalangeal joints		slight flexion	Maximal extension

CAPSULAR PATTERN—LOWER EXTREMITY

Joint	Limitation of Motion (Passive Angular Movements)
Hip (art. coxae)	Internal rotation > flexion = abduction = extension > other motions
Knee (art. genu)	Flexion > extension (±5:1)
Proximal tibiofibular joint (art. tibiofibularis proximalis)	No capsular pattern: pain at the end range of passive translatory movements
Talocrural joint (art. talocruralis)	Plantar flexion ≥ dorsiflexion
Subtalar joint (art. talocalcaneonavicularis)	Varus > valgus
Midtarsal joints (artt. calcaneocuboidea and talonaviculares)	Inversion (plantar flexion, adduction, supination) > dorsiflexion
Intertarsal joints (artt. intertarseae)	No capsular pattern; pain at the end range of translation movements
Tarsometatarsal joints (artt. tarsometatarseae)	See above: intertarsal joints
Intermetatarsal joints (artt. intermetatarseae)	See above: intertarsal joints
Metatarsophalangeal joints (MTP) (artt. metatarsophalangeae)	Flexion ≥ extension
Metatarsophalangeal I joint (artt. metatarsophalangeae hallucis)	Extension > flexion (±2:1)
Interphalangeal joints: Proximal Distal (artt. interphalangeae proximales and distales)	Flexion ≥ extension

END-FEEL AND STRUCTURES THAT CAUSE THE END-FEEL 1

The end-feel is specified on the visual analogue scale: ——————— The left end of the scale indicates the softest possible end-feel, the right end indicates the hardest possible end-feel. Given here are the average normal end-feels for normal joints.

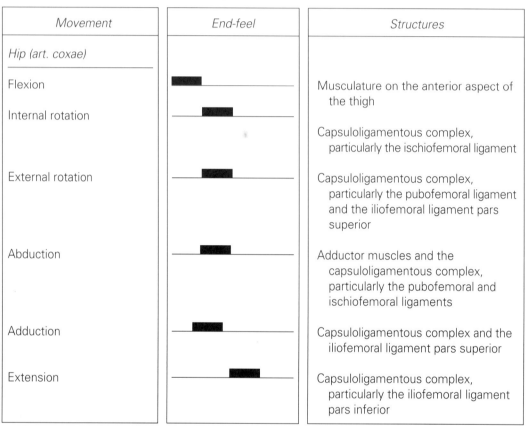

Movement	End-feel	Structures
Hip (art. coxae)		
Flexion		Musculature on the anterior aspect of the thigh
Internal rotation		Capsuloligamentous complex, particularly the ischiofemoral ligament
External rotation		Capsuloligamentous complex, particularly the pubofemoral ligament and the iliofemoral ligament pars superior
Abduction		Adductor muscles and the capsuloligamentous complex, particularly the pubofemoral and ischiofemoral ligaments
Adduction		Capsuloligamentous complex and the iliofemoral ligament pars superior
Extension		Capsuloligamentous complex, particularly the iliofemoral ligament pars inferior

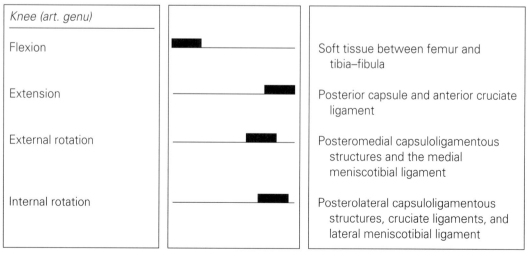

Movement	End-feel	Structures
Knee (art. genu)		
Flexion		Soft tissue between femur and tibia–fibula
Extension		Posterior capsule and anterior cruciate ligament
External rotation		Posteromedial capsuloligamentous structures and the medial meniscotibial ligament
Internal rotation		Posterolateral capsuloligamentous structures, cruciate ligaments, and lateral meniscotibial ligament

END-FEEL AND STRUCTURES THAT CAUSE THE END-FEEL 2

The end-feel is specified on the visual analogue scale: ——————— The left end of the scale indicates the softest possible end-feel, the right end indicates the hardest possible end-feel. Given here are the average normal end-feels for normal joints.

Movement	End-feel	Structures
Ankle (art. talocrural) Dorsiflexion (extension) Plantar flexion (flexion)		With extended knee: triceps surae and Achilles tendon With flexed knee: posterior capsuloligamentous complex Dorsal capsuloligamentous complex and extensor tendons

Subtalar joint *(art. subtalaris)* Varus Valgus		Lateral capsule and talocalcaneal ligaments Medial capsule and talocalcaneal ligaments

END-FEEL AND STRUCTURES THAT CAUSE THE END-FEEL 3

The end-feel is specified on the visual analogue scale: ————— The left end of the scale indicates the softest possible end-feel, the right end indicates the hardest possible end-feel. Given here are the average normal end-feels for normal joints.

Movement	End-feel	Structures
Transverse tarsal joint (art. talonaviculare and art. calcaneocuboidea)		
Dorsiflexion (extension)		Dorsal and plantar capsuloligamentous structures
Plantar flexion (flexion)		Dorsal and plantar capsuloligamentous structures
Abduction		Medial capsuloligamentous structures (talonavicular)
Adduction		Lateral capsuloligamentous structures (calcaneocuboid)
Pronation		All transverse tarsal capsuloligamentous structures
Supination		All transverse tarsal capsuloligamentous structures

Movement	End-feel	Structures
Toes (artt. metatarsophalangeae artt. interphalangeae proximales and distales)		
Extension		Plantar capsuloligamentous structures
Flexion		Dorsal capsuloligamentous structures

CLINICAL REVIEW OF PERIPHERAL MOTOR DEFICITS OF THE LOWER EXTREMITY

The most characteristic nerve root is indicated in boldface type.

Obturator nerve

Adductor muscles (mm)	L**2, 3. 4**
Obturator externus muscle (m)	L**2, 3, 4**

Gluteal nerves

Gluteal mm	L5, S**1, 2**
Piriformis m	L5, S1, 2

Femoral nerve

Iliacus m	L1, **2, 3,** 4
Iliopsoas m	L1, **2, 3,** 4
Sartorius m	L2, 3, 4
Pectineus m	L2, 3, 4
Quadriceps femoris m	L2, **3, 4**

Sciatic nerve

Obturator internus m	L4, **5,** S**1, 2**
Biceps femoris m	L5, S**1, 2**
Adductor magnus m	L4, 5
Piriformis m	L5, S1, 2
Semimembranosus m	L4, **5,** S**1, 2**
Semitendinosus m	L4, **5,** S**1, 2**
Quadratus femoris m	L4, **5,** S**1, 2**
Gemelli mm	L4, **5,** S**1, 2**

Peroneal nerve

Extensor digitorum longus m	L4, **5,** S1
Peroneus longus m	L4, **5,** S1
Peroneus brevis m	L4, **5,** S1
Extensor digitorum brevis m	L4, **5,** S1
Extensor hallucis brevis m	L4, **5,** S1
Extensor hallucis longus m	L4, **5,** S1
Tibialis anterior m	L**4,** 5

Tibial nerve

Popliteus m	L5, S**1, 2**
Gastrocnemius m	L5, S**1, 2**
Soleus m	L5, S**1, 2**
Tibialis posterior m	L**5,** S**1**
Flexor digitorum longus m	L**5,** S**1, 2**
Flexor digitorum brevis m	L**5,** S**1, 2**
Flexor hallucis longus m	L**5,** S**1, 2**
Flexor hallucis brevis m	L**5,** S**1, 2**
Plantaris m	L5, S**1, 2**
Abductor hallucis m	L5, S1, 2
Abductor hallucis m	L5, S1, 2
Abductor digiti minimi m	L5, S1, 2
Quadratus plantae m (accessory flexor m)	L5, S1, 2

Appendix D

Algorithms for Diagnosis and Treatment of the Hip

LIMITATION OF MOTION IN THE HIP

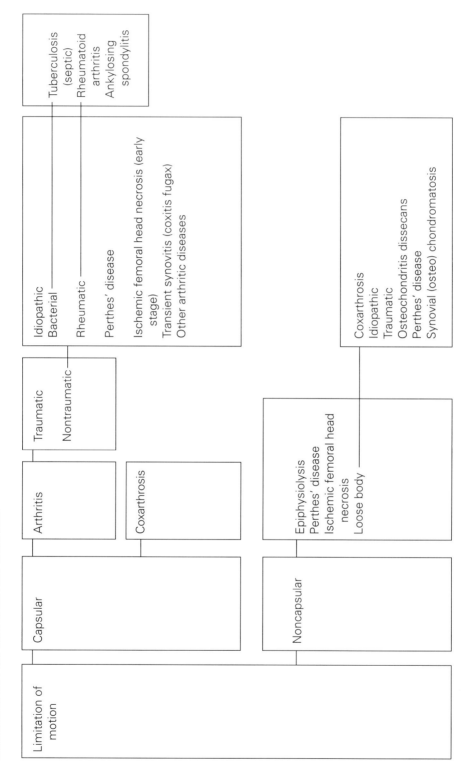

PREDILECTION AGE SPANS IN ARTHROPATHIES OF THE HIP

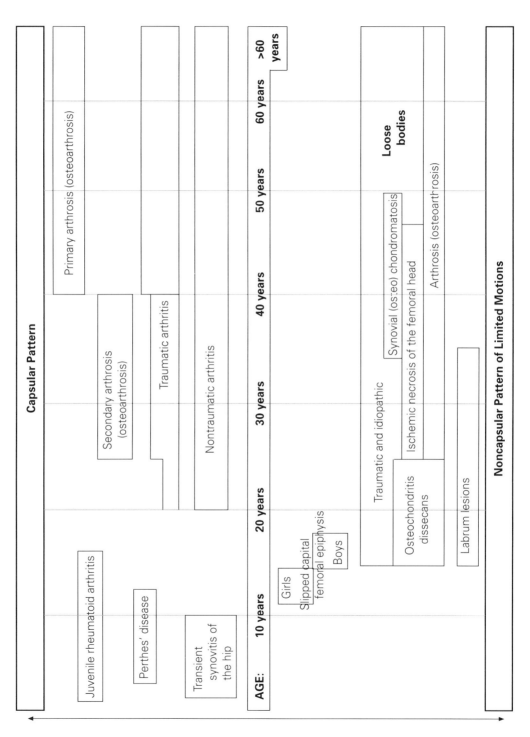

PUBALGIA

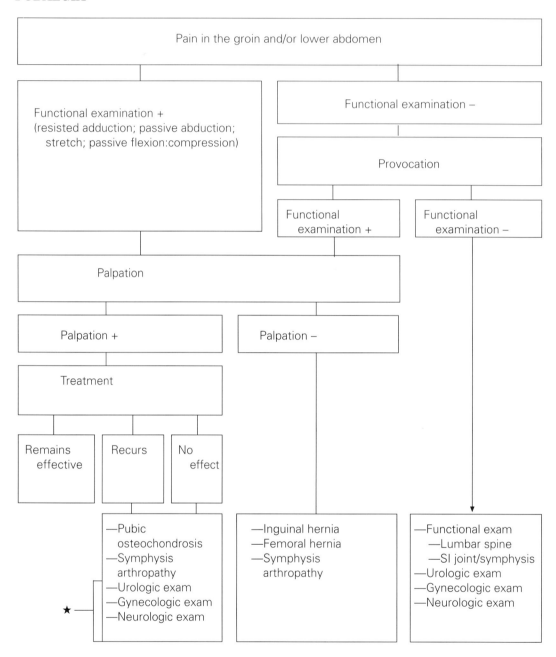

★ As a result of pain, an abnormal pattern of motion can develop in the hip with resultant overuse
   of the adductor muscles.
   SI, sacroiliac.

DIFFERENTIAL DIAGNOSIS OF PAIN IN THE REGION OF THE GREATER TROCHANTER

Pathology	Clinical Examination	Treatment
Gluteus maximus insertion tendopathy	Local tenderness to palpation of the posterior aspect of the greater trochanter *In extreme cases:* Resisted hip extension is painful; sometimes resisted external rotation and resisted abduction are also painful	Physical therapy of transverse friction and gentle stretching exercises If symptoms do not improve with physical therapy, injection with a local anesthetic is indicated; if the symptoms are relieved only temporarily, the injection is repeated, but with a corticosteroid In rare instances, surgery is required
Calcification at the insertion of the gluteus maximus	Same clinical findings as in gluteus maximus insertion tendopathy	Usually surgery is necessary
Subtendinous trochanteric bursitis	See gluteus maximus insertion tendopathy Often, passive hip flexion, external rotation, and/or adduction are also painful Patrick's sign is sometimes positive Combined motion of passive hip flexion, internal rotation, and adduction is most painful	injection with a local anesthetic; if the symptoms are relieved only temporarily, the injection is repeated, but with a corticosteroid
Intertendinous trochanteric bursitis	Same clinical findings as in subtendinous trochanteric bursitis	Same as subtendinous trochanteric bursitis
Gluteus medius insertion tendopathy, with or without calcification	Same clinical findings as in gluteus maximus insertion tendopathy; the most tender area is slightly more proximal on the posterior aspect of the greater trochanter	Same as gluteus maximus insertion tendopathy
"Snapping hip" (coxa saltans)	Usually no pain Snapping occurs during flexion from a position of extension or in alternating internal and external rotation from a position of hip flexion	In instances of pain: stretching If a secondary bursitis is present: injection
Lateral compartment syndrome of the thigh	Pain and local swelling of the tensor fasciae latae muscle in the area of the greater trochanter Pain during sitting as well as during activities	Surgery
Stress fracture of the greater trochanter	Local percussion pain	Rest, meaning avoidance of all pain-provoking motions for 6–8 weeks
Scar tissue after hip surgery in which a posterior incision was performed	Functional examination is usually negative Local tenderness	Surgery is sometimes indicated
Pain due to loosening of a hip endoprosthesis	Functional examination usually has vague findings Technetium (bone) scan is diagnostic	Surgical revision
Referred pain from L4 or L5	Examination of the lumbar spine or sacroiliac joints is positive	Depends on pathology

DIFFERENTIAL DIAGNOSES OF GROIN PAIN

Tests Performed	Articular lesion with a capsular pattern of limitation	Articular lesion with a noncapsular pattern of limitation	Lumbar spine L1–3 nerve root syndrome	SI joint lesion	Lesion of the pubic symphysis	Pubalgia	Compression neuropathy	Urologic disease	Gynocologic disease	Femeral hernia / Inguinal hernia
Active hip movements	● ●	● ●				○				○
Passive hip movements	●● ●●	●● ●●				●	○			○
Resisted hip tests						●●				○
Lumbar spine examination			● ●	○				Negative orthopedic examination	Negative orthopedic examination	
SI joint test				●●	○					
Symphysis palpation					●●	○				
Palpation of the hernia predilection areas										●

SI, sacroiliac

LESIONS OF THE ILIOPSOAS AND DIFFERENTIAL DIAGNOSES

Tests Performed	**Lesions** Sports injury: strain proximally in the medial femoral triangle	Complications from a coxarthrosis	Apophyseal avulsion fracture of the lesser trochanter	Iliopectineal bursitis	L3 nerve root syndrome	spondylolisthesis (anterolisthisis)	Malignancy in L3 nerve root area
Passive hip flexion	○	● ●	●	●●			
Passive hip external rotation		○ ○		○			
Passive hip internal rotation	○	● ●●(●)	○	○			
Passive hip extension	○	●● ●●(●)	●	○			
Resisted hip flexion	●(●)	●	●●	○	○	○	●(●)
Resisted hip external rotation	○	○	●				
Muscle length test of the iliopsoas	*	* ●●(●)	*	○		*	
Passive stretch test of the iliopsoas	●(●)	● ●●(●)	●●	○	○	○	●
L3 (femoral nerve) stretch test	●	● ●●(●)	●	○	●●	○	●●

DIAGNOSIS OF THE HIP

Functional Examination of the Hip	Lesions	Arthritis	Coxarthrosis	Perthes' disease	Transient synovitis (coxitis fugax)	Osteochondritis dissecans
1. Trendelenburg's test		(+)	(+)	(+)		
2. Quick tests for the lumbar spine		ext.	ext.			
3. Active hip internal rotation		● ● (●)	● (●●)	● ●	○ ○ (●)	
4. Active hip external rotation						○ ○
5. Straight leg raise						
6. SI test (supine)						
7. Passive hip flexion		● ○ (●)	● ○ (●)	● ○	○ ○ (●)	○ ○ (●)
8. Passive flexion into adduction		● ○ (●)	● ○ (●)			
9. Passive internal rotation		●● ●● (●)	●● ●● (●	●●(●)	○ ○ (●)	
10. Passive external rotation		○	○			○ ○ (●)
11. Passive abduction		● ○ (●)	● ○ (●)	●	○ ○ (●)	○ ○ (●)
12. Passive adduction		○ ○	○ ○			○ ○
13. Resisted flexion			○			
14. Resisted abduction						
15. Resisted adduction						

Ischemic femoral head necrosis	Slipped capital femoral epiphysis	Loose body	Iliopectineal bursitis	Subtrochanteric bursitis	Ischial bursitis	Pubalgia	Rectus femoris tendopathy	Sartorius lesion	Iliopsoas lesion	Tensor fasciae latae and iliotibial band lesion	Quadriceps lesion	Hamstrings lesion
(+)	(+)											
							ext.		ext.			
○ (●●)	● ○ (●●)	○ ○ (●)						○	○			
○ ○ (●)		○ ○ (●)	○	○				○	○			
					○							● ● (●)
○ ○ (●)	○	○ ○ (●)	● (●)	●		○	○ (●)	○	○			
		○ (●●) ○ (●)	● ●			● (●)						
○ (●●)	○ (●●)	○						○	○			
○ ○ (●)	○	○ (●) ○ (●)	●	●								
○ ○ (●)	○	○ (●) ○ (●)				● (●)						
○ ○ (●)	○	○ (●●) ○ (●●)		○ (●)						○		
			○			○	○	○ (●)	○ (●)			
				○						○		
						● (●)						

DIAGNOSIS OF THE HIP (continued)

Functional Examination of the Hip	Lesions	Arthritis	Coxarthrosis	Perthes' disease	Transient synovitis (coxitis fugax)	Osteochondritis dissecans
16. Passive extension		● ●(●)	● ●(●)	● ●	○ ○(●)	
17. L3 (femoral nerve) stretch test						
18. Passive internal rotation (prone)		●● ●●(●)	●● ●●(●)	●(●) ●●	○ ○(●)	
19. Resisted internal rotation						
20. Resisted external rotation						
21. Resisted extension						
22. Resisted knee extension						
23. Resisted knee flexion						

Ischemic femoral head necrosis	Slipped capital femoral epiphysis	Loose body	Iliopectineal bursitis	Subtrochanteric bursitis	Ischial bursitis	Pubalgia	Rectus femoris tendopathy	Sartorius lesion	Iliopsoas lesion	Tensor fasciae latae and iliotibial band lesion	Quadriceps lesion	Hamstrings lesion
○○ (●)	○	○○	○ (●)				○ (●)		○		○	
							● (●)				● (●)	
○ (●●)	○ (●●)	○○						○	○			
								○ (●)	○ (●)			
					○							○ (●)
							● (●)				● (●)	
												● (●)

Appendix E

Algorithms for Diagnosis and Treatment of the Knee

CAUSES OF LIMITATIONS OF MOTION IN THE KNEE

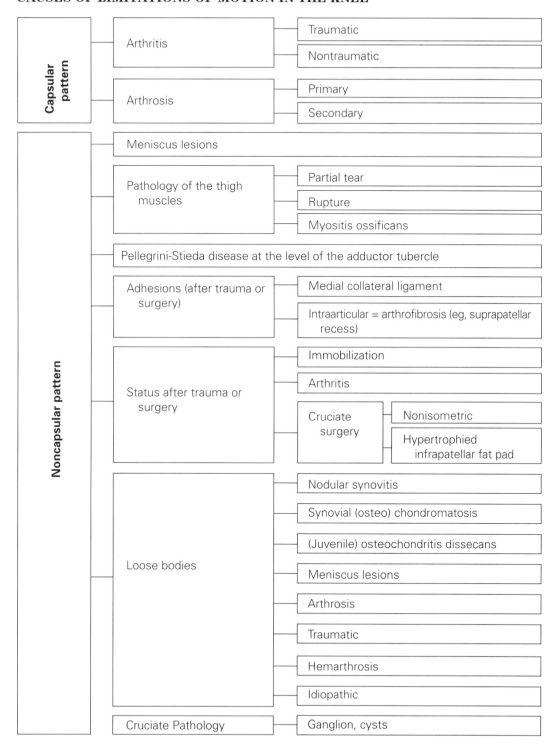

INTERPRETATION OF FINDINGS WITH RESISTED TESTS OF THE KNEE 1

Test	Location of symptoms	Further diagnostic tests	Diagnosis	Differential diagnosis
Extension	Anterior	Palpation (possibly injection with a local anesthetic)	Supra- or infrapatellar insertion tendopathy ("jumper's knee," apexitis patellae)	Infrapatellar bursitis Meniscus lesion (at the junction of the extensor mechanism with the menisci)
	Medial	Passive external rotation of the tibia In 30° flexion, passive shift of the patella medially Palpation	Medial parapatellar insertion tendopathy	Mediopatellar plica syndrome Medial meniscus lesion
	Lateral	Iliotibial band test Palpation	Lateral parapatellar insertion tendopathy	Iliotibial band friction syndrome Lateral meniscus lesion
Flexion	Posterior	Perform resisted tibial internal rotation and external rotation simultaneously with flexion as well as individually Palpation	In cases when only flexion is painful: Baker's cyst (CT scan or MRI) Posterior cruciate ligament sprain Posterior capsule sprain	Meniscus lesion

CT, computed tomography.
MRI, magnetic resonance imaging.

INTERPRETATION OF FINDINGS WITH RESISTED TESTS OF THE KNEE 2

Test	Location of symptoms	Further diagnostic tests	Diagnosis	Differential diagnosis
External rotation	Lateral	Palpation Joint-specific examination of the proximal tibiofibular joint	Usually biceps femoris insertion tendopathy at the head of the fibula	Lateral meniscus lesion Sprain of the capsuloligamentous structures of the proximal tibiofibular joint Iliotibial band lesion (resisted tests are seldom positive)
Internal rotation	Lateral	Palpation Injection with a local anesthetic	Usually meniscus lesion	Lesion of the (tendon from the) popliteus muscle
	Medial	Palpation Injection with a local anesthetic	Usually superficial pes anserinus insertion tendopathy	Superficial pes anserinus bursitis Medial meniscus lesion Semimembranosus (tendon) lesion

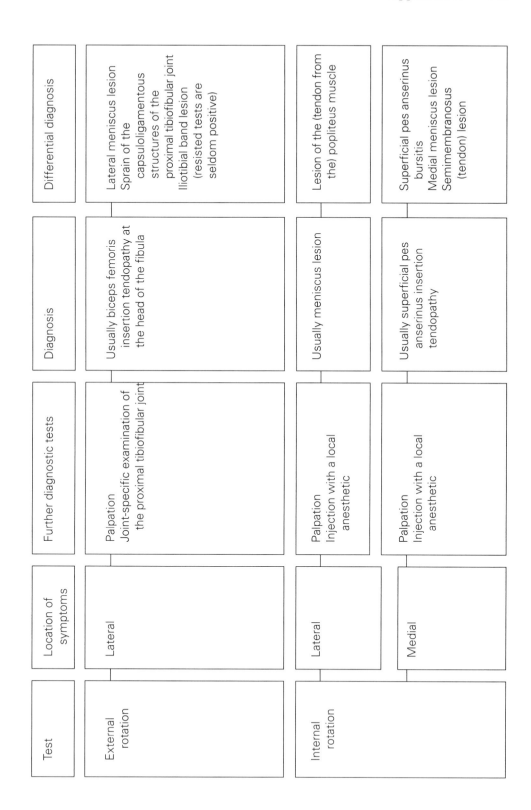

KNEE INSTABILITY

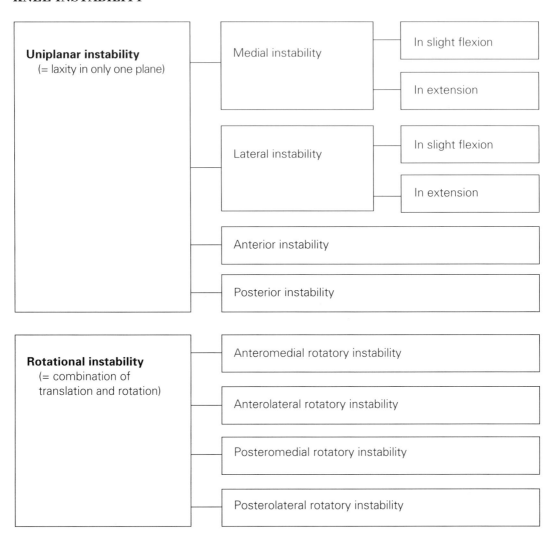

UNIPLANAR KNEE INSTABILITY 1

Affected structures

Medial, in slight flexion

1+	medial meniscotibial ligament (coronary ligament) (possibly medial meniscus)
2+	see 1+, and medial collateral ligament posterior oblique ligament
3+	see 2+, and anterior and/or posterior cruciate ligament

Medial, in extension

1+	posterior oblique ligament (possibly medial meniscus)
2+	see 1+, and medial meniscotibial ligament (coronary ligament) anterior and sometimes posterior cruciate ligament(s)
3+	see 2+, and posterior cruciate ligament

Lateral, in slight flexion

1+	lateral meniscotibial ligament (coronary ligament) (possibly lateral meniscus) lateral collateral ligament: sprain or partial tear
2+	see 1+, and iliotibial band anterior and or posterior cruciate ligament(s)
3+	see 2+, and lateral collateral ligament: rupture popliteal arcuate ligament popliteus tendon

Lateral, in extension

1+	popliteal arcuate ligament lateral meniscotibial ligament (coronary ligament) (possibly lateral meniscus) lateral collateral ligament: sprain or partial tear
2+	see 1+, and lateral collateral ligament: rupture popliteus tendon anterior and/or posterior cruciate ligament(s)
3+	see 2+, and iliotibial band

UNIPLANAR KNEE INSTABILITY 2

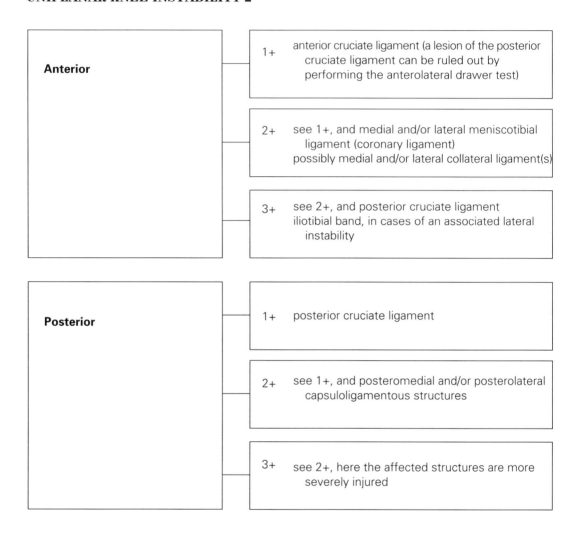

Anterior

1+   anterior cruciate ligament (a lesion of the posterior cruciate ligament can be ruled out by performing the anterolateral drawer test)

2+   see 1+, and medial and/or lateral meniscotibial ligament (coronary ligament)
possibly medial and/or lateral collateral ligament(s)

3+   see 2+, and posterior cruciate ligament
iliotibial band, in cases of an associated lateral instability

Posterior

1+   posterior cruciate ligament

2+   see 1+, and posteromedial and/or posterolateral capsuloligamentous structures

3+   see 2+, here the affected structures are more severely injured

ROTATORY KNEE INSTABILITY

Affected structures

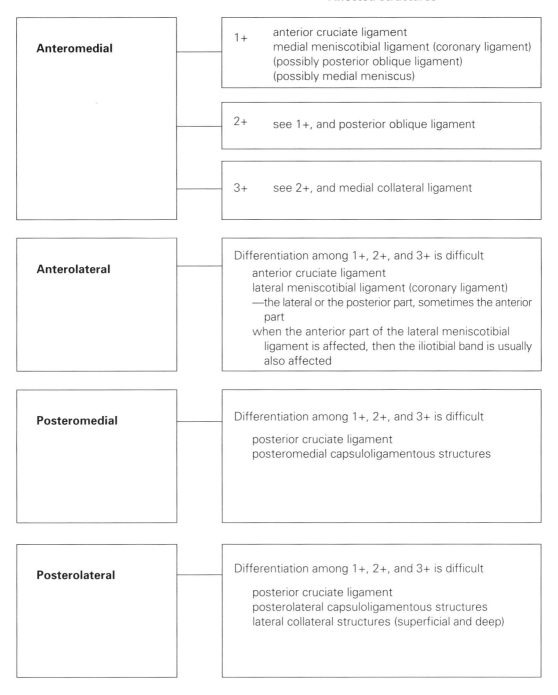

Anteromedial

1+   anterior cruciate ligament
medial meniscotibial ligament (coronary ligament)
(possibly posterior oblique ligament)
(possibly medial meniscus)

2+   see 1+, and posterior oblique ligament

3+   see 2+, and medial collateral ligament

Anterolateral

Differentiation among 1+, 2+, and 3+ is difficult
   anterior cruciate ligament
   lateral meniscotibial ligament (coronary ligament)
   —the lateral or the posterior part, sometimes the anterior
     part
   when the anterior part of the lateral meniscotibial
     ligament is affected, then the iliotibial band is usually
     also affected

Posteromedial

Differentiation among 1+, 2+, and 3+ is difficult

   posterior cruciate ligament
   posteromedial capsuloligamentous structures

Posterolateral

Differentiation among 1+, 2+, and 3+ is difficult

   posterior cruciate ligament
   posterolateral capsuloligamentous structures
   lateral collateral structures (superficial and deep)

DIFFERENTIAL DIAGNOSIS OF ANTERIOR KNEE PAIN

Pathology	Functional Examination
Lesion of the extensor mechanism	Painful resisted extension Sometimes painful passive flexion
Patellofemoral pathology	One or more of the following tests is painful: 1. Stand on affected leg and, while exerting pressure posteriorly against the patella, move from full extension to about 90° flexion 2. With the knee positioned in 30° flexion, passively shift the patella distally and hold it there during resisted extension 3. Resisted knee extension
All knee arthropathies	Limitation of motion in a capsular pattern (arthritis or osteoarthrosis) or in a noncapsular pattern
Meniscus lesion	Number of possibilities (see also diagrams for differential diagnoses of medial and lateral knee pain)
Mediopatellar plica lesion	Sometimes painful passive external rotation Sometimes passively shifting the patella medially with the knee positioned in 30° flexion is painful
Prepatellar bursitis	Usually the functional examination is negative, although sometimes passive flexion is painful Local swelling, fluctuation, and tenderness
Superficial or deep infrapatellar bursitis	Sometimes painful passive flexion and/or resisted extension, although usually the functional examination is negative Local swelling, fluctuation, and tenderness
Osgood-Schlatter disease	Sometimes painful passive flexion After activities, sometimes resisted extension is painful Local swelling and tenderness
Meniscotibial (coronary) ligament lesion	Sometimes painful passive flexion Medial ligament: painful passive external rotation Lateral ligament: painful passive internal rotation
Hoffa's disease (inflammation of the infrapatellar fat pad)	Sometimes painful resisted extension Local swelling and tenderness
Referred pain: L3	Negative functional examination of the knee Examination of hip or lumbar spine is positive

ANTERIOR KNEE PAIN SYNDROME 1

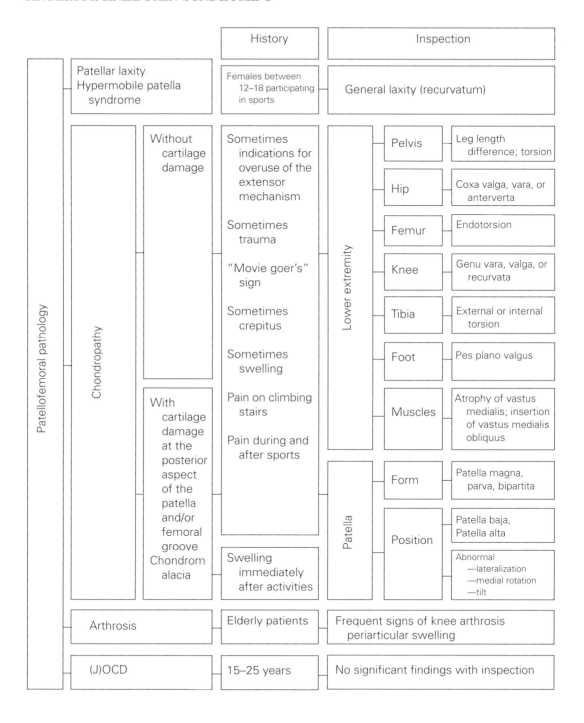

			History		Inspection		
Patellofemoral pathology	Patellar laxity Hypermobile patella syndrome		Females between 12–18 participating in sports		General laxity (recurvatum)		
	Chondropathy	Without cartilage damage	Sometimes indications for overuse of the extensor mechanism Sometimes trauma "Movie goer's" sign Sometimes crepitus Sometimes swelling Pain on climbing stairs Pain during and after sports	Lower extremity	Pelvis	Leg length difference; torsion	
					Hip	Coxa valga, vara, or anterverta	
					Femur	Endotorsion	
					Knee	Genu vara, valga, or recurvata	
					Tibia	External or internal torsion	
					Foot	Pes plano valgus	
		With cartilage damage at the posterior aspect of the patella and/or femoral groove Chondrom alacia			Muscles	Atrophy of vastus medialis; insertion of vastus medialis obliquus	
				Patella	Form	Patella magna, parva, bipartita	
					Position	Patella baja, Patella alta	
			Swelling immediately after activities			Abnormal —lateralization —medial rotation —tilt	
	Arthrosis		Elderly patients		Frequent signs of knee arthrosis periarticular swelling		
	(J)OCD		15–25 years		No significant findings with inspection		

ANTERIOR KNEE PAIN SYNDROME 2

	Examination	Treatment = management

Patellar instability	Knee hyperextension, increased external rotation
	Sometimes slight anterior drawer
	Normal or hypermobile patellofemoral motions
		Always treat conservatively first.
		Always:
		  1 Local
		    — Brace or taping to improve the tracking of the patella
		    — Strengthening and proprioceptive obliquus training of the vastus medialis

Chondro-pathy	I. Tests for pain provocation
	  — Resisted knee extension from various positions of knee flexion
	  — From 30° flexion, pull the patella up against resistance
	  — Sometimes percussion pain (in 30° flexion)
	  — In standing, knee flexion with pressure against the patella applied by the examiner; pain and crepitus are strong indications of chondromalacia
	  — A painful arc during knee flexion in weight bearing indicates a cartilage lesion
	II. Tests for possible causes
	  Movement of the patella
	  1 During active knee flexion–extension
	    —Amount of patella lateralization
	    —Presence of abrupt change in trajectory
	  2 Passive range of motion
	    —Medial shift
	    —External rotation
	    —Medial tilt
	    —Distal translation
	  Lower extremity
	  1 Joints
	    —Hip: eg, rotations
	    —Knee: eg, stability (posterior cruciate)
	    —Foot: eg, extension in talocrural and tarsal joints, mobility of the subtalar complex
	    —SI joint: locked
	  2 Muscles
	    —Rectus femoris
	    —Iliotibial tract
	    —Hamstrings
	    —Triceps surae
	III. Radiologic examination, to include tangential view
	IV. Arthroscopy
		If necessary:
		  1 Local
		    — Stretching the lateral retinaculum
		    — Stretching the iliotibial band (the retinacular part)
		    — Transverse friction, often at the superomedial pole and apex of the patella
		    — Patellofemoral mobilization, usually medial and inferior
		  2 Semilocal
		    — Stretching of the rectus femoris
		    — Stretching of the iliotibial band
		    — Stretching of the hamstrings
		    — Stretching of the triceps surae
		
		Causal:
		  — Mobilize joints (eg, talocrural joint, SI joint)
		  — Functional orthotic (eg, to correct a functional flat foot)
		
		Surgical:
		  — Arthroscopic "cleaning"
		  — Drilling
		  — Shaving
		  — Various operations are performed to influence the tracking of the patella, with variable results (to include Maquet, retinaculum releases)

Arthrosis	Usually capsular pattern of the knee Hypomobile patella	
(J)OCD	Radiologic	Rest

SI, sacroiliac.
(J)OCD, (juvenile) osteochondritis dissecans.

DIFFERENTIAL DIAGNOSIS OF MEDIAL KNEE PAIN

Pathology	*Functional Examination*
Medial meniscus lesion	Number of possibilities 　—Locking with pain on passive flexion and/or extension 　—Passive extension painful and/or limited 　—Passive flexion painful and/or limited 　—Painful passive external rotation 　—Painful varus and/or valgus test 　—Painful medial and/or lateral shear test 　—Painful resisted extension 　—Painful resisted flexion 　—Painful resisted internal rotation 　—Positive McMurray's test 　—Positive Steinmann's test
Medial meniscotibial (coronary) 　ligament lesion	Sometimes painful passive flexion Painful passive external rotation Sometimes painful valgus test in slight flexion
Medial collateral ligament lesion	In some cases, capsular pattern of limitation noted as a result of 　traumatic arthritis: limited and painful flexion more than extension Sometimes painful passive external rotation Valgus test in slight flexion is painful with a sprain or partial rupture Valgus instability noted with a total rupture
Pellegrini-Stieda disease	Progressive limitation of flexion Valgus test can be painful
Mediopatellar plica lesion	Sometimes painful passive external rotation Sometimes, with the knee positioned in 30° flexion, passively 　shifting the patella medially is painful
Pes anserinus superficialis bursitis	Usually the functional examination is negative Sometimes painful resisted flexion with external rotation Local swelling, fluctuation, and tenderness
Medial collateral ligament bursitis	Usually the functional examination is negative Local tenderness at the joint line or just proximal or distal to the 　joint line
Pes anserinus superficialis insertion 　tendopathy	Painful resisted flexion with internal rotation
Semimembranosus insertion 　tendopathy	Painful resisted flexion with internal rotation
Saphenous nerve compression 　neuropathy	Usually the functional examination is negative Local tenderness about 4 cm proximal to the medial femoral 　epicondyle

DIFFERENTIAL DIAGNOSIS OF LATERAL KNEE PAIN

Pathology	*Functional Examination*
Lateral meniscus lesion	Number of possibilities: —Painful passive extension —Painful passive flexion —Painful passive external rotation ⎤ combinations are also possible —Painful passive internal rotation ⎦ —Painful resisted extension —Painful resisted flexion —Painful resisted external rotation (due to biceps femoris) —Painful resisted internal rotation (due to popliteus) —Positive McMurray's test —Painful lateral and/or medial shear test
Lateral meniscotibial (coronary) ligament lesion	Sometimes painful passive flexion Painful passive internal rotation Sometimes painful varus test in slight flexion
Lateral collateral ligament lesion	Painful varus test in slight flexion with a sprain or partial rupture Varus instability noted with a total rupture
Biceps femoris insertion tendopathy	Painful resisted flexion and external rotation Sometimes painful passive internal rotation (in 90° flexion)
Popliteus insertion tendopathy	Painful resisted flexion and internal rotation Sometimes painful passive external rotation (in 90° flexion) Sometimes painful passive extension
Lateral parapatellar insertion tendopathy	Painful resisted extension Usually as a result of a patellofemoral problem: examine patellofemoral joint
Iliotibial band friction syndrome	Tenderness to palpation at the lateral femoral epicondyle between about 20° and 50° flexion
Proximal tibiofibular joint arthropathy	Painful resisted flexion and/or external rotation Passive varus test is sometimes painful
Referred pain: L4, L5	Negative functional examination of the knee Examination of the lumbar spine or SI joint is positive Seldom hip pathology

SI, sacroiliac.

ANTEROMEDIAL AND ANTEROLATERAL LOWER LEG PAIN

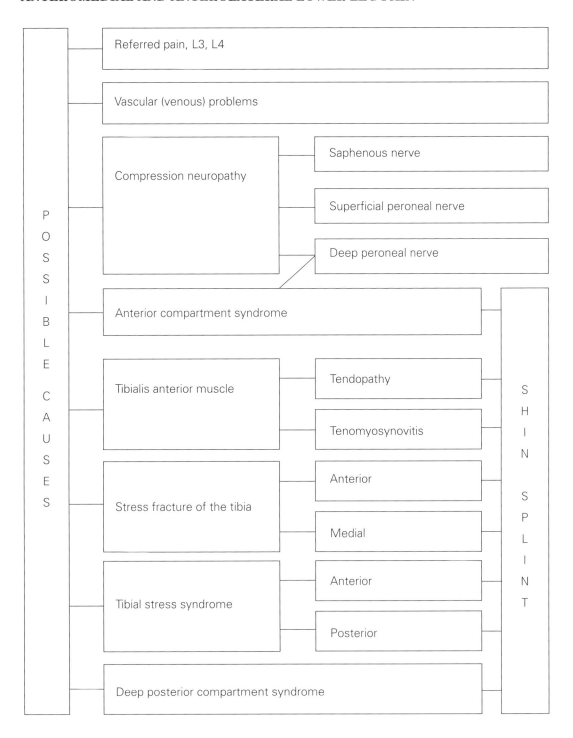

DIAGNOSIS OF THE KNEE 1a

Functional examination of the knee	**Pathology** Traumatic arthritis	Nontraumatic arthritis	Gonarthrosis (osteoarthrosis)	Hemarthrosis
1 Stand on the affected leg and, from full extension, bend the knee to about 90° flexion. The examiner exerts slight pressure posteriorly against the patella.	!			!
2 Patella ballotment (maximal effusion)	+	+	(+)	+
3 Test for moderate effusion	(+)	(+)	(+)	
4 Test for minimal effusion			(+)	
5 Passive extension	●●	●●	○	●●
6 Passive hyperextension	!	!		!
7 Passive flexion	●●●	●●●	●●(●)	●●●
8 Passive external rotation				○
9 Passive internal rotation				○
10 Passive varus test in slight flexion				○
11 Passive varus test in extension	!			
12 Passive valgus test in slight flexion	●(●)			○
13 Passive valgus test in extension	!			
14 Gravity test				
15 Anterior drawer test in 90° flexion				
16 Anterior drawer test in 90° knee flexion and maximal external rotation				

Osteochondritis dissecans	Loose body	Synovial (osteo)chondromatosis	Meniscus lesion	Plica syndrome	Intraarticular adhesions	Pellegrini-Stieda disease	Medial collateral ligament sprain	Medial meniscotibial (coronary) ligament sprain	Lateral collateral ligament sprain	Lateral meniscotibial (coronary) ligament sprain
		(+)								
(+)	(+)	(+)					(+)			
(+)	(+)	(+)	+				(+)	(+)		
○○	○○	○○	○○	○○			(○○)	○		
			○					○		
○○	○○	○○	○○	○○	○●●●	○●●●	●●			
			○	○			○	●		
			○							●
	○		○						●	○
			○			○	●(●)	○		

DIAGNOSIS OF THE KNEE 1b

Functional examination of the knee	Pathology	Traumatic arthritis	Nontraumatic arthritis	Gonarthrosis (osteoarthrosis)	Hemarthrosis
17 Anterior drawer test in 90° knee flexion and 50% internal rotation					
18 Anterior drawer test in 90° knee flexion and maximal internal rotation					
19 Posterior drawer test in 90° knee flexion					
20 Posterior drawer test in 90° knee flexion and maximal external rotation					
21 Posterior drawer test in 90° knee flexion and maximal internal rotation					
22 Anterolateral drawer test in 90° knee flexion					
23 Lateral shear test in 90° knee flexion					
24 Medial shear test in 90° knee flexion					
25 Lachman's test					
26 Pivot-shift test					
27 McMurray's test					
28 Steinmann's test					
29 Medial shift of the patella					
30 Lateral shift of the patella					
31 Distal shift of the patella					
32 Medial shift of the patella with the knee in 30° flexion					
33 Quadriceps contraction while the patella is held in a distally shifted position, knee in about 30° flexion					

Osteochondritis dissecans	Loose body	Synovial (osteo)chondromatosis	Meniscus lesion	Plica syndrome	Intraarticular adhesions	Pellegrini-Stieda disease	Medial collateral ligament sprain	Medial meniscotibial (coronary) ligament sprain	Lateral collateral ligament sprain	Lateral meniscotibial (coronary) ligament sprain
			○							
			○							
			● (●)	○						
			○							
				○						

DIAGNOSIS OF THE KNEE 1c

Functional examination of the knee	**Pathology**	Traumatic arthritis	Nontraumatic arthritis	Gonarthrosis (osteoarthrosis)	Hemarthrosis
34 Resisted knee extension		O	O		O
35 Resisted knee flexion		O	O		O
36 Resisted knee flexion and external rotation		O	O		O
37 Resisted knee flexion and internal rotation		O	O		O
38 Active or passive extension from 90° flexion while the examiner exerts pressure on the lateral femoral condyle					

Osteochondritis dissecans	Loose body	Synovial (osteo)chondromatosis	Meniscus lesion	Plica syndrome	Intraarticular adhesions	Pellegrini-Stieda disease	Medial collateral ligament sprain	Medial meniscotibial (coronary) ligament sprain	Lateral collateral ligament sprain	Lateral meniscotibial (coronary) ligament sprain
○			○							
○			○							
○			○							
○			○							

DIAGNOSIS OF THE KNEE 2a

Functional examination of the knee	Pathology	Medial instability in slight knee flexion (medial meniscotibial ligament, medial collateral ligament, and possibly medial meniscus)	Medial instability in knee extension (posteromedial capsule, medial collateral ligament, and possibly medial meniscus)
1 Stand on the affected leg and, from full extension, bend the knee to about 90° flexion. The examiner exerts slight pressure posteriorly against the patella.			
2 Patella ballotment (maximal effusion)			
3 Test for moderate effusion			
4 Test for minimal effusion			
5 Passive extension			
6 Passive hyperextension			
7 Passive flexion			
8 Passive external rotation		●□	
9 Passive internal rotation			
10 Passive varus test in slight flexion			
11 Passive varus test in extension			
12 Passive valgus test in slight flexion		●□	○□
13 Passive valgus test in extension			○□
14 Gravity test			
15 Anterior drawer test in 90° flexion			
16 Anterior drawer test in 90° knee flexion and maximal external rotation			

Lateral instability in slight knee flexion (lateral meniscotibial ligament, lateral collateral ligament, and possibly lateral meniscus)	Lateral instability in knee extension (posterolateral capsule, lateral meniscotibial ligament, lateral collateral ligament, and possibly lateral meniscus)	Anterior instability (anterior cruciate ligament and possibly medial meniscus)	Posterior instability (posterior cruciate ligament)	Anteromedial rotatory instability (anterior cruciate ligament, medial meniscotibial ligament, posterior oblique ligament, and possibly medial meniscus)	Anterolateral rotatory instability (anterior cruciate ligament, lateral and/or posterior part of lateral meniscotibial ligament, and possibly iliotibial band)	Posteromedial rotatory instability (posterior cruciate ligament, posteromedial capsuloligamentous structures)	Posterolateral rotatory instability (posterior cruciate ligament, posterolateral capsuloligamentous structures)
		○□		○□	○□		
				●□			
○	○						
○□	○□				○□		○□
	○□				○□		○□
						○□	
				○□		○□	
	□		□			□	□
	□○			○□	○□		
				○□			

DIAGNOSIS OF THE KNEE 2b

Functional examination of the knee	Pathology	Medial instability in slight knee flexion (medial meniscotibial ligament, medial collateral ligament, and possibly medial meniscus)	Medial instability in knee extension (posteromedial capsule, medial collateral ligament, and possibly medial meniscus)
17 Anterior drawer test in 90° knee flexion and 50% internal rotation			
18 Anterior drawer test in 90° knee flexion and maximal internal rotation			
19 Posterior drawer test in 90° knee flexion			
20 Posterior drawer test in 90° knee flexion and maximal external rotation			
21 Posterior drawer test in 90° knee flexion and maximal internal rotation			
22 Anterolateral drawer test in 90° knee flexion			
23 Lateral shear test in 90° knee flexion			
24 Medial shear test in 90° knee flexion			
25 Lachman's test			
26 Pivot-shift test			
27 McMurray's test		○	○
28 Steinmann's test		○	○
29 Medial shift of the patella			
30 Lateral shift of the patella			
31 Distal shift of the patella			
32 Medial shift of the patella with the knee in 30° flexion			
33 Quadriceps contraction while the patella is held in a distally shifted position, knee in about 30° flexion			

Lateral instability in slight knee flexion (lateral meniscotibial ligament, lateral collateral ligament, and possibly lateral meniscus)	Lateral instability in knee extension (posterolateral capsule, lateral meniscotibial ligament, lateral collateral ligament, and possibly lateral meniscus)	Anterior instability (anterior cruciate ligament and possibly medial meniscus)	Posterior instability (posterior cruciate ligament)	Anteromedial rotatory instability (anterior cruciate ligament, medial meniscotibial ligament, posterior oblique ligament, and possibly medial meniscus)	Anterolateral rotatory instability (anterior cruciate ligament, lateral and/or posterior part of lateral meniscotibial ligament, and possibly iliotibial band)	Posteromedial rotatory instability (posterior cruciate ligament, posteromedial capsuloligamentous structures)	Posterolateral rotatory instability (posterior cruciate ligament, posterolateral capsuloligamentous structures)
					□○		
			○□			○□	○□
							○□
						○□	
			○□			○□	○□
		○□		○□	○□		
		○□		○□	○□		
○	○	○		○			
○	○	○		○			

DIAGNOSIS OF THE KNEE 2c

Functional examination of the knee	**Pathology**	Medial instability in slight knee flexion (medial meniscotibial ligament, medial collateral ligament, and possibly medial meniscus)	Medial instability in knee extension (posteromedial capsule, medial collateral ligament, and possibly medial meniscus)
34 Resisted knee extension			
35 Resisted knee flexion			○
36 Resisted knee flexion and external rotation			
37 Resisted knee flexion and internal rotation			○
38 Active or passive extension from 90° flexion while the examiner exerts pressure on the lateral femoral condyle			

Lateral instability in slight knee flexion (lateral meniscotibial ligament, lateral collateral ligament, and possibly lateral meniscus)	Lateral instability in knee extension (posterolateral capsule, lateral meniscotibial ligament, lateral collateral ligament, and possibly lateral meniscus)	Anterior instability (anterior cruciate ligament and possibly medial meniscus)	Posterior instability (posterior cruciate ligament)	Anteromedial rotatory instability (anterior cruciate ligament, medial meniscotibial ligament, posterior oblique ligament, and possibly medial meniscus)	Anterolateral rotatory instability (anterior cruciate ligament, lateral and/or posterior part of lateral meniscotibial ligament, and possibly iliotibial band)	Posteromedial rotatory instability (posterior cruciate ligament, posteromedial capsuloligamentous structures)	Posterolateral rotatory instability (posterior cruciate ligament, posterolateral capsuloligamentous structures)
	○			○	○	○	○
	○				○		○
	○			○	○	○	○

DIAGNOSIS OF THE KNEE 3a

Functional examination of the knee

Pathology	Subluxation of the patella	Chondromalacia of the patella	Hoffa's disease	Superficial/deep infrapatellar bursitis	Prepatellar bursitis	Pes anserinus superficialis bursitis	Medial collateral ligament bursitis	Iliotibial band friction syndrome
1 Stand on the affected leg and, from full extension, bend the knee to about 90° flexion. The examiner exerts slight pressure posteriorly against the patella.		●●						
2 Patella ballotment (maximal effusion)								
3 Test for moderate effusion								
4 Test for minimal effusion		(+)						
5 Passive extension			○					
6 Passive hyperextension			●					
7 Passive flexion				○	○			
8 Passive external rotation								
9 Passive internal rotation								
10 Passive varus test in slight flexion								
11 Passive varus test in extension							Functional examination is negative	
12 Passive valgus test in slight flexion								
13 Passive valgus test in extension								
14 Gravity test								
15 Anterior drawer test in 90° flexion								
16 Anterior drawer test in 90° knee flexion and maximal external rotation								

	Baker's cyst	Parapatellar insertion tendopathy	Suprapatellar insertion tendopathy	Quadriceps tendon rupture	Infrapatellar insertion tendopathy ("jumper's knee")	Patellar ligament rupture	Pes anserinus superficialis insertion tendopathy	Semimembranosus insertion tendopathy	Biceps femoris insertion tendopathy	Popliteus muscle lesion	Saphenous nerve compression neuropathy	Common peroneal nerve compression neuropathy	Tibial nerve compression neuropathy	Osgood-Schlatter disease	Dislocation of the proximal tibiofibular joint	Popliteal artery compression syndrome	Soleus syndrome
	○						○	○	○	○					●		
	○						○	○	○	○							
	●	○	○		○									○			
	○																
										○							
															○		

Functional examination is usually negative; pain at the medial side of the knee particularly during activities when the knee is flexed more than 60°

Functional examination is usually negative

Functional examination is usually negative

DIAGNOSIS OF THE KNEE 3b

Functional examination of the knee	Pathology	Subluxation of the patella	Chondromalacia of the patella	Hoffa's disease	Superficial/deep infrapatellar bursitis	Prepatellar bursitis	Pes anserinus superficialis bursitis	Medial collateral ligament bursitis	Iliotibial band friction syndrome
17 Anterior drawer test in 90° knee flexion and 50% internal rotation									
18 Anterior drawer test in 90° knee flexion and maximal internal rotation									
19 Posterior drawer test in 90° knee flexion									
20 Posterior drawer test in 90° knee flexion and maximal external rotation									
21 Posterior drawer test in 90° knee flexion and maximal internal rotation									
22 Anterolateral drawer test in 90° knee flexion									
23 Lateral shear test in 90° knee flexion									
24 Medial shear test in 90° knee flexion									
25 Lachman's test									
26 Pivot-shift test									
27 McMurray's test									
28 Steinmann's test									
29 Medial shift of the patella									
30 Lateral shift of the patella			○						
31 Distal shift of the patella									
32 Medial shift of the patella with the knee in 30° flexion			○						
33 Quadriceps contraction while the patella is held in a distally shifted position, knee in about 30° flexion			● (●)						

Baker's cyst

Parapatellar insertion tendopathy

Suprapatellar insertion tendopathy

Quadriceps tendon rupture

Infrapatellar insertion tendopathy ("jumper's knee")

Patellar ligament rupture

Pes anserinus superficialis insertion tendopathy

Semimembranosus insertion tendopathy

Biceps femoris insertion tendopathy

Popliteus muscle lesion

Saphenous nerve compression neuropathy

Common peroneal nerve compression neuropathy

Pain and possibly sensory disturbances in the anterolateral aspect of the lower leg, dorsum of the foot, and first four toes; possible weakness of the foot evertors and dorsiflexors

Tibial nerve compression neuropathy

Sensory disturbances on the sole of the foot and from midcalf to and including the heel; possible motor deficit of the foot and toe flexors

Osgood-Schlatter disease

Dislocation of the proximal tibiofibular joint

Popliteal artery compression syndrome

Soleus syndrome

DIAGNOSIS OF THE KNEE 3c

Functional examination of the knee	**Pathology** Subluxation of the patella	Chondromalacia of the patella	Hoffa's disease	Superficial/deep infrapatellar bursitis	Prepatellar bursitis	Pes anserinus superficialis bursitis	Medial collateral ligament bursitis	Iliotibial band friction syndrome
34 Resisted knee extension		●		○				
35 Resisted knee flexion		○○					○	
36 Resisted knee flexion and external rotation								
37 Resisted knee flexion and internal rotation							○	
38 Active or passive extension from 90° flexion while the examiner exerts pressure on the lateral femoral condyle								● 30°–40° flexion

Baker's cyst	Parapatellar insertion tendopathy	Suprapatellar insertion tendopathy	Quadriceps tendon rupture	Infrapatellar insertion tendopathy ("jumper's knee")	Patellar ligament rupture	Pes anserinus superficialis insertion tendopathy	Semimembranosus insertion tendopathy	Biceps femoris insertion tendopathy	Popliteus muscle lesion	Saphenous nerve compression neuropathy	Common peroneal nerve compression neuropathy	Tibial nerve compression neuropathy	Osgood-Schlatter disease	Dislocation of the proximal tibiofibular joint	Popliteal artery compression syndrome	Soleus syndrome
	●	●	●	●	●								●			
						●	●	●	●					○		
								●	(●)					○		
						●●	● (●)		●	●)						

Appendix F

Algorithms for Diagnosis and Treatment of the Ankle and Foot

MOTIONS OF THE ANKLE AND FOOT 1

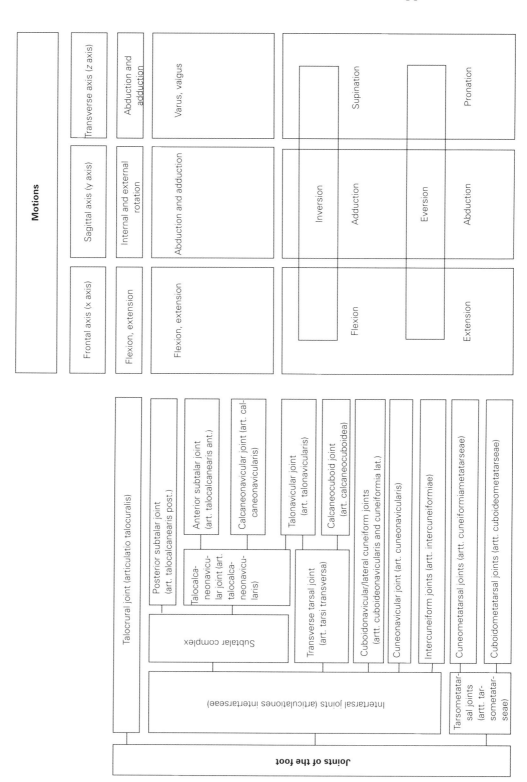

MOTIONS OF THE ANKLE AND FOOT 2

Joints of the foot	Motions		
	Frontal axis (x axis)	Sagittal axis (y axis)	Transverse axis (z axis)
Intermetatarsal joints (artt. intermetatarseae)	Flexion, extension	Abduction and adduction (2nd ray)	Pronation and supination
Metatarsophalangeal joints (artt. metatarsophalangeae)	Flexion, extension	Abduction and adduction (II–V) Abduction and adduction (I)	Pronation and supination
Interphalangeal joints (artt. interphalangeae)	Flexion, extension	Abduction and adduction (2nd ray)	Pronation and supination

PHASES OF WALKING

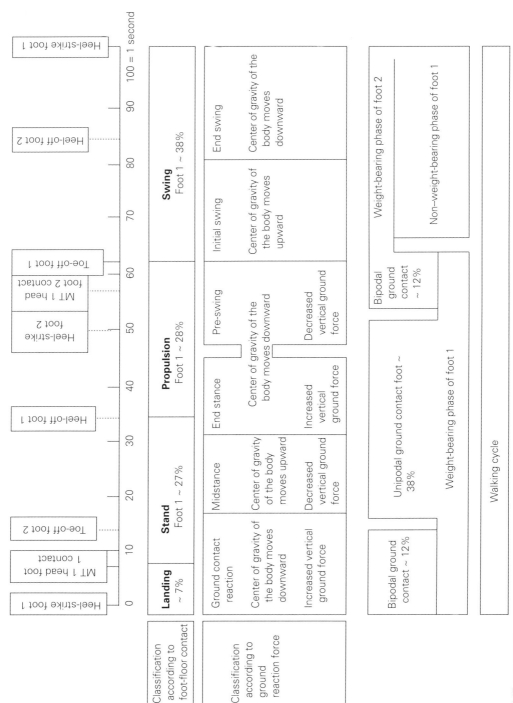

MT, metatarsal.

PHASES OF RUNNING

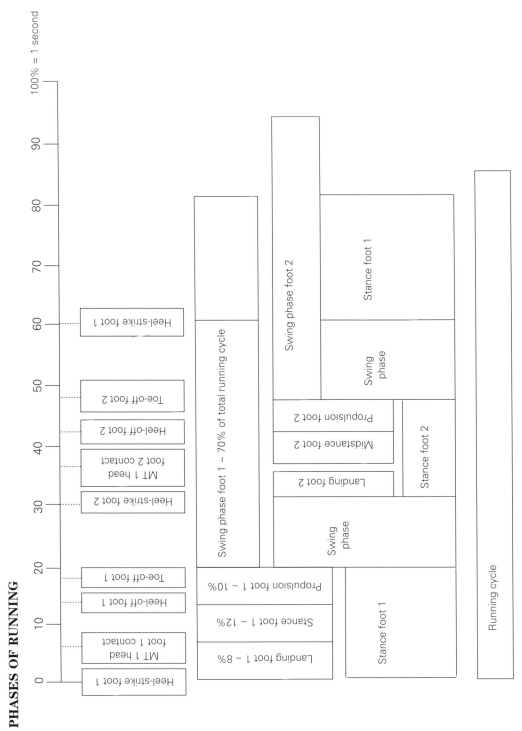

MT, metatarsal.

ANALYSIS OF FOOT MOTIONS DURING WALKING AND RUNNING 1

	0	10	20	30	40	50	60	70	80	90	100% = 1 second

Motions of the foot during walking

	Stance			Propulsion			Swing		
Landing	Ground contact reaction	Midstance	End stance	Preswing		Initial swing	End swing	

I — Subtalar joint, anterior and posterior

Relative valgus	Varus	Varus

II — Talocrural joint

Absolute plantar flexion	Dorsiflexion (extension)		Plantar flexion		Dorsiflexion (extension)	
	Relative	Absolute	Relative	Absolute	Relative	Absolute

III — Talocalcaneonavicular joint / Calcaneocuboid joint

Eversion	Inversion	Dorsiflexion (extension)
		Supination
		Adduction

ANALYSIS OF FOOT MOTIONS DURING WALKING AND RUNNING 2

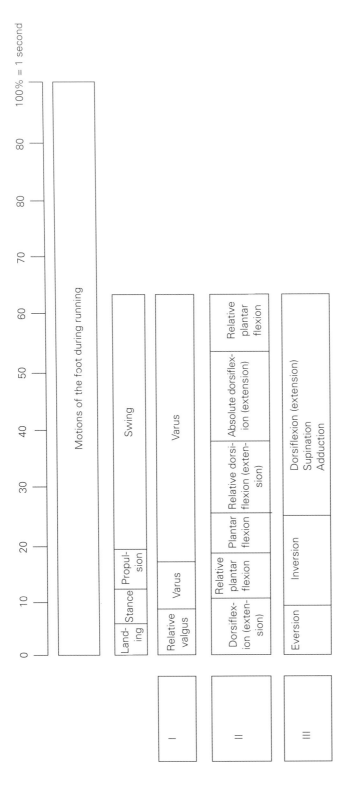

TYPICAL AGE SPANS FOR FOOT DISORDERS 1

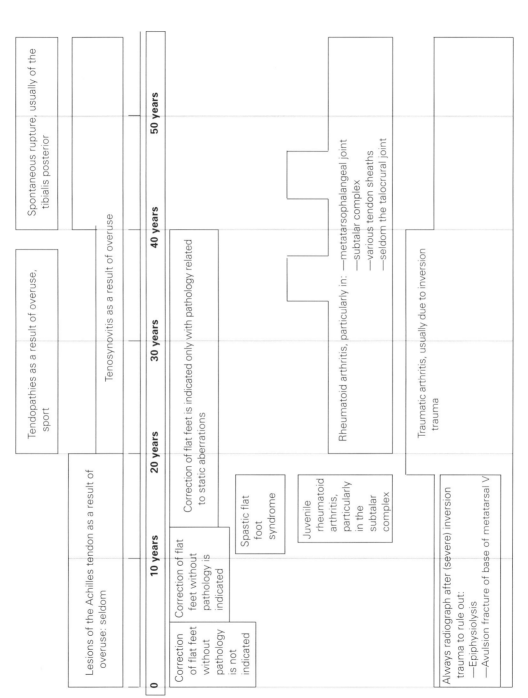

TYPICAL AGE SPANS FOR FOOT DISORDERS 2

0   10 years   20 years   30 years   40 years   50 years

Köhler I, aseptic necrosis of the navicular

Calcaneal apophysitis (Sever's disease)

Osteochondritis dissecans of the talus

Synovial (osteo) chondromatosis in the talocrural joint and the subtalar complex

Ankylosing spondylitis: —Chronic bilateral achillodynia without sports activity
—Heel pain!

Reiter's disease

Gout: in 50% of the acute cases does not occur in MTP I joint

Secondary osteoarthrosis

Primary osteoarthrosis: seldom

MTP, metatarsophalangeal.

INVERSION TRAUMA

	Grade I	Grade II	Grade III
	Sprain of the anterior talofibular and possibly calcaneofibular ligaments	Rupture of the anterior talofibular ligament, sprain or partial tear of the calcaneofibular ligament	Rupture of the anterior talofibular and calcaneofibular ligaments, possible rupture of the posterior talofibular ligament and/or other complications
Swelling	Minimal (effusion) Only lateral	Moderate	Severe (hemarthrosis) Lateral and medial
Pain	Localization: lateral and medial Weight bearing is possible	Mixture of findings from grades I and III	Localization: lateral Weight bearing impossible
Functional examination	Capsular pattern of the talocrural joint Anterior talofibular ligament stretch test is positive Calcaneofibular ligament stretch test can be positive	Mixture of findings from grades I and III	Initially, it is impossible to perform functional examination, except for the anterior drawer test
Course	Symptoms decrease after 4 days	Mixture of findings from grades I and III	No change in symptoms after 4 days
Anterior drawer test	Negative but painful	Positive and very painful when testing the end-feel	Positive but not painful
Talar tilt test	Negative	Negative	Positive
Arthrogram	Negative	Can be positive	Positive
	Treatment: immediate, conservative	Radiographic examination to rule out fractures	Radiographic examination to rule out fractures

INTERPRETATION OF THE VARUS CLICK TEST

Performed in instances of chronic pain after an inversion trauma of the ankle

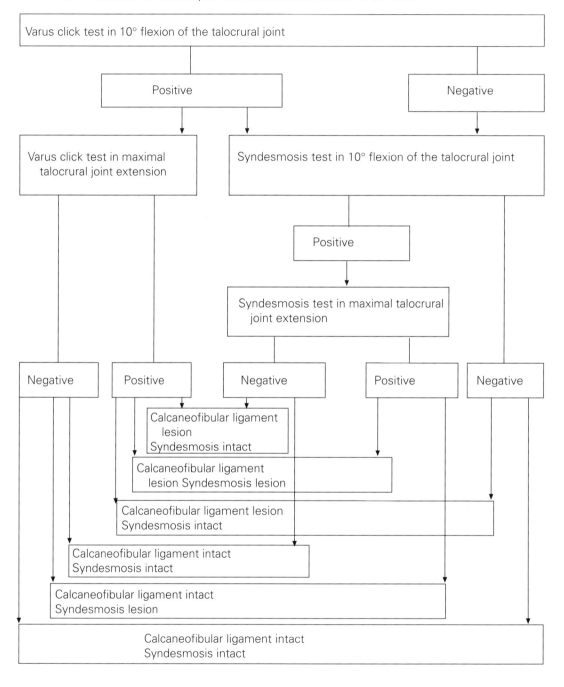

POSSIBLE COMPLICATIONS IN INVERSION TRAUMA OF THE FOOT 1

	Pathology	*Functional Examination*
Ligamentous	Lesion of the bifurcate ligament (calcaneocuboid and calcaneonavicular ligaments)	Painful passive adduction and supination of the TTJ
	Lesion of the cuboid–metatarsal V ligament	Painful passive adduction of the forefoot
	Lesion of the anterior tibiotalar and tibionavicular ligaments	Painful passive plantar flexion–abduction–pronation of the foot
Articular	Traumatic arthritis of the TCJ	Painful and limited plantar flexion and dorsiflexion of the TCJ
	Traumatic arthritis of the STJ	Painful and limited varus > > valgus in the STJ
	Traumatic arthritis of the TTJ	Painful and limited inversion > dorsiflexion of the TTJ
	Posterior tibiotalar compression syndrome	Very painful passive plantar flexion of the TCJ
	Sinus tarsi syndrome	Complaints of feeling of instability, but functional examination is negative
	Tibiofibular syndesmosis instability (anteroinferior and posteroinferior tibiofibular ligaments)	Syndesmosis stability test is positive (instability) Passive varus test of the STJ is positive (click and instability)
Muscular	Tenosynovitis of the peroneal muscles	Painful passive dorsiflexion-adduction-supination of the foot
	Tendinitis of the peroneal muscles	Painful resisted plantar flexion–abduction–pronation of the foot
	Rupture of the superior extensor retinaculum with a dislocation of the peroneal tendons ("snapping ankle")	Negative functional examination Dislocation ("snapping") of the peroneal tendons anteriorly during active dorsiflexion and pronation of the foot

TCJ, talocrural joint.
STJ, subtalar joint.
TTJ, transverse tarsal joint.

POSSIBLE COMPLICATIONS IN INVERSION TRAUMA OF THE FOOT 2

	Pathology	*Functional Examination*
Muscular	Achillodynia	Usually negative functional examination Sometimes painful resisted plantar flexion of the foot
	Tenosynovitis and/or tendinitis of the extensor hallucis longus muscle	Painful passive plantar flexion–abduction–pronation of the foot with passive flexion of the great toe And/or painful resisted dorsiflexion–adduction–supination of the foot with resisted great toe extension
	Tenosynovitis and/or tendinitis of the extensor digitorum longus muscle	Painful passive inversion of the foot with passive flexion of the toes And/or painful resisted foot eversion with toe extension
Neurologic	Overstretching of the common peroneal nerve, of the superficial peroneal nerve (particularly the intermediate ramus), or of the deep peroneal nerve	Passive inversion of the foot causes burning pain in the sensory area supplied by the particular nerve
Osseous	Avulsion fracture of the base of metatarsal V	Painful passive foot inversion Local pain and swelling
	Fracture of the shaft of metatarsal V	X-ray
	Avulsion fracture at the lateral calcaneus	X-ray
	Avulsion fracture at the cuboid and/or the base of metatarsal V	X-ray
	Fracture of the anterior calcaneal process	X-ray
	Osteochondral fracture of the talus	Painful and limited dorsiflexion of the TCJ X-ray
	Fracture of the lateral tubercle on the posterior process of the talus	Painful passive plantar flexion of the TCJ X-ray
	Navicular impression fracture	Painful passive foot inversion Local pain and swelling X-ray
	Talar neck impression fracture	X-ray
	Talar head impression fracture	X-ray

TCJ, talocrural joint.
STJ, subtalar joint.
TTJ, transverse tarsal joint.

PAIN AT THE MEDIAL ASPECT OF THE ANKLE WITHOUT A LIMITATION OF MOTION

As the result of inversion trauma	Especially by compression of the bony structures
As the result of valgus trauma	Passive maximal flexion-abduction-pronation motion and/or abduction-pronation from the resting position is painful Passive abduction-pronation movement in maximal extension (with straight knee) is seldom (solitarily) painful
Tibialis posterior tenosynovitis	Passive eversion is painful Resisted (isometric) inversion can be painful
Tarsal tunnel syndrome	Passive valgus motion sometimes provokes burning pain, especially passive eversion Local tenderness at the level of the tarsal tunnel
Compression neuropathy of the medial and lateral plantar nerves	Passive eversion is the most painful test Passive inversion can be painful Local tenderness at the level of the abductor hallucis
Referred pain, L4	The functional examination (even after provocation) is negative
Compression neuropathy of the saphenous nerve	The functional examination (even after provocation) is negative Pressure at the level of the entrapment (the width of four fingers above the medial femoral condyle) provokes local and radiating pain

HEEL PAIN 1a

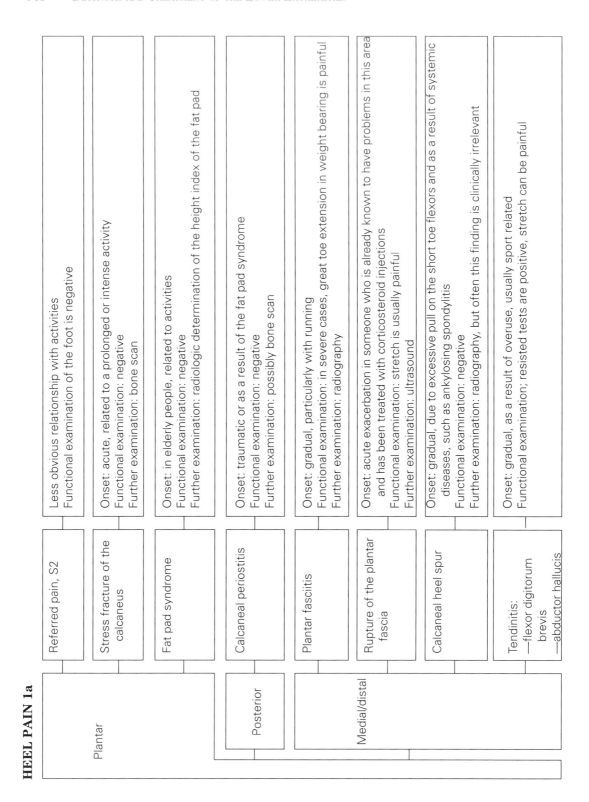

Plantar

| Referred pain, S2 | Less obvious relationship with activities
Functional examination of the foot is negative |

| Stress fracture of the calcaneus | Onset: acute, related to a prolonged or intense activity
Functional examination: negative
Further examination: bone scan |

| Fat pad syndrome | Onset: in elderly people, related to activities
Functional examination: negative
Further examination: radiologic determination of the height index of the fat pad |

Posterior

| Calcaneal periostitis | Onset: traumatic or as a result of the fat pad syndrome
Functional examination: negative
Further examination: possibly bone scan |

| Plantar fasciitis | Onset: gradual, particularly with running
Functional examination: in severe cases, great toe extension in weight bearing is painful
Further examination: radiography |

Medial/distal

| Rupture of the plantar fascia | Onset: acute exacerbation in someone who is already known to have problems in this area and has been treated with corticosteroid injections
Functional examination: stretch is usually painful
Further examination: ultrasound |

| Calcaneal heel spur | Onset: gradual, due to excessive pull on the short toe flexors and as a result of systemic diseases, such as ankylosing spondylitis
Functional examination: negative
Further examination: radiography, but often this finding is clinically irrelevant |

| Tendinitis:
—flexor digitorum brevis
—abductor hallucis | Onset: gradual, as a result of overuse, usually sport related
Functional examination; resisted tests are positive, stretch can be painful |

HEEL PAIN 1b

Medial

Tarsal tunnel syndrome
Onset: gradual
Functional examination: passive valgus can be positive

Arthritis of the posterior talocalcaneal joint
Onset: traumatic or nontraumatic (eg, systemic disease)
Functional examination: passive varus is painful and limited
Further examination: radiography or laboratory tests, depending on the cause

Flexor digitorum longus tenosynovitis
Onset: gradual, usually as a result of a static aberration
Functional examination: stretch test is positive

Flexor hallucis longus tenosynovitis
Onset: gradual, usually as a result of a static aberration
Functional examination: stretch test is positive

Stress fracture of the calcaneus
Onset: acute, related to long-lasting or intense activity
Functional examination: negative
Further examination: bone scan

Chronic overuse of the posterior talocalcaneal joint
Onset: gradual, pain during vigorous activities
Functional examination: passive plantar flexion is painful, varus can be limited
Further examination: radiography

Stress fracture of the medial tubercle of the posterior process of the talus
Onset: as a result of chronic overuse of the posterior talocalcaneal joint
Functional examination: negative
Further examination: radiography, bone scan

Plantar/distal

Compression neuropathy:
—lateral plantar nerve
—medial plantar nerve
—calcaneal nerves
Onset: often a combination of static aberration and vigorous activity
Functional examination: passive inversion can be painful, passive extension of the fourth and fifth or the first and second toes with the foot in maximal eversion can be painful

Plantar/posterior

Triceps surae insertion tendopathy
Onset: often a combination of static aberration and sports activity
Functional examination: depending on the stage, toe raises can be painful, stretch can be painful

HEEL PAIN 2a

Stress fracture of the calcaneus — Onset: acute, related to long-lasting and/or intense activities on hard ground/floor
Functional examination: negative
Further examination: bone scan

Lesion of the calcaneal insertion of the superior peroneal-retinaculum/calcaneofibular ligament — Onset: posttraumatic (inversion trauma)
Functional examination: pain by passive plantar flexion, adduction, supination with the talocrural joint in 10° plantar flexion

Compression neuropathy of the sural nerve — Onset: after surgery (eg, Achilles tendon) or local pressure
Functional examination: negative

Calcaneal periostitis — Onset: usually seen in elderly people, combination of fat pad atrophy and supination gait
Functional examination: negative

Triceps surae insertion tendopathy — Onset: combination of sports activities and static aberration
Functional examination: depending on stage, possibly painful against resistance, possibly painful with stretch

Lateral

Plantar/posterior

HEEL PAIN 2b

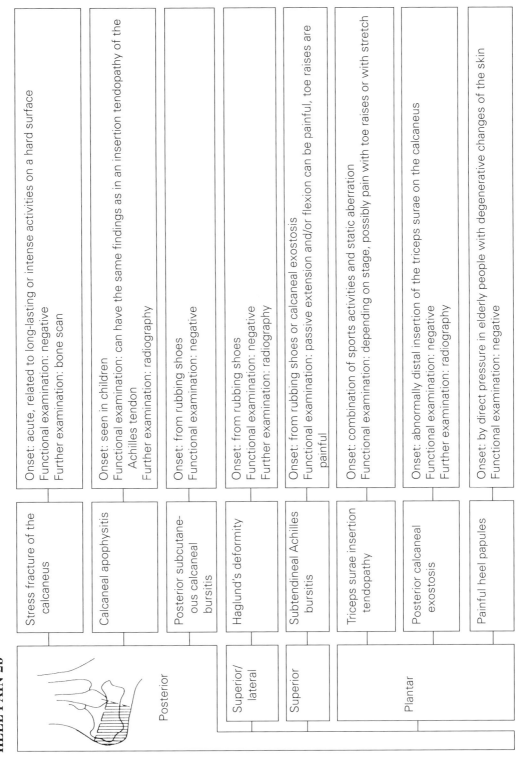

	Stress fracture of the calcaneus	Onset: acute, related to long-lasting or intense activities on a hard surface Functional examination: negative Further examination: bone scan
	Calcaneal apophysitis	Onset: seen in children Functional examination: can have the same findings as in an insertion tendopathy of the Achilles tendon Further examination: radiography
Posterior	Posterior subcutaneous calcaneal bursitis	Onset: from rubbing shoes Functional examination: negative
Superior/lateral	Haglund's deformity	Onset: from rubbing shoes Functional examination: negative Further examination: radiography
Superior	Subtendineal Achilles bursitis	Onset: from rubbing shoes or calcaneal exostosis Functional examination: passive extension and/or flexion can be painful, toe raises are painful
	Triceps surae insertion tendopathy	Onset: combination of sports activities and static aberration Functional examination: depending on stage, possibly pain with toe raises or with stretch
Plantar	Posterior calcaneal exostosis	Onset: abnormally distal insertion of the triceps surae on the calcaneus Functional examination: negative Further examination: radiography
	Painful heel papules	Onset: by direct pressure in elderly people with degenerative changes of the skin Functional examination: negative

Index